Economics

7 Day Loan

Su er

Heinemann

Heinemann Educational Publishers
Halley Court, Jordan Hill, Oxford OX2 8EJ
a division of Reed Educational & Professional Publishing Ltd

OXFORD MELBOURNE AUCKLAND
JOHANNESBURG BLANTYRE GABORONE
IBADAN PORTSMOUTH NH (USA) CHICAGO

Heinemann is a registered trademark of Reed Educational & Professional Publishing Ltd

First published in 2000

04 03 02 01
10 9 8 7 6 5 4 3

British Library Cataloguing in Publication Data
A catalogue record for this book is available from the British Library

ISBN 0 435 33111 6

Typeset by Wyvern 21 Ltd
Cover Design by Brian Melville, Big Red Hat
Printed and bound in Great Britain by The Bath Press Ltd, Bath

Acknowledgements

Copyright acknowledgements appear on page 372

The publishers would like to thank the following for permission to use photographs:
Format/Jenny Matthews for the cover photograph of men working in Rover factory, Cowley; Environmental Images/John
Morrison for the cover photograph of cows in front of power station chimneys; Tony Stone Images for the cover
photographs of racing yachts at sea and the New York Exchange trading floor; Camera Press for the TUC building on p. 6;
Rex Features for the chimneys belching out pollution in USSR on p. 96.

The publishers have made every effort to trace copyright holders. However, if any material has been incorrectly
acknowledged, we would be pleased to correct this at the earliest opportunity.

Tel: 01865 888058 www.heinemann.co.uk

Contents

Part 1 AS Economics

Section 4 Government policy

Part 1
AS Economics

Economics in Context - Specification Grid

AS LEVEL

Section / Unit	1	2	3	4	5	6	7	8	9	10	11	12	13	14	15	16	17	18	19	20	21	22	23	24	25	26	27	28	29	30
Section	1				2				3						4				5									6		
EXAM BOARD / Modules																														
AQA																														
Markets and Market Failure																														
The National Economy				✓	✓	✓	✓	✓	✓	✓	✓	✓	✓	✓	✓	✓	✓	✓	✓	✓	✓	✓	✓	✓	✓	✓	✓	✓	✓	✓
Markets at Work																														
Working as an Economist																												✓		
Business Economics and Distribution of Income															✓	✓	✓	✓											✓	
Government Policy																			✓	✓	✓	✓	✓	✓	✓	✓	✓			✓
Edexcel																														
Markets - How They Work	✓	✓	✓	✓	✓	✓	✓	✓	✓						✓															
Markets - Why They Fail														✓	✓	✓	✓	✓												
Managing the Economy										✓	✓	✓	✓																	
Industrial Economics																														
Labour Economics																														
Economic Development																														
The Global Economy																			✓	✓	✓	✓	✓	✓	✓	✓	✓			
OCR																														
The Market System	✓	✓	✓	✓	✓	✓	✓	✓	✓	✓	✓	✓	✓	✓	✓	✓	✓	✓												
Market Failure and Government															✓	✓	✓	✓												
The National and International Economy																			✓	✓	✓	✓	✓	✓	✓	✓	✓			
Economics of Work and Leisure																														
Transport Economics																														
Economics of Development																														
The UK Economy																														
Economics in a European Context				✓																										

A2 LEVEL

Section / Unit	1	2	3	4	5	6	7	8	9	10	11	12	13	14	15	16	17	18	19	20	21	22	23	24	25
Section	1				2							3							4				5		
The National Economy											✓														
Markets at Work													✓						✓						
Working as an Economist																									✓
Business Economics and Distribution of Income								✓	✓																
Government Policy	✓	✓	✓	✓	✓	✓	✓	✓	✓			✓	✓	✓	✓	✓	✓	✓	✓	✓	✓	✓	✓	✓	✓
Edexcel																									
Markets - How They Work																									
Markets - Why They Fail																									
Managing the Economy																									
Industrial Economics	✓	✓	✓	✓																					
Labour Economics							✓	✓	✓																
Economic Development				✓				✓																	
The Global Economy												✓	✓	✓	✓	✓	✓	✓	✓	✓	✓	✓	✓		
OCR																									
The Market System																									
Market Failure and Government																									
The National and International Economy					✓	✓	✓	✓	✓	✓	✓														
Economics of Work and Leisure										✓															
Transport Economics																						✓			
Economics of Development																								✓	
The UK Economy												✓	✓	✓	✓	✓	✓	✓	✓	✓	✓	✓			
Economics in a European Context													✓							✓				✓	✓

Section 1
Introduction to Economics

Introduction

This book is designed to help you progress through your economics course, and as importantly to enjoy economics. You will find that economics is a rewarding subject. It develops your ability to analyse and evaluate. It provides you with useful skills and tools to assess some of the most crucial current day issues such as unemployment, congestion, poverty and changes in the way countries are running their economies.

This book has been written to cover the new AS and A2 specifications with the first half of the book being devoted to the AS modules and the second half being largely devoted to A2 modules. The specification grid opposite shows where the subject content of each of the Examination Boards, AQA's, Edexcel's and OCR's modules are covered in the text of the book. However, the book also covers much of the content of HND and first year university economics courses.

The AS Section

The AS part is further divided down into sections. AS Section 1 explores the meaning of economics, introduces some important concepts and distinguishes, with examples, between micro and macroeconomics. AS Section 2 covers demand and supply analysis and explains how changes in the amount households want to buy and the amount firms want to sell influences the quantity and prices of products. In AS Section 3 influences on the behaviour of firms are explored. AS Section 4 explains why the way firms produce their output and the prices they charge does not always result in the best outcome for households. It also discusses how the government responses to the problems which arise including pollution and poverty.

In AS Section 5 attention switches to the operation of the whole economy. This section starts by discussing the key government objectives for the economy and how the performance of the economy is assessed. It uses aggregate demand and supply analysis, and assesses the causes and effects of inflation, unemployment, international trade performance and changes in total output. AS Section 6 explores three interesting topics, housing, the environment and sport and leisure. It shows how the key concepts covered in the earlier sections can be applied to these topics.

The A2 Section

The A2 section of the book builds on the AS part, and extends the analysis applied. A2 Section 1 explores the behaviour and performance of firms and government policies towards firms in some depth and explains, for example, why firms sometimes charge different people different prices for the same product. A2 Section 2 focuses on the world of work and leisure. It covers, for example, what influences our choice of job and the pay we receive. In A2 Section 3 the effect that contact with other countries has on the performance of the UK economy is discussed. The causes of unemployment, inflation and changes in output are also explored.

A2 Section 4 covers the nature and effects of government policies including changes in the rate of interest and the rate of income tax. A2 Section 5 explores three topical issues in some depth. The unit on transport discusses, for example, the problem of congestion and applies a number of microeconomic concepts. The economic development unit covers, among other related issues, an analysis of why some countries face widespread poverty. The final unit of the book concentrates on the performance of countries which are changing their economic systems and the main issues facing the European Union.

Questions and Activities

Each unit contains a number of questions and activities. These are intended to make you think, check your understanding and allow you to apply this understanding to a range of situations, mainly ones drawn from real world events. Some of the data response questions are based on past examinations. Others are original questions, based on articles and original material analysing current day issues. These increase the number of questions available for you to work through.

At the end of each section there is a also a range of other types of questions. In the case of the AS sections these include multiple choice questions which provide a quick way for you to assess a wide area of your understanding. Answers to these questions (with explanations) are provided at the end of the book. The AS and A2 sections include essay questions and suggestions for project work. Essays enable you to write at some length and analyse questions in some depth. Project work permits you to research topics and to gather evidence for key skills. Economics is a subject that develops all the key skills.

At the end of the book is a glossary that gives a succinct explanation of some of the key terms used in economics.

We hope that you will find this book useful in your studies and we welcome any comments or suggestions you may want to make.

What is economics?

Key concepts covered
- finite resources
- unlimited wants
- choices
- opportunity cost
- economic system
- decision-making
- knowledge and understanding
- technical vocabulary
- thinking like an economist

Introduction

Studying economics changes lives. It alters the way people see and understand the world around them. Watching TV, reading newspapers, listening and taking part in conversations will not be the same again. There are different ways in which it is possible to communicate an understanding of what economics is about. This unit considers economics from three different perspectives:

- Its existence as a subject.
- Its use.
- Differences between economics and other subjects.

Why does economics exist?

Economics deals with some of the fundamental forces which affect our lives. Our lifestyles, our friendships, our relationships will be strongly influenced by the job(s) that we do. Some people measure success by the things that they can afford to buy. Others have concerns about poverty and the inequalities that exist in the world. Many young people, especially those who go travelling, are fascinated by foreign cultures and ways of life. Some of us worry and brood about the future, especially when it comes to damaging and degrading our environment. Learning about economics will help you understand:

- why particular jobs are available
- why some people earn more than others
- why different goods are priced the way that they are

- why poverty exists
- what shapes the lives people live in different parts of the world
- will planet earth survive?

Studying economics should help you develop the skills to provide a better understanding of fundamental issues.

What is special about economics? Economics exists because we live in a world in which **resources are finite**. There are not endless supplies of energy, minerals, food stuffs and so on. On the other hand, we live in a world in which the vast majority of people are materialistic in the sense of always wanting more. Two-thirds of the world's population does not have enough to eat. Most of us aspire to improving our lifestyles by having more and better and newer and nicer things. In short, people have **unlimited wants**. Their needs outstrip the means of satisfying them. Put simply, three into two won't go. There is not enough to go round. Some people starve while others enjoy fantastic standards of luxury.

This is not a morality tale, rather it is a description of the world in which we live. Economists use this image to demonstrate the fundamentals of their subject. Economics is about making choices. People have virtually unlimited wants. Resources are finite. Economics is about making more informed choices. It is about understanding that if one choice is made others have to be forgone. For example, it can be argued that if we want cleaner air, then we need to use cars less. This sacrifice is called an **opportunity cost**, that is, what has to be given up as the result of a particular choice.

We can't always get what we want. Therefore, all societies need some kind of **economic system** in order to decide what gets produced, how it is produced and, crucially, who gets what. Unravelling and understanding these sorts of issues is what economics is all about, and learning about the subject gives a better understanding of the forces which have and will shape all our lives.

Economics in use

Looking at how economics is used provides another way of developing an understanding of what economics is all about. The following two case studies provide examples of how economics is used in two very different types of organisations.

Case study 1: Cheltenham and Gloucester Building Society

Cheltenham & Gloucester

Over the past decade the Cheltenham and Gloucester Building Society has become the third largest lender in the mortgage market. In 1995 it was taken over by Lloyds Bank but it still retains its own name and associated image.

The success of the Cheltenham and Gloucester (C and G) is attributable to a variety of reasons. It was run aggressively and competitively whereas many of its competitors were old-fashioned and stuck into a traditional pattern of mortgage lending. Building societies tended to be traditional. They waited for business to come through their doors and were slow to take advantage of new technologies.

C and G developed marketing strategies which led to a period of dramatic growth. In the late 1980s most building societies understood marketing as being concerned with promotional literature and redesigned logos. C and G was different as it wanted to grow nationally. It wanted to get a larger slice of the market. In order to do this it carefully analysed the mortgage market and selected that part which offered the greatest growth potential at the least possible risk.

The upshot of this was that C and G developed a very sophisticated view of its market segment. It was not interested in new buyers. It targeted people looking for second mortgages, or those moving house. C and G realised that those in its market segment were likely to move in three to five years. It was not trapped in the traditional belief that a mortgage was for life, and it restructured its organisation to make it most effective in pursuing this particular market. In particular, C and G:

- pioneered mortgage selling by phone
- established a ruthless policy towards those who fell into arrears
- used its power in the money markets to borrow as cheaply as possible
- streamlined its administrative systems to ensure that costs were minimised.

Case study 2: TUC

The Trades Union Congress (TUC) is an umbrella organisation of which most trade unions are

The TUC headquarters in London

members. It works to support union activity, and one of its functions is to act as a pressure group, seeking to influence and change government policies which affect union members. The TUC employs a number of economists specifically to help in this process.

Economists working for the TUC pay particular attention to 'macro economic variables', that is the latest data about unemployment, economic growth, inflation, earnings and the exchange rate. These are used to prepare forecasts of trends in the national economy, and used by individual unions to prepare for negotiations with employers. This kind of data is also used in an attempt to influence government decisions affecting trade union members, and to challenge what is called 'economic orthodoxy'. For example, the TUC has argued that many economists are wrong to assume that falling unemployment will lead to rising prices (inflation). Similarly, data are collected which can be used to assess the impact of the introduction of a statutory minimum wage.

The TUC works hard as a pressure group to influence government policy and law making. It is represented at various parliamentary select committees but considers that it is only worth being involved in such activity if it has got something to say that pushes the debate forward. The TUC has to use sound evidence and good economics to put forward arguments – if it does not, its arguments will be demolished. The current Labour government is sympathetic to union interests but is only convinced by sound economic argument.

ACTIVITY 1

a What do these two different organisations have in common?

b In what ways do they differ?

Using economics

Looking at the above organisations from an economic perspective shows that both employ people with particular **decision-making** skills. Decisions are made on the basis of a whole variety of factors but economists are expected to provide numerical evidence to back up findings that have been researched in some way. Thirdly, both organisations draw upon their knowledge and understanding about the possibility of the existence of particular economic relationships.

Making decisions

In their different ways the work of each of these organisations reflects the basic issues described at the beginning of this unit. The Cheltenham and Gloucester Building Society lacked the resources to sell mortgages to all possible buyers. It had to identify its particular market and concentrate its available resources on meeting the needs of this target group. It needed to decide how to focus the marketing and also to decide how best to organise itself to meet these objectives.

The TUC is working to argue that the minimum wage should be increased as one means to ensure that more resources are devoted to meeting the needs of its members rather than the better off. It aims to influence decisions which the government might or might not make.

Evidence

Although some economists delight in making their subject abstract and incomprehensible, most people know the basics of the subject. We are all consumers and producers. All of us argue, knowingly and unknowingly, about economic issues. People have views about immigration, the destruction of rain forests or restrictions on tobacco advertising. But economics is about more than having views on a range of controversial issues. The case studies above showed how evidence can be used in order to support arguments and make decisions. Thus, the C and G used data about the mortgage market to target its products at a particular market. The TUC submitted written evidence to the Low Pay Commission to support its contention that implementing the minimum wage would have a very limited effect on employment.

Often this requirement for evidence leads to the collection of numerical data. It is claimed that this use of quantitative methods means that economics is more objective and should be regarded as a science.

Not all economists would agree with this statement but most would share the view that the collection, interpretation and analysis of numerical data is a skill which economists need.

Knowledge and understanding

As with other disciplines, collective **knowledge and understanding** builds up over the years. Economics as we know it today has developed over the past 400 years. Some would argue that its origins are much older, but recent developments are linked with industrialisation and the development of capitalism. Adam Smith, who wrote *The Wealth of Nations* (1776), is seen as one of the first economists. He wrote about how specialisation in particular tasks could lead to greater production. Economists such as David Ricardo were involved in arguments about import duties, and the later nineteenth-century economists became much more scientific and mathematical. As with other disciplines, the subject has constantly evolved and successive generations of economists have argued and debated each other's work. In this way a body of knowledge and understanding associated with economics has developed. There is broad agreement about parts of this and dispute about others. As shown later in this book, most economists will agree about the nature of demand and supply, but differences exist when it comes to looking at the effectiveness of different government policies.

All economists draw upon this reservoir of knowledge and understanding. Thus it is well established that as people's incomes increase they tend to spend on housing, and the C and G deliberately targeted those most likely to become better off.

ACTIVITY 2

Compare economics with another subject which you take.
a   What do they have in common?
b   How do they differ?

Economics and other disciplines

Economics is different from familiar subjects like history and technology as only a minority of students study economics before they are 16. As with all disciplines economics has a **technical vocabulary** all of its own. Economists are also very precise in their use of particular terms. For example, in everyday usage people often refer to the *cost* of a cinema ticket when describing how much they have to pay to see a film. Economists would call this the price of a ticket and would use the term cost when talking about how much the cinema operator would have to pay out in terms of rent, rates, wages, film hire, etc.

This precise use of particular terms takes some getting used to but it is important especially in terms of clearly communicating your understanding of the subject and developing economic analysis and argument.

Economics is classified as a social science, which means that it has much in common with subjects like sociology and psychology. Each is concerned with different aspects of people's behaviour. Because of this social sciences can never be as exact and as accurate as some branches of physical sciences like physics and chemistry. You can't subject people to strict laboratory conditions but at the same time theories and concepts should be based on the careful collection of evidence. As indicated earlier, numerical data is very important as is the development of logical and ordered argument. Organisations such as the C and G and the TUC will also draw upon insights offered by other disciplines in order to be as effective as possible.

Finally, economics is about choices. It is often about controversial issues. Economic arguments are often used by politicians to support particular ideas. In fact economics and argument go hand in hand. Often there are no right or wrong answers; no clear-cut solutions to economic issues. Governments and political parties often disagree about economic issues and this means that economics often appeals to those who enjoy argument and debate, and also take an interest in current affairs and politics.

ACTIVITY 3

a What appeals to you about economics?
b What puts you off?
c Summarise your initial reactions on one side of A4.
d Compare and discuss with other members of your class. Make brief notes of the outcomes and file for future reference

Summary

Economics exists because in the world we live in we have to make choices. Wants are said to be infinite whereas resources are finite.

Learning about economics involves learning to **think like an economist**. Economists are employed in all kinds of jobs in the private, public and voluntary sectors. They try to aid the decision-making process by the careful consideration of evidence and making use of the accumulated wisdom of economists. To be effective economists like other scientists are always suspicious, always critical, always on the look out for new ways of understanding.

Economics is a social science which has a technical language of its own and in which analysis, argument and theory should always be supported by appropriate (often numerical) evidence.

The remainder of this book is devoted the development of a deeper understanding of how economists and economics work in the context of study of a range of economic issues. These include housing, the environment and Europe. Learning about economics involves understanding that all economic decisions involve choices, that economists are expected to provide evidence (usually numerical) and that economists make use in a sceptical and critical way of the accumulated wisdom which has been developed over the years.

Question

How might an economist contribute to the work of:
a a charity such as Oxfam
b Marks & Spencer
c your school or college?

UNIT 2 Key economic concepts

Key concepts covered

- macroeconomics
- microeconomics
- inputs
- outputs
- factors of production
- land
- labour
- capital
- production
- enterprise
- demand
- supply
- output
- households
- firms
- consumption
- subsistence
- surpluses
- trade
- barter
- money
- markets
- specialisation
- division of labour

Introduction

Economists use the same or similar concepts again and again. Most are easy to understand but practice needs to be gained in applying them to a range of different contexts. A broad distinction is drawn between **macroeconomics** which tends to deal with economic events and phenomena at a national and international level, and **microeconomics** which tends to focus on individual markets. This unit introduces five key concepts which can be used to analyse both micro and macro contexts. They are:

- factors of production
- demand and supply
- production possibilities
- circular flow of income
- specialisation and trade.

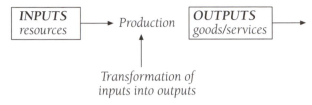

Figure 2.1 Simple input/output model

Factors of production

One way of looking at economics is that it is concerned with a study of how wealth is created. The creation of wealth involves taking resources and transforming them into a product or service which can then be consumed or used in some other way. This process can be illustrated diagrammatically, as is shown in Figure 2.1 with a simple input/output model.

Although simple the model captures a wide range of issues and concepts important to economists. The use of **inputs** encompasses environmental economics as it deals with the relationship between economic activity and the world's resources both renewable and finite. The middle part of the model is concerned with how resources are transformed. Business studies students call this process 'adding value', and it can include complex processes involving the use of highly sophisticated technology, or the more straightforward harvesting and packaging of an agricultural crop. Finally, the output part of the model is the bit concerned with 'shopping' and enjoying or using **outputs** in some ways to improve our lives.

ACTIVITY 1

As a class, produce posters showing the inputs, transformation and outputs involved in the production of a range of different goods and services.

Keep these for future reference. It may be amusing and informative to look at them again later in your course.

Types of resources

The simple input/output model outlined above can be expanded to identify and classify different types of resources. Economists call these **factors of production** and they are illustrated in Figure 2.2.

Figure 2.2 Factors of production

1 Land

Land includes all that which is locked up in the earth's surface. It includes not just land in the sense of farmland, building and factory sites, but what are often called 'natural resources', like minerals, fossil fuels and timber, and what can be grown and harvested. Land includes the products of the seas, the content of our atmosphere and by implication what has yet to be discovered in space.

2 Labour

Labour is a similar catch-all concept, which includes what we as people bring to the production process. These include personal attributes such as strength and particular aptitudes which we can learn and skills which we are able to develop.

3 Capital

Economists refer to **capital** as all those assets which are used to produce goods or services. This category, therefore, includes machinery and factories and equipment which is used to transform 'land' into some particular form of output. The term capital is often used in everyday conversation to describe the money that is used to set up and keep a business going. It is also used to describe savings in shares or such like. All these uses are linked directly or indirectly to the actual **production** process, but economists use the term capital in a more restricted sense. It could be said that they are not interested in money as such but the uses to which it can be put, and especially uses which result in economic activity.

4 Enterprise

This is often described as the fourth factor. Economic activity involves the combination of particular quantities of land, labour and capital to produce something. **Enterprise** is the process of managing and deciding how factors should be confined and to what end. Being enterprising may also involve taking risks and guessing what goods or services are likely to be in demand. It could be argued that the ability and desire to be enterprising is another personal attribute like strength or artistic skills falling under the

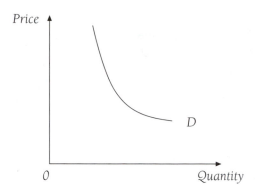

Figure 2.3 Demand curve

heading of labour. Nonetheless, identifying enterprise as a separate factor of production enables economists to emphasise the crucial contribution of deciding how resources are to be used towards the success or otherwise of economic activity.

As indicated in Unit 1, economics is partly about making decisions and choices, and the concept of enterprise recognises that there are different ways of producing the same good or service, and that changing factor inputs can have significant effects on other areas of economic activity.

Demand and supply

As is shown later in this book, the concepts of **demand** and **supply** are at the heart of the analysis of markets. Many people equate economics as a subject with demand and supply. Demand refers to the relationship between how much of a particular good or service people are prepared to buy in relation to different prices. Generally speaking, more will be bought if prices are low and less when prices are high. Demand can therefore be represented by a curve or schedule as shown in Figure 2.3.

Supply, on the other hand, refers to the willingness of producers to supply different amounts

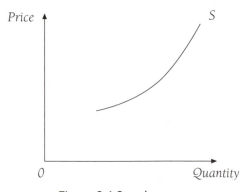

Figure 2.4 Supply curve

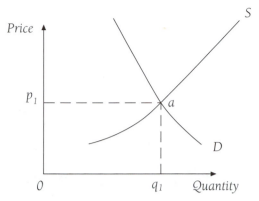

Figure 2.5 Demand and supply curves

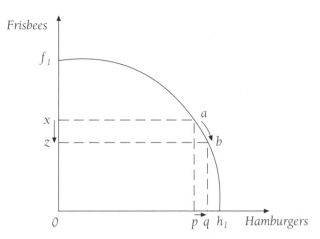

Figure 2.6 Production possibility curve

of a good or service in relation to different prices. Other things being equal, greater profits can be made if a good can be sold for a high price, therefore, producers will wish to produce more of a good if the price is high and vice versa. Supply theory is based on this set of generalisations and supply curves are drawn sloping upwards from left to right. This is shown diagrammatically in Figure 2.4.

Both demand and supply curves can be plotted on the same graph and this is shown in Figure 2.5.

Point a on the diagram is called an equilibrium as at this point demand is equal to supply. The balancing of demand and supply will determine the price that is charged for the product and this is shown as p_1. Similarly, the amount sold is shown as q_1.

ACTIVITY 2

The explanation above is a very brief and simplified version of demand and supply analysis which is developed much further in other parts of the book.

You might like to test the value of this model of how a market works by using it to predict what would happen to the price and sales if the following two separate events occurred:

a   There was a sudden increase in demand.
b   There was a sudden increase in supply.

Tip – show the effects on two separate diagrams. Check whether or not you got the right answers by asking whether or not your predictions make sense. If you are still in doubt the answers are given at the end of this unit.

Production possibilities

Another economic concept which is relatively easy to understand but has widespread applications,

especially for macroeconomics, is that of production possibility curves. As with other models, these are a simplification of how the real world is thought to work. In Figure 2.6 it is assumed that an economy is capable of producing just two goods: hamburgers and Frisbees. If it were to use all its available factors of production to produce hamburgers it would produce h_1. Alternatively, if all resources were devoted to making Frisbees, f_1 would be made. The line between f_1 and h_1 is called a production possibility curve as it shows all the different combinations of Frisbees and hamburgers that could be produced. It also illustrates opportunity cost, i.e. what has to be given up as the result of a particular decision. The movement from a to b on the production possibility curve would indicate an increase in the production of hamburgers from p to q. If all resources are being used this can only be achieved by cutting the production of Frisbees from x to z. This is the opportunity cost of increasing the **output** of hamburgers.

This diagram can be used to represent a variety of changes. Thus, if a new technique were discovered which meant that more Frisbees could be produced with the same amount of resources there would be a movement in the curve from f_1h_1 to f_2h_1 (Figure 2.7).

This new production possibility frontier indicates a higher possible standard of living. This country could now produce both more Frisbees and hamburgers using the same amount of resources.

Point x in Figure 2.7 also illustrates an economy which is not making full use of all its resources. Both more Frisbees and more hamburgers could be produced. This failure to use all resources can be described as unemployment of resources.

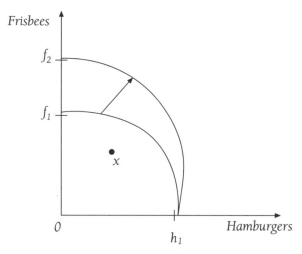

Figure 2.7 Shifting production possibility curve

Circular flow of income

The circular flow of income model is used to understand and analyse how the whole economy works. It is assumed that there are two important components, **households** and **firms**. Households represent the owners of factors of production, and firms represent all those organisations who transform factors of production into goods and services. Households provide firms with factors of production and this is represented by the 1 arrow in Figure 2.8. Firms pay households incomes for the supply of factors shown by the 2 arrow. These incomes are used by households to buy goods and services. This **consumption** is represented by the 3 arrow. Goods and services are produced by firms and these flow to households as shown by the 4 arrow.

This model provides clear insights into the processes that are at work when economies boom or slump. If, for some reason, firms decide to produce more goods, greater supplies of factors of production will be required; firms will have to pay out more in income in order to obtain additional factors of

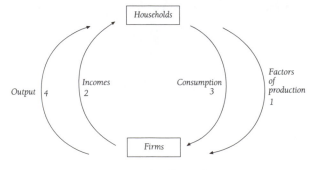

Figure 2.8 Circular flow of income

supply. Households will have more to spend. Their demand for goods and services will rise, firms will produce more, pay out more in incomes and the economy will expand. Unfortunately, this virtuous cycle would not continue indefinitely. Sooner or later some factors of production will become scarce, and firms will be unable to meet the extra demands of households. Prices could start rising. In other words, inflation would be stimulated.

ACTIVITY 3

a   Use the simple circular flow model in Figure 2.8 to describe how a slump might occur.
b   Present your findings to the rest of the class.

Specialisation and trade

It is helpful to have an understanding of how economies have developed and continue to change over time. Much economic activity in the past could be described as **subsistence**, whereby small groups within societies attempted to produce through their own labour sufficient food and basic products in order to survive. The survival of many subsistence economies was fragile. Poor harvests could mean that there would not be enough food. Natural disasters could wipe out possessions and shelter. Many people still live like this and famine and natural disaster are still commonplace.

Subsistence economies which became more successful were able to produce more food and other goods than were needed for immediate survival. They were able to store unused produce, perhaps to provide a buffer against unforeseen disasters. These **surpluses** could also be traded with other groups producing surpluses of other products. **Trade** would therefore permit greater prosperity and higher standards of living. It is likely that early trade would have been by **barter** by which one group of people with a surplus of, say, fish would swap with another group able to produce more grain than it needed. Growing trade would have exposed the limitations and inconvenience of barter and there is considerable archaeological evidence of particular tribes using a variety of more portable commodities to simplify the process of trade. Shells and other small precious items were used as early forms of **money**, and by 3000 years ago coins were being used as we use them today.

The combination of surpluses, money and growing trade provided the foundations for the development of **markets** which, in turn, provided a

The rise and fall of the Incas

'The Spanish defeat of the Inca Empire … was more than simply another conquest. It did not just impose another set of rulers in the succession of Andean civilisations. It tore up by the roots the co-operative agrarian society of the Andean ayllus. The old heart of the Inca Empire in what is now Peru and Bolivia was reorganised for the extraction of precious metals. A way of life that today we would call 'sustainable' was destroyed.' (Neil Macdonald, *The Andes: A Quest for Justice*)

The Incas were a pre-literate 'stone-age' people who didn't even use the wheel. Their great engineering feats were achieved by superb organisation and an enforced labour system called the mita.

The Inca Empire was a rigid hierarchy, a pyramid stretching down from the Inca himself. At the base of this pyramid was a much older Andean social unit; the village clan or ayllu. The ayllus allowed co-operation on large communal tasks, such as the building of an irrigation canal. The Inca formalised this into the mita, but retained the principle of communal welfare.

The Spanish destroyed the ayllu. They divided the land into estates, called encomiendas, each owned by a Spanish encomendero. Indians within each estate had to support their new Lord. The Spanish crown piously instructed the encomenderos to take less from the peasants than the Incas, but in far-away Peru this half-hearted request was ignored, and the encomenderos worked 'their' Indians to death. The only duty required of them in return was to teach Christianity.

Before the Conquest, the Peruvians had few animals except the llama. But as farmers they were unsurpassed. Using the different micro-climates created by varying altitudes, they cultivated a greater range of plants and medicines than anywhere on earth. Beans, 20 varieties of maize, 240 types of potato, chocolate, peanuts, cashews, avocados, pineapples, squashes, peppers, tomatoes … so many common foods come from Peru that it's hard to imagine what we ate in Europe before the Conquest.

The Spanish brought farming techniques developed for Europe's temperate climate to a land of mountains, deserts and jungle, ignoring 12,000 years of local knowledge. They ignored the need for terracing to prevent erosion of steep Andean valleys, or irrigation systems to water the coastal desert. They introduced animals that grazed away fragile pastures. They farmed monocrops – cash crops such as coffee – instead of letting the land recover by mixed planting, crop rotation and fallow years. They destroyed the collective ownership system in which communities farmed both valleys and hillsides at once to guard against floods or droughts at one level.

The effect was disastrous. Today, Peru grows less food than it did before the Spanish arrived.

Mark Mann, *The Gringo Trail* (Somersdale, 1999).

further impetus for the development of economic activities that resulted in economic growth and development.

Trade meant that an individual group no longer needed to attempt to produce all its requirements. Other groups might be better at producing particular commodities. Some could specialise in the production of those products or groups they were best or most efficient at producing. Hence, **specialisation** took place enabling increased trade and the development of larger surpluses.

Similarly, within tribes and societies different tasks were increasingly delegated to particular individuals and groups. Through this **division of labour** people were able to improve their skills and increase productivity such that more was produced. In this way past empires and dynasties grew and developed. Those which were most successful were able to use their surpluses to finance buildings, public works, religious celebrations and the like (see box).

Western dominance

Growth and expansion of specialisation, trade and the amassing of surpluses occurred in western Europe from the twelfth and thirteenth centuries. Agricultural production gradually rose, and European travellers and explorers were able to develop new trade routes with the east. World domination was aided by the voyages of Columbus and the conquests by Europeans of most of the Americas. From the fourteenth century onwards technological advances created an accelerating process of industrial and social change.

The nineteenth and twentieth centuries were characterised by conflicts between nations about world dominance. These continue but it is increasingly apparent that we now live in a global economy. Economic development has shifted from subsistence, to the development of locally based markets, through to international trade and now to a world in which major companies have more economic assets and power than many countries.

Summary

This unit has been devoted to a series of short introductions to major economic concepts which are useful in helping develop an understanding of both how our economy works and how it has developed. The graphical analysis covered in demand and supply and production possibilities are developed in later units. More sophisticated analysis of trade and national economies are also the subject of further consideration. Globalisation is a theme which is considered in greater depth in the second half of this book.

Question

Use each of the following to exemplify and explain possible changes to our economy during the last century.

- Factors of production
- Demand and supply
- Production possibilities
- Circular flow of income
- Specialisation and trade

Answers to Activity 2

a Both price and sales increase.
b Price falls and sales increase.

Microeconomic issues

Key concepts covered

- prices
- demand
- supply
- markets
- profits
- government intervention
- market failure

Introduction

Learning about how markets work is one of the major steps that needs to be undertaken to develop an understanding of economics. In this unit consideration is given to the initial effects of the British beef crisis. These effects are described in two ways: the first using everyday terminology and the second using the more specialist language of economics. Finally, there is an introduction to other features of markets and their importance in our lives.

The British beef crisis described

47 nations still ban our beef

As the smoke clears from French farmers burning barricades in Calais, British beef is still off the menu across the world.

The French government may have been humiliated when European Union scientists declared British beef among the safest in the world, but it remains barred from 47 countries.

The worldwide ban has destroyed a £520m export industry and ruined thousands of farmers. The government has spent £3.5 billion on the BSE crisis since the start in 1996.

Add to that £2 billion in lost exports – a cost which will be added to for many years yet.

On Wednesday EU Commissioner David Byrne will make recommendations to the other 19 commissioners about whether to launch legal action against the ban by France.

But last night the French consumers' association urged its government to keep it in place.

A spokeswoman said: 'History has shown that we are never too prudent.'

Ian Kirby in the *Mail on Sunday*, 14 November 1999

European Countries			
Importer	Metric tonnes 000s	1995 value £m	Now £m
France	81.4	179.0	0
Italy	43.5	126.0	0
Ireland	34.6	52.0	0
Netherlands	20.8	49.4	0
Spain	7.1	17.4	0
Denmark	7.0	12.0	0
Belgium	3.6	10.0	0
Portugal	3.0	7.0	0
Sweden	0.9	3.0	0
Greece	0.4	0.6	0
Germany	0.2	0.6	0
Finland	0.0	0.0	0
Austria	0.0	0.0	0
Total	202.5	457.0	0

Meat and Livestock Commission

Rest of the World			
Importer	Metric tonnes 000s	1995 value £m	Now £m
South Africa	35.2	23.8	0
Mauritius	3.2	4.0	0
Ghana	3.0	2.5	0
Angola	2.3	1.5	0
Malta	2.2	2.2	0
Saudi Arabia	2.2	1.7	0
Hungary	2.1	1.8	0
Philippines	2.1	1.5	0
Gabon	2.1	1.7	0
Hong Kong	1.6	1.8	0
Other Non-EU	15.4	20.5	0
Total	71.5	63.0	0

USA – banned in 1991
Argentina – banned in 1995

Meat and Livestock Commission

In 1996 the UK government announced that there could be a link between a disease in cattle, BSE and its human variant, Creutzfeld-Jakob disease. Most countries immediately banned imports of British beef. The following summarises the immediate effects of the beef crisis:

- Sales of beef products fell.
- Consumers became better informed as to which products contained beef and substituted other products to replace the beef.
- The **prices** of beef products fell.
- Food retailers devoted less shelf space to beef products.
- Some groups of people called for a total ban on beef sales.

■ Butchers and meat wholesalers bought less beef.

■ Farmers sold fewer cows.

These were some of the initial responses to the emergence of new information about eating beef and health.

A whole range of other consequences occurred. Cattle are not only raised to provide beef. The production of male cows is partly a by-product of milk production. If fewer beef cattle are demanded, fewer calves are likely to be born and this may mean that less milk will be produced. Similarly, the supply of other British produced by-products such as leather, and cat food, and old-fashioned glue and fertilisers could have been reduced. There was less **demand** for straw, silage, and veterinary products. The prices of all these products tended to fall.

The repercussions of the beef crisis went on. The fall in demand for meat products also meant that there was a fall in demand for workers who are involved in the production of beef and related products. Again, generally speaking, if the demand for something falls it would be reasonable to expect that the price of those items would also fall. Thus, wages of farm workers fell. Similarly, the incomes of farmers specialising in beef production fell. These effects were not contained within the UK. The initial health warnings were known worldwide. Consumers elsewhere responded with reduced consumption of beef and related products. Those areas of the world dependent upon beef production suffered.

In the preceding analysis of the immediate responses to the beef crisis only one aspect or side of the problem has been considered. Consumers did not simply eat less beef, they switched to alternative products. Some switched to lamb and pork while others gave up meat eating and became vegetarians. The increase in demand for these products had similar but opposite repercussions to those outlined earlier. The demand for lamb rose leading to a rise in price of lamb, an increase in **supply** of lambs, an increase in supply of related products like wool, and an increase in demand for hay, sheep concentrate, veterinary products and the like. Sheep workers and farmers could have become better off.

In short, a complex set of interrelated events was set off.

This example may be considered to be somewhat extreme but it takes little imagination to realise that every minute of every day in every part of the world people's behaviour changes for a whole variety of reasons. These changes have impacts that are far ranging and difficult to predict.

The beef crisis from an economist's perspective

Economists have developed ways of getting a better understanding of complex chain reactions such as these. The principal way in which the beef crisis has been analysed is by reference to what might occur in markets. Economists visualise the effects of the beef health crisis in terms of its impact on a whole series of different but interconnected markets.

The original impact of the health warning was in the market for beef products. That in itself is made up of a whole series of smaller markets for a range of individual products. Any market consists of three elements:

■ buyers

■ sellers

■ some means by which these two groups might meet.

Buyers are generally expected to try to get as much of something as possible for as little as possible. Sellers want to sell as little of something for as much as possible and the market is simply the place where buyers and sellers attempt to make a deal. In most markets, making a deal involves arriving at a mutual agreement as to 'the right price'. In the case of rump steaks butchers will cut their prices until they can sell all or most of their steaks. Buyers or customers will tend to buy more steaks if they become cheaper. In this way the actions and the objectives of both buyers and sellers will determine the price of rump steaks.

A fall in the price of rump steaks will, in turn, have an impact on a whole range of related markets. As was indicated earlier, if this is part of a broad switch away from beef products, falling prices will act as stimuli for changes in other markets. For example, meat retailers will stock more alternatives to beef products, dead-weight and live-weight prices of cows will fall, milk may cost more, chicken may become more expensive and eggs may become cheaper. Silage may go down in price while hay gets cheaper.

These price changes are also significant because both **profits** and incomes in particular jobs are tied up with the prices of the goods or commodities in question. Falling prices and sales, other things being equal, will mean falling profits or surpluses, while rising prices and increasing sales will mean increasing profits.

Changing profit levels are also very significant especially in economies in which many economic decisions are taken by privately owned and run firms.

Such businesses require some level of profit in order to survive. Successful businesses are often those that make the highest level of profits. Businesses which go to the wall often do so because they are not profitable. Business people in both large and small firms are often motivated to increase profits, and one way to do this is to move into businesses in which profits are likely to rise and move out of those businesses which are expected to be less profitable.

Thus, changing prices lead to changing levels of profit and these will lead to the expansion of more profitable industries and the contraction of those which are less profitable. Seen in this way markets can be visualised as pulsating, changing and dynamic. Any shocks to this system of interconnected and interrelated mechanisms will cause ripples and waves of further changes.

Market failure and government intervention

Market changes such as those associated with the beef crisis are real and painful and life changing. Jobs are gained and lost. There are few people in this country who over the past decade have not experienced or known others who have suffered unemployment. Others have experienced vast improvements in living standards. We are not victims of fate, but rather, subject to the effects of the economic mechanisms and forces which affect our lives.

As was indicated earlier, markets are not necessarily benign institutions. They are social constructions. They have been made by people, and people make them work. Some people benefit. Others don't. The outcomes of some market solutions are seen in our kind of society as being desirable while others are not. Thus, it is likely that most people in Britain value the choice and chance of a possible bargain provided by the major food retailers. They operate in a range of related markets and a strong element of competition does something to ensure that prices are kept down, improved customer service is provided and that product improvements take place.

However, most people in this country would recoil from the idea that health care should be marketed in much the same way that supermarkets sell cola, soap powder or cat food. Would we be better off if doctors charged for their services? Would the population like the opportunity to choose between hospital beds provided at budget prices by, for example, Kwik Save, or appreciate the high level of service provided at a higher price by, say, Marks & Spencer? To many

people the application of market solutions to questions of health care would be unacceptable. The logic of such an approach would be that if you were too poor you would get inferior or no treatment, and if doctors and hospitals failed to make expected levels of profit, they would be shut down.

Such callousness is not currently acceptable in British society and **government intervention** takes place to change the way in which the health market might otherwise work. Health services still have to be paid for, but for many they are financed by general taxation and are free to whoever needs them. This system doesn't mean that there is still not a problem caused by finite resources and unlimited wants. Decisions still have to be made as to who gets what. In the National Health Service queuing is used to keep demand and supply in balance. Cynics might argue that if the queues are long enough potential patients might die before they receive treatment.

As is demonstrated in later sections of this book, there are many other examples where **market failure** occurs. Failing in the sense that market solutions are not always socially acceptable. The remedy that is usually applied in circumstances of market failure is government intervention, and because this occurs in all modern economies, economists are also keen to study both the causes and effects of such actions.

ACTIVITY 1

Research task. Find out as much as you can about recent changes in the beef market.
a Who has suffered most?
b Who has gained most?
c Has the government intervened wisely?

Summary

This unit has considered the ever-changing world of economics with which most people are familiar. The same issue of the dynamic effects of changing patterns of demand for beef products has been described into two slightly different ways. The first relied on an intuitive understanding of some of the economic forces which affect us. Greater emphasis was given in the second description to the concepts of the market, price and profits. The end of the unit considered social aspects of the working of markets including the concepts of market failure and government intervention.

Question

Choose one of the following:

a recent rises in the price of crude oil

b the merger of Glaxo and SmithKline Beecham

c an intensification of the war in Chechnya

d any other significant contemporary event.

Produce a written report outlining what economic outcomes might occur. Present your findings to the rest of your class.

C3.1(b), C3.3

UNIT 4 Macroeconomic issues

Key concepts covered

- command economy
- free market economy
- mixed economies
- infrastructure
- privatisation
- barter
- inflation
- unemployment
- balance of payments
- economic growth

Introduction

This unit is devoted to an examination of some of the issues relating to societies undergoing major change in their political and economic systems. Eastern European countries have all been affected by the collapse of the USSR and communist political systems which occurred in the late 1980s and early 1990s. The Czech economy has been chosen for closer study as an example of transformation from a communist-run command economy to one in which much greater importance is attached to the private ownership of resources and the development of a market based economy.

The main features of command and free market economies are outlined. This is followed by a summary of the Czech Republic's historical and geographical contexts, an examination of the problems facing the Czech economy in transition and an introduction to macroeconomic measures to assess progress.

Command, market and mixed economies

Economists use the distinction between market and command economies to highlight differences between the economic systems favoured by communist-run states and those more common in the west. A pure **command economy** has the following features:

- All resources are owned by the state.
- The state is responsible for deciding what is to be produced, how it is to be produced and who consumes production.

A pure **free market economy** is completely different:

- all resources are owned by individuals
- there is no government intervention
- economic decisions are taken by individual households
- markets bring together these individual decisions and determine what is actually produced and who consumes production.

In practice, there have been few, if any, examples of countries which have adopted totally free or command economies. Most economies are **mixed economies** and what differs is the amount of government intervention. Thus, about 30 per cent of the output of the US economy is determined by government and the remainder by markets. In the UK and other western European countries governments determine 40–50 per cent of national output and in North Korea 90 per cent.

In practice, command economies have been shown to:

- be effective in times of national crisis, for example the British economy was a command economy during World War II
- be capable of transforming backward economies, for example the USSR in the 1930s
- have the potential to be more equal and fair.

However, the failure of command systems to survive in the late twentieth century indicated that these possible gains can only be met at enormous social and economic costs, including the following:

- Personal freedoms are sacrificed.
- Individual consumer demands are not met.
- Economic planning is bureaucratic, complicated and often inefficient.
- Political considerations dominate economic decision-making.

ACTIVITY 1

What features of the UK economy are characteristic of a command economy, and what features are characteristic of a free market economy?

Figure 4.1 Location of the Czech Republic within Europe

The Czech Republic: historical and geographic context

The Czech Republic, comprises the historic regions of Bohemia, Moravia, and part of Silesia, in central Europe (see Figure 4.1). It is bordered on the north by Poland, on the east by Slovakia, on the south by Austria, and on the west and north by Germany. Formerly part of Czechoslovakia, the Czech Republic emerged as an independent republic on 1 January 1993.

Until World War I Czechoslovakia was part of the Austro–Hungarian Empire. Although there had been a nationalist movement since the middle of the nineteenth century, independence was delayed until 1918.

The new state prospered but was weakened by tensions between Czechs and Slovaks and other ethnic groups, including 3 million Germans. When Hitler seized power in 1933 he demanded that self-government be given to these Germans. Germany invaded Austria in 1938 and forced the Czechs into giving up large parts of their country. They were eventually invaded by the Germans having received no help from the British or French who were meant to be their allies. After World War II Czechoslovakia turned more to the USSR for protection.

Elections were held in 1946 and the communists won a third of the seats in government. During the next two years of great instability the communists took more and more power. Opponents were killed or exiled. Industries were nationalised. The state took

over education, and the media. Christians were persecuted. Land was taken over by collectives and closer and closer links were formed with the USSR.

In the 1950s Czechoslovakia became one of the most highly centralised and repressive eastern European countries. There was no private ownership of any resources. The state was all-powerful. Russian troops were used to put down any resistance, and occupied the country from 1968. In spite of the oppression various groups argued for greater freedom. The power of the USSR declined in the 1980s and in November 1989 the communist government was finally overthrown in a bloodless coup known as the 'velvet revolution'. On 1 January 1993 separate Czech and Slovak republics were created.

The Czech Republic: from command to market economy

Changing from a command to a market-based economy involved many challenges. These can be identified under the following headings:

- Ownership.
- **Infrastructure**.
- Competition.

Ownership of resources

Prior to 1989 all resources were owned by the state and controlled through a series of state-owned companies. One of the first tasks of the democratic government was to develop a programme of **privatisation** – the process by which ownership of resources is transferred from the state to private individuals. This is being achieved through the following three programmes:

1 Loans have been provided to enable workers in small businesses to buy the companies for whom they worked.
2 All citizens have been entitled to a number of vouchers which can be turned into shares in companies formally owned by the state.
3 The government has attempted to find foreign partners to be involved in and/or take over large Czech companies. In this way, vehicle manufacturer Volkswagen has taken over Skoda, Daewoo (South Korean) owns 51 per cent of shares in Avia, a truck manufacturer, and Bass the British brewers own Staropramen.

These policies have been partially successful, but the Czech government has been worried about the extent of foreign ownership, and the dangers of social unrest arising from the fundamental changes. It has, therefore, maintained ownership of some companies, including banks, and has kept some businesses going which have made huge losses. Some economists would argue that the process of privatisation has not gone far enough and that there needs to be more economic reform.

Infrastructure

Under communist rule priority was given to investment in those infrastructure projects that were considered to be politically important. Thus, the new Czech Republic has inherited a relatively effective system of public transport, reasonably equipped and run schools, and good levels of health care.

On the other hand, the state tolerated and ignored harmful externalities such as pollution. Waste and various effluents have polluted both land and rivers. Most electricity was produced by coal-fired power stations whose emissions have caused acid rain in many parts of the country. Atmospheric pollution is a major problem in cities like Prague. Similarly, there was little incentive to modernise and improve key areas of the economic structure. Road and communication links with western European countries were poor as most trade was directed towards the USSR in the east.

The communists left a legacy of under investment in key areas of the economy, and this has placed pressure on the democratic government to find ways of financing infrastructure improvements.

Competition

Under communism the Czech economy was largely insulated from competitive forces both at home and abroad.

Imports and exports were controlled by the state. Although communist rule had been brutal and oppressive the Czech economy had made some progress in the 1950s to 1970s. As with other east European countries international trade was dominated and controlled by the USSR which favoured the development of **barter**. Thus Czech beer, cars and trucks were swapped for buses from Hungary, and oil and gas from the USSR. These deals tended to be made on terms dictated by the USSR. Trade with the West had occurred. This included Skoda cars, chemical products and beer.

Nonetheless, the ending of communist control and the break up of the USSR has fundamentally changed Czech patterns of international trade. Western companies can now freely export to the new

republic, and Czech firms need to find new markets for their products. This exposes them to international competition and helps illustrate some of the weakness of the old command economy:

■ Workers had little or no motivation to be productive or quality conscious.

■ There were few incentives for workers or managers to show initiative.

■ Managers had little experience of dealing with the challenges and risks of the market place.

■ Investment in modern technology had been poor.

On the positive side, skill and education levels were high by eastern European standards, and labour costs were low.

The Czech government hoped that a mixture of foreign investment, the development of business skills and improvements to education and training would all contribute to the increased competitiveness of the economy.

Have the Czechs succeeded?

The success of the new democratic governments can be judged by how well the economy has performed. The following are key indicators of economic performance:

■ Inflation.

■ Unemployment.

■ Balance of payments.

■ Economic growth.

Inflation

Inflation or rising prices has been a major problem in most of the former communist states. When they were command economies, governments set most prices. In this way the Czech government kept the price of basic foodstuffs, public transport, and rents very low. Items considered to be luxuries were expensive. Wages were fixed by the government. The ending of price controls, and the creation of freely operating markets, coupled with shortages of goods and services in high demand, were all potentially inflationary. In countries such as Russia prices rose by as much as 1000 per cent per annum.

Inflation was a potential problem because if it was allowed to get out of hand the prices of exports would rise very quickly, making them unattractive to foreign buyers. Also those people on low and fixed incomes would be faced with hardship and suffering.

Unemployment

As with inflation, unemployment did not exist in communist times. All those of working age were given a job. State-owned companies produced not according to demand but in response to orders from the Ministry of Economics. Many companies employed far too many workers by western standards.

The shift to a market-based economy meant that newly privatised companies were exposed to competition. There was little to stop imports coming in from abroad. As with inflation, unemployment posed a big threat both to the economy and social stability.

Balance of payments

The balance of payments is a financial record of all flows of money coming in and out of a country. In communist times these would be strictly controlled by the government. In the absence of such controls the Czech economy could have been subject to a balance of payments deficit. Imports of attractive consumer goods could have flooded into the country. Given the disruption to traditional Czech markets in eastern Europe, export earnings would have fallen, creating a potential deficit. This could have led to a balance of payments crisis and increasing foreign debt.

Economic growth

This is the main measure of how well or badly an economy is doing. Economic growth refers to the change in national income usually measured over yearly intervals. National income is a measure of how much wealth has been created. If an economy is doing well it is likely to have growth rates of anything over 2.5 per cent. If the rate is negative the economy is actually in decline and people generally are becoming worse off (see Table 4.1).

Table 4.1 The performance of the Czech economy

	1995	1996	1997
Inflation	9.1%	8.8%	8.5%
Unemployment	2.9%	3.5%	5.2%
Balance of payments (current account) (US$ millions)	−1369	−4292	−3155
Economic growth	5.9%	4.1%	1.0%
Foreign debt (US$ billions)	16.5	20.8	21.0
Base interest rate	9.5%	10.5%	13.0%

A C T I V I T Y 2

Use the data in Table 4.1 to assess the progress of the Czech economy in its transformation from a command economy

Summary

The communist-run Czech state was very highly centralised. The government owned all resources. The population was supplied with a range of services which ensured that education, public transport, sport and culture were well provided. However, individual freedoms were limited and there were few incentives for individuals or government owned companies to improve or become quality conscious.

The sudden collapse of the state-run economic system could have led to rapid and difficult social change but the democratic governments have tried to minimise social disruption, caused by excessive inflation or widespread unemployment. Data on the performance of the Czech economy indicate that some economic progress has been made.

This mixture of commentary and numerical data is typical of macroeconomic issues which are dealt with in much greater detail in later sections of this book.

Question

Use electronic and other data sources to research and identify the key features of the transformation policies of another eastern European economy. Compare its economic performance to that of the Czech Republic.

N3.1, N3.3

Section 1 questions

Essay questions

1 Suggest how an economist might advise:
   a a local council on its responses to a planning application to build new houses on a large green-field site (8)
   b a company planning on the provision of a wide range of budget-priced organic products (8)
   c a trade union representing media workers worried about the merger of companies to create a global communications network. (9)

Project

Select any of the issues identified above and collect

copies of relevant news stories. What do these tell you about different responses to this issue?

Multiple-choice questions

1 A man bought a car for £8000, but never uses it. A similar car would now cost £9500 new, but his would fetch only £3500 second hand. His present opportunity cost of owning the car is
A £1500
B £3500
C £6000
D £8000

2 The diagram shows a straight line production possibility boundary.

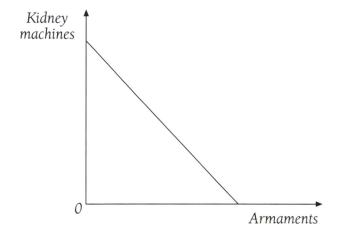

It indicates that, as more armaments are produced, the cost of producing armaments in terms of kidney machines
A falls
B rises
C remains constant
D exceeds the benefits

3 Economics is concerned with
A studying how unlimited resources are or may be used for the satisfaction of unlimited wants
B indicating the social/political goals which limited productive resources should be used to achieve
C studying how unlimited wants are or may be met by varying allocations of relatively scarce resources
D indicating the social/political environment in which the best use of the available productive resources will be made

4 The diagram shows the production possibility frontiers for an economy.
The movement from point X to point Y could represent

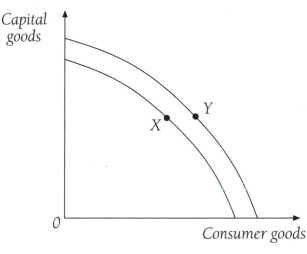

A the use of previously unemployed resources
B reallocation of resources from producing capital goods to producing consumer goods
C an improvement in technology which results in more consumer and capital goods being produced
D an increase in efficiency in the production of consumer goods

5 Opportunity cost means
A the price of a good
B what has to be given up as the result of buying a particular product
C the minimum cost of production
D what a product should cost

6 A demand curve is drawn to indicate
A that demand rises as price rises
B that demand rises as price falls
C that demand falls as price falls
D that demand rises as costs rise

7 The simple circular flow of income model indicates that rising incomes will be associated with
A falling output
B falling demand for factors of production
C rising unemployment
D rising consumption

8 Which of the following would you most associate
   with a subsistence economy?
A Barter
B Regular production of surpluses
C Extensive use of money
D Division of labour

9 Which of the following is least likely to happen as
   a result of the BSE crisis?
A Increases in sheep farmers' income
B Increases in demand for organic products
C Increases in prices for agricultural machinery
D Decreases in agricultural rents

10 Which is not usually a feature of a command
   economy?
A Government ownership of resources
B Black markets
C Share ownership
D Shortages of consumer goods

Section 2
Markets

Introduction

This section is devoted to an examination of how markets work and involves further consideration of demand and the various factors which cause demand to change. Supply is treated in a similar way and, finally, demand and supply are brought together to illustrate how markets might work in a range of contexts to determine both the price of goods and the level of sales.

UNIT 5 Demand

Key concepts covered

- wants
- effective demand
- demand
- model building
- substitute
- complements
- tastes
- disposable income
- normal goods
- inferior goods

Introduction

This unit is devoted to a more detailed treatment of demand and is illustrated by reference to the housing market. Those factors (variables) which influence demand are identified and explained. They are:

- price
- prices of other goods
- incomes
- tastes of consumers.

Economists use graphical analysis to help understand demand and this approach is used to predict how the demand for a good or service will be affected by changes in the variable identified above.

The housing market

. . . the housing market continues to recover with prices on average 10% higher across Britain than a year ago. The recovery in London has been particularly dramatic with some prime areas seeing price increases of up to 14.5% in three months. As parts of the capital experience chronic shortages of available properties, some agents have been exploiting desperate buyers, according to the Office of Fair Trading . . .

Housing is a key market in the economy. For many people spending on housing is the largest single item in their budget. Rapid fluctuations in house prices in the late 1980s and early 1990s are thought to have had a significant effect on consumer confidence, and spending on a wide range of products. Predicting likely future trends on house market prices is useful not only to those involved in buying and selling houses but also to a wide range of other interest groups. This unit introduces how economists might seek to analyse demand and shows how this way of thinking provides an understanding of those factors which affect the price and sales of houses.

The housing market is like any other market. It is a notional place where buyers and sellers meet in order to make a transaction or transactions. In this case the potential transaction will involve someone selling a house and receiving a (large) payment in return. This market is notional in the sense that it is not necessary for buyers and sellers actually to meet. It is possible to conceive of a situation in which an estate agent and solicitor handle all aspects of the transaction and that the buyer and the seller would not have to meet each other. Each market tends to have its own characteristics and it is often helpful to ask a simple question – if a person wanted to buy or sell something, in this case a house, where would he or she go? The most obvious answer in this case is to an estate agent. Estate agencies exist to bring together buyers and sellers, communicating through advertisements, shop fronts, and a wide array of other promotional techniques.

In the UK estate agents earn revenue, and hence potential profits from the commissions they charge house sellers. This encourages them to try to get as high a price as possible for each sale. At the time the opening extract was written the demand for housing in parts of London was rising more quickly than the supply, and this enabled some estate agents to encourage sellers to ask for higher prices for their property. A government agency – the Office for Fair Trading – was concerned that this practice of forcing up house prices exploited buyers.

Estate agencies exist to bring together buyers and sellers

Wants and effective demand

One of the first stages in developing a fuller understanding of how markets work is to develop a good working knowledge of how both buyers and sellers of houses go about their business in an attempt to 'make a deal'. The focus of this unit is on buyers and it is important to establish a clear definition of this term, which can mean different things in different contexts. Economists consider that it is very important to distinguish between those customers who might like to purchase a particular good or service and those who actually have the means to do so. The general aspirations of people in terms of what they might like to have are called **wants**. While the size and characteristics of people's wants are important, economists focus their attention on examining consumer behaviour which combines two related factors:

1 wants
2 the ability to purchase the means by which such wants might be satisfied.

If consumers meet these criteria, then they are said to exercise **effective demand** – the 'effective' refers to the ability to pay. This term is usually shortened simply to **demand**.

In the example of the housing market, being able to get a mortgage is likely to be a crucial factor in making an individual's demand effective. Currently, anyone living in London and earning less than £25 000 a year is unlikely to qualify for a mortgage large enough to buy a house or flat.

Demand theory

Demand theory is based on a simple generalisation about customer behaviour that has been observed for centuries, that most people would regard as 'common sense'. Generally speaking, if a good or service becomes more expensive, consumers are less likely to buy it. Rising house prices *are likely* to depress demand and lower prices *are likely* to provide a boost to sales. Economists strive to be both precise and accurate by developing the skill of saying exactly what they mean and no more – the words 'are likely' are very significant as they emphasise the caution needed when broad generalisations about consumer or any other kind of economic behaviour are made. More thorough research of the housing market is likely to show that cutting house prices does not always bring an increase in demand. Indeed, in the example given at the beginning of the unit it may be possible to observe rises in house prices happening at the same time as rising demand. Economists will want to try and untangle cause and effect, and often use phrases like 'other things being equal' in an attempt to freeze out or exclude the impact of other factors. Thus, it is possible to find examples of demand rising in response to an increase in price but, in general, if a particular brand of make-up, washing powder, or banking service becomes cheaper sales are likely to increase. On the other hand, rising prices are likely to lead to reduced demand.

The next stage in developing an understanding of demand represents an attempt to build up a model which can be used to represent consumer behaviour in relation to house buying. **Model building** is part of the essential toolkit of economists. In this case a useful model would be one which could be used to predict how consumers in general would behave and react to changes in various factors. Its value can then be assessed by testing its ability to predict what might happen.

Modelling can provide a powerful tool as it is likely that the factors which influence the demand for house buying are likely to be similar to those factors which affect consumer behaviour for other products and services. Price has already been identified as a key influence. Also, the discussion about effective demand included consideration of the ability to pay for a particular product or service. Thus, consumer income is also likely to be important. However, a model developed in which these were the only two factors thought to influence demand would be a gross simplification of consumer behaviour and would be of little use in understanding the complexities of the housing or any other market.

Traditional demand theory

The processes outlined above could be applied to each and every product and service which exists. Fortunately, we can take advantage of research, argument and discussion in which economists have already engaged. Practically all economists agree on the validity of the model outlined in the next section as being applicable to all markets. As long as it is recognised that economists themselves are human and capable of making mistakes, it makes sense to take advantage of the consensus which suggests that four sets of factors (variables) are always likely to be important in determining the demand for a particular product or service. These are:

■ the price of the good or service in question
■ the price of other goods and services

ACTIVITY 2

a Consider the demand for housing. List all those factors which are likely to influence an individual's decision whether or not to buy a new house.

b Compare your list with that of another student in your group.

c Modify your list to make it apply to both of you.

d Compare your joint list with that of another pair of students.

e Work on your own or in groups and attempt to prioritise those factors you have identified. This is likely to involve argument and discussion and you may have to compromise. Such compromise might be impossible and your group may produce a number of different prioritised lists.

f Take each factor on your list and try to identify those additional factors which are likely to affect those originally chosen.

g What conclusions can you reach about the demand for housing?

This process illustrates the first stage of model building, and, as in any other science, this should be followed by research to test the validity of such initial (or *a priori*) thinking

h Design a questionnaire and survey potential house buyers to check on the validity of the conclusions you reached in h above. This is called empirical research.

■ consumers' tastes
■ consumers' incomes.

The price of the good or service

The potential impact of changes in the prices of houses on their demand has already been discussed. Thus, if a good becomes more expensive demand is likely to fall, and if price falls then demand is likely to rise.

The price of other goods and services

Clearly, the decision to buy or not to buy a house is not made simply on the basis of its price. As earlier analysis showed buying a house is not a straightforward decision. What kind of house? New? Second hand? What about the option of renting? Houses can be rented in the public, private and voluntary sectors. Even if the decision is narrowed down a prospective buyer will then have to choose which individual house meets his or her needs. Changes in house rents are likely to have an impact on demand for houses to buy. In this context rented property is described by economists as a **substitute** good. If rents were to rise it is likely that the demand for rented accommodation will fall. On the other hand, higher rents would lead to an increase in demand for houses to buy.

In some cases the demand for one good is likely to be jointly related to the demand for another good. In this case a fall in the cost of a mortgage might lead to a rise in demand for mortgages and this might in turn lead to an increase in demand for houses to buy. Such a pair of goods are known as **complements**.

Consumers' tastes

This term is used by economists to capture a whole range of other influences on demand. At one level we all like and dislike different things and these personal preferences are likely to affect what we wish to buy. These individual differences are hard for economists to model, but it is easier to identify broad trends and changes in **tastes**. There is widespread evidence that, unlike many other Europeans, the British place great importance on home ownership in preference to living in rented accommodation. This cultural difference might be attributable to the advertising and promotional activities of companies like Bovis, Wimpey and Westbury Homes which each spend a great deal to promote and advertise new housing developments.

Tastes and social influences are likely to have a big impact on the demand of individuals for different types of housing. Some areas are considered by some people to be better than others are. Some house buyers will choose to live in a particular area because they perceive local schools to be better. Other areas will be considered by some to be 'rough'. The importance of these factors can have a big impact on potential demand for particular houses in particular areas.

The concept of tastes can be stretched in this context to include 'consumer confidence'. Buying a house is such a major decision that it is affected by what has been called the 'feel good factor', which is a shorthand way that journalists have developed to describe the positive psychological frame of mind which may have more influence over the decision to buy a house than any other factor.

Consumer income

As indicated earlier, the ability to buy a house will be strongly influenced by the ability of a potential customer to pay. The main factor affecting this is likely to be income. Economists further refine this and use the term **disposable income** to describe the amount of money available for spending. Rising incomes are likely to increase both the demand for houses in general and for particular types of houses. As demand is likely to rise as incomes rise housing is described as a **normal good**.

Other products are classified as **'inferior' goods**, in the sense that as consumer incomes rise demand falls, and vice versa. Terraced houses in some areas of northern cities can be described in this way. As owners of such houses become better off they are more likely to purchase more expensive substitutes.

In summary, economists usually analyse the demand for a particular good or service in terms of four variables. Each of these variables can be analysed in further detail (see Table 5.1).

Although most of the information in Table 5.1 will appear to be common sense, what has been described is a complex set of relationships. It is difficult to model or analyse phenomena which are subject to many influences which may be changing all the time. This is described as a multi-variate situation. In order to try to make sense of what could be potentially confusing economists make a judgement, based on evidence, about which variable is most important. This process of identification is called 'making a simplifying assumption'. In terms of the analysis of demand it is assumed that price is the most important variable. The significance of this assumption is shown in the following section which shows how economists use graphs to make their model building clearer, and visual. This assists analysis.

ACTIVITY 2

Compare the outcomes of your attempts at this first stage in model building with those developed over the years by economists.
a Did you reach the same conclusions?
b Is your way of looking at consumer demand better than that traditionally presented by economists?

Note: There is a tendency for students to take for granted the accuracy of what they read in books or are told by teachers. Remember that economists, however experienced, do not have all the answers. Economics is dynamic and ever changing. It is quite possible that in this activity or others you will reach conclusions or make discoveries that do not fit with economics as presented in this text or others. Don't assume that you are wrong. In a social science the only way of resolving who may be right and who may be wrong is by reference to evidence.

ACTIVITY 3

Choose another market and use the model described above to present a written analysis of the relative importance of various factors influencing the demand for the product or service.

Table 5.1 Analysis of variables

Demand for a given good depends on:	Variable	Subset of variable	Effect on demand of good or service in question
	Price	Increase Decrease	Fall in demand Rise in demand
	Prices of other good	Substitutes Complements	Decrease in demand if price of substitute increases and vice versa Increase in demand if price of a complement falls and vice versa
	Incomes	Normal goods Inferior goods	Demand increases as income rises and vice versa Demand decreases as income rises and vice versa
	Tastes	Favourable change Unfavourable change	Increase in demand Decrease in demand

Demand curves

Economists use graphs to help illustrate and analyse changes in markets. Table 5.2 has been derived from market research undertaken by an estate agent to assess the likely demand for particular houses assuming that the price that consumers might pay is the most important factor influencing demand. The table shows what appears to be a relationship between sales of houses and different prices.

Table 5.2 House price data

House price £000	Anticipated enquiries per month
40	30
50	20
60	10
70	2
80	0

The numerical data can also be illustrated in the form of a graph. Figure 5.1 shows that if the price is £50 000 the quantity demanded will be 20 houses. A price decrease from £50 000 to £40 000 will lead to a rise in demand from 20 to 30 houses. Economists describe a change such as this as a movement along a curve.

The demand curve can also be used to illustrate another concept of particular importance to both economists and business people. In Figure 5.2 p_1 is a price which would result in sales of q_1. Multiplying the price by the quantity gives the total amount of spending or revenue on a particular good. The shaded rectangle, therefore, indicates the revenue

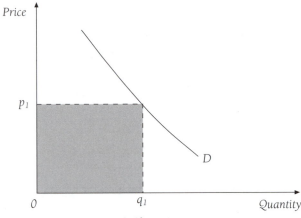

Figure 5.2 Changing revenue

that would be earned by the suppliers of this good if it sold at a price of p_1.

Note: Graphs are useful ways in which numerical data can be represented and are part and parcel of an economist's toolkit. In this case it is the convention to measure price on the vertical axis and possible levels of demand on the horizontal. Students of maths and the physical sciences might recognise that this approach differs to that with which they are familiar.

The graph in Figure 5.2 can be used to model consumer behaviour, and to answer a series of 'what if?' questions. What if the prices of substitutes or complements change? What if incomes change? What if tastes change?

Substitutes

A change in the rents of privately owned accommodation may have a direct effect on the demand for houses to buy. If rents rise, it is likely that demand for houses at each price level would increase. This is illustrated in Table 5.3.

Table 5.3 Demand for housing

Price of houses to buy	Demand for houses to buy	Demand for houses to buy given a 20% increase in rents in the private sector
£35 000	100	120
£40 000	95	116
£45 000	85	100
£50 000	75	80
£55 000	60	64
£60 000	30	32
£65 000	20	21

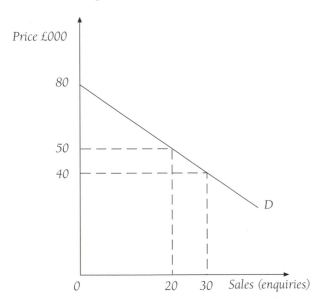

Figure 5.1 Demand curve for houses

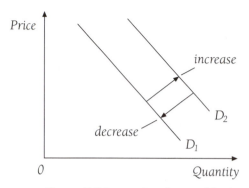

Figure 5.3 Increasing demand for houses

These possible effects can be added to the original graph and the shift to the right indicates that the demand for houses for purchase at all possible prices is likely to increase (see Figure 5.3).

Complements

Buying a house is a complex decision. Houses might be cheap but interest rates high. If interest rates rise mortgage repayments would become more expensive and the demand for houses for purchase will fall. On the other hand, competition between banks and building societies means that a range of discounts in the form of 'cash back offers' and 'discounted fixed rates' are on offer. These represent possible reductions in the cost of borrowing which may result in an increase in demand for houses. These possibilities are illustrated in Figure 5.4, where the shift to the left indicates a decrease in demand and the shift to the right an increase.

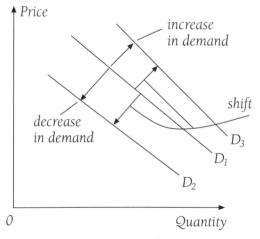

Figure 5.4 Increasing and decreasing demand for houses

Incomes

All available evidence points to the fact that most houses are normal goods. This means that demand is likely to increase as people become better off, and fall if people's incomes drop. The effect would be shown diagrammatically in the same way as in Figure 5.4.

Tastes

The significance of both sociological and psychological factors as important influences on house buyers has already been considered. Economists might describe the purchase of particularly attractive houses as examples of conspicuous consumption. In other words, some people feel that their status is improved if they live in a particular neighbourhood. These subjective factors are used in marketing and promoting houses. New estates are often given country sounding names to give the impression of rural tranquillity. Over the past 20 years there have been increases in demand for houses in rural locations near prosperous urban areas and falling demand for those in poor urban areas.

ACTIVITY 4

Explain and illustrate using graphs what might happen to the demand for country cottages of the following:
   a   rise in price
   b   increase in the price of petrol.
   c   fall in urban land prices.
   d   greater prosperity
   e   growing concerns about the harmful health effects of urban pollution.

Summary

Economists have developed models to analyse consumer behaviour. Demand and supply provide an excellent example of this form of diagrammatic modelling. Economists agree that the demand for any product or service is likely to be affected by changes in its price, the price of other goods, consumer tastes and consumer income. Moreover, there is broad consensus that the price of the good is usually the most important of these variables. Graphs can be used to explore the effects of changes in any of these variables on demand.

Data response question

EMI shares bobbed up almost 2% yesterday, but whether the rise owed more to a report that Germany's Bertelsmann has the British group in its sights or to an uprating by Commerzbank analysts is open to question.

EMI displayed the straightest of bats in responding to the report in *Der Spiegel,* which linked Bertelsmann with EMI or Sony Music.

'We don't comment on these sort of reports,' was the only reaction from EMI's head office . . .

The AOL-Time Warner merger is expected to mean more music being delivered via the net, but Commerzbank Global Equities says the deal has also highlighted the value of consumer content relative to internet distribution.

Music retailers are seeking to sell at CDs at lower prices via the internet, and Commerzbank reckons that 'cutting out the bricks and mortar, the retailer lowers the price and increases record company margins'.

Its note said: 'Lower prices would be more than compensated for by increased volumes.'

Upgrading its investment to 'buy', Commerzbank valued EMI at 698p and said that net alliances or the prospect of EMI content being offered for streaming raises this value to 767p.

Source: Datastream Primark

EMI share price, pence

Mark Milner, 'EMI attracts some upbeat attention' in the *Guardian*, 18 January 2000

1 Use the concepts below to provide possible explanations for fluctuations in the demand for EMI shares between 1998 and 2000.
   a Substitutes
   b Complements
   c Tastes (6 marks)

2 What other factors are likely to influence the demand for EMI shares? (6 marks)

3 What are the implications of expected changes in how music might be sold in the future? (8 marks)

UNIT 6 Demand elasticities

Introduction

This unit further develops an understanding of demand by explaining the concept of elasticity. Elasticity is a measure of responsiveness which has many applications in economics. It measures how much one variable changes in response to a change in another variable. Consideration is give to three types of elasticity of demand, as follows:

- price
- income
- cross.

In 1999 interest rates were at their lowest for over 20 years, yet estate agents reported the market to be sluggish. In other words many people were reluctant to take advantage of the lower price of mortgages to buy houses.

Price elasticity of demand

Economists are not content with the observation that if the price of buying a home falls there is likely to be a rise in demand. They and estate agents like to specify the extent to which demand is likely to change. Economists use the concept of elasticity to measure the responsiveness of one variable to a change in another. Unit 1 considered the response of demand to changes in a number of different variables, but especially to changes in price. The two diagrams in Figure 6.1 show very different responses in demand to identical reductions in price.

In the case of (a) a cut of around 10 per cent in house prices leads to a rise in demand of about 50 per cent. In (b) the same price cut causes a much smaller rise in demand – about 5 per cent. In (a) demand is very responsive to changes in price, whereas in (b) demand is much less responsive. Given the use of the same axis the slope of the demand curve will indicate the degree of responsiveness to changes in price.

It is also possible to be more precise and mathematical about this relationship. As indicated earlier, the slope or gradient of the demand curve indicates its elasticity. This can be represented by the following formula:

Price elasticity of demand (PEd) =

$$\frac{\text{Percentage change in quantity demanded}}{\text{Percentage change in price}}$$

In Figure 6.1(a) the price went down by 10 per cent and demand increased by 50 per cent. Using the formula above:

$$\text{PEd} = \frac{+50}{-10}$$

$$= -5$$

And solving the same formula for (b) would give the following result:

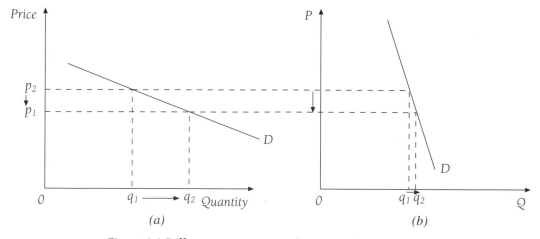

Figure 6.1 Different responses to the same change in price

$$PEd + = \frac{+5}{-10}$$
$$= -0.5$$

These answers or values are called co-efficient and they give an instant insight into the responsiveness of demand for a product to a change in price. Any value which is less than –1, for example –0.6 or –0.2, indicates that demand for the product is not very responsive to changes in price. To be more precise, any given percentage change in the price of the product will result in a smaller proportional change in quantity demanded. Economists describe this kind of demand response as relatively inelastic.

On the other hand, a value which is larger than –1, for example –2.5 or –6, represents a demand which is very responsive to a change in price. The percentage change in quantity demanded for such a product will exceed the percentage change in price. Economists would describe this kind of demand response to be relatively elastic.

ACTIVITY 1

a   What conclusions would you make if you were told that the price elasticity of demand for a product was +2?
b   Is the price elasticity of demand constant along the whole of a straight-line demand curve?
c   What does it mean if the price elasticity of demand for a product is always –1?
d   What would a graph of such a demand curve look like?

(Answers are given at the end of this unit.)

Elasticity and revenue

Understanding about elasticity can help house sellers, especially large companies like Bovis, gauge whether or not price cuts would be an effective strategy. If price elasticity of demand is greater than –1 a cut in price will generate a proportionally larger increase in demand. The additional revenue from increased sales would more than compensate for the smaller revenue gained from each individual house sale. If the price elasticity of demand were less than -1, sales would increase by a smaller percentage, leading to a reduction in revenue from house sales. These two situations are shown in Figure 6.2.

ACTIVITY 2

a   Devise a simple questionnaire designed to find out the price elasticities of demand for:
   i   Bovis or another company producing new homes
   ii   homes in general.
b   Use your questionnaire to collect data from a cross-section of potential house buyers.
c   Present your findings in the form of
   i   graphs
   ii   co-efficients.
d   Complete the activity by explaining your findings, noting any conclusions, and providing a commentary on the reliability of your research methodology.

Why elasticities differ

The demand conditions for no two products are the same and this applies to their price elasticity.

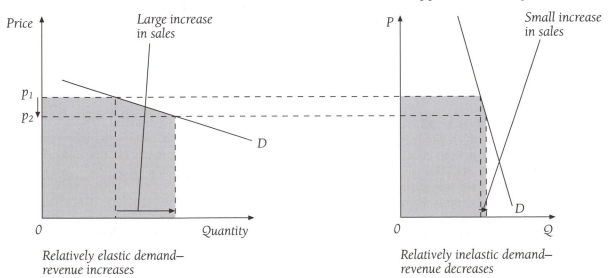

Relatively elastic demand–
revenue increases

Relatively inelastic demand–
revenue decreases

Figure 6.2 Elasticities and revenue

Elasticities will differ according to how the product in question is defined. The demand for specific branded products, such as Bovis homes, is likely to be relatively elastic, whereas the demand for more generic groupings – houses in general – is likely to be less elastic. Once a product has been clearly defined it is likely that the following factors will have the strongest effect on the elasticity of demand for a product:

- the existence or otherwise of substitutes
- the proportion of disposable income spent on the product in question
- consumer knowledge
- time.

Substitutes

The demand for Bovis homes is likely to be relatively elastic because other companies such as Wimpey produce and market similar products. In other words, more **competition** means more substitutes and greater consumer choice. Thus, the most important factor in influencing price elasticity of demand is whether or not close substitutes exist for the product in question. A substitute is a product which customers are prepared to buy as an alternative to a given product. Greater competition in a given market should lead to greater choice between similar or substitute products which will make the price elasticity of demand relatively elastic.

Some house buyers have a much more restricted choice. The supply of housing in some areas of London is very limited relative to the demand. Houses and flats sell quickly and if job requirements limit living out of London buyers are likely to be forced to pay more. In this case there are few substitutes, and less competition. If estate agents decide to cut prices they are unlikely to create extra 'sales' but, on the other hand, if they were to increase prices desperate house and flat hunters would have to pay up.

Proportion of disposable income spent on the product

If consumers spend only a small fraction of their disposable income on a given product it is probable that they will be less sensitive to changes in the price of that product. Thus, a small change in the price of potatoes is unlikely to have a significant impact on their sales. But buying a house is for most people the largest item of expenditure they are ever likely to undertake, which helps explain why, even if other factors like changes in income are favourable, the decision to buy or not to buy is so much more acute. Thus, the demand for mortgages is likely to be very

sensitive to changes in their price as represented by changes in interest rates.

Customer knowledge/ignorance

Customers will be influenced by changes in the price of a good or service if they have a good knowledge about how prices might have changed and the price of possible substitute goods. House prices in particular areas or for particular types are generally well known. This cannot always be said about the cost of buying a mortgage as banks and building societies often confuse customers by having complicated pricing structures, which often include hidden costs. In other cases, where purchases are infrequent, customers are less likely to know the 'going price'. For example, it would be unrealistic for supermarket shoppers to know in advance the prices of all 15 000 items stocked by the average large supermarket.

Time

If the price of a good or service changes significantly it may take time for customers to adjust their spending to meet the changing circumstances. In the short term customers may be less willing to switch products or services. Over a longer period of time it may become easier for buyers to find alternatives or to change their spending patterns. This will probably not apply to house buyers but it is an important factor in other related purchases. Thus, the price in the UK of domestic fuel oil has fallen over the last three years, yet it takes time and convincing for home owners to switch from other fuels such as gas, especially if heating systems have to be changed.

Income elasticity of demand

This concept is similar to price elasticity of demand. Income elasticity of demand measures the responsiveness of the demand for a product to changes in incomes. It is represented by the following:

Income elasticity of demand =
$$\frac{\text{Percentage change in quantity demanded}}{\text{Percentage change in income}}$$

Note: Only the bottom of the formula is different.

The housing market in the late 1980s was affected significantly by increases in earnings by certain income groups. Cuts in personal taxation, coupled with relatively low interest rates and increasing competition between lenders resulted in a big surge in demand for houses. Incomes of some people rose and their demand for improved housing rose even more. Their income elasticity of demand for houses measured more than 1.

On the other hand, the demand for lower-quality housing in some areas actually fell. The co-efficient for income elasticity of demand would in this case be negative. Economists call goods such as these **inferior goods**. As has been illustrated, changing life styles have a big impact on the degree to which demand for a product or service is likely to be influenced by changes in income. Goods such as social housing, and cars such as Ladas which are associated with poverty are likely to be rejected by those whose income rises, while the demand for goods and services which are perceived to be associated with status is likely to rise in proportion or more than in proportion to changes in income. There may be lags or delays before this response occurs.

Cross elasticity of demand

This further application of the concept of elasticity is used to measure the responsiveness of demand for one good in relation to a change in the price of another. As indicated in Unit 5, two types of these kinds of relationships are useful to economists. Goods, like those produced by two rival building companies, are classified as **substitutes** whereas products and services like houses and mortgages which may be purchased jointly are **complements**.

The formula which is used to work out the co-efficient of **cross elasticity** of demand is similar to those used earlier in this unit.

The cross elasticity of demand for Bovis homes in respect to changes in the prices charged by Wimpey is expressed as follows:

Cross elasticity of demand =

$$\frac{\text{Percentage change in quantity demanded of Bovis homes}}{\text{Percentage change in the price of Wimpey homes.}}$$

Note: The product in question, in this case Bovis homes, will appear on the top half of the equation and whatever is considered to be the potential cause of change goes on to the bottom half of the equation.

In this case it might be reasonable to suggest that if the price of Wimpey homes were to be cut then this is likely to result in a fall in demand by some customers for the Bovis alternative. Thus, a 10 per cent price cut by Wimpey may lead to a fall in demand for Bovis by 20 per cent. Translated into the formula above this means that the cross elasticity of demand is:

$$\frac{-20}{-10}$$
$$= +2.$$

The size of the co-efficient indicates how substitutable the two products are for one another. If there were little brand loyalty and a high degree of customer knowledge the value of the co-efficient would be much larger. If few customers switch house brands it will be smaller.

If two sets of goods are complements, the co-efficient of the cross elasticity of demand of one good in respect of a change in the price of another will always be negative. For example, a fall in the mortgage rate is likely to lead to an increase in the demand for homes. Thus, a cut in interest rates of 1 per cent may lead to a 10 per cent increase in demand for houses giving a value of -10.

The relatively large negative figure would indicate that the demand for houses is very sensitive to changes in the mortgage interest rates. If two goods are complements their co-efficient for their cross elasticities will always be negative and, as with all the other uses of the concept of elasticity, the smaller the value the less responsive the relationship.

ACTIVITY 3

Investigate cross elasticity of demand.
a   Select two clothing brands which you believe to be close substitutes.
b   Devise a suitable questionnaire to collect data to test whether or not you have made a good choice.
c   Select a suitable sampling frame, i.e. one which should give you unbiased results and be large enough for you to draw conclusions.
d   Collect your data.
e   Collate your findings.
f   Present the outcomes of your research.
g   Replicate the above process choosing two goods which you consider to be complements.
h   Discuss the outcomes of your research.

Summary

This unit shows how the different elasticities of demand can be calculated and indicates how the co-efficients can be used in different ways. Larger values always indicate greater degrees of responsiveness of negative and positive values show the direct of particular relationships.

Data response question

This task is based on a question set by the University of Cambridge Local Examinations Syndicate (Cambridge Modular Economics) in a specimen paper in 1994. Study the tables and then answer the questions that follow.

Table A Number of goods vehicles* by size in the UK in 1984 and 1990

Gross vehicle weight in tonnes	Thousands of vehicles	
	1984	1990
3.5–7.5	146.9	166.4
7.5–12	27.1	20.1
12–16	51.7	29.3
16–20	82.3	89.5
20–24	2.0	3.4
24–28	31.5	36.3
28–32	19.2	22.4
32–38	76.4	92.2
All goods vehicles	437.1	459.7

*excludes vehicles under 3.5 tonnes gross vehicle weight

a **i** How has the distribution of the stock of goods vehicles changed between 1984 and 1990? (1)

ii Explain **one** likely effect of these changes on:
- the railways (2)
- the production costs of manufacturing firms. (2)

b **i** For which product group has road's share of the market shown the greatest increase? (1)

ii In which product group has rail increased its share of the market? Has the *volume* of rail freight increased in this product group? Explain your answer. (4)

c **i** Explain what is meant by 'cross-elasticity of demand'. (2)

ii Discuss how cross-elasticity of demand can be applied when a firm is making its choice between road and rail transport. (4)

iii In which commodity group might you expect the highest cross-elasticity of demand? Explain your answer. (4)

Answers to Activity 1

a To get an answer of +2 to the formula PEd = Percentage change in quantity demanded/Percentage change in price would require two negative or two positive values in the equation. Thus + 40/+20, or –30/–15 would give and answer of +2. In the first case a 20 per cent increase in price is associated with a 40 per cent increase in demand, and in the second a 15 per cent fall in price is linked to a 30 per cent fall in quantity demanded. Such relationships are unusual but they can occur. Some firms deliberately raise the price of the products to create an impression of greater quality or higher status. If such strategies succeed increased prices can lead to greater demand and vice versa.

b The answer to this is no. Take three different price changes: one near the top or vertical axis of the demand curve, one in the middle and one near the bottom. Solve the PEd equation for each and you should find that the co-efficient gets small as you move from left to right along the demand curve. In other words, the demand becomes relatively less elastic as you move down the demand curve.

Table B Tonne-kilometres carried by commodity and means of transport 1984 and 1990

Commodity	1984			1990		
	Billion tonne-km	% road	% rail	Billion tonne-km	% road	% rail
Food, drink & tobacco	25.4	98	2	32.8	99	1
Building materials & aggregates	23.2	88	12	12.3	76	24
Coal & coke	9.4	37	63	9.2	46	54
Chemicals & fertilisers	9.4	91	9	9.6	98	2
Iron & steel products	13.0	78	22	11.5	80	20
Other products (inc. crude oil)	47.0	69	31	71.0	92	8
All commodities	127.4	83	17	146.4	89	11

Source: Central Statistical Office, *Transport Statistics*, 1992

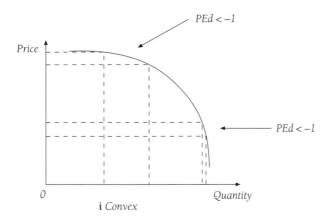

i *Convex*

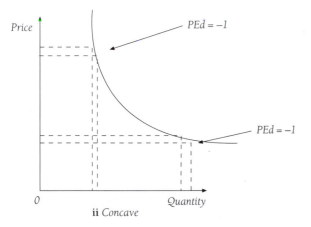

ii *Concave*

Figure 6.3

c Working back through the equation to get a value of −1, the percentage change in quantity must be equi-proportional to the percentage change in price. Thus, a 10 per cent cut in price will lead to a 10 per cent increase in quantity.

d The solution to b shows that this can't be a straight line. Therefore, it must be a curve – concave or convex – to the origin? The two examples illustrated in Figure 6.3 show that it must be the latter – in fact, a demand curve of unitary elasticity must be a rectangular hyperbola.

U N I T

7 Supply

Key concepts covered

- supply
- costs of production
- stocks
- (influence of) price
- technology
- profitability
- other factors
- elasticity of supply

Introduction

In this unit supply is analysed in a similar way to the way demand was in the previous unit. Supply refers to the willingness to supply goods to a market and price is considered to be the most important variable. This unit focuses on the willingness of companies to supply new cars. The supply of a product will depend on the following factors:

- stocks
- price
- costs of production
- technology
- relative profitability.

The new car market

The new car market is a very significant part of the UK economy. Although most motor manufacturers are foreign-owned, employment in the industry is high and particular parts of the country are highly dependent on the fortunes of car makers. The British car market has been insulated from similar markets in other countries and, as will be discussed in later units, this has been seen as an abuse of monopoly power resulting in higher UK prices for the same cars sold in Belgium, the Netherlands and other European Union (EU) countries. The car manufacturing industry tends to respond to booms and slumps in the economy. More new cars are sold when the economy is expanding whereas purchasing decisions are postponed if the economic outlook is less optimistic. Producers of cars have to decide how to respond to various outside events such as these. Should production be cut? Should it be expanded? Should new products be introduced? Economists investigate these decisions and the outcomes of these

decisions under the general heading of **supply**.

Supply is analysed in similar ways to demand but it is important to remember that the study of supply is focused on the decisions which producers take, whereas the study of demand concentrates on the behaviour of consumers.

Supply theory

Price, costs, stocks and profit

What drives a company to produce and sell cars? Broadly speaking, goods are brought to market for one of two interrelated reasons – to enable someone to make money, or to be more precise, a profit. Thus, motor manufacturers strive to ensure that their businesses are profitable. However, goods and services will only be sold if they are needed, or to be more precise, if there is an effective demand for them. Other business and organisations exist for a variety of social reasons and because they may improve people lives. Thus, the NHS exists in an attempt to ensure that all members of society get medical treatment, most schools are not run for profit, and in the voluntary sector people give up time and money to help those they perceive to be less fortunate than themselves. However, all businesses whether in the private, public or voluntary sectors need to ensure that their income or revenue is at least sufficient to cover their costs. Businesses which succeed in this way can grow while those that are unsuccessful are likely to decline and may go out of business. Thus, it can be argued that all businesses exist to make some kind of profit, and practically all businesses have a 'bottom line', i.e. the need to ensure that revenue at least covers costs. The focus of the analysis which follows is on businesses in the private sector, but the principles used can also be applied to the public and voluntary sectors.

Economists argue that three factors are most important in affecting how much of a good or service is produced. They are:

- **costs of production**
- revenue
- **stocks**.

Costs

Costs refer to all payments which have to be made in order to produce a good. All businesses estimate potential costs and then set this against revenue which is simply the money coming into a business in order to determine profitability.

Revenue

Sales revenue refers to monies earned by a firm and will be determined by the **price** multiplied by sales. Other things being equal, the higher the price that something can be sold for, the higher the sales revenue and the bigger the potential profit. On the other hand, the lower the price, the lower the revenue and the smaller the potential profit. If more profit can be made by providing a particular product or service then more will be produced. In the example given at the beginning of the unit increasing incomes are likely to lead to an increase in the demand for new cars, and bigger sales mean bigger profits especially for those companies that produce more of the type of cars which people are prepared to buy.

Stocks

Those cars which have been built but not yet sold form **stocks**. As cars are a relatively bulky product large unsold car stocks are often highly visible. If firms carry large stocks supply can be increased quickly in response to increases in demand and price. But there are opportunity costs attached to holding large stocks and motor manufacturers would probably prefer to avoid having stocks of unsold cars. Ideally, they would like to produce cars to meet individual orders. In the analysis which follows it is assumed that stocks of unsold cars are minimal.

Suppliers will increase output if they think profits will rise, and profits will rise, other things being equal, if the price of a product rises. Conversely, falling demand will lead to falling prices, and if profits fall, supply is likely to drop. This generalisation enables a supply curve to be drawn

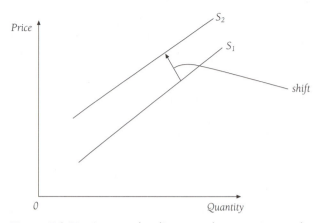

Figure 7.2 Rise in costs leading to a decrease in supply

using the same axis as used when drawing a demand curve. Price is represented on the vertical axis and quantity sold on the horizontal. Supply curves usually slope upwards from right to left showing that higher prices will result in more being supplied but lower prices will lead to a reduction in supply. This is shown in Figure 7.1 where, other things being equal, 2000 Ford Escorts would be built each month if each could be sold for £10 000.

Changes in the costs of producing cars will have an impact on how many cars are planned to be built. Other things being equal, increases in component costs, labour and the like will push up the cost of producing each car. This increase in costs will reduce profits and make car production less attractive. Such changes are illustrated by an upward shift in the supply curve. This is shown in Figure 7.2 where the shift from S_1 to S_2 represents an increase in costs leading to a fall in supply at every possible price level.

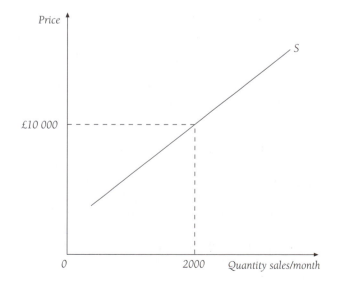

Figure 7.1 Supply of Ford Escorts per month

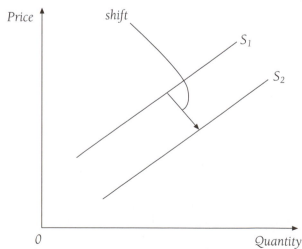

Figure 7.3 Rise in costs leading to a decrease in supply

On the other hand, if costs of production are reduced then the supply curve shifts downwards to the right showing a greater willingness to produce cars (see Figure 7.3).

Changes in technology

Improvements in the way in which things are made or how services are provided can have a major impact on supply. Car producers have reduced both production and running costs by using plastic components rather than those made of metal. Certain production processes have been speeded up and made more efficient by the use of robotics. Rapid innovation in other uses of information and computer technology (ICT) has made the complicated process of car manufacture easier to organise, plan and manage. Improvements in **technology** are often associated with reductions in the cost of production and they can be illustrated in a similar way. The adoption of better and cheaper ways of making cars will shift the supply curve downward to the right (see Figure 7.4).

Relative profitability

The importance of profits has previously been considered but a further issue, especially for those firms that have an easy choice between producing different products or providing different services, is the relative **profitability** of producing different goods or services. Thus, a car manufacturer may choose to reduce production of saloon cars if the profits from producing off-road vehicles were greater. If supplying an alternative product becomes more profitable the supply of the good in question will fall as illustrated

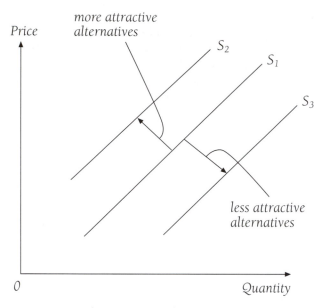

Figure 7.5 Changes in supply relating to changes in profits in related products

in Figure 7.5 by the leftward shift from S_1 to S_2. On the other hand, if the supply of an alternative becomes less profitable there could be shift to S_3, showing an increase in supply.

Other factors

In a similar way to the effect of changes in tastes and fashion on demand, a whole set of human **factors** can affect the decision of what and how much to produce. As will be shown in Unit 10, different firms often have different objectives. Some owners of small firms may not wish their businesses to grow so large that they lose control. In this case rising prices might not lead to increased output, or improvements in technology might allow the same level of profit in return for working less hard. Growing sensitivity to environmental issues may lead some firms not to expand production if resources near to depletion are required. Thus, some car firms have invested in producing engines which are more efficient and less polluting.

Economists need to be sensitive to the particular interplay of different factors when they are analysing supply. This is especially true, as there are costs associated with changing levels of production. Cutting supply may involve making skilled workers such as engineers and designers redundant. This kind of labour may be difficult to recruit if output needs to be increased at some time in the future.

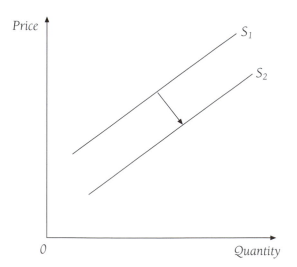

Figure 7.4 Improved technologies resulting in increased supply

What motivates decision-makers in local businesses? Could incentives be provided which would encourage expansion? Work with others to collect primary evidence which should help provide possible answers to this key problem:

a Interview the owners of local businesses.

b Devise a questionnaire designed to reveal the relative importance of the factors considered in this unit to be the major determinants of supply.

c Collect data.

d Compare and discuss your responses.

e How far does your research support or contradict the theory of supply outlined in this unit?

Elasticity of supply

The responsiveness of supply to changes in price is measured using the concept of elasticity of supply. The formula for working out the co-efficient is very similar to that relating to price elasticity of demand. It is:

Elasticity of supply =

$$\frac{\text{Percentage change in quantity supplied}}{\text{Percentage change in price.}}$$

Thus, if the price of cars rises by 10 per cent but the supply increases by 2 per cent the co-efficient would be +0.2. If, on the other hand, manufacturers have large stocks of unsold cars and can change output quickly in response to a price rise the co-efficient is likely to be larger than 1. It is very unlikely for a negative co-efficient to occur, as this would mean that producers expand production in response to a fall in price or cut output in response to a rise in price.

Given the use of the same axis the gradient or slope of the supply curve indicates its elasticity. A supply curve with an elasticity of +0.5 is illustrated in Figure 7.6 by S_1, whereas S_2 is less steep and has an elasticity of +3.

The rule is that the steeper the curve, the more elastic the supply and vice versa.

Factors affecting the elasticity of supply

Different products are likely to have different elasticities of supply. If prices rise producers are likely to want to respond by increasing production. Their ability to do so will be constrained by a range of factors. The simplest way of increasing supply is to release any unsold stocks on to the market. Firms could pay workers to work longer hours and additional shifts. But once existing plant and machinery (capital) is used to the full, production can only be increased by expanding productive capacity.

It is possible to make some generalisations from about those factors which will have most effect in determining the elasticity of supply of a product or service:

■ Availability of stocks, and raw materials – if there are stocks of unsold cars, components and other materials it will be relatively easy to expand the production and sales of cars. Expansion could be checked by the unavailability of one small component.

■ Unused productive capacity – if existing factories

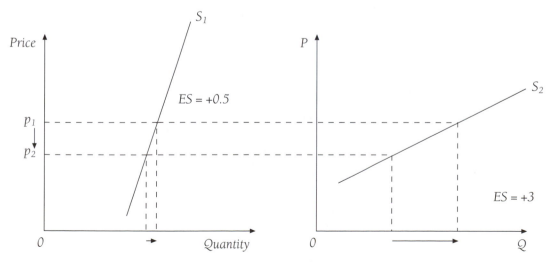

Figure 7.6 Supply curves of differing elasticities

and production lines are not being used all the time supply is likely to be more elastic

- Availability of imports – car manufacture is a global industry and companies can switch supplies from contracting markets to those that are growing.

- Availability of suitably trained labour – the difficulty and extra costs of attracting skilled workers will limit the responsiveness of a car manufacturer to meeting increases in demand.

- Capital intensity – car production tends to be capital rather than labour intensive so this factor will be crucial.

The significance of these factors can be viewed in a different way by using the concept of 'time' – the supply of most products and services is likely to become more elastic over a longer time scale. Changes in elasticity of supply over time are shown in Figure 7.7 where S_1 represents the elasticity of supply in a very short time scale as unused stocks of materials and under-utilised labour is used, S_2 for a longer period in which existing productive capacity can be brought into production and S_3 over an even longer period to allow for the acquisition of new plant and machinery along with the training of new workers.

ACTIVITY 2

What factors are likely to affect the elasticity of supply in the following markets:
a   wheat production
b   electrical generation
c   T-shirt manufacture?
Which supply is likely to be most responsive to changes in demand/price?

ACTIVITY 3

Investigate the supply conditions in a different market, using the concepts developed in this unit.

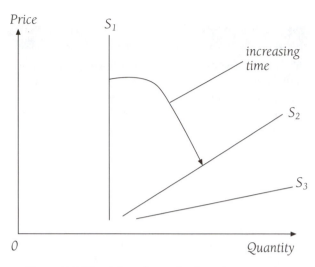

Figure 7.7 Elasticity of supply changing over time

Summary

This unit has presented a brief introduction to the theory of supply. The supply of any good will depend on a range of factors. Firms will be more likely to produce more of a good or service if they expect prices to rise. The interplay between prices, profits and costs of production is crucial in affecting supply. Firms may be less responsive if large stocks exist. Elasticity of supply measures the responsiveness of producers to changes in price and is likely to vary according to both 'time' and technical factors affecting production.

Data response question

1   How might the supply of digital services described in the advertisement opposite be influenced by changes in:
   a   technology   (2)
   b   costs of production   (2)
   c   future profit forecasts for Telewest?   (2)
2   What other factors are likely to influence the expansion of supply by Telewest?   (6)
3   What are the implications of this kind of development for the future of the telecommunications industry?   (8)

Telewest Active Digital is born

(And it gives you exactly
what you want.)

Now you can select the channels to suit you.

You know the wonders of digital television. That great choice of channels, clearer pictures, sharper sound. Well Active Digital Cable is even better, because you can actively pick the individual channels you want. Here are the bare facts. First pay your £50 connection fee* and then enjoy all 60 channels free for the first month. Then you're free to choose. For instance, you can keep all 60 channels for just £24 a month** including a phone line. Or you can design your own package by adding the individual channels you want. Whatever you do, you've got the run of the whole toyshop. Call us free for more information.

Now it's your choice, not just more choice

Telewesc

*Initial Connection Charges: Supply of digital television and telephone is subject to an initial charge of £50. The £50 charge quoted is an introductory offer. Telewest reserves the right to terminate this offer at any time. The initial charge includes telephone line rental, use of one Digital Smartbox for 30 days, connection of digital TV, telephone and stereo hook up/video connection. You will receive the Main Zone package free of charge for the first month. After this first month the Main Zone package with telephone line rental is £24 per month. This includes one Digital Smartbox, additional Digital Smartboxes are £15 per month each. If you do not nominate an alternative digital TV package, you will receive and be charged for the Main Zone package after the introductory offer finishes. Digital TV packages, with cable telephone, start from £15 a month. Digital TV channels once ordered, must be retained for a minimum of 30 days. **Payment Price quoted includes VAT and is for payment by Direct Debit. Payment by any other method will incur a £2 monthly administration charge. General: Digital Smartbox: You do not own the Digital Smartbox and you will be liable to pay repair/replacement costs if you damage or lose the Digital Smartbox. Information is correct at time of going to press and is subject to change. All offers and services are subject to status and availability. To maintain high standards, calls to sales and services are randomly recorded.

8 Markets at work

Introduction

In this unit demand and supply are brought together to provide an introduction to how markets might work. The analysis of markets is a key element in the economist's toolkit. Markets exist wherever those who demand products or services meet those who supply goods or services, and they provide a mechanism by which these separately determined sets of intentions are resolved. Price changes provide a mechanism by which demand and supply can be brought into equilibrium. This unit uses four examples to illustrate how different markets might respond to changes in demand and supply: the housing market, the market for tickets to the Wimbledon Tennis Championships, the market for organic vegetables and that for personal computers.

Markets

Many different kinds of markets exist. The earliest markets moved around the country and were often celebrated as fairs and special events when all kinds of resources were traded. Some were devoted to selling surplus production at harvest time, while others involved selling labour to the highest bidders. Cattle markets retain some of the features of these earlier trading events. Towns and city centres now take on many of the functions of traditional markets and the sellers of products and services use a wide variety of strategies to appeal to consumers. There are many other forms of market, including the following:

■ classified advertisements in newspapers
■ speciality global commodity markets such as those for oil and gold
■ the stock market where shares are traded
■ wholesale markets
■ futures market
■ auctions
■ flea markets
■ black markets
■ grey markets
■ the Internet.

This list could easily be extended but irrespective of the form and frequency of such markets they all share common elements:

■ Buyers are involved.
■ Sellers are involved.
■ There is some mechanism by which buyers and sellers reach an agreement and make a transaction.

As markets share common features it is possible for economists to model their behaviour and to use such models to predict outcomes to a series of 'What if?' scenarios.

Putting demand and supply together

As demand curves and supply curves are drawn against the same axes, it is possible to superimpose one on top of another as illustrated in Figure 8.1 for the market for new houses.

The demand for new houses slopes downward to the right. It is relatively inelastic, as there are not many close substitutes. This factor is likely to outweigh the significance of housing as taking up a very large portion of most customer's budgets. Supply slopes upward to the right and for the new houses this is also relatively inelastic, as it is not always easy for producers to change output quickly in response to changes in demand and price.

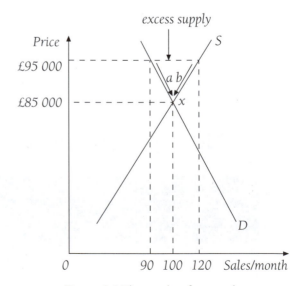

Figure 8.1 The market for new houses

The point x, where the supply and demand curves cross, shows the price at which demand and supply are equal. In this example the average price of a new house coming on the market will be £85 000 and 100 houses would be sold each month. This is called the **equilibrium** price and in a free market this will be established automatically. If the price were for some reason to be £95 000 demand would equal 90, whereas supply would be 120. The producers of new houses would be attempting to sell more than could be sold. This **excess supply** of 30 homes would mean that some houses were being built but not sold. Stocks of unwanted houses would build up and sellers would be tempted to cut prices. Falling prices would make new houses more attractive to some consumers, for example those on lower incomes would find that they were able to borrow enough money to buy, while some builders may find house building less attractive, and seek alternative building contracts. Demand would rise as supply would fall. According to price theory, this process would stop when the equilibrium price was reached. This pincer movement to the establishment of an equilibrium is shown by the two movements a and b along the demand and supply curves. The process by which markets are brought into equilibrium is called **market clearing**.

The same logical analysis can be applied to a situation in which new houses were being sold for £75 000 each. In this case demand **excess demand** would apply and some prospective house buyers would be forced to go without. New houses coming on to the market would be snapped up quickly, and enterprising estate agents might well attempt to take advantage of shortages of new houses by raising their prices. This process would set a similar pincer movement in operation. Rising prices would put off some potential house buyers but would also make house production more attractive. Demand would fall and supply would rise until equilibrium is reached.

The key point is that as long as demand curves slope downwards to the right and supply curves slope upwards to the right, and as long as they both cross there will be one equilibrium, that price where demand is equal to supply.

Demand changes

If one of the key variables which determine the demand for any product changes the equilibrium will change. These variables are as follows:

- the prices of other goods – substitutes and complements
- incomes
- tastes of producers.

Change in the price of a substitute

The effect of this is investigated using the market for seats at the Centre Court for the Wimbledon All-England Open Tennis Championship as a example. In this case the supply is fixed and would appear as a vertical line, as shown by S_1 in Figure 8.2. Demand is represented by D_1 giving an equilibrium price of p and ticket sales of q. Those thinking of buying a ticket will not only consider the price of the ticket they are also likely to consider the prices of alternatives. This would include prices of tickets for other courts or a whole range of other leisure products. If, for example, a cricket Test Match was being staged in London at the same time and seat prices for that were reduced it is conceivable that some people may be attracted to cricket rather than tennis and this would cause the demand for Wimbledon tickets to fall, as shown by the shift from D_1 to D_2 in Figure 8.2.

D_2 shows the lower level of demand for tickets at all possible prices. If the price were to remain at p there would be disequilibrium between demand and supply. Supply would exceed demand by tq. As in the earlier analysis excess supply would exist. If the price stayed at p some tickets would be unsold. The managers of Wimbledon may consider cutting prices to r in order to make sure all seats were sold. This change in price would be described by economists as being the outcome of 'market forces' at work.

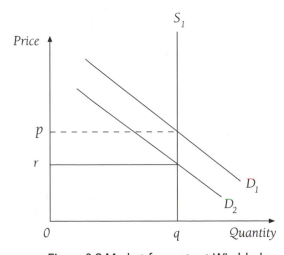

Figure 8.2 Market for seats at Wimbledon

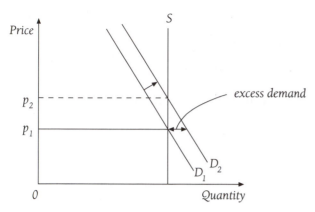

Figure 8.3 Effects of a fall in the price of a complement

Change in the price of a complement

A number of other products or services are likely to be jointly consumed by visitors to Wimbledon. Travel to the courts, the famous strawberries and cream, perhaps having something new to wear might all fall within this category. If, for example, travel to Wimbledon were to become free from any part of London this might lead to an increase in demand for seats. This possibility is illustrated in Figure 8.3.

In this case demand increases as indicated by the shift to the right from D_1 to D_2 and the earlier analysis would be reversed. The old equilibrium would become a disequilibrium. If prices remained at p^2 excess demand would occur. This would give Wimbledon's managers the opportunity to raise seat prices p^2. If they didn't opportunities would arise for ticket touts to exploit the situation by selling tickets at inflated prices.

Changes in income

If the country as whole becomes better off potential ticket sales at Wimbledon are likely to rise. Studies show that the income elasticity of demand for 'products' such as this is highly positive and if incomes in general rise it is likely that demand for tickets will rise and the effects of this would be similar to those illustrated in Figure 8.3.

Changes in tastes

In this example it appears that tennis as a spectator sport is becoming more and more popular especially as leading players receive extensive publicity. If a longer time period were considered this rising popularity could be represented by a series of shifts in the demand curve from D_1 to D_2 to D_3 and so on as shown in Figure 8.4. Taking a longer view might also reveal efforts by the owners of Wimbledon to take advantage of growing demand by expanding

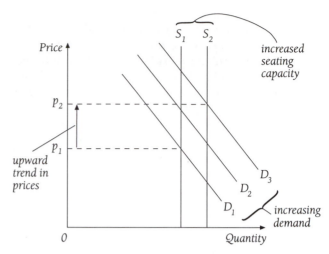

Figure 8.4 Effects of favourable change of tastes on tennis ticket prices

seating capacity at the Centre Court as shown by the shift from S_1 to S_2. In this case the long-term trend in ticket prices is upwards.

ACTIVITY 1

a Analyse the effect on the price and sales of tennis rackets of:
  i a rise in membership fees for tennis clubs
  ii a reduction in income tax.
b Why might an understanding of income elasticity and cross elasticity of demand be helpful in attempting to answer a?

Changes in supply

Changes in supply factors are considered in the context of the demand for organically grown vegetables. In this case supply is likely to be affected by:

- changes in the price of organic vegetables
- changes in costs of production
- technological changes
- changes in the objectives of producers.

Prices of organic vegetables

In this market, compared to Wimbledon, suppliers or producers will have much less influence over the price charged for their product, and the supply of organic vegetables is likely to slope upwards from left to right showing a greater willingness to produce if prices are high and vice versa. A possible supply curve S_1 for organic carrots is

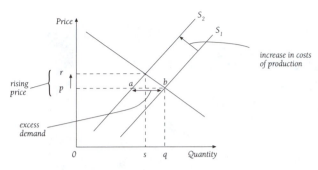

Figure 8.5 Effects of increased costs faced by organic carrot producers

shown in Figure 8.5. To this is added a demand curve D1 giving an equilibrium of price of p, and sales of q.

Effect of changes in costs

Organic producers face additional costs in order to assure buyers that their produce is really organic. Thus, the Soil Association operates a certification scheme to guarantee the organic origins of products. If it were to increase its registration fees, organic carrot producers would be faced with an increase in costs. This is shown in Figure 8.5 by the leftward and upward shift in supply to S_2.

If the price were to remain at p/kilo demand will now exceed supply by a-b. **Excess demand** means that some potential buyers might have to go without; enterprising green grocers might raise their prices. The price is likely to rise until a new equilibrium is reached. In this case demand will be equal to the reduced supply at r/kilo, and sales will fall to s.

Technological changes

Alternatively, an improvement could be made in the production process which reduced costs of supply. Potential profits would be higher. Production would be more attractive and the supply curve would shift downwards to the right. If the old price were maintained disequilibrium would arise in which supply was greater than demand. Prices would fall until a new equilibrium was established showing both a lower price and higher sales. This is illustrated in Figure 8.6.

Objectives of producers

An increasing number of farmers are turning away from heavy reliance on non-organic methods of farming and are choosing for ethical reasons to adopt organic techniques. This trend is likely to lead to an increase in the supply of organic products as shown in Figure 8.7. The long-term effect of these trends is that the supply and sales of organic carrots and other products should increase and prices should fall relatively.

Using demand and supply analysis in another context

The personal computer market

How might an economist analyse the personal computer market? Firstly, demand would be considered. There is nothing special about the demand for PCs that would challenge the generalisation that, other things being equal, lower prices will lead to higher sales and vice versa. Thus, the demand curve for a given PC is likely to be downward sloping from left to right. Moreover, there are many producers of very similar looking and performing products which should mean that the market

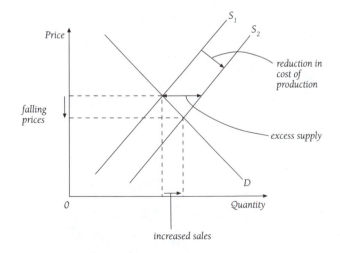

Figure 8.6 Effects of technological improvements on the organic carrot market

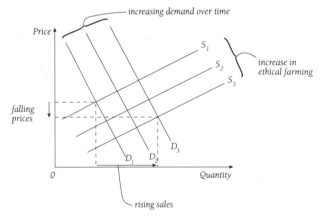

Figure 8.7 Long-term effects of ethical producer objectives in favour of organic production

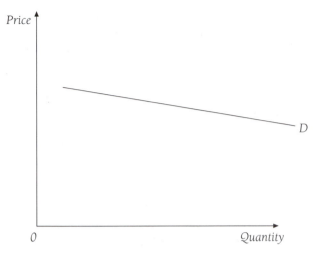

Figure 8.8 Demand for Viglen PCs

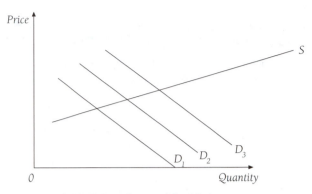

Figure 8.10 Rising demand for Viglen computers

is very competitive. This means that the demand for, say Viglen PCs, is likely to be relatively elastic as there are a fair number of relatively close substitutes. If these assumptions and observations are accurate the demand curve for an entry-level Viglen PC is likely to look something like that illustrated in Figure 8.8.

Secondly, what can be said about the supply of PCs? Although individual components are very sophisticated most PCs are relatively simple to make as all that is required is that a particular set of components is linked together and put into a box. Another key supply factor is the very rapid changes in technology. Sometimes it seems that new faster processors are brought on to the market on a weekly basis. Faster machines with larger and larger memories are being continually developed. In short, PCs can be made relatively easily, in a short period of time, but their technical specification changes very quickly. As this is a fast moving market, stocks are likely to be small. The

supply curve for an entry-level Viglen PC might therefore look like the one shown in Figure 8.9.

So can demand and supply analysis help us to understand why the price of this kind of PC has fallen so dramatically over the past 12 months? Looking at demand first it is likely that the demand for this kind of PC has increased significantly. This is known to be a growing market for business and home users, income elasticities of demand tend to be high and positive, expenditure on advertising is high, the price of complementary products and services such as access to the Internet continue to fall. It is likely that demand curves have been shifting steadily to the right as illustrated in Figure 8.10.

Such developments would normally lead to rising prices but they ignore changes which might be happening to supply. Competition between the suppliers of components is intense, and the costs of many PC components have fallen significantly. Some have been over supplied, and those imported from countries in the Far East have become cheaper with the fall in value of their currencies. The effect of this is that there has been a massive increase in supply which is illustrated in Figure 8.11. The graph shows that prices have fallen dramatically while at the same time sales have increased.

Figure 8.9 Supply of Viglen computers

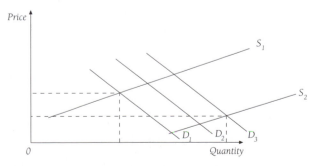

Figure 8.11 Effects of large increases in supply of Viglen computers

ACTIVITY 2

Use demand and supply diagrams to offer a possible explanation for each of the scenarios below.

a Adopt the role as a promoter of musical events. You have hired a venue with a capacity of 2000. Show the effects of
   I   overpricing tickets
  ii underpricing tickets.

b The market for grapes shows widespread fluctuations at different times of the year – prices can vary from £2 per kilogram to £6.58 per kilogram. Why might this be so?

c In some countries in order to try to protect the less well off, governments impose fixed prices for basic foodstuffs like oil, flour and rice. Show the possible effects of these policies.

d In the UK some firms use various means to ensure that the prices of consumer goods like CDs, cars and more expensive perfumes are kept artificially high. Will such policies always work?

ACTIVITY 3

Use the tools of economic analysis developed in this unit to analyse market forces at work in a market of your choice. You may wish to focus on sport and leisure, transport, or markets for 'green' products. Use demand and supply analysis to explain trends in prices in this market over the past five years? Present your findings in report format and use at least one graph, one chart and one diagram.

Summary

Markets bring demand and supply together to determine price and sales. Changes in demand or supply will lead to changes in price and sales. Demand and supply conditions always differ between different markets and it is advisable to always try to consider what might make one set of demand and supply conditions differ from another set.

Data response question

For the first time since Saddam's tanks rolled into Kuwait in 1990 the price of North Sea Brent crude oil broke the level of $25 a barrel. This is significantly higher than the average $15 a barrel many analysts were predicting at the start of the year. An oil expert said: 'This has been a year of extraordinary development in the oil market and a windfall year for OPEC'. The Organisation of Petroleum Exporting Countries accounts for 25 million of the 72 million barrels a day the world consumes. Its members are estimated to have made an additional $25bn in revenues this year. Economists are beginning to worry about the inflationary pressure exerted by higher oil prices.

UK motorists have already seen petrol – a major derivative of crude – rise several times in the past three months. Price competition between petrol companies has kept the rise to 9% this year, even though crude prices have jumped by 40%. The price of aviation fuel has increased by 30% since the middle of July. As a result, British Airways last week put prices up by 2.5% on European routes and is considering a rise on long-haul routes. There are reports that other airlines are considering introducing plastic cutlery to save weight, and fuel.

Production from non-OPEC countries such as Norway and the UK has fallen below expectations. The hurricane that hit Mexico and its oil production facilities last year was also significant. The country lost 40 million barrels – the equivalent of OPEC cutting production by 600 000 barrels a day for six months. But while uncertainty surrounding supply in producer countries is normally to blame for sharp oil price rises, this time the demand side has surprised the industry experts. There was a colder winter in the northern hemisphere and a much greater thirst for oil from emerging markets.

But the developed world has thrown up its surprises. The rule of thumb for mature economies was that for every percentage point rise in GDP, oil demand went up by between 0.5 and 0.75%. Evidence from the UK and Japan suggests this has increased to 1%.

Source: Adapted from A. Barnett, 'Surge in oil prices has government over a barrel', in *The Observer*, 20 October 1996

1 Using evidence from the passage, what can be inferred about the price elasticity of demand for oil? (2 marks)

2 Analyse two effects of higher oil prices mentioned in the passage. (6 marks)

3 Explain why the rise in the price of petrol has been significantly less than the increase in the price of oil. (3 marks)

4 Using supply and demand analysis, explain why oil prices rose in 1996. Illustrate your answer with a diagram. (6 marks)

5 What does the passage suggest about the income elasticity of demand for oil? (3 marks)

The interrelationships between markets

Key concepts covered

- local markets
- national markets
- global markets
- product markets
- factor markets
- derived demand
- factor immobility
- government intervention

Introduction

Many economists consider that the housing market is one of the most important in terms of affecting how the whole UK economy works and performs. From 1986 to 1989 there was a boom in the housing market. As has already been shown, this was caused by rapid increases in demand fuelled by falling interest rates, lower personal taxes, rapid economic growth and rising incomes. The effects of these changes were not confined to the housing market.

But no market works in isolation from other markets. Changes in one market will lead to changes in others which will have further effects. These chain reactions have a big impact on our lives. They can cause us to become richer or poorer. They impact on the environment. They can change the way we see things.

In this unit links between product markets and factor markets are explored.

Local market interrelationships

The housing boom was first triggered by changes in the south east of England. In the mid-1980s there was a dramatic expansion in the financial services market. Insurance, banking, share dealing and related activities, especially those connected to information technology developments, grew rapidly, and the earning of key workers, especially those in short supply, grew very rapidly.

House buying has a high positive income elasticity of demand, and the demand for houses in London and the south east grew rapidly. The supply of houses in the short run is relatively inelastic resulting in a rapid rise in regional house prices. People planning to move away from the area found they could profit greatly from selling in London and buying relatively cheaper property elsewhere. Land prices rose. There was an immediate increase in the demand for workers with building skills. The earnings of bricklayers rose dramatically enabling many to buy their own homes. Estate agents found both sales and high profits easy to earn. Their growing prosperity added to the local boom. The demands for all kinds of building materials rose. Earnings of workers and the profits of the owners of such businesses also climbed.

Rising house prices in London forced some potential house buyers to look further afield pushing up the demand for housing in the counties around London, and causing a similar chain reaction as increases in demand in one market rippled over into closely related markets.

It would be possible to construct an ever-growing web of relationships and interrelationships as partially illustrated in Figure 9.1

It is easy to see how such ripples and waves would set off further reactions, and that it is possible to visualise the rise in property prices in the south east of England reaching out and affecting the whole local economy.

It is possible to envisage that any local economy consists of thousands and thousands of interconnected **local markets**, each with their own demand and supply curves shifting and adjusting to change after change. The key links between these individual markets are price changes.

Thus, the rise in the price of houses is a signal to those who supply associated products like paint, and nails, and furnishings, and washing machine products that they should consider increasing their supplies and raising their prices.

Rising incomes in the building trade were also a signal which would have attracted more workers to move to the region, and more young people to undertake training.

Rising profits would also have led to increases in the share prices of leading building firms.

The demand for water, electricity and other utilities also rose.

National interrelationships

The impact of the property boom was not confined to the South East. It spread to **national markets**. Brickmakers in Bedford, timber suppliers in Scotland, screw-makers in Birmingham would have all

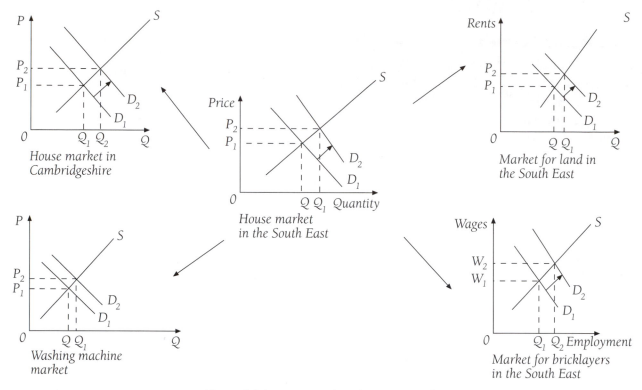

Figure 9.1 Interconnections between markets

experienced growing order books. Demand for their products would have risen as well as demand for their labour, and other resources. A whole series of demand curves shifted to the right and prices and outputs rose.

Ever-growing congestion and rising land prices in the South East encouraged some employers to relocate to other parts of the country. Business activity spread out from London along the main motorways and rail links. Cities like Bristol benefited from the further expansion of the financial services market.

ACTIVITY 1

a   Did the boom carry on?
b   What happened between 1989 and 1994?
c   Interview people who experienced the changes in the property market between these years.
d   Compare your findings.
e   What were the effects of these changes? Were the eventual effects global?

Global effects

The effects of the property boom spread beyond the UK into **global markets**. Foreign suppliers of building materials, furnishings, and white goods (fridges, washing machines and the like) enjoyed increased demand for their products. Workers from Ireland, Spain, Italy and other southern European countries were attracted to Britain because of labour shortages especially in the hotel and catering industries. The property boom spread to northern France and southern Ireland as those in high earning jobs in England spent part of the increased incomes on holiday and weekend homes.

Factor markets

The earlier analysis has tended to treat all markets in much the same way but economists place importance on the distinction between markets for final products (or services) and those for factors of production. Whereas customers can express their demands in **product markets**, and these can be translated by firms into the provision of particular goods and services, **factor markets** exist to help ensure that factors of production are used in order to meet demands expressed in product markets. Thus an increase in demand for organic products could have the effects shown in the Figure 9.2.

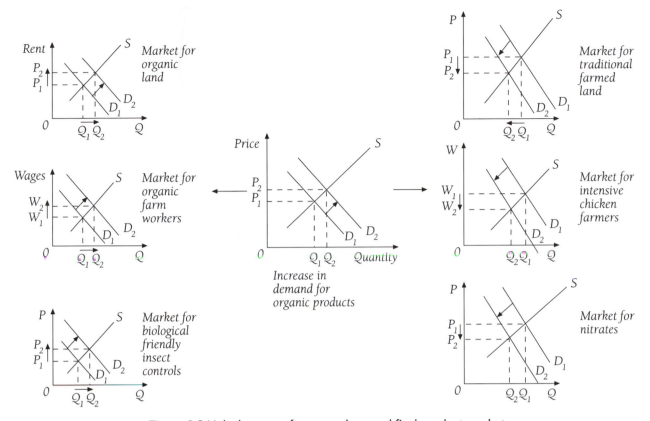

Figure 9.2 Links between factor markets and final product markets

Demand

Factor markets can therefore be analysed using similar concepts to those used to help understand the market for a final good or service. These include:

- demand
- supply
- government intervention.

But there are some important differences which modify how these concepts are applied. These include:

- **derived demand**
- **factor immobility**.

Demand

Factors of production are in many senses like any other product that is traded. They have a price. The price, for example, of labour is the wage or salary that has to be paid. Rent is the return earned by the owners of land. Profit is a reward for enterprise, and interest or dividends can be seen as the price of money or capital. In the case of labour this is called wages. If factors of production, other things being equal, are expensive then the demand is likely to be low. If, on the other hand, they are cheap demand

will be high. Thus, the demand for a factor can be illustrated as in Figure 9.3, where wages per week are shown on the vertical axis and numbers employed on the horizontal.

Derived demand
However, factor markets and those for final goods differ in a very important respect. Final goods like cars or houses are demanded for what they are. Factors are demanded not for what they are but because they are required to produce something else. The nature of the

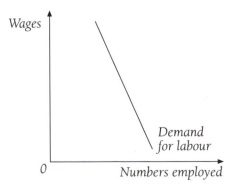

Figure 9.3 A hypothetical demand for labour

demand for that final product will impact on the demand for the factors required to produce that product. Therefore, the demand for pesticide-free land will increase as a result of the increase in demand for organic foodstuffs, while the demand for meat-processing equipment falls because the demand for meat products has fallen. Premier League footballers command enormous salaries because they contribute to the success and earnings of top clubs.

If the demand for the final product is highly price elastic, then it is likely that the demand for factors such as labour will also tend to be relatively elastic. This has implications in those industries in which responsiveness to customer demand is significant. Firms working in such fields as fast food, fashion and leisure activities are likely to want a flexible labour force. Hence the attraction for companies such as McDonald's to employ students.

If the demand for the final product is relatively inelastic, factor use is likely to be more stable. Moreover, if high prices can be charged for the final product, the rewards to factors in that industry are likely to be higher. Part of the attraction of working in the City of London is attributable to the existence of very high salary levels because the value of the final products is so high.

Supply of factors

If it is assumed that the owners of factors of production are materialistic, then it is possible to regard the supply of land, labour, capital or enterprise in much the same way as the supply of any commodity. If the price is high then, other things being equal, the supply will be greater. Alternatively, if the price is low, then the supply is likely to be low. This means that a supply curve for any factor will slope upwards to the right as is illustrated in Figure 9.4, with hourly wage rates on the vertical axis and numbers employed on the horizontal.

Factor immobility

The elasticity of the supply of factors is very significant. In the case of footballers or other top sports people the supply is very limited. Alternatively, it may take a long time to equip a person with the skills and experience to do a particular job: for example, it takes four years to train a nurse.

Moreover, people may not work solely for monetary reward. Some jobs are more attractive than others irrespective of wages or salary levels. Some people are loath to leave some parts of the country for others even though wages and salaries might be higher.

The use of other factors of production may be even less flexible because some may be fixed in supply. Thus, in the UK the amount of land for new housing developments tends to be fixed for a mixture of reasons. Land itself is finite. It can't really be moved from one part of the country to another.

The mobility of factors of production refers to the ease or otherwise in which they can be switched from one use to another, and is reflected diagrammatically in Figure 9.5.

ACTIVITY 2

How far can the concepts of demand and supply be used to explain the differences in earning between successful pop bands and those who struggle to make ends meet?

Government intervention

This is considered in much greater detail in Section 3 of this book but there tends to be more **government intervention** in factor markets than in those for final goods. Planning controls have a major impact on land use, and legislation about minimum pay and health and safety significantly affect the market for labour.

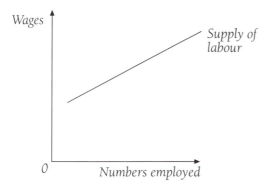

Figure 9.4 Supply of shop workers in Gloucester

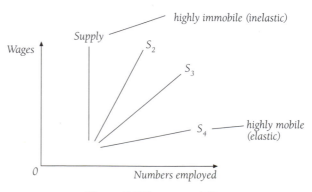

Figure 9.5 Factor mobility

Summary

This unit brings together key concepts which provide very powerful and useful ways of analysing the main factors that affect key economic phenomena. Price changes can bring about the equilibrium between demand and supply, therefore, determining many aspects which affect our lives. What we pay for the goods and services we buy, what happens if shortages occur, which jobs are most rewarding, and how the limited resources of our planet might be used.

Data response question

1 Use your understanding of factor markets to explain:
   a why the Futon Company is recruiting Sales Managers and Sales Advisors   (2)
   b why managers are paid more than advisors?   (2)
   c Futon Company's payment system.   (2)
2 Assess the relative importance of three economic factors which are likely to determine the success or otherwise of the Futon Company's efforts to recruit sales staff.   (6)
3 Investigate the relative attractiveness of two alternative jobs available in your area.   (8)

Roll Up! Roll Up!

Sales Managers – £15,000 – £21,000 (including commission and bonus)
Sales Advisors – Up to £12,000 (including commission)

Futon is the Japanese word for bed roll.

And the English word for amazing career opportunities with one of the fastest-growing retailers in Britain - we already have 25 stores and open a new store every 8 weeks!

If you love selling, have a passion for customer service and the enthusiasm and drive to play a full part in the bedroom revolution that we have created, then this is your chance to get your career on a roll.

Please send your CV to Irene Levin at FREEPOST FUTON COMPANY or fax it to her on 020 7243 1258 by the 17th January 2000. For further information call her on 020 7792 9119.

FUTON COMPANY ❧

SOUND SLEEPING ARRANGEMENTS

Changes in the British Labour Market

Extract 1

Table 1 shows the distribution of earnings as a percentage of the median pay of men and women in 1979 and in 1995. The median pay is the mid-point of the earnings distribution – in 1995, for example, the median pay for men was £304 per week and for women £222 per week. Consequently as the table shows, 10% of men earned at least 186% of the median wage in 1995, while 90% of men earned at least 57% of the median wage.

Table 1
Distribution of Earnings as a Percentage of Median Pay

	Men		Women	
	1979 % of Median pay	1995 % of Median pay	1979 % of Median pay	1995 % of Median pay
top 10% earned more than	157	186	159	181
top 25% earned more than	125	137	125	140
top 50% earned more than	100	100	100	100
top 75% earned more than	80	74	82	76
top 90% earned more than	66	57	69	61

Note: The figures relate to gross weekly earnings of full-time employees whose pay was not affected by absence in April each year.

Source: Department of Employment, *New Earnings Survey*, 1997, Part A, HMSO

Extract 2
Wages Councils and Minimum Wages

The Trade Union Reform and Employment Rights Act in the early 1990s brought at least a temporary end to the 84 year old system of legal minimum wages. Until that date it was the role of Wages Councils to determine them. At abolition, the 26 Wages Councils determined minimum rates of pay for 2.4 million workers, mostly non-union women working in the service sector – in shops, restaurants, hairdressers etc – but also in some parts of manufacturing. (10)

The Wages Councils did little to raise the relative pay of the low paid, but they may have prevented it from falling. The government's precise reason for abolishing the councils was unclear. Ministers sometimes implied that minimum wages priced unskilled workers out of jobs and led to higher unemployment. In defending abolition of the councils, however, former Employment Secretary, Gillian Shepherd, argued that they were irrelevant, since most workers covered by the Council's Wages Orders earned more than the minimum rates of pay being set. (22)

If the latter claim proved true, abolition would have had little effect other than to save the money spent on the councils' administrative machinery. If the Councils did serve to price some workers out of jobs, however, reform should have led to more jobs, but with the consequence of even lower pay for some of the weakest groups in the labour market. (29)

Source: Adapted from 'The Labour Market' by John Philpot in Focus on Britain. Edited by Phillip Allan, John Benyon and Barry McCormick. Published by Perennial Publications.

1 (a) Give **two** reasons which might explain the fact that the median earnings of men and women differed in 1995 (lines 5–7). [4]

   (b) (i) Using the data in Table 1, show how the pay gap (i.e. the gap between the highest paid and lowest paid) widened between 1979 and 1995. [3]

   (ii) Explain **one** reason why this pay gap may have widened. [2]

   (c) (i) Use supply and demand analysis to explain why it could be argued 'minimum wages priced unskilled workers out of jobs' (lines 23–24). [2]

   (ii) Explain the likely impact of the abolition of the Wages Councils on the pay gap for women. [3]

(d) Discuss one policy which might be used to reduce earnings differences between men and women. [6]

Questions

1 If the income elasticity of demand for a product is +0.3 then;
   a a fall in real incomes will lead to a proportionally larger fall in demand.
   b a rise in real incomes will lead to a proportionally larger rise in demand.
   c a fall in real incomes will lead to a proportionally smaller fall in demand.
   d a fall in real incomes will cause a rise in price.

2 Under which of the following circumstances would an increase in the price of product X result in a fall in the demand for product Y?
   a The demand for Y is income inelastic
   b Y is an inferior good.
   c X and Y are complementary goods.
   d X and Y are substitutes.

3 If the price elasticity of demand for coffee is −0.7 and the cross elasticity of demand between tea and coffee is +1.1, then a 10% increase in the price of coffee will cause the quantity demand of coffee to;
   a fall by 7% and the demand for tea to fall by 11%.
   b rise by 0.7% and the demand for tea to fall by 1.1%.
   c fall by 0.7% and the demand for tea to fall by 1.1%.
   d fall by 7% and the demand for tea to rise by 11%.

Source: Edexcel sample paper, 2000

4 Since the UK bus industry was privatised in 1986 fares have gone up by 80% and passenger journeys have gone down by 22%. Revenue for the bus companies has gone up by 40%.

Given the above information the price elasticity of demand for bus travel in the UK can be said to be
   a relatively elastic.
   b perfectly elastic.
   c unit elastic.
   d relatively inelastic.

5 The table shows the income and cross-elasticities of demand for two commodities, **X** and **Y**.

	income elasticity	cross-elasticity in relation to each other
commodity **X**	+0.5	+0.5
commodity **Y**	0	+0.5

Income rises by 10% and the price of **Y** falls by 10%.

If the price of **X** remains unchanged, what will happen to the quantity of **X** demanded?

a It will fall by 10%.
b It will remain the same.
c It will rise by 10%.
d It will rise by 20%.

Source: WJEC sample papers, 2000

6 Incomes are most likely to be higher in occupations where
a Derived demand is low
b Labour costs are a relatively small proportion of total costs
c Skills shortages exist
d trade unions are not recognised

Essay questions

1 The estimated price elasticity of demand for peak period air travel between London and Paris is −0.8, while at off-peak (weekend) times it is −2.4.
 a Explain the difference between the two price elasticity of demand estimates.
 b Discuss the business significance of these estimates for airlines and for other providers of transport services between London and Paris.

Source: Adapted from UCLES March 98 Market Systems and Market Failure Paper.

2 a Outline the factors which might determine the demand for foreign holidays by households in the UK
 b Discuss the impact of a reduction in air fares on the demand for holidays abroad and in the UK

Source: UCLES March 97 Market Systems and Market Failure Paper.

3 a Explain with the aid of a diagram how the pay and employment of unskilled hotel workers may be influenced by the introduction of the national minimum wage (10)
 b Discuss how an increase in the number of bookings for hotel rooms may affect the pay and employment of unskilled hotel workers (15)

Source: UNCLES March 97 Market Systems and Market Failure Paper.

Project

Identify a particular type of market e.g. retail fashion, fresh fruit and vegetables, DIY and collect data to illustrate how each of the following operates.
 a Demand
 b Supply
 c Market clearing
How does the operation of the market you have studied impact on
 a consumers
 b producers
 c workers
for the product or service in question.

C3.1a, C3.1b, C3.2, N3.1, N3.2, N3.3, IT3.1, IT3.2, IT3.3

Section 3
The market system

Introduction

This section is devoted to explaining how a free market economic system might work to decide the what, how and who questions which economics seeks to answer. What should be produced? How should goods and services be produced and who should consume what is produced? Strengths and weaknesses of this system are considered as an introduction to Section 4 which is devoted to closer examination of how the market system might be considered to fail.

The following topics are covered in this section:

- objectives of firms
- costs
- revenue
- profits.

Key concepts covered

- objectives
- plcs
- privately owned firms sector
- profit
- public sector
- voluntary sector
- profit maximisation
- profit saticficing
- stakeholder analysis

Introduction

This unit considers the importance of **objectives** in helping understand the behaviour of firms. It relates differing objectives to different types of organisations:

- plcs
- privately owned firms
- public sector
- voluntary sector.

Finally, consideration is given to assumptions that economists have traditionally made about the objectives of firms.

Large companies (plcs)

In the UK most large firms are public limited companies – **plcs**. They are allowed to sell shares to the general public, and are legally obliged to publish their accounts in the form of an annual report. These publications are usually freely available to the public and are a useful source of information about larger companies as they can reveal their objectives.

The 1997 annual report of the Kingfisher Group, which consists of Woolworth, B&Q, Comet and Superdrug and other well-known names, contains details of aims and objectives. The former is called a mission statement and is as follows:

'Building shareholder value by making the customer king'

This is further explained:

'Our objective is to deliver consistent and superior returns to our shareholders by being one of Europe's most profitable volume retailers.'

Kingfisher wants its shareholders to get better dividends than they would by owning other shares, and it intends to achieve this by selling large amounts of retail goods to customers in Europe.

The company also identifies those factors which are going to be important in helping meet their objectives:

'Throughout Kingfisher our people are of crucial importance and we aim to recruit and retain high quality people wanting challenging and satisfying careers . . .

Our suppliers are also important and our continuing policy is to develop long term relationships of mutual trust and benefit' . . .

Within the communities where we operate we are involved corporate citizens, initiating or supporting socially and environmentally beneficial projects. We are also working to continually achieve higher environmental standards throughout our operations.

In all our dealings with shareholders, customers, colleagues suppliers and the general community our aim is to be open, honest, straightforward and fair.'

Kingfisher plc, Annual Report and Accounts 1997

These statements contain a wealth of information about Kingfisher and how its board of directors would like their company to be run and organised. The mission statement and objectives will be used by the company to train and inform staff, to set individual objectives for managers, to organise marketing and purchasing, and as a means to judge how effective the company has been. It appears that Kingfisher places greatest value on ensuring that its shareholders receive 'superior' returns by concentrating on markets which it understands, being better than competitors, placing great value on its workforce, developing long-term relationships with suppliers, having regard to the community and the environment, and in being open, honest and fair. The value of such statements to an economist is that the information they contain might help to clarify the similarities and differences which may exist between this and other firms.

ACTIVITY 1

Use the Internet to obtain annual reports or other promotional material and summarise the objectives and performance of three different plcs. Present your findings to the rest of the class electronically.
Try the following web sites:
www.tutor2u.com/
www.fp.ebea.f9.co.uk/
www.ioe.ac.uk/eeeg/belinks.html
What differences and what similarities do you find?

What plcs have in common

As indicated earlier, Kingfisher and other similar firms are likely to be public limited companies. They tend to describe their objectives in terms of dividends to shareholders, meeting customer needs and achieving significant market share. Other common factors may include references to community service, the environment and supply chains. Although large companies are usually very conscious of their public image most place profitability very high on their list of priorities. However, the existence of other objectives may indicate that profits are not the only priority.

Privately owned companies

Companies in the **privately owned firms sector** tend to be smaller and their shares cannot be traded on the stock exchange. They have fewer legal obligations and are not compelled to publicise their accounts. It is, therefore, harder to find out and research the aims and objectives of this type of firm. It is, however, possible to make some broad generalisations about key objectives. In order to survive privately owned companies must pay their way. They have to pay their workers, their suppliers and others. In order to do this they need to generate income or revenue. Also it is likely that the owners of such companies expect to be compensated for the risks that they are taking by being in business. It is reasonable to deduce therefore that making some level of profit is important for this type of firm. What is likely to differ between different privately owned firms is the extent to which their owners want their businesses to grow.

The public sector

In the UK about 42 per cent of national income is spent by national and local government. This includes spending by government departments such as the Department of Trade and Industry, local government, the armed forces, the police and such like. These organisations are not usually regarded as firms, but just as with the private sector, they receive and spend income in different ways. In some parts of the country local councils, hospitals and the police are the largest employers. Clearly, knowing about the behaviour of these organisations is important for economists, and central to this is having an understanding of the objectives of different **public sector** organisations. Developing this understanding is probably harder than when dealing with privately owned businesses.

For example, consider the activities of a Health Trust. The Gloucester Royal Hospital employs 1500 workers and has 430 hospital beds. Is its primary objective to make everyone in the area well? Should it care for the dying? Should it make a profit? Need it worry about the costs of treatment? Should it be getting bigger?

The Severn NHS Trust is an example of a public sector organisation which is likely to have more complicated objectives than those in the private sector and they are more likely to include reference to service to the community.

ACTIVITY 2

Use the Internet to identify three different public sector organisations and find out as much as you can about the aims, objectives and strategies of each. Compare your findings with the rest of your class.
You might like to start at www.open.gov.uk/
What conclusions can you draw from your findings?

The voluntary sector

Organisations as diverse as the Citizens Advice Bureau, the League Against Cruel Sports and Harrow Hill Football Club are all examples of **voluntary sector** organisations. They differ from the other types of firms which have been described in that they rely to varying degrees on voluntary labour and funding. Some are legally constituted as charities, others are friendly societies, some trusts, while some have little or no legal status at all. It would, however, be a mistake to underestimate the contribution which the voluntary sector makes to the economy as a whole.

It is likely that voluntary sector firms emphasise some form of service as their prime objective.

ACTIVITY 3

Select a club, society or other voluntary sector organisation and find out about its aims and objectives. How does it try to ensure that these are met? Present your findings to the rest of your class.

Profit

Most economists would agree that the need or desire to make a profit in some form is common to practically all businesses, even those which exist most obviously to provide some kind of service. For example, the Terrence Higgins Trust provides support to Aids patients. In order to exist the Trust has to ensure that it has enough income to fund its services. If its spending exceeds its income it will be forced either to cut down the help it provides or seek new sources of funding. In this way the Terrence Higgins Trust is as much a business as Virgin Records or Vodaphone. It employs specialists to manage its cash flow. Raising funds is a key objective. Costs have to be carefully controlled. If these business functions were not undertaken the Trust would be less effective in its vital work.

Economists, however, have differing views as to the importance of profit in shaping and determining the behaviour of large privately owned business.

In classical economic theory, the pursuit of profit was seen to be the very engine which drove all business and the economy as a whole. Traditionally, economists have considered that firms seek to earn as large a profit as possible and that this objective overrides all others. This is called **profit maximisation**, and economists have for many years used this generalisation as the basis for arguing that a business which seeks to maximise its profits will choose that output of goods which gives the greatest possible profit. Economic models were developed, and are still widely used, in which profit maximisation is a key assumption. In later units of this book this concept is considered in greater detail.

Some economists consider that the assumption of profit maximisation is too restrictive. It has been argued that large companies may set out to gain enough profit to keep their shareholders happy and then pursue other objectives. This is called **profit saticficing**. Other economists, believe that **stakeholder analysis**, by which competing expectations about how firms behave are considered, is a more appropriate tool of analysis. These concepts are considered in greater detail in the second half of this book.

Summary

Considering the objectives of any firm is often the starting point for economic analysis. There is broad consensus between economists that making a profit is one of the most important objectives facing all firms.

Results summary

	1998	1997	% change	
			As reported	At constant exchange rates
Sales (a)	£4106m	£4173m	−2%	+4%
Trading profit before exceptional items and restructuring costs (a)	£642m	£642m	+3%	+8%
Trading margin before exceptional items (a)	15.3%	14.5%	+0.8pts	+0.8pts
Profit before tax, exceptional items and disposals	£609m	£575m	+6%	+11%
Basic earnings per share	35.0p	68.7p	N/A	N/A
Underlying earnings per share (b)	39.4p	37.2p	+6%	+11%
Net dividend per share	19.0p	18.0p	+6%	+6%
Capital expenditure (a)	£162m	£209m	−22%	−18%
Marketing expenditure (a)	£726m	£706m	+3%	+6%
Free cash flow	£157m	£157m	Nil	N/A
Total Group employees	38 656	41 320	−6%	N/A

(a) From continuing operations

(b) Represents Basic earnings per share adjusted to exclude exceptional items and gains and losses on disposals of subsidiaries and investments

Cadbury Schweppes plc, Summary Financial Statement 1998

Traditional classical economists assumed that profit maximisation was the most important motive for owners and managers of firms. This view has been challenged by some economists who have given more attention to other objectives. Stakeholder analysis is a modern development of this kind of thinking. The concept of profit, therefore, provides a good example of the degree to which economists both most agree and disagree. Clearly, profit is important to all types of businesses but whether or not it is more important than other objectives is debatable. There is no right or wrong answer.

Data response question

Our primary objective: To grow the value of the business for our shareowners.

Managing for value: This is the business philosophy which unites all our activities in pursuit of this objective.

The objective is quantified: We have set three financial targets to measure our progress:

1   To increase our earnings per share by at least 10% every year
2   To generate £150 million of free cash flow every year
3   To double the value of our shareowners' investment within four years.

Our approach: Our approach to this task is holistic.

We seek simultaneously to develop better strategies, upgrade our business culture and align our reward structure with the interests of our shareowners.

Cadbury Schweppes plc, Interim Report 1999

1   What are Cadbury Schweppes' objectives?   (3)
2   Why have these objectives been chosen?   (3)
3   What other objectives might a company such as this pursue?   (4)
4   Assess the success of Cadbury Schweppes in meeting its objectives in 1998.   (10)

Costs

Key concepts covered

- costs
- profit
- fixed costs
- short run
- variable costs
- total costs
- average (total) cost
- long run
- law of diminishing marginal returns
- long run average costs
- diseconomies of scale
- economies of scale
- internal and external returns to scale

MARKS & SPENCER'S recovery looked a long way off yesterday after the retailer announced a sharp fall in half-year profits alongside highly disappointing current trading figures.

Peter Salsbury, chief executive, admitted 'there is no quick fix' as he acknowledged that the competitive climate had worsened since the company's full-year results in May. He said: 'Since May, there has been a huge amount of change in our business, but meanwhile competitive developments in international retailing have accelerated so we have to move faster to catch up and get ahead.'

Profits before tax fell by 58% to £114.4m after £78.4m of exceptional charges, including redundancies and the cost of store closures in France and Germany. Underlying profits fell by 43%. Like-for-like sales over the half fell by 7.9pc with clothing and home furnishings down 11.8% and foods 1.6%.

Mr Salsbury admitted the much-heralded autumn clothing range failed to deliver a sales uplift. He said 'Although there was a good reception to previews of our autumn ranges, this was not reflected in the September sales performance, which was affected by the exceptionally warm weather.'

Robert Colvill, finance director, said sales would have to rise by 3% in the first full year of credit cards ' to compensate for the costs of introducing credit cards and for the effect they could have on the M&S store card'. M&S admitted it was 'disengaging' from its supply relationship with Daks Simpsons, which unions believe puts 800 jobs at risk. This is on top of the 4,300 UK jobs at risk after M&S sacked William Baird.

Mr Salsbury insisted M&S would still be 'the biggest purchaser of UK clothing'. Savings would be reinvested in cutting prices. He said: 'The savings we make will give us the margin to enable us to drive the top line.' M&S said it also planned to raise £400m from the selling or securitising 'non-operational' properties, including The Gyle Shopping Centre.

Mr Salsbury stressed that despite M&S's problems, 'we have had no takeover approaches'. One analyst said: 'The problem is Peter Salsbury sounds like John Major when what you really need in there is a Margaret Thatcher.' The shares fell 5 to 278p.

Alistair Osborne, "No quick fix" for ailing Marks' in the electronic *Telegraph*, 3 November 1999

Introduction

All firms, irrespective of their mission statements, objectives, ownership and what they might say about themselves have to make decisions about two key factors: **costs** and revenue. The current problems facing high street retailer Marks & Spencer are partly attributable to its high costs of production of clothing. If firms are going to survive they need to ensure that one way or another their revenues are at the very least the same as their costs. Most businesses will strive to ensure that revenue exceeds costs and this positive difference is described by economists as **profit**. Should costs exceed revenue, a loss is made. The economic analysis contained in this section is based on this very simple reasoning.

Thus, examination of data about costs and revenue is of crucial importance to developing a better understanding of the behaviour of firms. This applies just as much to organisations which are not primarily motivated to make profits, for example government agencies and voluntary groups. This unit is devoted to developing an understanding of how economists look at costs of production and the factors which are likely to cause costs to change both in the short and in the long run. The following unit provides an introduction to those factors which affect the revenue which firms can earn.

Costs of production

All payments made by a firm in the production of a good or provision of a service are called costs. Economists make use of the convention followed by many businesses of distinguishing between overheads and running costs. Overheads are costs of production which businesses have to pay irrespective of their level of output. Thus, a bookstore is likely to be faced with bills for rent, business rates and repayment of loans which will remain the same irrespective of how many books are sold. These expenditures are classified as **fixed costs** and the convention is that these do not change in the **short run**, which is defined as that period of time in which it is not possible to change the quantity of an input of a particular factor of production (usually called factor input). Running costs, such as payment of wages, stock purchases and the like, which will change as sales change in the short run, are classified as **variable costs**. In practice, it is not always easy to decide whether a particular cost should be classified as fixed or variable. For example, contracts and salaries might be agreed to cover a particular length of time, making them fixed, whereas maintenance costs might change considerably as output changes making them variable.

The addition of fixed to variable costs gives **total costs**, which include all the costs faced by a firm in the production of a good or a provision of a service.

The total cost divided by the output of the business gives the short run **average total cost** which is usually abbreviated to short run average cost, or even **average cost**. This is probably the most useful of these measures as it indicates the cost of producing each item or providing a service. The average cost is sometimes referred to as the unit cost.

Finally, economists and business people make use of the concept of marginal cost, which is the additional cost of producing an extra unit of output of a particular good or service. Thus, if a clothing manufacturing company were to produce an extra suit, it would be faced with the costs of additional materials and labour but would not have to pay out any more for design or machine setting costs.

Short run costs

Economic analysis of the behaviour of firms focuses on either the short or the long run. In the short run, as has already been indicated, a firm can change only the input of variable factors such as labour. In the long run it can change the inputs of any factor. This section is concerned with the analysis of changes in the short run, and a series of logical deductions can be made on the basis of this classification. The data contained in Table 11.1 are based on the actual costs of running a bookshop and illustrate how short run costs are likely to behave.

Table 11.1 Average monthly costs of Forest Bookshop (March 1999)

Fixed costs	£	Variable costs	£
Rent	2000	Purchase of new stock	2000
Uniform Business rate	1000	Postage	300
Bank loan repayment	1000	Telephone	200
Depreciation of computer and other equipment	50	Overtime	500
Insurance	50		
Wages	2000		
Total fixed cost	**£5850**	**Total variable cost**	**£3000**
			Total cost £8850

From Table 11.1, it is easy to compute the monthly total costs (total variable cost plus total fixed cost) of running the bookshop (column 2 plus column 4). From this, it is possible to derive the average cost of selling convenient bundles of books. In this example 2500 books were sold in March. If this figure is divided into the total costs of £8850, the average cost of selling each book is £3.54.

ACTIVITY 1

Assume the Forest Bookshop was able to sell twice as many books in April. Construct your own table of data reflecting these higher sales. What will be the effect on:

a   fixed costs

b   variable costs

c   average costs

d   and, by implication, potential profits?

An important deduction should follow from your analysis. As sales rise, fixed costs are shared by larger levels of output and, thus, become progressively less significant as a proportion of total costs. This is known to all business people who often speak of the benefit of expanding sales to allow overheads to be more widely spread.

Graphing average costs

If it were possible to continue to collect cost data relating to different levels of output or sales, then it would be possible to construct graphs illustrating the relationship between costs and different levels of sales.

Thus, to take an agricultural example, farmers are likely to have a fair idea of the best number of livestock to keep given the acreage and quality of their farmland. In Table 11.2 average costs of producing each lamb on a 250-acre farm are related to different 'outputs' of lambs.

Table 11.2 Costs of producing lambs

Annual sales of lambs	Fixed costs £	Variable costs £	Total costs £	Average costs £
0	5000	0	5000	
50	5000	1000	6000	120
200	5000	4000	9000	45
500	5000	14 000	19 000	38
1000	5000	60 000	65 000	65
1500	5000	105 000	110 000	73

Table 11.2 shows what a good farmer would know without having to make such calculations, i.e. the most appropriate number of ewes to keep given the size of farm and cost of different factor inputs. In this example, if no lambs were sold the farmer would still be faced with certain fixed costs which will probably be dominated by fencing, rent and repayment of loans. A small flock of around 30 ewes might be expected to produce 50 lambs. Variable costs for feed, veterinary and abattoir costs would be incurred, but given the relatively high level of fixed costs it would cost £120 to rear and slaughter each lamb. Production of 200 lambs would be more 'economic' as better use would be made of the available land, but each lamb would still cost £45 to produce. Increasing the flock size to around 300 ewes could produce 500 lambs and even better use would be made of the farm, giving an average cost of £38 per lamb. Continued expansion of the flock would, however, push up average costs to £65 a lamb when 1000 are produced and £73 if 1500 were raised. Breeding more and more lambs would put pressure on the available grass, lead to the purchase of more and more hay, and concentrates, and probably lead to a greater incidence of disease.

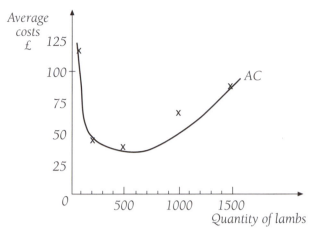

Figure 11.1 Short run average costs of sheep farmer

In short, if this farmer wanted to be most efficient and keep short run costs to a minimum he or she should produce around 500 lambs a year. The average cost data contained in Table 11.2 is illustrated in Figure 11.1.

Output is measured on the horizontal axis and average costs of production on the vertical. This (short run) average cost curve is U-shaped. As output expands efficiency increases and short run average costs fall. They reach a minimum or 'optimum' point and beyond that short run costs rise indicating declining efficiency. This will apply to the short run costs of any firm, and is known by economists as the **law of diminishing marginal returns** which will always occur if the use of a variable factor is increased while another factor input remains fixed. In the example of the sheep farmer, more and more fodder and concentrates were purchased to feed an expanding flock of sheep but the size of the farm remained the same. Similarly, if a factory manager wanted to increase production in the short run he or she would not be able rapidly to expand the size of the factory, or immediately buy new machines. Employees could be asked to work overtime, and more workers could be taken on. If this process were to be continued a point would be reached when overcrowding and the sheer mass of workers would contribute to rising short run average costs.

Graphing marginal costs

As indicated earlier, any change in costs brought about by changing production by an additional unit is described as a marginal cost. These can be calculated by looking at how total costs change according to changes in output. Table 11.3 relates to total costs incurred on a daily basis by a garage specialising in undertaking MoTs.

Table 11.3 Calculating costs

Daily number of MoT tests	Total daily costs £	Average costs £	Marginal costs £
0	150		
1	150	150.00	150
2	180	90.00	30
3	196	65.30	16
4	211	52.75	15
5	224	44.80	13
6	236	39.30	12
7	247	35.30	11
8	257	32.10	10
9	266	29.50	9
10	274	27.40	8
11	280	25.40	6
12	285	23.75	5
13	292	22.50	7
14	301	21.50	9
15	311	20.70	10
16	331	20.70	20
17	355	20.90	24
18	385	21.40	30
19	423	22.30	38
20	471	23.60	48

In the example, the garage owner is faced with fixed costs of £150 a day – rent, business rates, wages, loan repayment and so forth. As more and more MoTs are carried out, resources are used more efficiently which is reflected in both falling average cost and marginal costs. As with the sheep farmer, the garage owner will find that costs will bottom out and then begin to increase. In this example, undertaking 16 rather than 15 MoTs causes a big rise in costs – perhaps because extra labour is required. As work increases the garage becomes more crowded and congested and both average and marginal costs rise.

The data contained Table 11.3 are illustrated graphically in Figure 11.2. Marginal costs are plotted against the midpoint of each unit change in output, and the marginal cost curve will cut the lowest point of the average cost curve.

What is important is in the short run, average and marginal cost curves will always have the same relationship to each other. The application of the law of diminishing marginal returns means that any attempt to increase output by changing the use of one factor while the use of others remains fixed will initially lead to falling average and marginal costs. An optimum will then be reached where average costs are at a minimum, and thereafter growing inefficiency will lead to rising average costs, This observation, that

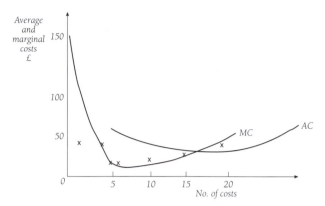

Figure 11.2 Marginal and average costs

short run average cost curves are U-shaped, is one that all students of economics become familiar with.

Long run costs

Economists define the long run as that period of time in which it is possible for a firm to alter any or all of its factor inputs. Thus, the sheep farmer could purchase more land, the bookseller expand his or her premises and the garage install new car testing machinery. The effect of expanding production on **long run average costs** is less clear cut than is the case with the short run and is likely to depend on a number of factors.

The following three scenarios are linked to the sheep farmer doubling the size of his or her farm.

Scenario 1

Suppose the cost of a loan to purchase additional land was the same as was already being paid for the original 250 acres. Assume that there will be proportionately similar increases in costs for labour, winter feed, fencing and veterinary fees. In this situation the average short run cost of producing each lamb would not be very different from the short run cost on the smaller farm. Thus, at the optimum level of output each lamb would cost about £38 to produce. However, the farmer can now produce 1000 lambs a year whereas on the smaller farm diminishing returns occurred if more than 500 lambs were produced.

Scenario 2

In this case suppose the farmer had to borrow relatively more money to buy less productive land. At the optimum level of output the short run average costs of producing each lamb would be greater than was the case with the optimum level on the smaller farm.

Scenario 3
In contrast to the previous scenario, the newly acquired land might be cheaper and more productive. It may pay the farmer to transport his or her own livestock and suppliers of winter feed might be prepared to supply larger orders at a discount. In this case optimum short run costs of production would fall and not only would the farmer be able to produce more lambs he or she would be able to produce each one more cheaply.

Returns to scale
The three scenarios exemplify the concept of returns to scale, which is the concept used to judge the impact on costs in the long run of changing any or all factor inputs. Scenario 1, where average costs of production remain the same, is described as an example of constant returns to scale and is illustrated by a graph in Figure 11.3

Scenario 2 involves rising long run costs which can also be described as **diseconomies of scale**. This is shown in Figure 11.4.

Finally, scenario 3 is about **economies of scale** which are falling long run costs as illustrated in Figure 11.5.

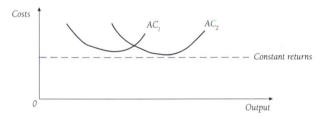

Figure 11.3 Constant returns to scale

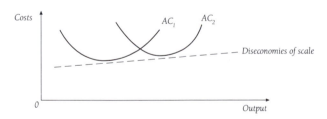

Figure 11.4 Diseconomies of scale

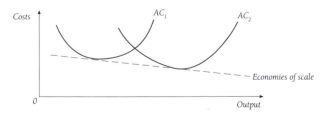

Figure 11.5 Economies of scale

Factors affecting returns to scale
The behaviour of long run average costs is important to all businesses and there are a number of factors which will determine whether or not they tend to rise or fall. They can be subdivided into **internal and external returns to scale**. Internal relate to a growth in the size of the individual firm and include the following:

- Technical factors. As firms grow they may be able to sell larger outputs which make it 'economic' to use particular production techniques which are more efficient. For example, a wide-bodied plane such as the Airbus 300 series has lower running costs per passenger mile compared to a smaller plane such as the Boeing 707. The most significant factor leading to this is that larger planes are more fuel efficient. Similarly, as manufacturing firms grow and produce larger saleable outputs they are more likely to be able to afford more expensive but more efficient computer-driven automated production methods.

- Organisational factors. The growth of firms and production of larger outputs enables firms to apply the division of labour and principles of specialisation. Those who work for small firms may have to undertake a range of jobs and will find it hard to develop cost saving skills and expertise in particular fields. As firms grow they can afford to employ specialists in finance and marketing and the like and this can result in cost savings leading to falling long run average costs.

- Growth and higher revenues can allow firms to invest more heavily in research and development. This is especially important in those industries in which the rate of change is rapid, for example electronics and pharmaceuticals. These sectors of the global economy tend to be dominated by giant firms such as Sony, and Glaxo Wellcome – their growth leads to greater research efforts, which lead to the development of new products and the establishment of new sources of competitive advantage.

- On the other hand, growing size can be associated with more bureaucracy. Communications in larger firms can be slower and less effective. Small businesses may be more responsive to their customers. In this case growth can lead to rising long run costs or diseconomies of scale.

■ Market power. Firms that grow larger can exercise more power in the various market places in which they operate. Expanding output can allow companies to negotiate larger discounts from suppliers. In the UK the major supermarkets are said to be able to compel prospective suppliers of food stuffs to accept ever lower prices while maintaining ever higher quality standards.

External returns relate to changes in long run costs which are associated with the expansion of a particular industry rather than an individual firm. Long run costs might fall if an industry expands in a particular area such that suppliers are attracted, leading to a reduction in the transport costs of components. Alternatively, the grouping of related businesses in urban areas such as London generates additional costs of congestion and pollution.

Conclusions

There is no automatic formula which can be applied to firms as they grow in size. In some industries, such as motor car manufacture, potential economies of scale that benefit firms able to produce in large scale for a global market are enormous. In others, especially where more traditional methods of production are used, diseconomies of scale may be more significant.

ACTIVITY 2

Choose a business which you are confident you can find out more about. Identify its main fixed costs, variable costs, the length of time it takes to vary inputs of land, labour and capital, and the existence of significant economies or diseconomies of scale.

Present your main findings to the rest of your class.

Discuss with your class how far you are able to make generalisations about the firms you have studied.

Modern approaches to costs

Some economists have questioned the wisdom of making a rigid distinction between short and long run costs, while others have researched the actual nature of costs faced by firms in different industries. Two broad themes have been derived from this research:

■ In many modern businesses, flexible working and modern technological developments mean that the distinction between the short and the long run can become blurred. Thus, modern technologies can link factories in one country to others in the world. If more machine parts are needed it is not necessary to construct a new factory or plant; new orders can be subcontracted to other suppliers in most parts of the world very easily. Similarly, improvements in the transportation of materials mean that individual components can be shipped around the world quickly and relatively cheaply. These developments are tied in to the globalisation of production and business.

■ Many firms find that initial growth in output and sales is accompanied by dramatic cost savings, i.e. economies of scale are significant. Thereafter unit or average costs remain similar irrespective of output, until a point is reached at which average costs rise dramatically.

If these two sets of research findings are applied to traditional approaches of classifying costs they have a significant effect on how the behaviour of firms is analysed. Figure 11.6 illustrates this. There is no short run average cost or long run average cost, there is just an average cost 'curve' which might be 'trench'-shaped.

ACTIVITY 3

Research, by using other texts and journal articles, different approaches to modelling average costs. Is the modern approach outlined above more helpful to you in making sense of the behaviour of firms? You may find www.bizednet.bris.ac.uk helpful in locating suitable articles.

Summary

This unit presented two different ways of treating costs faced by firms. Traditional economic analysis is based on a rigid distinction between the short and

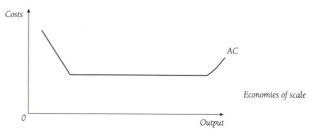

Figure 11.6 Modern approaches to average cost curves

the long term, and this provides a rationale for the existence of the U-shaped average cost curve, and the concept of returns to scale. Alternative treatments regard the distinction between short and long run as artificial, and consider that firms can be much more flexible and responsive in their reactions to changing market conditions.

Data response question

Two students, Sue and Emma, have decided to investigate the possibilities of setting up an Internet-based travel agency aimed at people in their age group. They have £10 000 to put into the business – see Travel – and estimate that they will need to find £4000 to set up and equip a suitable office. Their web site will cost about £2000 to create and they plan to pay themselves £800 each per month. Suppliers of holidays and flights are prepared to pay see Travel commissions of 10 per cent for each booking made. Market research shows that they can expect on average ten customers per week in the first year of operation, and that the average spend per customer will be £400. They have yet to identify and quantify other running costs such as telephone bills and office costs. They are not sure whether or not their plans are viable.

1 Identify and estimate other running costs (3)
2 Use these and see *Travel*'s own figures to estimate the company's total costs for the first six months of operations. (3)
3 Calculate the average cost of each typical holiday. (3)
4 Will see *Travel* be profitable after the first year of trading? (3)
5 Are the various assumptions that have been made realistic? (4)
6 Would Sue and Emma do better if they put their £10 000 in a savings account? (4)

UNIT 12 Revenue

Key concepts covered

- revenue
- price elasticity of demand
- movements along a demand curve
- shift of the demand curve
- monopolistic markets
- competitive markets
- price makers
- price takers
- market entry
- barriers to entry

Introduction

Revenue is the term used by economists to describe those flows of money which are received by a firm, as distinct from costs which refers to those payments made by firms. Different firms earn 'revenue' in different ways. For example, private sector business revenues will be largely determined by the value of sales of goods and or services. Charities largely depend on donations made by the public. Schools and colleges rely on funding provided by government agencies according to formulas based on student numbers. In short, all firms need revenue from somewhere. The analysis in this unit is based on an example of a firm operating in the private sector but it can also be applied to public and voluntary sector organisations.

Revenue in the private sector

Price wars

At different times in the 1990s price wars have broken out among newspapers. These have been triggered by attempts by Rupert Murdoch and his company Newscorp to gain larger shares of the different sectors of the market. In 1994 he slashed the price of *The Times* to 20p. He was accused of predatory pricing, i.e. setting artificially low prices to drive out competitors. The *Daily Telegraph*, the *Guardian* and *The Independent* were most directly affected by Murdoch's tactics. *The Independent* was almost forced out of business, but the *Daily Telegraph* decided to retaliate by cutting its price. The effects of this are illustrated in the table below:

Price	Date	Sales
48p	March 1994	993 395
40p	November 1995	1 052 340
35p	July 1995	1 059 503
30p	August 1994	1 091 658

ACTIVITY 1

To what extent was the fight back by the Daily Telegraph successful?

Calculating revenue

Calculating revenue is straightforward. The price of a good or service is multiplied by the number of items which are sold. This information is captured by a demand curve. Thus, the data in the table in the newspaper article can be translated into a demand curve as illustrated in Figure 12.1. Reading off the vertical axis at 35p gives a sales level of 1 059 503. Price × quantity sold = revenue; therefore, the shaded area abcd represents the total sales revenue earned.

Changes in revenue

Revenue will change if prices and/or demand changes.

Price changes

Demand curves provide a way of analysing the effects of price changes on revenue. Changing the price up or down will have an immediate effect on revenue. In the example above, reducing the price of the *Daily*

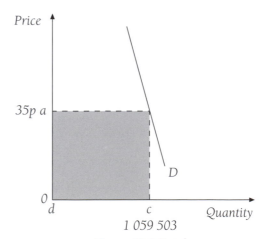

Figure 12.1 Total revenue

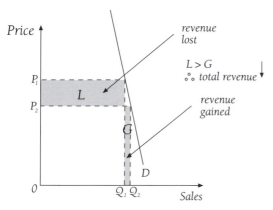

Figure 12.2 Revenue falls as price is cut

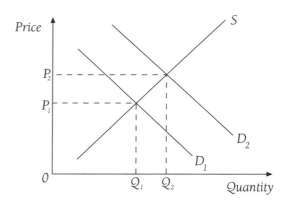

Figure 12.4 Increased demand leading to increased revenue

Telegraph results in a fall in revenue. The effects of any change in price on revenue will be determined by the **price elasticity of demand** for the product or service. (See Unit 6). The data about the *Daily Telegraph* show that demand was relatively inelastic. In other words, the percentage increase in sales is smaller than the percentage fall in price – more revenue is lost through the reduced price than is gained from increased sales. This is illustrated in Figure 12.2.

Where the demand for a product or service is relatively elastic the reduction in price would lead to an increase in revenue. This is shown in Figure 12.3.

Changes in price such as those illustrated above are referred to as **movements along a demand curve**.

Demand changes

Revenue will also change if demand shifts. Figure 12.4 represents a situation in which the Daily Telegraph responded to competition by offering reduced airfares to popular destinations. This move attracted additional sales and is illustrated by the shift of the demand curve to the right shown in Figure

12.3. If prices were kept at 40p revenue would increase.

If the demand for the *Daily Telegraph* were to fall for some reason, for example the launch of a new newspaper, the demand curve would shift to the left resulting in falling revenue irrespective of the price charged. This would be the reverse of that shown in Figure 12.4.

Competition, and revenue and corporate power

If firms wish to boost profits they need to raise revenue or cut costs or ideally do both. The previous section provides some clues as to broad strategies which firms could use to boost revenue. In terms of the demand for their good or service they need to shift the demand outwards to the right, and/or, more subtly, twist their demand curve to make it more inelastic. These approaches are illustrated in Figure 12.5.

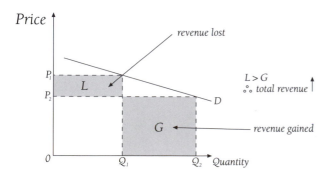

Figure 12.3 Revenue increases as price is cut

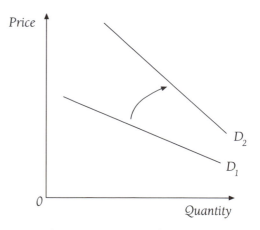

Figure 12.5 Strategies aimed at increasing revenue

The ability of an individual firm to achieve such objectives will be strongly constrained by the characteristics of the market within which it operates. Economists distinguish between **monopolistic markets** and **competitive markets**.

Monopolistic markets

A strict theoretical definition of a monopoly is when the production and/or sales of a good or product is in the hands of one producer. Thus, as British Airways (BA) is the only airline to fly between Bristol and Newcastle, it would be said to have a monopoly of direct flights between these two cities. Railtrack has a virtual monopoly of railway lines in the UK (a few are privately owned, often by railway enthusiasts). Those living in a village may be dependent on one local store.

Firms who operate within monopolistic markets have considerable freedom to charge relatively high prices for their products. The return airfare between Bristol and Newcastle is £275 (late 1999). However, it is a mistake to think that a monopolist can charge what it likes for a product. Forcing prices up will force potential customers to reconsider their purchase of a particular product or service. Thus, travellers between Bristol and Newcastle may consider using rail services or driving if airfares are increased further. Economists use the term **price makers** to describe firms such as BA who have the power to set prices.

Another way of illustrating the existence of a monopoly is by examination of the demand curve for such a product. By definition, a monopoly has no direct competitors. In other words, there are few close substitutes. The demand for a product which has few if any substitutes is likely to be relatively inelastic. This is illustrated in Figure 12.6.

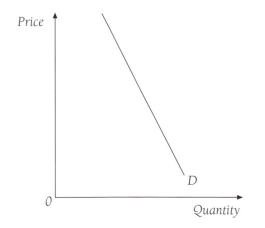

Figure 12.6 Likely demand facing a monopolist

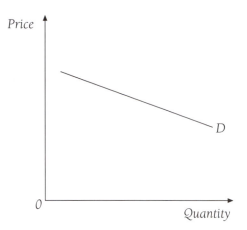

Figure 12.7 Likely demand facing a firm in a competitive market

Competitive markets

Competitive markets are those in which there are a wide range of similar goods or services on offer to the customer, who needs to be aware of such choices. Currently, there is fierce competition between Internet service providers (ISPs). There is almost always a high level of competition between small builders, hairdressers and second-hand car sales businesses. In these markets individual firms have to take great care in setting the price of their particular product or service. If they pitch prices too high they will lose many customers who will buy cheaper substitutes; if they set prices lower than their competitors they run the risk of being over run by eager customers. In very highly competitive markets the individual firm will have little or no scope in charging a price different to its competitors. Economists refer to such firms as **price takers**.

Unlike a monopoly for which there are few close substitutes, a firm facing strong competition is likely to have many substitutes, and this can be represented by the gradient or slope of the demand curve facing the individual firm. In Figure 12.7 the individual firm has virtually to accept the price set by the market.

ACTIVITY 2

Collect evidence from monopolistic and highly competitive markets which illustrates how the behaviour of firms is influenced by the degree of competition they face.

Discuss and compare your findings.

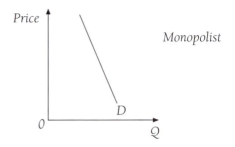

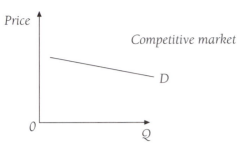

Figure 12.8 Continuum of competition

Degrees of competition

Economists recognise that most firms do not fall into extreme categories of being absolute price makers or total price takers. Most firms have some degree of market power which enables them to have some influence on the price for which their good or service sells. A 'continuum' of competition is illustrated in Figure 12.8.

Most firms are likely to fall into the middle of this continuum, and this is examined in greater theoretical detail in Unit 2 of Part 2 of this book.

Competitive or monopolistic?

What makes a market competitive or monopolistic? Economists make use of the concept of market entry to help explain why market characteristics differ. This is defined as the ease or otherwise of firms to enter or leave a market. The following five factors are considered to be crucial:

■ capital requirements

■ legal framework

■ scale of production

■ branding

■ uncompetitive behaviour.

Capital requirements

Some industries are said to be highly capital intensive. In other words, successful production depends on considerable investment in machinery. The manufacture of motor vehicles, ships and planes all fall into this category. Similarly, research and development in electronics and pharmaceuticals requires heavy investment. This will make it very costly for new firms to enter such industries and, conversely, it is more costly for firms to leave or exit such industries. Competition is likely to be more limited.

On the other hand, if capital requirements are

modest, the initial investment will be lower, ease of entry and exit will be greater, and more competition is likely to exist. Thus, it is often easier to set up a new firm in retailing than it is in manufacture, and competition will be greater.

Legal framework

As will be shown later in this book the law is a very important factor in shaping business behaviour. Some companies are protected from competition by patents, which restrict the copying of new ideas or processes. They are given to companies by governments anxious to encourage innovation. Planning restrictions may limit the development of new firms. The monopoly of the Post Office to deliver mail for less than £1 is protected by law. Similarly, rules and regulations can make it harder for new firms to enter particular industries.

Scale of production

The preceding unit considered the behaviour of long run average costs, and in some industries those firms which are able to produce high levels of output may enjoy significant economies of scale enabling production of low levels of unit cost. A new entrant to such an industry will find it harder to achieve large enough market share to be able to enjoy economies of scale. Unit or average costs would be higher and it would be possible for established firms within a market to drive out new competitors by starting a price war.

Branding

Many firms attempt to create, through marketing activities, a strong brand image. Advertising and promotion are used, usually over an extended period of time, to make particular brand names common-place. For example, Hoover, Marmite and Adidas are so well known to be valuable simply for their 'name'. It is harder and more costly in terms of advertising and image building for a new entrant to break into a market that is dominated by strong brands.

Uncompetitive behaviour

Many firms prefer to minimise risks and avoid competition. For example, Microsoft has grown quickly by taking over firms that develop potentially useful software. The world's airlines have been going through a phase of 'alliance building' whereby they share ticketing systems and other approaches to develop larger market share, and make the entry of new airlines more difficult. Some companies produce a range of products which are designed to foster the illusion of competition. The detergent market in the UK is dominated by two companies, Procter & Gamble and Unilever, but they market their products under a wide variety of brand names, for example Ariel, Persil and Bold, and various own-name brands of the major supermarkets.

Some firms break the law to maintain barriers against the entry of new companies. In the UK it is illegal for most manufacturers to set the retail price of the goods which they make. Similarly, it is illegal for firms to enter into secret agreements to restrict trade or divide up markets. However, there have been many examples of firms operating illegally in order to maintain some degree of monopoly power.

Barriers to entry

If it is hard for firms to join or leave an industry barriers to entry are said to exist.

ACTIVITY 3

Choose two contrasting industries, identify the main barriers to entry, and assess their impact on consumers.

Summary

The revenue earned by a firm will be determined by the interaction of price on the demand for its good or service. Firms can attempt to increase revenue by changing the price charged and/or by attempting to influence demand. Their ability to bring about such changes will be strongly influenced by the amount of competition in the markets within which they operate. Various factors will affect the degree of competition and economists place particular emphasis on the ease of entry/exit from a market.

Data response question

Car insurance market

Traditionally, car insurance was bought from insurance brokers. Even small towns would have had one or two brokers. The job of brokers was to find the best deal from insurance companies for their clients who generally speaking would remain loyal customers. In the event of a claim brokers would sort things out. This system survived for many years.

In the mid-1980s major insurance companies followed the lead of Direct Line, a company which cut out the brokers and sold direct to customers. They were able to undercut brokers. Selling insurance by telephone has since taken up a major share of the car insurance market.

In the 1990s there was increasing merger activity which resulted in the establishment of larger and more powerful insurance companies.

1. Identify three trends which helped facilitate the growth of direct selling of care insurance. (3)
2. What evidence is there to suggest that this market is becoming
   a more competitive (4)
   b less competitive? (4)
3. Assess the relative importance of three barriers to the entry of new firms into the car insurance market. (9)

UNIT 13 Profits

Key concepts covered
- normal profits
- supernormal profits

Introduction

This unit integrates concepts developed in the previous three units and develops an understanding of profit that links the behaviour of individual firms to how a market economy might operate.

Profits

If a business knows how much it will cost to produce a particular output and can calculate the revenue that such an output will earn if it is sold, it can estimate whether a profit or a loss will be made. If planned total revenue exceeds expected total costs, profit will be made. On the other hand, if costs exceed revenues a loss will follow.

Economists refine this approach by distinguishing between **normal profits** and **supernormal profits**.

Normal profits

Normal profits are defined as that level of profit which a firm considers is just enough to continue in production in the long run without changing levels of output. If a firm is earning normal profits it will not be inclined to increase or decrease production.

What constitutes normal profit varies between different industries. Those in which risks are higher tend to have higher levels of normal profit, while lower risks are usually associated with lower levels of normal profit. It is argued that high potential profits will be required when the risks of failure are greater in order to attract risk-taking entrepreneurs. An indication of the existence of different levels of normal profit can be gained from examining how mark-ups differ. Mark-ups are the percentage added to cost prices. They roughly equate to gross profits from which overheads and other expenses have to be deducted to get net profits. Thus, it is common for the fashion retail industry to work on 100 per cent mark-ups on new or popular styles, whereas greengrocers are happy to work to 30 per cent margins.

Recent research has indicated that supermarkets in the UK expect comparatively higher levels of profit than do similar firms operating in the rest of Europe or the USA.

Supernormal profits

Profits above a normal level will have three important effects. Firstly, economists believe that they will encourage firms earning supernormal profits to expand production. Secondly, they will tempt new firms to enter those industries in which supernormal profits are being made. Finally, supernormal profits can provide internal finance for further expansion. All these factors should lead to expanded production.

Losses

Economists treat losses in a similar way, distinguishing between levels of loss which will merely cause firms to cut production and those which will make firms cease production altogether.

If a firm is making losses in the short run, yet has revenues which are larger than its variable costs, it will carry on producing in the short run, as it will be able to make a contribution to its fixed costs. If it ceased production in the short run it would be faced with the full amount of its fixed costs. Therefore, it minimises losses by continuing production. On the other hand, if revenues are less than variable costs, losses will be minimised by cutting production completely. Paying out for fixed costs in the short run will be cheaper than paying for them and that portion of variable costs not covered by revenue.

Firms and profits

It follows from the treatment given to the objectives of firms in Unit 10, that all firms, irrespective of ownership and objectives, will have an interest in the levels of profit which they earn. Firms which are able to increase levels of profitability are able to expand, diversify, pay their workers more, gain greater market share and give larger returns to shareholders. How they actually behave will depend on their objectives, and on the degree of competition which they face. Firms operating in competitive markets with low barriers to the entry of other companies will be forced to be very responsive to changes in profit levels. Higher potential profits make gaining greater market share possible by price-cutting or other promotional activity. Similarly, the fear of losses is likely to act as negative sanction for firms in competitive markets. They will do all that they can to avoid losses in order to survive and to prevent the possibility of being taken over by a competitor.

Firms operating in monopolistic markets will be more insulated from having to respond quickly to market changes affecting profitability. Competition is less direct and the existence of barriers to entry is likely to limit the emergence of new competitors.

The differences in competitive pressures between monopolistic and competitive markets leads economists to predict that:

■ normal profits are likely in highly competitive industries

■ supernormal profits are more likely in monopolistic markets.

Profits in competitive industries

It can be argued that for competition to exist one firm within an industry must have a reasonable idea of how other firms are behaving. There will be common levels of understanding as to the suitability of different production methods, alternative approaches to marketing and production can be copied. Skilled workers and managers can be poached by firms who are faced with particular recruitment problems.

If an individual firm successfully innovates by tapping into a new market the demand for its product will rise relative to that for its competitors. Other things being equal, increased demand will lead to increased revenue and the possibility of higher levels of profit – supernormal profits could be earned. These, it can be argued, will only be temporary. Supernormal profits in a competitive industry will last only in the short run. This is a result of the relative transparency that exists within competitive markets. In short, other firms within the industry will copy the firm which has innovated. Moreover, other new firms may be attracted by the existence of supernormal profits to enter the industry, introducing still more competition. Larger outputs by the industry as a whole will reduce the market share of the original innovator and squeeze supernormal profits back to normal.

ACTIVITY 1

How might a monopolistic firm respond if a government attempted to tax its supernormal profits?

Profits in monopolistic markets

The behaviour of firms that have monopoly power is likely to be less obvious. Such companies will generally be larger, more powerful and more secretive about their behaviour. They may be given monopoly power by the granting of patents.

Thus, an individual firm which introduces a profit boosting innovation could earn additional profits. Other firms might find it harder to copy the change or improvement. New firms will find that barriers to entry make it more difficult to join the market and share extra revenues and profit. For these reasons economists agree that firms which operate in monopolistic markets are more likely to earn supernormal profits and that these supernormal profits are more likely to persist in the long run.

It can be argued that this means that monopolistic firms can exploit customers by charging higher prices, and earning larger profits than would be the case for firms operating in more competitive markets. This is a possible source of 'market failure' which is considered in greater detail in Unit 15, as are the possible effects of government intervention to promote competition and limit the powers of monopolists.

Profits and the market system

In the previous sections of this unit consideration was given to how firms might respond to changes in profit, especially in competitive markets. Greater potential profits are likely to lead to greater production and will encourage new firms to enter industries which are relatively more profitable. Profits are said to be a signal which guides the use of resources into the production of those goods or services which are most valued by customers.

In the last few years of the twentieth century most commentators considered that the overall UK economy was growing at about 2.5 per cent per annum. However, that growth was not uniform across the country. Industries such as financial services and those associated with computing have grown more rapidly than many traditional manufacturing industries. There was a higher concentration of the latter in the north of the country than in the south east. Similarly, the South East contained a disproportionate number of firms in banking, insurance and computing.

The contrasting fortunes of these industries have affected the job market. There are more job vacancies in the South East than in the North and other regions. Hence there has been a shift in population to the South East, leading to projections of soaring demand for new housing as outlined in the newspaper article.

Report destroys Prescott pledge on countryside

John Prescott's attempts to curb house building in the countryside were in ruins last night.

A panel of inspectors he appointed recommended a near doubling of the number of homes to be built in the South East, outside London, over the next 16 years.

The panel concluded that 1.1 million new homes need to be built between 1996 and 2016 instead of the 668 000 homes originally proposed by Serplan, the regional conference of planning authorities, to which Mr Prescott had devolved the task of devising a regional draft plan.

The extra homes are the equivalent of five cities the size of Southampton. The panel said that more were needed for people moving to the South East and to ensure that homes were affordable to all income groups. The region was 'an engine of growth in the national economy'.

The panel, led by Professor Stephen Crow, a former Chief Planning Inspector, calls for the building of four new towns of between 80 000 and 100 000 homes at Stansted, Ashford, Milton Keynes and Crawley.

Surrey, which would have to absorb a 120 per cent increase in housing numbers, said the report was 'sheer madness' and would mean it alone would have to build the equivalent of two new towns the size of Guildford.

John Redwood, the Tory environment spokesman, described it as a 'massacre' of greenfield sites.

If Mr Prescott approves the panel's recommendations, the number of houses to be built in Surrey over the next 16 years would increase by 120 per cent, from 34 937 to 77 000. Those in Hampshire would have to rise by 66 per cent, from 101 900 to 169 000. Hampshire, with the largest number of houses to build, would be building 8450 a year for 20 years.

The panel clashed with the finding of the government's Urban Task Force, chaired by Lord Rogers, that 60 per cent of the new homes needed over the next 20 years could be built on recycled land, bringing about an 'urban renaissance'.

It said that regional planning guidance, when finalised, should seek only to achieve

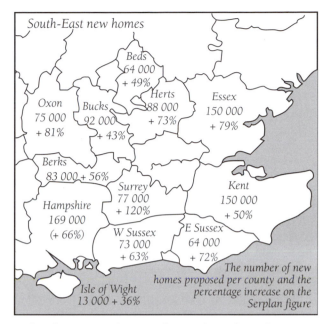

South-east new homes: the number of new homes proposed per county and the percentage increase on the Serplan figure

50 per cent of new development on already developed land in the South East.

The Council for the Protection of Rural England said the report, which Mr Prescott has until the end of the year to approve or reject, would lead to 'a nightmare future of urban decay, traffic congestion and sprawling development which should be firmly rejected by the government'.

Tony Burton, the CPRE's assistant director, said: 'This is quite the most devastating report I've seen. The government's whole approach to planning has been shot to pieces. John Prescott has agreed that "predict and provide" planning is dead and yet this report flatly contradicts this and blindly follows market demands.'

He added: 'It proposes a level of development which the Urban Task Force concluded could not be contemplated and which is 430 000 houses higher than that agreed by local authorities.'

Mr Redwood, who introduced a policy at this week's party conference of councils setting housing numbers, said: 'It is even worse than I feared. Labour came to power promising that it would relieve the pressure on our green fields. It has revealed it intends to massacre them.'

Tony Bosworth, a Friends of the Earth's housing campaigner, said: 'If John Prescott consents to plans for 1.1 million new homes in the South East, nearly 200 000 more homes will have to be built in some of Britain's most beautiful areas.

'It will provoke huge opposition in marginal constituencies. It could be an electoral nightmare for Labour.'

Marc Cranfield-Adams, for the House Builders' Federation, said: 'The independent panel has produced a responsible report that recognises the importance of the South East to Britain's economy.'

Charles Clover in the Daily Telegraph, 9 October 1999

The increase in demand has led to rising house prices in the South East compared to the rest of the country. Profits gained by companies building houses in the South East will rise, builders are likely to build more houses, and more building firms are likely to enter the market in the South East.

The net effect of these changes is that building resources, labour, materials and machinery are likely to be attracted to the South East away from other parts of the country. The chances of increased profits are a 'green' signal for builders to build in the South East, and the fear of reduced profits is a 'red' signal telling builders to build less in other parts of the country.

ACTIVITY 2

How might the economy be affected if a government attempted to tax its supernormal profits of all types of businesses?

Summary

Changing levels of profits will affect the behaviour of all firms, especially those operating in competitive

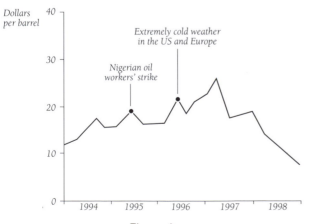

Dollars per barrel

Extremely cold weather in the US and Europe

Nigerian oil workers' strike

Figure 1

markets. Increased profits are likely to stimulate firms into increasing output, and falling profits are likely to lead to falling output.

The levels of profits received by firms operating in monopolistic markets are likely to be higher than those of firms operating in competitive markets.

Profits act as a signal. Rising profits will attract new firms into existing markets. Falling profits are likely to act as a disincentive for new firms to enter markets. These processes will be limited if barriers to entry exist.

The expansion and contraction of both firms and industries in response to changes in profit levels will have a dynamic effect on the whole economy, causing resources to be attracted to uses where profits are greater and to move away from uses in which profits are less or losses are made.

Data response question

Extract A

Surge in oil prices has governments over a barrel

The price of crude oil last week broke the psychologically important level of $25 a barrel. UK motorists have already seen petrol, produced from crude oil, rise several times recently, and, in the skies, jet fuel has leapt by 30%. In the USA, Germany and France, where many homes are heated with oil or diesel, the situation is reaching crisis point. Prices have risen 65% in the past year.

On the supply side, production from non-OPEC countries, such as Norway and the UK, has consistently undershot expectations. Refiners, facing a squeeze on profit margins, have been forced to keep much lower crude oil stocks. The hurricane that hit Mexico and its oil production facilities last year was also significant. The country lost 40 million barrels – the equivalent of OPEC cutting production by 600 000 barrels a day for six months.

But while uncertainty surrounding the supply of producer countries is normally to blame for sharp oil price rises, this time the demand side has fooled the industry experts. Demand was boosted by two factors: a colder winter in the northern hemisphere and a much greater thirst for oil from the emerging market economies. Consumption here rose by more than 3% this year.

Adapted from The Observer, 20 October 1996

Extract B

OPEC over a barrel

This week, the oil price sank below $10 a barrel, its lowest price in real terms since the oil crisis of 1973 – a price which makes North Sea rigs unprofitable.

The days when the Organisation of Petroleum Exporting Countries (OPEC) held the West to ransom have long since disappeared. High prices encouraged new sources of supply to be opened up, notably in the North Sea. Together, Norwegian and British oil production of 10 million barrels per day now exceeds even that of Saudi Arabia, to make it the world's biggest oil producing area.

OPEC was hurt when the West reduced its consumption of energy and embarked on massive diversification into nuclear power (France), domestic oil and gas production (Britain, the United States) and technical measures to slash oil bills (Japan). Technology has played a key role in breaking the back of the oil price – it has allowed the apparently inaccessible North Sea fields to be opened up and exploited in a manner few foresaw 20 years ago.

Extraction rates are rising for similar reasons elsewhere in the world. At the same time, high prices have made every economy more energy efficient, which on top of low growth in Europe and Japan, has restrained the growth in oil demand. The result – an oil price below $10 a barrel. There simply seems to be too much oil about.

Adapted from *The Observer*, 1 April 1998, and the *Guardian*, 13 December 1998

a Using Figure 1 (see page 82), describe the change in the crude oil price from 1994 to 1998.

(5 marks)

b Extract A refers to the change in oil prices up to late 1996. Use this item to

  i identify *two* demand-side and *two* supply-side factors which have influenced this change; (4 marks)

  ii explain, using diagrams, how *one* of these demand-side factors and *one* of these supply-side factors would affect the price of oil. (6 marks)

c In a market economy, prices act as a rationing device, provide incentives and give signals to consumers and producers.

Make use of the data and economic analysis to discuss the impact of changes in oil prices on the allocation of society's resources. (20 marks)

UNIT 14  Free markets

Key concepts covered

- free market
- invisible hand
- productive efficiency
- allocative efficiency
- consumer sovereignty
- price mechanism

Introduction

In this unit the workings of free markets are explained and analysed. The importance of the influence of Adam Smith is considered and two criteria for assessing the effectiveness of free markets are explained. These are:

- allocative efficiency
- productive efficiency.

Adam Smith's hidden hand

Adam Smith, said by some to be the first economist, has given his name to the Adam Smith Institute, a think tank which advocates **free market** solutions to economic problems:

Bus stop

'Bus services would be much better if local transport officials stepped out of the way and allowed private bus operators to manage things freely.' This is the view of Professor John Hibbs in the ASI report 'Don't Stop the Bus'. As you might expect, the opposite is happening. Many transport officials, claims Professor Hibbs, are rejecting the deregulation of the last decade and bringing in a highly regulated European-style franchise system, like that in London.

Unlike a fast food franchise, which faces daily competition and therefore has to offer good service and keen prices, a typical bus franchise has 5–7 years' security of tenure against any rivals. There is therefore little incentive to improve services.

The problem is that transport planners yearn for the pre-privatisation culture of top-down controls. They think their job is to run buses, rather than to move people.

www.adamsmith.org.uk

In his book *The Wealth of Nations* (1776) Adam Smith argued that if all members of society pursued what they perceived to be their selfish interest, then:

'The uniform, constant and uninterrupted effort of every man to better his condition, the principle from which public and national, as well as private opulence is originally derived, is frequently powerful enough to maintain the natural progress of things toward improvement, in spite both of the extravagance of government, and of the greatest errors of administration'.

In other words, society would improve if its individual members were left to their own devices. They would be driven, as if by instinct, to make profits from their activities. Those who were most successful would make the greatest profit. Those who were less successful would fail. Smith argued that an **'invisible hand'** linked producers to consumers and society as a whole. That invisible hand would help ensure that what is actually produced is what people want. His arguments provide much of the basis of the previous units but he argued that this ideal world could be distorted by two factors:

- too much government interference
- monopoly.

Discussing the role of the government Adam Smith said:

'Little else is requisite to carry a state to the highest degree of opulence from the lowest barbarism but peace, easy taxes, and a tolerable administration of justice: all the rest being brought about by the natural course of things.'

And as to the dangers of monopoly:

'A monopoly granted either to an individual or to a trading company has the same effect as a secret in trade or manufactures. The monopolists, by keeping the market constantly under-stocked, by never fully supplying the effectual demand, sell their commodities much above the natural price, and raise their emoluments, whether they consist in wages or profit, greatly above their natural rate.'

Similar analysis is used today to argue that governments should play a much smaller role in the economy. It was suggested above that bus services in London would improve if there were less regulation.

ACTIVITY 1

Divide into two groups. One group should develop further arguments to support the notion that bus services in London would improve if there were fewer regulations. The other group should develop counter arguments.

Discuss the rival viewpoints.

Note any conclusions reached. Is there a consensus?

A free market economy

Economists such as those who are members of the Adam Smith Institute believe in the benefits of a free market economy, which would be one in which all resources are owned privately, and all members of society would be free to engage in any kind of business activity. All economic decisions are taken by individuals who all pursue their own self-interest. Thus, the owners of factors of production are free to sell their resources, but self-interest should ensure that factors are sold to the highest bidder. Some people will choose to be entrepreneurs and take risks in combining particular factors of production in order to produce goods or services in order to earn a good a return as possible. People will also act in this system as customers or consumers whose motive will be to consume as much as possible of chosen products for as little an outlay as possible. The interaction of the independent actions of these economic agents will determine which resources are used to produce which goods or services and also who will consume them. Adam Smith's invisible hand will, it is argued, ensure that this web of independent yet interdependent actions produces outcomes which will be to the benefit of society. To be more precise **productive** and **allocative efficiency** will be maximised.

Allocative efficiency

This relates to the central questions which a study of economics is meant to answer. What gets produced? How is it produced? And who gets what is produced? In a free market it is argued that the consumer rather than the producer or anybody else is 'king'. In other words, customer preferences will determine what is produced. **Consumer sovereignty**, as this concept is known, means that the free market will adapt and change to ensure that what is produced is what customers want. This outcome will be achieved by means of the **price mechanism** which should work as in Figure 14.1.

Figure 14.1 Price mechanism in a free market

> Consumers receive income.
> ↓
> This income is spent to reflect the tastes of individual consumers.
> ↓
> If a good or service is in high demand then consumers will be willing to pay more for it.
> ↓
> Conversely, if a good or service is out of fashion and demand is low consumers will only be willing to pay relatively less.
> ↓
> The market as a theoretical meeting place for producers and consumers 'gathers up' the demands of individuals which are communicated to producers as a set of prices which consumers are prepared to pay.
> ↓
> Producers strive to meet these demands.
> ↓
> Successful producers will meet customer demand and, other things being equal, make larger profits.
> ↓
> Producers who fail to produce what the market wants will make smaller profits and if they completely misjudge demand, they will go out of business.
> ↓
> Firms earning high revenues will be able to pay more for factors of production – land, labour and capital.
> ↓
> Owners of these factors will sell to the highest bidder.
> ↓
> Resources will be diverted to the production of goods which are most in demand.

In other words, freely operating markets ensure that consumers decide which resources are devoted to which uses. Competition ensures that firms will be striving to meet changing customer demands and that those firms which fail to respond effectively to changing patterns of demand will go out of business.

ACTIVITY 2

'Denim is going out of fashion.' How might this change in tastes reported in the late 1990s be translated into changing the way that resources are used?

Figure 14.2 Price mechanism in a freely operating market

Assume one firm operating in one industry discovers a new, more efficient way of making what it produces.

↓

Its average cost of production will fall.

↓

If no other variables change this firm will now earn additional profits.

↓

If these exceed those regarded as normal, competitors will find out and copy the new production technique.

↓

Other firms will enter the industry.

↓

Output in the industry will rise.

↓

Rising output (supply) will cause the price of the product to fall.

↓

Falling prices will reduce the revenue earned by the original firm.

↓

Profits in that firm will fall until normal profits are earned.

↓

Alternatively, if the demand for a particular product or service falls:

↓

Reduced demand leads to a fall in price.

↓

Falling prices will reduce revenues for some firms below what are considered to be normal profits.

↓

Some firms in the industry will cut output.

↓

The least efficient firms will cease production and effectively leave the industry.

↓

Those firms which remain will receive greater market share – rising demand for their products.

↓

Revenues will rise.

↓

Profits will revert to normal.

Productive efficiency

If markets are truly competitive individual producers will be forced by market pressures to produce outputs at which average costs of production are minimised. This concept relates to the basic question 'How are goods and services produced?' and it follows that if markets are competitive and if there is relative freedom of entry and exit, that costs of production for an individual firm will be squeezed to a minimum. The reasons for this have been given earlier but freely operating markets should enable the price mechanism to work as in Figure 14.2.

In short, the forces of competition are such that any tendency by one firm to be more efficient and to cut costs will be copied by competitors, and any contraction in demand will be accompanied by the disappearance of the least efficient producers. This is a continuing process which should result in ever growing efficiencies in those markets which are truly competitive.

ACTIVITY 3

a Use other texts and journals to research the answers to the following questions:

 i How accurately does this free market model describe how our economy actually works?

 ii Are consumers sovereign?

 iii Are firms compelled to be as efficient as possible?

 What conclusions did you reach?

b check whether or not the economy works in the ways described in this unit?

c government interference were both threats to the efficient and effective working of the economy. Why?

Summary

A competitive economy in which the role of the government is minimised and in which there are no monopolies should ensure that customers determine what is produced, and that competitive pressures compel firms to be as efficient as possible.

Section 4 is devoted to exploring why free market solutions to the economic problem:

■ may not work

■ may be inappropriate

■ may be considered socially unacceptable.

Data response question

Beverages

Our key beverages businesses performed well in the first half of 1999 against a strong comparable period in 1998. At constant exchange rates, sales of £929 million were up 4% and trading profit at £169 million was up 9%. Trading margin increased by a point to 18.2% and marketing investment grew by 8%.

In the US, Dr Pepper/Seven Up, for the first time since acquisition, outperformed the total market with volumes up 3% for the first half generating a trading profit increase of 9%. The Dr Pepper brand is, for the fifteenth consecutive year, growing ahead of the market. 7 UP's overall performance was held back by competitive conditions in a few key markets. Encouraging progress was made by our key flavour brands in the US, particularly Sunkist, Welch's, Canada Dry, A&W Root Beer and Country Time Lemonade.

Elsewhere in North America, The American Bottling Company is undertaking a major restructuring programme which impacted on second quarter profits. Mott's had a difficult first quarter but a substantial sales increase in the second quarter gives confidence for the remainder of the year.

Our operations in Europe recorded an 8% increase in trading profit.

An excellent performance in Australia saw market share gains and leadership in non-cola beverages achieved for the first time, driving a 9% increase in trading profit in the Pacific Rim.

In Africa and Others, a 29% increase in trading profit was led by South Africa and Bromor's performance in particular.

Confectionery

Good performances from our largest chocolate businesses in the UK and Australia with market shares ahead contributed, at constant exchange rates, to a 1% increase in sales to £961 million and trading profit up 2% at £106 million. Most of our other confectionery businesses also recorded good results but a small number of markets experienced short-term trading issues, mainly in the first quarter, which diluted overall performance.

Cadbury Ltd in the UK achieved a trading profit growth of 6% and a market share increase of one percentage point for the half year. Cadbury Australia grew trading profit 12% and recorded a strong market share gain of 2.5 percentage points.

Elsewhere we saw robust contributions from our businesses in Spain, Ireland, Argentina, our chocolate operation in Canada, and also India, New Zealand and Malaysia which is making a very strong comeback after the problems in Asia last year.

Group trading profit (half year)

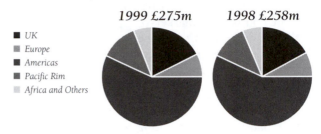

- ■ UK
- ■ Europe
- ■ Americas
- ■ Pacific Rim
- ■ Africa and Others

Cadbury Schweppes plc, Interim Report 1999

Both China and Russia reduced their operating losses. We anticipate breakeven in China in 2000 and our Russian business is performing in line with revised expectations.

Weaker businesses included Trebor Bassett in the UK which experienced some trade destocking and was affected by a major internal reorganisation in the first half, now successfully completed.

Our Continental European confectionery businesses continued to be affected by the Russian economic collapse in the second half of 1998; this has particularly impacted our German business, Piasten.

New product launches and increased marketing contributed to improving performances in the second quarter, which augurs well for the second half.

1 Identify five products produced by Cadbury Schweppes. (4)
2 How might Cadbury Schweppes have increased its trading profit by 9 per cent with an increase in sales of 4 per cent? (4)
3 Assess the relative success of Cadbury Schweppes' US beverage brands. (6)
4 Assess the relative success of Cadbury Schweppes' European confectionery business. (6)

Section 3 questions

Essays

1 Examine the significance of elasticity in decisions relating to:
a the decrease in the price of petrol by Tesco (6)
b an increase in the tax on tobacco (6)
c the pricing of long-haul holidays. (6)

2 To what extent can demand and supply analysis be used to explain:
a the falling cost of long-distance phone calls (6)
b the earnings of top footballers (6)
c the failings of the NHS? (6)

3 Are there advantages gained from having less competitive markets or disadvantages from having more competitive markets? (10)
What might be the consequences of the Post Office losing its monopoly to collect and deliver letters for less than £1. (10)

4 Assess the economic implications of proposals to:
a privatise the NHS (10)
b nationalise the rail operating companies. (10)

Project
Work with others to undertake the following:
a Select an area accessible to your home/school/college
b Survey local firms as to:
i size
ii ownership
iii industrial sector
c Carry out a sample survey within each of these sectors to determine:
i market share
ii competitiveness
iii performance.
d Use your findings to assess likely economic developments in your chosen area.
e Assess the significance of your research findings to your understanding of economic theory.

Multiple choice questions
1 If research identified a clear link between the consumption of beef products and the disease CJD, the consumption of beef would be likely to fall. The effect on price would be greatest if the supply of beef was
A perfectly inelastic
B perfectly elastic
C elastic
D of unitary elasticity.

2 A normal good can be distinguished from an inferior good because a normal good has
a positive price elasticity of demand
b negative price elasticity of demand
c positive income elasticity of demand
d negative income elasticity of demand.

3 An industry's supply curve is more likely to be elastic if
a firms are operating below full capacity
B producers have low levels of stocks
C new firms are unable to enter the market
D workers are highly trained with specialised skills.

4 If the elasticity of supply of steel is 0.75, an increase in the price from £20 to £22 per tonne will increase the quantity produced per week from 2000 tonnes to
A 2750 tonnes
B 2420 tonnes
C 2200 tonnes
D 2150 tonnes.

5 The diagram shows two supply curves (S1 and S2) and two demand curves (D1 and D2) for product X.

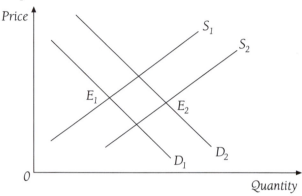

A movement from E_1 to E_2 could be caused by
A a fall in the price of raw materials with an increase in the price of substitutes for product X
B a tax on the output of the product with an increase in consumer incomes
C a fall in production costs with an increase in the price of complements for product X
D a subsidy on the product with a change in consumer tastes away from the product.

6 Which one of the following would be the most probable consequence of an increase in the supply of butter, the supply curve of margarine remaining unchanged?
A A decrease in the price of butter and an increase in the price of margarine
B An increase in the price of butter, bread and margarine
C An increase in the demand for margarine leading to an increase in its price
D A decrease in the price of butter and possibly of margarine also

7 What would be the long run effect on the price and output of natural rubber in the free market if consumers' preferences switched to synthetic rubber?
A Price will rise and output will fall
B Price will rise and output will rise
C Price will fall and output will fall
D Price will fall and output will rise

Section 4
Market failure and government intervention

Introduction

Market failure is a blanket term used by economists to describe situations in which markets might not work and/or markets might work to produce socially undesirable outcomes. The existence of such undesirable outcomes has provided governments with a justification for market intervention.

This section focuses on why markets might be considered to fail and what might be done to minimise the ill-effects of such failure. It deals with three sources of possible market failure and outlines government attempts to correct or ameliorate the worst effects of market failure.

15 Monopoly power

Key concepts covered

- price discrimination
- productive efficiency
- allocative efficiency
- Competition Commission
- the public interest
- privatisation
- barriers to entry

Introduction

The existence of monopolies can distort the workings of the free market system in the following ways:

- Prices can be higher than they would be in more competitive markets
- Choices can be restricted or illusionary.

This unit considers how and why monopolies might behave and whether or not they are acting in the public interest. Consideration is also given to how the UK government intervenes in an attempt to protect the wider interests of society.

Higher prices

Those companies that have monopolistic power can be price makers. Unit 12 explained that such firms have much greater freedom to push up the price charged for their products or services than firms operating in more competitive markets. This is illustrated in Figure 15.1.

The demand facing a firm having monopolistic power will tend to be more inelastic than that facing a firm in a more competitive market. In Figure 15.1 firm A has more scope in raising prices as customers have fewer alternative products which they can buy. However, if firm B raises prices even by a small amount such as p_1 to p_2, most of its potential customers will turn to substitute products.

Up to 50% off the price of your new car		
Make	**Price – UK**	**Europe**
Alfa 156	£17 800	£13 000
Audi Cab 2.8	£31 000	£24 000
BMW 318I	£19 950	£16 000
BMW 328I	£28 000	£21 000
Ford Focus	£14 000	£10 000
LandRover Free	£18 500	£15 000
Mazda 323	£11 770	£6 900
Peugeot 106	£13 200	£8 000
Porsche Boxter	£35 000	£29 000
Renault Clio	£10 505	£7 000
Seat Ibiza	£15 700	£8 000
VW Polo	£11 730	£8 100
Volvo S40	£16 600	£11 700
These prices are for identical cars!		

Source: Eurobuyers Guide

Firms with monopoly power can also charge different sets of customers different prices for the same product. Thus, in the advert for *Eurobuyers Guide* (see above) a Mazda 323 appears to be nearly £5000 more expensive in the UK than in the rest of Europe. Traditionally, car manufacturers have used the excuse of different specifications to charge different prices for the same

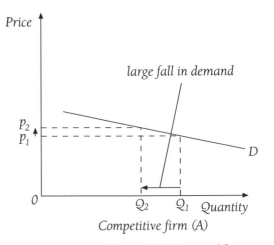

Competitive firm (A)

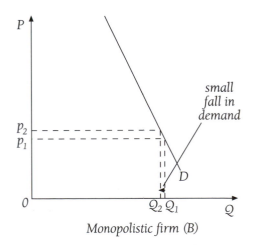

Monopolistic firm (B)

Figure 15.1 Demand for competitive market compared to monopolistic market

products across Europe. This particular form of monopoly power is called **price discrimination** and companies have used this technique to boost profits by charging higher prices to those with more inelastic demands and lower prices to those whose demand is relatively more elastic. This is becoming an increasingly common practice and there is evidence that companies deliberately create slightly different prices for the same or similar products in order to confuse customers.

Restricted choice

Monopolies can exploit the dependence of their customers on their products by restricting choice. Henry Ford was famous for saying that customers could buy a Model T Ford in any colour as long as it was black. More modern forms of this kind of behaviour include limiting the number of retailers allowed to sell particular products. Some electrical goods manufacturers do this, arguing that particular expertise is required to sell their products. Such practice makes it easier for manufacturers to ensure that retailers do not cut prices.

ACTIVITY 1

Survey prices of TVs in local stores. What evidence does this reveal of competition in this particular market?

Another company Birds Eye Wall's Ltd, a subsidiary of the Unilever group supplies 70 per cent of wrapped ice-cream to the UK market. It distributes ice-cream through wholesalers with whom it has contracts which do not allow them to distribute products made by competitors. Birds Eye Wall's operates a complex set of deals which means that those retailers who stocked only their products are given better deals than those who also stock competitors' products. The sheer size and scale of Birds Eye Wall's production, the strength of its brand name and its high expenditure on advertising and promotion all combine to give the company the power to undertake anti-competitive activity.

It could, however, be argued that the size and economic power of Birds Eye Wall's are such that it can afford to develop and market a product range wide enough to meet the needs of customers with different tastes and preferences, and also to enjoy economies of scale which allow the company to remain internationally competitive.

A challenge to the market system

Firms, through the exercise of monopolistic power, can raise prices and/or restrict customer choice. Both of these features distort the market system into producing a further set of outcomes which could be claimed to be socially undesirable:

- **productive inefficiency**
- **allocative inefficiency**.

Productive inefficiency

Firms in a competitive market are pressured into becoming productively efficient. They have an incentive to minimise average costs of production. Supernormal profits are competed away in the long run and firms that fail to make normal profits will find that it is difficult to carry on production. One way of boosting profits is to innovate and improve product design, either to capture a larger market share or to reduce costs of production. Both strategies will boost profits in the short run. If an industry is both truly competitive and dynamic products will be continually improved and prices should be driven down.

On the other hand, a monopolist is insulated from competition. Supernormal profits can be earned as long as demand is high relative to costs, and in an absolute monopoly barriers to entry would prevent competition from new businesses. For these reasons there is less incentive for a monopolistic firm to be efficient, by keeping costs to a minimum productivity.

If monopoly power is common within an economy then it is likely that that economy will be less dynamic and will produce more expensive goods and services.

Allocative efficiency

As has already been demonstrated a monopolist has more power to determine the price or output of a product, and can also use market power to restrict choice, and to use strategies such as price discrimination to confuse potential customers and boost profits. These approaches take power away from consumers which can mean that an economy in which there is considerable monopoly power will produce goods and services which monopolies choose to produce rather than those which consumers indicate that they want. This will reduce allocative efficiency. This means that resources will not necessarily be allocated according to customer preferences which is meant to be one of the benefits of having competitive markets.

Government responses to monopoly power

The UK and most other world governments pursue the following two strategies in order to reduce the possible distortions to the economy caused by the existence of monopoly power:

- Limit non-competitive behaviour by various constraints and controls.
- Encourage competitive behaviour by trying to create competitive conditions in markets.

Limiting the power of monopolists

All western countries have policies which are intended to protect customers from exploitation by the exercise of monopoly power, and in the UK these are the responsibility of the Secretary of State for Trade and Industry. There is considerable legislation which is designed to protect the interests of consumers and possibly limit the power of monopolists. In law, a monopoly exists if 25 per cent of sales in a given market are in the hands of one firm. There is a legal framework by which mergers that would result in gaining a similar market share are investigated. These and other laws to protect customers are 'policed' by the **Competition Commission** which was created on 1 April 1999 by the government in an attempt to strengthen consumer protection. This government body took over from the Monopolies and Mergers Commission and is responsible for undertaking investigations made possible by various legislation.

The role of the Competition Commission
The Competition Commission's role is to investigate and report on matters referred to it relating to mergers, monopolies, anti-competitive practices, the regulation of utilities and the performance of public sector bodies. The Competition Commission cannot initiate its own inquiries. Most referrals were made by the Director General of Fair Trading (DGFT), the Secretary of State for Trade and Industry and the regulators of utilities. In almost all cases, the Competition Commission is asked to decide whether or not the matter referred was against the public interest.

www.competition-commission.gov.uk

Table 15.1 Sources of Competition Commission investigations

Type of inquiry	Governing legislation	Referral made by
Monopoly	Fair Trading Act 1973	Director General of Fair Trading, Secretary of State or certain Utility Regulators
Merger	Fair Trading Act 1973	Director General of Fair Trading, Secretary of State or certain Utility Regulators
Newspaper merger	Fair Trading Act 1973	Secretary of State
Anti-competitive practices	Competition Act 1980	Director General of Fair Trading or certain Utility Regulators
Public sector references	Competition Act 1980	Secretary of State
General references	Fair Trading Act 1973	Secretary of State
Restrictive labour practices	Fair Trading Act 1973	Secretary of State
Broadcasting	Broadcasting Act 1990	Independent Television Commission or holder of regional Channel 3 licence
Utility references		
Telecommunications	Telecommunications Act 1984	Director General of Telecommunications
Gas	Gas Act 1986 and 1995 Gas (N Ireland) Order 1996	Director General of Gas Supply Director General of Gas Supply for Northern Ireland
Water	Water Industry Act 1991	Director General of Water Services
Electricity	Electricity Act 1989 Electricity (N Ireland) Order 1992	Director General of Electricity Supply Director General of Electricity Supply for Northern Ireland
Railways	Railways Act 1993	Rail Regulator
Water merger	Water Industry Act 1991	Secretary of State
Airports	Airports Act 1986 Airports (N Ireland) Order 1994	Civil Aviation Authority Civil Aviation Authority

Table 15.1 summarises the extent of recent legislation relating to the control of monopolies. The Competition Commission is a quasi-legal body which considers evidence prior to making judgements as to:

1   whether or not a particular firm or group of firms has acted in such a way as to violate any of the laws or regulations relating to that firm
2   whether a firm or group of firms has, for example, acted in an uncompetitive way, and its actions are against **the public interest**.

The notion of the public interest is a legal recognition that although firms may be judged to be uncompetitive there may be off-setting benefits to the public.

The Competition Commission reports directly to the Secretary of State for Trade and Industry and it is up to the government to decide on what action needs to be taken. The Commission also has powers to investigate mergers, which would have the effect of creating monopoly power.

ACTIVITY 2

Explore the web site www.competition-commission.gov.uk and produce a summary of current investigations by the Competition Commission. Why do you think these particular firms are under investigation?

Promoting competitive behaviour

UK governments have in recent years used a range of strategies in order to try to make markets more competitive. These policies are particularly associated with the Conservative government in power from 1979 to 1997, and there is every indication that the present Labour administration will continue to promote competition. There have been three main ways in which competition has been encouraged:

- through privatisation
- through removal of barriers to entry preventing the entry of new firms to some industries
- through promotion of entrepreneurial activity.

Privatisation

Privatisation refers to the transfer of ownership from the public to the private sector. This process is also called de-nationalisation and includes the 'selling off' of such diverse organisations as British Rail, the water boards and parts of the British airplane and motor vehicle industries. It is argued that if these organisations are freed from government control and interference that they will behave more competitively. There is an intense political and economic debate as to whether or not these strategies will produce such outcomes. Some have argued that privatisation merely replaces public sector monopoly power with private sector monopoly power, but time and more evidence will provide a better basis for making such judgements.

Removing barriers to entry

Policies to remove **barriers to entry** are designed directly to attack one of the main sources of monopoly power – legal, financial, historical and institutional barriers which prevent movement of firms in and out of an industry. Thus, opticians have had their exclusive right to sell spectacles to the public removed. Private firms are encouraged to compete for national and local government contracts, and various schemes have been designed to make it easier to get enough venture capital to start new businesses. The fact that there are now an increasing number of small businesses in the economy may provide evidence that these strategies have had some success.

Encouraging enterprise

Some argue that UK society provides less encouragement of entrepreneurial activities than some of our competitors, notably the United States. It has been argued that British people avoid risk taking, and look unfavourably at those who have made money by being entrepreneurial. Successive governments have tried to make it easier for people to start up their own businesses. Grants have been given to make this easier and support networks such as Business Link have been created to provide advice to small businesses. As indicated earlier, there has been a growth in the number of small businesses in recent years, but it is also noteworthy that business failure is greatest in the early years of new businesses.

ACTIVITY 3

Assess the strengths and weaknesses of the strategies used by the UK Government to promote competition.

Summary

Since the end of World War II, the UK government has enacted legislation designed to limit the abuse of monopoly power, especially in respect of protecting consumers from over pricing and a restricted choice of products. It has been argued that the existence of monopoly power tilts the balance of the economy away from meeting the interests of consumers to meeting those of large powerful companies. The existence of monopolies may, therefore, also make an economy less efficient both in terms of costs of production and in terms of customers being able to buy the goods and services which they demand.

Although the UK government has extensive powers to investigate large firms, monopolistic behaviour is common in our economy. This may reflect the inadequacy of controls or the sheer impossibility of governments to police the activities of large firms. The government does appear to have greater success in encouraging the set up of small firms and the creation of more competitive behaviour in some markets.

Data response question

Torn off a strip

Football supporters and parents of young fans should benefit from lower prices for replica kits after Premier League clubs, the Football Association (FA) and the Scottish FA promised to take action to prevent price fixing.

They have agreed that licensing contracts with manufacturers will include a requirement that retailers will not be prevented from discounting replica kits. Where contracts are already in place, manufacturers will have to tell dealers they can sell kits at whatever price they choose.

The move follows an OFT investigation prompted by complaints from retailers that shirt makers were threatening to hold back supplies if prices dropped below a set minimum.

'I have no doubt that both supporters and parents have been paying artificially high prices,' said Director General of Fair Trading John Bridgeman. 'Retailers are now free to set their own prices, and I hope we will soon see a variety of discounts.'

The OFT investigation found that several clubs had encouraged manufacturers to prevent discounting. Although the clubs are not considered to be suppliers and so have not themselves breached the law, the Director General of Fair Trading was keen to stress that any involvement in price maintenance was totally unacceptable.

During the OFT's two-year investigation, manufacturers Puma UK, Asics (UK) Ltd and Gilbert and Pollard Sports Ltd all gave assurances that they would not attempt to enforce minimum resale prices.

From 1 March next year [2000], the Director General will be able to impose penalties of up to 10 per cent of UK turnover on any party involved in price fixing – even if it is only through informal cooperation.

Office of Fair Trading, *Fair Trading News*, October 1999 (www.oft.gov.uk)

1 To what extent have football kit manufacturers attempted to distort a competitive market? (4)

2 Why might football clubs also be involved in fixing the prices of replica kit? (4)

3 Assess the likely economic outcomes of this example of government intervention. (6)

4 What evidence is offered that the government intends to try to make markets more competitive? (6)

UNIT
16 Externalities

Key concepts covered

- third-party effects
- negative externalities
- private costs
- social costs
- positive externalities
- private benefits
- social benefits
- cost benefit analysis
- 'government failure'
- public goods

Introduction

Externalities are defined by economists as **third-party effects** of any transaction between a consumer and a firm. Externalities can be either positive or negative. It can be argued that if markets are left to themselves too many goods and services will be produced which have harmful third-party effects and too few goods and services will be produced which have beneficial third-party effects. This unit examines these arguments and provides an introduction to discussion as to methods, which may be used by governments to correct this form of market failure.

The potential existence of externalities is illustrated in Figure 16.1.

Negative externalities

A whole range of industrial and commercial activities can give rise to **negative externalities**.

The photograph below captures the energy and activity which was said to characterise the industrial

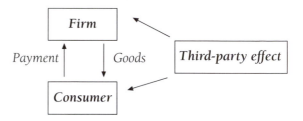

Figure 16.1 Third-party effects

revolution. Manufacturing was revolutionised by the use of steam power and the mechanisation of productive processes. Many firms paid scant regard to the effects of their activities on others. Smoke and other effluents poisoned the air. Clear and pure water was used to cool and clean and wash and was then returned to rivers and watercourses as pollution. Little attention was paid to the health and well-being of workers. Over time, efforts were made to remedy these unpleasant effects of the industrial revolution. Laws were passed governing health and safety. Town councils intervened to provide supplies of clear water and some factory owners decided that profits were better earned if proper regard was paid to the health and well-being of workers.

Negative externalities and market failure

Negative externalities are, however, still created today. Industrial practices common in Europe 160 years ago are now commonplace in the third world. Opponents of experiments in the production of genetically modified crops claim that their introduction will have significant effects on traditional farming. Anti-social behaviour by consumers of alcohol, and tobacco, can affect the well-being and health of 'innocent' third parties.

Negative externalities are significant to economists especially in the context of consideration of the strengths and weaknesses of the market system because their existence places additional costs on other members of society. Thus, there are links between smoking tobacco and a range of serious diseases. Treatment of patients with these diseases means that the National Health Service and private health insurance companies are faced with additional expenditure. If markets operate freely and effectively the price that a customer pays for a product or service should represent the actual costs involved in the production of that product or service. If this production generates additional costs which are incurred by other members of society the market system can be said to have failed. This can be

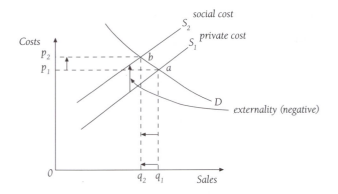

Figure 16.2 Private, external and social costs

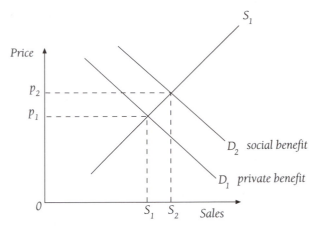

Figure 16.3 Positive externalities

illustrated in graphical form. In Figure 16.2 S_1 represents the costs of production faced by the producer of a good. These are known as **private costs**. S_2 represents the additional external costs which the production of this product creates. Private costs + external costs = **social costs**, i.e. the full costs to society of making the product.

If there were no government or other intervention, equilibrium would be reached at a and p_1 would be the price charged for the product and q_1 would represent the quantity sold. However, if it were possible to calculate the external costs, these could be added to the private costs. If consumers were required to pay the full social cost of production, a different equilibrium would prevail at b, giving a higher price of p_2 and reduced sales of q_2. In other words, a freely operating market would lead to lower prices and higher outputs of goods which have harmful environmental and/or social consequences.

Positive externalities

Unintended external effects do not necessarily lead to greater costs for society as a whole. Some economic transactions generate more beneficial third-party effects. Thus, the provision of clean piped water will directly benefit those who are directly supplied but may also contribute to better standards of health, less illness and disease, and greater productivity. Similarly,

improvements to education and training may benefit society as a whole, as well as those individuals who are directly concerned with the improvements.

The existence of **positive externalities** can also be illustrated graphically. In Figure 16.3 D_1 represents the demand from individuals, i.e. the **private benefits** gained from purchasing a particular good or service and S_1 represents the costs of providing that good or service.

The market equilibrium is given at c with a price of p_1 and sales of S_1. If, however, it were possible to quantify the positive externalities associated with the provision of this good or service, these could be represented by D_2 showing the full **social benefits** that would benefit society as a whole. If these additional benefits were to be taken into account the equilibrium would be at d with outputs S_2 selling for p_2. In other words, more would be produced. In this case freely operating markets would said to be failing because less would be produced of socially useful goods which would sell at higher prices.

Cost benefit analysis

Economists have long recognised the existence of externalities and have developed a range of statistical techniques in an effort to quantify both negative and positive externalities. This approach is called **cost benefit analysis** and involves attempting to give a monetary value to externalities.

Cost benefit analysis can be applied to new investments and also to existing markets. For example, there has been a long running enquiry into the building of a new terminal at Heathrow airport. Supporters claim that it will aid economic growth not just of those directly concerned but also for firms and employees dependent upon the continued growth and expansion of Heathrow. On the other hand, a range of interests opposed to the development have argued that noise pollution, congestion and the like will impose additional costs on the local community. As part of the process to decide whether or not permission should be given for this new development, cost benefit analysis has been undertaken. This is designed to reveal the full costs to society, i.e. social cost of the new development, and the full benefits, i.e. social benefit. Undertaking this calculation involves the following stages:

1 Identification and quantification of all private costs.
2 Identification and quantification of all external costs.
3 Calculation of social cost – these are the private and external costs added together.
4 Identification and quantification of all private benefits.
5 Identification and quantification of all external benefits.
6 Calculation of social benefit – these are the private and external benefits added together.
7 Comparison of social costs with social benefits. In theory, if the social benefit exceeds the social cost, society as a whole would benefit from the development, and if this relationship were reversed society would be economically worse off.

The challenge to those undertaking cost benefit analysis is to put a financial valuation on external costs and benefits. For example, it is difficult to quantify the monetary value of noise pollution. One approach might be to calculate the extent to which house prices and/or rents in the surrounding area might be affected while another might involve working out the costs of additional soundproofing. Assessing the impact on environmental factors such as the disturbance to particular plants or animals is even more problematical. Similarly, valuing indirect benefits such as those which might accrue to local businesses requires a mixture of approximations, forecasts and guesswork.

Government intervention

Negative externalities

Governments have traditionally used one of three broad approaches to try to reduce the impact of negative externalities:

■ The price mechanism.
■ Direct controls.
■ Persuasion.

Price mechanism

This approach can be illustrated diagrammatically as shown in Figure 16.4

A government could use the outcomes of cost benefit analysis to estimate external costs and if the government introduced a tax equal to the vertical distance a-b, then consumers of this product would be forced to pay a price, p^2, which represented the full costs to society of its production. Output would be reduced to Q^2 and a source of market failure would be reduced. If the government wished to control the harmful effects of negative externalities in this way it would have to overcome two major problems:

■ calculating the external costs of producing the good or service
■ calculating exactly the amount of tax which equates with the external costs of producing the good or service.

The first of these problems was considered in more detail in the previous section on cost benefit analysis and difficulties of setting a precise tax place great pressure on a government and can give rise to 'government failure'. This is a concept which recognises that governments can make mistakes and that the political process can distort the outcomes of planned government intervention. In this case if the

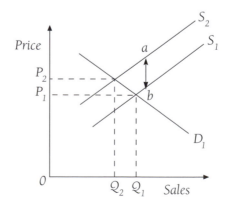

Figure 16.4 Taxing away negative externalities

tax is set too high or low the market distortion caused by this kind of market failure will not be corrected.

Direct controls

Governments can choose to pass laws and use the existing legislative framework in an attempt to control and constrain the behaviour of firms and industries which generate negative externalities. Thus, in the UK emissions of potentially dangerous chemicals are controlled by various regulations. Advertising by the tobacco industry is limited and car safety is promoted by annual car tests.

The main problems in getting direct controls to work are:

■ the possibility of '**government failure**'

■ evasion.

Government failure can occur especially as a result of the pressure which can be put upon government by various pressure groups and lobbyists. Thus, in 1999 the government announced that not all cigarette advertising was to be banned as quickly as originally intended. It has been argued that groups such as those promoting Formula 1 racing have been able to persuade the government to change its policies.

The introduction of any control or regulation provides scope for evasion. Policing emission controls is very difficult and in many cases the penalties for non-compliance are not very strong deterrents. Black markets can grow if government controls attempt to stifle significant consumer demands. Some negative externalities are global and this presents individual governments with additional difficulties in controlling and enforcing direct controls.

Persuasion

Some consider that changing customer and producer behaviour to ensure that greater account is taken of externalities is so complex and difficult that it is more effective in the long term to change the attitudes of those who demand and those who supply products and services which create negative externalities. Thus, the UK government part funds the Health Education Authority whose role includes that of encouraging people to eat healthier diets. If this approach is successful the effects will be fed through the market system. It is possible to argue that the demand for organic produce is a result of greater awareness of the importance of a healthy diet.

The problems with this approach to minimise the effects of negative externalities is that achieving attitudinal change is

■ long term

■ unpredictable.

Discussion and debate about the benefits of the production of organic foodstuffs have been going on for upwards of 50 years. For many years such arguments were dismissed as eccentric and inappropriate. However, in the late 1990s the major supermarkets started to devote increasing amounts of shelf space to the display of organic foods.

Changing the behaviour of people involves affecting complex and deep-rooted attitudes. Public relations campaigns do not always work in the ways in which they were intended. Some are far more successful than anticipated. Many depend upon the coincidence of other events. The problems that the British government faced in 1998–9 trying to gather more evidence as to the effectiveness of genetically modified crops is an example of a government attempt to change attitudes that has not worked.

Positive externalities

A similar framework can be used to explore options for governments to intervene to try to ensure that economic activity which has positive externalities is undertaken. The government could use the same techniques:

■ Price mechanism.

■ Direct controls.

■ Persuasion.

Price mechanism

Figure 16.5 illustrates the possible existence of positive externalities.

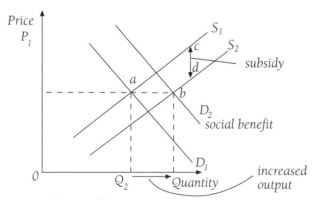

a = market equilibrium
b = equilibrium after government intervention
   in form of a subsidy

Figure 16.5 Using subsidies to account for positive externalities

If the government wished to work through the price mechanism to try to boost production of a product or service which a free market would over price and under produce, it could use cost benefit analysis to calculate the positive externality and it would need to pay a subsidy to producers equal to the vertical distance cd. The outcome would be production rising to q_2.

The problems of pursuing such a policy would be the same as those identified in the treatment of government intervention to reduce the effects of negative externalities.

Direct controls

In addition to the approaches outlined in the section about controlling negative externalities, a government might decide that the production of a particular good or service has significant positive externalities which society would not benefit from if markets were left to operate freely. Thus, in many market-based economies governments intervene to provide education, health and other public services. Such goods are dealt with in more detail in Unit 17 which is concerned with aspects of equity or fairness.

Persuasion

It could be argued that much of any government's work is concerned with the function of persuasion in the form of advertising, political campaigning and the like.

ACTIVITY 3

Undertake an investigation of a market in which you consider there are significant positive or negative externalities. Indicate how cost benefit analysis might be used in order to place a monetary value on such externalities. Consider the strengths and weaknesses of this approach.

Suggest possible government intervention strategies to take account of the externalities you have identified.

The Internet will provide you with evidence which you can use for this investigation. Start by looking at the following web sites:

www.foe.co.uk
www.oneworld.org
www.wiredforhealth.gov.uk

Summary

This unit has been devoted to consideration of both positive and negative externalities. The existence of these 'third party' effects and distort the price mechanism and lead to socially undesirable outcomes providing a rationale for government intervention. Governments may seek to encourage the greater production where positive externalities exist and limit production if negative externalities are identified. Devising effective interventionist policies is not easy and can involve international discussions and agreement.

Data response question

Some may have judged London 'the coolest city in the world' last year but the capital is winning few prizes for the state of its tube network. Griping about the underground has long been a favourite commuter pastime. But further cuts in government funding and a rush of disturbing accidents raise fears that the network is heading for an all-out collapse. (lines 1–7)

After a summer of strikes Mr Kenneth Clarke, the chancellor, must have considered London Underground a soft target for spending cuts in this year's budget. But the public tends to be less concerned by planned stoppages than those which occur by accident. Twice last year power failures brought almost the entire network to a standstill for several hours. Escalators are collapsing, embankments and tunnels are crumbling. (lines 8–16)

Not all the mishaps can be put down to under-investment. But the visible deterioration in the quality of the system adds weight to the warnings from London Underground and transport pressure groups that the system is approaching breaking point. (lines 17–22)

Reversing this year's cuts, as the grounds demand, might prevent the network deteriorating even further. But the problem goes well beyond a few years' funding. London First, a consortium of businesses pushing for better transport, calculates that 40 years of under-investment have produced a £1.2 bn backlog of projects needed to maintain and modernise the system. (lines 23–30)

The true figure required to give London a half-decent modern underground network may be significantly less than this. But even so, direct funding by government is unlikely to meet much of the shortfall. Nor should it. It would be grossly unfair for the country's

Figure 1   *Road traffic growth*

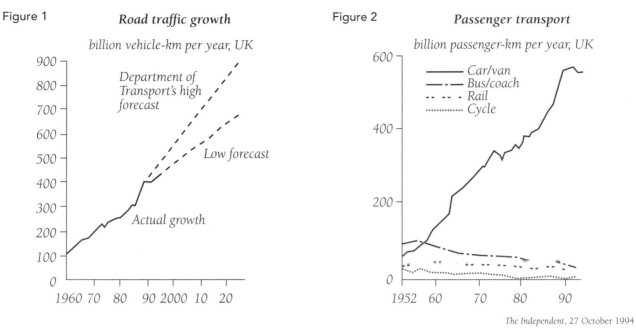

billion vehicle-km per year, UK

Department of Transport's high forecast

Low forecast

Actual growth

Figure 2   *Passenger transport*

billion passenger-km per year, UK

—— Car/van
—·—· Bus/coach
– – – Rail
········ Cycle

The Independent, 27 October 1994

Figure 3   *Road transport costs and revenue, 1993*

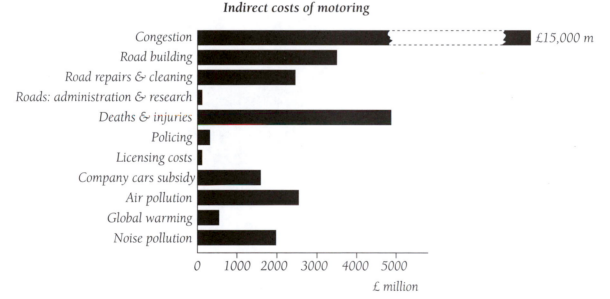

Indirect costs of motoring

Congestion	£15,000 m
Road building	
Road repairs & cleaning	
Roads: administration & research	
Deaths & injuries	
Policing	
Licensing costs	
Company cars subsidy	
Air pollution	
Global warming	
Noise pollution	

0 1000 2000 3000 4000 5000

£ million

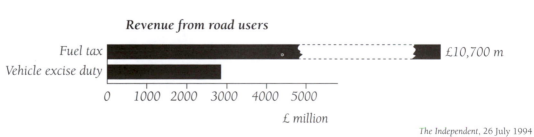

Revenue from road users

Fuel tax	£10,700 m
Vehicle excise duty	

0 1000 2000 3000 4000 5000

£ million

The Independent, 26 July 1994

richest region to get a large increase in investment funds at the general taxpayer's expense. The cost, rather, should be met by the local beneficiaries. (lines 31–9)

This does not just mean the direct users, who last week had to swallow yet another above-inflation rise in ticket prices. London as a whole – particularly its businesses – would gain from the reduced congestion and higher property values. (lines 40–4)

One solution would be finally to introduce some form of road-pricing to bring the personal cost of car use within the city closer to the true, social cost. (lines 45–7)

'Future going underground' in *The Financial Times*,
9 January 1997

1 Outline the problems associated with under-investment in the London Underground network. (2 marks)

2 **a** Explain what is meant by the term 'external benefits'. (2 marks)
b Identify two external benefits of a modern, efficient underground network in London. (2 marks)

3 Examine the case for and against the improvements to the London Underground being financed out of general tax revenues. (6 marks)

4 With reference to Figures 1 and 2 and any other relevant information, explain the growth in road traffic since 1960. (10 marks)

5 **a** With reference to Figure 3 and to the statement below, explain what is meant by the part of the following statement which is underlined:

'One solution would be to introduce some form of road pricing <u>to bring the personal cost of care use within the city closer to the true, social cost</u>' (lines 45–7).

Illustrate your answer with a diagram. (8 marks)
b With reference to the data and other material, examine the case for and against a system of road pricing. (10 marks)

Key concepts covered

- equity
- income distribution
- merit good
- public goods
- demerit goods

Introduction

Because of fears of undesirable outcomes, governments rarely allow markets to operate without intervention. Even Adam Smith advocated a role for governments to ensure that markets worked. Today, all governments play an active role in influencing how economies operate. The form and purposes of government intervention differ in different economies. Most governments develop policies and pass laws and regulations designed to limit the ability of free markets to create:

- inequalities
- the under production of socially desirable goods
- the over production of socially undesirable goods.

This unit examines how freely operating markets might lead to these socially undesirable outcomes and considers the effectiveness of government intervention in attempting to create **equity**.

Inequalities

There are two ways in which free markets might contribute to increasing inequalities in society. Firstly, the market mechanism allocates different rewards to the owners of different factors of production. In other words, it rewards those who own factors in short supply and penalises those who own factors which are relatively more plentiful. It creates both winners and losers.

Winners and losers

Freely operating markets depend on the existence of different price and income levels in order to signal changes in demand and supply. This means free markets can contribute to increasing inequalities in society. The free market punishes 'losers' and rewards 'winners'.

Losers

The unconstrained working of free markets can create losers. If consumer choices are to result in resources being shifted from those uses which are less in demand to those for which the demand is greater, there are likely to be winners and losers. Thus, many British and other European farmers are currently losers as they are finding it increasingly difficult to compete with cheaper imported foods and cope with changes in customer tastes away from products such as meat. Similarly, the coal industry in the UK is shrinking rapidly because of the greater use of alternative energy sources and the availability of cheap imports.

These changing patterns of demand and supply lead to changes in the structure of the UK economy. They will have two directly related outcomes:

- Decreases in incomes for those employed in affected industries like agriculture.
- Increases in unemployment in affected industries.

Other members of our economy can also be described as losers. These include some older people whose skills are no longer in demand, young people who lack both skills and qualifications and owners of businesses which have become uncompetitive. All these groups are likely to earn less.

ACTIVITY 1

Assess the validity of economic arguments that the government should intervene to protect the incomes of those working in the agricultural sector.

Winners

The price mechanism rewards those owners of resources who are able to produce goods and services in anticipation of changes in demand. Similarly, those who have skills for which there is relatively high demand can bargain for higher wages. Currently, electricians working on a variety of projects in London are alleged to be able to earn £1000 per week. Owners of property and land in the south east of England are currently earning higher rents from rising demand for housing, shopping and factory space.

These rewards are vital if free markets are going to work. Rising wages and salaries indicate relative shortages while falling pay levels signal the over supply of particular skills. It is likely, therefore, that free markets will result in inequalities and that one of the outcomes of these inequalities might be the existence of poverty for losers and the creation of material benefits for the winners. Outcomes such as these might not be socially acceptable.

The distribution of rewards

Not only do free markets create inequalities in income but they also allocate resources to those members of society who are prepared to pay the most. Some economists have likened the price mechanism to a system of votes. Each pound of income is the equivalent of one vote. Those with the most votes will determine not just what is produced for society but also who consumes such production. If there is a shortage of a good or service competition between buyers will force up prices until an equilibrium between buyers and sellers is reached. Those who cannot afford the market price of the good or service will go without.

Those members of society who have larger incomes will be able to consume more resources than those with relatively smaller incomes. Some people would regard such inequalities as unfair, and those economies in which there is an uneven **income distribution** might be considered to be less fair or

just than those societies in which incomes are relatively equally distributed.

The richest 20 per cent of households earn over 50 per cent of the national income, whereas the poorest 20 per cent earn only a little over 2 per cent of national income.

These income differences exist for a variety of reasons which include:

- occupations
- retirement.

Occupations (wage and salary differences)

Wages and salaries provide 56 per cent of all household incomes, and as Figure 17.1 shows there are wide variations between rates of pay in different jobs. These reflect different supply and demand conditions in different occupations, and show that those with few skills and qualifications are likely to earn less than those with more.

Retirement

The proportion of retired people in the UK population is rising and within this group there are considerable variations in income (see Figure 17.2).

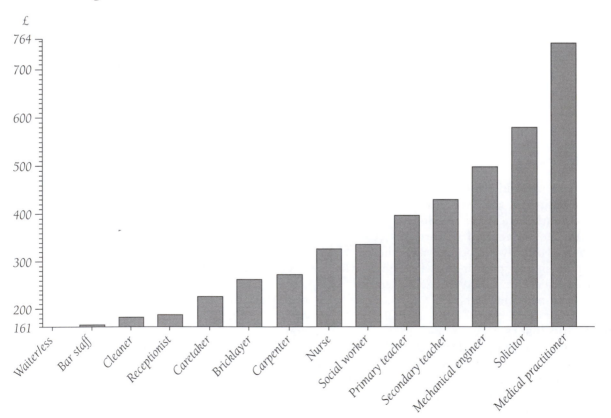

Figure 17.1 Real gross weekly earnings by occupation, Great Britain, 1995

Statistics for Education, SECOS database

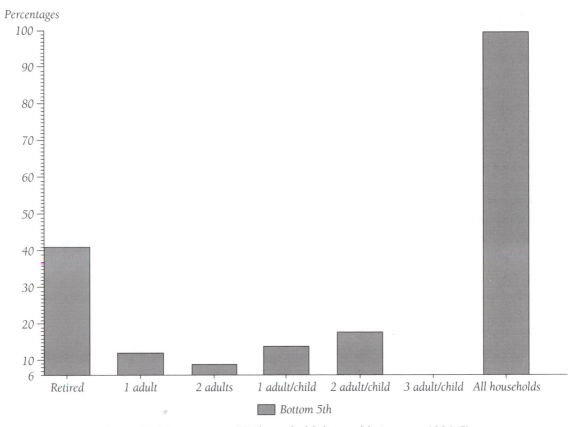

Figure 17.2 Low earners (UK household disposable income, 1994–5)

Geography

Figure 17.3 Income differences by region (personal disposable income)

Statistics for Education, *SECOS* database

Statistics for Education, *SECOS* database

Under production

The market system may lead to the under production of particular goods or services. Thus, poor people may not be able to afford to purchase goods or services which are regarded by most in society as a right. Until 1947 health services in this country were provided by a free market. Those needing a doctor had to pay, and poor people often suffered ill health because of this financial barrier. The Labour government which was elected in 1945 was committed to the notion of a health service which was free at the point of use. Economists call this type of provision a **merit good**. Other merit goods include the provision of library services, job centres, state education and health and recreational services. Not all of these are provided free. In some cases, such as the arts, sports and public transport, the government provides subsidies to ensure that particular services are provided.

Another class of goods and services which is likely to be under provided by a free market system is **public goods**. Public goods are products or services for which it is difficult to identify who benefits most. In a free market those who derive the greatest satisfaction from the consumption of a good or service are thought likely to be prepared to pay the most. In this way, resources are rationed out to those who believe they will benefit most. Thus, it is unlikely that a freely operating market would provide a national police force. It is impossible to predict who needs the police and when, and it would be hard to work out a means by which consumers of police services would actually pay for the resources used for their benefit.

Another way of looking at the same issue is to argue that the social benefits of an effective police force are enormous and much larger than any private benefit. This provides a justification for the government to intervene and provide not just the police but other public services such as road and rail building, and the provision of recreational facilities.

Economists argue that public goods have two important features which differentiate them from other goods. These are non-rivalry, which means that if one person consumes a good or service others are not prevented from doing the same. Thus, one person enjoying Snowdonia will not stop someone else having a similar experience. Secondly, public goods are non-excludable, which is a related concept that means than once a public good is provided to one person it is not possible to stop others from enjoying it.

ACTIVITY 2

Divide your class into two to debate the merits of the free market.

One group should develop arguments to support the contention that we would be better off if we left the provision of health care to free market forces.

The other group should develop arguments opposed to this contention.

Over production

Left to its own devices a free market could lead to the production of goods and services which a society might judge to be socially harmful. Consideration has already been given to circumstances in which companies will over produce if private costs are far less than social costs. The existence of **demerit goods** is related to that of negative externalities. These are goods which society believes to be harmful and various measures are taken by governments to reduce the consumption of commodities such as alcohol and tobacco. The provision of other goods and services such as cannabis, prostitution and offensive weapons is banned.

ACTIVITY 3

Consider and evaluate the economic arguments for the legalisation of cannabis or prostitution.

Government intervention – income inequalities

There are many measures used by governments to reduce the harmful effect of income inequalities. They can be subdivided into two areas of policy:

- Actions to reduce the impact of poverty.
- Policies aimed at redistributing income.

Reducing the impact of poverty

The welfare state is designed to provide a safety net to all those groups whose low incomes are likely to suffer from the ill-effects of poverty. Income support, child benefit, pensions, disability payments, free school lunches, free prescriptions and housing benefits are all examples of government measures to try to ensure that all members of UK society enjoy a minimum acceptable standard of living.

There is considerable debate about the effectiveness of these measures. Some like child benefit are 'universal' in that they are paid to all mothers with children. Thus, both high and low income earners receive the same benefit and it can be argued that payments are made to those not in need. Most welfare payments, however, have to be applied for and this limits their take up. Often those most in need fail to claim their entitlements. Some payments are discretionary which also leads to lower take-up rates.

Other programmes to reduce the impact of poverty include a strong element of compulsion. Those in work have to pay National Insurance contributions which are then used to finance sickness benefits and pensions.

Some economists argue that welfare payments in themselves contribute to poverty. They claim that welfare payments increase the dependence of claimants and provide a disincentive to work.

Redistributing income

There has been a long tradition of using the tax system to shift income from the better off to the worse off. The largest source of government revenue is income tax. The amount paid by any individual is worked out having taken account of a complicated system of allowances and different tax rates. All single people earning less than £80 per week pay no income tax. Tax benefits are given to families with children and, until April 2000, to those with mortgages. Tax rates for high earners are higher than those for low earners. In theory, those with higher incomes pay a higher proportion of their incomes in the form of tax than do those on low incomes. If the government then spends these revenues in such a way that poor people benefit more than rich people the government will have succeeded in redistributing income in favour of the less well off.

Other measures which might have a longer term effect in redistributing income include government expenditure on education and training, improving nursery and pre school provision, better housing, improved health services and developing more caring attitudes towards those who are less well off.

Government intervention – over and under production

Government attempts to limit the capacity of free markets to over produce goods which may be socially damaging, or under produce goods and services which may be socially beneficial, are dealt with in Unit 16 dealing with externalities.

Summary

The unconstrained action of Adam Smith's hidden hand can lead to socially unacceptable outcomes. Agreement as to what is acceptable and what is unacceptable in terms of inequalities, the over production of socially harmful goods and services and the under supply of socially valued outputs, is very difficult. Nonetheless, all governments intervene to change the outcomes that free markets would otherwise produce. The effectiveness of such interventions to make societies more just and fair is difficult both to judge and to measure.

Data response question

The challenge facing the government

Over the past two decades, inequality and its visible impact in the UK have increased dramatically. Major economic and social changes have contributed to this process and to escalating problems in the most deprived communities. In the past, policies have often been slow to react, and uncoordinated in the solutions they sought to offer. The result: too many people are poorer than they should be, and dependent on benefits when the need not be.

- The proportion of people living in households with relatively low incomes more than doubled between the end of the 1970s and the beginning of the 1990s.

- One in three children live in households below half average income.

- Nearly one in five working-age households has no one in work.

- The poorest communities have substantially more unemployment and experience higher levels of poor housing, vandalism and crime.

www.dss.gov.uk

1 Why has poverty increased in the last 20 years? (2)
2 Identify and explain three economic consequences of the existence of poverty? (3)
3 Suggest three market-led strategies which might reduce the problem of poverty. (3)
4 Suggest three strategies based on government intervention. (3)
5 Assess which strategies are likely to be most successful. (9)

UNIT 18 Market imperfections

Key concepts covered

- factor (im)mobility
- (im)perfect knowledge
- imperfect competition
- price controls
- minimum price
- maximum prices
- indirect taxes
- subsidies

Introduction

Unit 14 was concerned with the theory of how free markets might work, and might lead to socially desirable outcomes, for example efficient production and consumer sovereignty. The existence of monopoly and externalities can also prevent free markets from working to the advantage of society as a whole. Similarly, markets may help create unacceptable levels of inequality. This unit is devoted to consideration of other issues, which might limit the effective working of markets. Economists refer to market imperfections when considering those factors which might inhibit markets from working as efficiently and effectively as has been argued earlier.

Consideration is given to four concepts which economists have developed to understand why markets might not always work. These are:

- factor immobility
- imperfect knowledge
- imperfect competition
- price fixing.

In addition, the unit focuses on how government action might also stop markets from working effectively. The following examples of government action are analysed:

- indirect taxes
- subsidies.

Factor immobility

Free markets require **factor mobility**. Land, labour, capital and enterprise are all meant to be attracted by the prospect of better returns and repelled by the threat of worse returns. There are many reasons why this might not be the case.

Land

Economists define land to include not just farms, factory sites and building lots but also to include those resources which are contained within the earth's crust. Whereas natural resources such as timber, minerals and energy can be relatively easily transported, and switched from use to use, particular sites with particular qualities are more likely to be locked in time and space.

Labour

Free market theory requires that workers work primarily for money and that changes in wage and salary levels not only signal to workers that they should consider changing employment, but that they should also be geographically mobile. In spite of higher wages elsewhere some workers are reluctant to leave areas of high unemployment such as Cornwall, Merseyside and Teeside. Family and community links are hard to break. The evidence as to what primarily motivates workers is not clear.

In love with the job

How can employers motivate and satisfy their workers? The usual and easy answer is to pay them more. How can trade unions enthuse or at least retain their members? The usual and easy answer is to fight for higher pay. Yet this conventional wisdom on both sides of industry is probably wrong.

According to a Mori poll conducted for GMB, the municipal and engineering trade union, pay ranks well down the list of criteria by which employees judge their well-being. When more than a thousand workers from all walks of life were asked to pick six out of 21 qualities which were important for them in their jobs, only a third mentioned pay. The factors which came out overwhelmingly ahead, and the only two that were listed by more than half the respondents, were job security and 'finding the job interesting and enjoyable'.

Such findings, which have emerged from similar recent surveys in many other industrialised countries, are consistent with economic theory as well as psychological observation and common sense. As society becomes richer, an additional pound of pay is worth steadily less to all but its poorest members. As people leave the bread line far behind, non-material sources of satisfaction and security begin to gain the upper hand over money.

The diminishing importance of money as the sole reason for working has obvious implications for industrial relations, business management and even economic policy – or would, were it not that people do not act as they tell the survey-merchants they feel. Never has that paradox been more evident than in the current recession.

The government keeps warning that excessive pay increases will mean job losses. But many workers do not believe there is a direct connection between their own job security and their pay; and they are not entirely irrational in this respect. Not only do the jobs destroyed by excessive pay rises usually belong to other people, there have also been cases the world over where workers in declining and uncompetitive industries have accepted deep pay cuts but have still ended up losing their jobs.

Lower wages alone will not make a declining industry or a badly managed company competitive. A combination of wage restraint, product innovation and efficient improvement is usually required. In order to achieve this combination, a company obviously needs a cooperative and flexible workforce. But it also needs a management which knows how to enthuse its workers and is seen to protect the longer term security of their jobs by using their talents to best advantage. That is why personnel management is a central executive skill, wrongly subordinated to that of accountancy in the hierarchy of so many British companies.

The Times, 9 May 1991

Some workers indicate that 'job satisfaction' is more important than financial return, while others value 'status'. Given the complexity of human behaviour economists have to be very careful in making assumptions about motivations.

Capital

Finance capital has become a much more mobile factor of production compared to land and labour. Governments have historically tried to control international flows of finance capital but such intervention has become increasingly difficult and ineffective, especially as global capital markets have developed. If investments in a particular sector, or in a particular country, become more attractive relative to those in others, finance capital is likely to flow to that new use away from uses where the returns are less.

Enterprise

Enterprise should by definition be the most mobile of all factors. If enterprise is about taking risks and identifying where greatest profits can be made it follows that entrepreneurs will be mobile in pursuit of profit. However, as with labour, human factors are likely to influence decisions of entrepreneurs. Thus, owners of small businesses may be reluctant to make workers redundant when orders fall. Alternatively, there is evidence to suggest that some owners forgo greater sales and profits associated with growth as such expansion may threaten lifestyles and informal relationships with employees.

ACTIVITY 1

Discuss how far the following applies to you: 'When you finish your education, would you be prepared to go anywhere, and do anything provided the pay was better than you could get elsewhere?'.

Imperfect knowledge

If consumers are to make informed and effective choices of those products and services which they may wish to purchase, they need knowledge and understanding of the prices and qualities of potential purchases. In theory, they need **perfect knowledge**, which is the term used by economists to describe a total and all-encompassing knowledge. Numerous studies indicate, however, that consumer knowledge is far from perfect. Customers perceive there to be differences between products when there are none, and knowing the prices of competing products is too demanding for all but the most expert buyers.

Similarly, it is assumed that customers base purchases on rational decisions, that they are consistent and not swayed by irrational considerations. However, in many ways customer choices are unpredictable. Fashions and tastes change as do perceptions as to what represents good quality.

A similar consideration applies to producers of goods and services. As was outlined in Unit 12, producer knowledge of the behaviour of competitors is also imperfect.

Imperfections in customer and producer knowledge imply that markets may not respond quickly to changes in demand or supply conditions. They also give advertisers the opportunity to create illusions of quality, status or value for money which may inflate the demand for particular goods at the expense of demand for alternative products.

How rational a consumer are you? Have you ever been swayed by advertising?

Imperfect competition

Imperfect competition is said to be when firms are able to have some degree of influence over the price that is charged for their product or service. To develop the term used in Unit 12 firms become price makers rather than price takers. Firms spend considerable sums on advertising and promotion to encourage customer loyalty and repeat custom. Branding is used to create particular images for products. Psychological factors are exploited to promote sales. Some firms bewilder potential customers with choices of complicated tariffs or alternative prices.

Rail users face £660 county line penalty

A FARES scheme on a busy rail route means that some commuters face having to pay £660 a year more than their fellow passengers to make the same daily journey from the same station.

The 700 daily travellers from Manningtree station in Essex to London's Liverpool Street are divided by the new fares structure which provides more favourable discounts to residents of the county than to those passengers who live just across the border in Suffolk.

Essex-dwellers are being offered monthly season-tickets to London for £225, whereas their northern neighbours must pay £280, an annual 'penalty' of £660, or 24 per cent. If travelling first-class, Manningtree's Suffolk-based customers face extra costs of £1,200 a year compared with their counterparts from the south of the Stour.

Derek Monnery, the vice-chairman of the Manningtree Rail Users Association, said yesterday: 'It is a ridiculous anomaly, creating a situation which is very unfair on people who don't live in Essex.'

Anglia Railways said the 'commuter club' scheme offered reduced prices to all passengers on the Norwich-London line, with different rates set for residents of each of the three counties along the route. The firm accepted there was a 'particular problem' at Manningtree because of its proximity to the county border, and promised to regard 'flexibility' complaints from Suffolk customers

Paul Marston, 'Rail users face £660 county line penalty' in the electronic Telegraph, 12 January 1999

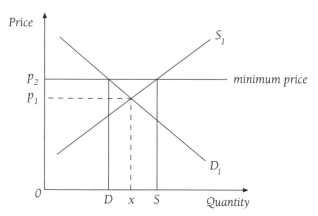

Figure 18.1 Price fixing above the equilibrium

Price fixing

Firms may distort markets and prevent them from operating effectively by trying to set prices for goods which may differ from the equilibrium or market price. Such practice in the UK is generally meant to be illegal but there is evidence that manufacturers of cars and electrical goods have in recent years forced retailers to sell goods at artificially inflated prices. The effects of such actions can be demonstrated by using demand and supply analysis as shown in Figure 18.1.

In Figure 18.1 the horizontal line drawn at p_2 illustrates a **minimum price** set by a manufacturer above the market clearing equilibrium. The effect is to create disequilibrium as supply will be S but demand will be D, whereas if market forces had been allowed to work, the x cars would have sold at p_1 price.

Governments also intervene by using price controls. These are usually **maximum prices**, which limit what can be charged for a good or service. A number of third world governments impose maximum prices for basic foodstuffs in order to ensure that poor people avoid going without. The effects of this type of price fixing are illustrated in Figure 18.2 where the price has been capped at p_2, which is below the market-clearing price of p_1.

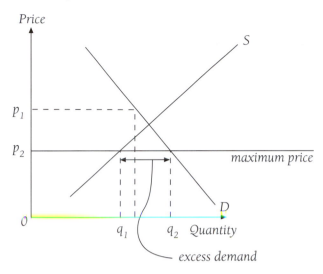

Figure 18.2 Maximum price set below equilibrium

In this case intervention will create a shortage. Demand will be q_2, whereas supply will be q_1.

Grey and black markets

The existence of both minimum and maximum price controls provide incentives for people to take advantage of distorted markets. In the UK major retailers have from time to time challenged manufacturers who set artificially high minimum prices.

'Tesco to sell "label" wear worth £8m'

TESCO is to put an extra £8 million worth of cut-price designer clothes, including Levi jeans and Calvin Klein underwear, on sale after a huge customer response to a European Union ruling banning the store importing the goods from outside the EU without the maker's permission.

A Tesco spokesman said the goods had been bought from unofficial outlets within the EU.

from the electronic *Telegraph*, 18 July 1998

Companies such as Tesco have bought in stocks of goods from abroad and undercut the manufacturer's set prices. Currently, it is possible to import British-made cars from abroad, saving several thousands of pounds on the prices charged in the UK. These practices are not illegal and are called **grey markets**.

Black markets arise when maximum prices are set such that shortages of products or services are created. Some customers are prepared to pay more than the set price and this also creates a new or black market for such products. They also occur at sporting and musical events. If governments introduce maximum prices as in war times they usually outlaw black markets.

Black Market could develop on Euro 2000 tickets

IT IS EXPECTED that a large number of tickets for the European Football championships will be sold on the black market. These are already being offered over the Internet and through other outlets.

The organisers of the event have warned agencies of the possible legal consequences of reselling tickets. The governments of the two host countries, Belgium and The Netherlands, have passed legislation making it a criminal offence to resell tickets, even at face value. Anyone caught may face a fine up to 1000 guilders (£277). The tickets are due to go on sale in May when it is expected that demand will greatly exceed the supply.

Indirect taxes

Governments can have a distorting effect on freely operating markets if they decide to impose **indirect taxes** on particular goods or services. The imposition

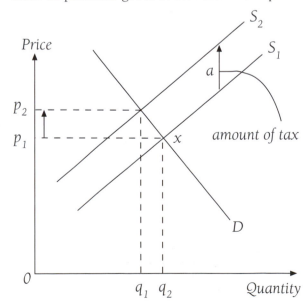

Figure 18.3 Effects of the imposition of an indirect tax

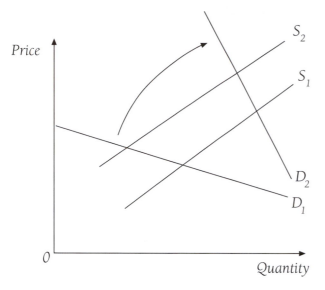

Figure 18.4 Significance of elasticity of demand on the impact of indirect taxes

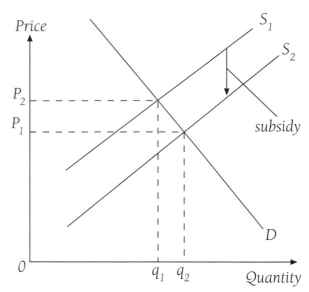

Figure 18.5 Effects of the imposition of a subsidy

of a tax can be illustrated by an upward shift of a supply curve. The vertical distance a in Figure 18.3 illustrates the imposition of a tax.

Without a tax, the market equilibrium would settle at x, giving a price of p_1 and sales of q_2. The effects of imposing a tax are to push up the price paid by consumers to p_2, and cut the amount sold to q1. The final impact on price and sales will be determined by the price elasticity of demand for the product. This is shown in Figure 18.4 where prices will increase more if demand is D^2 rather than D^1.

Subsidies

Economists treat **subsidies** as reverse taxes on the basis that they are amounts paid to a producer to provide a product or service. In this case the provision of a subsidy is illustrated in Figure 18.5 by a vertical shift downwards of the supply curve, y, leading to a fall in price from p_2 to p_1 and a rise in sales from q_1 to q_2.

ACTIVITY 3

What would be the implications on the agriculture industry of moving towards a much more market-based economy by ending government indirect taxes and the provision of subsidies?

Summary

Many factors can contribute to market imperfections. Factors of production are not always supplied to the highest bidder. Labour and land can be particularly immobile, leading to the under supply of some factors and the over supply of others.

Moreover, both consumers and producers may have imperfect knowledge of markets. This can lead both into decisions about consumption and production which may be based on irrational or an incomplete understanding of what might be supplied or demanded.

Many industries in our economy are characterised by imperfect competition, where a limited number of suppliers produces products or services which are similar but different. Consumers may be manipulated into buying more expensive products. Some companies may attempt to gain extra revenue by fixing minimum prices for their products, leading to artificially raised prices and limited sales.

Governments can contribute to market imperfections by imposing maximum prices for particular products. They may also distort freely operating marketing by the imposition of indirect taxes and subsidies.

Data response question

Unions urge fight to save jobs at Ford

BRITAIN'S two biggest unions reacted with fury yesterday when Ford refused to deny reports that it would axe production at Dagenham East, with the potential loss of more than 3,000 jobs.

The latest threat to manufacturing provoked angry union bosses to call on the Government to 'fight to the death' to save jobs.

The threat of closure at Dagenham comes in spite of reduced losses for the company in Britain and record profits worldwide.

Unions accuse the Government and its wait-and-see policy on the single currency of failing to recognise sterling's impact on manufacturing.

The GMB said the reported closure would be a 'catastrophe' and called on the Government to take direct action. Union colleagues at the TGWU made thinly-veiled threats of industrial action which would damage Ford's European business.

John Edmonds, general-secretary of the GMB, said: 'We keep hearing about all this activity going on behind the scenes but the Department of Trade and Industry's German equivalent is explicitly protecting jobs. The DTI here appears to see its role as ensuring that regulations ensuring a free market are upheld.'

'Ford has made it clear to the Government that its present review is looking at the problems of overproduction and excess capacity across its operations throughout Europe. This review is not centred on issues which solely affect the UK. We expect an announcement from Ford . . . within the next few weeks.'

The GMB believes Blair's approach to the single currency and the strength of the pound is putting off potential rescuers such as Volkswagen, reportedly interested in parts of Ford's UK operations.

The pound makes British products 20 per cent more expensive than European-made goods – but industry's pleas for a cut in interest rates have so far failed. The Bank of England's monetary policy committee is expected to put rates up after its next meeting in order to keep inflation low.

London mayoral candidate Ken Livingstone backed demands for government action. He said: 'This is vital for the future of manufacturing in London. Thousands jobs are at stake in the plant and tens of thousands in related industries in one of the poorest areas of London. Dagenham was Ford's most productive plant last year.'

sarah.ryle@obverver.co.uk, 23rd April 2000

1. Identify and explain three possible reasons for job losses at Dagenham. (6)
2. To what extent is this an example of market failure? (4)
3. Evaluate one government strategy to respond to this problem. (10)

Section 4 questions

Essay questions

1a Explain why road congestion can be described as a form of market failure. (7)

b Evaluate two alternative strategies which a government might use to deal with the problem of road congestion. (18)

2a In what sense is the depletion of the ozone layer an economic problem? (15)

b What are the economic implications of policies to reduce the depletion of the ozone layer? (20)

3a Explain why the persistence of poverty can be described as a form of market failure. (8)

b Evaluate government policies to reduce poverty. (17)

4a Why might the existence of market imperfections limit the effectiveness and efficiency of a market economy? (10)

b Discuss the contention that all markets are imperfect. (15)

Project

Work with others to present proposals to your local council to help tackle the problem of social exclusion. You should:

a Identify the extent and nature of social exclusion in your area.

b Interview those working for public sector and voluntary agencies to collect evidence as to the cause of social exclusion.

c Assess existing local council initiatives to tackle social exclusion.

d Present to the leader of your local council a set of strategies to tackle social exclusion. These strategies need to be costed, and you should indicate how their success might be evaluated.

C3.1a, C3.1b, C3.2, N3.1, N3.2 N3.3, IT3.1, IT3.2, IT3.3.

Multiple-choice questions

1 The *main* reason why the government provides public goods is because

A excessive profits would be earned if private firms were allowed to supply them

B if private firms were allowed to charge for public goods, it would lead to inequalities in the distribution of income

C the government wishes to regulate the conditions in which public goods are consumed

D it is unlikely that they would be provided by the private sector because not enough people would be willing to pay for them

2 Which one of the following provides the best definition of a merit good?

A merit good is a good which

A is provided free of charge by the government

B provides benefits which are not fully appreciated by the prospective user

C has strong negative externalities

D cannot be supplied by the market

3 If waste from a chemical factory kills fish in a river, this is best classified as

A an opportunity cost

B a private cost

C a negative externality

D a public good

4 A firm engaged in producing a certain good has private costs which are not equal to social costs. In order to increase economic welfare the government could

A tax the firm if social costs are less than its private costs

B subsidise the firm if social costs exceed its private costs

C tax the firm if social costs exceed its private costs

D subsidise other firms in the same industry if their private costs are less than their social costs

5 If the government established a guaranteed minimum price of P the effect would be that

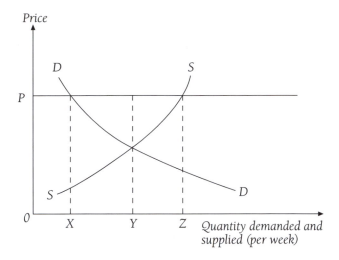

A there would be a shortage of supply equal to XZ

B price would be forced down towards the equilibrium

C the government would have to purchase quantity XZ at price P

D there would be an excess supply of quantity YZ

6 The imposition of an indirect tax designed to reduce the consumption of demerit goods will be most successful when

A demand is price elastic

B supply is price elastic

C demand is price inelastic

D demand is income elastic

7 The diagram represents the supply and demand for wheat.

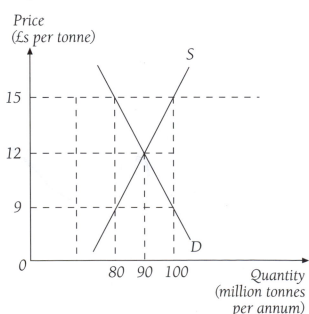

If the government wished to maintain a guaranteed price to farmers of £15 per tonne of wheat it could purchase

A 10 million tonnes at £12 per tonne and destroy it

B 20 million tonnes at £9 per tonne and release it at the same price to the home market

C 10 million tonnes at £12 per tonne and sell it at a subsidised price overseas

D 20 million tonnes at £15 per tonne and hold it as a buffer stock

8 Which one of the following is likely to result from a decrease in subsidies for public transport in cities?

A A reduction in traffic congestion

B A decrease in the standard of living of city dwellers who use public transport

C An increase in distances travelled to work

D An increase in the number of bus operators

Section 5
The national economy

Introduction

This section is concerned with the key issues of macroeconomics. These issues affect all of our lives, including the prices we pay, the goods and services we enjoy and our chances of gaining a job.

In Unit 19 the main objectives that governments have for the economy are identified and discussed. The key indicators which are used to assess an economy's performance in achieving the objectives are covered in Unit 20. This unit also explains how these indicators are measured.

The concepts of aggregate demand and supply are used in examining and explaining the performance of economies. These form the focus of Unit 21. In Unit 22 aggregate demand and supply analysis is used to explain how the level of output and general price level in an economy are determined.

Increases in output are the topic of Unit 23. The nature, causes and effects of economic growth are covered. In Unit 24 inflation is discussed. Different measures of inflation are explained and the causes and consequences of inflation are considered. While one possible cause of inflation is high and increasing aggregate demand, one possible cause of unemployment is falling aggregate demand. Unemployment is the topic of Unit 25.

In Unit 26 a number of issues relating to the UK's balance of payments position are examined, including the UK's performance in goods and services, the pattern of UK trade and the causes and consequences of a country spending more abroad on goods and services than it earns.

Finally, in Unit 27 government policies which can be used to influence the country's balance of payments position, unemployment, inflation and economic growth are discussed. These policies include fiscal, monetary and supply-side policies.

Government policy objectives

Introduction

'We will provide stable economic growth with low inflation and promote dynamic growth and competitive business and industry at home and abroad.'

This is a quote from the 1997 Labour Party manifesto. It states some of the economic objectives of the Labour government elected in May 1997. This unit explains the role of economists in influencing, implementing and assessing government economic objectives. It identifies the main government macroeconomic objectives, explains what these mean, discusses the desirability of achieving them and examines recent UK performance. It also identifies some other possible objectives and touches on the need to have a separate policy instrument to achieve each objective.

Economists and objectives

When the Labour Party was in opposition, it sought the advice of City and academic economists on the viability of its objectives and how to achieve them. Now in government, Labour draws on the advice of economists working for the government and independent city and academic advisers, including Martin Weale from the National Institute of Economic and Social Research, DeAnne Julius, former chief economist of British Airways and Professor Wynne Godley of Cambridge University. The government also receives advice from economic journalists, for example David Smith of *The Sunday*

Times and Samuel Brittan of the *Financial Times* on what its objectives should be and which objectives should receive priority.

Economists employed by the government are involved in implementing government policies used to achieve the government's objectives, while economists working for private sector firms provide advice to their employers about how government policies will affect their markets, costs and revenue.

The success of the government in achieving its stated objectives is assessed by economists working in the media, universities, the City and in government service.

So economists are involved in:

- advising on the government's economic objectives
- implementing the policies to achieve them
- interpreting the objectives and policies
- assessing how successful the policies are in achieving the objectives.

Main objectives

Government **macroeconomic policy objectives** and, even more commonly, the emphasis placed on the objectives can change as administrations, circumstances and economic theories change. However, the four main objectives for the economy (macroeconomic objectives) pursued by most governments are:

- **full employment**
- low and stable **inflation**
- stable economic **growth**
- a satisfactory **balance of payments** position.

Full employment

As Figure 19.1 shows the rate of unemployment has fluctuated over the past 30 years. Throughout this period all administrations have sought to achieve as high employment, and as low unemployment, as possible. However, what has changed over time has been how economists and politicians have interpreted what the highest employment rate is, the priority they have given to achieving it, the policies they have used and world economic conditions.

The highest possible employment may be referred to as full employment. However, this term is somewhat misleading as it does not mean zero

ACTIVITY 1

In the second half of 1999 the UK economy was generally thought to be in good shape. Economic growth was high, unemployment had fallen to its lowest level since 1980 and inflation was low. However, a number of economists, including Charlie Bean, an adviser to the Treasury and Professor at the London School of Economics, were concerned that inflation might rise.

a   Does the paragraph above suggest that the government was meeting the macroeconomic objectives outlined in the quote at the start of the unit?

b   Identify the main government macroeconomic objective not mentioned in the passage.

c   In 1999 Charlie Bean worked for the Treasury and for a university. Identify two other types of organisation which employ economists.

d   i   Using a CD-Rom or the Internet find and print off an article from a broadsheet newspaper for a particular month in which an economic journalist comments on which of the four macroeconomic objectives should be given priority.

   ii   Discuss your findings with others in your group and decide on the extent to which the views of the journalists you have selected agree.

unemployment. In the period 1945 to 1970 it was thought to be approximately 2–3 per cent unemployment. This figure was based on the view that even during periods of high economic activity and when the number of registered unemployed equals the number of vacancies, some people will be out of work. These will be people who have left one job and are spending some time seeking a new job (i.e. people in between jobs).

In the 1980s a group of economists, known as new classical economists, redefined full employment as the level of employment existing when the labour market is in equilibrium and those willing and able to work at the going wage rate can find employment. Some suggested that in the UK in the early 1980s this would occur when approximately 8 per cent of the workforce were out of work. However, they suggested also that this 'natural rate of unemployment' can change over time. For instance, they argued that a fall in unemployment-related benefits will reduce the time people spend searching for jobs and thereby reduce unemployment.

At the turn of the millennium economists and politicians again began to talk about the possibility of economies returning to unemployment levels of 2–3 per cent or even below.

High employment confers a number of important advantages, including the possibility of high output and high living standards, while unemployment involves a waste of resources, a loss of potential output and gives rise to a number of social problems.

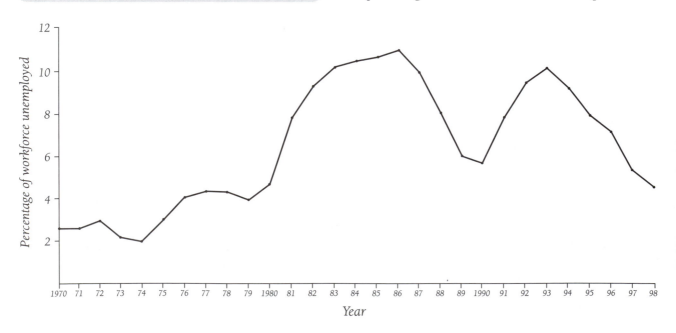

Figure 19.1

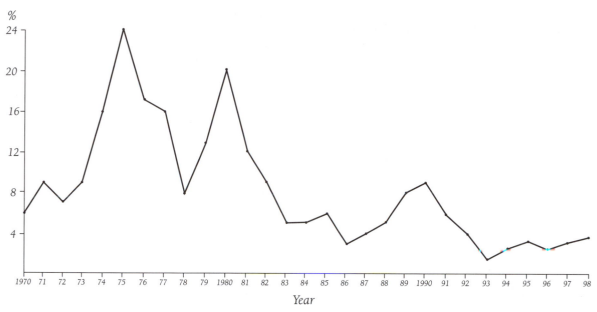

Figure 19.2

Low and stable inflation

As Figure 19.2 shows inflation reached high levels in the mid-1970s. It was considered to be a significant problem in the 1970s and 1980s. Indeed, reducing the rate of inflation was the main objective of Conservative administrations in the 1980s. However, in more recent years inflation has been relatively low.

Low inflation may be taken to mean that the general level of prices is rising at no more than, for example, 2.5 per cent a year. Stable inflation refers to the general price level rising at a consistent rate rather than at an accelerating rate, for example 3 per cent this year and 3 per cent or near next year and not 3 per cent now and 10 per cent next year.

A high and accelerating rate of inflation can be harmful to an economy because it may reduce the international price competitiveness of the country's goods and services, may reduce the real value of people's incomes and savings and is likely to cause uncertainty making planning difficult.

However, zero inflation, with the general price level remaining unchanged, has always been regarded as difficult to achieve and many economists now question whether it is even desirable. A low level of

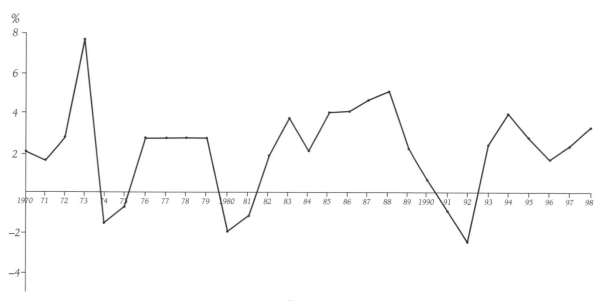

Figure 19.3

inflation, rather than zero inflation, may bring benefits. For example, it may enable firms to reduce their costs by not raising wages in line with inflation rather than by making some workers redundant.

When economists refer to price stability they usually mean low and stable inflation rather than zero inflation.

Stable economic growth

Stable economic growth refers to a steady increase in the output of goods and services a country produces. The UK has tended to grow at a rate of approximately 2 per cent a year since 1950. However, as Figure 19.3 shows, the rate of growth has not been steady. In some years output increased by more than 2 per cent, for example 1973 and 1987, while in other years, such as 1980 and 1991, the amount produced actually declined. These fluctuations in economic growth cause uncertainty and make it difficult for the government, firms and households to plan for the future.

A steady rate of economic growth may provide a number of advantages in an economy, including increasing material living standards. It also enables a government to reduce poverty without having to lower the living standards of the rich and middle income groups. This is because higher output will mean higher total income, some of which can be used to increase the employment opportunities of the poor by, for example, training, and some can be given to the poor in the form of increased benefits. On the other hand, if

total income does not rise the only way to increase government spending to reduce poverty is to increase taxes on the rich and middle income groups.

However, economic growth does not catch the headlines to the same extent as unemployment and inflation do. So it is sometimes given lower priority. Indeed, it may be sacrificed, in the short term, to achieve lower inflation and a satisfactory balance of payments.

Satisfactory balance of payments position

The **balance of payments** is a record of a country's transactions with other countries over the period of a year. It shows the amount of money which has come into the country and the amount which has left. It is divided into a number of sections. The section which receives the most attention in the media is the current account. This, in turn, is divided into four sections. The two best known are trade in goods and trade in services. These record the amount of money the country has earned from selling goods and services abroad and the amount it has spent on buying goods and services abroad.

Figure 19.4 shows the UK's current account position from 1970 to 1998. During this period there have been a number of phases in the performance. At the start, the current account position was in surplus (revenue exceeding expenditure). Then in the mid-1970s it went into deficit (expenditure exceeding revenue). From the late 1970s until 1986 it was mostly in surplus. From 1987 until 1993 there were large deficits, particularly in 1989. From 1994 until 1998 it was

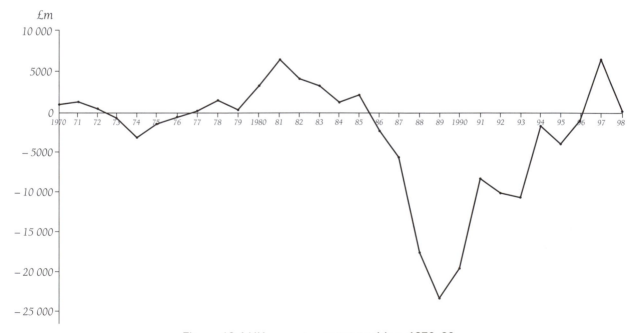

Figure 19.4 UK current account position, 1970–98

roughly in balance, with the exception of 1997 when a record surplus of £6.6 billion was recorded.

In the long term a government is likely to aim to match revenue from expenditure on goods and services. However, in the short term it may be content, or indeed desire, to see a deficit or a surplus. For example, a deficit may be offset by a surplus in another section and it will mean that people are enjoying more goods and services than the country is producing.

Some economists argue that the balance of payments position is more of a constraint on a government's other objectives than an objective in itself. For example, if the UK is experiencing a deficit the government may be reluctant to increase government spending to help reduce unemployment. This is because it may believe that the higher spending will increase incomes and that some of this increase will be spent on imports of goods and services. If more is spent on imports the size of the deficit will get larger.

ACTIVITY 2

Select a country from Germany, Italy, Japan, Netherlands or the USA.

a   Find out from **The Economist** newspaper, or other appropriate source, the country's current unemployment and inflation rates and its current account position.

b   Compare the country's recent economic performance with that of the UK.

c   Decide what further data would be useful in enabling you to make a more confident judgement on this.

Internal and external goals

Internal goals refer to the objectives a government is seeking to achieve within the domestic economy. They will include full employment, low inflation and growth. These are also sometimes called primary goals as they are desirable in their own right.

In contrast, **external goals** are the objectives a government is seeking to achieve in relation to the balance of payments and the exchange rate. These are known as secondary goals since they are sought not for their own sake but to avoid the external balance acting as a constraint on the internal goals.

Other objectives

Governments may have a number of other objectives. For example, a government may seek to reduce poverty, achieve a more even distribution of population and employment between regions and to improve **the environment**. It may also seek to **redistribute income** from the rich to the poor by means of taxation and benefits.

ACTIVITY 3

In November 1999 the Labour government stated that 'its central economic objective is to achieve high and stable levels of growth and employment'. It also set out four long-term economic ambitions for the next decade:

■   from a platform of stability, Britain will have a faster rise in productivity than its main competitors, as it closes the productivity gap

■   school and college leavers will gain the highest possible qualifications they can with the majority going on to higher education for the first time

■   there will be a higher percentage of people in employment than ever before, and

■   child poverty will be reduced by half, as the government moves towards its aim of abolishing child poverty in Britain within the next 20 years.

The government has also stated that as it meets its economic goals it 'is committed to meeting its environmental targets'.

Adapted from Pre-Budget Report, HM Treasury, November 1999.

a   Identify:
  i   which of the four main government objectives are referred to in the extract
  ii   which additional objectives are mentioned.

b   Make a list of the benefits an economy will gain from raising the qualifications of school leavers and compare your findings with others in your group.

c   In a group discuss how you would assess the extent to which the objectives mentioned in the extract have been achieved.

Policy instruments

To achieve its objectives a government will use policy instruments. These are government policy measures. A government has a range of measures it can employ, for example taxation and the rate of interest. These measures are discussed in AS Unit 27. Jan Tinbergen, a Dutch economist, argued that for each objective a government wishes to achieve it should use a separate policy instrument. This is known as **Tinbergen's rule**.

For example, a government wishing to reduce inflationary pressure may reduce government spending and to increase employment it may reduce employers' National Insurance contributions.

Summary

Economists working in industry, government, the media and universities are involved in drawing up, implementing and assessing government macroeconomic objectives. The four main macroeconomic objectives are full employment, low and stable inflation, stable economic growth and a satisfactory balance of payments position. Full employment can be taken to mean 2–3 per cent unemployment. Low and stable inflation occurs when the general level of prices rises by a small, non-accelerating rate. The lower unemployment is, the greater output is likely to be. Stable economic growth makes it easier for governments and firms to plan and the higher output enables material living standards to rise. A satisfactory balanced of payments position is one which is, in the long term, in balance so that deficits and surpluses do not build up. A government may also seek to achieve other objectives for the economy, including creating a more equal distribution of income and wealth. Tinbergen's rule states that for each of the government's objectives there should be a separate policy instrument employed.

Data response question

It might appear that it would be easy for a government to achieve all its macroeconomic objectives. It has a range of policy instruments it can use and experienced civil servants and outside advisers to provide information and advice.

However, governments find it difficult to achieve all their objectives precisely and simultaneously, so in practice governments compromise. Rather than setting a specific target for inflation of, say, 2.5 per cent, a government may set a target rate of 2.5 per cent but with a margin either side. It will also seek to get a balance between objectives but, at any given time, will be likely to give greater priority to a particular objective. Under the Conservative administrations of the 1980s and 1990s control of inflation was the main objective.

Table 19.1 Main macroeconomic objectives

Year	Economic growth %	Inflation %	Unemployment %	Current account balance £bn
1991	-1.0	5.9	8.0	-5.8
1992	-2.6	3.7	9.7	-7.4
1993	2.3	1.6	10.3	-6.7
1994	3.9	2.5	9.4	-4.6
1995	2.7	3.4	8.1	-2.8
1996	1.6	2.4	7.4	-4.2
1997	2.2	3.1	5.6	0.0
1998	3.2	3.5	4.8	-8.0

1 Identify two government policy objectives not discussed in the passage. (4)
2 What do you think is the main policy objective of the current government? Explain your answer. (7)
3 Calculate the average growth, inflation and unemployment rates and current account positions for:
   a the period 1991–94
   b the period 1995–98. (6)
4 Using the information calculated in 3 discuss in which period 1991–94 or 1995–98 were more of the main government macroeconomic objectives achieved. (8)

Indicators of economic performance

Key concepts covered

- errors and omissions
- relative inflation
- index numbers
- real and nominal (values)
- productivity
- the black economy
- quality of life indicators
- the Human Development Index
- the Human Poverty Index

Introduction

At any one time some economies will be performing better than others. For example, towards the end of the 1990s most economic commentators regarded the French economy to be in a healthier state than Germany's. France's economic growth was higher and its unemployment was lower. However, in assessing the performance of an economy care has to be taken in interpreting the indicators.

In this unit the main indicators of economic performance are discussed. They are:

- unemployment
- employment
- balance of payments position
- inflation
- economic growth.

Some of the factors which have to be taken into account when interpreting figures on these variables are discussed. The construction of index numbers, which are used in making comparisons, is explained and illustrated. The difference between real and nominal gross domestic product (GDP) and production and productivity are identified. The limitations of GDP as an indicator of changes in living standards and the meaning of sustainable economic growth are discussed and then three other indicators of performance are covered. These are quality of life indicators, the Human Development Index and the Human Poverty Index.

Unemployment and employment

Economists measure the number and percentage of people unemployed and employed. On the surface, a country with a higher percentage of its workforce in employment would appear to be doing better than one with a smaller percentage. However, as well as taking into account the quantity of jobs it is also important to consider their quality.

People in temporary jobs may feel very insecure and the quality of some workers' lives may be adversely affected by the long hours they work (resulting in poor health and difficult family relationships). Some of the jobs may be poorly paid and of a low-quality, unskilled nature. There may also be people in part-time jobs who would rather be in full-time employment. So just because employment may be high and unemployment is low in a country it cannot be assumed that its citizens are happy with their work and pay.

Balance of payments

Care has also to be taken when measuring and interpreting a country's balance of payments. There are a vast number of activities which result in money entering and leaving a country. It is a time-consuming process to collect all the information. Mistakes can be made and some transactions may not be reported in time. For this reason governments include a section in their balance of payments for **errors and omissions**.

A country's balance of payments may show that the country earns more from goods and services than it spends on goods and services from other countries. However, closer examination may show that the country's earnings have come mainly from tourism. Indeed, tourism is the fastest growing industry in the world. However, tourism tends to create mainly unskilled, low-paid jobs, and the presence of tourists may also create negative externalities, including congestion and pollution at tourist spots, environmental damage and clashes with native culture and traditions.

Inflation

In assessing a country's inflation performance it is important to consider inflation over time and in comparison with other countries, i.e. **relative inflation**. For example, if a country is experiencing 6 per cent inflation whereas in recent years it has experienced 9 per cent inflation, its performance is improving. If other countries are encountering inflation of 10 per cent it is also becoming more price competitive.

Index numbers

In examining a country's performance in terms of inflation and the other main indicators, economists use **index numbers**. These provide a measure of the relative change in a set of figures. They enable users of the data to assess quickly the percentage change on some previous year without having to undertake any calculations. The year against which such comparisons are made is known as the base year. It is given a value of 100. The year should be one in which nothing unusual happened.

Converting data into an index form
To convert data into an index the following formula is used:

$$\frac{\text{Current year figure}}{\text{Base year index}} \times 100$$

For example:

'Raw data': Year	Real GDP (£m)
1994	693 177
1995	712 548
1996	730 767
1997	756 430
1998	773 380

Using 1995 as a base year, the index numbers would be calculated as:

1994: $\dfrac{693\ 177}{712\ 548} \times 100 = 97.3$

1995: $\dfrac{712\ 548}{712\ 548} \times 100 = 100.0$

1996: $\dfrac{730\ 767}{712\ 548} \times 100 = 102.6$

1997: $\dfrac{756\ 430}{712\ 548} \times 100 = 106.2$

1998: $\dfrac{773\ 380}{712\ 548} \times 100 = 108.6$

So the index for real GDP is:

Year	Index of real GDP
1994	97.3
1995	100.0
1996	102.6
1997	106.2
1998	108.6

Using the index it can be seen that output rose by 6.2 per cent between 1995 and 1997 and 8.6 per cent between 1995 and 1998. This is straightforward as the comparison is with a year in which the index is 100. To calculate the percentage change from one year to the next, for example from 1994 to 1995, it is necessary to use the following formula:

$$\frac{\text{Change}}{\text{Earlier year figure}} \times 100$$

For example:

$$\frac{2.7 \times 100}{97.3} = 2.8 \text{ per cent}$$

So between 1994 and 1995 real GDP rose by 2.7 index points and 2.8 per cent.

ACTIVITY 1

a   Convert the following data on exports into an index (using 1995 as the base year):

Year	Total exports (£m in 1995 prices)
1994	184 873
1995	202 412
1996	217 600
1997	236 283
1998	241 123

b   Decide in which year there was the greatest percentage rise in exports.

Economic growth

Economic growth is measured as the percentage change in GDP. GDP is the total output of a country. It can be measured by totalling up the output, income or expenditure of the country. Care has to be taken when undertaking these calculations.

When using the output measure, it is important to avoid double counting, that is counting the same output twice, for example including the output of raw materials and then including them again in the value of the finished products. In the income measure, only incomes which have been earned in return for providing goods and services are included, so, for example, pensions and job seekers' allowance are not included. With the expenditure measure it is important to remember to include exports (as they are produced by domestic firms) and to exclude imports (as they are produced by other countries' firms).

Real and nominal (money) GDP

In discussing index numbers we made use of **real** GDP. A real figure (which can also be described as one measured in constant prices) is one which has been adjusted for inflation. For example, the GDP of a country measured in the prices operating in the year in question (current prices) may rise from, say, £500 000 million in 2000 to £550 000 million in 2001. This would appear to suggest that output has risen by:

$$\frac{£50\ 000m}{£500\ 000m} \times 100 = 10\%$$

So **nominal** GDP has risen by 10 per cent. However, at least part of this increase may be due to the prices of the goods and services being produced rising. To assess the rise in volume, the effects of price rises are taken out by using the following formula:

$$\text{Current year figure} \times \frac{\text{Current year price index}}{\text{base year price index}}$$

So, if the price index in 2000 was 100 and 106 in 2001, real GDP was:

$$£550\ 000m \times \frac{100}{106} = £518\ 867.92m$$

In real terms GDP has risen by:

$$\frac{£18\ 867.92m}{£550\ 000m} \times 100 = 3.4\%$$

From this, it can be seen that the economic performance was not as good as the nominal figures suggested. Other real figures, for example real interest rate and real wages, have been adjusted for the effects of inflation.

Production and productivity

GDP is a measure of the total output of the economy. Output of a country, firm, area or other unit is the same as its production, whereas **productivity** is output per worker hour. Changes in productivity can be used to assess a country's economic performance. If productivity rises by more than wages then labour costs will fall and a country can become more price competitive. It is, of course, possible for production and productivity to move in opposite directions. When an economy is expanding production will rise. If less skilled workers have to be recruited to make the extra output, productivity may fall. This would indicate that while the economy may appear to be doing well its ability to sustain rises in output may be in doubt.

Changes in real GDP and living standards

On the surface, an increase in real GDP may appear to suggest that living standards are increasing but this may not be the case.

One problem of interpretation that economists can eliminate is that a rise in output may be exceeded by a rise in population. If there is, for example, 4 per cent more output and 7 per cent more people to share the output between, on average each person will be worse off. So what economists often assess is real GDP per head (or per capita). This is found by dividing real GDP by population.

However, there are other problems involved in comparing a country's real GDP over time and between countries. One is the existence of the **black economy**. This term covers undeclared economic activity. The output of a country is likely to be higher than its official real GDP figure suggests. Some people selling goods and services may not include all the money they have earned on tax returns and those engaged in illegal activities, for example selling non-prescribed drugs, will not be declaring any of their income from such activities. The size of the black economy is influenced by social attitudes to tax evasion, penalties involved, the risk of being caught, tax rates and the range of activities which are declared illegal. For example, in a country with high marginal tax rates the size of the black economy may be high.

It is also not simply the size of the real GDP and its increase which are significant. What is also important in deciding how the level and changes in real GDP affect people's living standards is the composition of real GDP. If more is produced but the extra output consists of capital goods, people will not immediately feel better off, although they will in the long run. If the rise in real GDP has been accounted for by increasing the police service to match rising crime people may actually feel worse off.

A rise in real GDP may not benefit many of the population if income is very unevenly distributed. Higher output may also result in people feeling the quality of their lives has not improved if they are working longer hours or working under worse conditions. These are factors which the official figures do not take into account.

The official figures also do not include positive and negative externalities. So, for example, if pollution rises real GDP does not fall, even though people will experience a lower quality of life. Indeed, if measures have to be taken to cope with the higher pollution, for example extra cleaning, real GDP will rise.

Sustainable economic growth

Economists and governments are increasingly showing an awareness of the significance of the environment in influencing the quality of people's lives. In assessing an economy's performance economists judge not only the rate of a country's economic growth but also whether it is sustainable. Sustainable economic growth is economic growth which is achieved in such a way as not to damage future generations' ability to produce more. For example, a country may, in the short run, grow very rapidly by chopping down rainforests, using intensive farming methods which erode the soil and fertilisers which are washed into rivers causing pollution. However, these methods will reduce a country's ability to produce in the future.

ACTIVITY 2

Farmers have a problem. After 100 years of higher productivity, rice farmers in Japan have been unable to increase yields for more than 10 years. In the American mid-west wheat farmers have been struggling to boost yields since 1983, despite intensive use of fertilisers and genetic engineering.

The implications are clear. Far from being able to treat the soil as a machine farmers have found there are limits to what the land can take, and the dust bowl beckons unless it is recognised that agriculture is governed by ecological constraints. Modern industrial farming methods boost short-term profitability but at the expense of long-term, and perhaps irreparable, damage.

Few people would now doubt that environmental sustainability matters.

Larry Elliot, 'Ease up, before the workforce cracks up' in the *Guardian*, 23 August 1999

In a group discuss whether:

a 'few people now doubt that environmental sustainability matters'

b it is possible to increase labour efficiency indefinitely

c the introduction of genetically modified crops will increase or reduce the rate of sustainable economic growth.

Quality of life indicators

In 1998 the Labour government introduced a series of 13 new headline main indicators, covering 120 separate categories. These allow the government's performance to be judged not only by economic growth rates but also by the effect of policies on the environment and social welfare. The 13 **quality of life indicators** are:

- economic growth
- social investment, for example investment in buses, hospitals and schools
- employment

- health, including life expectancy
- education and training
- housing quality
- climate change
- air pollution
- transport
- water quality
- wildlife
- land use
- waste.

Human Development Index

The **Human Development Index** (HDI) is a measure of the quality of people's lives, in the form of human development, first published by the United Nations in 1990. It takes into account longevity, knowledge and 'a decent standard of living', and is measured by life expectancy, educational achievement and real, per capita GDP (see Table 20.1).

Table 20.1 The 1998 HDI top twenty rankings

1	Canada	11	Spain
2	France	12	Belgium
3	Norway	13	Austria
4	USA	14	United Kingdom
5	Iceland	15	Australia
6	Finland	16	Switzerland
7	Netherlands	17	Ireland
8	Japan	18	Denmark
9	New Zealand	19	Germany
10	Sweden	20	Greece

The Human Poverty Index

Human Poverty Index (HPI) measures how progress is distributed in a country and takes into account the proportion of people who are left behind – the extent of deprivation.

HPI -1

This measures poverty in developing countries. It takes into account:

- the percentage of people expected to die before the age of 40
- the percentage of adults who are illiterate
- the percentage of people without access to health services and safe water
- the percentage of underweight children under 5.

See Table 20.2.

Table 20.2 HPI-1: lowest ten countries, 1998 (starting with the lowest)

1	Niger	6	Burundi
2	Burkina Faso	7	Guinea
3	Sierra Leone	8	Yemen
4	Ethiopia	9	Senegal
5	Mali	10	Mozambique

HPI-2

This measures poverty in rich, industrial countries and accepts that human deprivation varies with the social and economic conditions of the country. It takes into account:

- the percentage of people likely to die before the age of 60
- the percentage of people whose ability to read and write is far from adequate
- the percentage of people with disposable income of less than 50 per cent of the median
- the percentage of long-term unemployed (12 months or more).

ACTIVITY 3

'… the Netherlands and the United Kingdom have similar average incomes but very different human poverty levels, at 8.2 per cent and 15 per cent. One might expect that the higher a country's GDP the fewer poor people there would be. But comparing GDP per capita with the HPI-2 suggests the opposite; poverty rates in higher income countries are the same as – or higher than – rates in lower industrialised countries.'

United Nations, *Human Development Report 1998*

a Explain why one 'might expect that the higher a country's GDP the fewer poor people there would be'.

b Explain the difference between GDP, HDI, HPI-1 and HPI-2.

Summary

Signs of a good economic performance include low unemployment with a high proportion of the country's workforce being in high-quality jobs, a balance of payments equilibrium, relatively low and stable inflation and stable economic growth.

Economic growth is measured in terms of changes in real GDP, i.e. changes in output adjusted for the effects of inflation. Output may rise as a result of the employment of more workers and/or higher output per worker hour. The latter is referred to as higher productivity. Improvements in productivity are taken to be an important cause of economic growth. Higher output may raise living standards but this does not have to occur if, say, the size of the black economy falls, the extra goods and services produced do not add to the quality of people's lives, income becomes more unevenly distributed and pollution increases. Most countries now aim for sustainable economic growth which is economic growth achieved in a way that does not endanger future generations' ability to increase output.

Among the other measures of performance are the Labour government's quality of life indicators (which include a number of social and environmental indicators, for example education, training, health, pollution and waste) and the UN's Human Development Index (taking into account real GDP, life expectancy and educational achievement) and the Human Poverty Index (taking into account life expectancy, illiteracy, access to clean water and percentage of under-weight young children).

Data response question

'Economic growth has been rejected as the main measure of how good life is in Britain and has been replaced with 120 indicators of quality. If life is going downhill the government promises to take action to correct the problem.'

'The issues revealed by some of the indicators are already causing severe problems for the government – for example, average journey lengths have increased, along with congestion and pollution caused by cars. Access to services for those without cars is more difficult.'

'On the economy, the government says that while growth has been 2.2 per cent above the rate of inflation over 18 years, this is not as good as other countries, and investments in skills have gone down.'

'The government's aim is to make life sustainable so one of the measures is what percentage of new houses are built on green fields and how much on previously used land, known as brown field sites.'

Extracts from Paul Brown, 'Outlook darkened by waste and congestion' in the *Guardian*, 9 December 1999

Quality of life

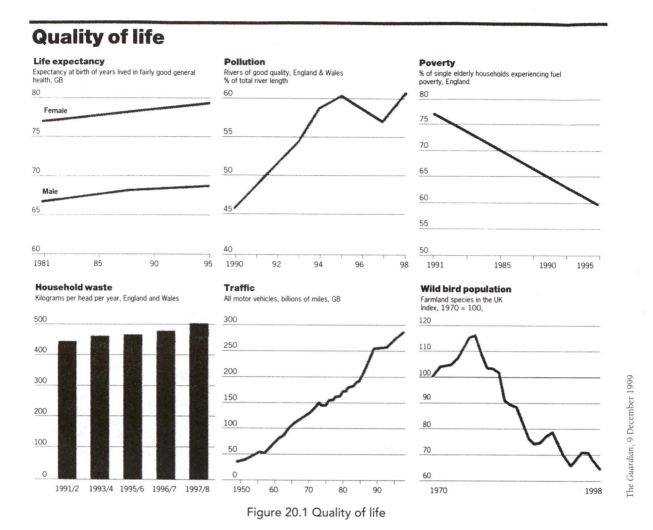

Figure 20.1 Quality of life

1 On the basis of the charts and the information in the extracts, discuss whether the quality of life of UK citizens improved from 1990 to 1998. (7)

2 Is the 2.2 per cent economic growth rate given in the extract a figure for the change in real or nominal output? Explain your answer. (2)

3 Explain what is meant by making 'life sustainable'. (3)

4 Discuss the effect of an increase in car production on real GDP and living standards. (6)

5 Discuss whether a higher real GDP per head necessarily means a higher quality of life. (7)

UNIT 21 — Aggregate demand and supply

Key concepts covered

- aggregate demand
- consumption
- investment
- net exports
- gross investment
- net investment
- government spending
- aggregate supply
- short run aggregate supply
- long run aggregate supply

Introduction

In studying the workings of individual markets economists make extensive use of demand and supply analysis. When they investigate the workings of the world economy they frequently make use of aggregate demand and supply analysis.

For example, in 1998 and 1999 economists and politicians in Japan expressed concern about the low level of aggregate demand. They were particularly worried about the low level of consumption, even though there had been hopes that the wealth effect from a rising stock market would encourage people to spend more. However, a lack of consumer confidence caused total spending to fall. This, in turn, provoked a decline in aggregate supply.

In this unit aggregate demand and aggregate supply are defined. The factors which influence the four components of aggregate demand are discussed and the reasons why an aggregate demand curve slopes down from left to right and the causes of shifts in the aggregate demand curve are explained. Attention then moves to aggregate supply. A distinction is made between short run and long run aggregate supply and between the Keynesian and new classical economists' view of the shape of the long run aggregate supply curve. Causes of shifts in short and long run aggregate supply curves are also discussed.

Aggregate demand

Aggregate demand is the total demand for a country's goods and services at a given price level. Demand comes from:

- people buying goods and services such as clothing and food – **consumption** (C)
- firms buying capital goods, for example machines, delivery vehicles – **investment** (I)
- the government buying goods and services, for example educational materials, medicines – government spending (G)
- foreigners buying the country's goods and services (X) minus domestic demand for foreign goods and services (M) – **net exports** (X – M).

Aggregate demand (AD) is often expressed as: AD = C + I + G + (X – M).

Consumption

Consumption is the largest component of aggregate demand. The main influence on consumption is income. As income rises, consumption is likely to increase, although the proportion spent usually declines when people become richer. This is because they are able to save a higher proportion of their income. Other influences on consumption include the age structure of the country, inflation, the rate of interest and optimism about the future. For example, a fall in the rate of interest will encourage some people to spend more. This is because they will gain less from saving, it will be cheaper for them to borrow and they will have more money left to spend when they have paid their mortgages.

Investment

Investment is the most volatile component of aggregate demand. **Gross investment** is the total amount spent on capital goods. It is sometimes referred to as gross domestic fixed capital formation. It includes depreciation (or capital consumption) which is spending on capital goods to replace existing ones which have either physically worn out or have become out of date. **Net investment** is spending on extra capital goods, bought to increase the stock of capital goods. Net investment is gross investment minus depreciation.

Again, the main influence on investment is income. When income is high, increasing demand for consumer goods and services is also likely to be high and rising. Firms are likely to want to expand their capacity to meet this higher demand.

Investment is also influenced by expectations. These feelings of optimism and pessimism about the future were called 'animal spirits' by John Maynard Keynes. Keynes was a British economist who wrote extensively on macroeconomics in the 1920s, 1930s and 1940s. He favoured government intervention in the economy to ensure that full employment was achieved. He also argued that shifts in expectations made private sector investment very volatile. Demand may be high and rising but if firms believe that the increase in demand will slow down or reverse in the near future, they will not buy capital goods to expand capacity and they may not even replace all the capital goods which wear out.

Other influences on investment include the level of profit, corporation tax, the cost of capital goods, the rate of interest and changes in technology.

If profit is high firms will have the money available and incentive to purchase extra capital goods in order to expand capacity. Lower corporation tax (the tax on firms' profits) will mean that firms can keep more of their profits. This again will increase the finance and incentive to invest. A fall in the rate of interest will reduce the cost of borrowing funds to spend on capital goods and will reduce the opportunity cost of using retained profits for investment purposes.

Firms will also be encouraged to buy capital goods if advances in technology make them more productive than existing ones.

Government spending

A UK government purchases a range of goods and services, including equipment and books for state schools, equipment and materials for National Health Service (NHS) hospitals and equipment for the armed services.

The amount of **government spending** depends on a number of factors. These include its views on the extent of market failure and the ability of state intervention to correct it, the electorate's demand for health, education and roads, and the level of activity in the economy.

For example, if there is a high level of unemployment a government may increase its own expenditure to stimulate demand, output and employment. In recent years in the UK the increase in the average age of the population, advances in technology and increased expectations of good health have pushed up government spending on the NHS.

Net exports

Demand for a country's exports, relative to its demand for its imports, is influenced, for instance, by the price and quality competitiveness of its goods and services, incomes at home and abroad, marketing and the exchange rate.

For example, demand for exports is likely to be high and demand for imports low if the country's products are of a higher standard and a lower price than its competitors.

ACTIVITY 1

What effect would you expect the following to have on a country's net exports:

a a recession in foreign countries

b a rise in the price competitiveness of foreign countries

c a major sporting event, for example the Olympic games, being held in the home country?

The aggregate demand curve

The aggregate demand curve shows the total quantity demanded at different price levels.

In Figure 21.1 the curve slopes down from left to right indicating that aggregate demand will be higher the lower the price level. This is because a fall in price will have the following effects:

■ It will make the country's goods and services more price competitive internationally. People will buy more domestically produced products and fewer foreign products. So net exports will rise.

■ The amount that people's wealth can buy will increase. This will encourage them to spend more and so raise consumption. This is sometimes referred to as the wealth effect.

■ Lower prices cause interest rates to fall, and lower interest rates encourage a rise in consumption and investment.

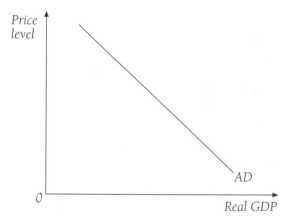

Figure 21.1 Aggregate demand curve

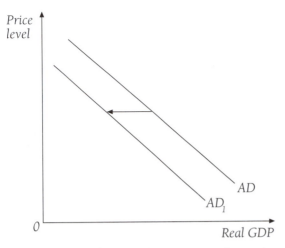

Figure 21.2 A decrease in aggregate demand

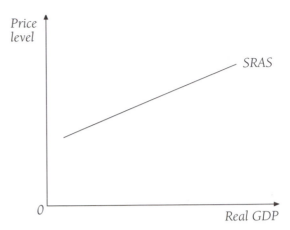

Figure 21.3 Short run aggregate supply curve

Shifts in aggregate demand

If the aggregate demand curve shifts to the right it means that the total demand for goods and services has increased for some reason other than a change in the price level. A shift to the left represents a decrease in aggregate demand as shown Figure 21.2.

We have already touched on some of the reasons why the components of aggregate demand may change. For example, advances in technology will encourage firms to demand more capital goods. Other causes of changes in aggregate demand are changes in the size of the population and changes in the money supply.

Explain whether you would expect the following to shift the aggregate demand curve to the left or right:

a a rise in expected future profits
b a fall in income tax
c a fall in foreign income.

Aggregate supply

Aggregate supply is the total quantity of goods and services that the country's firms and government concerns produce at a given price level. An aggregate supply curve shows the quantity of goods and services that would be produced at different price levels.

Economists distinguish between short run aggregate supply and long run aggregate supply.

Short run aggregate supply

Short run aggregate supply is the total quantity which will be supplied at different price levels when

the prices of factors of production are assumed not to be changing. Figure 21.3 shows a short run aggregate supply (SRAS) curve.

This curve slopes up from left to right. There are two ways of looking at this. One is to explain why the price level rises when output goes up. The reason is because while, for example, the wage rate is assumed not to be changing, average costs may rise with output. This is because to increase output overtime rates may have to be paid and machinery may have to be worked at a faster rate, leading to more breakdowns. The other is to explain why aggregate supply should rise when the price level goes up. If prices of products sold do increase while the prices of factors of production remain constant, production becomes more profitable.

Shifts in short run aggregate supply

A movement to the left of the SRAS curve shows a decrease in aggregate supply whereas a shift to the right shows an increase. Figure 21.4 illustrates an increase in short run aggregate supply.

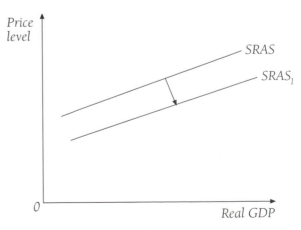

Figure 21.4 Increase in short run aggregate supply

The main causes of changes in short run aggregate supply are:

- changes in import prices
- changes in the productivity of factors of production
- changes in taxation on firms.

These, of course, all change firms' costs of production.

Long run aggregate supply

Long run aggregate supply (LRAS) is the total quantity supplied at different price levels over a time period when the prices of the factors of production can change. For instance, the wage rate can move up or down.

Different views on the shape of the long run aggregate supply curve

Keynesian economists believe that the shape of the long run aggregate supply curve can be perfectly elastic at low levels of economic activity, less elastic at higher levels and perfectly inelastic when full employment is reached. Their view is illustrated in Figure 21.5 where y represents output (income).

When the level of output is very low, and hence unemployment very high, between 0 and y, any increase in output can be achieved by offering unemployed workers jobs at the going wage rate and paying the going price for materials and capital equipment. Between y and y_1 shortages of workers, particularly skilled workers, and materials and equipment cause firms to compete for their services by offering to pay more for them. This raises costs and the price level. At y_1 all resources are employed and it is not possible to produce any more, however high the price level rises.

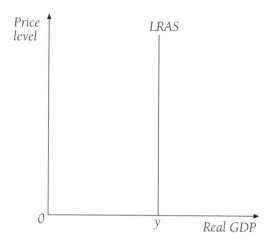

Figure 21.6 New classical long run aggregate supply curve

In contrast, new classical economists believe that in the long run the economy will operate at the full employment level and the LRAS curve will be vertical as illustrated in Figure 21.6.

They argue that if, in the short run, aggregate demand falls the workers who are made redundant will accept pay cuts and so price themselves back into employment in the longer run. So when the economy is operating at the long run equilibrium position no one who is prepared to work at the going wage rate will be unemployed.

Shifts in long run aggregate supply

An increase in long run aggregate supply is illustrated by a shift to the right of the LRAS curve and a decrease by a shift to the left.

Figure 21.7 illustrates both the Keynesian and the new classical views of an increase in LRAS.

A move to the right of the LRAS curve shows that the productive potential of the economy has increased (compare this with a move to the right of the production possibility curve). With its resources fully employed, an economy is capable of producing more goods and services. There are two main reasons why

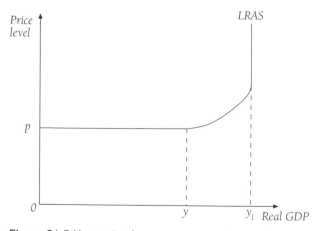

Figure 21.5 Keynesian long run aggregate supply curve

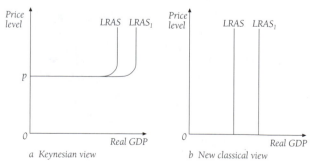

Figure 21.7 An increase in long run aggregate supply

LRAS could increase. One is an increase in the quantity of resources. For instance, an increase in married women's participation in the labour force will increase the supply of potential workers and net investment will increase the quantity of capital goods available. The other is an increase in the quality and hence the productivity of resources. So, for example, advances in technology and improvements in educational achievements will increase the quality of capital and labour and thereby raise their potential output per unit.

ACTIVITY 3

Explain whether you would expect the following to shift the long run aggregate supply curve to the left or right:

a a reduction in the retirement age

b negative net investment

c a higher proportion of people entering higher education

Summary

Aggregate demand is the total demand for domestic goods and services at a given price level. It is composed of consumption, investment, government spending and net exports. Consumption is the largest component and the main influence on consumption is income. Investment is the most volatile component. Again, it is influenced by income, in particular changes in the rate of growth of income and expected future changes. Government spending is influenced by deliberate government policies and by changes in economic activity. Net exports will rise if a country becomes more internationally competitive.

A movement along an aggregate demand curve is caused by a change in the general price level, whereas a shift in the curve is caused by any other factor affecting aggregate demand, for example, a rise in optimism.

Aggregate supply is the total output at a given price level. The short run aggregate supply curve shifts when firms' costs of production change, whereas shifts in the long run aggregate supply curve arise as a result of changes in the quantity or quality of resources. Keynesians argue that the long run aggregate supply curve is perfectly elastic at low levels of output and employment, then elastic and, when full employment is reached, perfectly inelastic. As new classical economists believe the economy always works at full employment, they argue the long run aggregate supply curve is vertical.

Data response question

'The US economy expanded in the third quarter at an annual rate of 5.5 per cent, raising fresh concerns about labour shortages and another rise in interest rates early next year.'

'The buoyant economy has been powered by the American shopper, made confident by the rosy employment picture, increases in real wages and wealth gains from the stock market. In the third quarter, consumer spending – accounting for two-thirds of economic activity – increased at an annual rate of 4.6 per cent, up from 4.3 per cent estimated last month.'

Extracts from Nancy Dunne, 'America goes shopping and growth hits 5.5 per cent' in the Financial Times, 25 November 1999

1 At what point on its LRAS curve might the US economy have been producing? (7)

2 What effect would a rise in interest rates be likely to have on aggregate demand? (6)

3 Discuss the factors that were causing consumption to rise in the USA in 1999. (6)

4 According to the extracts, how significant was consumption as a component of aggregate demand? (3)

5 What are the other components of aggregate demand? (3)

UNIT 22 Output and price determination

Key concepts covered

- equilibrium output
- spare capacity
- demand-side shocks
- supply-side shocks
- new economic paradigm

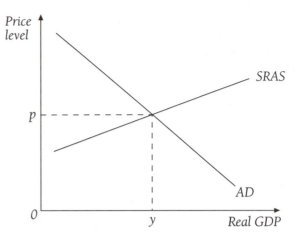

Figure 22.1 Short run equilibrium output

Introduction

In 2000 the output of Russia was below that of the United States, even when the size of the populations was taken into account, and the price level in Russia was rising more rapidly than in the USA.

The output a country produces and the price level it encounters are determined by its aggregate demand and supply. In this unit equilibrium output is explained and a distinction is made between short run and long run equilibrium, including different versions of where long run equilibrium will occur. The effects of changes in aggregate demand and aggregate supply, including demand-side and supply-side shocks are discussed and the significance of the new economic paradigm for the position of the long run aggregate supply curve is touched on.

Equilibrium output and price level

Equilibrium output and price level occur where aggregate demand and aggregate supply are equal. In this case there would be no reason for output to change. However, if, for example, aggregate demand is higher than aggregate supply there would be a tendency for output to increase and/or the price level to rise.

Short run equilibrium

The short run equilibrium of output occurs where aggregate demand equals short run aggregate supply (see Figure 22.1).

At the price level of P all the output produced by domestic firms is sold and there is no reason for producers to increase or reduce their output and there are no pressures pushing up or lowering the price level.

Long run equilibrium

The long run equilibrium output and price level of an economy take place where aggregate demand equals the long run aggregate supply. However, economists disagree about what this level of output will be.

New classical economists argue that in the long run the economy will operate with full employment. As we saw in Unit 21 they believe that the long run aggregate supply curve is vertical. Figure 22.2 illustrates their view on long run equilibrium.

Keynesians argue that aggregate demand may be equal to long run aggregate supply at any level of employment. They believe it is possible for an economy to be operating with **spare capacity**, i.e. with unused resources. Figure 22.3 shows long run equilibrium output occurring well below the full employment level.

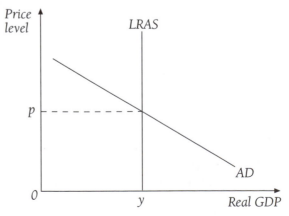

Figure 22.2 Long run equilibrium output

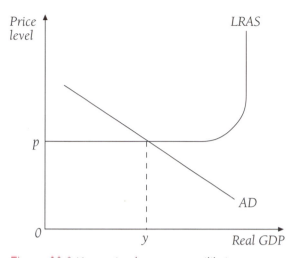

Figure 22.3 Keynesian long run equilibrium output below full employment

Both groups of economists accept that an economy can be in short run equilibrium but not in long run equilibrium. If, for example, aggregate demand rises to a very high level, in the short run domestic output may rise as a result of workers being prepared to work longer hours and low-quality resources being used. However, in the longer run the rise in costs which results will cause the short run aggregate supply curve to shift to the right and output to fall. Figure 22.4 uses the new classical version of the long run aggregate supply curve to illustrate this.

The economy is initially in short run and long run equilibrium at y. The increase in aggregate demand, illustrated by the shift in the aggregate demand curve from AD to AD_1 causes output to rise in the short run. The economy moves to a new, higher level short run equilibrium output of y_1 and a higher price level

of p_1. However, in the longer run the higher costs which result from firms competing for increasingly scarce labour and raw materials raise costs of production. The short run aggregate supply moves to the left, and firms realising that in real terms, with the price rises they gained being offset by higher prices, they are no better off, reduce their output back to y.

Effects of a shift in aggregate demand

As Figure 22.4 suggests, new classical economists believe that an increase in aggregate demand will cause a rise in output and the price level in the short run, but in the long run the only effect will be on the price level. Similarly, in the long run a fall in aggregate demand will lower the price level but leave output unchanged. Figure 22.5 illustrates a fall in aggregate demand. Output initially falls to y_1 and the price level to p_1. However, they argue, that in the long run the workers made unemployed when output is cut back will be prepared to accept lower wages. This fall in costs encourages firms to expand their output and, as a result, output rises back to y but now with lower unit costs and price level.

However, Keynesians argue that the effects of an increase in aggregate demand will depend on where the economy was initially operating. If it was producing at the full employment level then the long run effect will be purely inflationary. Figure 22.6 shows aggregate demand rising from AD to AD_1 which pushes up the price level but leaves output unchanged at y.

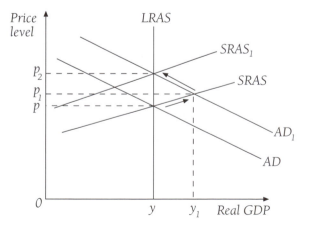

Figure 22.4 New classical view of the effects of an increase in aggregae demand

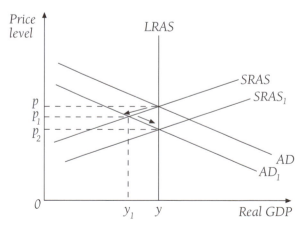

Figure 22.5 New classical view of the effects of a decrease in aggregate demand

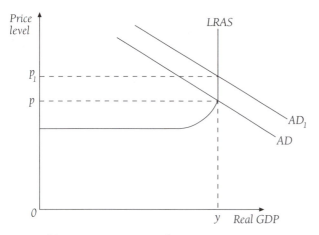

Figure 22.6 Keynesian view of an increase in aggregate demand occurring at the full employment level of output

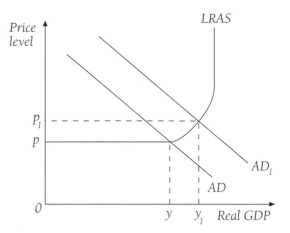

Figure 22.8 Keynesian view of an increase in aggregate demand occurring at a level of output where shortages start to be experienced

If, in contrast, the economy is producing with a high level of unemployment an increase in aggregate demand will cause output to rise from y to y_1 and have no effect on the price level as illustrated by Figure 22.7.

The third possibility is that, before the rise in output, the economy may be experiencing some shortages of resources, for example skilled workers. In this case an increase in aggregate demand will raise both the price level and output as shown in Figure 22.8.

It is interesting to note that an increase in aggregate demand will have a greater final effect on the economy. This is because when households, firms, the government and importers spend money that money becomes the income of the people who sell

them the goods and services. They, in turn, will spend some of the money they receive. So there is a knock-on effect, with aggregate demand rising by more than the initial amount.

Effects of shifts in the short run aggregate supply curve

Economists agree that a decrease in short run aggregate supply will raise the price level, whereas an increase in short run aggregate supply will reduce the price level. For example, a rise in the cost of imported raw materials will raise firms' costs of production. This will shift the SRAS curve to the left and push the price level up to p_1 and reduce output to y_1 as illustrated in Figure 22.9.

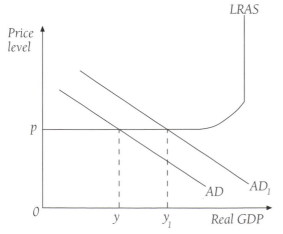

Figure 22.7 Keynesian view of an increase in aggregate demand occurring at a low level of output

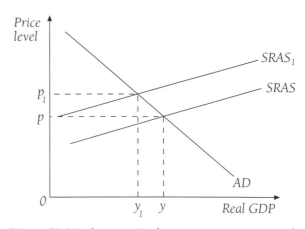

Figure 22.9 A decrease in short run aggregate supply

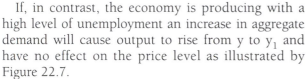

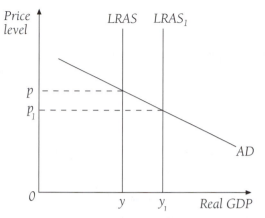

Figure 22.10 New classical view of an increase in long run aggregate supply

ACTIVITY 1

In Spain in 1999 consumer confidence was high and this contributed to a 5 per cent rise in consumer spending. The Spanish government also increased its spending without raising taxes.

a   Illustrate the likely effect on output and the price level of the events mentioned using:
  i   the new classical version of the LRAS curve
  ii the Keynesian version of the LRAS curve.
b   Discuss what factors may cause a rise in consumer confidence.

The effects of a shift in long run aggregate supply

Again, there is disagreement among new classical and Keynesian economists about the effects of a shift of the LRAS curve. New classical economists argue that it will cause the economy to move to a new equilibrium position with a higher output and lower price level. This is shown in Figure 22.10.

Keynesians, however, argue that it depends again on where the initial equilibrium position is. If the economy is operating at a low level of economic activity the increase in LRAS will increase the productive potential of the economy, but the lack of aggregate demand will mean that it will not be used and output will remain at y. Figure 22.11 shows the LRAS curve moving to the right but the price level and output staying at their initial levels.

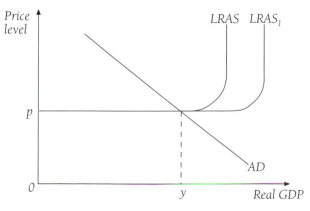

Figure 22.11 Keynesian view of an increase in long run aggregate supply occurring at a low level of output

Demand-side shocks

Demand-side shocks are unanticipated events that effect domestic aggregate demand, shifting the AD curve and affecting the economy. These can be external or internal.

External shocks start in other countries. For example, in 1997 and 1998 a number of East Asian countries ran into significant difficulties with some of their banks and other firms going out of business. The decline in economic activity in, for example, Japan, Indonesia and Thailand reduced their demand for imports from Europe and the USA. As a result, Germany and the UK, among others, exported less to the Far East and this put downward pressure on their aggregate demand and reduced their economic growth rates.

There can also be internal shocks. For example, households may become more optimistic about the future and as a result increase the amount they spend – a consumer boom.

Supply-side shocks

Supply-side shocks are again unanticipated events but this time ones which affect aggregate supply. For example, if key groups of workers gain a pay rise this may spread to other groups. Wage costs will rise and the short run aggregate supply curve will shift to the left and the price level will rise.

The sudden changes in aggregate supply may also result from external events. If the price of oil increases those countries which buy their oil from abroad will face higher costs of production.

ACTIVITY 2

In 1999 the prices of gold and cocoa fell. This hit the economy of Ghana which is a major exporter of gold and cocoa. Its export earnings fell dramatically and thousands of workers were laid off by the gold mining and cocoa companies.

a Illustrate the likely effect on output and the price level in Ghana of the decline in its export earnings using:

  i the new classical version of the LRAS curve

  ii the Keynesian version of the LRAS curve.

b Discuss the effect on the output and the price level in Ghana of a decision by the Ghanaian gold mining companies to close down their gold mines.

The new economic paradigm

At the end of the twentieth century some economists began to argue that microeconomic changes in the economy mean that it is possible for economies to continue to grow at high and steady rates without causing the price level to rise. They argue that increasing global competition, increasing use of the Internet for shopping and lower expectations of inflation are putting downward pressure on the price level and that, in particular, advances in information technology are increasing the productive potential of economies. Thus, as aggregate demand shifts to the right the higher level of aggregate demand is met by higher long run aggregate supply. This is shown in Figure 22.12. The suggestion is that economies have changed and

that a **new economic paradigm** or model is needed to explain how economies now operate.

ACTIVITY 3

Argentina experienced a recession, i.e. a fall in output, at the end of the twentieth century. Among the causes of this downturn in activity were a fall in exports and a lack of investment. Some economists suggested that the Argentine government should raise economic activity by increasing government spending.

a Using aggregate demand and supply diagrams, discuss whether an increase in government spending would raise output.

b Using newspaper articles from *The Times*, *Guardian*, *The Independent* and/or the *Daily Telegraph* CD-ROMs or the Internet, discover the current state of the Argentine economy.

Summary

Equilibrium output and price level occur where aggregate demand is equal to aggregate supply. Keynesians believe long run equilibrium output can occur at any level of employment, whereas new classical economists believe it will occur at the full employment level of output. These different views lead the two groups to believe that shifts in the aggregate demand curve may have different outcomes in the long run. Both agree that if the economy is operating at full employment the long run effect will be to raise the general price level but to leave output unchanged. However, Keynesians argue that at less than full employment an increase in aggregate demand will raise output and will also raise the general price level when the economy begins to experience shortages of resources.

A decrease in short run aggregate supply will raise the price level and reduce output. New classical economists argue that an increase in long run aggregate supply will raise both potential and actual output. Keynesians, however, believe that the effect will again depend on at what level of economic activity the economy was first operating.

Demand-side shocks are unexpected events which shift the aggregate demand curve, whereas supply-side shocks shift the short run aggregate supply curve.

The new economic paradigm suggests that the long run aggregate supply curve is being moved outwards as a result of improvements in information technology, productivity and international competitiveness.

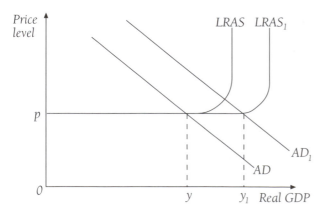

Figure 22.12 The new economic paradigm

Data response question

'Suddenly the economic news is all heading in the same up beat direction. In a week in which America's third-quarter growth was revised up to a 5.5. per cent annualised rate, the European Commission lifted its growth forecasts for the European Union sharply higher.'

'In Britain, as in America, the driving force for growth has been the consumer. Spending was weaker than expected in the third quarter because car buyers were reluctant to go for new V-registered vehicles in September (the expectation of imminent price costs held back sales), but the consumer has kept the economy growing through a period when it could have been hit hard by the Asian crisis.'

'Asian economies, after an appalling 1998 and in many cases a poor 1999, are rapidly returning to growth, with rates of 5 per cent to 6 per cent typical of countries such as Malaysia, the Philippines and South Korea.'

'As in America, the notable factor (in the UK) has been that economic growth has strengthened without triggering higher inflation. In many sectors, indeed, competitive pressures appear to be increasing. As growth returns, it is natural for economists to look for the normal inflationary side effects. This time, perhaps, policy makers have discovered the secret of non-inflationary growth.'

Extracts from David Smith, 'World economy fires on all cylinders' in *The Sunday Times*, 28 November 1999.

1 What was the European Commission predicting would happen to the level of output in the EU? (2)
2 What was causing output to rise in the UK in the last quarter of 1999? (3)
3 What effect would you expect the difficulties experienced by Asian countries to have had on the output of western countries and why?(6)
4 In what circumstances would higher output be associated with inflation? (7)
5 Explain how it may be possible to increase output without inflation occurring. (7)

Economic growth

Key concepts covered

- actual growth
- potential growth
- trend growth
- the output gap
- overheating
- the opportunity cost of economic growth

Introduction

Shi Guangshen, China's foreign trade minister, in late 1999 predicted that China's economy would grow by 7 per cent in 2000. This would match the expected 1999 figure. By international standards 7 per cent is a high rate. However, it is below the high rates China achieved in the early 1990s and is lower than the country's trend growth rate. Some economists have expressed concern that if the country's economic growth rate declines it would mean that some of the ever-increasing numbers of school leavers would not find jobs and the long-term unemployed would feel increasingly frustrated.

In assessing a country's economic growth performance, economists first have to measure its growth rate, then compare it with the rate it is capable of and then seek to understand its causes and consequences.

In this unit these key aspects of economic growth are explained. A distinction is made between actual and potential growth. Trend growth, which is referred to above and which you may come across in a number of articles, is defined. Linked to trend growth are the concepts of an output gap and overheating and these are explained. Then the causes of economic growth are explored in broad terms and in terms of differences in economic growth rates between countries. Finally, the benefits and costs of economic growth are assessed.

Actual growth

As noted in Unit 19, economic growth refers to an increase in the output of a country. It is measured as the rate at which real GDP (gross domestic product) is changing. This can be referred to as **actual growth**. An economy may produce more as a result of using previously unemployed resources or using resources more efficiently. This is illustrated on a production

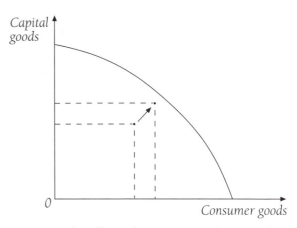

Figure 23.1 The effect of using previously unemployed resources

possibility diagram by a movement of the production point on or towards the production possibility curve as shown in Figure 23.1.

It may also produce more as a result of using more or higher quality resources. This time, both the production point and the curve will move to the right as shown in Figure 23.2.

Potential growth

The increase in the quantity and/or the quality of a country's resources raises the productive potential of the country and can be referred to as **potential growth**. Figure 23.2 shows both potential and actual growth occurring. Of course, it is possible for potential growth to occur without actual growth taking place. For example, the labour force of a country may increase but if there is no demand to use this resource, output will not rise.

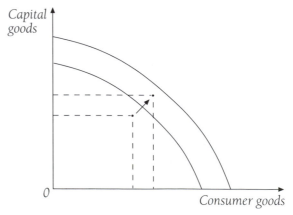

Figure 23.2 Potential and actual growth

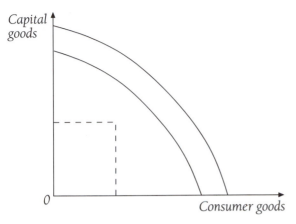

Figure 23.3 Potential but not actual growth

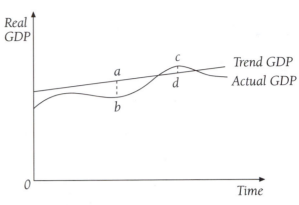

Figure 23.4 Trend and actual GDP

Figure 23.3 shows potential but not actual growth occurring with the production possibility point being unchanged.

In the long run, for economic growth to continue the productive potential of the economy must rise. If not, the economy will hit a supply constraint, unable to produce any more with the given quantity and quality of resources.

Trend growth

In practice the productive potential of most economies increases each year. In industrial economies this is due mainly to improvements in educational standards and technology. In some developing economies it is also due to rises in the size of the labour force.

Trend growth is the expected increase in potential output over time and is a measure of how fast the economy can grow without generating higher infla- tion. It is sometimes referred to as 'the economy's speed limit'. In late 1999 the UK government revised upwards the economy's trend rate of sustainable growth from 2.25 per cent to 2.5 per cent a year. This rise, if achieved, would increase output by £2 billion a year. The reasons for the upward revision were:

■ an increase in productivity growth

■ a rise in employment

■ improvements in education and training

■ increase in competitive forces putting downward pressure on prices – particularly in food retailing.

Output gap

When aggregate demand matches the full employment level of aggregate supply, actual output will match potential output. The economy will be making the maximum output it is capable of producing. However, when there is a lack of aggregate demand there will be unemployed resources and an **output gap**. Figure 23.4 shows the growth in potential output and actual output over time.

The distance ab represents the output gap. When the economy has been producing below its potential output there is the possibility that its actual output will grow at a faster rate than its potential output. In this case the output gap will narrow.

For short periods of time the high levels of aggregate demand may push rises in output above the trend growth rate. Some of the extra output may be achieved by workers working overtime, and machines being worked flat out without pauses for maintenance. However this is not sustainable. It is likely to lead to inflation and is referred to as overheating. The distance cd in Figure 23.4 shows the economy **overheating**.

Causes of economic growth

If an economy is operating below its potential output, an increase in aggregate demand will cause a rise in national output. Figure 23.5 shows an increase in aggregate demand, leading to a rise in real GDP from y to y_1.

Aggregate demand will increase if consumption, investment, government spending or net exports rise, or any combination of these rise. Increases in investment and some forms of government spending, for example spending on education and research and development will also shift the aggregate supply curve to the right.

In the long run, for economic growth to continue aggregate supply must increase. For this to take place

A C T I V I T Y   1

'If I am right, we will look back on early November 1999 as the time when the belief that "this time it will be different" that the economy has embarked on some kind of new era or new paradigm, finally started to have an impact on official thinking.

The first inkling of this came when, on the eve of Gordon Brown's pre-budget report last Tuesday, the Treasury published a paper revising up Britain's trend rate of sustainable growth from 2.25 per cent to 2.5 per cent a year.'

David Smith, 'Brave New World' in *The Sunday Times*, 14 November 1999

a   Explain what the new economic paradigm is.
b   What is meant by the trend rate of economic growth?
c   Discuss, in a group, whether you think we have entered a 'brave new world' of economic prosperity and stability.

either the quantity and/or quality of resources must increase. For example, a country may be able to produce more because it has more capital goods and/or because the capital goods it has are of a higher quality, incorporating advanced technological features.

Causes of differences in countries' economic growth rates

Generally, industrial countries grow at a more rapid rate than developing countries. However, some

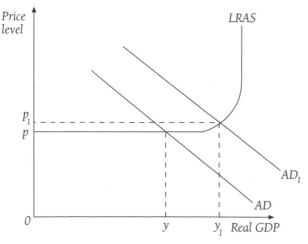

Figure 23.5 Economic growth caused by a rise in aggregate demand.

developing countries have grown at a fast rate and have narrowed the gap between their level of real GDP per head and the real GDP per head of industrial countries.

Economists seek to understand what enables a country to grow at a high and stable rate. So far, no magic formula has been found. However, among the significant factors are thought to be the following:

■   Stability, including a stable growth of aggregate demand and government policy in terms of, for example, tax rates. Producers will make more goods and services if they believe that demand will continue to rise. What will discourage economic growth is fluctuations in demand. An uneven growth in aggregate demand will discourage firms from expanding as they will be uncertain that they will be able to sell extra output in the future.

■   High levels of expenditure on good quality investment. The use of extra machines, buildings and other capital equipment will increase the productive capacity of a country. Investment levels are usually higher in industrial countries than in developing countries. Poor countries have low income levels and so their people are not able to save much. This reduces the funds available for investment.

■   Technological progress. Advances in technology, including improvements in the methods of production and the quality of capital goods, raise productivity and reduce costs. Advances in information technology are currently being credited with the increase in the growth rate of the USA and a number of EU countries.

■   Good quality education and training. Improvements in education and training should increase labour productivity. In poor countries very few people go on to higher education and in some countries the majority of children do not even receive secondary education. It has been estimated that the average five-year-old in sub-Saharan Africa can expect to receive four to six years of education. This is in contrast to a child growing up in the west. He or she will receive 15 to 17 years of education.

■   A good export performance. If a country performs well both at home and abroad the size of its firms' markets will be larger, enabling them to take greater advantage of economies of scale. It will also mean that if demand falls in the home market its firms may still be able to sell to other countries and so may not have to reduce their output. To perform well in export markets firms have to be competitive in terms not only of price but also quality.

■ Strong manufacturing (secondary) and services (tertiary) sectors. Some economists argue that the rate of economic growth tends to be most rapid when a high proportion of the labour force is employed in the manufacturing and tertiary sectors. The argument is that economies of scale are most significant in the manufacturing sector and that demand is more income elastic and less prone to wide fluctuations for the products produced by firms operating in the secondary and tertiary sectors. A number of developing countries still have a high proportion of their labour force employed in low productivity agriculture.

■ Appropriate government policies. There are differences of opinion on what are the appropriate government policies. However, it is agreed that in some countries governments have not always adopted policies which have promoted stability and economic growth.

■ A low level of international debt. A number of poor countries, which have borrowed in the past in an attempt to improve their economic performance, are now paying back more to rich countries in the form of interest payments than they are receiving in the form of foreign aid.

■ Manageable changes in population. In some developing countries the high rise in the birth rate means that resources which could have been devoted to the production of capital goods have to be devoted instead to the building and maintenance of new schools and hospitals.

Benefits and costs of economic growth

Economic growth can have both benefits and costs.

Benefits

The main benefit of economic growth is likely to be a rise in people's material standard of living. If real GDP per head rises the population can enjoy more goods and services. Poor countries are desperate to raise their output so that their people have enough food, housing and other necessities. Rich countries have already seen most of their citizens obtaining not only basic necessities but also an increasing range of luxury goods and services.

Economic growth enables poverty within a country

ACTIVITY 2

'Over very long periods, growth in GDP can be attributed to growth in the input of capital, growth in the input of labour, and productivity growth – where that is "total factor productivity" including the efficiency of capital as well as labour.'

'Total factor productivity has been the biggest contributor to economic growth in most countries at most times. And there certainly seems to be a rapid pace of technological innovation.'

Extracts from Diane Coyle, 'Hurdles on the road to sustained growth' in *The Independent*, 10 November 1999

a Explain what is meant by productivity.
b Use both a production possibility and a long run aggregate supply curve to illustrate the effect of an increase 'in the input of capital'.
c Discuss, in a group, what technological innovation you are aware of in:
  i consumer products
  ii capital goods and methods of production in firms where you may undertake part-time work and in your educational institution.

to be reduced without having to redistribute existing income. Higher output raises tax revenue without having to increase tax rates, and some of this can be used to finance schemes to help the poor. Some of the higher tax revenue can also be used to improve public services, such as education and health care and to tackle pollution and improve the environment.

Economic growth raises the level of a country's real GDP and can thereby increase its status and power in international organisations and international negotiations. The USA, which has a very high level of real GDP and real GDP per head, is a very powerful member of the United Nations (UN), the International Monetary Fund (IMF) and the World Trade Organisation (WTO).

Costs

Economic growth, depending on a country's circumstances and how it is achieved, can have costs. If an economy is currently using all its resources, and so producing on its production possibility curve, the only way it can increase output is to switch resources from making consumer goods and services to making capital goods. Thus, in the short run, fewer consumer goods and services will be produced. However, in the long run the extra capital goods will enable more consumer goods and services to be made. If economic growth is achieved in a way that is not sustainable, for example by the expansion of heavy industry without regard to controls on pollution, there will be damage to the environment. There is also the risk that economic growth may result in the depletion of non-renewable resources.

Economic growth may also reduce the quality of some people's lives. A growing economy is one which requires some people to acquire new skills and some to change jobs. The pace of work may also increase. Some people may find these changes stressful.

While economic growth has the potential to reduce poverty, it may make some of the poor worse off. This is because a more prosperous economy may produce fewer goods and services for the poor. The gap between the rich and the poor may also increase.

The quality of life of a range of people may be adversely affected by the increase in the quantity and range of goods and services. For example, the production and use of more cars has increased people's flexibility of travel but has also resulted in more accidents, an increase in breathing-related illnesses and has reduced the ability of children to play in their local streets.

In addition, having more goods and services does not guarantee happiness. Indeed, it can create a desire for even more goods and services and a feeling of discontent. Some years ago most households were happy with one television, now many have two televisions and some would like to more.

ACTIVITY 3

In India, since 1992 real incomes per head have been rising at over 4 per cent a year. If this rate is sustained, real income per head will have doubled by 2008.

a   Using *The Economist* newspaper, compare India's current economic growth rate with that of China and the UK.

b   In a group compare the benefits that economic growth may provide for the citizens of India and for the UK.

c   In pairs carry out a survey asking ten people you know over the age of 40 in what ways they believe the quality of their life has improved, in what ways it has got worse and whether they are happier now than they were 15 years ago. Pool your findings and decide what conclusions you can draw about the benefits of economic growth.

Summary

Actual growth refers to increases in output, whereas potential growth is increases in a country's ability to produce goods and services. Trend growth is the expected increase in productive potential over time. When an economy grows below its trend growth there is an output gap. If it grows above it, the economy is said to be overheating. In the short run the main cause of economic growth is increases in aggregate demand, whereas in the long run it is increases in aggregate supply. Among the factors thought to be important in fostering economic growth are high levels of investment, good quality education and training, technological progress and appropriate government policies.

The main benefit of economic growth is higher material living standards. However, economic growth will clearly be less desirable if it is bought at the cost of damage to the environment and increased stress levels.

Data response question

Dr Klaus Topfer, the head of the United Nations Environment Programme, presented the UN programme's GEO-2000 report at a launch in London in September 1996.

He said: '… the gains by better management and technology are still being outpaced by the environmental impacts of population and economic growth. We are on an unsustainable course. Time is rapidly running out for a rational, well-planned transition to a sustainable future.'

The two major causes of environmental degradation, he stressed, were the continued poverty of the majority of the planet's inhabitants and excessive consumption by the well-off minority.

'The global environment has never before been under such pressures,' he said. 'It is little wonder that it is becoming the worse for wear. Full-scale emergencies now exist on a number of issues.'

After climate change, water was the most serious. By 2025 as much as two-thirds of the world's population would be subject to 'water stress' meaning difficulty of access to water supplies or to clean water. Already, he said, 20 per cent of the world's population lacked access to a safe drinking water and half the world lacked access to a safe sanitation system.

'The global water cycle is unlikely to be able to cope with the demands that will be made of it in the coming decades,' he warned.

Michael McCarthy, 'UN report warns of Earth's unsustainable future' in *The Independent*, 16 September 1999

1   Discuss why economic growth may result in environmental problems. (7)
2   Explain what is meant by sustainable economic growth. (5)
3   What are the main threats to the environment? (4)
4   What is meant by water stress? (2)
5   Discuss whether it is possible to achieve both economic growth and an improvement in the environment. (7)

Key concepts covered

- Retail Prices Index (RPI)
- RPIX
- RPIY
- harmonised index of consumer prices
- demand-pull inflation
- cost-push inflation
- hyperinflation
- menu costs
- shoe leather costs
- inflationary noise
- fiscal drag
- zero inflation
- Monetary Policy Committee

Introduction

The effects of inflation are influenced by its level, whether it is accelerating or not, whether it was anticipated or not and what caused it.

In 1999 Russia experienced an inflation rate of above 50 per cent while the UK had an inflation rate of only 2 per cent. The high average rise in prices caused considerable difficulties, especially to the poor, whereas the citizens of the UK benefited from relatively stable prices. It has not always been like this. In the 1970s and 1980s UK inflation, although never reaching levels comparable to those in Russia in 1999, was regarded as the main problem facing the economy.

In this unit inflation and its measurement are discussed in more depth than in Unit 19 of this section. The causes of inflation are discussed and the consequences of inflation are explained.

Definition

Prices are changing all the time. For example, the price of personal computers may be falling while the price of petrol may be rising. Inflation is an increase in the price not of a few individual goods and services and not a one-off increase but a continuous rise in the general (average) price level. Thus, if the lower prices of personal computers are accompanied by a rise in the price of most other goods and services the average change in prices will be upwards and inflation will occur.

When inflation does take place the value of money must fall. Each unit of the currency, for example each pound, will be able to buy less if prices are higher. Table 24.1 shows how inflation reduced the purchasing power of the pound between 1980 and 1998. So, for example, by 1991 a £1 would have been able to buy the equivalent of what could have been purchased for 50p in 1980.

Table 24.1 The purchasing power of the pound

Year	Pence	Year	Pence
1980	100	1990	53
1981	89	1991	50
1982	82	1992	48
1983	79	1993	48
1984	75	1994	46
1985	71	1995	45
1986	68	1996	44
1987	66	1997	42
1988	63	1998	41
1989	58		

Measurement of inflation

To assess what is happening to prices governments construct price indices (or indexes). These include producer price indices, which measure changes in the price of inputs and outputs, and the general domestic product (GDP) deflator, which measures changes in the price of capital and consumer goods made in the home country.

However, the price index which receives most media attention in most countries is the consumer price index. In the UK the main consumer index is the **Retail Prices Index** (RPI). This shows changes in the price of consumer goods and services purchased in the UK.

Steps in constructing the Retail Prices Index

The RPI is a weighted price index. This means that changes in the prices of goods and services which people spend more on are given more importance than those on which they only spend a small amount.

Government officials first seek to find out what people spend their money on. They do this by carrying out a Family Expenditure Survey. This involves asking 7000 households to keep a record of what they buy and which bills they pay over a period of two weeks and to give details of their major purchases over a longer period.

From this weights are given to different items of expenditure. In the UK there are 14 main categories:

food
fuel and light
motoring expenditure
catering
household goods
fares and other travel costs
alcoholic drinks
household services
leisure goods
tobacco
clothing and footwear
leisure services
personal goods and services
housing.

If it is found, for instance, that 10 per cent of people's expenditure goes on food, this will be given a weighting of 10/100 or 1/10, whereas if 5 per cent is devoted to leisure goods and services, this category will be given a weight of 5/100 or 1/20.

Then officials from the Office for National Statistics (ONS) check how the prices of a variety of items have changed. To do this each month they visit a number of shops throughout the country and gain information about changes in the prices of electricity, gas and rail fares from the head-quarters of the companies and from the government. In total they obtain more than 100 000 prices for approximately 600 types of goods and services.

The expenditure of two groups is omitted from the Family Expenditure Survey to make it more representative of the typical household: low-income pensioner households and the households of the very rich. The reason for this is that it is thought their expenditure patterns are significantly different from the majority of the population.

The final stage is to multiply the price changes by the weights in order to find the inflation rate.

Example

Category:	Weight ×	Price change =	Weighted price change
Food:	4/10 ×	10% =	4%
Housing:	3/10 ×	20% =	6%
Motoring expenditure:	2/10 ×	5% =	1%
Leisure goods:	1/10 ×	−1.5% =	−1.5%
			9.5%

ACTIVITY 1

a A Family Expenditure Survey indicates that 5/10ths of people's expenditure goes on food, 2/10ths on housing, 2/10ths on clothing and footwear and 1/10th on alcoholic drink. The price of food rises by 4 per cent, the price of housing rises by 10 per cent, the price of clothing and footwear falls by 5 per cent and the price of alcoholic drinks rises by 30 per cent.
Calculate the rate of inflation.

b

'Britons now spend more on fun than on any other household expenditure, as spending on leisure outstrips that on housing and food for the average family for the first time.

Spending on holidays, home computers, sporting events and other leisure goods and services now forms the largest share of household outgoings, according to official figures published today.

Until now, spending on food and non-alcoholic drinks has taken the largest slice of the household's budget.

The average household now spends a total of £350 a week, with £60 going on leisure goods and services, £59 on food and £57 on housing costs such as rents or mortgages, the government's annual survey of household spending reveals. A year ago the same household spent £329 a week with £55 spent on leisure, £56 on food and £51 on housing.'

Julia Hartley-Brewer, 'Fun-loving Britons splash out more on leisure' in *The Guardian*, 25 November 1999

i Comment on how spending patterns have changed.
ii Calculate the weighting which would have been given to leisure goods and services in 1999.
iii Identify two categories of expenditure not mentioned in the extract.

Limitations of the Retail Prices Index

The RPI aims to give a representative picture of what is happening to prices in the UK. However, there are a number of reasons for believing that it may not give a totally accurate picture. These include the following:

■ To assess whether prices are rising the prices of the same goods and services should be compared over time. However, over time goods and services change, often improving in quality. So, for example, if the price of a vacuum cleaner rises by 6 per cent this may reflect a higher charge to cover improvements in the model rather than the same vacuum cleaner becoming more expensive.

■ Government officials do not monitor prices in sales, charity shops, or car boot sales. In addition, not all Internet purchases are included. A limited range of Internet purchases, those of toys and books, were included for the first time in February 2000. The intention is to increase the range of products over time. Thus, the RPI may overstate the price rises which people face.

■ One of the main categories in the RPI is housing which includes mortgage interest rate re-payments. When a central bank raises interest rates in a bid to lower inflation this raises the cost of mortgage interest rate repayments and so, at least in the short run, raises the inflation rate.

Other measures of inflation

RPI is often referred to as the 'headline' rate of inflation as it has traditionally received so much media attention. The government uses the data it collects in its compilation of the RPI to construct two measures of the underlying rates of inflation, **RPIX** and **RPIY**. These seek to provide a picture of the inflationary pressures building up in the economy.

RPIX is RPI minus mortgage interest payments and RPIY is RPI minus not only mortgage interest payments but also minus indirect taxes. RPIX is also known as the target rate as this is the one on which the government's target for inflation is based. RPIY is also known as the core inflation rate.

Other countries' consumer price indices often do not include mortgage interest payments and to make comparisons with other EU countries, the UK government now also publishes the **harmonised index of consumer prices** (HICP) (see Table 24.2). This measure was created after the Maastricht Treaty of 1991 so that EU countries would have a directly comparable measure of inflation. It is based on consumer price indices collected in the countries of the EU using a similar basket of goods and services.

Table 24.2 Harmonised indices of consumer prices, July 1999

	%		%
UK	1.3	Finland	1.4
Irish Republic	1.9	Portugal	1.9
Austria	0.3	France	0.4
Italy	1.7	Spain	2.1
Belgium	0.7	Germany	0.6
Luxembourg	- 0.3	Sweden	0.2
Denmark	2.0	Greece	1.8
Netherlands	1.8	EU average	1.1

The causes of inflation

There are thought to be two main causes of inflation. One is known as **demand-pull inflation** and the other is **cost-push inflation**. Demand-pull inflation arises from aggregate demand increasing at a faster rate than aggregate supply. Figure 24.1 shows aggregate demand increasing from AD to AD_1 when the economy is operating at full employment.

With the existing quality and quantity of resources it is not possible to increase output and so the higher aggregate demand causes the price level to rise.

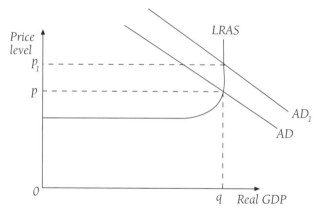

Figure 24.1 Demand-pull inflation at full employment

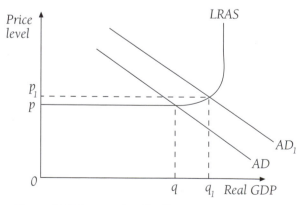

Figure 24.2 Demand-pull inflation occurring as the economy approaches full employment

Inflation can also occur when output is approaching the full employment level. Figure 24.2 shows an increase in aggregate demand causing both output and the price level to rise.

As output rises, shortages of skilled workers and capital equipment begin to build up. Firms wanting to expand compete with each other for these scarce resources by bidding up their prices.

One cause of demand-pull inflation is a consumer boom. When consumers are very confident about the future, perhaps because of falling unemployment, they tend to spend more. Firms seeking to raise their output to meet this higher demand may experience higher costs due to competition for resources. The higher demand will make them more confident about passing these higher costs on to consumers. Indeed, they may raise their prices by more than the rise in their costs in buoyant markets in order to raise their profit levels.

As we have seen, increases in aggregate demand can have an effect on costs of production. However, the starting point of the inflation is an excessive growth of aggregate demand.

In contrast, the other main cause of inflation is increases in costs of production. This is referred to as cost-push inflation and is a rise in the general price level caused by, for example, a rise in the price of imported raw materials, independent of any change in aggregate demand.

Cost-push inflation is illustrated by a decrease in the short run aggregate curve as shown in Figure 24.3.

For example, a rise in wages will increase the costs of production. This will shift the short run aggregate supply (SRAS) curve to the left which, in turn, raises the price level. This can set off a period of inflation as the higher wages are likely to cause an increase in aggregate demand. This, in turn, may cause a rise in

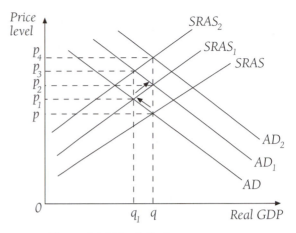

Figure 24.4 The inflationary process

costs of production and so on. The inflationary process is shown in Figure 24.4.

Deciding on the causes of inflation

Once inflation is under way it can sometimes be difficult to decide whether it was caused by sustained increases in aggregate demand or sustained increases in the costs of production. However, on other occasions the starting point is clear. For example, in Brazil in the late 1990s the inflation experienced was caused by cost-push. The value of the Brazilian currency, the real, fell, which caused the price of imported raw materials to rise. The inflation which occurred in the UK in the late 1980s was of a demand-pull nature. Consumers feeling optimistic about the future, due to falling unemployment and rising house prices and finding it easy and cheap to borrow, increased their spending significantly.

How economists assess the causes

To assess what factors are causing inflation economists study data and surveys on the key influences. For example, economic theory suggests a direct relationship between changes in earnings and inflation. If earnings rise by more than increases in productivity, costs of production will rise and so cost-push inflation will occur, as was shown in Figure 24.3.

The inflationary process will be reinforced by the increase in spending which will arise from the increase in earnings.

However, economists have to study the relationship carefully because the line of causation might run the other way. An increase in inflation is likely to stimulate an increase in earnings as workers press for wage rises to maintain their real wages.

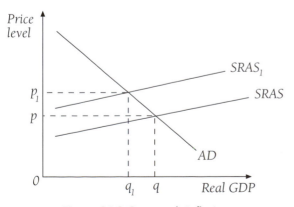

Figure 24.3 Cost-push inflation

Table 24.3 Inflation rate and change in average earnings

Year	Inflation rate (changes in RPI)	Change in average earnings*
1990	9.5	9.8
1991	5.9	8.1
1992	3.7	6.3
1993	1.6	3.3
1994	2.5	3.0
1995	3.4	2.3
1996	2.4	2.1
1997	3.1	4.4
1998	3.5	4.8

* earnings = wages + overtime payments

Examining the data in Table 24.3 shows that inflation and the increase in earnings were highest at the start of the period. Inflation and the increase in earnings then fell from 1990 to 1993. From 1995 to 1997 the general price level and earnings started to rise rather more rapidly. For most of the period inflation moved in the same direction. However, earnings and inflation moved in the opposite direction in 1994 and 1996. The percentage growth in earnings was higher than inflation in all but one year, which was 1995. If the rise in earnings was contributing to inflation this might be expected, as, for example, an 8 per cent increase in earnings will cause costs to rise by less than 8 per cent – earnings are only one of the costs of production.

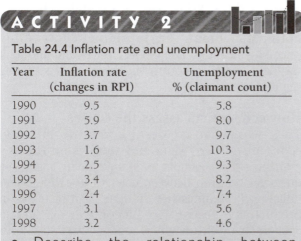

ACTIVITY 2

Table 24.4 Inflation rate and unemployment

Year	Inflation rate (changes in RPI)	Unemployment % (claimant count)
1990	9.5	5.8
1991	5.9	8.0
1992	3.7	9.7
1993	1.6	10.3
1994	2.5	9.3
1995	3.4	8.2
1996	2.4	7.4
1997	3.1	5.6
1998	3.2	4.6

a Describe the relationship between unemployment and inflation shown in the data.
b Discuss, in a group, what type of relationship you would expect to find and why.

The consequences of inflation

Inflation can cause the downfall of governments. However, it may also promote economic activity. The outcome largely depends on the rate of inflation, whether the rate has been correctly anticipated or not and whether it is accelerating or stable.

High inflation

A high rate of inflation can cause many problems. A very high rate of inflation is referred to as **hyperinflation**. When the price level is rising so rapidly that people loose confidence in the value of money, it can be difficult for an economy to operate. In Germany in the 1920s inflation reached phenomenal levels. Money became worthless and people asked to be paid in a range of items, including cigarettes, which they believed would prove to be more acceptable when it came to paying for goods and services. Barter also made a comeback with people directly exchanging goods and services. The disruption caused to the economy and people's lives led to political unrest and contributed to the rise of Hitler.

Even when inflation is not at hyperinflation levels but is at levels which would be regarded as high it can still impose costs on an economy. These include menu, shoe leather and administrative costs.

Menu costs are the costs involved in changing prices in, for example, catalogues and advertisements and in changing slot machines and coin telephone boxes. The term **shoe leather costs** can be applied to two adverse effects of high inflation. One is the extra time which has to be spent searching round for the lowest prices of goods and raw materials. Inflation creates what is called 'an **inflationary noise**'. This term refers to the distortionary effect which inflation causes. Without inflation, if the price of, for instance, one model of television rises it can be concluded that it has become relatively more expensive. However, with inflation consumers will be uncertain whether the rise in price does actually reflect a relative price rise or whether it is just in line with inflation. Now, to see whether the particular model has become relatively more expensive the price of other models will have to be checked out.

The other meaning of shoe leather costs is the extra time and effort companies have to spend moving money into and out of financial institutions such as banks. If money is losing its value at a high rate it cannot be left idle. So firms receiving payments are likely to try to gain interest on the money even if they are going to pay it out in a few days time. The time of their staff has to be taken in account assessing where the highest interest is being paid and moving the money around.

There are also administrative costs. Staff time also has to be spent on adjusting accounts, assessing raw material costs, negotiating with unions about wage rises and estimating appropriate prices.

Unanticipated and anticipated inflation

Even when inflation is not high, there can still be costs involved if the government, firms and households do not correctly anticipate the rate of inflation and make appropriate adjustments for it. These costs may include some people experiencing a fall in their real income. For example, if the rate of interest does not rise in line with inflation the real rate of interest will fall and lenders will not be able to buy as much with the interest they receive. Some workers' wages may also fail to gain wage rises which keep pace with inflation and some private pensions may not be indexed-linked, i.e. not adjusted automatically in line with changes in inflation. Of course, others may gain as a result of inflation. These include home buyers, since the value of property tends to rise by more than the rate of interest, other borrowers and workers with strong bargaining power.

The government is also likely to gain from inflation. This is because it is usually a large net borrower and if tax rates are not adjusted in line with inflation it may gain extra tax revenue. The tendency for people's income to be pushed into higher tax brackets as a result of inflation is referred to as **fiscal drag**.

One of the most serious disadvantages of unanticipated inflation is the uncertainty it creates. For example, households will not know whether it is better to take out a fixed rate or variable rate mortgage. Even more seriously, if firms are uncertain what their costs will be and what prices they will gain from selling their products they may be reluctant to invest. This, in turn, will slow down economic growth and may even result in a fall in output.

However, when inflation is anticipated tax rates can be adjusted and pensions and wages can be raised in line with inflation.

Whether inflation is anticipated or unanticipated it can have a harmful effect on a country's international trade position. What is important here is the country's inflation rate relative to other countries' inflation rates. If the country's inflation rate is above that of its main competitors its goods and services will become less price competitive. This is likely to result in fewer exports being sold and more imports being purchased.

Zero inflation versus price stability

The target the government has set the Bank of England is not **zero inflation** but price stability. This is defined as a $2\frac{1}{2}$ per cent target for inflation on the RPIX measure, with a 1 per cent point margin either side.

There are four main reasons why the government does not aim for zero inflation:

1 Measured inflation may exceed true inflation due to, for example, RPI and hence RPIX not fully reflecting new products, quality improvements and the prices being paid for some products purchased on the Internet. So measured inflation might mean that the general price level is actually falling.

2 A low and stable level of inflation allows some flexibility in firms' costs. Workers usually resist reductions in their money wages. So without inflation firms may have to cut employment in order to get their costs down. However, with inflation real wages can be reduced by either not raising money wages or not raising money wages by as much as the rate of inflation.

3 A low and stable inflation rate permits real interest rates to fall which can lower firms' costs and increase demand for products and thereby stimulate investment and output.

4 A climate of optimism may be created by a low and stable inflation rate of a demand-pull nature.

The Monetary Policy Committee

The **Monetary Policy Committee** (MPC) is a committee of the Bank of England set up in 1998. It has been given responsibility for meeting the government's inflation target and uses interest rate changes to try to prevent aggregate demand increasing more rapidly than the underlying trend rate of growth of output.

There are nine members of the MPC, five Bank of England employees including the Governor, and four members appointed by the Chancellor of the Exchequer.

The MPC meets each month. It hears reports from Bank of England staff, including the Bank's regional agents. These reports cover evidence on current and future retail sales, changes in firms' stocks, wage rises, the strength of the currency, employment changes, borrowing, house price changes and developments in other economies.

If the MPC, having studied the economic indicators, believes that the inflation rate will move outside its target it will change the rate of interest. If, for example, it thinks that inflation will rise above the target rate it will raise the rate of interest. A higher rate of interest can reduce inflation by lowering aggregate demand in a number of ways including:

- by encouraging saving
- by reducing borrowing
- by reducing the spending power of those with mortgages.

Those with savings will enjoy higher incomes but savers tend to spend a smaller proportion of their income than borrowers. So the net effect is likely to be for spending to fall.

ACTIVITY 3

In July 1999 unemployment reached an 18-year low. This encouraged consumers to borrow and to spend more. The rise in retail sales also prompted firms to spend more on capital goods, raise profit margins and concede wage rises above productivity increases.

In a group decide:

a whether the inflationary pressures being experienced in July 1999 were of a demand-pull or cost-push nature

b whether you would have recommended that the MPC should have raised the rate of interest, left it unchanged or lowered it. Also comment on other information which would have been useful in reaching your decision.

Summary

Inflation is a rise in the general price level and so a fall in the value of money. Measures of inflation include the Retail Prices Index, RPIX (RPI minus mortgage interest payments), RPIY (RPIX minus indirect taxes) and the harmonised index of consumer prices. These are weighted consumer price indexes which take into account the different amounts spent on items.

Inflation can be caused by excessive increases in aggregate demand (demand-pull inflation) or increases in the costs of production (cost-push inflation). However, once under way it can be difficult to decide what started the inflation.

Inflation has more harmful effects if it is high, accelerating and unanticipated. These costs include uncertainty, administration costs, lack of

international competitiveness and a redistribution of income from, for example, lenders to borrowers. The government aims for low, stable inflation rather than zero inflation. This is because measured inflation is thought to be greater than true inflation and because low inflation creates some flexibility. The MPC has been given the task of meeting the government's inflation target of 2.5 per cent on the RPIX measure.

Data response question

Last week I was in a shop and on the point of taking something to the till when I thought 'Hang on, I can buy this a lot cheaper over the internet'. So I did. But such decisions are not being picked up in official inflation figures. The price I would have paid in the shop is reflected in the retail prices index (RPI), which last week showed inflation edging up from 1.1 per cent to 1.2 per cent. Net prices are not and will not be for some time.

The RPI advisory committee would first require evidence of the extent of net spending from the Family Expenditure Survey, and this will not be available for two years. In the meantime, there is the danger the RPI will be biased upwards. Last month, for example, one of the upward influences on the RPI was from motor-insurance premiums. But many people now buy cover over the net, I do.

But how big is the likely net effect? There will, in fact, be two separate effects. The direct effect comes because of lower prices for online goods. The indirect effect arises because, to avoid losing business to e-tailers, shops will cut prices. This is already happening, as the latest retail sales figures, showing rising volumes but falling prices suggest, and is hopefully being reflected in the RPI. Boots achieved publicity last week when it cut CD prices, a move said to be in response to online competition.

David Owen, a Dresdner Kleinwort Benson economist, suggests that within three years these direct and indirect effects will be knocking about 0.5 per cent off inflation. But he warns that this is probably a conservative estimate and that, when these net effects come through, it will be in the form of an 's-curve' – that is, sudden rushes of net activity and price reductions, rather than as a steady progression. This is one to watch.

David Smith, 'Industry's heroes engineer a productivity miracle' in
The Sunday Times, 21 November 1999

1 Explain the role of the Family Expenditure Survey in compiling the RPI. (5)

2 Why does the development of Internet shopping mean that the RPI, as currently compiled, overestimates inflation. (4)

3 Discuss one other reason why the RPI may overestimate the rate of inflation? (4)

4 Explain why the Internet is likely to reduce inflation as measured by the RPI. (6)

5 Distinguish between the RPI, RPIX and RPIY. (6)

UNIT 25 Unemployment

Introduction

In this unit unemployment is defined and the two main measures of unemployment used in the UK are explained. The link between unemployment and employment is discussed and then attention is focused on the effects of unemployment. These effects are examined from the perspective of the unemployed and society. The unit finishes with a brief discussion of the causes of unemployment.

The changing employment situation

At the Labour Party Conference in September 1999 Gordon Brown, the Chancellor of the Exchequer, held out the promise of reaching full employment. He said that 648 000 jobs had been created since Labour came into power in 1997 and that Labour would get rid of unemployment within a generation. However, at the same time that unemployment was indeed falling nationally some UK companies were announcing redundancies. These included banks which were closing some branches in response to the shift in demand from their customers away from the traditional branch towards post, telephone and Internet banking.

At any time in an economy some jobs are being created while others are being lost. What can become a serious situation is when the number of jobs being lost is greater than those being created. If those made redundant from the banks found new jobs quickly the disruption to their lives might have been relatively small. However, if they did not, the costs to them and to society might have been high.

The meaning of unemployment

Unemployment exists when potential workers are without jobs. Some people aged between 16 and 65 are not in the labour market because, for example, they are homemakers, disabled or have retired early. These people are said to be **economically inactive** and are not regarded as unemployed.

However, there are other people who would classify themselves as being unemployed. Some of these are not prepared to take the jobs on offer. This may be because they are hoping a better job will come along or because the money they are receiving on unemployment benefit (job seekers' allowance) is greater than they would be paid in employment. These people are said to be **voluntarily unemployed**.

Others are **involuntarily unemployed**. This means that while they would be willing to work for the going wage rates on offer they are unable to find employment.

Measuring unemployment

To assess how the economy is performing and whether unemployment is a problem it is important to measure the number of people who are unemployed. In practice this is not as easy as it might appear. It can be difficult to decide which groups should be included and to assess who is genuinely looking for employment.

There are two main measures of unemployment in the UK and both seek to record as unemployed those who are involuntarily unemployed. One measure is the **claimant count**. This includes as unemployed anyone who is receiving job seekers' allowance. However, it misses some of those who are involuntarily unemployed. This is because some of those who are willing to work and who are seeking employment are not receiving job seekers' allowance, for example those aged over 55 (who are given income support instead) and those on government training schemes.

The other measure, which now receives more government attention, is the **Labour Force Survey** (LFS) measure. As its name suggests, this is based on a survey. It is a household survey which collects a range of information on the labour force including employment, earnings of workers, personal characteristics such as age, sex and educational qualifications as well as unemployment. In deciding who is unemployed from the responses given to them, this measure uses the International Labour Office (ILO) definition (and so is also sometimes referred to as the **ILO measure**). This defines as unemployed anyone who:

- is without a job
- was available to start work in the two weeks following the LFS interview; and
- either had looked for work in the four weeks prior to the LFS interview or was waiting to start a job they had already obtained.

This is a more inclusive measure and as it is used in many countries, it makes international comparisons easier.

The unemployment rate

As well as publishing the number of people unemployed the government also publishes the **unemployment rate** – the percentage of people who are out of work. This is calculated by dividing the number of people unemployed by the labour force (i.e. those in employment and those unemployed – the **economically active**). For example, if there are 2 million people unemployed out of a labour force of 28 million the unemployment rate is:

$$\frac{2m}{28m} \times 100 \qquad = 7.1 \text{ per cent}$$

ACTIVITY 1

Table 25.1 Unemployment rates in the EU (per cent)

Country	1999	2000*	2001–5*
Austria	4.4	4.2	3.8
Belgium	9.1	8.9	8.5
Denmark	4.7	4.5	4.3
Finland	10.2	9.7	9.7
France	11.1	10.4	9.6
Germany	9.0	8.8	8.7
Greece	9.6	9.2	8.7
Ireland	6.8	6.0	5.8
Italy	12.0	11.6	11.4
Netherlands	3.4	3.1	3.9
Portugal	4.4	3.9	3.7
Spain	16.2	14.6	12.8
Sweden	6.9	6.0	4.4
UK	6.1	6.0	6.3

* forecasts

National Institute of Economic and Social Research, *National Institute Economic Review*, October 1999

a i Calculate the average unemployment rate for the EU in 1999.

ii Identify which countries had an unemployment rate above the average.

b Comment on the predicted changes in unemployment from 2000 to 2001–5 for Austria, Finland, the Netherlands and Spain.

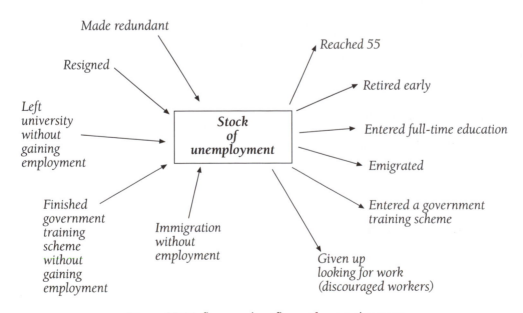

Figure 25.1 Inflows and outflows of unemployment

Unemployment and employment

When the number of people unemployed goes down the number of people employed usually increases. Similarly, when the number of people employed falls the number of people unemployed usually increases. However, this does not have to occur and while, in practice, the figures usually do move in opposite directions they frequently do not move proportionately. For example, unemployment may fall by 30 000 one month while employment rises by only 25 000. This situation can occur because there are a number of reasons why people cease to be unemployed. For example, some of the unemployed may decide to re-enter full-time education in order to improve their employment chances. Figure 25.1 shows a number of reasons why people may enter or leave the state of unemployment.

Unemployment increases whenever the inflow into unemployment exceeds the outflow from it.

ACTIVITY 2

'The rate of unemployment fell sharply over the last quarter from 6.2 per cent to 5.9 per cent, the lowest rate since the ILO measure began in 1984.'

'The claimant rate also fell to a new 19-year low, hitting 4.2 per cent and putting it in sight of rates of 3.9 per cent not seen since Harold Wilson's Labour administration of 1974. The number of people in work hit a fresh all-time high, with an extra 54 000 flowing into the workforce, taking the total to 27 412 million or 74 per cent.'

Extracts from Philip Thornton, 'Pay rises and fall in jobless spark fears over inflation' in *The Independent*, 16 September 1999

a   Explain the difference between the ILO and claimant measures of unemployment.
b   Explain how the rise in employment can be greater than the fall in unemployment.
c   In a group discuss the benefits of unemployment falling.

Duration of unemployment

As well as examining the number of people unemployed the government is also concerned about how long people are out of work. This is because the longer people are out of work the greater the costs involved. An unemployment rate of 6 per cent with

people on average being out of work for two years will create more problems than an unemployment rate of 9 per cent with people being unemployed for an average of two months.

The costs of unemployment to society

The main cost of unemployment to an economy is the opportunity cost of lost output. If, for example, 2 million people are out of work the output they could have produced is forgone for all time. When a country has unemployed workers it is not using all its resources and so is not producing the maximum output it is capable of (not reaching its potential output). Figure 25.2 shows the production possibility curve of a country experiencing unemployment.

As some of the labour force is unemployed it is producing inside its production possibility curve at point A. With full employment it could produce at point B, C or any other point on the curve.

As well as lost output, there are a number of other costs that unemployment imposes on a country. When people are out of work they spend less so the government receives less revenue from indirect (expenditure) taxes such as VAT and excise duty. Total income will also be below what it would be if there was full employment and so revenue from income tax will be lower than its potential level.

While tax revenue will be less, government expenditure will have to be higher. This is because the government will have to spend money on job seekers' allowance. If there was less unemployment the government could spend more on other areas such as education and health or have lower tax rates.

Unemployment also generates other pressures on government expenditure. When people are out of work they are more likely to suffer from poor

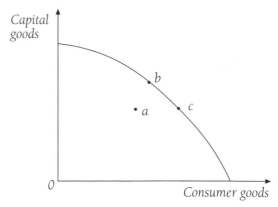

Figure 25.2 Production points

physical and mental health. People with higher incomes enjoy better physical health than those with lower incomes. For example, the poor suffer more from tuberculosis than middle and high income groups. Financial worries and the loss of status can also contribute to mental ill health, in some cases resulting in suicide and the breakdown of relationships. So unemployment can increase government expenditure on health services and supporting lone parents.

The fall in income can reduce the health and educational performance of the children of the poor with long-term implications for health care needs and the quality of the labour force.

There is also some evidence of a link between the level of unemployment and crime. Young men are particularly prone to unemployment. When they are out of work they may feel alienated from society and turn to crime to gain a higher income and perhaps even a certain form of status.

The costs of unemployment to the individual

Of course, the people who bear the main burden of unemployment are the unemployed themselves. Most people who become unemployed experience a fall in income, loss of status and pressure on their relationships.

Unemployment also involves financial costs. When people are out of work they may spend more time at home. This will increase, for example, their heating and lighting costs. Applying for jobs and going for interviews also involves paying out money. These costs build up the longer people are out of work.

In addition, the longer people are unemployed the more they miss out on training, updating and promotion and the more difficult they will find it to gain employment.

The benefits of unemployment

Being unemployed may enable some people to reappraise their skills and ambitions and to gain a more rewarding job. Firms may also find that the existence of unemployed workers will keep wage rises down and make workers more willing to accept new production methods. However, most politicians and economists believe that the costs of unemployment outweigh any benefits.

ACTIVITY 3

'Once a town develops one industry, perhaps by pure chance, success tends to breed success. There is a virtuous circle of growth as jobs give local people money to spend, which encourages other new business, which expands because there is a suitable labour force.'

'Just as success can become embedded, so it can decline. An absence of local jobs fosters crime and drug-taking, young people lack the experience of work and therefore the basics of employability (such as the ability to turn up on time and be polite to their colleagues), the housing stock deteriorates, local businesses including bank branches and post offices close or move out.'

Extracts from Diane Coyle, 'Richer and poorer; Britain's cities have their own north-south divide' in *The Independent*, 23 August 1999

a   Explain the costs of unemployment mentioned in the extract.

b   In a group decide whether your area is currently experiencing a virtuous circle of growth or decline.

Causes of unemployment

As unemployment can impose significant costs it is important to understand what causes it. There can be occasions when there is unemployment but also a high number of vacancies. Indeed, the number of vacancies may exceed the number of unemployed. In this case those who are unemployed may lack the necessary skills, may live in areas away from the vacancies and may be unable or unwilling to move, may be unaware of the vacancies or may be unwilling to take up the vacancies.

Large-scale unemployment arises when aggregate demand is below the full employment level of aggregate supply. Figure 25.3 shows the equilibrium level of real GDP to be y. This is below the level (y_1) which could be produced with all the labour force in work.

Over time if aggregate demand grows more slowly than the increase in the productive potential of the economy there will unemployment. Figure 25.4 shows the long run aggregate supply curve shifting to the right (perhaps as a result of an increase in the

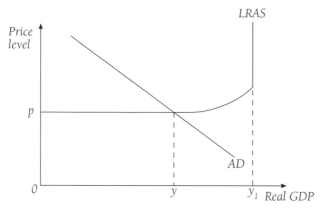

Figure 25.3 Unemployed resources due to a lack of aggregate demand

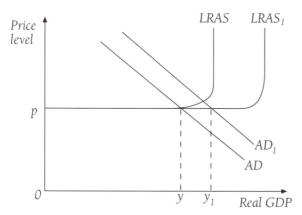

Figure 25.4 A widening of the gap between actual and potential output

number of people in the labour force). Aggregate demand also shifts to the right but by a smaller amount, which will result in unemployment.

Summary

Unemployment occurs when potential workers are without jobs. In the UK unemployment is measured by the claimant count (those receiving job seekers' allowance) and the Labour Force Survey (the ILO measure which includes those actively seeking work). People may cease to be unemployed because they have found jobs. However, it may also be for other reasons, for example they have entered full-time education, gone on a government training course or have retired. The main cost to society of unemployment is lost output. To the individual the costs include loss of status, income and work and training experience.

Unemployment can arise because people are unaware of vacancies or lack the skills or ability to move home to take them up. Large-scale unemployment can arise as a result of a lack of aggregate demand.

Data response question

What kind of job market do we have when 1.2m unemployed people (1.7m on the Labour Force Survey measure) co-exist with nearly 1m vacancies? And, do vacancies tell us the labour market is about to overheat dangerously?

Having so many vacancies and so much unemployment tells us several things. We know that, even if there are thousands of vacancies in every region, including 200 000 in London and the South East, they are not necessarily in the right places.

It is easy to forget, when looking at the big picture, that some of the biggest economic differences occur within regions rather than between them. Jobs in full-employment Newbury are not much use to people in high-unemployment Thanet or Hastings, yet both are in south-east England.

In London, full employment in Kingston does not appear to mean much for the unemployed of Lewisham, Hackney or Tottenham, where more than one in eight are jobless.

This locational mismatch between vacancies and people who could fill them is cumulative. The local spending power of full-employment areas generates jobs and lifts house prices, which makes it more difficult for the jobless from poor areas to move in.

There is also a mismatch between skills of the unemployed and the skills employers want. It is no longer true that former miners or steelworkers can never expect to work again. In Rotherham they man call centres. But it is true that some of the unemployed, possibly a disturbingly high proportion, have no meaningful skills or aptitude to offer employers.

David Smith, 'Jobs galore but in the wrong places' in
The Sunday Times, 3 October 1999

1 By how much did unemployment exceed vacancies? (2)
2 Explain what is meant by full employment. (5)
3 How would you have expected wage rates in Kingston and Hackney to compare? (6)
4 Explain the causes of unemployment the writer discusses. (6)
5 Why, even in prosperous times and prosperous areas, may some people still remain unemployed? (6)

Balance of payments

Key concepts covered

- current account
- capital and financial accounts
- net errors and omissions
- trade in goods
- trade in services
- pattern of trade
- investment income
- current account deficit

Introduction

The balance of payments is a record of a country's economic transactions with the rest of the world. It contains a fascinating collection of information and enables us to see, for example, what products the country buys and sells, what countries it trades with and which countries are buying factories and shares in the country.

In this unit the sections of the balance of payments are discussed, with particular attention being paid to the trade in goods and trade in services parts of the current account section. The products and the countries the UK trades with and the UK's performance on the current account are looked at. The UK usually spends more overall on foreign goods and services than it earns from selling goods and services abroad. This means it is usually in deficit, so the causes and consequences of a current account deficit are explored.

The sections of the balance of payments

The main sections of the balance of payments are:

1   The **current account**. This includes trade in goods and services, income earned by residents from shares, companies and property held in other countries and income earned by foreign residents from assets held in the UK.
2   **Capital and financial accounts**. This shows the movement of: direct investment, for example the purchase of a farm, factory or 10 per cent of the shares in a company in another country, portfolio investment, such as the purchase of shares and government securities.
3   **Net errors and omissions**. If all the transactions were recorded accurately the difference between credit items (ones which bring money into the country) and debit items (ones which take money out

of the country) would be zero. However, as noted in Unit 20 the balance of payments is based on information relating to a vast number of transactions. In some cases the data used to measure the credit and debit sides are drawn from different sources and some transactions and the corresponding payments are recorded in different years. To ensure that the balance of payments balances, a net errors and omissions item is included. This shows whether credit or debit transactions are needed to balance the accounts. It does not show where the errors and omissions have occurred. However, it is usually the capital and financial accounts section which has the most errors and omissions.

Trade in goods

Trade in goods records the earnings from exports and expenditure on imports. There is a wide collection of goods which countries trade in, for example cars, food, oil and chemicals. In recent years the UK has had a deficit in trade in goods. This means that it has spent more on imports of goods than it has earned from selling goods to other countries. Indeed, the UK has not achieved a surplus on its trade in goods since 1982.

As Table 26.1 shows, in 1998 the UK earned more from its exports of oil, chemicals, capital goods and unspecified goods than it spent on imports. However, in all the other categories it spent more on imports than it earned on exports.

Table 26.1 Trade in goods, 1998

Category	Balance (£ million)
Food, beverages and tobacco	−6027
Basic materials	−3110
Oil	3059
Other fuels	−423
Semi-manufactured goods	
Chemicals	4716
Precious stones and silver	−1187
Other semi-manufactured goods	−5305
Total semi-manufactured goods	−1776
Finished manufactured goods	
Motor cars	−4959
Consumer goods	−9354
Intermediate goods	−1267
Capital goods	3456
Ships and aircraft	−444
Total finished manufactured goods	−12 568
Unspecified goods	80
Total	−20 765

UK Balance of Payments, *The Pink Book*, 1999 edition, Office for National Statistics

ACTIVITY 1

a   Find out where ten items you have recently purchased were produced.

b   Pool your findings with others in the group.

c   Estimate what percentage of your items were imported.

d   Discuss what influences whether you buy a domestically or foreign produced product.

Trade in services

Services include travel (tourism), insurance, financial (banking) and computer and information services. The UK performs well in services. Since 1966 it has recorded a surplus every year. As Table 26.2 shows, seven of the services categories showed surpluses in 1998.

Table 26.2 Trade in services, 1998

Category	Balance (£ million)
Transportation	-2144
Travel	-5623
Communications	-244
Construction	177
Insurance	2624
Financial	6147
Computer and information services	1074
Royalties and licence fees	365
Other business	10 022
Personal, cultural and recreational	250
Government	-395
Total	12 253

UK Balance of Payments, *The Pink Book*, 1999 edition, Office for National Statistics

ACTIVITY 2

At the end of 1999 the UK manufacturing sector improved significantly. Its increase in output was attributed to a buoyant domestic economy and improving demand in overseas markets.

a   Explain why a buoyant domestic economy may raise or lower exports.

b   Discuss what may cause a rise in demand for exports.

Pattern of trade

As Table 26.3 shows, the UK's main trading partners are the USA, Germany, France and the Netherlands.

Eight of the most important buyers of our exports are European Union (EU) members and seven of the countries from which we buy most of our imports are also from the EU. We buy from and sell to the same countries, which are industrial countries and with which, in the main, we have economic and social ties.

Table 26.3 Main destination of UK exports and main source of imports, 1998

		Exports £ million
1	USA	35 805
2	Germany	24 839
3	France	19 778
4	Netherlands	15 539
5	Irish Republic	12 022
6	Italy	10 450
7	Belgium and Luxembourg	10 145
8	Spain	8593
9	Sweden	5479
10	Japan	5395
		Imports £ million
1	USA	34 926
2	Germany	28 232
3	France	22 795
4	Netherlands	15 188
5	Italy	11 775
6	Belgium and Luxembourg	10 655
7	Japan	10 615
8	Spain	9757
9	Irish Republic	9388
10	Switzerland	5767

The UK Balance of Payments, *The Pink Book*, 1999 edition, Office for National Statistics

The UK's performance

There are a number of industries in which the UK is very internationally competitive. These include pharmaceuticals, business services, computer software, civil aviation and financial services. The industries in which the UK is least competitive tend to be those heavily dependent on heavy capital investment or cheap labour and which are facing strong competition from developing countries. They include footwear, iron and steel and textiles.

Investment income

The UK usually has a surplus on **investment income**. This means that its residents earn more in terms of profits, interest and dividends on their assets held in other countries than foreigners earn on their investments in the UK.

The causes of a current account deficit

A **deficit on the current account** occurs when the country's expenditure abroad exceeds its revenue from abroad. This situation can arise because the country has spent more on goods or more on services and/or there has been a net outflow of investment income. In the UK's case the most common reason for the current account to be in the red is for there to be a deficit on the trade balance.

That deficit may arise because the country is importing raw materials. This may be self correcting as the raw materials may be converted into finished goods, some of which are exported.

It may also arise because the purchasers of the country's goods and services are experiencing economic difficulties and are not able to afford to buy as many goods and services. When their economies improve the deficit may disappear. In contrast, the domestic economy may be booming and the high demand may suck in more imports and cause goods and services to be diverted from the export to the home market.

What is more serious is if the deficit is caused by a lack of price or quality competitiveness. If the country is charging too much for its goods and services, producing poor-quality goods and services or making goods and services which consumers do not want to buy the deficit will not be corrected without steps being taken to improve the performance of the country's firms.

The consequences of a current account deficit

The effects of a current account deficit will be influenced by its cause, its size and its duration. A small deficit which will be self correcting is obviously of less concern than one which is large and which results form poor performance.

When a country spends more than it earns it is enjoying a higher living standard than it can afford. This will have to be financed by borrowing.

Summary

There are three main sections of the balance of payments. These are the current account, capital and financial accounts, and net errors and omissions. Two of the items in the current account which receive considerable attention from economists are the trade in goods and trade in services sub-sections.

The UK usually spends more on imported goods than it earns on its exports of goods. However, while it usually has a deficit on its trade in goods balance, it usually has a surplus on its trade in services balance, earning more from exporting services than it spends on imported services.

The UK's main trading partners are the USA, Germany, France and the Netherlands, and the main area it trades with is the European Union.

The UK is internationally competitive in a number of products, including business services and computer software. Nevertheless, it usually has a current account deficit. There are a number of reasons why a country may spend more abroad than it earns from selling goods and services abroad. These include short-term situations such as incomes falling abroad or more serious causes such as a lack of competitiveness in terms of quality and price. A deficit enables a country's inhabitants to enjoy more goods and services than the country is producing, but the deficit has to be covered.

Data response question

'There may be more to Cool Britannia than slick government marketing. Official figures published yesterday showed explosive growth in the creative industries has helped the UK overtake Germany and France to become the world's second biggest exporter of services.

Fashion, film, pop music and advertising are among the fastest growing sectors of the UK economy. An expanding appetite in other countries for a taste of British style and culture is outpacing overseas demand for core services such as transportation and travel.'

ACTIVITY 3

In 1999 the United States of America had a deficit on the current account of its balance of payments of $339 billion. Alan Greenspan, the Governor of the Federal Reserve Bank of America warned that the USA could not continue to run up ever-increasing current account deficits.

a   Explain what is meant by a current account deficit.

b   Discuss why the USA cannot 'continue to run up ever-increasing deficits'.

'Rapid growth in the financial services, computing and information technology industries have also boosted exports.'

'The largest single consumer of British films and television programmes is the US, which accounted for £330m or just over a quarter of the industry's export revenue in 1997. Sweden, Germany and France follow some way behind.'

'The US is also the UK's biggest trading partner in all services. Services trade with Europe moved from a deficit of £1.69bn in 1992 to a surplus of £534m in 1997.'

Extracts from Christopher Adams, 'UK is world's second biggest services exporter' in the *Financial Times*, 12 February 1999

1 How significant is the UK as an exporter of services? (3)
2 According to the extracts, which were the fastest growing services? (3)
3 Discuss what may cause a rise in demand for UK services. (7)
4 Why do you think the USA purchases such a high value of services from the UK? (7)
5 Explain one other section of the current account balance. (5)

27 Government policy

Introduction

Having discussed government macroeconomic objectives, this unit focuses on the policies that a government can implement to achieve its objectives.

A report by the Organisation for Economic Co-operation and Development (OECD) published in November 1999 commented on the chances of the UK government reaching its objectives. It stated that the UK economy would experience higher economic growth and lower inflation in the next millennium. It forecast that unemployment would continue to fall and inflation would stay low despite increases in household wealth and pay. It also predicted that the trade deficit would disappear by 2001. However, to ensure that this 'golden scenario' would be achieved it recommended that the UK government should avoid raising government expenditure by too much and should ensure that, if necessary, there was a rise in the rate of interest to keep inflation close to the government's target.

Changes in government expenditure are a fiscal policy instrument. This is the first government policy discussed. In addition to government expenditure, taxation and the effects of changes in fiscal policy are covered. Interest rate changes are a monetary policy instrument and this is the second government policy to be discussed. The effects of both interest rate changes and exchange rate changes are covered. The third policy area examined is supply-side policies. The unit concludes with a discussion of possible conflicts between policy objectives.

Fiscal policy

Fiscal policy is changes in taxation and government spending. To influence economic activity and to improve the workings of individual markets a government can change the rate of taxes, the types of taxes it imposes, the level of government expenditure, its composition and its timing.

Taxation

Governments impose taxation for a number of reasons including:

- to raise revenue for expenditure
- to discourage the consumption of demerit goods
- to convert external into private costs in the case of, for example, pollution
- to discourage the purchase of imports
- to redistribute income
- to influence the level of aggregate demand
- to influence the level of aggregate supply.

In the financial year 1999/2000 the source of UK government revenue was as shown in Table 27.1.

Taxes can be categorised in two main ways. One is into **direct** and **indirect taxes**. Direct taxes are taxes on the income of people and firms and are collected by the Inland Revenue, for example income tax and corporation tax. Indirect taxes are taxes on spending and are collected by the Department of Customs and Excise, for example VAT and excise duty. The other way of categorising taxes is into **progressive**, **proportional and regressive taxes**. A progressive tax is one which takes a higher percentage of the income of the rich, a proportional tax takes the same percentage of the income of all income groups and a regressive tax takes a greater percentage of the income of the poor.

Government expenditure

Governments spend in order to:

- provide merit and public goods, either free or at subsidised prices
- pay interest on government debt
- redistribute income
- influence aggregate demand
- influence aggregate supply.

In 1999/2000 the main items of government expenditure were as shown in Table 27.2.

Table 27.1 Sources of government tax revenue

Type of tax	Revenue raised	What it taxes
Income tax	£91bn	Income tax is a tax on people's gross income after certain allowances have been deducted
VAT (value added tax)	£56bn	VAT is a percentage tax on the sale of a range of goods and services
National Insurance contributions (NICs)	£56bn	NICs are a tax on employers and employees to cover National Insurance benefits, including pensions, child benefit and sickness benefit
Excise duty	£34bn	Excise duty is a specific tax imposed on alcohol, cigarettes and petrol
Corporation tax	£34bn	Corporation tax is a tax on the profits of companies
Business rates	£16bn	Business rates are local authority taxes on firms
Council tax	£13bn	Council tax is a local authority tax on people based on the value of their houses
Other	£50bn	Other taxes include inheritance tax, capital gains tax and air passenger duty, etc.

Table 27.2 Government expenditure

Area of expenditure	£ billion
Social security (which includes spending on pensions and job seekers' allowance)	100
Health	61
Education	41
Debt interest	26
Defence	22
Law and order	19
Industry, agriculture and employment	15
Housing and environment	13
Other	44

In recent years there have been a number of pressures causing the UK and other European governments to spend more. One of the main ones is the ageing population. With people living longer, there is an increasing demand for National Health Service treatment, pensions and residential care. Others include the increased length of time people spend in education, increased expectations of the range and quality of health care treatment and advances in technology which increase the number and complexity of operations which are possible and the capital requirements of educational institutions.

The effects of changes in fiscal policy

Higher government spending on, for example, computers in schools will increase demand for the products of a range of information technology companies. The companies which receive this extra income are likely to take on more staff and promote some of their existing staff. The companies' employees will, in turn, spend some of their extra income. This knock-on effect will create more jobs in areas such as retailing and entertainment.

The extra aggregate demand resulting from the higher government spending is also likely to cause a rise in output and so contribute to economic growth. Figure 27.1 shows an increase in aggregate demand causing a rise in real gross domestic product (GDP).

In contrast, if a government wants to reduce demand-pull inflation or reduce a balance of payments deficit it may choose to cut aggregate demand by lowering government spending or raising taxation. For instance, a rise in taxation would reduce people's disposable income and so their ability to buy goods and services would be less. Changing the level of aggregate demand to influence economic activity is referred to as demand management.

The Budget

The Chancellor of the Exchequer outlines government spending in its spending reviews and taxation plans in the **Budget** held each year. In the March 1999 Budget Gordon Brown announced a number of changes, including:

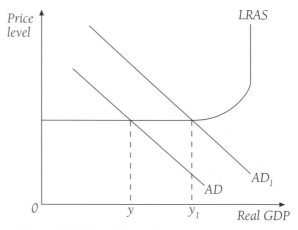

Figure 27.1 The effect of an increase in aggregate demand

- a reduction in the basic rate of income tax from 23 per cent to 22 per cent to take effect from April 2000

- the introduction of a new 10 per cent starting rate of taxation from April 1999

- a reduction in corporation tax from 31 per cent to 30 per cent and a reduction in small companies tax from 21 per cent to 20 per cent, with the introduction of a new 10 per cent rate for start-up companies

- increases in the tax on leaded petrol by 4.25p a litre and unleaded petrol by 3.79p

- an extra £100m to be spent on school computers

- every state school to get £2000 to spend on books

- new investment in university science laboratories of £100m

- an extra £500m to spend on upgrading hospital accident and emergency units

- an extra £170m on crime prevention.

The overall effect of the budget was to increase aggregate demand.

ACTIVITY 1

In most EU countries VAT is imposed on food but at present VAT is not charged on most food sold in the UK.

a   Using a diagram explain the effect of the imposition of VAT on food.

b   In a group decide whether VAT is a progressive, proportional or regressive tax.

c   In a group discuss the effect of the imposition of VAT on:
i   aggregate demand
ii   the distribution of income.

Monetary policy

The instruments of **monetary policy** include changes in the money supply, the rate of interest and the exchange rate.

The main instrument now used is the interest rate. As noted in Unit 24, the Monetary Policy Committee (MPC) of the Bank of England sets the interest rate with the objective of keeping inflation close to the government's target level for RPIX of 2.5 per cent.

The operation of interest rate changes

The rate of interest which the MPC sets is called the **repo rate** (sale and repurchase rate). This is the rate of interest which the Bank of England charges on loans to financial institutions, including retail (high street) banks such as Lloyds TSB and Barclays. If the Bank of England raises the repo rate the banks, because they are having to pay more, are likely to raise the rates they charge their customers. So the decision by the MPC to change the repo rate will have a knock-on effect throughout the financial system.

The ways in which changes in interest rates affect the economy

As discussed briefly in Unit 24, a rise in interest rates can reduce inflation in a number of ways. The process by which changes in interest rates can affect prices, output and employment is referred to as the **transmission mechanism**. This process is explored in more depth below.

The effects on consumer expenditure

Higher interest rates are likely to reduce consumer expenditure for a number of reasons:

- Higher mortgage rates will reduce the amount of money people have to spend on other items.

- Higher mortgage rates will also be likely to reduce demand for residential property. Lower demand will reduce the price of housing. For most people their house is their most valuable asset. A fall in house prices will make them feel poorer and discourage them from spending. It will also mean that the value of the security on which they can borrow will fall.

- Lower house prices will reduce activity in the housing market. People often buy new carpets and new furniture and spend on decorating materials when they move. So a decline in residential property sales will be likely to reduce expenditure on curtains, carpets and wallpaper and so on.

- Higher interest rates will encourage savings. People tend to reduce the proportion of their income that they spend and increase the proportion that they save.

- Higher interest rates are often accompanied by a fall in the value of financial assets, including shares. This again will make people feel worse off and discourage them from spending.

The effects on firms' expenditure and costs

Higher interest rates are likely to reduce firms' expenditure, as follows:

- Higher interest rates will increase the costs of firms which have borrowed in the past.

- Borrowing for future investment will become more expensive and may be discouraged.

- The expected lower consumer demand resulting from higher interest rates is also likely to discourage investment.

- The higher exchange rate which may result will reduce domestic companies international price competitiveness and thereby lower their profits and ability to spend.

However, it should be noted that a higher exchange rate will reduce the cost of imported raw materials.

The effect on net exports
A higher exchange rate will raise the price of exports and lower the price of imports. This is likely to reduce revenue from exports and increase expenditure on imports. So demand for the country's products will fall.

The exchange rate
A government may decide to allow the exchange rate to be determined by the free market forces of demand and supply. This is referred to as operating a **floating exchange rate**.

On the other hand, it may decide to set an exchange rate at which the price that its currency exchanges for other currencies is fixed. This is referred to as operating a fixed exchange rate. Stability in the value of the currency is maintained by the government buying and selling its currency and changing the rate of interest. A government may also seek to keep its exchange rate within certain limits or to move it in a particular direction. This is referred to as a managed exchange rate.

ACTIVITY 2

At the end of 1999 the chief of Japan's Economic Planning Agency expressed concern about the low level of aggregate demand in the economy. Consumption had fallen by one per cent during the quarter to September and investment was sluggish.

a What effect might low aggregate demand have on a government's policy objectives?

b Discuss what fiscal and monetary policy measures the Japanese government could have taken to raise aggregate demand.

c Use the Internet to find out details about the current performance of the Japanese economy and compare them with the information provided above.

- To reduce inflationary pressures a government may raise the exchange rate. This may succeed in lowering inflation by:

- reducing the price of imported raw materials and so reduce firms' costs of production

- reducing aggregate demand

- putting pressure on domestic firms to keep their prices low in order to remain competitive.

Supply-side policies

Supply-side policies seek to increase aggregate supply by raising the efficiency of markets. The term covers a range of measures.

Education and training
Improvements in education and training will raise the productivity of labour. Output per worker hour will increase and the potential output of the economy will rise. This will shift out the long run aggregate supply curve as shown in Figure 27.2.

Reduction in direct taxes
As well as increasing aggregate demand, lower direct taxation may also increase aggregate supply. This would be achieved by increasing incentives to firms, workers and potential workers. A cut in corporation tax will increase the funds which firms have available to invest and the return from any investment undertaken. If investment does increase the aggregate demand curve will shift to the right, but so will the long run aggregate supply curve as new capital will increase the productive capacity of the economy.

Some economists believe that a cut in income tax will encourage some existing workers to undertake

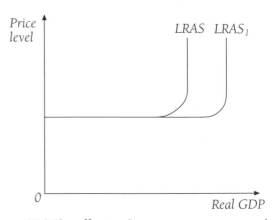

Figure 27.2 The effect on long run aggregate supply of improvements in education and training

overtime, be more willing to accept promotion and to stay in the labour force for longer. In addition, they believe it will persuade more of the unemployed to accept employment at the going wage rate as their disposable income (income after taxation has been deducted and state benefits have been added) will rise. However, others argue that lower income tax rates may encourage some workers to take more leisure time as they can now gain the same disposable income by working fewer hours. It is also argued that what stops the unemployed from gaining employment is not a lack of willingness to work at the going wage rate but a lack of jobs.

Reduction in unemployment benefit

Those economists who believe that market failure is a significant problem and favour government intervention do not support a cut in job seekers' allowance. They believe that what this will do is to reduce aggregate demand as the unemployed will have less money to spend. The lower demand will cause output to fall as shown in Figure 27.3 and the reduction in output will result in a rise in unemployment.

However, supporters of free market forces argue that lowering job seekers' allowance will, by widening the gap between paid employment and benefits, force the unemployed to seek work more actively and to accept employment at lower wage rates.

Reduction in trade union power

Those who favour the operation of free market forces believe that reductions in trade union power will reduce imperfections in the labour market. They argue that trade unions reduce employment by pushing the wage rate above the equilibrium level and by encouraging workers to engage in restrictive practices. These economists suggest that reducing the power of trade unions will increase labour productivity and reduce the cost of employing labour. As a result, firms will be encouraged to employ more workers and to raise output.

Again, some economists disagree. They argue that trade unions act as a counterbalance to the market imperfection of very powerful employers. They also claim they reduce firms' costs by acting as a channel for communication between employers and workers on issues such as health and safety and because it is cheaper to negotiate with one body than with individual workers.

Privatisation and deregulation

Supporters of free market forces argue that government intervention in the economy should be reduced. They believe that firms are in the best position to make decisions about what to produce, how to produce and what to charge. This is because they are subject to the discipline of the market. If they do not provide the goods and services which consumers want at competitive prices, it is argued, they will go out of business. So these economists favour the removal of rules and regulations on firms and the transfer of firms from the public to the private sector.

However, again other economists disagree. They argue that rules, regulations and/ or government ownership of firms is beneficial in a number of circumstances, for example, where there is a risk of external costs arising.

Supply-side policies and government objectives

Although there is disagreement about the merits of some of the supply-side polices, economists do agree that if the supply-side performance of the economy can be improved it will be easier for a government to achieve its objectives.

A higher quality of resources will raise productivity. This will make domestic firms more price and quality competitive, which should improve the country's balance of payments position. Also, as noted in Unit 23, in the long run GDP grows as a result of supply-side factors such as technological advances, capital accumulation and increases in the size and quality of the labour force. Increasing

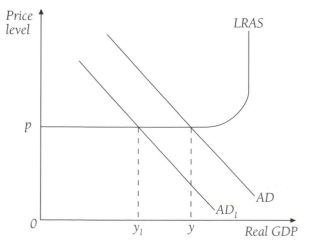

Figure 27.3 Keynesian view of the effects of a cut in job seekers' allowance

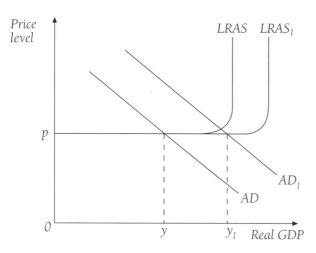

Figure 27.4 Non-inflationary growth

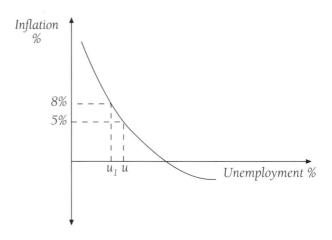

Figure 27.5 The Phillips curve

aggregate supply enables aggregate demand to continue to rise over time without inflationary pressures building up. Figure 27.4 shows both aggregate demand and aggregate supply rising and the price level remaining at P.

ACTIVITY 3

UK firms have been criticised for being slow at developing new technologies, processes and products. A number of factors have been blamed for this shortcoming, including tax and regulatory policies, lack of management skills, poor educational performance and firms being more concerned with short-term profits than long-term gains.

a   What effect does innovation have on aggregate supply?

b   Discuss, in a group, how educational standards could be raised.

c   Explain two measures a government could implement, apart from improved educational standards, to encourage innovation.

Conflicts between objectives

In deciding on what policy instruments to implement governments take into account possible conflicts between their objectives. For instance, if a government wishes to reduce unemployment by increasing demand it has to appreciate that the higher demand may cause inflation and may result in more imports being purchased and goods and services being diverted from the export to the home market.

A government may decide that to achieve one objective it is prepared to sacrifice, to a certain extent, another objective. To reduce unemployment it may be willing to see inflation rise by a small amount. This trade-off is shown on a diagram which is called the **Phillips curve** (see Figure 27.5).

Increased government expenditure causes a fall in unemployment from u to u_1. This is accompanied by a rise in inflation from 5 per cent to 8 per cent as the lower unemployment raises aggregate demand and pushes up wage rates.

The new economy

The new economy (or new economic paradigm), as discussed in Unit 23, suggests that advances in information technology by increasing aggregate supply may mean that governments will now find it easier than in the past to achieve all their objectives simultaneously.

Summary

A government may use a range of policies in managing an economy. These include fiscal, monetary and supply-side policies.

Fiscal policy covers changes in taxation and government spending. Direct taxes are taxes on incomes, whereas indirect taxes are taxes on spending. Taxes may also be progressive (taking a higher percentage of the income of the rich), proportional (taking the same percentage of the income of the rich and the poor) or regressive (taking a higher percentage of the income of the poor). The main source of UK tax revenue is income tax, followed by VAT. The main item of government expenditure is social security payments. Increases in government spending and cuts in tax raise aggregate demand which may cause output to rise and unemployment to fall.

Monetary policy instruments include changes in interest rates, the money supply and the exchange rate. Rises in interest rates and the exchange rate tend to reduce aggregate demand.

Supply-side policies are measures designed to increase aggregate supply. These include improving education and training, cutting direct taxes and job seekers' allowance, reforming trade unions, privatisation and deregulation.

The Phillips curve suggests there is a trade-off between two of the government's policy objectives, i.e. unemployment and inflation.

Data response question

In November 1999 the American Federal Reserve (the central bank of the USA) raised the rate of interest. It did this in order to reduce inflationary pressure.

A number of factors were perceived to be contributing to the build up of inflationary pressure. One was the serious labour shortages being experienced. Firms were increasingly having to take on marginal workers who had low skill levels and little employment experience. Some of these people had been forced into work by the government's welfare reforms.

Consumer spending was also very high. US retailers reported a rise in retail sales of 8.5 per cent in October 1999 above the previous year's levels. Consumer confidence was high because of the ready availability of jobs. Rising share prices were also making people feel better off and encouraging them to spend more. The buoyant consumer market and resulting rise in profits was encouraging firms to undertake more investment.

Improvements in the performance of other economies was causing an increased demand for goods and services. The effect of this was to raise demand for US exports but also to raise the price of its imports, including the price of imported raw materials.

1 Explain why labour shortages may cause inflation. (5)
2 What was happening to aggregate demand prior to the rise in interest rates and why? (4)

3 Discuss the effect of using marginal workers on productivity and firms' costs of production. (5)
4 Discuss the possible effects of a rise in interest rates on employment and economic growth. (6)
5 Explain one other measure a government could take to reduce inflation. (5)

Section 5 questions

Essay questions
1a Explain the main government macroeconomic policy objectives. (10)
b Discuss how an increase in aggregate demand may affect these objectives. (15)
2a Distinguish between actual and potential economic growth. (10)
b Discuss the main benefits and costs of economic growth. (15)

Project
Prepare a report assessing whether it is possible for a government to achieve full employment and price stability simultaneously. This should cover:

a definitions of full employment and price stability
b a discussion of economists' views on the possibility of achieving full employment and price stability
c a discussion of the benefits of full employment and price stability
d the implications of full employment for price stability
e an analysis of the UK's and another country's recent unemployment and price stability record
f a list of sources.

You should make use of appropriate economic theory, including demand and supply analysis, throughout your report.

C3.1a, C3.1b, C3.2, N3.1, N3.2, N3.3, IT3.1, IT3.2, IT3.3

Multiple-choice questions
1 Which is a government macroeconomic objective?
A Balance of payments equilibrium
B High unemployment
C Unsustainable economic growth
D Zero inflation

2 What does Tinbergen's rule state?
A A government cannot achieve all of its objectives simultaneously.

B A government's main objective should be full employment.

C A government has to use a separate policy instrument for each of its objectives.

D The measures a government implements to reduce inflation are likely to increase unemployment.

3 Why may a rise in real GDP per head have been accompanied by a fall in the quality of life? There is an increase in:

A inflation

B population

C pollution

D life expectancy

4 In which circumstance would production fall but productivity rise?

A Employment falls and output is unchanged.

B Employment rises by more than output.

C Output falls and employment rises.

D Employment is unchanged and output falls.

5 Which would cause an increase in aggregate demand?

A A decrease in net exports

B A decrease in the rate of income tax

C An increase in the labour force

D An increase in the rate of interest

6 What would result in a shift to the right of the short run aggregate supply curve?

A A decrease in wage rates

B A decrease in labour productivity

C An increase in indirect taxes

D An increase in the quantity of capital goods

7 Figure 1 shows the equilibrium output of an economy.

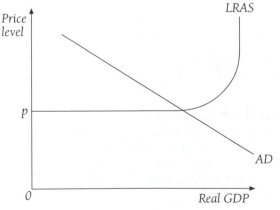

Figure 1

What effect would an increase in aggregate demand have on the price level?

A Increase it

B Leave it unchanged

C Uncertain

D Reduce it

8 According to the new classical model, what effect would a decrease in aggregate demand have on output and the price level in the long run?

	Output	Price level
A	Reduce	Reduce
B	Leave unchanged	Reduce
C	Reduce	Leave unchanged
D	Leave unchanged	Leave unchanged

9 Figure 2 shows the economy producing at point T. What does the movement of the production possibility curve from WX to YZ indicate?

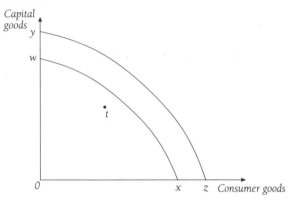

Figure 2

A Actual economic growth

B Potential economic growth

C Actual and potential economic growth

D A reduction in the output gap

10 An economy currently operates at the full employment level. What effect would a rise in the number of resources devoted to producing capital goods be likely to have on the output of consumer goods in the short and long run?

	Short run	Long run
A	Reduce	Reduce
B	Reduce	Increase
C	Increase	Increase
D	Increase	Reduce

11 Which event could cause demand-pull inflation?

A A cut in income tax rates

B A rise in interest rates

C An increase in wage rates above productivity gains

D A reduction in the exchange rate which results in a rise in the cost of imported raw materials

12 What must occur as a result of inflation?

A Fiscal drag

B A fall in the value of money

C A reduction in the country's international price competitiveness

D A transfer of income from savers to borrowers

13 Which item is included in the RPI measure of inflation but not the RPIX measure?

A VAT

B Council tax

C Foreign holidays

D Mortgage interest payments

14 What is the main opportunity cost of unemployment to society?

A Tax revenue

B Output

C Job seekers' allowance

D Health care expenditure

15 Which group is in the labour force?

A Those who have retired early

B The unemployed

C Full-time home makers

D The severely disabled

16 Why may unemployment and a high level of vacancies exist at the same time?

A The unemployed are geographically mobile.

B Wages on offer are above the level of job seekers' allowance.

C There is perfect knowledge of the vacancies.

D There is a mismatch of skills between the unemployed and the jobs available.

17 Which would appear in the current account of a country's balance of payments?

A Capital investment

B Portfolio investment

C Errors and omissions

D Trade in goods

18 In which section of the current account does sea transport appear?

A Trade in goods

B Trade in services

C Investment income

D Current transfers

19 Which is a monetary policy measure?

A Income tax

B Government expenditure

C The rate of interest

D Privatisation

20 The Phillips curve shows the relationship between

A inflation and unemployment

B unemployment and economic growth

C economic growth and the balance of payments

D the balance of payments and economic growth

Section 6
Economics in context

Introduction

The final section of AS Economics is devoted to the application of economic concepts, and ways of thinking to three contexts: housing, the environment and sport and leisure. In each case key concepts have been identified and students are offered an introduction into the analysis of key issues within each context. You may wish to concentrate your study based on one of these units or you may wish to develop your skills of economic analysis by consideration of all three.

UNIT 28 Housing

Key concepts covered

- demand
- supply
- price elasticity of demand
- income elasticity of demand
- externalities
- equity
- barriers to entry
- merit good

Introduction

While people talk about the housing market, it is more appropriate to consider a large set of interconnected markets which collectively bring together suppliers of housing and those who demand housing. These markets are like any other market and they can be analysed using concepts such as:

- price elasticity of demand
- income elasticity of demand
- externalities
- equity.

In this unit the special nature of housing markets and how each of these concepts might be used in this special context is discussed.

The principal housing markets

Housing is usually broken down into three interconnected markets:

- owner occupation
- social housing
- private renting.

Owner occupation

This is the most common form of housing tenure in the UK. House buying is for most people the largest individual item purchased. The overwhelming majority of house purchases are financed by mortgages. Thus, in order to purchase a house, a customer must first satisfy the demands of the bank, building society or other financial institution in order to obtain a mortgage. Generally speaking, lenders are prepared to advance a mortgage equal to three times the salary of the main breadwinner. They also require the survey and valuation of prospective properties,

and have a range of other rules which have to be followed. Repayment of mortgages is usually monthly and the main influence on the size of repayments will be the interest rate.

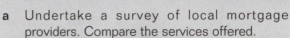

ACTIVITY 1

a Undertake a survey of local mortgage providers. Compare the services offered.
b What will be the minimum income needed to purchase a house in your area? Does this exclude any groups from becoming owner occupiers?

The supply of homes for owner occupation

There are two interconnected subsets of this sector:

- new houses
- second-hand houses.

The production of new houses for owner occupation is dominated by nationally known companies such as Bovis, Wimpey and Westbury, but barriers to entry are relatively low and smaller regionally based companies exist as do one-person firms.

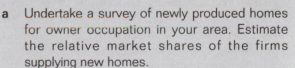

ACTIVITY 2

a Undertake a survey of newly produced homes for owner occupation in your area. Estimate the relative market shares of the firms supplying new homes.
b What conclusions can you make of the competitiveness of your local market for new homes?

Second-hand homes

The majority of properties coming on to the national housing market are second hand. They are almost exclusively owned by their occupiers, whose motivations in deciding whether or not to offer their property for sale are very complicated. Anticipated sale price is a key factor and recent trends indicate that rising house prices are associated with greater preparedness to sell. In fact, the decision to sell is often tied up with the decision to buy another property.

The owner-occupier property market

Although it is possible for individuals to sell and buy second-hand houses themselves, the majority of sales are made through estate agents. Barriers to entry in this particular sector are relatively low. Agents usually charge a commission of between 1 per cent and 3 per cent of the final selling price to the sellers of houses and, as this is only paid when the deal finally goes through, estate agents have to take considerable risks.

Social housing

Social housing is the name now given to both local authority owned and housing association owned housing. Both sub sectors are or have been government funded and decent housing has been seen over the past 100 years as a merit good – something which the free market will not necessarily supply but is socially desirable. It could also be argued that decent housing provides considerable external benefits as it might contribute to a healthier, better educated and more productive workforce, and that this too provides a rationale for government intervention.

Early examples of social housing were built over 100 years ago by various charitable trusts. Their work was largely taken over by local authorities between the 1920s and the 1980s, who undertook extensive provision of council houses, flats and estates to replace slums and raise living standards for the less well off. Conservative governments in the 1980s restricted the capability of local authorities to build new council houses but provided finance to housing associations to provide decent accommodation at 'affordable' rents. Housing associations developed in the 1960s as charitable trusts to modernise and improve old houses as another means of providing decent housing to those in need.

Social housing is not then a market in the way that other markets have been described in this book. There are those who demand social housing, and there are those organisations that provide social housing. The refurbishment of old property and the building of new is paid for largely by the rents paid by tenants, yet the ability and preparedness to pay is not used as a means of allocating social housing. Councils and housing associations work very closely together to allocate newly available property according to need. In most cases the needs of potential tenants are assessed and points are given according to various criteria, for example number of children, state of existing accommodation. Available housing is then, theoretically, allocated to those in greatest need.

ACTIVITY 3

Research the availability and allocation of social housing in your area. Are the needs of all potential tenants being met? If not, why not?

The private rented sector

This is less significant in the UK compared to most other European countries. Activity in this sector of the housing market tends to be dependent on conditions in the other sectors. Thus, in the 1990s there was an increase in the supply of rented accommodation from individual homeowners who had decided to rent out their property rather than sell at what they perceived to be poor prices.

Some of the demand for housing in this sector comes from those excluded from other housing sectors. Thus, low incomes prevent some applicants from consideration for a mortgage limiting the option of owner occupation. In some areas the demand for social housing creates long waiting lists for council and housing association accommodation and the private rented sector is the only option.

Both the demand and supply of privately rented accommodation are likely to be sensitive to changes in its price, i.e. rents, and this sector contains a relatively high proportion of housing which is poor, overcrowded, or even unfit for habitation.

Price elasticity of demand

Housing markets contain a wide spectrum of differing degrees of competition. Major builders compete head to head offering similar products at similar prices. It is likely that small changes in the price of one particular 'brand' of housing will lead to relatively large changes in demand. In more specialist areas of the market, such as sheltered housing for the elderly elasticity of demand may be less significant.

Income elasticity of demand

The demand for particular types of housing in many parts of the country is highly sensitive to changes in income. Mortgage offers are usually worked out as multiples of an individual or couple's income. A rise in salary will, therefore, increase their buying power. Poor quality housing, on the other hand, is likely to be regarded as an inferior good, and currently significant numbers of houses in some northern cities lie empty or can be bought for next to nothing.

Externalities

From the middle of the nineteenth century the existence of positive externalities associated with good housing and negative externalities associated with poor housing have been identified. Philanthropic families such as Cadburys provided decent housing for their workers because they recognised that well-housed workers were more productive. Bad housing is associated with illness and disease which imposes additional costs on the rest of society.

For these reasons, the provision of housing by the private sector has been seen to be a source of market failure, giving a rationale for the intervention of local and national governments and the voluntary sector. Some people would argue that housing should be regarded as a merit good.

Equity

The existence of significant externalities coupled with an imbalance between demand and supply of housing has created significant inequalities within housing markets. In the UK there has been a long-term under supply of housing in those areas in which needs are greatest. This contributes to the use of bed and breakfast accommodation as emergency housing, and to the considerable problem of homelessness. On the other hand, the well off can afford to live in large, under utilised and luxurious accommodation. Some would argue that the existence of such inequalities is not morally justifiable.

ACTIVITY 4

Undertake a joint research project into housing provision in your area.

a Assess the extent of each sector of the local housing market.

b Analyse how each market works in order to equate demand and supply.

c Judge each market in terms of productive efficiency, allocative efficiency, externalities, equity and government intervention.

d What recommendations would you make to improve housing provision in your area? What would be the implications of these recommendations? What conclusions can you make?

Summary

Housing markets are probably the most important markets in which we participate. The quality of our housing has a direct bearing on our health, and children growing up in poor housing conditions are likely to be less productive and more costly to society as a whole to keep healthy and well. Housing markets are also very significant as spending on housing forms the biggest proportional outlay of any expenditure for most people in the UK. Changes, therefore, in mortgage payments or local authority/housing association rents have a indirect effect on many other areas of economic activity.

Data response question

Extract A

Low inflation and the property market

In the 1980s, in a period of high inflation everyone thought they were making a fortune out of the house they lived in. People buying houses believed that any increase in inflation would more than cover the interest rate on their mortgages. Although the nominal interest rates house buyers paid was quite high and positive, the real interest rate was negative. Housing provided a protection against inflation and house purchase was regarded as a good investment.

In the late 1980s, the government significantly increased interest rates to try to control inflation and as a result the economy moved into a serious recession in the early 1990s. Unemployment rose, consumer confidence fell and house prices collapsed. The number of properties on the market rose as house builders found it difficult to find buyers and some existing home-owners, who could no longer afford their mortgage repayments, tried to sell.

In the 1990s, the low rate of general inflation transformed the property market. Nominal interest rates fell considerably, but real rates of interest became positive. Furthermore, the rate of house-price inflation was much lower than it had been in the 1980s.

Householders now treat home ownership more as a consumer purchase than a financial investment. Lower inflation has cancelled the advantage of home ownership and increased the debt burden for borrowers. During a period of lower inflation, with house prices rising more slowly, smaller capital gains are likely to be made from owning property.

Adapted from *The British Economy Survey*, Autumn 1996

Extract B

House prices and the wider economy

Some economists have argued that changes in real house prices causes changes in total consumption, via changes in housing wealth. During periods of rapid inflation, the price of houses rise and the

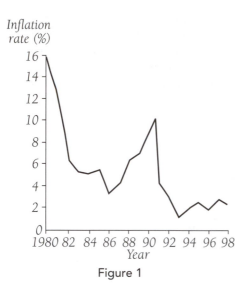

Inflation rate (%)

Figure 1

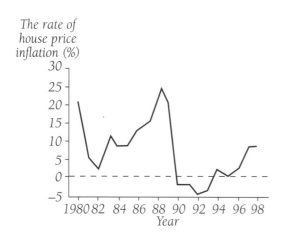

The rate of house price inflation (%)

Figure 2

repossessions, 'negative equity' has an opposite effect on consumption spending to that resulting from equity withdrawal.

Adapted from *Bank of England Quarterly Bulletin*, August 1995

1 What is meant by:
   a 'inflation' (Extract A, line 1) (4 marks)
   b 'capital gains' (Extract A, line 29) (4 marks)
2 Distinguish between 'nominal' interest rates and 'real' interest rates (Extract A, lines 5–7) (4 marks)
3a Compare the general rate of inflation and the rate of house-price inflation in the UK, between 1980 and 1998 shown in Figures 1 and 2. (4 marks)
   b Explain how a difference between the two inflation rates can lead to EITHER 'equity withdrawal' OR 'negative equity' mentioned in Extract B. (7 marks)
4 Explain *two* ways in which the changes in house prices between 1980 and 1998 may have affected aggregate demand. (9 marks)
5 Discuss the various factors which may have caused house prices to fall in the early 1990s. (18 marks)

real value of mortgage debt falls as it is eroded by inflation. As a result owner-occupiers grow wealthier, even though their wealth is locked up in the bricks and mortar or 'equity' of the houses they live in. But as their net wealth increases, many house owners decide to convert part of their wealth from illiquid bricks and mortar into money which can then be spent on consumption. This process, which is know as 'equity withdrawal', involves taking out bigger mortgages on existing properties, and spending the amount borrowed on general consumption.

But for a large number of UK households, falling house prices in the early 1990s, resulted in the value of their properties falling below the size of their outstanding mortgages and the problem of negative equity. Along with other symptoms of housing distress, such mortgage arrears and house

to the recovery ... otherwise have ... so creates new ... mountains of ... ling to turn into ... oblem stems from ... of recycling has ... ans have simply ... bins and the over-

expensive industrial ... involving transport ... ke glass for example, ... ials to recycle, despite ... s. If a household recy- ... uld save about 6.2 kg ... would soon be lost if ... bank. Installing low ... e, for example, is over ... an recycling. If paper is ... or four times, the fibres ... r newspapers.

4 Explain how the information in the last paragraph of **Extract C** illustrates both the incentive and rationing functions that prices perform in a market economy. *(9 marks)*

5 Making use of the information in **Extract D** and your knowledge of economics, discuss the reasons why the recycling of waste products may do little to help conserve the world's natural resources. *(18 marks)*

Key concepts covered

- market failure
- externalities
- social costs and benefits
- cost benefit analysis
- government intervention
- economic growth
- sustainable development

Introduction

Environmental economics is newly emerging as an important area of study and research. It has developed from the 1960s. Before this time economists tended to ignore the environmental effects of economic activity. Resources such as air and water tended to be regarded as free goods. Notions of non-renewable resources were ill developed.

Environmental economics attempts to compensate for the shortcomings of traditional approaches by using and applying many of the concepts developed earlier in this book:

- market failure, especially externalities and the extent to which market prices and outputs accurately reflect actual social costs and benefits
- the use of cost benefit analysis in an attempt to account for the environmental impact of economic activity
- consumer and producer responses to environmental issues
- the effectiveness of government intervention in dealing with environmental issues
- the effects of globalisation on the environment

Moreover, environmental economists have developed additional analytical tools to take better account of the environmental impact of economic activity:

- alternative measures of economic growth and development
- new microeconomic tools of analysis to take account of environmental degradation.

Market failure

One of the challenges to economists when dealing with environmental issues is to devise ways of fully accounting for the impact of economic activity on the environment. Does the price paid by consumers for equatorial hardwoods accurately reflect the possible long-term costs which may arise from erosion, the destruction of species and possible climate change? Similarly, does the price paid by motorists include the long-term costs of global warming?

ACTIVITY 1

Consider any local economic activity:

a Assess its environmental impact. Is it sustainable?
b Are there positive or negative externalities?
c Are there global implications?
d Does the price paid for the product or service reflect its full environmental costs?

Cost benefit analysis

Cost benefit analysis can be used in an attempt to place a monetary value on the environmental effects of any economic activity. It is hard to place a value on particular plants or animals that may be faced with extinction. Similarly, it is hard to place a current value on costs and benefits which are likely to impact over hundreds or thousands of years.

ACTIVITY 2

a How would you use cost benefit analysis to assess the environmental impact of nuclear power stations?
b How might you measure the possible costs of the negative externalities. Are there positive externalities?
c How sure can you be of your analysis? What assumptions would you have to make?
d Had cost benefit analysis been used would nuclear power stations have been built?

Government intervention

Most people probably agree that it is quite legitimate for a government to intervene in order to reduce or eliminate the harmful effects of economic activity on the environment. There is, however, little consensus on how this might be best achieved. Broadly, two approaches can be used:

- using the price mechanism
- direct controls.

Using the price mechanism refers to policies considered in Unit 16. The government can impose taxes or give subsidies in order to try to find market-based solutions to environmental problems.

Alternatively, governments can use their legal powers to control and limit the production of environmentally harmful products.

ACTIVITY 3

Discuss the relative merits of these two approaches to restricting private car use in urban areas.

Globalisation

Environmental issues are not limited by political boundaries, and the emergence of global rather than national markets has increased the pressure on the world's resources. This makes finding solutions even harder as international cooperation is required if possible solutions are given the chance to work. Increased air travel, and the growth of global tourism, have made the world a smaller place but also more fragile in terms of sustainability.

Alternative measures of growth and development

The traditional and still commonly used measure of macroeconomic performance, gross domestic product (GDP) aggregates the money values of all final goods and services produced in the domestic economy during a year and excludes valuation of most environmental goods.

Traditional economics has made analysis of the environmental impact of economic activity even harder as depleting a stock of natural resources (for example oil, minerals and forests) increases GDP, since it results in new sales. Thus, an economist has recalculated Indonesia's growth rate to include the consumption of natural capital. Allowing for the degradation of resources such as timber lowers the growth rate from 7 per cent to 4 per cent.

One response to the failure of traditional methods of measuring economic growth has been to adjust GDP to account for natural resources – 'Green GDP'.

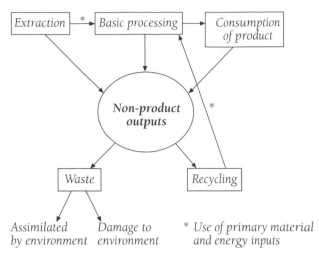

Figure 29.1 Input and output analysis applied to environmental degradation

Turner, Pearce and Bareman, *Environmental Economics*, Harvester Press, 1994, pp. 18 and 20

Microeconomic tools of analysis

In Figure 29.1 a simple input/output model is amended to take account of the production of waste, which is, in turn, subdivided into that which can be absorbed by the environment, that which causes damage and that which can be recycled.

Not all economists agree with approaches which attempt to account for the environmental effect of economic activity. Some economists have argued that devoting resources to environmental regulations distorts the market system and diverts inputs from the production of output to other goals, such as reducing emissions. Since environmental benefits are not measured in GDP, diverting resources leads to a fall in GDP, and economic growth, as traditionally measured, slows. Some US economists have estimated that: environmental regulations have caused a 2.6 to 6 per cent reduction in US GDP.

Nonetheless, there are positive effects of the environment on the economy, as environmental resources are an input to production. For example, if clean water is not available, it cannot be used. Environmental regulations that protect water thus benefit GDP. Also environmental quality affects the quality of other inputs. For example, reduced air pollution makes agriculture more productive and provides healthier workers. Health care provision consumes a large portion of GDP spending; therefore, reducing the number of sick people reduces the costs of treating them.

ACTIVITY 4

a Undertake a joint rese... environmental issues in ... those issues which are mos...

b Use the tools of economic a... the likely future impact of thes...

c Assess the extent to whic... intervention might be appropria...

d What recommendations would... future action? What would be th... of these recommendations?

e What conclusions can you mak... significance or otherwise of env... issues?

Summary

Environmental economics is one of the growing research areas, especially as sci... produce gloomy forecasts of future pollution... ozone depletion and global warming. The exi... of such global issues provides a challeng... economists and their traditional ways of work... The interdisciplinary nature of approaches to try... deal with ensuring that the planet survives prov... another challenge to compartmentalising thinkin... and analysis between particular disciplines... Nonetheless, economists are likely to have an... increasing role to play in devising strategies which promote sustainable development.

What a load of old rubbish!

The recycling of products can lea... of natural resources that would... been wasted but recycling a... problems. All over Germany... rubbish which no-one of the pr... something else. Much of the pr... the fact that the collection sid... been too successful. Germ... overstuffed their yellow rubbish... supply is now rotting uselessly...

Recycling itself is also an... process, consuming energy... costs and producing waste. T... one of the most difficult mater... the popularity of bottle bank... cled 52 bottles a year, this w... of carbon, but these savings... people drove to the bottle... energy lighting in the hom... 200 times more effective th... recycled more than three... become too short to use f...

Extract A

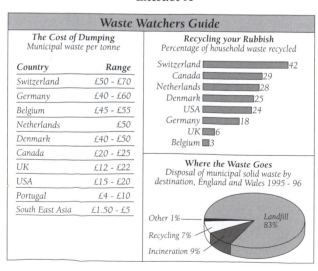

Waste Watchers Guide	
The Cost of Dumping Municipal waste per tonne	**Recycling your Rubbish** Percentage of household waste recycled

Country	Range
Switzerland	£50 - £70
Germany	£40 - £60
Belgium	£45 - £55
Netherlands	£50
Denmark	£40 - £50
Canada	£20 - £25
UK	£12 - £22
USA	£15 - £20
Portugal	£4 - £10
South East Asia	£1.50 - £5

Percentage of household waste recycled:
Switzerland 42
Canada 29
Netherlands 28
Denmark 25
USA 24
Germany 18
UK 6
Belgium 3

Where the Waste Goes
Disposal of municipal solid waste by destination, England and Wales 1995 - 96

Landfill 83%
Incineration 9%
Recycling 7%
Other 1%

Figure 29.1

2 L...
'r...
ma...

3 Fig...
per...
perc...
recycl...

a Des...
dum...
of tot...

b Expla...

30 Sport and leisure

Key concepts covered

- demand and supply
- market failure
- government intervention
- black market
- competition
- barriers to entry
- merit goods
- exchange rates

Introduction

The economics of sport and leisure is a developing area of applied economic study. It includes holidays and travel, film, TV, the theatre and other forms of entertainment. Over the past decade this has been one of the fastest growing sectors of the economy. Analysis of trends and developments in this sector can involve the application of a wide range of economic concepts, including:

- demand and supply
- different market characteristics
- market failure and government intervention
- impact of changes in macroeconomic factors.

Demand and supply

The sport and leisure markets, like any others, can be analysed through the application of demand and supply analysis. This can be particularly useful as the prices of most sporting and cultural events have to be fixed prior to the event. Moreover, the capacity of venues is always limited. Thus, in recent years the relevant local authorities have limited sales to the Glastonbury Festival to 80 000 tickets. Prices have been set at about £80. This can be illustrated in Figure 30.1

Could the organisers have set a higher price? A possible answer is given in Figure 30.2. In 1999 tickets sold out a month before the event. It is likely that the actual demand was as illustrated in Figure 30.2.

Setting a price below the market clearing equilibrium resulted in both a black market in tickets and a number of ingenious attempts to gain entry without paying.

ACTIVITY 1

Choose a band/DJ and a suitable local venue. What would be your market clearing price of tickets?

Different market characteristics

Sport and leisure consist of many linked and interrelated markets. Competition and barriers to entry vary widely. It is relatively easy to form a band and fiercely competitive to book reasonably paying gigs. Joining the successful elite of top bands is much harder.

Success in sport can involve the creation of immense economic power. The world's major soccer clubs use this to ensure that their earnings are maximised. They are able to charge high prices to see

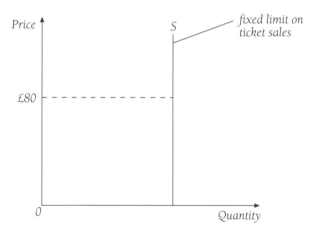

Figure 30.1 Setting a price for tickets to Glastonbury

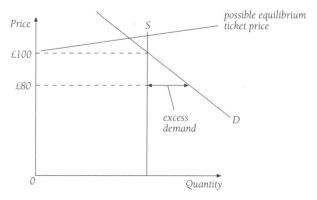

Figure 30.2 Excess demand for tickets to Glastonbury

games, negotiate lucrative TV contracts and sell club merchandise at inflated prices. They are monopolists in the sense that there is only one Manchester United.

ACTIVITY 2

a Discuss the contention that the power of the top soccer clubs in Britain will eventually contribute to the decline of football as the national sport. Consider the financial positions of those teams in the Premier League compared to those in Division 3.

b How significant is the floating on the stock market of major clubs. Is this now a global market? What about the links with media and communication companies?

Market failure and government intervention

Should the government subsidise the arts? Traditionally, most governments have decided that the provision of cultural activities is worthy of government intervention in the form of subsidies. Similarly, governments tend to regulate the degree of competition in the provision of different forms of media.

ACTIVITY 3

Is the opera a merit good?

Macroeconomic factors

Some third world countries are heavily dependent on tourism. The popularity of different tourist destinations can be volatile. Changes in exchange rates can have a significant effect on flows of tourists to particular countries. A rise in the value of the US dollar in comparison to other currencies is likely to make US citizens more likely to take foreign holidays. A movement in the other direction is likely to have an opposite effect.

Changes in the flows of tourists will, in turn, have an effect on those countries most dependent upon tourism. Nepal is one of the poorest countries in the world and receives most of its foreign earnings from tourism. Even a small fall in the number of tourists could have a damaging effect on living standards.

ACTIVITY 4

a Undertake a joint research project into sport and leisure needs in your area. Identify those needs which are most important.

b Use the tools of economic analysis to assess the likely future consequences if these needs are not met.

c Assess the extent to which government intervention might be appropriate.

d What recommendations would you make for future action? What would be the implications of these recommendations?

e What conclusions can you make about the significance or otherwise of sport and leisure issues?

Summary

Sport and leisure is one of the fastest growing sectors of the economy. Its growth provides many new jobs to replace those lost in declining sectors of the economy. The development of this sector has other implications, not least the impact of worldwide tourism on fragile economies and eco structures. Sport and leisure provision has historically been provided by the voluntary and public sectors but increasing commercialisation means that private sector involvement is now significant. This development may involve changed priorities and objectives which may have implications in accounting for externalities and raise issues of fairness and equality.

Data response question

Extract A

For the 1998/99 season, Chelsea Football Club raised the price of season tickets by well above the rate of inflation. Some season ticket prices rose by 47 per cent in nominal terms, or by over 44 per cent in real terms. The fact that the demand for a product, such as Chelsea, is highly price inelastic increases clubs' ability to raise prices. Worse could be to come. If anything, football clubs have been historically under pricing their products. In the past the higher prices at football matches have not been that high, and clubs have not exploited the willingness of wealthier individuals to pay. Clubs should be charging a wider range of prices

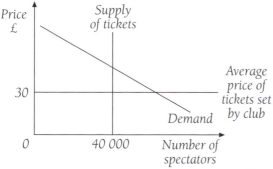

Market conditions for a typical game at a leading premier league club

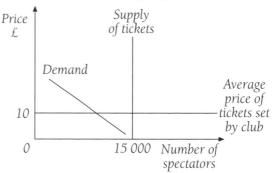

Market conditions for a typical game at a lower league game

Figure 1

so that 16-year-olds can get in while wealthier supporters are charged the £40 a game they are willing to pay.

Football compares unfavourably to other leisure events in terms of the range of prices on offer. Taking the price of the most expensive ticket available as a multiple of the cheapest, the most accessible leisure activity available is opera: the price range for the English National Opera is 850 per cent. A West End musical has a comparatively wide range, at 558 per cent. The same differential for a Premier League club is a mere 188 per cent. Only cinema has a similar range (120 per cent). Cinema is currently doing well, and not because of better films. Ticket sales have gone through the ceiling because cinemas have good facilities, good parking and good pricing structure, and the prices are within reach of the family pocket.

Football may have more in common with theatre than the cinema and should be priced accordingly. Cinema audiences all see exactly the same film, mainly at a distance and angle that is acceptable and enjoyable. They all use the same entrance and exit, have access to the same refreshments and book tickets in the same way. By contrast, theatre audiences see a live performance, which means that positioning in the theatre is a much more important element in enjoying the show. Finally, customers are dealt with in different ways, with theatre members of friends having special privileges. This allows theatregoers to pay for what they want, with London theatre tickets ranging from £5 to £45 for the same performance.

Adapted from the *Guardian*, 18 February 1998

Extract B

Tackling monopolies

TV sports broadcasters are exercising monopoly power. Money is pouring into sport because television

viewers are willing to watch it, but viewers are paying over the odds because sporting authorities are able to use their control over the supply of games to force up the price of TV rights.

Monopoly power can be curbed by injecting competition but this is hard to do in the case of sports. Although team owners often assert that they compete not just with other teams but with other forms of entertainment, that is true only to a limited extent. Football fans are unlikely to find cricket, much less the film Titanic, an acceptable substitute for a soccer match. Competition between authorities within a particular sport is also a non-starter. Fans prefer a single World Cup because they want to know which country's football team is the best in the world.

Adapted from *The Economist*, 7 February 1998

1 What is meant by:
a the rate of inflation (Extract A, lines 2–3) (4 marks)
b demand being highly price inelastic (Extract A, lines 5–6). (4 marks)

2 Distinguish between prices rising in 'nominal terms' and prices rising in 'real terms' (Extract A, lines 3–4) (4 marks)

3 Figure 1 shows supply and demand conditions facing two football clubs, one in the Premier League and one in a lower league. The average price charged by the Premier League club is £30 a ticket, while that charged by the lower league club is £10.

a What would be the equilibrium price for match tickets at each club? Briefly explain your answers. (4 marks)

b Discuss whether at the prices set by the two clubs, tickets are under priced in the two markets. (7 marks)

4 Explain how competition might be injected into the market for sport on television (Extract B, lines 6–7). (9 marks)

5 Making use of the data and your economic knowledge, evaluate the case for charging a much wider range of prices to spectators watching live football matches. (18 marks)

Part 2
A2 Economics

Section 1
Firms and their behaviour

Introduction

AS Unit 10 provided an introduction to the importance of understanding the objectives of firms and their influence on the behaviour of firms. Economists differ as to the importance attached to particular objectives but there is a broad level of agreement that:

- small firms operating in competitive markets are unlikely to survive if objectives other than maximising profit are not pursued
- larger firms, operating in less competitive markets are likely to have greater freedom in pursuing a range of objectives
- significant microeconomic decisions are taken by government, charities and voluntary bodies. Organisations such as these are likely to have social objectives.

However, if all types of firms are to survive they need to consider the impact of strategic decisions in terms of costs, revenue and, although they may use other terms, of profit – just as privately owned competitive firms do.

This section provides an introduction to the detailed theoretical framework used by economists to illustrate the consequences of decision-making by firms. Understanding what has become known as 'Industrial Economics' requires the development of skills of graphical analysis by which the impact of different objectives is examined in terms of their effect on:

- prices
- sales
- profits.

This section also builds on the descriptive treatment given to costs, revenue, and profits in AS Section 3 of this book.

Before reading this section, check that you can recall the meaning and use of the following key concepts:

- profit maximisation
- profit saticficing
- stakeholder analysis
- fixed costs
- variable costs
- total costs
- average (total) costs
- revenue
- monopolistic markets
- competitive markets
- price makers
- price takers
- normal profits
- supernormal profits.

Introductory theory of the firm

Key concepts covered

- perfect competition
- monopoly
- average revenue
- marginal revenue
- profit-maximising rule
- homogeneous product
- perfect knowledge

Introduction

This unit develops and expands concepts introduced in AS Units 12 and 13 to develop an understanding of how graphical analysis can be used to predict sales, prices and profits of firms operating with different objectives and in two highly contrasting theoretical market structures. Firstly, the use of graphs to illustrate how different outputs may be associated with differing objectives is discussed. This is then expanded to include further modelling of both perfect competition and monopoly.

Objectives of firms

AS Unit 10 considered the range of different objectives which firms may pursue. The following were identified:

- profit maximisation – the individual firm will choose that output which produces the maximum possible profit

- sales maximisation – where individual firms attempt to gain the largest possible level of sales while ensuring that average costs are covered

- particular social objectives which may be pursued by government, voluntary and charitable organisations

- multiple or conflicting objectives as analysed through the use of stakeholder analysis.

It is possible to use graphical analysis to predict the sales, price and profit levels of following each of these alternative strategies. Such analysis builds on the treatment given in AS Unit 11 of different costs facing firms on the short run. This is summarised in Figure 1.1.

Similar analysis can be applied to the concept of revenue described in AS Unit 12. Economists distinguish between:

- **average revenue** (AR), and
- **marginal revenue** (MR).

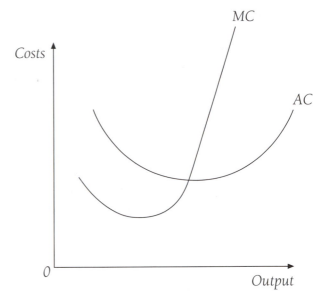

Figure 1.1 Average and marginal costs in the short run

Average revenue

Average revenue is total revenue gained from selling a product divided by the number of items sold. Average revenue is usually referred to as the price of the product and will, therefore, be determined by the demand for the product in question. In most cases the demand for a product is likely to be high when the price is low and vice versa. A typical demand curve is illustrated in Figure 1.2.

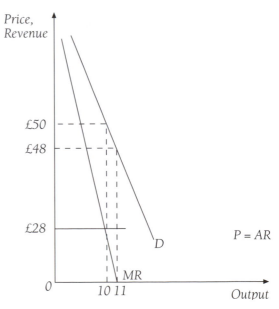

Figure 1.2 Typical demand curve

Marginal revenue is defined as the change to revenue which occurs if sales are changed by one unit. In Figure 1.2 if sales are increased from 10 units to 11 units, revenue will rise by £28 (10 units sold for £50, each giving a total revenue of £500, but to sell 11 units the firm has to accept a lower price of £48 per unit, giving a new total revenue of £48 × 11 = £528). If sales are further increased the marginal revenue will continue to decline. In other words, if the demand curve is downward sloping to the right more goods can only be sold at a lower price, which means that MR will always be less than AR. Thus, if the demand curve for a product or service is represented by a straight line, then the marginal revenue curve will bisect the angle formed by the average revenue (or demand) curve and the vertical axis as illustrated in Figure 1.2. Note that the marginal revenue is plotted against the midpoints of sales represented on the horizontal axis.

The two diagrams representing the costs facing a firm and possible levels of revenue can be superimposed one on top of the other as shown in Figure 1.3, which can be used to determine possible levels of output and sales according to:

- the market conditions facing the firm – this will be represented by the position and shape of the demand curve
- the objectives of the individual firm, which will determine target levels of output or price.

Social objectives

The key feature of Figure 1.3 is that this firm will cover its costs by choosing any output between n and

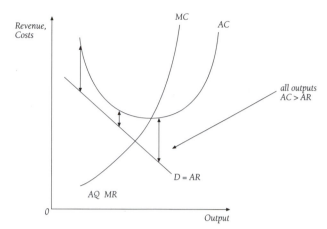

Figure 1.4 Firm making a loss at all possible outputs

m. Data such as these would be useful to a firm or organisation pursuing social objectives. Producing less than n or more than m would create a loss, which if not financed by a grant, subsidy or charitable contribution would threaten the viability of the organisation.

On the other hand, demand conditions might be such that irrespective of the output chosen the firm would be making a loss. This is shown in Figure 1.4.

Sales maximisation

This form of graphical analysis can be used to predict the output chosen by a firm wishing to maximise sales. In other words, to achieve the highest possible level of sales while at the same time avoiding a loss. This is shown in Figure 1.5 by output t and price p.

Profit maximisation

Using graphical analysis to identify the profit maximising output is slightly more complicated.

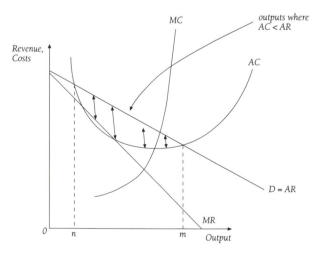

Figure 1.3 Hypothetical demand and cost conditions facing a firm

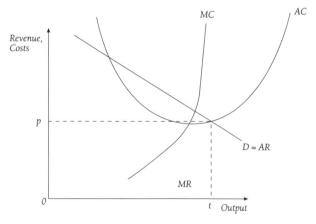

Figure 1.5 Output of a firm seeking to maximize sales

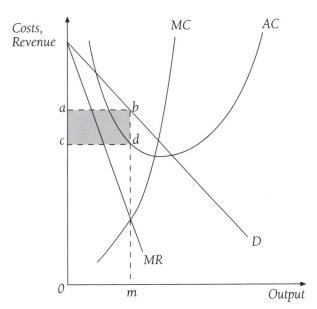

Figure 1.6 Output of profit-maximising firm

Perfect competition

Perfect competition is the name given to a theoretical construction useful in helping understand the behaviour of small firms operating in highly competitive markets. Economists have developed this model on the basis of a series of simplifying assumptions. They consider that a perfectly competitive market consists of a large number of small firms, each:

1 producing an identical or **homogeneous product**
2 contributing only a tiny proportion of the final output of the industry
3 selling to customers who also have a **perfect knowledge** of the behaviour of all the firms operating in the industry
4 having perfect knowledge of the behaviour of other firms in the industry with absolute freedom to enter or leave the industry.

The combined effect of the first three of these assumptions is that a firm operating in a perfectly competitive market will have to be a price taker. In other words, because there are so many firms producing an identical product, each individual firm will have to accept the price that is set by the market. This is illustrated in Figure 1.7.

If the firm were to attempt to sell for more than the market price p, customers would switch to cheaper alternatives, and selling for less p would make little sense as the market would be prepared to pay more.

This means that the demand or average revenue curve facing a perfectly competitive firm will be horizontal and will be identical to the marginal revenue curve. It follows from the assumptions outlined above that the individual firm can sell

Profit maximisation quite simply means producing the largest profit possible and this output is found by applying the **profit-maximising rule**. This means choosing the output at which marginal costs and marginal revenue are equal. This is illustrated in Figure 1.6.

At output m the gap between average revenue and average costs is maximised. If a firm chose this output, total profits equal to the shaded area abcd would be earned. As AR > AC these would be called supernormal or abnormal profits as distinct from normal profits earned if AR = AC.

If the firm decided on an output to the right of m, marginal costs would exceed marginal revenue; in other words, expanding production beyond m would raise costs by a larger amount than any increase in revenue, reducing total profits. On the other hand, any point to the left of m would mean that marginal costs were less than marginal revenue, meaning that if output were expanded, revenue would grow by more than costs. Only at the point at which MR = MC will profits be maximised.

In AS Units 14 and 15 the main features of competitive and monopolistic markets were described. These concepts have been derived from models developed by economists to analyse the behaviour of firms operating under different market conditions. In this unit the following models are developed:

■ **perfect competition**
■ **monopoly**.

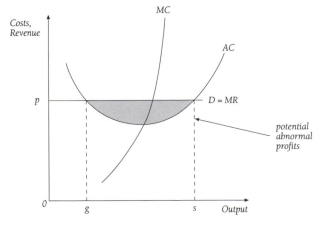

Figure 1.7 Short run market price and individual demand curve for perfectly competitive firm

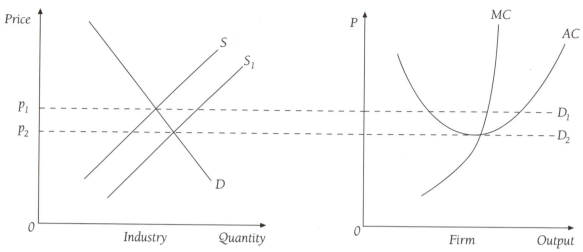

Figure 1.8 Long run equilibrium of perfectly competitive firm

whatever it produces as long as it is prepared to accept the market price. If it sells an additional unit it will receive the market price which will be the same for each unit of production.

Normal profits

The final two assumptions are important as they combine to ensure that in the long run a perfectly competitive firm:

■ is obliged to attempt to maximise profits

■ can earn only normal profits.

In Figure 1.7 the demand for the product is such that between outputs g and s average revenue exceeds average costs, i.e. abnormal profits can be earned. The existence of these abnormal profits will be known to competitors and other potential market entrants. The former are likely to increase production and new entrants will also boost supply. The long-

term effect will be an increase in market supply which will depress price as shown in Figure 1.8.

The converse of this is also true. If prices are below average costs, as illustrated in Figure 1.9, then some firms will leave the industry and total output will fall.

The long-term effect of this is shown in Figure 1.10.

Thus, market forces will ensure that costs and revenues are in the long term kept in balance and Figure 1.11 shows the long-term equilibrium of the perfectly competitive firm, in which AC = AR and normal profits are earned.

If perfect competition were to exist and if such an industry and its firms were in long run equilibrium, the following would occur:

■ There would be efficiency in terms of minimising the average costs of production.

■ Excessive profits could only be earned in the short run.

■ Firms would have to attempt to maximise profits.

■ Firms would have to respond to changes in demand.

■ The desire to survive should ensure that firms are continually competing in order to try to gain competitive advantage over other firms.

However, these predictions apply only if the assumptions required to build up the perfectly competitive model are met in the real world.

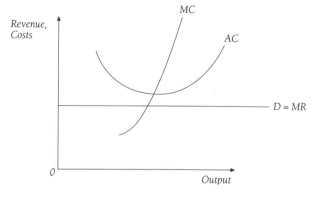

Figure 1.9 Short run equilibrium of loss making perfectly competitive firm

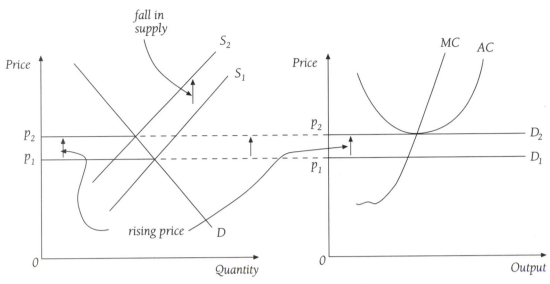

Figure 1.10 Establishment of long run equilibrium

 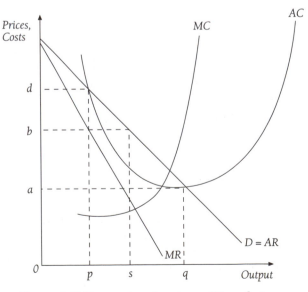
Monopoly

Economists have built up a theoretical model of monopoly in a similar way to that of perfect competition. The foundation of this model relies on a related series of two simplifying assumptions:

■ Production of an whole industry is in the hands of one firm.

■ Complete barriers prevent the entry and exit of firms.

These assumptions mean that the demand curve for

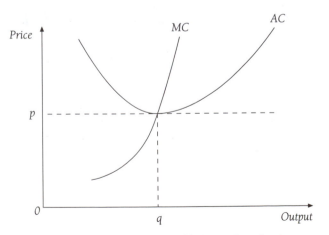

Figure 1.11 Long-term equilibrium of perfectly competitive firm

Figure 1.12 Demand and cost conditions facing a monopolistic firm

the individual firm will be the same as that for the industry as a whole. Moreover, there is no distinction, as there is with perfect competition, between the short and the long run. Barriers to entry are absolute, which prevents other firms from competing away excess profits, and the monopolist will be a price taker with a greater degree of freedom to pursue particular economic and social objectives.

Possible price, sales and output levels can be analysed graphically as in Figure 1.12 where demand and average revenue are above average costs at outputs between p and q, which means that the monopolistic firm could set the price anywhere between a and d and make more than normal profits.

In this case a profit-maximising monopolist would produce at s, a sales maximiser at q, and one looking for a quiet life at p. Barriers to entry would ensure that this short run situation was also the long run position.

If monopolies existed which conformed to this model, the following would occur:

- Average costs of production would not necessarily be minimised.

- Excessive profits could be earned in the long run.

- Firms would not have to attempt to maximise profits.

- Firms would not necessarily have to respond to changes in demand.

- There would be little incentive to innovate.

- Customer choice could be restricted.

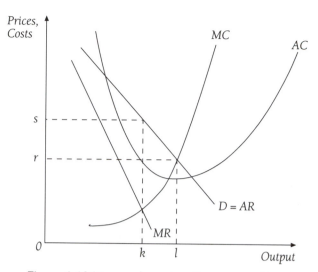

Figure 1.13 Monopoly and perfect competition compared

competitive pressures to produce where MC equals price. If this applied to a whole industry perfectly competitive output would be at l and price r, whereas a profit-maximising monopolist would charge s for an output of k.

This conclusion depends on one implicit assumption – that both monopolist and perfectly competitive firms would be faced with the same average and marginal cost conditions. One argument that has been used to justify the existence of monopolies is that they are able to enjoy the benefits of economies of scale that may arise in increasing size which then leads to falling long run average costs. The effects of this possibility are illustrated in Figure 1.14 where AC_2 and MC_2 represent lower long run costs arising from economies of scale enjoyed by the monopolist

ACTIVITY 2

a Which of the following are closest to being monopolies as defined in this unit?
  i Microsoft
  ii Railtrack
  iii Littledean Village Store
b How useful is the monopolistic model in helping us understand how businesses operate in the 'real ' world?

ACTIVITY 3

a In which of the following markets might the consumer benefit from monopoly provision?
  i Local bus services
  ii Nuclear power generation
  iii Computer operating systems
b Consider the contention that the development of a global economic will inevitably lead to greater monopoly power.

Comparisons with perfect competition

Graphical analysis can be used to demonstrate that in the short run prices under monopoly will be higher than those if perfect competition were to apply and that output would be lower. This is illustrated in the Figure 1.13.

Under perfect competition firms are forced by

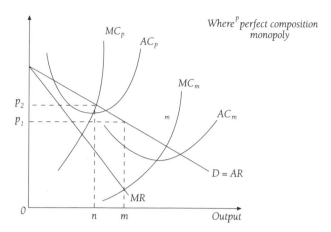

Where p perfect composition monopoly

Figure 1.14 Monopolist benefiting from economies of scale

Summary

This unit built on the descriptive treatment of monopoly and competition developed in AS Unit 14. Graphical analysis was used to compare output, prices and profits under the two extremes of perfect competition and monopoly. The use of this analysis indicates that prices might be lower and outputs higher under conditions of perfect competition than under monopoly. However, this simple comparison ignores the existence of economies of scale and the greater freedom that a monopolistic firm has to pursue differing objectives.

Data response question

In its 10-year history of policing large, cross-border mergers, the European Commission has blocked only 12. The twelfth was Airtours' £950m bid for rival package holiday company First Choice, turned down yesterday by Mario Monti, the new competition commissioner.

Although the rejection was widely expected, the commission's reasons for doing so point to a new trend in merger policy which is not to everyone's liking.

'There is a danger that this case is going to set a precedent,' said one Brussels-based diplomat.

Airtour's hostile bid for First Choice was turned down because it would have created 'a market structure in which the remaining three vertically integrated companies would collectively have a dominant position', said Mr Monti.

Retailers and broadcasters are likely to greet today's decision with particular trepidation. The Commission has been sensitive to concentration in the broadcast market, vetoing a disproportionate number of merger and take-over bids in that sector. Signor Monti has also made it clear that he is worried about the current spate of merger activity in the retail sector. At his European Parliament confirmation hearings earlier this month he singled out the negative impact of merger activity on the supply chain. If a take-over in the British holiday market can be vetoed because of its impact on the whole supply chain, European retailers must be vulnerable to the same logic.

A successful bid by Airtours would have left 80 percent of the market under the control of the three companies, according to the commission's analysis.

'It looks very much as if the commission is trying to roll back the barriers of collective dominance,' said the diplomat. 'What will be next? Four players with 80 percent? Two players with 70 percent?'

Mr Monti, holding his first press conference as competition commissioner, hinted that this was indeed a landmark case.

'It is not unlikely that we face more and more such cases,' he said. 'In a number of sectors firm regulatory action by national governments and the Commission to maintain and promote competition has undermined the basis for pure monopoly . . . we have to ensure that

SHARE PRICES
Relative to FTSE All-Share index since initial bid approach to First Choice

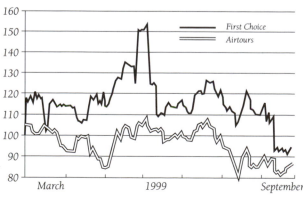

UK PACKAGE HOLIDAY MARKET SHARE
1998

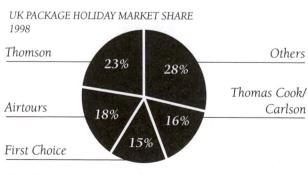

Air-inclusive tours
Sources: Primack Datastream; CAA/Atol

other forms of market dominance which are maybe less obvious but just as disruptive do not emerge.'

While competition experts recognise the dangers of collective dominance, many believe the Commission is treading uncertain terrain.

'In proving collective dominance the Commission cannot look at past known facts but has to evaluate what might happen in certain circumstances in the future,' says Dan Goyder, visting professor in law at King's College, London. 'It is not saying that the companies will collude, but that they will probably not compete fully because it is not in their interests to do so until one or other of them decides to break the mould.'

For Mr Goyder, there is no question but that the Commission is trying to build up a record on collective dominance: 'It is very keen to have the precedent.'

The trend reflects changes in market structures, increasingly characterised by two to four groups that have a high market share and which are therefore able, without colluding illegally, to act in parallel.

But even if the commission is right to pursue collective dominance as a fertile new field for competition policy, was Airtours/First Choice the right case?

'The joint dominance theory is fine, but they have taken a very poor market in which to apply it,' said Simon Holmes, a lawyer at SJ Berwin. 'Experience suggests that the UK travel market is highly competitive.

The Commission recognises that yesterday's case was contoversial, and has promised to hold a discussion on the issue of collective dominance. The case also sets another procedural precedent – that companies must respect the deadlines by which remedies to a deal have to be offered during a merger investigation,

Since Kirch and Bertelsmann dropped new concessions on the Commission's desk on the very day it was due to block their merger, Brussels has toughened its stance. It spelled out then that companies had to offer concessions within three months of the four-month merger investigation. Mr Monti said the last offers from airtours had not come in time to be taken into consideration. Even if they had, they were unlikely to have been accepted he added.

1 Which market structure best describes the UK package holiday market? With the aid of the data explain your answer. (10 marks)
2 Analyse the view that although the UK package holiday market is competitive it has significant barriers to entry. (20 marks)
3 'Sectors such as brewing, retailing, and banking are dominated by a small number of large firms.' Discuss whether the UK and EU competition authorities should prevent mergers between such large firms. (20 marks)

Imperfect competition

Key concepts covered

- monopolistic competition
- product differentiation
- oligopoly
- interdependence
- sunk costs
- game theory
- maximin strategy
- maximax strategy
- dominant strategy game
- kinked demand curves
- collusion

Introduction

Unit 1 was devoted to the development of two theoretical models of widely contrasting market conditions, perfect competition and monopoly. It is hard to find industries and firms to which it is possible to apply the assumptions that underpin each model. However, it is taken for granted that some businesses do have considerable market power and are price makers, while others compete vigorously in order to survive. Common sense tells us that most markets lie between these two extremes. This view is supported by the many economists who have sought to develop theories which are modelled more accurately on the characteristics of businesses operating in the 'real' world.

This unit is devoted to theories which provide closer models of typical business behaviour. These are examples of imperfect competition – a term used to describe market structures which lie between the theoretical extremes of perfect competition and monopoly. Two further models of behaviour are considered:

- monopolistic competition, which is said to apply in markets where there is a relatively large number of firms each producing similar products
- oligopoly, in which a relatively small number of firms produce similar products.

Monopolistic competition

The model of monopolistic competition was developed in the 1930s by US economist Edward

Chamberlain, and his theorising can be seen as an attempt to marry different elements of perfect competition and monopoly. The following underpinning assumptions are made:

1 There will be freedom of entry and exit – as with perfect competition, it is assumed that there are no barriers preventing firms from joining or leaving the industry in question.

2 Both producers and customers will have perfect knowledge.

3 Firms will make independent decisions, i.e. individual firms decide about sales levels, product design and the like without reference to the behaviour of potential competitors. In this respect, firms are expected to behave in a similar way to perfectly competitive firms.

4 Each firm operating under conditions of monopolistic competition will seek to make its product or service different to that of its competitors, i.e. product differentiation. Such differences might be in packaging or branding, but could also include more fundamental differences in design or construction. This characteristic has more in common with monopoly than it does with perfect competition.

Equilibrium under conditions of monopolistic competition

The third assumption above means that the demand curve facing the monopolistically competitive firm will slope downwards to the right (like monopoly). This means that the marginal revenue curve will also slope downwards to the right (also like monopoly). In other words, a firm operating in these conditions is to some degree a price maker rather than a price taker. Both these features are illustrated in Figure 2.1.

If market conditions are like those illustrated in Figure 2.1 there will be a range of profitable outputs between q and s, and prices between M and T, between which average costs would exceed average revenue. A profit-maximising firm would choose to produce at R, where MC = MR, and abnormal profits equivalent to the area abcd would exist.

Long run equilibrium of the firm under conditions of monopolistic competition

The situation in the long run will be determined by the application of the first two assumptions made in building up this model. Other firms will realise that

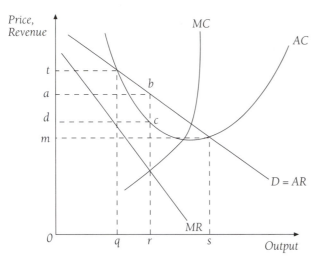

Figure 2.1 Short run equilibrium of a monopolistically competitive firm

abnormal profits can be made by copying the behaviour of the firm managing to produce with AR>AC. They too will increase production or be attracted into the industry, leading to a long-term increase in supply which will result in a decrease in the price. Prices will fall and the short run abnormal profits will be eroded away until a situation occurs as depicted in Figure 2.2.

Monopolistically competitive firms

If firms in an industry satisfy the assumptions of this model, then the following is likely:

■ Supernormal profits can only be earned in the short run.

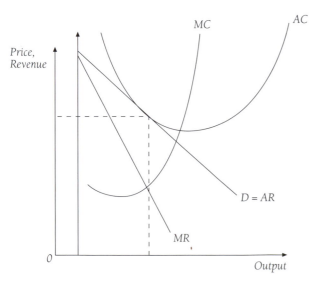

Figure 2.2 Long run equilibrium of monopolistically competitive firm

■ There is a constant incentive for firms to innovate and differentiate their product from that of competitors. This could include the use of advertising and branding.

■ In the long run firms will not be maximising their efficiency as they will not be producing at the lowest point on their average cost curve. In fact, output will be lower and a monopolistically competitive firm will have spare or excess capacity.

■ If firms are to survive in the long run they are obliged to maximise profits.

ACTIVITY 1

a   Which of the following industries comes closest to satisfying the assumption of monopolistic competition?
   i   PC manufacture
   ii   Low-cost airlines
   iii Pubs selling food
b   How useful is the model of monopolistic competition in understanding the behaviour of businesses in the real world?

Oligopoly

Oligopoly literally means competition among the few, and there are two principal assumptions which underpin this model, as they are:

1   The existence of barriers of entry to and from the industry. These will vary from industry to industry but their existence makes oligopoly more similar to monopoly than to monopolistic competition.

2   The **interdependence** of decision-making. The assumption is unique to this model and means that individual firms make decisions about prices, marketing, product design, etc. with reference to how they perceive their competitors will respond. Each firm is affected by the actions of others.

Barriers to entry

The first assumption has especial importance in understanding the likely behaviour of oligopolists. In theory a monopolist's market dominance is secure. Barriers to the entry of other firms are absolute. Perfectly and monopolistically competitive firms can, in theory, try to maintain short run barriers but in the long run the assumption of perfect knowledge should ensure that any form of product differentiation could be copied. Oligopolists, on the other hand, are protected by barriers and are likely constantly to erect new barriers in order to maintain long-term market share and profits. Barriers to entry and exit are likely to include the following:

- capital costs, especially in capital and technology intensive industries, for example Sony Music

- high levels of **sunk costs**, i.e. those fixed costs attributable to capital equipment which cannot be transferred to other uses, for example the Channel Tunnel

- national and global branding, for example Nike, Adidas and other leisurewear firms have spent billions on promoting a global image which would be both costly and difficult for a newcomer to match

- patent and copyright, especially important in pharmaceuticals, for example Glaxo Wellcome

- technological expertise, especially when backed up by large research and development expenditures, for example Nokia

- takeover – dominant firms often respond to the threat of new entrants by taking them over, for example Microsoft.

Interdependence

The second assumption is very significant because it makes it much more difficult for economists to model the behaviour of an oligopolistic firm. The behaviour of one firm will depend upon its perceptions of how other firms will react to changes. The responses of other firms will depend upon their perceptions of the responses of others. It is harder, therefore, to predict how oligopolistic firms are likely to behave. Economics have developed further limiting assumptions about the objectives of oligopolists to make their work easier. They include:

- competition, i.e. that oligopolistic firms will wish to compete with their rivals to gain greater market share

- collusion, which refers to firms coming together to avoid the risks associated with competition. Colluding firms may seek to set common prices or levels of output for each.

Competitive oligopolists

As indicated above, predicting the outcomes of decision making by oligopolists is difficult. For example, Volkswagen needs to decide on the recommended selling price for its new Polo. It is currently selling a basic version of the Polo for £7999, but some competitors like the Nissan Micra are available more cheaply while others like the Vauxhall Corsa are more expensive. There are fears in the automobile industry that car prices are likely to fall. What should Volkswagen do? If it cuts its price and competitors follow suit, it will end up with the same market share. If it cuts its price and competitors fail to respond, its market share may increase. What if Vauxhall or Nissan make larger price cuts? One approach used by economists to try to make sense of such competitive behaviour is by use of game theory, first developed by psychologists when trying to predict human responses in a similarly unpredictable situation. At a simple level this can be restricted to looking at the behaviour of one firm and the possible responses of another. Figure 2.3 illustrates a **game theory** matrix.

To start with, assume that the market for small cars is shared equally between Volkswagen and Nissan. They charge the same price of £7999 for cars with similar specifications, and they both equally share the total 'industry' profit of £200 million. This is depicted in box A of the matrix. The outcomes of Volkswagen cutting £1000 from its recommended price will depend upon the responses of Nissan. If Nissan keeps its original price, Volkswagen will gain a bigger market share and a larger proportion of the industry profit. This is illustrated in box B. Alternatively, Nissan could copy Volkswagen, leaving both with an equal market share but reduced profits because of the price cut. This is shown in box D. A fourth alternative is that Volkswagen maintains its price at £7999 but Nissan cut its price to, say, £6999. In this case both Volkswagen's market share and profits will be cut as shown in box C.

This approach to the analysis of the behaviour of oligopolists yields an important prediction. For Volkswagen option B would give the best possible return

	Micra	
	£7999	£6999
Polo £7999	A Each shares market earning £200m profit	C Nissan takes larger market share + £300m profit
Polo £6999	B VW captures larger market share + £350m profit	D Equal market shares, each with profit of £100m

Figure 2.3 Game theory matrix

but is also the most risky. It depends on Nissan ignoring an aggressive price cut. Option C is the worst outcome, while D and A are the least risky. Logic dictates that Volkswagen ought to collude with Nissan.

The essence of game theory is that there is a range of possible outcomes in response to market changes or changes in the behaviour of firms. Game theory focuses on alternative strategies which firms may pursue. Cautious firms will elect for a strategy which is least risky. This is called a **maximin strategy**, whereas an approach which involves taking greater risks to gain higher levels of profit is called a **maximax strategy**. If both approaches lead to the same outcome firms are said to be playing a **dominant strategy game**.

ACTIVITY 2

Construct a matrix to predict possible outcomes of interdependent decision-making in an industry of your choice.

Kinked demand curves

An alternative theoretical treatment of the behaviour of oligopolists is that associated with another US economist, Paul Sweezy. He observed that even if oligopolists were in competition with each other, prices in such markets tended to be stable. He used a simplified form of game theory by reasoning that as pricing decisions by oligopolists were interdependent, an individual firm would be very reluctant to raise its prices as it would fear that none of its competitors would follow suit. On the other hand, he argued that an individual firm would be reluctant to cut its prices as this decision would be copied by competitors. In other words, the oligopolist would be faced with an elastic demand curve in terms of price rises and an inelastic curve for price cuts – a **kinked demand curve**. This is illustrated in Figure 2.4.

This theory has been attacked by a number of economists as lacking in any empirical evidence.

Collusive oligopolists

Game theory can be used to demonstrate that it is in the interests of oligopolistic firms to collude, i.e. form agreements to reduce the risks attached to competition, especially price competition. **Collusion** can take the following three forms:

- Open, when firms make a formal collective agreement. This is called a cartel and will usually bind its signatories to agreed price levels and/or production quotas. Cartels, with some

exceptions, are illegal in the UK and in most other western countries.

- Informal, by which firms find ways of evading legal restrictions in order to maintain common prices. It is thought that informal agreements are common in the UK, especially in the markets for electrical goods, cars and perfumery but, as this form of activity might be the target of government investigation and intervention, it is hard to find evidence of secret agreements.

- Tacit behaviour by which individual oligopolists arrive at common policies without formal or informal agreements. Some industries are dominated by a particular firm and others will follow its pricing decisions. In the UK ESSO is seen as the leader in terms of petrol prices, Kellogg's for breakfast cereals and Nike for trainers. Common prices and other apparent collusion can arise when firms in industries follow common pricing formulas and pay similar amounts for factor inputs. Most pubs mark up the price of beers and lager by 100 per cent, local stores add 40 per cent to the cost price of confectionary and similar products, while restaurants add 500 per cent to the cost of ingredients to price their menus. This can lead to competitive firms charging similar prices for the same meals.

Collusion, though attractive to oligopolists as a means of reducing risks and safeguarding profits, has particular dangers. Stable relationships between firms can be upset by:

- the development of new technologies, for example in printing and publishing

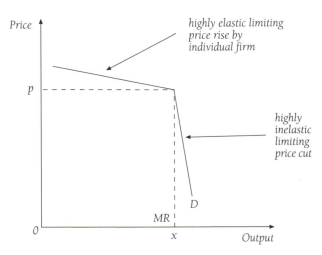

Figure 2.4 Kinked demand curve

changes in ownership – most oligopolists are plcs and takeovers and mergers can rapidly lead to changes in objectives, for example gaining greater market share at the expense of competitors

the temptation of firms which collude to break ranks and establish competitive advantage by cutting prices or raising output.

The behaviour of oligopolists

Analysing the behaviour of oligopolists is far more complex than for firms operating in other market structures. Graphical analysis is less helpful as outcomes in terms of pricing, output and profits are less predictable. Particular industries may be characterised by high levels of competition while in others tacit agreements result in high levels of price stability and little or no competition. Some industries may alternate between periods of intense competition and periods of stability and collusion. However, a number of generalisations can be made about the behaviour of oligopolists:

There will be strong incentives to collude.

Price competition will generally be avoided as non-price competition in terms of advertising and customer service is less risky.

Agreements, whether overt or tacit, can easily be broken, leading to price wars and market instability.

Oligopolistic firms will tend to maintain and strengthen barriers to entry to their industry.

ACTIVITY 3

a Which of the following industries comes closest to satisfying the assumptions of oligopolistic competition?
  i   Brewing
  ii   Airlines
  iii Electricity generation
b How useful is the model of oligopoly in understanding the behaviour of businesses in the real world?
c What evidence would you search for to try to establish the validity of the following models to analyse the behaviour of large firms?
  i   Monopolistic competition
  ii   Game theory
  iii Kinked demand curves

Summary

This unit has been devoted to examination of two further forms of market structure, monopolistic

competition and oligopoly. Both provide models which conform more closely to the behaviour of businesses in the UK and other western countries. It is more difficult to model and predict the behaviour of oligopolists but economic theory indicates that they may have both the power and incentive to collude to safeguard market share and profits. They are also able to maintain barriers of entry and exit which are difficult to break down. Whether the behaviour of oligopolists is in the public interest or not is an issue which is of major concern to both economists and governments, and this is explored in more detail in the following units.

Data response question

Henderson's Travel Ltd is a small tour operator situated in a prosperous suburb of Manchester. The business organises package tours to a variety of European, North American and African holiday destinations. The directors of the company estimate there are approximately 75 businesses in the North West of England offering a similar service.

Most of its customers live within a 25-mile distance of Manchester, and 75% of its customers have used the business more than once. In the past few months Henderson's Travel has attracted new customers from other parts of the North West area, suggesting that a recent newspaper advertising campaign has been successful.

The directors of the business place considerable emphasis on long-term profitability, and to achieve this aim they have identified three main strategies:

i   to continue to improve its customer service in order to build up its reputation and encourage repeat business
ii to expand its share of the independent tour operators' market through advertising
iii to develop its tour operations into more profitable markets.

A market research company has recently published estimates about UK consumers' demand for holidays in certain countries. A summary of the main findings is given below.

Table 1

Holiday destination	Price elasticity of demand	Income elasticity of demand
Spain	−1.8	−0.1
USA	−1.2	1.3
South Africa	−0.5	2.0

The directors of Henderson's Travel have studied these findings but feel that further research is required before they decide on the future policies of the company.

1 a Describe the characteristics of monopolistic competition. (5 marks)
   b To what extent does Henderson's Travel appear to be operating in a monopolistically competitive market? (5 marks)
2 With reference to Table 1:
   a Explain the difference between normal and inferior goods. (4 marks)
   b Explain how an increase in consumers' income might affect the demand for each of the holiday destinations. (4 marks)
   c Advise the directors of Henderson's Travel on what further research might need to be carried out before they decide on the future stategy of the company. (6 marks)
3 Using the information from the case study comment on the pricing policies that the directors of Henderson's Travel could adopt to increase the **revenue** of the business. (6 marks)
4 Discuss, with the aid of appropriate diagrams, what affect an increase in advertising expenditure might have on the **profits** of the business:
   a in the short run (10 marks)
   b in the long run. (10 marks)

UNIT 3 Assessing market power

Key concepts covered

- internal growth
- external growth
- merger
- demergers
- concentration ratios
- contestable markets
- takeover
- price discrimination
- consumer surplus
- producer surplus

Introduction

Economic theory demonstrates that firms which are monopolies or oligopolies have considerable market power to set prices, determine customer choice, limit competition and prevent new market entrants. These firms are also often very large, commanding turnovers greater than most countries in the world, and able to use their economic power to influence the behaviour of governments. Economists differ in their assessments of the impact of such large firms but have developed further theories and techniques to help measure market power and advise governments of possible intervention strategies. This unit is devoted to examining:

- why and how firms grow to gain market power
- the measurement of competition
- price discrimination
- consumer and producer surplus.

The growth of firms

Firms can get bigger in two different ways. They can grow by:

- internal expansion
- external growth.

Internal expansion

Firms grow in size by increasing total sales or turnover. This can be achieved by out competing rivals and gaining greater market share or by being part of an expanding market. Both approaches require development of greater productive capacity. These growth strategies can to some degree become self-financing as retained profits can be used to provide the finance for expansion. **Internal growth** can lead to economies of scale and lower long-term costs of production which can provide greater competitive advantage and therefore help further growth.

Firms that successfully pursue such policies will also usually find it easier to raise additional funds, either from banks or from the stock market. Most oligopolistic firms are plcs but this also makes expanding companies liable to take over, especially if they are competing in the same market as larger better-resourced firms.

Merger and takeover

Firms can also grow in size and economic power by **merger**, when two businesses agree to collaborate to form one, i.e. **external growth**. More commonly one business takes over another, either by outright purchase or by the accumulation of a controlling interest of shares. Both external forms of growth are usually referred to as mergers. These take three forms:

- *vertical*, by which one firm merges with another involved in different stages of the production chain, for example electricity supply companies buying into electricity generation
- *horizontal*, when mergers take place between companies at the same stage of the production chain, for example Wal-Mart and Asda
- *conglomerate*, where firms from different industries merge, for example Lloyds TSB's takeover of the Cheltenham and Gloucester Building Society.

Merger activity provides a rapid means of building up market share, helps protect firms from competition, and helps ensure greater control over the productive process but, as will be outlined in the next section, can reduce customer choice and increase monopoly power. Merger activity tends to be greatest towards the peak of the economic cycle. Successful companies generate profits which can be used to part finance further acquisitions.

Demergers

Contrary to the developments outlined above, there has been an increase in **demergers** over the past decade. Increasing competition and globalisation can leave large conglomerates at a disadvantage compared with firms more clearly focused on a particular economic activity. Improvements in technology, especially information and computer technology (ICT), the further development of subcontracting, multiskilling of workers and the development of flatter, more customer-focused organisations are combining to reduce the cost advantages enjoyed by conglomerates. The fashion in business is increasingly to 'concentrate' on core activities. Selling off non-core activities is another way of financing further growth and development focused on particular activities. An example of this process is the restructuring of GEC, its defence-related business was sold off to British Aerospace, and the company has been renamed Marconi to concentrate on the growth of the ICT sector.

Measuring competition

Economists use a number of techniques in order to measure the amount of competition which exists in different industries. These include:

- the use of **concentration ratios**
- assessing the **contestability of markets**.

Concentration ratios

The calculation of concentration ratios involves the calculation of the share of output of the leading firms in a given market. Thus, a three-firm concentration ratio would involve adding together the market shares of the three largest firms. The government uses a five-firm ratio to produce a measure of competitiveness in key economic sectors. The results are shown in Table 3.1.

Table 3.1 Five-firm concentration ratio by industrial sector

Industrial sector	Five-firm concentration ratio (%)
Tobacco	99.5
Iron and steel	95.3
Motor vehicles	82.9
Cement	77.7
Water supply	49.7
Footwear	48.2
Bread and biscuits	47.0
Carpets	21.8
Clothing	20.7
Plastics processing	8.8

Examination of the ratios in Table 3.1 reveals the possible existence of two interrelated influences determining levels of competitiveness:

- differing levels of economies of scale, for example iron and steel and cement

- differing extent of barriers of entry, for example clothing and water supply.

However, national ratios such as these do not indicate the level of global competitiveness, for example motor vehicle manufacture, nor do they account for the existence of local monopolies, for example water supply.

Contestable market theory

This is an alternative approach based more on the adaptation of traditional theory to assess the degree of competition which may occur within an industry. The theory of contestable markets is based on the premise that firms will operate competitively if they fear competition in some way. There are a number of variants of this theory but generally it is argued that a monopolist will behave like a competitive firm if:

- there is a fear of **takeover**
- barriers to entry and exit are minimised.

No plc is free from the fear of takeover, and senior managers of such firms have to compete with other businesses on the stock market. Rising share prices are associated with business success and will be fed by stock market perceptions of potential profits, levels of customer service, responsiveness to changes in demand, etc. Monopolistic and oligopolistic firms which fail to pursue those and other objectives associated with competitive behaviour will, the theorists argue, be punished by the stock market and share prices will fall, making such firms more liable to takeover. It could be argued that this describes the current (early 2000) position of Marks & Spencer.

A market is said to be perfectly contestable if barriers to entry and exist are zero. This assumption resembles that of monopolistic competition. Other firms would be attracted to those industries in which supernormal profits exist in the short run. In order to prevent increased competition, firms operating in a contestable market will keep prices down, and ensure that profits are kept to normal levels. Exit barriers need also to be minimised. If sunk costs are significant firms already in an industry will be deterred from leaving as they cannot transfer such resources to other uses. Moreover, new entrants will be deterred if they were unable to transfer capital elsewhere.

The significance of contestable market theory for policy makers is considered in the following unit.

Price discrimination

Another means of assessing the degree of power which any firm has in the market place is to establish the degree to which it is able to charge different customers different prices for the same product or service. This is called **price discrimination** and is an aspect of market power used by firms to boost revenue and profits. Most of us are used to being charged a range of different prices for particular goods or services. Airfares are a good example as customers flying from London to New York can pay anywhere between £200 and £1000 for the same seat in the same aircraft. In order to benefit from price discrimination, airlines need to ensure that the following conditions are fulfilled:

- The firm must have some degree of market power and be a price maker.
- Demand for the good or service will be spread between different customers, each with differing price elasticities of demand for the product or service.
- These different market segments have to be separated from each other.
- The proportion of fixed to total costs is likely to be high.

Market power

Only those firms which are facing a downward sloping overall demand curve for their product or service will be able to charge different prices to different customers. The more monopoly power a firm enjoys, the more it can price discriminate. On the other hand, those firms who are closer to being perfectly competitive will have only a limited opportunity to charge different prices to different customers. Clearly, there are only a limited number of airlines flying between London and New York and those that offer the most flights will be able to set prices rather than having to accept the 'market' price.

Differing price elasticities of demand

A discriminating monopolist will wish to charge higher prices to some of its customers and will be prepared to sell the same product or service to others at a lower price, as long as this boosts overall revenue. Airlines exploit this by charging those who have to fly at particular times and those whose airfare is likely to be part of an expense account much higher fares. Other market segments such as young people travelling around the world are likely to be much more price sensitive and will only be attracted by lower fares. Another important segment for some airlines is the holiday market. Holiday companies may make block bookings of seats but will expect significant discounts. Finally, seats which are hard to sell can be sold through 'bucket shops' and those travel agencies dealing in last-minute bookings.

Separation of markets

Elaborate strategies such as those outlined above will only work if it is impossible for one set of airline customers to sell on its cheaper tickets to passengers who would otherwise be prepared to pay higher fares. This is relatively easy for the airlines as tickets are usable only by a named person. Other price discriminators use time to separate markets. Train tickets bought at different times of the day cost different amounts and can be used only on specified trains.

Relatively high fixed costs

The bulk of the costs of flying from London to New York are fuel, maintenance and debt repayment. Once committed to the flight the airline has low levels of variable costs. Put another way, marginal costs of carrying additional passengers are low. It costs very little more to carry 350 passengers than it does to carry 349. Hence, the airline will add to its profits once it has covered the costs of extra meals, ticketing and costs associated with the 350th passenger.

If variable costs are relatively more significant, marginal costs will be higher and a profit-seeking company would be more limited in its opportunities to discount.

Consumer and producer surpluses

Another way in which economists attempt to assess the impact of non-competitive behaviour by firms is by the use of two concepts:

■ **consumer surplus**

■ **producer surplus**.

Consumer surplus

This concept uses graphical analysis to illustrate the benefits that customers gain from consuming a particular product or service. Figure 3.1 illustrates consumer surplus and p represents an equilibrium price with the level of sales at s.

The last customer is prepared to pay the market price for the product but all earlier customers would have been prepared to pay more. For instance, r customers would have been prepared to pay more at q, and t customers would have been prepared to pay still more. The vertical distances indicate how much more some customers would have been prepared to pay. Taken together the shaded area represents an additional benefit enjoyed by consumers of this product. This is referred to as consumer surplus.

Producer surplus

A similar analytical approach can be made to gains made by producers of a good or service. In Figure 3.2

producers receive a for their total output of x, but producers would have been prepared to supply anything less than x for less.

J producers were prepared to supply for b, whereas k producers were prepared to accept even less at c. The shaded area, therefore, represents producers' surplus.

This concept is applied to understanding the impact of monopoly power. Figure 3.3 illustrates that a profit-maximising oligopolist or monopolist will produce at q and charge p for its output, whereas a perfectly competitive industry facing the same cost structure will produce at 0r and charge q for its output. Consumer surplus under monopolistic conditions will be the equivalent of area a, but under perfect competition it would be larger and equal to a + b + c. Producer surplus, on the other hand, has is

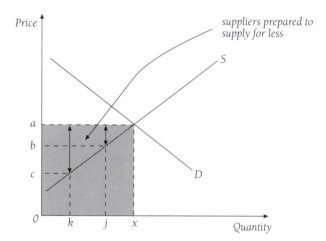

Figure 3.2 Producer surplus

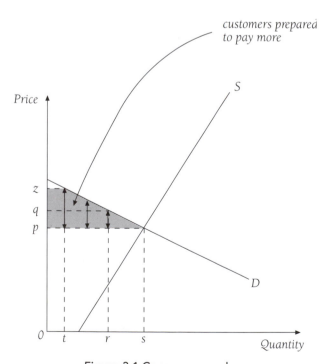

Figure 3.1 Consumer surplus

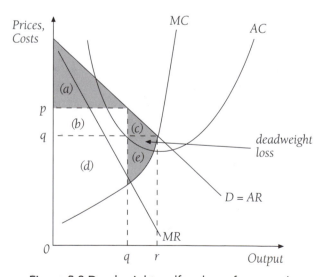

Figure 3.3 Deadweight welfare loss of monopoly

bigger under monopoly consisting of d + b compared with a perfectly competitive producer surplus of d + e. In other words, this graphical analysis shows that producers gain while consumers lose. Overall c + e represents losses under monopoly of both producer and consumer surpluses. This area is known as deadweight welfare loss of monopoly.

ACTIVITY 3

How might consumer and producer surplus be affected by the following?
a Reduction of barriers of entry in an industry
b The establishment of a cartel in an industry

Summary

This unit has been devoted to an explanation of some of the techniques, which economists use to measure the extent and possible effects of the exercise of monopoly power. The tendency of firms to gain greater monopoly power through internal and external growth has been described. Concentration ratios were explained as a crude means of assessing the possible extent of monopoly power, and the ability of firms to charge different prices to different sections of their markets was also considered as a way of assessing monopoly power. Finally, graphical analysis has been used to indicate the possible harmful affects of monopoly power.

Data response question

Extract A

The United Kingdom car market
'There are around 40 vehicle manufacturers and importers operating in the UK. Around two million new cars are sold per year, mainly through a network of around 7000 authorised dealers. Car manufacturers enter into 'selective and exclusive' distribution agreements with their dealers. These allow the manufacturers to set standards which dealers must meet in return for an exclusive territory within which to operate.

In February 1998, the European Commission (EC) reported that the UK was the most expensive market for 61 of the 72 best-selling models in the European Union. The current price differentials between the UK and other EU countries are far beyond those regarded by the EC as acceptable. We believe that price discrimination might be resposible for some of these differences.

Price discrimination is possible because 'parallel importing', which occurs when consumers buy cars from dealers in other EU countries rather than from a manufacturer's authorised UK dealer, is more difficult in the UK than in most other EU countries. This is partly because of the difficulties consumers face in importing cars due to the right-hand drive specification. UK consumers are also discouraged from buying their cars from other EU countries by the obvious practical inconvenience, primarily distance as they cannot drive over a border to take advantage of lower prices as some other European consumers can. Also, a recent ruling of the European Court of Justice limits 'grey imports' into the UK. 'Grey imports' include cars which are brought into the country through channels not approved by the manufacturers.

UK car buyers who wish to 'parallel import' may find that a request for a right-hand drive car from a continental dealer causes delay and difficulties. In February 1998, the EC stated that it was "*receiving continual complaints from British consumers who wished to purchase right-hand drive vehicles in the cheaper markets*". It went on to remind manufacturers that they must supply right-hand drive cars to any EU dealer wishing to sell them. Recently, VW was fined £67 million in January 1998 by the European Commission for forcing its dealers in Italy to refuse to sell cars to foreign buyers. Circumstantial evidence at least would indicate that this is not a practice peculiar to VW.

The car manufacturers deny that price discrimination occurs and argue that other factors are responsible for price differences. These factors include exchange rates, tax rates, delivery costs, and the fact that a car sold in the UK is different from a car sold on the continent. The UK is unusual in two further respects. Firstly, the company car or fleet car market represents over 70% of new car sales. Manufacturers charge much higher prices and make much larger profits on cars sold to private motorists than they do on fleet cars sold to companies. Secondly, the UK has the biggest used car market in Europe, in part because of the size of the UK fleet sector. Lower list prices for new cars in the UK would have an adverse effect on the used car market. Manufacturers are keen to keep high prices for new cars to protect second-hand values since high second-hand values improve the attractions of the car for consumers. Part of the new-car pricing policy involves 'protecting' second-hand car prices.

Adapted from the 1st Report on Vehicle Pricing of the House of Commons Select Committee on Trade and Industry, November 1998

Extract B

UK New Car Registrations 1997

% Share		% Share	
Ford group (Ford, Jaguar)	18.7	Renault	7.3
General Motors (Vauxhall, Opel, Saab)	14.3	Nissan	4.4
BMW group (BMW, Rover)	12.9	Fiat Group (Fiat, Alfa Romeo)	4.3
Peugeot group (Peugeot, Citroen)	11.4	Toyota	3.3
Volkswagen group (VW, Audi, Seat, Skoda)	8.7	Others	14.7
		Total Market	**100.00**

Extract C

EU Car Price Differences

Price disparities in ECUs at 1 May 1998

Small Segment		Medium Segment		Large Segment	
	%		%		%
Opel Corsa	24.0	VW Golf	43.5	BMW 318i	12.0
Ford Fiesta	44.7	Opel Astra	26.0	Audi A4	13.0
Renault Clio	33.8	Ford Escort/ Orion	33.8	Ford Mondeo	58.5
Peugeot 206	21.1	Renault Megane	27.9	Opel Vectra	18.2
VW Polo	36.7	Peugeot 306	46.2	VW Passat	36.4

Source: *Financial Times*, 12 November, 1998

1 a Making use of Extracts A and B, describe the market structure of the car industry in the United Kingdom. (4 marks)

b Using Extract A, identify two entry barriers and briefly explain how they affect the structure and competitiveness of the UK car market. (6 marks)

2 a Explain how price discrimination might be resposible for some of the differences in car prices between the UK and other EU countries. (10 marks)

b Discuss whether price discrimination provides an adequate explanation of the different prices charged in the UK car market compared with other EU countries. (30 marks)

Public policy

Key concepts covered

■ public interest
■ restrictive trade practices
■ privatisation
■ natural monopolies
■ X inefficiencies
■ regulators

Introduction

AS Section 4 was devoted to examining how markets might be considered to fail and what remedies might be open to governments. The preceding units in this section contained a more detailed theoretical treatment of the significance of market structures. This analysis tends to indicate that, subject to crucial assumptions, customers and societies will be better off if markets are competitive rather than monopolistic. However, there is growing evidence that concentration ratios in key industries tend to be increasing and that many firms develop strategies to avoid competitive pressures. This divergence between what might be seen as socially desirable and the actual behaviour of an increasing number of larger firms provides a challenge both to economists and to governments. This unit explores how governments, especially those in the West, have attempted to promote competition and limit the adverse effects of firms able to exercise monopoly power.

The case against monopolies is summarised in the first part of the unit. This is followed by a discussion of anti-monopoly policies, those to promote competition, and a review of policies towards public ownership and privatisation.

The case against monopoly

Economic theorists have argued that monopoly power can result in:

■ higher prices
■ lower outputs
■ less customer choice
■ fewer innovations
■ less efficient production both allocatively and productively.

On the other hand, it can be argued that firms with large market shares:

■ are able to exploit economies of scale
■ can compete more effectively in the global market place
■ have the resources to devote to research and development
■ can be socially responsible.

The economic arguments against monopolistic power are not conclusive and they provide a particular challenge to governments in developing policies which guard against the potential excesses of monopolistic power while trying to ensure that possible benefits are not lost.

UK government policies towards monopolies

The UK government has not always been suspicious of the motives and behaviour of firms perceived to have monopoly power. In the 1930s the government promoted development of larger and more powerful companies as it was considered that they would provide a more secure business environment. However, since the passing of the Monopolies and Restrictive Practices Act in 1948, successive governments have looked more critically at the activities of large firms. The Act which has been amended, and strengthened by the addition of further powers, has provided the basis of government control which continues today. The Secretary of State for Trade and Industry is advised by the Office of Fair Trading. In particular, the Office of Fair Trading recommends cases of possible abuse of monopoly power which should be investigated more fully. This function is carried out by the Competition Commission (formally known as the Monopolies and Mergers Commission). The Commission is a quasi-legal body which hears evidence prior to coming to a judgement about suspected abuses of monopoly power. Its findings are reported to the Secretary of State, who is then responsible for taking or not taking action. The Secretary of State, therefore, has the final say.

The law defines a monopoly as being any firm which has a 25 per cent or more share in a local or national market, or two or more firms supplying 25 per cent of the total market if it is suspected that they are colluding informally. The 1980 Competition Act identified various types of uncompetitive behaviour which included the following:

- price discrimination
- selective distribution, by which a firm may refuse to supply particular companies
- predatory pricing, when firms deliberately cut prices below costs in an attempt to force competitors from a market.

The job of the Competition Commission is to establish whether or not uncompetitive behaviour is taking place and to balance this against possible benefits in order to make a judgement as to whether or not the firm in question is acting in the **public interest**. The Commission, and its predecessor, has investigated many different possible instances of the abuse of monopoly power. These include the control of public houses by major breweries, high profit levels earned by the major supermarkets, selective distribution by Birds Eye Wall's, and retail-only agreements by Rank Xerox. Various recommendations have been made which have included:

- price cuts
- reduced expenditure on advertising
- reducing barriers of entry.

Control over mergers

In 1965 Parliament enacted legislation which strengthened government controls over the potential abuse of monopoly power by compelling companies to give notice to the Office of Fair Trading of any proposed merger which would result in the creation of a monopoly as defined by the legislation. The Office of Fair Trading can recommend to the Secretary of State that conditions may be attached to giving permission for the merger to take place or reference can be made to the Competition Commission to investigate the likely outcomes of the merger in terms of the framework developed for investigating the abuses of monopoly power. The Commission, having considered evidence, recommends to the Secretary of State whether or not the merger should proceed.

In practice, only a tiny minority of mergers have been referred to the Commission. Practically all of these proposals have been rejected by the Secretary of State or abandoned by the companies in question. This apparent contradiction may indicate that government policies towards mergers have lacked consistency. It is not clear on what basis referrals are made to the Secretary of State and analysis of the outcomes indicates that mergers tend not to be in the public interest.

The Labour government in November 1999 published a green paper on reforms to its policies towards mergers. It proposes to give greater powers and independence to the Office of Fair Trading. Its Director would be empowered to decide which mergers be investigated by the Competition Commission and it is also suggested that the Director-General of the Office of Fair Trading should take responsibility from the Minister in making the final decision as to whether or not a proposed merger should take place.

Control over monopolistic and oligopolistic abuses

The legal framework used to curb the abuse powers of monopolists and oligopolists is tougher than that relating to their existence and creation. **Restrictive trade practices** is the legal terminology used to describe various forms of collusion. All such agreements have to be registered with the Office of Fair Trading and they are banned unless the participants can prove that they are in the public interest. The law recognises that collusion can bring benefits such as:

- protecting employment
- promoting exports
- ensuring safety standards are met.

But even if it is possible to prove the existence of such benefits before the Restrictive Practices Court, firms still have to demonstrate that possible benefits outweigh any harmful effects.

Similarly, a tough stance is taken towards limiting the power of manufacturers to set and enforce minimum retail prices for their products. Over the years formal price fixing agreements have been ended, and only currently exist for some medical products.

European Union competition policy

The development of the single European market has meant that member states have been forced to adopt a common approach to competition policy, especially in respect of those firms which have monopoly power within the European Union (EU). There is no minimum market share which triggers investigation. Firms which behave unfairly towards consumers by their pricing policies or other activities can be referred to the European Court of Justice, and if found 'guilty', they can be fined as well as being debarred from acting uncompetitively.

EU policies towards mergers and collusive behaviour are similar. The focus is on investigation of uncompetitive behaviour rather than market share or such like.

Public ownership and privatisation

The first half of this unit has been concerned with government policies designed to limit the abuses of market power by monopolists and oligopolists. Successive governments have also intervened in order actively to promote competition by trying to create more competitive structures. This has been done in two ways:

- privatising firms and industries, which involves transferring the ownership of resources from the public to the private sector
- creating more competitive structures within the public sector.

Transferring the ownership of resources from the public to the private sector – **privatisation** – is a policy which is associated with Margaret Thatcher and the economic policies followed by Conservative governments in the 1980s. Such policies had been applied earlier and in other countries, but their popularity also coincides with the collapse of command economies as outlined in AS Unit 4 about changes in the Czech Republic.

The growth of the public sector

The first three Labour governments after World War II increased the size of the public sector for a variety of reasons which included:

- social and political objectives
- the provision of merit and public goods
- employment.

Social and political objectives

The depression of the 1930s, followed by the sacrifices and disruption of World War II led to fundamental ways in which western governments used and applied economic policies. Unemployment and the collapse of world trade prior to the war were seen as a failure of the market system and of capitalism. The experience of running a planned or command economy and winning the war provided an alternative model for economic policies. Finally, in 1945 the Labour government won an overwhelming general election victory pledging to create a welfare state, free education for all, the National Health Service (NHS), and to ensure that everyone who wanted could work. These policy objectives were to be achieved through a mix of the public and private sectors. The Labour Party believed that in order to create a fairer and more just society 'a land fit for heroes', the state needed to control the 'governing heights of the economy'. This provided a rationale for state or public ownership of key British industries, including:

- coal
- iron and steel
- railways
- electricity generation and supply
- road haulage
- BOAC and BEA (British airlines – forerunners to British Airways)
- ports
- airports.

These industries could be seen as providing the essential infrastructure to British industry, and it was argued that under private ownership investment had been inadequate. In terms of earlier discussion, these industries had large positive externalities which would not be reflected in the returns earned under private ownership. Consequently, there would be under supply. These arguments were strengthened in the case of electricity generation, gas supply and the railways which were considered to be **natural monopolies**. In other words, massive economies of scale occur when there is only one firm controlling supply. The national electricity grid is a good example of a natural monopoly. There would be little point in producing alternative grids, given the high level of sunk costs. Public ownership, or nationalisation, of these industries allows economies of scale to be realised and also, in theory, ensure that prices and outputs were set in the public interest to benefit society as a whole, rather than in the interest of shareholders whose main objective would be dividends and profits.

The provision of merit and public goods

In addition, such institutions as the BBC, the Bank of England, Thomas Cook and the Royal Mint were publicly owned while, during the late nineteenth and twentieth centuries, local authorities took responsibility for the provision of a wide range of services, including swimming pools, public baths, libraries and the supply of water and gas. These activities could be seen as examples of the provision of both public and merit goods. It can be argued that many people and organisations benefit from the appropriate and efficient supply of notes and coins and having the Royal Mint in the state sector ensures that the public interest rather than private profit is pursued. The British government has also taken responsibility for the provision of a range of activities which can be classed as public goods and which we take for granted: the police, other emergency services, and air traffic control.

Public libraries, like education, are seen as a 'good thing' by which the quality of our lives is enriched and could, therefore, be classified as merit goods and provided 'free' by the state but funded through general taxation.

Employment

Finally, at different times in the 1960s and 1970s, Labour governments nationalised or brought into public ownership industries which were on the verge of collapse. They feared the loss of jobs in key industrial sectors and the multiplier effects of redundancies, especially in regions dependent upon particular industries. These included:

- Rolls Royce
- British shipbuilders
- parts of British Leyland (cars and trucks)
- parts of British Aerospace.

Thus, in the 1960s and 1970s, a range of different types of organisation were publicly owned, for a variety of reasons.

The performance of the public sector

It was, and still is, hard to assess the performance of the public sector. Some elements such as public libraries have always been run as 'public services', others such as British Rail were expected to 'break even', while others such as the NHS were expected to meet any demands. Some like the Coal Board found it difficult to make a profit, whereas British Gas was highly efficient. It is clear, however, that firms operating in the public sector:

- were insulated from market pressures
- suffered varying degrees of political interference.

Market pressures

Managers of firms operating in the private sector have to have a high regard for the profitability of their businesses. Those who ignore 'the bottom line' are unlikely to keep their jobs, and privately owned businesses which consistently make losses will go out of business, be taken over, or reorganised. Those working in the public sector have traditionally been insulated from concerns about profitability. They have been able to take decisions without reference to revenue, costs and profit. In the past schools, hospitals and other public services were run with little control over expenditure. Instead, local authorities and central government provided funding to ensure that each covered its costs. Employees in the public sector considered that their jobs were secure and there was, therefore, less incentive for them to be productive and cost efficient. These factors have been called **X inefficiencies** and could be represented by higher average costs of production which can occur if firms are insulated from competitive or market pressures.

Political interference

Although firms in the public sectors were theoretically given varying degrees of independence from government interference, it was inevitable that politicians had some say in key decisions:

- Major spending decisions had a direct effect on jobs and the popularity of both MPs and the government. Many firms in the public sector found government finance more generous immediately before elections than after.
- Some MPs were more effective than others in lobbying for government support for particular industries, for example major steelworks were built at Newport and Port Talbot.
- Profits from the public sector were taken by the Treasury to boost government revenues.

ACTIVITY 2

Assess the validity of political and economic arguments used in the period 1945–79 to justify public ownership and supply of goods and services.

Changes in the 1980s – the Thatcher factor

Industrial relations, production and the international competitiveness of the UK economy in the late 1970s were seen to be poor. Margaret Thatcher came to power in 1979 with the slogan 'Getting Britain back to work'. She was strongly influenced by 'right-wing' economists who argued that the performance UK economy would improve if:

- monetarist polices were followed
- trade union power was reduced
- government intervention in markets was reduced
- enterprise and market-based strategies were encouraged.

Market-based strategies

The Conservatives favoured market-based strategies in an effort to improve the performance of the UK economy. Two aspects of their policies related to the control and influence of monopolistic and oligopolistic power:

- Privatisation and the transfer of the ownership of some firms from the public to the private sector.
- The introduction of competitive forces with those organisations which remained in the public sector.

Privatisation

Firstly, businesses such as BP, ICL (computers) and British Sugar operating in competitive markets were transferred from public to private ownership. In the mid-1980s, Sealink, Jaguar, British Telecom and British Gas were sold. At the end of the decade and in the early 1990s more complicated sell-offs, such as the water, electricity and rail industries, were undertaken. The Labour government elected in 1997 has indicated that it will continue these Conservative policies by privatising Air Traffic Control, but it has backed away from selling off the Post Office.

In addition to fitting in with the overall policy of promoting the private sector and the expense of the public sector, privatisation created additional government revenue which has been estimated to exceed £60 billion.

The privatisation process

Transferring ownership from the public to the private sector has usually followed the process outlined below:

1 Valuation of assets to be sold off.
2 Publication of prospectus, detailing the form and nature of the share offer, including the determination of number of shares to be issued.
3 Setting an individual share price.
4 Publicising the sell-off.

5 Flotation, i.e. selling shares.

From the government's point of view stage 3 is crucial. If the business is undervalued the government loses potential revenue, but if it is overvalued the actual flotation could fail.

The Conservative governments in the 1980s recognised that the transfer of ownership from the public to the private sectors would not be sufficient to protect the public from the abuse of monopoly power. In order to safeguard the public interest, legislation to permit privatisation also contained provision for the creation of **regulators**. These are independent bodies such as OFTEL (Communication), OFWAT (water) and OFGEM (Gas and Electricity) with powers to regulate the actual behaviour of these industries by imposing pricing formulas, insisting on customer service targets and levels of investment. The most important sanction available to most regulators is over pricing. In many cases the freedom of newly privatised firms to raise prices is limited by formulae. Although its application varies between industries, the regulator's formula can be represented as RPI - X + Y + K where RPI stands for the Retail Prices Index, X a percentage representing costs saving which the regulator expects to be reflected in lower customer prices, Y unavoidable cost increases and K applies to the water companies as an allowance to cover the costs of environmental improvements, for example, cleaner rivers.

These regulatory powers are in addition to the legal constraints outlined earlier, and are particularly relevant in the case of natural monopolies.

Natural monopolies

Industries such as water, electricity supply and the railways can be described as natural monopolies and it has been more difficult to sell them off in such as way as to promote competition and the other benefits that private ownership is meant to bring.

Privatising British Rail

This was one of the Conservative government's last privatisations and one that was especially problematical. The government, on the advice of economists, created an imaginative plan to try to introduce competition into this natural monopoly. This split the industry into three:

- the railway and station network
- rolling stock provision
- train operating companies.

Each section was privatised differently.

Railtrack

The government accepted that this was a natural monopoly which could not be broken up and sold it into private ownership for slightly less than £2 billion in 1996. Its market value in January 2000 was £3.25 billion.

Rolling stock

Three rolling stock companies were created whose job was to compete in order to supply engines and carriages to the train operating companies.

Train operating companies

Investors were encouraged to bid for franchises to run trains over regional and intercity routes. Successful companies would then pay Railtrack to use 'its' stations and track, and lease rolling stock as required. At the end of seven to 14 years new bids would be invited to run services.

Regulation

A powerful independent regulatory regime was introduced to ensure that minimum service levels were met, that profits were not excessive and that government guidelines were followed.

Assessing performance of the privatised rail network

The general perception of the public, as revealed in surveys, is that the privatisation of the railways has yet to be successful:

■ Train operating companies have used their market power to introduce complicated discriminatory pricing policies.

■ Prices on some services have been dramatically increased.

■ Punctuality and customer service are thought to have deteriorated.

■ Safety may have been given less priority.

The long-term test of the success of this particular privatisation will be the degree to which a natural monopoly re-establishes itself through merger and takeover within the industry. This has already started to occur in the electricity generation and supply industry.

Competition within the public sector

In the 1980s the Conservative government realised that the total privatisation of the public sector would be both politically unacceptable and very difficult to implement. It chose instead a variety of strategies designed to introduce or mimic market forces within industries and organisations. These included:

■ the creation of internal markets in the BBC and NHS

■ compulsory competitive tendering (CCT) for a range of central and local government functions

■ greater freedom for educational institutions to control their own budgets.

Internal markets

The creation of internal markets involves the creation of individual cost centres and greater independence in financial decision-making. Thus, in the NHS budget-holding doctors were given the freedom to purchase medical care from those hospitals providing the most attractive service. Hospitals were expected to compete for business from GPs. This represented a radical change in established procedures which could have had devastating political effects had the government been prepared to allow failing hospitals to go 'bust' and close. The incoming Labour government abandoned these policies in 1997.

A version of an internal market still exists within the BBC in which independent programme makers have the freedom to employ camera operators, directors, costume designers, etc. from within the BBC or from outside contractors.

Compulsory competitive tendering

Local and central government departments were compelled by legal changes to put the provision of services out to tender. Thus, rather than local authorities employing refuse collectors, they were required to invite private companies to bid for contracts to collect domestic and commercial refuse. The rules relating to tendering have now been relaxed to permit councils to tender for the provision of their own services.

Education

The Conservative governments in the 1980s also tried to apply market disciplines to education. Universities were further encouraged to compete with each other. Schools were encouraged to become independent of local authority control, and it was believed that educational standards would benefit if schools competed with each other for students.

A C T I V I T Y   3

Would competition improve health care and educational standards?

Summary

Public policy associated with trying to prevent the abuses of monopolistic and oligopolist power has traditionally been based on a legal framework which has focused attention on ownership and structural aspects of large companies. Merger and monopoly policy has not been strictly or consistently applied in the UK, and few sanctions have been used against firms whose actions have been judged to be against the public interest. More recent developments in European law and the developing role of regulatory bodies place greater emphasis on examining unacceptable behaviour by large firms, backed up by the use of fines and direct controls.

In recent years governments in the UK have also attempted to encourage the development of more competitive markets through privatisation and the introduction of internal markets and other structures within the public sector. Some of these policies appear to have been more successful than others but it is too early to assess the long-term impact of these changes on society as a whole.

Data response question

The UK brewing industry

The price of a pint of beer	
Retail price	£1.44
Pub profit	21p
Pub costs	27p
VAT	26p
Wholesale price of which:	
Duty	24p
Brewer's profit	6p
Corporate overhead	3p
Advertising/Marketing	5p
Distribution	15p
Labour	11p
Raw materials	6p

The Mail on Sunday, 19 February 1995

'*Since a recent judgement by the monopolies and mergers commission, major brewing companies such as Bass and Whitbread have had to sell a number of the public houses that they owned; these are called tied pubs. No single brewer could now own more than 2,000 public houses. There are now many more*

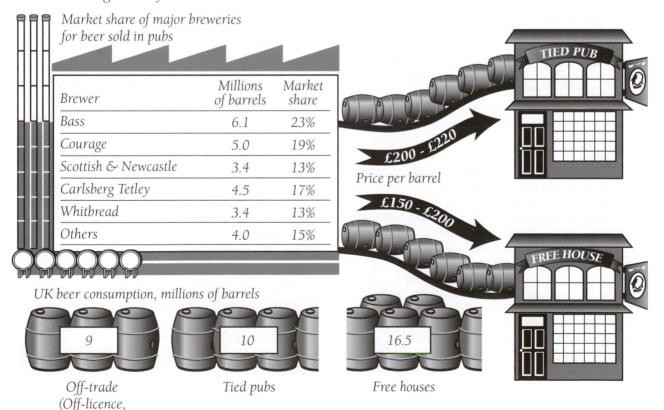

Market share of major breweries for beer sold in pubs

Brewer	Millions of barrels	Market share
Bass	6.1	23%
Courage	5.0	19%
Scottish & Newcastle	3.4	13%
Carlsberg Tetley	4.5	17%
Whitbread	3.4	13%
Others	4.0	15%

Price per barrel
£200 – £220
£150 – £200

TIED PUB
FREE HOUSE

UK beer consumption, millions of barrels

9 — Off-trade (Off-licence, supermarket, etc.)

10 — Tied pubs

16.5 — Free houses

"free houses" which can buy their beer from any brewer they wish.'

The Mail on Sunday, 19 February 1995

1 **a** Using the above information, calculate the five firm concentration ratio in the UK brewing industry. (2 marks)

b What does this suggest about the market structure in this industry? (2 marks)

2 **a** What type of integration is illustrated in the following circumstances:

i a merger of Bass and Carlsberg Tetley:

ii brewers which own public houses? (3 marks)

b Examine the economic implications for both consumers and producers of beer of the ownership of public houses by brewing companies. (8 marks)

Section 1 questions

Essay questions

1 **a** 'British pig farms are good examples of firms which are perfectly competitive.' Evaluate the validity of this statement. (10 marks)

b Discuss the extent to which it might be possible for the government to intervene in order to ensure the British pig meat industry survives. (15 marks)

2 **a** Explain how a monopolist maximises its profits in the long run. (10 marks)

b Discuss the extent to which profit maximisation is a realistic managerial objective for firms. (15 marks)

3 **a** 'A hot food take-away shop is an example of a firm operating in a monopolistically competitive market.' Discuss this statement. (10 marks)

b Comment upon the extent to which economic efficiency is likely to be achieved in this market structure. (15 marks)

4 'Once a market such as the telecommunications market or the gas market becomes sufficiently contestable, regulation is no longer needed.'

a Choosing a utility industry, such as the telecommunications or water industry, explain the factors which may affect the contestability of the market. (20 marks)

b Assess the case *for* and *against* abolishing the agency, such as OFTEL or OFWAT, which is currently responsible for regulating the industry. (30 marks)

Project

Produce a submission to the Competition Commission recommending how one of the following monopolies might be investigated:

■ Microsoft

■ Birds Eye Wall's

■ Vodaphone

Explain how you would judge whether or not the company you have chosen is acting in the public interest.

Evaluate the potential impact of policies to protect the public interest against potential monopoly abuses by the company under consideration.

C3.1a, C3.1b, C3.2, N3.1, N3.2, N3.3, IT3.1, IT3.2, IT3.3

Key Skill Planning

You may wish to use this activity to develop and or accredit key skills. The following guide may be helpful in assisting your planning. If you want accreditation for wider key skills you will need to work with others.

Stage 1

Work with other students and divide research tasks between you. (WO3 1,2 and 3)
Each member of your group would be required to report their findings to other group members. (C3.1(a) and (b))

Stage 2

Individual members your group should choose a particular area of study and undertake more detailed research involving the use of both numerical and written data.
(LP3 1,2 and 3, C3.2, N3.1)

Stage 3

Individual members of your group would be required to formulate a more precise title/hypothesis and to plan how they are going to organise and present their findings.
(PS 3 1,2,3 and 4)

Stage 4

Write up final report using appropriate IT packages (C3.3, N3 2 and 3, IT3 1,2 and 3)

Key skill opportunities

C 3.1a, C3.1B, C3.2, N3.1, N3.2, N3.3, IT3.1, IT3.2, IT3.3.

Section 2
Labour markets

Introduction

AS Section 2 and Section 3 covered the operation of markets and market failure. This section focuses on the workings of labour markets.

A labour market consists of all those seeking to sell their services as workers and all those including households, firms and the government seeking to buy those services.

This section examines a number of the key aspects of labour markets. It first examines the influences on the demand and supply of labour, then explores the operation of labour markets concentrating on how wages are determined and why they differ between different groups. Reasons why free market forces may not result in an efficient allocation of resources and the government policies which seek to improve the performance of the markets are examined. Differences in wages are one reason why income levels vary. The issue of the distribution of income and wealth is discussed and the topic of poverty explored. The opportunity cost of work is leisure and this is covered in the last unit in the section.

Before reading this section, check that you can recall the meaning and use of the following concepts:

- derived demand
- elasticity of demand
- elasticity of supply
- monopoly
- oligopoly
- perfect competition
- monopolistic competition
- average cost
- marginal cost
- marginal revenue
- market failure
- externalities
- merit goods
- public goods.

The demand and supply of labour

Key concepts covered

- derived demand
- aggregate demand for labour
- marginal productivity theory
- marginal revenue product of labour
- elasticity of demand for labour
- aggregate supply of labour
- economic activity
- participation rate
- elasticity of supply of labour
- occupational mobility
- geographical mobility
- backward sloping supply curve
- income and substitution effects

Introduction

This unit examines the features of labour markets on different levels – including aggregate, occupational and individual firms. In analysing the influences on demand and supply use is made of the key concepts of marginal productivity theory, elasticity of demand and elasticity of supply. Recent trends in labour markets are also examined.

Derived demand

As with the demand for all the factors of production, demand for labour is a **derived demand**. Factors of production are not wanted for their own sake but for what they can produce. So the number of workers that firms wish to employ depends principally on the demand for the products produced. If demand rises, firms will usually seek to employ more workers.

The aggregate demand for labour

The **aggregate** (total) **demand for labour** depends mainly on the level of economic activity. If the economy is growing and firms are optimistic that it will continue to grow in the future, employment is likely to be rising. However, if output is declining or even growing at a slower rate and firms are pessimistic about future levels of aggregate demand, employment is likely to be falling.

A firm's demand for labour

How many workers, or working hours, a firm seeks to employ is influenced by a number of factors. These include:

- demand and expected future demand for the product produced – this is again the key influence
- productivity – the higher the output per worker hour, the more attractive labour is
- complementary labour costs – as well as wages, firms incur other costs when they employ labour, so, for example, if National Insurance contributions rise, demand for labour is likely to fall
- the price of labour – a rise in wage rates above any rise in labour productivity will raise unit labour costs and is likely to result in a contraction in demand for labour
- the price of other factors of production which can be substituted for labour – if capital becomes cheaper firms may seek to replace some of their workers by machines.

Marginal productivity theory

Marginal productivity theory suggests that demand for any factor of production depends on its marginal revenue product (MRP) and that the quantity of any factor employed will be determined by where the marginal cost of employing one more unit of the factor equals the marginal revenue product of that factor.

The marginal product of labour is the change in total output which results from employing one more worker. As more workers are employed, output may initially rise rapidly as increasing returns are experienced, so marginal product may increase. However, once a certain level of employment is reached marginal product may fall as diminishing returns set in. **Marginal revenue product of labour** is the change in a firm's revenue resulting from employing one more worker. It is found by multiplying marginal product by marginal revenue. In a perfectly competitive product market marginal revenue will be equal to price. Table 5.1 shows how marginal revenue product is calculated.

If the wage rate is constant at £400 the firm will

Table 5.1 Marginal revenue product

Number of workers	Total output	Marginal product		Marginal revenue (price £)		Marginal revenue (product)	Total revenue (£)
1	20	20	×	10	=	200	200
2	80	60	×	10	=	600	800
3	160	80	×	10	=	800	1600
4	220	60	×	10	=	600	2200
5	260	40	×	10	=	400	2600
6	280	20	×	10	=	200	2800

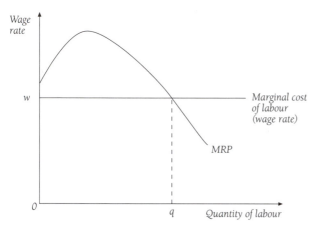

Figure 5.1 Marginal revenue product

employ five workers since this is where the marginal cost of labour equals MRP. At this level of employment the total cost of workers will be 5 × £400 = £2000. This level of employment is the one where the gap between total revenue and total cost of labour is greatest, i.e. £2600 – £2000 = £600.

The marginal revenue product of labour curve shows the quantity of labour demanded at each wage rate as shown in Figure 5.1.

So the marginal revenue product curve of labour is the demand curve for labour.

The MRP and hence the demand curve for labour will shift out to the right if the marginal product of

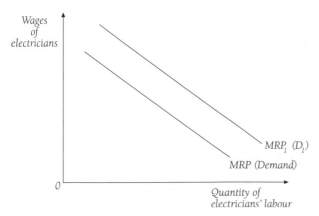

Figure 5.2 An increase in MRP

labour and/or marginal revenue increase. For example, the demand for electricians will increase if the productivity of electricians rises, perhaps due to increased training and/or if the price of their services rises due to, for example, a switch from gas to electrical appliances. This increase in MRP is illustrated in Figure 5.2.

ACTIVITY 1

A firm operates in a perfectly competitive product market. It sells the good it produces for £6 and pays a wage rate of £480. The figures below show how total output changes as employment rises.

Number of workers	Total output
1	40
2	100
3	200
4	280
5	340
6	380
7	400

a Calculate the number of workers the firm will employ.

b Calculate the number of workers the firm would employ if the price of the product rises to £12.

In practice, it can be difficult to measure MRP. This is because workers often work in teams so it can be difficult to isolate the contribution one worker makes to changes in output. In addition, it is difficult to measure the marginal product of a number of people who work in the tertiary sector. For example, is a surgeon who treats 20 people in a day for varicose veins more productive than one who carries out one multiple-organ transplant?

The elasticity of demand for labour

While a change in marginal productivity or marginal revenue will shift the demand curve for labour, a change in the wage rate will cause a movement along the demand curve for labour. The extent to which demand will contract or extend as a result of a change in the wage rate is measured by the **elasticity of demand for labour**. The formula is:

Elasticity of demand for labour =
$$\frac{\text{Percentage change in demand for labour.}}{\text{Percentage change in wage rate}}$$

There are a number of factors which influence the elasticity of demand for labour. These include the following:

- The price elasticity of demand for the product produced. If demand for the product is inelastic, demand for the labour that produces it is also likely to be inelastic. This is because the rise in the price of the product that will result from a rise in the wage rate will cause a smaller percentage fall in demand for the product. So as output will not change by much, employment will not fall significantly.

- The proportion of wage costs in total costs. If wages account for a significant proportion of total costs, demand will be elastic. The reason is because a change in the wage rate will have a large impact on total costs. If the wage rate falls, total costs will fall by a noticeable amount and demand for labour will rise by a greater percentage.

- The ease with which labour can be substituted by other factors. If it is easy to substitute capital for labour, demand for labour will be elastic. A rise in the wage rate will cause workers to be substituted by machines. Demand for labour will fall by a greater percentage than the rise in the wage rate.

- The elasticity of supply of complementary factors. If wages fall and it is easy to obtain more of the factors that are used alongside labour, demand for labour will be elastic.

- The time period. Demand for labour is more elastic in the long run when there is more time for firms to reorganise their production methods.

The aggregate supply of labour

The aggregate (total) **supply of labour** is influenced by three key factors: the size of the population, the size of the labour force and the hours worked.

Population

The larger the population size, the greater the potential supply of labour. So, for example, the USA with a population of 272 million has a greater supply of labour than France with a population of 59 million. As well as the total size of population, the age distribution of the population, school-leaving age and retirement age influence the size of the labour force. The higher the proportion of the population in the working age range, the greater the supply of labour. In the UK the population of working age consists of those aged between 16 and 65. This proportion could rise as a result of a rise in the birth rate that occurred 16 or more years before, net immigration (since most immigrants are aged between 20 and 40), a lowering of the school-leaving age or a raising of the retirement age. In a number of countries including the UK, USA, Germany, France and Japan, the proportion of people of working age is declining as a result of the population ageing.

The labour force

The labour force consists of those in employment and those seeking employment. This is not the same as the population of working age. Some of those who are older than the school leaving age and younger than the state retirement age may not be economically active. The main groups who are not actively participating in the labour force are those still in full-time education, those who have retired early, those who are long-term sick or disabled and those who are homemakers.

There are various factors which influence the **participation rate** of the population of working age in the labour force. They are as follows:

- Wage rates. Higher wage rates will tend to encourage more people to seek to enter or stay in the labour force.

- Employment opportunities. The greater the number and quality of jobs on offer, the higher the participation rate is likely to be.

- Social attitudes to women working. Countries in which it is acceptable for women and, in particular, married women to work have a large pool of workers to call on.

- Provision for the care of the very young and the elderly. Those countries in which there is state and private provision will tend to have a higher participation rate than those in which the very young and the elderly are looked after solely by relatives at home.

The hours worked

As well as the number of workers, the hours they work influences the supply of labour. The number of hours worked in turn is influenced by the length of the working week, the number of days' holidays and the number of days lost through industrial action. The more hours worked, the greater the supply of labour in terms of quantity. However, when workers work long hours, with few holidays, the quality of what they produce may decline.

Workers in the UK work longer hours than those in most other European Union (EU) countries. On 1 October 1998 the Working Time Regulations came into force. This requires employers to 'take all reasonable steps' to ensure that employees do not work, against their will, more than an average of 48 hours a week. Despite this, in 1998 more than a fifth of UK workers worked more than 48 hours a week in their main jobs.

The supply of labour to a particular occupation

The number of people willing and able to work in a given occupation is influenced by the following:

■ The wage rate. The higher the wage rate, the more people are likely to want to do the job. For example, a relatively high number of people seek to become accountants because of the high wages on offer.

■ The convenience and flexibility of hours. Long and unsociable working hours are likely to discourage potential workers, whereas flexibility of hours may attract people to a given occupation. For example, nursing homes may find it difficult to recruit night-time nursing staff, while sales representatives may be able, to a certain extent, to decide when they work.

■ Status. The high status achieved in some jobs such as pilots makes them attractive.

■ Promotion chances. Some people are prepared to work initially for relatively low wages, for example in the media, in the hope that they will progress to high-paid jobs.

■ Flexibility of location. It is becoming increasingly possible in certain occupations, for example architects and designers, to work at least some days from home. This increases the attractiveness of the occupations.

■ Qualifications and skills. The higher the qualifications and skills required, the fewer the number of people who are able to undertake the occupation. While the supply of sales assistants is relatively high, the supply of brain surgeons is low.

■ Job security. The more secure a job, the more

attractive it is likely to be. University lecturers and professors in the UK used to be given tenure for life. This made some people willing to enter an academic life even though pay was not very high. However, security of tenure has now ended and this has coincided with a decrease in the numbers wanting to become university lecturers.

■ Pleasantness of the job. Everything else being equal, more workers will be attracted to more pleasant jobs. It might be expected that the supply of, for example, sewage workers would be low as it is not a particularly pleasant job. However, the unpleasantness is more than offset by the low level of qualifications required. Some sewage workers may not be particularly keen to work in the occupation but they may not have the qualifications to switch to alternative jobs.

■ Holidays. Long holidays are likely to attract workers. Some people may be encouraged to become teachers because of the relatively long holidays on offer. However, this benefit is likely to diminish. Already lecturers in further education have experienced reductions in their holiday entitlement.

■ Perks and fringe benefits. Company cars, paid trips abroad, profit-sharing schemes, free private health care, good company pension schemes are likely to make a given occupation more attractive. For example, pilots receive a number of benefits, including very cheap flights for their families, good company pension schemes and the opportunity to retire early.

ACTIVITY 2

In 1999, while many people were waiting for operations, some hospital beds were lying empty. This was due to a lack of nursing staff. It was estimated that staff shortages were running at as many as 13 000 jobs.

a   What factors influence demand for nurses?
b   Discuss what would cause an increase in the supply of nurses.

The supply of labour to a particular firm

Some of the same influences as in the case of the supply of labour to a particular occupation come into play here including:

■ the wage rate offered
■ the length and convenience of the hours

- promotion chances
- flexibility of location
- job security
- working conditions
- holidays
- perks and fringe benefits.

In addition, supply is influenced by the following:

- The quality and quantity of training on offer. The greater the quality and amount of training that workers can gain from the firm, the greater the number of workers that are likely to be attracted.

- The location of the firm. Firms based in major cities have a greater pool of labour to select from.

- The level of employment. Firms often find it difficult to recruit workers when there is a low level of unemployment.

- The reputation of the firm. This is similar to the status of an occupation.

- The recent performance of the firm. Potential workers are encouraged to apply to firms which are doing well and expanding. This is linked to previous influences, as an expanding firm may be expected to offer higher wages, more training, greater promotion chances and more job security than static or declining firms.

- The opportunity to work overtime. Some people are keen to raise their incomes by working extra hours at higher rates.

The elasticity of supply of labour

As already noted, the wage rate on offer is a key influence on the supply of labour. The extent to which the supply of labour changes as a result of a change in the wage rate is measured by the **elasticity of supply of labour**. The formula is:

Elasticity of supply of labour =

$$\frac{\text{Percentage change in supply of labour.}}{\text{Percentage change in wage rate}}$$

The factors which influence the elasticity of supply of labour are as follows:

- The qualifications and skills required. The supply of skilled workers is more inelastic than the supply of unskilled workers as there are fewer skilled than unskilled workers. For example, the supply of vets is more inelastic than the supply of pet-shop assistants.

- The length of training. A long period of training may discourage some people from undertaking the occupation, so a rise in the wage rate will not attract many new workers.

- The level of employment. If there is high unemployment, supply of labour to many occupations is likely to be elastic. This is because the wage rate will not have to be raised by much to attract a high number of applicants from people seeking employment.

- The mobility of labour. The easier workers find it to switch jobs (**occupational mobility**) and the easier they find it to move from one area to another (**geographical mobility**), the more elastic supply will be.

- The time period. As with demand, supply will be more elastic the longer the time period involved. A rise in the wage rate of barristers, for example, may not have much effect on the supply of barristers in the short run. However, in the long run it is likely to as more students will be encouraged to study law and undertake the necessary training.

The individual supply of labour

The number of hours a worker decides to work is influenced by the number of hours on offer and the relative importance that the worker attaches to income and leisure.

Many workers are unable to alter the number of hours they work in their main jobs. They are contracted to work, say, 38 hours a week and are not offered the opportunity to vary these hours. However, with increasing flexibility in labour markets, more workers are now being provided with a choice as to how many hours they work.

It is thought that at low wages a rise in the wage rate will cause an extension in supply with a worker being prepared to work more hours. However, after a certain wage is reached when a higher wage rate is offered a worker may choose to work fewer hours. He or she may decide that a given income is sufficient to meet his or her financial requirements and may be keen to have more leisure time in which to enjoy his or her earnings. For example, a worker may currently work 40 hours at £15 per hour. This gives a gross income of £600 per week. A rise in the wage rate to £20 would enable the worker to earn the same wage rate by working 30 hours, giving 10 hours more leisure time. This change in response to an increase

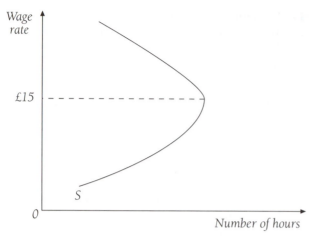

Figure 5.3 The backward sloping supply curve

in the wage rate gives rise to the backward sloping supply curve as illustrated in Figure 5.3.

Up to the wage rate of £15 the supply of labour extends, but any rise above £15 causes supply to contract.

The behaviour of the worker can be explained by the **income and substitution effects**. The income effect of a wage rise is to reduce the number of hours a person works. This is because as the wage rate rises he or she buys more of most goods and services, including leisure. In contrast the substitution effect of a wage rise is to increase the number of hours worked. A higher wage rate increases the return from working and increases the opportunity cost of leisure, so the worker selects to work more hours.

At a low wage rate it is thought that the substitution effect is likely to outweigh the income effect. The worker will work more hours in order to raise his or her material living standard. However, once the wage rate has reached a certain level, in our example £15, the income effect may outweigh the substitution effect. The worker is now able to afford to buy more leisure time.

Present trends in the labour market

In recent years there have been some noticeable changes in the labour market in the UK and many other industrial countries. These include a rise in part-time employment, a rise in the participation of women, a continuation of differences in the participation rates of people from different ethnic backgrounds, a rise in self-employment, temporary employment and second jobs and a fall in the proportion of workers employed in manufacturing.

Part-time employment

While most people still work on a full-time basis the number of people working part time increased by 30 per cent between 1986 and 1998. More women than men work part time. The reasons why men and women work part time also differ. Most women choose to work part time in order to spend time looking after their children. However, surveys indicate that only about a quarter of male employees in part-time employment have chosen to do so. Most are working part time while seeking to gain full-time employment.

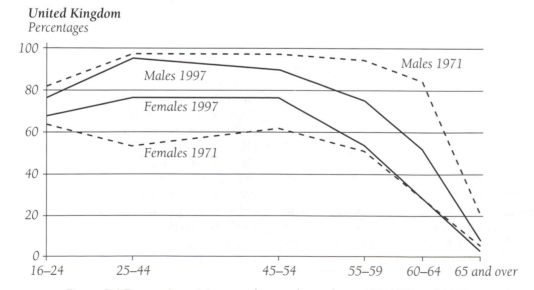

Figure 5.4 Economic activity rates by gender and age, UK, 1971 and 1997

Chart 4.1 Social Trends 29, 1999, Office for National Statistics

Participation rate of women and men

Women are continuing to form an increasing proportion of the UK's labour force. This reflects an increase in the participation rate of women and a decline in the participation rate of men. In 1986 88 per cent of males of working age were economically active and 68 per cent of females. By 1998 this had changed to an economic activity rate for males of 84 per cent and 71 per cent of females.

The major rise in the participation rate of women has come in the 25–44 age range. In 1971 just over half were economically active. This had risen to more than three-quarters by 1997. There are a variety of reasons why women are participating more. These include increased job opportunities for women, increased pay, changing social attitudes and increased expectations of living standards. Women are also tending to have children later and returning to work more quickly.

As Figure 5.4 shows the main change in the participation rate of men has come in the age range 60–64. The number of economically active men in this age range fell by nearly half between 1971 and 1997. The main reason for this has been the rise in early retirement.

ACTIVITY 3

Table 5.2 Economic activity rates by ethnic group, gender and age, Great Britain, 1997–98

Economic activity rates[1]: by ethnic group, gender and age, 1997–98[2]
Great Britain   Percentages

	Males				Females			
	16–24	25–44	45–64	16–64	16–24	25–44	45–59	16–59
White	79	93	78	85	71	76	70	73
Black Caribbean	68	92	72	82	65	78	72	75
Black African	57	85	76	77	..	62	..	56
Other black groups	68	85	..	78	..	71	..	71
Indian	54	94	73	81	53	70	48	61
Pakistani	54	88	60	72	41	28	..	32
Bangladeshi	58	90	..	70	..	..	..	21
Chinese	40	87	75	71	..	63	..	60
None of the above	54	84	83	76	49	58	63	56
All ethnic groups	77	93	78	85	69	75	69	72

Table 4.7, *Social Trends 29*,1999, Office for National Statistics

Using Table 5.2, compare the economic activity rates for men and women from the different ethnic groups and comment on your findings.

Self-employment

The proportion of the labour force who are self-employed continues to rise. A report from the Department of Trade and Industry published in 1999 predicted that four out of ten workers will be self-employed by 2015. The three main industrial categories in which people are self-employed are:

- construction
- distribution, hotels and restaurants
- banking, finance and insurance.

However, the fastest growth is in artistic and literary creation, hairdressing and other beauty treatment.

Temporary employment

Although the proportion of workers in temporary employment in the UK is increasing it is still below that of most of the other EU countries. For example, in 1997 12.2 per cent of all EU employees were in temporary work. The percentage was very high in Spain, 33.6 per cent. In the UK it was 7.4 per cent, and only Belgium and Luxembourg had smaller percentages, 6.3 per cent and 2.1 per cent respectively. In every EU country the percentage of female employees in temporary employment was higher than males. In the UK's case it was 6.5 per cent of men and 8.4 per cent of women.

The rise in temporary employment is a reflection of increased flexibility in the labour market. Employers wishing to increase their responsiveness to changes in demand are offering more jobs on temporary contracts.

Second jobs

More women than men have second jobs and most of those with a second job work part time in their main job. The growth in the number of second jobs rose in the period 1992–95 and has fallen slightly since. In 1998 approximately 500 000 male workers had a second job and 700 000 female workers.

Sectors and occupations

The proportion of workers employed in manufacturing continues to decline while the proportion employed in the tertiary sector increases.

Table 5.3 shows that the percentage of people employed in craft and related occupations declined from 1991 to 1998 while the proportion of managers and administrators, professional, associate professional and technical and personal and protective services increased. The table also shows gender differences. For example, a higher proportion of women than men are engaged in clerical and secretarial and selling work but a smaller proportion work as managers, administrators and professional workers. However, the gender difference is declining slightly.

Table 5.3   UK employees by gender and occupation, 1991 and 1998

| | Percentages | | | |
| | Males | | Females | |
	1991	1998	1991	1998
Managers and administrators	16	19	8	11
Professional	10	11	8	9
Associate professional and technical	8	9	10	11
Clerical and secretarial	8	8	29	26
Craft and related	21	17	4	2
Personal and protective services	7	8	14	17
Selling	6	5	12	12
Plant and machine operatives	15	15	5	4
Other occupations	8	8	10	9
All employees (=100%) (millions)	11.8	12.2	10.1	10.6

Social Market Trends 29, 1999, Office for National Statistics

Summary

Demand for labour is a derived demand. Marginal productivity theory states that demand for labour depends on the productivity of labour and the price that can be obtained for the products produced. Demand for labour is also influenced by the price and availability of the substitutes and complements to labour. In the case of both the demand and supply of labour the wage rate is a key influence. Because of this economists measure the elasticity of demand and supply of labour. The supply of labour is influenced by both monetary and non-monetary factors. In recent years the UK labour market has seen an increase in the participation of women and the development of a more flexible labour force.

Data response question

The Federal Bank's Beige Book economic report last week detailed the tightest US job market in 30 years, with national unemployment dipping to 4.1 per cent of the workforce.

The report highlighted labour shortages across the country, including the shortage of carpenters in Cleveland and the lack of entry-level employees in Kansas City. Retail stores in Boston, Philadelphia, Chicago, Minneapolis and San Francisco also reported difficulties in finding temporary workers for the holiday period.

The chase for entry-level workers – a mainstay of retailers – has become so fierce that some retailers in Texas, Oklahoma and Louisiana have 200 per cent worker turnover rates, said Diane Swonk, chief economist at Bank One. In many regions, she said, the labour market is becoming the primary constraint on growth.

Perhaps more important in the new retail atmosphere is the hiring difficulties for shipping and trucking companies. Trucking is the life-blood pumping through the arteries of e-commerce as well as more traditional retail.

Shippers are now struggling to fill jobs, especially with the nationwide scarcity of truck drivers. The shortage of US truck drivers is acute and getting more serious by the day, said Peter Lytle, chief executive of United Shipping and Technology, a same-day delivery company in Minneapolis.

To get good new drivers to work for United Shipping, the company offers signing bonuses of $500–$1000, he said. However, competitors have snatched away drivers with offers of bigger bonuses, creating a situation where new employees jump ship for a second bonus. The situation has 'just gone haywire', Mr Lytle said. 'Everybody raises the bar every day.'

Christopher Bowe, 'Workers urgently wanted: employees switch jobs for yet another bonus' in the *Financial Times*, 17 December 1999

1   Why do retailers employ a significant number of temporary staff? (4 marks)
2   What effect does a fall in unemployment have on the elasticity of supply of labour? (5 marks)
3   Explain why the labour market may be a constraint on growth. (5 marks)
4   What may cause a shortage of truck drivers? (6 marks)
5   How might a firm seek to reduce labour turnover. (5 marks)

UNIT 6 Wage determination and wage differentials

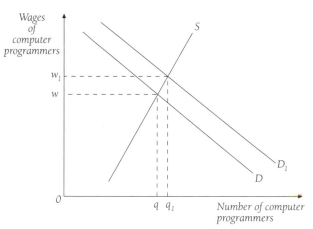

Figure 6.1 An increase in demand for computer programmers

Introduction

In Unit 5 the demand and supply of labour were discussed. The interaction of demand and supply is a key determinant of the level of wages, but they are not always the only determinants.

We are all interested in how much we earn, or will earn in the future, and why we earn more or less than others. This unit seeks to explain how wages are determined and why wages differ. These reasons are then applied to explain the differences in the wages earned by particular groups.

Wage determination

The wages paid in a particular labour market, for example the market for journalists or the market for footballers employed by Manchester United, are influenced by a number of factors. These include demand and supply, trade unions and employer organisations, government intervention and social convention.

Demand and supply

The market forces of demand and supply play a key role in **determining relative wages**. The wage rate of a group of workers will rise if either the demand for their services increases or their supply decreases. For example, the wages of computer programmers have risen as the spread of information technology has increased demand for their services. This effect is shown in Figure 6.1.

In contrast the wage of clerical workers has fallen relative to other groups as their supply has increased and demand for their services has fallen.

Economic rent and transfer earnings

The level of demand and supply and their elasticities determine not only the level of wage rates but also the proportion of wages which consist of **economic rent** and the proportion which consist of **transfer earnings**.

Transfer earnings are what a worker can earn in his or her next best paid job – the opportunity cost of performing the current job. They are the equivalent to the minimum which has to be paid to keep the worker in his or her current job.

Economic rent is the surplus over transfer earnings and is total earnings minus transfer earnings. For example, a woman may earn £580 a week as an optician. If the next best paid job she is willing and able to do is as an advertising executive earning £494 a week, her economic rent is £86 and her transfer earnings are £494.

Figure 6.2 shows that the total earnings received by the workers is 0wxq. Of this, ywx is economic rent and 0yxq is transfer earnings. This figure shows that economic rent is the area above the supply curve and below the wage rate. The amount of economic rent earned by the workers will vary. The first worker employed would have been prepared to work for considerably less than the wage rate actually paid, so a relatively high proportion of his or her earnings will be economic rent, whereas the last worker employed would have be prepared to work only for the going wage rate and so earns no economic rent.

The proportion of earnings which constitute economic rent depends on the elasticity of supply. Eco-

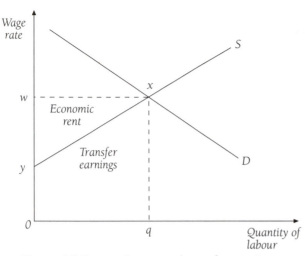

Figure 6.2 Economic rent and transfer earnings

nomic rent will form a large proportion when supply is inelastic. For example, many of the footballers playing in the premier leagues of England and Scotland are thought to earn a large amount of economic rent. Supply is inelastic since most footballers enjoy playing football and would continue to play even if their wage rate was cut, as most would earn considerably less in their next best paid jobs. These footballers are also highly paid. Demand for their skills is high since they attract not only large attendances at matches but also promote high merchandise sales, whereas the supply of skilled players is limited. Figure 6.3 shows the market for premier league players, with the wage rate at the high level of W.

The influence of trade unions and professional organisations

In practice, many wages are not determined in competitive labour markets. For example, there may not be many buyers and sellers. Workers may sell their labour through one body. This may be a trade union or a professional organisation. If all the workers in a labour market are members of a trade union or a professional organisation, the body will act as a monopoly seller. This will alter the supply curve of labour.

Figure 6.4 shows the effect of a trade union forcing the wage rate up from w to w_1. The supply curve now becomes w_1xS. All workers would be prepared to work for w1 or above.

The diagram also shows employment falling from q to q_1. This may occur if trade unions force up the wage rate paid by firms producing under conditions of perfect competition or monopolistic competition in the product market. In these two market structures firms earn only normal profit in the long run. So a rise in their costs will cause marginal firms to leave the industry causing output and employment to fall.

The trade union may seek to avoid loss of jobs by supporting measures to increase labour productivity (for example participating in training initiatives) or measures to increase demand for the product (for example participating in an advertising campaign). In both cases if the measures are successful, the marginal revenue productivity and hence the demand curve for labour will shift to the right.

A union may be in a stronger position to raise the wage rate of its members if the employer operates under conditions of monopoly or oligopoly in the product market. This is because the firms may be earning supernormal profits in the long run.

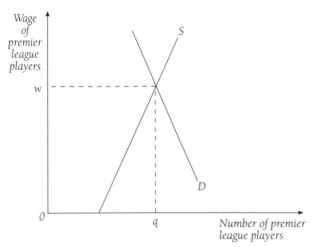

Figure 6.3 The market for premier league football players

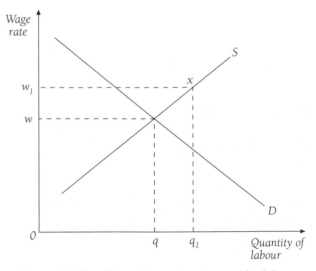

Figure 6.4 The effect of a trade union on the labour market

Employers with labour market power

Those employers who employ a high percentage of workers in a particular labour market can influence the wage rate. In a labour market a **monopsonist** is a firm which is the only buyer (i.e. employer) and an **oligopsonist** is one of a few dominant firms buying a certain type of labour. Examples would be the Ordnance Survey, which is the main employer of map-makers in the UK, and in some areas veterinary practices where there are only a few.

Monopsonists and oligopsonists are price makers. They influence the wage rate. To employ more workers they have to raise the wage rate. So the marginal cost of labour (MCL) will exceed the average cost of labour (ACL) which is equivalent to the wage rate.

Table 6.2 shows how the average cost of labour exceeds the marginal cost of labour. For example, to attract a fourth worker costs the employer an extra £25 since he or she not only pays that worker £16 but also pays an extra £3 to each of the first three workers employed.

Table 6.2 Cost of labour per hour

Number of workers	Average cost of labour (wage rate) per hour (£)	Total cost of labour per hour (£)	Marginal cost of labour per hour (£)
1	10	10	10
2	1	22	12
3	13	39	17
4	16	64	25
5	20	100	36
6	25	150	50

In this circumstance a union can raise the wage rate without causing unemployment.

Figure 6.5 shows that in the absence of union action the number of workers employed will be q (where MRPL equals MCL) and the wage rate will be w (found from the ACL) curve.

The union may then raise the wage rate to W_1. This then becomes the new marginal cost of labour (MCL_1) as there will be one wage rate for all union members. Employment now rises to q_1.

A union can prevent a monopsonist driving the wage rate down by limiting the number of workers employed. It also means, however, that once the wage rate has been settled by negotiation the monoposonist will not have to increase the wage rate to attract labour.

When a monopoly trade union negotiates with a monopsonist employer, the situation is referred to as a bilateral monopoly. In this case the wage rate will be

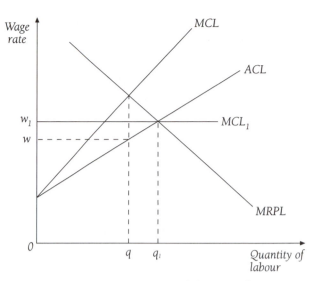

Figure 6.5 A monopsony labour market

determined by the relative **bargaining strengths** of the two sides. If the monopsonist is very powerful the outcome will be a wage rate close to that which the monopsonist would have chosen to pay without any trade union intervention. The upper limit will be the maximum the monopsonist can pay without threatening the existence of the firm. The stronger the trade union is, the closer the wage rate will be to this limit.

Figure 6.6 shows the lower limit and a possible upper limit.

Factors influencing a trade union's (professional organisation's) bargaining strength

A union will be stronger, the:

■ greater the financial reserves of the union

■ higher the proportion of workers in the trade union

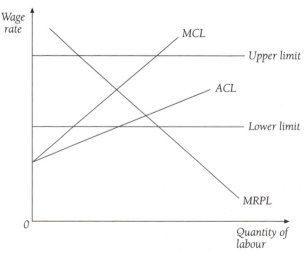

Figure 6.6 Bargaining limits

- more inelastic the demand for the firm's product
- lower the degree of substitution between capital and labour
- lower the proportion of labour costs in total costs
- lower the rate of unemployment
- greater the support the workers have from the general public
- more legislation favours the rights of workers
- more disruption any industrial action would cause.

Factors influencing an employer's bargaining strength

An employer will be stronger, the:

- greater the financial reserves it has with which it can last out any dispute
- lower the proportion of its workers are in the union
- greater the degree of substitution between capital and labour
- higher the rate of unemployment since this will mean it can substitute existing workers with unemployed workers
- lower the support workers have from the general public
- lower the disruption any industrial action would cause to the productive process
- the more branches the firm has which employ either non-union labour or labour in different unions – so that production can be moved in the case of a dispute
- the more legislation favours employers.

Government policy

Government policy influences wages in a variety of ways. Despite the major privatisation programmes of the 1980s and 1990s the government remains a major employer. The pay of people working in the public sector, for example nurses, civil servants and teachers, is affected by the level of government expenditure and the government's attitude to pay rises. If the government is concerned about the inflationary effects of pay rises, it is the pay of its own workers that it can restrain most directly.

The government also places orders with the private sector. If the government increases its spending on, for example, road building contracting firms will receive more revenue. To increase output

they may raise wages in order to attract more workers. A government may also discourage firms from awarding very high pay rises during periods of inflation or indeed paying very low wages by not placing contracts with them.

In addition, the government operates macro and microeconomic policies. Government measures which increase aggregate demand will tend to stimulate employment and raise wages and measures which reduce aggregate demand will tend to constrain wage rises.

Changes in tax rates and welfare benefits can affect wage rates. New classical economists believe that cuts in tax rates and benefits will stimulate a rise in the supply of labour and reduce upward pressure on gross wages. In contrast Keynesians believe that the effects of tax cuts are more uncertain and that reductions in benefits may reduce employment by lowering aggregate demand.

Government policies on particular markets can affect wage rates in those markets. For example, raising tax rates on cigarettes is likely to result in a fall in demand for cigarettes and thereby put downward pressure on wages. The government also passes legislation affecting labour markets. For example, the National minimum wage introduced in 1999 has raised the wage rate of some of the low paid.

The government also operates the Advisory, Conciliation and Arbitration Service (ACAS) which conciliates in disputes between employers and employees. It has, in addition, in the past acted directly as an arbitrator in wage disputes between employers and trade unions.

Social convention

Attitudes towards 'what people deserve to be paid' influence wages via the amounts that workers and unions ask for and what employers offer. Public opinion tends to value highly sacrifice in the form of being prepared to undergo long periods of training and study and certain groups. In many societies work dominated by white, middle-class males is held in higher esteem than work undertaken mainly by the working class or women or people from ethnic minorities. For example, most top barristers who are highly paid are still mainly middle class, male and white. This is known as **social convention**.

Wage differentials

Wage differentials are differences in wages. Wage differentials occur between occupations, industries,

Remember when we had an industrial cavalry? In the Seventies and Eighties – the Advisory, Conciliation and Arbitration Service – was forever called in to intervene in heated stand-offs between large employers and powerful unions. It would lock battling sides in different rooms, rushing between the two in an effort to keep the lights on or ensure that cars rolled off the production line.

Of course, things have changed. Industry is more global and cannot afford lengthy fights that halt production. The unions are not as powerful, nor as combative.

But ACAS has never been busier. Its work is cut out mainly because the world of work is getting more litigious.

Employees may not now be fighting en masse to any greater extent, but they are much keener to fight individually. Armed with more laws protecting and empowering workers, and with a growing awareness of those laws, we are taking to the employment tribunals in our droves.

Christine Buckley, 'Tough job for the referee as more workers pick a fight' in *The Times*, 2 September 1999

1 Discuss why workers and employers were less 'combative' in 1999 than in the 1970s and 1980s.
2 According to the extract, how has the role of ACAS changed?

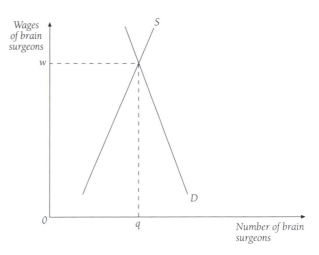

Figure 6.7 The market for brain surgeons

viable substitute. Figure 6.7 shows the market for brain surgeons.

In contrast the supply of waiters and waitresses is high and elastic. The job requires no qualifications and the minimum of training. So there is a large number of people capable of doing the job, and a rise in the wage rate will attract a greater percentage extension in supply. The marginal revenue productivity of waiters and waitresses is also low and so demand is low. Figure 6.8 shows the market for waiters and waitresses.

Relative bargaining strength

Most brain surgeons are members of the British Medical Association (BMA), a strong professional organisation. The Association has large funds and has built up a close relationship with Ministers of Health. Any industrial action it may take would have significant consequences and brain surgeons cannot

firms and regions and within these categories. These differences can be explained by the factors influencing the determination of wages.

Demand and supply

Wages are likely to be high when demand is high and inelastic and supply is low and inelastic. In contrast wages are likely to be low where supply is high relative to demand and both demand and supply are elastic.

For example, brain surgeons are paid considerably more than waiters and waitresses. The supply of brain surgeons is low relative to demand. It is limited by the long period of training involved and the high qualifications required to start that training. These features also make supply inelastic. A rise in the wage rate will not attract many new brain surgeons in the short run. Demand is also inelastic as brain surgeons are a vital part of an operating team and there is no

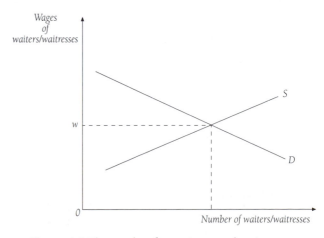

Figure 6.8 The market for waiters and waitresses

be replaced by capital equipment or other types of doctors. By contrast waiters and waitresses have low bargaining power. Very few belong to a trade union and they can usually be replaced by unemployed workers.

Government policy

An ageing population, increasing technology and increasing expectations have increased public spending on health care and increased demand for brain surgeons. The government has also granted relatively large pay increases for surgeons.

Government policy has also recently had an impact on the pay of waiters and waitresses via the introduction of the National minimum wage. This has raised the wage rate of some waiters and waitresses but not all of those aged under 18.

Social convention

Surgeons are held in high public esteem. They are perceived of as providing a vital service, of having undergone a long period of training and of being well qualified and highly skilled. Most of the top surgeons are still male and middle class, whereas a high proportion of the people who serve on tables are female. A significant proportion are also from ethnic minorities. The job they perform is not held in particularly high regard and it is generally thought that anyone could do the job.

ACTIVITY 2

The independent civil service watchdog warned in 1999 that British universities were facing a crisis because academics were being underpaid. It recommended substantial pay rises to prevent lecturers and professors moving overseas and into rival professions.

a   In a group discuss in what sense academics might have been regarded as being underpaid in 1999.

b   What does the passage suggest about how academics' pay was composed in terms of economic rent and transfer earnings?

Wage differentials between particular groups

■   Skilled and unskilled workers. Skilled workers are paid more than unskilled workers principally because the demand for skilled workers is higher and their supply is less. The marginal revenue productivity of skilled labour is high because the skills possessed by the workers will lead to high output per worker. The supply of skilled labour in many countries is below that of unskilled workers. It is also more difficult to substitute skilled labour with machines and unemployed workers than is the case with unskilled labour. Figure 6.9 shows the markets for skilled and unskilled workers.

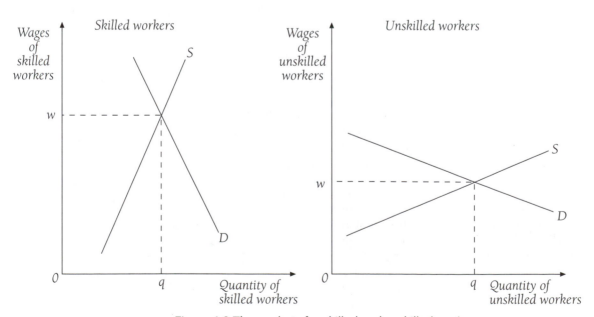

Figure 6.9 The markets for skilled and unskilled workers

■ Male and female workers. Despite equal pay legislation men are still paid more than women. When comparing weekly pay part of the explanation lies in the fact that more women work part time than men. However, even when hourly paid rates are compared men still earn more than women. This is true throughout the European Union as shown in Table 6.2.

Table 6.2 The EU wage gap – women's wages calculated as a percentage of men's (gross hourly full-time earnings, excluding any bonuses)

	%
East German part of Germany	89.9
Denmark	88.1
Sweden	87.0
Luxembourg	83.9
Belgium	83.2
Finland	81.6
West German part of Germany	76.9
France	76.6
Italy	76.5
Spain	74.0
UK	73.7
Austria	73.6
Ireland	73.4
Portugal	71.1
Holland	70.6
Greece	68.0

Cherry Norton, 'Women earn 73 per cent of men's salaries' in *The Independent*, 10 June 1999

There are a number of reasons why women still earn less than men. One is that on average the marginal revenue productivity of women is lower than that of men. In the past a significant reason was that the qualifications of men were greater than that of women. More males went to university than females. The gap in the qualifications and hence the marginal productivity of the genders is now narrowing. However, the marginal revenue productivity of women remains below that of men because women are disproportionately concentrated in low-paid occupations which generate low marginal revenue. In addition, a smaller percentage of women belong to trade unions and professional organisations and so have lower bargaining power. Some women also lose out on promotion chances because of leaving the labour markets at crucial times in their career in order to have and raise children. Another factor which still exists is discrimination, with some employers undervaluing the services of female workers.

■ Part-time and full-time workers. Part-time workers, on average, receive less pay per hour than full-time workers. Again there are a number of reasons which explain this. One is that the supply of people wanting to work part time is relatively high relatively to the demand. Part-time work is convenient for a number of people bringing up children, pursuing university studies and other interests and careers. Part-time workers are also less likely to receive training, both on and off the job, than full-time workers so their productivity tends to be lower. In addition, a smaller proportion of part-time workers belong to trade unions and professional organisations and a higher proportion are women.

■ Ethnic groups. Those from ethnic minorities tend to be lower paid than white workers. One particular group which receives low pay is workers of a Bangladeshi origin. There are a number of reasons for this. One is that a high proportion of Bangladeshis work in the catering industry which is low paid. Another is that the qualifications of Bangladeshis, particularly Bangladeshi women, are currently, on average, below those of the rest of the population. Another factor is discrimination.

ACTIVITY 3

In January 2000 pay awards were announced for NHS workers. Consultants were given an increase of more than 6 per cent or almost £4000 on a typical consultant's salary of £61 605. Most nurses were awarded a rise of 3.4 per cent and ancillary workers received 3.25 per cent or £300 whichever was greater.

a What effect would the pay awards have had on wage differentials between NHS workers?

b What factors may the government have taken into account when deciding on these awards?

Summary

Wages are influenced by the forces of demand and supply. In general, workers whose skills are in high demand and short supply will be well paid. However, demand and supply are not the only determinants. The relative bargaining power of employee and employer organisations, government policy and social convention usually play a part. Workers with strong bargaining power and who benefit from government policy and who society holds in high esteem are likely to be well paid.

Data response question

The growth of the 24-hour economy is shifting jobs from industry to the services sector, and sucking in an army of women workers to what are often poorly paid part time jobs according to pay experts, Incomes Data Services.

Using official government pay data in a report published today, the research company finds that female workers are far more likely to be employed in low-paid jobs, despite rising opportunities for women in the professions.

One in five women earns less than £200 a week, compared to just 8% of men. And just 12% of women earn more than £500 a week, compared to 27% of men.

'The labour market has changed enormously over the last 20 years, with a decline in the manufacturing jobs traditionally done by men and a huge growth in service sector employment, where women are most likely to work,' the IDS report says.

The average women worker earned just 62% of the average male salary 20 years ago. Today the gender pay has narrowed, but women still earn just 73.8% of the male weekly salary even though younger women are increasingly likely to be better qualified than their male counterparts.

While the growth of knowledge industries and expansion of higher education has created thousands of well paid jobs for women, the fastest growth has been in the low-paid end of the female labour market.

'Overall, the gender pay gap has not closed quickly because the growth in earnings of women professionals is offset by the expansion in the number of women in low-paid jobs,' the IDS report says.

There are two dimensions to the gender pay gap, according to the report. Firstly men and women do different jobs with women far more likely to be employed in low-paid occupations like cleaners and sales assistants. And secondly, when women do the same jobs as men, they are paid less for their work.

The average female solicitor earns £661 a week before tax, while a male solicitor earns £788 on average. Female bar staff bring in just £171 a week before tax, while male bar workers earn £195.

Even in occupations where women dominate, such as primary school teachers, where females outnumber males by six to one, women's hourly earnings are still only nine-tenths of men.

'In every occupation women are less likely to reach the highest paid levels – primary head teachers for example,' the report notes.

Charlotte Denny, 'Women still bottom of earnings pile' in *The Guardian*, 13 December 1999

1 Discuss the effects changes in the labour market have had on the participation rate of women workers. (5 marks)

2 According to the article why do women earn less than men? (6 marks)

3 According to the chart which occupation had the greatest actual gender gap and which had the greatest percentage gender gap? (4 marks)

4 What may cause women to fail to 'reach the highest levels' in occupations? (5 marks)

5 Why may the gender gap close in the future? (5 marks)

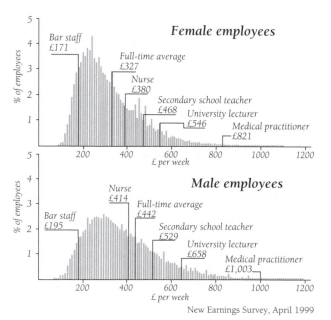

New Earnings Survey, April 1999

Distribution of gross weekly earnings of full-time employees, April 1999

UNIT 7 Labour market failure

Key concepts covered

- labour market failure
- geographical immobility
- occupational immobility
- discrimination
- negative discrimination
- positive discrimination
- Becker's theory
- statistical discrimination

Introduction

In this unit the reasons for labour markets performing inefficiently are examined, including immobility of labour, monopoly and monopsony power, lack of information, inertia, attachment between buyers and sellers and externalities. Particular attention is paid to discrimination, including both the consequences of discrimination and two theories which seek to explain it.

Labour market failure

Labour market failure occurs when the market forces of demand and supply do not result in an efficient allocation of resources. Evidence of labour market failure occurs in a number of forms. The most obvious is unemployment. Other examples include shortages of skilled labour, workers being in jobs that they are not best suited for, a lack of training and wage rates being above or below their equilibrium rate.

Causes of labour market failure

There are a number of causes of labour market failure. These, of course, are closely linked to the causes of market failure in product markets. The causes include the following:

- Labour immobility. This comes in two main forms. One is **geographical immobility** which is the obstacles workers experience in moving from jobs in one area to jobs in another area. When this occurs shortages of workers in one area and surpluses in other areas will not be corrected and regional unemployment and geographical wage differentials will continue to exist. Geographical immobility arises for a number of

reasons. These include differences in the availability and price of housing in different areas and social ties.

- The other type of immobility is **occupational immobility**. This is the obstacles which workers experience in changing occupations and which contribute to occupational wage differentials and structural unemployment. Occupational immobility arises because of differences in qualifications, skills and social barriers.

- Trade unions. Trade unions may push the wage rate above the equilibrium and thereby cause unemployment. They are unlikely to push up the wage rate indefinitely since such a policy would result in one highly paid member. Trade unions may also engage in restrictive practices such as job demarcation in which workers will only undertake tasks outlined in their job descriptions. This will influence the flexibility of the labour force.

- In the UK trade union membership fell from 1979 to 1998. One reason for this was the high level of unemployment in the 1980s and first half of the 1990s – there were fewer workers to belong to trade unions. Another reason was the reduction in the power of trade unions caused by the Trade Union Acts implemented by the Conservative governments.

- Monopsonist and oligopsonist employers. In labour markets with employers who have the power to determine the wage rate and employment, both are likely to be lower than in a perfectly competitive labour market.

- Lack of information. Workers may be in jobs which are less well paid and which they enjoy less than other jobs they are capable of doing because they are unaware of suitable vacancies. Similarly, employers may not appoint the most productive workers because they are not in touch with all the potential workers. Obtaining information on job vacancies and potential workers, applying for jobs and interviewing workers involves a variety of costs. For workers, it takes time and effort and money to look for a new job, fill out application forms and attend interviews. Employers incur costs in advertising jobs, assessing applications, interviewing people and inducting new staff, So both groups have to consider the benefits of searching for a better situation against the costs of searching.

■ Attachment between workers and employers. Some workers may stay in less well-paid jobs because they like working for their employers – they have a good working relationship. Employers may also feel a sense of loyalty to their existing workforce. This attachment reduces the mobility of labour and makes supply more inelastic.

■ Inertia. Workers may not move to higher paid jobs and employers may not seek to replace less productive by more productive workers out of laziness.

■ Externalities. Training is a merit good. It has positive externalities and if left to market forces too few resources would be devoted to it. This is because some workers and some firms take a short-term view and underestimate the benefits of training. In addition, some firms are afraid that other firms may reap the benefits of their expenditure by poaching their staff.

■ **Discrimination**. Discrimination is when a group of workers and potential workers is treated differently than other workers in the same job in terms of pay, employment, promotion and training opportunities and work conditions.

ACTIVITY 1

'[The government's Skills Task Force] will say Britain is suffering a "significant competitive disadvantage" because 30 per cent of workers do not have GCSE qualifications or the vocational equivalent.

In a report to Mr Blunkett the taskforce warns that these workers face exclusion from the jobs market over the next 20 years as GCE A-levels and the vocational equivalents become the minimum qualifications sought by most employers.

It says there is 'a worrying trend' for workers who already have skills to extend their qualifications and competence while those with skills fall further behind.'

Kevin Brown, 'Incentives to boost workplace training' in the *Financial Times*, 12 January 2000

a In a group discuss why some workers do not seek to improve their skills and qualifications.

b What are the implications for the wage differential between skilled and unskilled workers and the performance of UK labour markets of the predicted situation described by the Skills Task Force?

Negative discrimination

Discrimination can be negative or positive. **Negative discrimination** is when a group is treated less favourably than other workers. Groups which experience negative discrimination include black workers, women, the disabled, the old and the young.

If an employer believes because of prejudice that the marginal revenue productivity of black workers is lower than it actually is, the wage rate paid to these workers and their employment will be below the allocatively efficient level as Figure 7.1 shows.

This discrimination is likely to have an effect throughout the labour market. Those who cannot gain employment with the discriminating employer/employers will seek employment with those employers who do not discriminate. This will increase the supply of labour to the non-discriminating employers and lower the wage rate as shown in Figure 7.2.

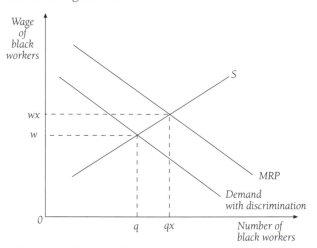

Figure 7.1 A discriminating employer labour market

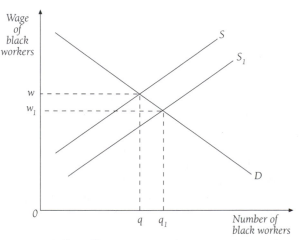

Figure 7.2 The effect on a non-discriminating employer labour market

Negative discrimination can also occur on the part of consumers and fellow workers. If consumers would boycott shops which have black workers or other workers are racist, an employer may feel forced into not employing black workers.

The costs of negative discrimination

Negative discrimination can impose costs on a number of groups:

- The group discriminated against clearly suffers. The people within it are likely to be paid less than other workers doing the same job and to find it harder to gain employment. In addition, some may have to settle for less demanding jobs than they are capable of undertaking, may be overlooked for promotion and may not be selected to go on training courses. The existence of discrimination may also discourage members from the discriminated group from applying for well-paid jobs and from seeking to gain higher qualifications.

- Producers who discriminate have a smaller pool of labour to select from. They may also not make the best use of any black workers they do employ. This will raise their costs of production and make them less competitive against rival firms at home and abroad.

- Consumers will experience higher prices if producers discriminate. They will also experience higher prices and less choice if they themselves discriminate against firms which employ workers from a particular group.

- The government may have to pay out more welfare benefits to groups which are discriminated against and may have to spend time and money introducing and monitoring legislation to end discrimination and tackling social tension.

- The economy will lose out as a result of the misallocation of resources. Output will be below the potential output which could be achieved if the group were not discriminated against in terms of employment, pay, promotion and training.

Theories of negative discrimination

Various theories have been put forward to explain negative discrimination, including the following:

- **Becker's theory**. Gary Becker, Professor of Economics at Chicago University, argues that some people may be prepared to experience

higher costs rather than come into contact with members of a particular group. In effect, the individuals pay in the form of lower profits to avoid employing, for example, women workers and in the form of higher prices to avoid buying from firms employing female workers.

- **Statistical discrimination**. This arises because of imperfect information. Some economists argue that employers discriminate as a result of seeking to reduce their costs. They do not know in advance the productivity of job applicants and may find it difficult to measure the productivity of existing workers. So when deciding who to employ, how much to pay and who to promote and train they make decisions on generalisations about groups of workers. For example, an employer may assume that workers aged 50 and over are less productive and will have a shorter time with the firm than younger workers. As a result he or she may use age as a screening device when deciding on job applicants, may not promote older workers or send them on training courses and if deciding on redundancies may select older workers first.

Positive discrimination

Positive discrimination is when a group of workers and potential workers are treated more favourably than other workers. Employers may overestimate the marginal revenue productivity of a particular group, for example workers who have degrees from particular universities or who attended particular schools. This will result in them paying a higher wage and employing a greater number of the particular category than the allocatively efficient levels.

Consumers may also discriminate. For example, consumers may prefer to eat in Indian restaurants which employ waiters and waitresses of Indian origin, believing that this means that the food is authentically Indian. In this case consumers may be prepared to pay higher prices to eat in the restaurant than in other restaurants serving Indian food but not employing waiters and waitresses of Indian origin. Of course, what the consumers are unlikely to know is the ethnic origin of the owner, chef and other kitchen staff.

The government may also engage in positive discrimination in order to offset negative discrimination. It may itself seek to employ members of a group which is discriminated against and/or it may set minimum quotas for the employment of workers in private sector firms.

ACTIVITY 3

In the UK in 1998 solicitors on average earned £680 a week while secondary school teachers earned £470.

As a group, draw up a list of reasons why, in the light of this wage differential, most teachers did not become solicitors.

Summary

When left to market forces, labour markets do not usually achieve an allocatively efficient allocation of resources. This is due to a number of reasons. There are frequently dominant buyers and sellers, workers are not perfectly mobile, there is not perfect knowledge on either the part of workers or employers and there can be attachment between the two. In addition, the employment, promotion and training opportunities and wages offered to different workers is not always based on their marginal revenue productivity. This because employers' offers can be influenced not only by imperfect information but also by discrimination. Negative discrimination imposes a range of costs. Two significant ones are higher costs and lower output.

Data response question

The government is bracing itself for the publication of a damning report on sex discrimination in universities, where women are being systematically underpaid at every level and for all types of academic, administrative

and manual work.

The inquiry team, including vice-chancellors and union representatives, commissioned research from the Office of Manpower Economics to provide the first up-to-date statistics on earnings across all types of university employment.

It discovered that full-time male academics in the older universities were paid on average £4259 a year more than their female counterparts.

The salary figures (excluding clinical academics who are paid at NHS rates) showed women were less likely to be promoted to senior grades. But even within each grade women earned less than men. For example, a male lecturer on the bottom grade got £238 a year more on average than a female counterpart.

The gender gap for senior lecturers was £541 and for professors was £1807. Women were also more likely to be on fixed-term contracts with less job security.

'In all institution types and all non-clinical academic grades, the average salary for women was lower than that for men. Conversely, more men than women were bunched at the top of their respective pay scales,' the OME report concluded.

It found that 'average full-time salaries of female researchers over all grades lagged behind those of men by £900 in pre-1992 universities and £700 in post-1992 universities.' The gender gap for technicians was almost £2000, for administrative and professional staff just over £1800, and for manual staff £250.'

Gender gap: pay differentials at the older universities

	Men	Women
All academic posts	£32 118	£27 859
Professor	£42 999	£41 192
Senior lecturer	£32 971	£32 430
Researcher	£20 403	£19 480
Manual	£8089	£7839

John Carvel, 'Universities underpay women' in the *Guardian*, 6 May 1999

1 Using the table estimate at what level the gender gap was greatest in percentage terms. (3 marks)
2 Illustrate on an appropriate diagram women being underpaid. (4 marks)
3 Why do you think the gender gap was greater in pre-1992 than post-1992 universities? (6 marks)
4 Apart from pay, what other evidence is provided in the extract of discrimination against women workers? (5 marks)
5 Discuss two costs which universities may have experienced as a result of engaging in discrimination. (7 marks)

UNIT 8 Labour market policy

Key concepts covered

- regional policy
- human capital
- national minimum wage
- discrimination legislation
- trade union reform
- Social Chapter
- supply-side policies
- flexible labour
- primary labour market
- secondary labour market
- ageing population

Introduction

Unit 7 showed there are a number of reasons why labour markets may not operate efficiently. Keynesians believe that government policy measures should be used to offset labour market failure. In contrast new classical economists believe that problems in labour markets arise because of previous intervention.

This unit examines both interventionist measures designed to offset labour failure and supply-side measures designed to allow free market forces a greater reign. It also discusses some recent developments in the labour market.

Measures to offset labour market failure

These include the provision of labour market information, regional policy, the provision and encouragement of training, the provision of state education, minimum wage legislation, discrimination legislation, trade union reform and acceptance of the EU's Social Chapter.

Labour market information

To offset the lack of labour market information the government provides information in a variety of forms. There is a state-funded careers service which provides details about requirements, working conditions and pay of a variety of occupations. Careers education is also part of the curriculum of state schools and most private sector (public) schools. Government job centres provide information about job vacancies and welfare benefit officials discuss with the unemployed what jobs are on offer and how to apply for them.

Regional policy

Regional policy seeks to influence the distribution of firms and people. To reduce the problem of geographical immobility of labour and regional unemployment governments employ a variety of measures. Financial assistance may be given to workers to relocate to areas where there are vacancies requiring their particular skills. More commonly, however 'work is taken to the workers' by providing financial assistance for firms to locate and relocate in areas of high unemployment.

Training

A government can seek to raise the level of training to the allocatively efficient level in a variety of ways. It can provide training itself directly to its own employees and to the unemployed and those changing jobs, it can subsidise individuals to engage in training and/or firms to provide training and it can pass legislation requiring firms to engage in a certain level of training.

Education

Increases and improvements in state educational provision should raise the qualifications and skills levels of workers. This should increase the occupational mobility of the labour force, reduce the shortage of skilled labour and raise the productivity of labour.

Measures to raise the qualifications and skills of workers are referred to as investment in **human capital**. If there is investment in developing the abilities of a wide range of people the problem of social exclusion (people not feeling a part of society) should also be reduced.

Minimum wage legislation

Minimum wage legislation is introduced to help raise the pay of low-paid workers. To have any effect the minimum wage has to be set above the market equilibrium wage rate.

New classical economists argue that such government intervention in the operation of free market forces raises firms' costs of production and results in higher unemployment. Figure 8.1 shows that the setting of a minimum wage of wx above the equilibrium wage rate of w causes an extension in the

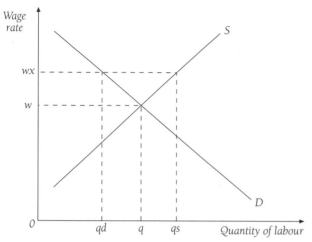

Figure 8.1 The effect of the introduction of a minimum wage

supply of labour but also a contraction in the demand for labour causing a shortfall of employment of qS-qD. Compared to the situation before the intervention of the government, employment falls from q to qD.

However, some Keynesian economists argue that the introduction of a national minimum wage may not result in higher unemployment. Low-paid workers often have low bargaining power relative to their employers, some of which are monopsonists and oligopsonists. In these cases the introduction of a minimum wage could raise both the wage rate and employment. Figure 8.2 shows that a minimum wage of wx becomes the new marginal cost of labour and raises employment from q to q_1.

There are other reasons why a **national minimum wage** may not cause unemployment. One is that the

first effect of its introduction is to raise wages. This, in turn, raises demand for goods and services which, in turn, may increase demand for labour. The higher wages may also raise the morale and productivity of those affected. Productivity will also increase if employers seek to gain higher returns from the now higher-paid workers by providing more training. Rises in demand for products and increases in productivity will shift the marginal revenue productivity (demand for labour) to the right and increase employment as illustrated in Figure 8.3.

A national minimum wage was introduced in the UK in April 1999. The minimum pay for adults was initially set at £3.60 per hour, £3.00 for 18–21-year-olds (which rose to £3.20 in June 2000). Workers aged 16 and 17 were made exempt.

Discrimination legislation

A government can pass legislation making discrimination against a particular group illegal. In the UK the Equal Pay Act of 1970, which was implemented in 1975, sought to end differences in pay between men and women undertaking the same or broadly similar work or for work rated as equivalent under a job evaluation study. The Sex Discrimination Act made unequal treatment on the grounds of gender or marital status in aspects of employment other than pay, which was already covered, illegal. In 1983 both Acts were consolidated and broadened under the Equal Pay (Amendment) Regulation. The Race Relations Act of 1976 makes it illegal to discriminate on the grounds of colour or race. In 1995 the Disability Discrimination Act came into force which made discrimination on the grounds of disability illegal.

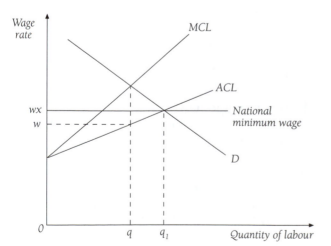

Figure 8.2 The effect of a minimum wage in a monopsony labour market

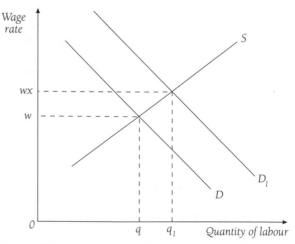

Figure 8.3 An increase in demand resulting from the introduction of a minimum wage

Such **discrimination legislation** may change attitudes over time. Employers may find that a group which they had previously discriminated against is more productive than they first thought. However, at least in the short run, employers may seek to get round any such legislation by, for example, claiming that workers from a certain group are less well suited than others for the jobs on offer and redefining jobs undertaken by workers from different groups. In practice, it can often be difficult to prove that discrimination has occurred.

Trade union reform

If it is thought that the power of trade unions has been weakened by **trade union reform** through previous legislation and that bargaining power had been reduced too much in relation to that of employers, a government may repeal some of the legislation. The Labour government that came to power in May 1997 changed a number of the measures that previous Conservative governments had introduced. For example, it removed the ban on government employees at GCHQ at Cheltenham from joining a union.

Agreement on the Social Chapter

In 1997 the newly elected Labour government reversed the UK's opt out from the **Social Chapter** of the Maastricht Treaty. It adopted various EU directives on employment legislation such as the right to paternity leave and paid holidays, maximum working hours and minimum standards of health and safety at work.

ACTIVITY 2

A paper by Professor Patrick Minford and Andrew Haldenby of the Centre for Policy Studies published in 1999 argued that new rules on trade union recognition would raise union membership by around 1 million from 6.8 million to 7.8 million. The outcome of this, they suggested, would be to raise unemployment by about half a million as trade unions would push up wages and slow the introduction of cost-reducing technology.

a Would a rise in wages necessarily lead to a rise in unemployment?

b Why might trade unions seek to slow the introduction of cost-reducing technology?

Supply-side policies

Supply-side policies seek to raise the productive potential of the economy by increasing the quantity and quality of resources available. Such measures affecting labour markets include reducing marginal tax rates, cutting unemployment benefits and reducing the power of trade unions.

Cutting marginal tax rates

New classical economists believe that reducing marginal direct tax rates will raise the incentive for existing workers to increase the number of hours they work, for the unemployed to seek work more actively and for those considering retiring early to stay in the labour force for longer.

They argue that the substitution effect of any rise in net pay resulting from a tax cut will exceed the income effect. However, studies have shown that a large proportion of workers are not free to alter the hours that they can work and of those who can as many choose to work fewer hours as work more hours.

However, cuts in marginal tax rates do seem to have some influence on people's decision as to when they will retire if they have some choice in the matter.

The effect on unemployment is a controversial matter. Keynesians believe that the main cause of unemployment is a lack of aggregate demand and hence job vacancies. They do not think that people remain unemployed because they are not prepared to work for the going wage rate.

Reducing unemployment benefit

Some new classical economists have suggested that in addition to cutting marginal tax rates, the gap between paid employment and benefits (for example job seekers' allowance) should be increased by reducing benefits. They believe that this makes unemployment a less attractive prospect and so reduces the time that the unemployed spend searching for a job.

Again, Keynesians argue that the unemployed are not voluntarily unemployed. They also believe that cutting job seekers' allowance will actually increase unemployment by reducing aggregate demand. The unemployed spend a high proportion of their income. A cut in their benefits will reduce their spending which will have a knock-on effect on the spending of the people they buy goods and services from and so on.

Trade union reform

New classical economists believe that trade unions can cause unemployment by pushing the wage rate above the equilibrium level and engaging in restrictive practices, so they consider that reducing the power of trade unions will result in a more efficient allocation of resources. The Conservative administrations of 1979 to 1997 passed a number of Acts limiting the power of trade unions, for example the 1980 Employment Act and the 1993 Trade Union Reform and Employment Rights Act. The former required unions to put closed shop agreements to a secret ballot and limited unions' ability to take secondary action against a firm not directly involved in a dispute by allowing employers to take legal action against them. The latter effectively ended closed shop agreements (arrangements whereby employment is restricted to those who belong to a certain union) by giving employees the right to join any union, required union ballots to be conducted by post and ended the remaining wage councils which had been protecting the pay of low-paid workers.

Flexibility of the labour force

Supply-side economists have encouraged the development of a labour force which adjusts more easily in terms of the number of hours worked and the amount of pay received to changes in market conditions. **Flexible labour** is normally perceived to include workers who work part time, have temporary contracts or are self-employed. It can also be interpreted more widely in terms of temporal flexibility (ability to change the hours people work), locational flexibility (ability to change where people work – at home or their place of employment) and functional flexibility (ability to change the tasks workers perform).

Flexibility allows firms to respond to increased demand without encountering capacity constraints and without putting upward pressure on wages and it allows them to adjust smoothly and quickly to falls in demand. However, it can create greater insecurity for workers. For example, if they are working on a casual contract they may find it difficult to obtain a mortgage.

The high level of unemployment in the 1980s and 1990s resulted in a growth in part-time and temporary jobs at the expense of full-time jobs. This was particularly true in terms of low skilled jobs. The reduction in trade union power contributed to this trend. Some economists discuss these developments

in terms of a **primary and a secondary labour market**. The primary labour market consists of workers on full-time contracts who have a high degree of attachment to the labour force. These workers are sometimes called core workers. The secondary labour market involves those workers on temporary and part-time contracts. These move in and out of the labour market, for example students and mothers, and are sometimes called peripheral workers.

ACTIVITY 2

'The announcement that British Telecom aims to have a tenth of its 100 000 employees working from home is just the latest development in a chain of events that has seen workers in organisations as varied as local authority and IBM spending increasing amounts of time working away from their offices. BT itself says that about 3000 to 4000 of its employees regularly work from home already.'

Roger Trapp, 'IT is transforming the world of work' in *The Independent*, 13 May 1999

In a group discuss:

a the advantages and disadvantages for employees of working from home
b the reasons why a number of firms are promoting locational flexibility
c the effects of locational flexibility on pollution and congestion.

Ageing population

In many developed economies falls in the birth rate and increases in life expectancy are causing the average age of the population, including the working population, to rise. This trend has a number of implications for the labour market and for the government.

Older workers used to be regarded as less adaptable to change and more geographically and occupationally immobile. While they are probably more geographically immobile than younger workers there is increasing evidence that they are just as occupationally mobile and adaptive to change.

As the number of young people entering the labour force continues to decline firms will increasingly have to draw on the services of older workers. To attract people to stay in the labour force longer and to encourage some of those who have retired early to re-enter the labour force, firms will have to offer flexible work patterns. They will also have to engage in regular retraining of their workforce.

The **ageing population** also has implications for governments. As the number of retired people dependent on working age adults increases governments are having to consider how the increasing burden can either be reduced or financed. One possible solution, thought to be being considered by a number of governments, is to raise the retirement age in line with rising life expectancy. This would simultaneously reduce the number of dependents and raise the size of the working population. Ways of coping with the burden are to encourage the development of private pension schemes and/or to raise income tax rates.

ACTIVITY 3

'Peter Peterson, an investment banker, points out there were 6.8 working-age adults to support each person over 65 in the member countries of the Organisation for Economic Co-operation and Development in 1960. Today this is 4.5. By 2030, it will be 2.5. Between 1995 and 2050, the number of taxpayers per retired person will fall from 4.2 to 2.3 in the US, from 2.7 to 2.1 in the UK, from 2.5 to 1.4 in France, from 2.3 to 1.2 in Germany and from 1.3 to a terrifying low 0.7 in Italy.'

Martin Wolf, 'Older but no wiser' in the *Financial Times*, 4 January 2000

a   Explain why the number of people over 65 and the number of retired people are not the same.

b   Discuss how the potential increase in the burden of the over-65s in the UK compares with the USA, France, Germany and Italy.

c   In a group discuss:
   i   what has been happening in recent years to the age at which people retire.
   ii a measure, other than increasing the retirement age, of reducing the burden.

Summary

This unit has discussed some of the measures which governments can take to improve the performance of labour markets. These policies can be based on the view that government intervention is necessary to correct the effects of labour market failure. One such policy is a national minimum wage which is introduced to help those who would otherwise receive very low wages. The effects on employment

are disputed. While Keynesians argue that unemployment may not rise, new classical economists claim that it will. New classical economists also believe that labour market policies should be designed to remove previous legislation and reduce taxation and benefits which have interfered with the signals and incentives created by the operation of free market forces. One aim of new classical supply-side policies is to create a more flexible labour force. The UK's labour force is indeed becoming more flexible in terms of when they work, the tasks they perform and where they work. The population is also becoming older and this has implications for future labour market policy including deciding what the retirement age should be.

Data response question

Six months after the introduction of national minimum wage legislation, illegal employment practices, in-sufficient enforcement and a climate of fear among low-paid workers mean that thousands are still not receiving the minimum hourly rate of between £3 and £3.60.

Among those workers least likely to be receiving the minimum wage are women, particularly those for whom English is not a first language, and the young.

For workers aged 18 to 21 the minimum wage is £3. It goes up to £3.60 for those aged over 21. The legislation does not apply to workers under 18.

The problems of workers not receiving the minimum wage is particularly acute in the north-west of England, which has a high concentration of low-paid workers.

A conference in Manchester to mark the first six months of the national minimum wage, organised jointly by the TUC, the National Association of Citizen's Advice Bureaux (Nacab) and the Greater Manchester low pay unit, heard yesterday that in addition to overt non-payment of the minimum salary, employers had adopted various sharp practices to avoid paying the rate.

It also heard that in the majority of cases, workers were too frightened of losing their jobs to make a formal complaint against an employer.

A TUC submission to the government's low pay commission, which will report in December, includes cases in which employers avoided paying the rate by understating hours on pay slips to make it appear as if the minimum had been paid.

This raised problems of enforcement, in that pay slips and employers' books would show that the rate was being paid, when in reality it was not.

Workers had also been told they were not eligible for the minimum because they were self-employed, part-time or on piece rates. In fact they were due the rate.

The low pay commission reported that a 'significant number' of workers had been dismissed as a result of demanding the rate, while some 23% of callers to its minimum wage advice line said they had either been flatly refused the rate, or suffered some reduction in terms and conditions as a result of receiving £3 to £3.60 per hour.

Paul Kelso, 'Workers still losing out on minimum wage' in the *Guardian*, 2 October 1999

1 According to the extract why are some 'workers still losing out' on the national minimum wage? (6 marks)

2 Why do some women 'for whom English is not a first language' receive a low wage? (5 marks)

3 Why may an area have a 'high concentration of low paid workers'? (5 marks)

4 What sharp practices have some employers used to get round the legislation? (4 marks)

5 Discuss the effect the national minimum wage may be having on the employment of 17-year-olds. (5 marks)

The distribution of income and wealth

Introduction

Units 5–8 have discussed how differences in employment opportunities and differences in wages arise and the influence that government policy has on these. This unit goes further in examining how differences in income from employment and other sources arise, why differences in wealth occur and how government policy affects these.

Throughout most of the twentieth century income and wealth became more evenly distributed. However, the last two decades of the twentieth century saw a reversal of this trend and, now, at the start of the twenty-first century a quarter of the UK population live in households with incomes below half the national average.

Wealth

Wealth is a stock of assets that have a financial value. Economists distinguish between marketable and non-marketable wealth. **Marketable wealth** is wealth that can be transferred to another person, for example houses and shares. **Non-marketable wealth** is wealth which is specific to a person and cannot be transferred, for example pension rights.

The **distribution of wealth** can be considered in terms of how it is distributed between the population (size distribution), the forms in which it is held and

according to the characteristics of those holding wealth.

The size distribution of wealth

Wealth is very unequally distributed among the UK population. Table 9.1 shows the size distribution of marketable wealth in the UK in 1986 and 1995.

Table 9.1 Distribution of wealth in the UK

	Percentages	
	1986	1995
Marketable wealth		
Percentage of wealth owned by:		
Most wealthy 1%	18	19
Most wealthy 5%	36	39
Most wealthy 10%	50	52
Most wealthy 25%	73	74
Most wealthy 50%	90	93
Total marketable wealth (£ billion)	955	2042

Social Trends 30, 2000, Office for National Statistics

Table 9.1 shows that wealth has become more unequally distributed between 1986 and 1995. It also shows the extent of inequality. In both years the wealthiest 10 per cent of the population owned half of the country's wealth.

Wealth distribution between assets

Wealth can be held in a variety of forms including life assurance and pension funds, property, securities and shares, banking and building society deposits and cash.

Life assurance and pension fund holdings have in the past accounted for the largest percentage of wealth held, forming more than a third of all household wealth in 1997. This form of wealth is more evenly distributed than property, securities and shares.

The proportion of a particular asset in the wealth of the household sector is influenced not only by the amount accumulated but also by changes in its value. For example, in the late 1980s the share accounted for by property in the form of residential houses rose as a result of increases in owner-occupation and rises in the price of houses, whereas in the early 1990s the fall in property prices was reflected in a decline in property as a percentage of the wealth of the household sector.

ACTIVITY 1

Wealth in Britain has soared to record levels. Forty years after Harold Macmillan declared that Britons never had it so good, the country is richer than ever.

Household wealth rose by 15% last year to top £4000 billion for the first time, according to estimates by Salomon Smith Barney, the investment bank. The rise in wealth in 1999, the biggest in any year in the 1990s, means that each individual in Britain is worth an average of £72 000.

The surge in wealth reflects two factors; house prices, which increased by 13.6% in the 12 months to last month, and the booming stock market, which rose by 21%.

Total household wealth at the end of last year was £4267 billion, according to the new estimates. Of this, just over £1300 billion is in houses (after allowing for the amount owed in mortgages) and the remainder in shares, bank deposits, pensions and other financial assets.

David Smith and Trushar Barot, 'Boom makes Mr. Average worth £72,000' in *The Sunday Times*, 9 January 2000

a What were the main causes of the increase in wealth in 1999?

b In 1997 23 per cent of the wealth of the household sector was accounted for by houses. What percentage was it in 1999? What may have accounted for this change?

c Discuss the effect a rise in wealth is likely to have on consumption.

Wealth distribution between different groups

As would be expected, wealth is unevenly distributed between age categories. For example, people in their 40s and 50s have had more time to accumulate savings than people in their 20s and 30s and do indeed have greater wealth.

However, the amount of wealth held also varies between ethnic groups and genders. White adults have more wealth than adults from ethnic minorities. The group which currently has the lowest holding of wealth per head is people of a Bangladeshi background. Men also have more wealth than women.

Source of wealth

A person can become wealthy in four main ways:

■ Through inheritance. This is the main way someone becomes wealthy.

■ Through saving. A person could accumulate wealth by saving. However, to achieve significant wealth saving has to be on a large scale. This is easier to achieve by people with high incomes that may themselves be generated by significant holdings of wealth. Indeed, wealth creates wealth.

■ Through the use of entrepreneurial skills. Some people are self-made millionaires as a result of building up a business. For example, Bill Gates of Microsoft has built up a fortune in excess of £36.25 billion.

■ Through chance. Lottery winners receive a considerable amount of publicity and a number of people are made 'instant millionaires'. However even a £2 million lottery win pales into insignificance when compared with the approximately £1750 million that the family of the Duke of Westminster stand to inherit.

Causes of the inequality of wealth

The causes of the inequality of wealth are obviously linked to the sources of wealth and include the following:

■ The pattern of inheritance. In the UK significant holdings of wealth have traditionally been passed on to the next generation on the basis of primogeniture (the right of the eldest son to inherit to the exclusion of others). In the UK major estates and the connected titles are still passed on to the eldest son, whereas in countries where property and other assets are distributed among the children on the death of the parents, wealth becomes more evenly distributed over time.

■ Marriage patterns of the wealthy. The wealthy tend to marry other wealthy people. This further concentrates wealth in the hands of the few.

■ Inequality of income. As already noted, people with high income are more able to save and earn interest.

■ Different tendencies to save. Those who save a higher proportion of their income will accumulate more wealth than those who save a smaller proportion.

■ Luck. This plays a part in terms of the success of businesses which people start and in terms of who wins money.

Wealth and income distribution

Wealth is more unevenly distributed than **income**. While a person can survive without owning any assets by, for example, renting a house, it is not possible to survive without any income. In addition, due to inheritance the highest amount of wealth a person can hold at any one time exceeds the highest amount a person can earn.

Distribution of income

Within a country the **distribution of income** can be considered in terms of how income is shared out between the factors of production (functional distribution of income), between households (size distribution) and between geographical areas (geographical distribution of income).

The functional distribution of income

Income is a flow of money over a period of time. Income can be earned by labour in the form of wages, by capital in the form of interest, by land in the form of rent and by entrepreneurs in the form of profits. In the UK wages still account for the largest percentage, but the percentage is falling. In 1987 61 per cent of household income came from wages but by 1997 it was down to 56 per cent. By contrast income from dividends, interest and rent (collectively known as investment income) has been rising.

In addition to earned income and investment income, households can receive income in the form of social security benefit. The relative shares of earned income, investment income and transfer payments depend on a variety of factors but principally on the level of employment and the relative power of labour and capital.

Measuring the size distribution of income

A common method of measuring the degree of inequality of income and wealth distribution between households is the **Lorenz curve**. This is named after the US statistician Max Otto Lorenz.

As well as measuring the extent of industrial concentration, Lorenz curves can be used to compare the distribution of income and wealth over time and between countries. The horizontal axis measures the percentage of the population starting with the poorest. In the case of income distribution, the vertical axis measures the percentage of income earned. A 45° line is included. This is called the line of income equality as it shows a situation in which, for example, 40 per cent of the population earned 40 per cent of the income and 80 per cent of the population earned 80 per cent of the income. The actual cumulative percentage income shares are then included on the diagram. In practice, this will form a curve which starts at the origin and ends with 100

per cent of the population earning 100 per cent of income but which lies below the 45° line. The greater the degree of inequality, the greater the extent to which the curve will be below the 45° line. Figure 9.1 shows that income is more unevenly distributed in Country A than in Country B.

For example, in country A the poorest 20 per cent of the population earn only 5 per cent of the income, whereas in country B they earn 12 per cent. The distribution can be measured in terms of, for example, fifths of the population (quintiles) or deciles (tenths).

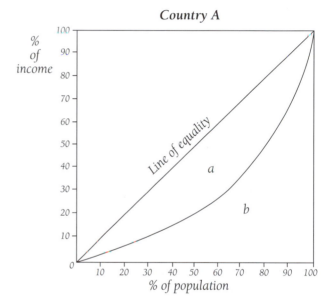

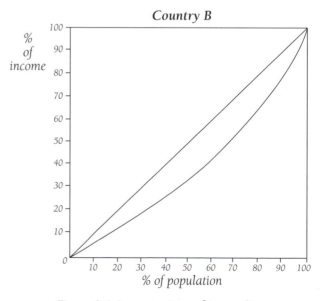

Figure 9.1 A comparison of inequality

The **Gini coefficient** measures precisely the degree of inequality shown on a Lorenz curve. It is the ratio of the area between the Lorenz curve and the line of inequality and the line of income inequality to the total area below the line. In Figure 9.1a this is the ratio of a/a+b. Complete equality would give a ratio of 0 and complete inequality 1. So, in practice, the ratio will lie between 0 and 1, and the nearer it is to 1, the more unequal the distribution of income.

ACTIVITY 2

a Using the information given in Table 9.1 plot a Lorenz curve for the distribution of marketable wealth in 1995.

b In 1966 the figures for the distribution of marketable wealth were:

Percentage of wealth owned by:	%
Most wealthy 1%	33
5%	56
10%	69
25%	87
50%	97

Plot these figures on a separate Lorenz curve.

c Comment on how the degree of wealth inequality changed between 1966 and 1996.

The size distribution of income in the UK

In recent years the distribution of income has become more unequal. The widening of the gap between those with high incomes and those with low incomes was particularly noticeable between 1980 and 1990.

There were a number of reasons for this rise in income equality. One was the cut in the top tax rates which, of course, benefited the rich most. Another was the rise in top executive pay which was sparked initially by privatisation. At the other end of the income range there was a decrease in the real value of benefits, particularly job seekers' allowance, and a rise in the number of lone parents. The percentage of families with dependent children that are headed by lone parents more than doubled between 1971 and 1996. The lack of support in bringing up the children means lone parents are often not in work or only in part-time jobs.

The causes of income inequality between households

These include the following:

■ Unequal holdings of wealth. As wealth generates income in the form of profit, interest and dividends, differentials in wealth cause differences in income.

■ Differences in the composition of households. Some households may have, say, three adults working, whereas other households may contain no one in employment. Indeed, low income is closely associated with a dependency on benefits.

■ Differences in skills and qualifications. Those with high skills and qualifications are likely to be in high demand and hence likely to be able to earn high incomes.

■ Differences in educational opportunities. Those who have the opportunity to stay in education for longer are likely to gain more qualifications and develop more skills and so, as indicated above, are likely to increase their earning potential. Indeed, lifetime earnings of graduates are noticeably higher than those of non-graduates.

■ Discrimination. The income of some groups is adversely affected by discrimination in terms of employment opportunities, pay and promotion chances.

■ Differences in hours worked. Most full-time workers earn more than part-time workers and those who work overtime earn more than those who work the standard hours.

The geographical distribution of income

Income is unevenly distributed between the regions of the UK. For example, in 1997 the average disposable income per head was £11 084 in London, £8661 in Scotland and only £8464 in Northern Ireland.

Table 9.2 shows how GDP per head compares in the different regions of the UK.

Table 9.2 Regional comparison of GDP per head in 1997

Region	GDP per head (UK Index = 100)
North East	83
North West	91
Yorkshire and Humberside	89
East Midlands	96
West Midlands	93
East	102
London	125
South East	118
South West	98
Wales	82
Scotland	96
Northern Ireland	80

Social Trends 30, 2000, Office for National Statistics

Regional income differences are even greater in Germany and Italy. Germany has a very wide gap between the former East Germany and the former West Germany. There is a North-South divide in Italy, where the Southern Mezzogiorno region is much poorer than the North.

There are a number of causes of differences in the geographical distribution of income, including differences in:

- unemployment rates
- the proportion of the population claiming benefits
- the qualifications and the skills of the labour force
- industrial structure
- occupational structure
- living costs, for example London allowances.

Of course, there are variations within regions. Even though London as a whole has a high income per head, it has some of the most deprived districts in the UK.

Government policies

The extent to which a government intervenes to affect the distribution of income and wealth depends on the extent to which it believes that the free market distribution would be inequitable, the effects such inequality will have on society and the effects it believes any intervention will have on incentives and efficiency.

New classical economists do not favour significant intervention. This is because they believe that differences in income act as signals encouraging workers to move jobs and differences in wealth promote saving and investment.

They also argue that the provision of benefits above a minimum level for those who cannot work such as the disabled and sick can encourage voluntary unemployment.

In contrast Keynesians believe that intervention is justified as market forces will not ensure an efficient allocation of income and wealth and that low levels of income and wealth can cause considerable problems for the households involved, including having a detrimental effect on the educational performance of the children. They also think that significant differences in income and wealth can cause social division with the poor feeling socially excluded.

Ways in which governments affect the distribution of income and wealth.

Governments influence the distribution in a number of ways, including the following:

- Taxation. To assess the effects of taxation on the distribution of income and wealth, pre- and post-tax distribution can be compared. In the UK the overall effect of the tax system is to reduce inequality. However, while progressive taxes, such as income tax, which take a higher percentage of the income or wealth of the rich make the distribution more equal, regressive taxes, such as VAT, which take a higher percentage of the income of the poor make the distribution more unequal.

- The provision of **cash benefits**. There are two types of cash benefits – means tested and universal. **Means-tested benefits**, for example family credit, are available to those who claim them and who can prove their income is below a certain level. **Universal benefits** are available to everyone in a particular group irrespective of income, for example families with young children receive child benefit. Means-tested benefits reduce inequality and universal benefits form a larger percentage of the income of the poor.

- The provision of **benefits in kind**. These include the provision of, for example, health care, education and school meals. The take up of these benefits depends on the age composition of the household (for example the elderly make the most use of the National Health Service) and attitudes and opportunities to access the provision (with, for example, more middle-class children staying on in education after 16 than working-class children).

- Labour market policy. The Minimum Wage Act of 1999, the anti-discrimination acts and government subsidising of training reduce income inequality.

- Macroeconomic policy influences the distribution of income and wealth in a number of ways. For example, measures to reduce unemployment may benefit low-income households and regional policy reduces geographical inequalities of income and wealth.

Table 9.3 shows that income tax and benefits in kind reduced income inequality in the UK in 1997–98.

Table 9.3 Redistribution of income through taxes and benefits, UK, 1997–98

£ per year

	Quintile group of households					
	Bottom fifth	Next fifth	Middle fifth	Next fifth	Top fifth	All households
Average per household						
Wages and salaries	1510	4680	12 090	20 780	35 110	14 830
Imputed income from benefits in kind	10	30	90	320	1010	290
Self-employment income	320	570	1070	1700	5580	1850
Occupational pensions, annuities	300	940	1500	2060	2770	1520
Investment income	220	340	610	920	2980	1020
Other income	160	210	170	180	160	170
Total original income	2520	6780	15 530	25 960	47 610	19 680
plus Benefits in cash						
Contributory	2010	2510	1910	1150	760	1670
Non-contributory	2770	2490	1680	900	360	1640
Gross income	7300	11 780	19 120	28 000	48 720	22 980
less Income tax and NIC	320	960	2710	5090	10 530	3920
less Local taxes (net)	430	540	660	770	910	660
Disposable income	6550	10 280	15 760	22 140	37 280	18 400
less Indirect taxes	2010	2550	3570	4680	5770	3720
Post-tax income	4540	7730	12 180	17 460	31 520	14 690
plus Benefits in kind						
Education	1750	1280	1190	1040	640	1180
National health service	1910	1870	1850	1530	1320	1700
Housing subsidy	90	80	40	20	10	50
Travel subsidies	50	60	60	70	110	70
School meals and welfare milk	80	20	10	-	-	20
Final income	8430	11 030	15 330	20 120	33 590	17 700

Source: Table 5.18 *Social Trends 30*, 2000, ONS

ACTIVITY 3

Using Table 9.3, calculate the effect of indirect taxes on the distribution of income.

Summary

This unit has examined the forms in which wealth is held. For many people the most important forms of wealth they hold are their house and their pension rights. Wealth is very unevenly distributed in the UK. The most wealthy 10 per cent of the population own 50 per cent of the wealth. The main cause of this inequality is inheritance. Differences in holdings of wealth give rise to differences of income. Other causes of the inequality of income are differences in earnings ability (which, in turn, reflect differences in skills and qualifications) and differences in the composition of households. Income is more evenly distributed than wealth, although the last two decades have witnessed a rise in inequality.

The degree of inequality of income and wealth distribution can be measured using a Lorenz curve which plots the cumulative percentage of population on the horizontal axis and the cumulative percentage of income or wealth on the vertical axis. Income and wealth would be more unevenly distributed in the absence of government intervention in the form of taxation, benefits, macroeconomic and labour market policies.

Data response question

The Prime Minister was always on a hiding to nothing if he thought he could convince the nation there is no North-South economic divide. Inequality is pervasive in capitalist economies and one of the varieties of inequality is regional. Britain is not very different from the US or France or Italy, or any other country, in this respect. Each has regions that seem unable to cast off their heritage of decline and failure. In the case of the UK it is the industrial North, some of the once-mighty cities that generated the national wealth are economic no-go zones at the turn of the 21st century.

Mr Blair is right to point out that London has the country's worst pockets of poverty and deprivation, cheek by jowl with its most ostentatious wealth; and some measures of the regional divide, such as unemployment rates, have indeed narrowed. Of course, government policies must tackle these problems, no matter where they occur. An anti-poverty policy makes sense in the way that a 'pro-North' policy would not.

'There is inequality, but hand-outs will not solve the North's problems', *editorial, The Independent, 7 December 1999*

Table 9.4 Income in different regions in 1995–98

Region	Average gross weekly income (=100%)	
	per household	per person
	£	£
North East	333	145
North West	84	158
Yorkshire and the Humber	360	152
Eas Midlands	401	166
West Midlands	381	155
East	419	177
London	491	204
South East	474	207
South West	405	173
Wales	360	151
Scotland	371	158
Northern Ireland	336	126
United Kingdom	408	171

Regional Trends, 1999, Office for National Statistics

1 Explain why 'inequality is pervasive in capitalist economies'. (6 marks)
2 Identify one other variety of income inequality. (2 marks)
3 Apart from the industrial structure, discuss two other reasons why income per household may vary between regions. (4 marks)
4 Give an example of 'ostentatious wealth' and explain what may cause an increase in the inequality of wealth distribution. (6 marks)
5 The North East and Northern Ireland have similar household incomes but a greater difference in income per head. What could explain this? (2 marks)
6 Does Table 9.4 indicate a North-South economic divide? Explain your answer. (5 marks)

Introduction

Unit 9 discussed how income and wealth are unequally distributed. This unit examines the position of those who are at the bottom end of the distribution. In the last two decades the number of households with incomes below half of average income has risen. It is estimated, for example, that in the UK a third of children, 4.5 million, live in poverty. This unit discusses the meaning, measurement and consequences of poverty. It also covers some of the policy measures that a government can take to reduce poverty.

Absolute poverty

Economists distinguish between **absolute poverty** and **relative poverty**. People are said to be in absolute poverty when their income is insufficient for them to be able to afford basic shelter, food and clothing. Even in rich countries there are some people who still do not have any housing. It has been estimated that in England in 2000 there were 1600 people sleeping rough. Of course, the problem of absolute poverty is more extensive in poor countries.

Relative poverty

While people in the UK may consider themselves to be poor if they are living in poor accommodation, have a television but no video recorder and can only afford to go out once a week, people in, say, Mali might regard themselves as well off if they had the same standard of living. This reflects the difference between absolute and relative poverty.

People are relatively poor when they are poor in comparison to other people. They are those who are unable to afford a certain standard of living at a particular time. As a result, they are unable to participate in the usual activities of the society they live in.

Table 10.1 is based on three items which most people in the European Union might have expected to be able to afford in 1995.

Table 10.1 Percentage of households that did not feel that they could afford certain items: EU comparison, 1995

	Percentages		
	Eat meat every other day	New clothes	A week's holiday
Portugal	6	47	59
Greece	35	32	51
Spain	2	9	49
United Kingdom	10	15	40
Irish Republic	4	7	38
Italy	6	15	38
France	5	10	34
Belgium	4	10	26
Austria	8	10	24
Denmark	2	5	16
Netherlands	2	13	15
Luxembourg	3	5	14
Germany	5	15	12

Social Trends 29, 1999, Office for National Statistics

Table 10.1 gives some indication of differences in living standards across the European Union. The UK does not compare well with the other countries. The UK, Portugal and Greece had a relatively high percentage of households who did not appear to be enjoying a high living standard. Of course, if the same items were considered for most developing countries the figures would be much higher.

Relative and absolute poverty

Relative poverty varies between countries and over time. Someone who is regarded as poor in the USA might be regarded as relatively rich in, for example, Ethiopia. Fifteen years ago in the UK a personal computer might have been regarded as something of a luxury for a household, but now to participate in the activities of society it might be viewed as a necessity.

If a country experiences a rise in income, absolute poverty may fall. However, if those on high incomes benefit more than those on low incomes relative poverty may rise.

Measuring poverty

To assess the extent to which poverty is a problem, it has to be measured. Whereas there are measures which the government uses in terms of inflation (for example RPIX) and unemployment (for example the Labour Force Survey (LFS) measure), there is no official measure of poverty.

ACTIVITY 1

'Income inequality continued to grow in the final years of the last Conservative government and the first few months under Labour.

Figures released by the Social Security department yesterday showed that between 1994–95 and 1997–98, people in the bottom 10 per cent saw no growth in income before housing costs.

Against that, the population as a whole saw on average a 6 per cent rise in their real income, matched, or possibly slightly bettered, by those with incomes in the top 10 per cent, according to the Households Below Average Income series.'

Nicholas Timmins, 'Gap between rich and poor widened during Labour's honeymoon months' in the *Financial Times*, 15 October 1999

According to the extract what happened to absolute and relative poverty in the UK in the second half of the 1990s?

However, economists often define as poor those whose income is less than half the average income (adjusted to take account of family size). Indeed, the European Union has developed a poverty standard set at 50 per cent of the average disposable income before housing costs per equivalent household. The current Labour government, has set itself the task of eradicating child poverty within a generation, and now publishes a **poverty audit**. This includes poverty statistics and assesses the government's performance against a set of indicators in the form of targets. The first poverty audit came out in September 1999. It found that:

- a quarter of the population were living in households with incomes below the poverty line of £132 a week – half the national average income

- a third of all children, 4.5 million, lived in poverty – three times the number in 1979

- more than half of the 5.6 million people claiming income support, jobseekers' allowance and incapacity benefit had been on benefits for more than two years

- one fifth of children lived in households where nobody worked – which was twice the 1979 level

- the proportion of families with dependent children that are headed by lone parents increased from 8 per cent to 21 per cent in 1996.

Among the targets included are:

- an increase in the proportion of working-age people with a qualification

- improving literacy and numeracy at age 11

- reducing the proportion of older people unable to afford to heat their homes properly

- reducing the number of households with low incomes

- reducing homelessness

- reducing the number of children in workless households.

The poor

Particular groups are more prone to poverty than others. These include the old, the disabled, the sick, lone parents with children, the unemployed and those from ethnic minorities. For example, in 1996–97 42 per cent of lone parent families were in the bottom fifth of the income distribution and in 1995–96 66 per cent of Pakistani/Bangladeshi households were in the bottom fifth.

Causes of poverty

Essentially, the amount of poverty experienced depends on the level of income achieved and how it is distributed. The reasons why particular people are poor include the following:

- Unemployment. This is a major cause of poverty, with some households having no one in employment.

- Low wages. Some workers in unskilled, casual employment earn very low wages. For example a significant proportion of workers in Northern Ireland and the North East are on low wages. However, just because someone earns low wages does not necessarily mean they are poor. It is possible that they could live in a household with a high-income earning partner or parents.

- Sickness and disability. Most of the long-term sick and disabled are dependent on benefits and this takes them into the low-income category.

- Old age. For pensioners state benefits are the largest source of income. However, occupational pensions and investment income are forming an increasing proportion of the income of some of the old.

- **The poverty trap**. This arises when the poor find it difficult to raise their disposable income because any rise in gross income results in them having to pay more in taxes and receiving less in benefits.

- Being a lone parent. Not having a partner to cope with the raising of a child may make it difficult for someone to obtain full-time employment.

- Reluctance to claim benefits. A number of people, either because they are unaware of their entitlements or because of fear of social stigma, do not claim benefits which could help to supplement their incomes.

The effects of poverty

Poverty, especially absolute poverty, has a number of serious adverse effects on those who experience it. The poor tend to suffer worse physical and mental health and indeed have a lower life expectancy.

The children of the poor suffer in terms of receiving less, and often a lower quality of, education. They are less likely to stay in full-time education post-16, have few books at home and attend low-performing schools. They are also less likely to have a personal computer in the home and to travel abroad. All these factors tend to result in them gaining fewer qualifications and a vicious circle of poverty developing.

The poor can also feel cut off and even alienated from society, unable to live the type of life that the majority can experience.

ACTIVITY 2

Human poverty, a concept introduced in the Human Development Report 1997 sees impoverishment as multi-dimensional. More than a lack of what is necessary for material well-being, poverty can also mean the denial of opportunities and choices most basic to human development. To lead a long, healthy, creative life. To have a decent standard of living. To enjoy dignity, self-esteem, the respect of others and the things that people value in life. Human poverty thus looks at more than a lack of income. Since income is not the sum total of human lives, the lack of it cannot be the sum total of human deprivation.

United Nations, *Human Development Report 1998*, Oxford University Press

a Explain how the definition of human poverty differs from absolute poverty as it is usually defined.

b Discuss how easy you think it is to measure human poverty and absolute poverty.

c What is included in the UN's Human Poverty Index (HPI)?

Government policy measures to reduce poverty

Governments may seek to reduce absolute policy by introducing measures which raise the income of the poorest groups. They may also try to reduce relative policy by introducing measures which also reduce the gap between the rich and the poor. Among the various measures which they might use are the following:

- Operating a national minimum wage. If set above the equilibrium rate this will help the low paid who stay in employment. However, there are disputes about the effect that such a measure may have on the employment of unskilled workers. Also, as mentioned above, not all the low paid are poor and, of course, not all the poor are in low-paid jobs, for example the old and the disabled. In addition, if over time the minimum wage is not raised in line with earnings it will cease to have any effect.

- Cutting the bottom rates of income tax. This is something the Labour government has done in order to reduce the extent of the poverty trap and provide a greater incentive for people to work. Although in addition to the incentive there also has to be the jobs available.

- Increasing employment opportunities. This is thought to be significant as a major cause of poverty is unemployment. However, economists disagree about the best methods of increasing the number of jobs on offer.

- Improving the quantity and quality of training and education. This is a long-term measure but again is an important one as it will increase the productivity and potential productivity of those affected and thereby improve their job prospects and earning potential.

- Making use of the trickle-down effect. This is a more controversial measure favoured by some supply-side economists. The idea is to cut the rate of corporation tax and the high rates of income tax with the intention of encouraging entrepreneurs to expand and thereby create employment for the poor. It is also thought that the higher spending which the rich may undertake may also stimulate the economy. However, it can be debated how the rich will react and whether the poor will benefit from any expansion that does occur. For example, will they have the skills for any new jobs created and what about the poor who are unable to work?

■ Increasing benefits. Economists differ on their views about the effects of raising benefits for the unemployed. Keynesians think that it can raise aggregate demand and thereby create jobs, while new classical economists believe it will increase voluntary unemployment. However, there is more agreement on increasing benefits for those unable to work or who are retired. Those dependent solely on state sickness or disability benefit or the state pension fall into the lowest quintile of income and many of these would be unable to take out private insurance or invest to raise their income.

■ Increasing the provision of affordable child care. This would enable more lone parents to undertake full-time employment and raise themselves out of poverty.

A C T I V I T Y 3

[The government is considering introducing a] 'system of loans funded by banks which employers will take on to finance training …

Under the proposal, groups of companies will organise the loans on behalf of individual employees.

Should the person move job, debts will be transferred to the new employer.'

Kevin Brown, 'Incentives to boost workplace training' in the *Financial Times*, 12 January 2000

a Explain why such a loan system may encourage firms to train their workers.

b Discuss one other measure which the government could introduce to raise the skills of workers.

Summary

Absolute poverty is experienced by those whose income is below that needed to achieve a minimum standard of living, whereas people experience relative poverty when they are poor relative to others. Most economists define as poor those whose income falls below half of average income. Most of the poor are dependent on benefits and a major cause of poverty is that no one in the household is in employment. The poor are less healthy and their children's educational prospects are adversely affected. A range of measures have been suggested to reduce poverty, including increasing employment opportunities, reducing marginal tax rates, increasing benefits and the long-term measure of raising educational performance.

Data response question

[The government's] report backs up the government's belief that worklessness, not family structure, is the main cause of child poverty. In 1997–98, children of lone parents were more likely to be in poor families, but that is because lone parents were less likely to work. Of the 2.9m children in lone-parent families, 1.8m had no working parent, compared with only 1m of the 8.3m children of couples. Children of couples where both parents worked were more likely to be in well-off households. But children of couples where only one worked, or where none worked, were just as likely to be rich or poor as children of lone parents in similar circumstances.

Ministers have said that they do not want to alleviate poverty simply by increasing benefits. They want to help those on low incomes to haul themselves up. One part of the report sheds light on how far this has happened, by tracking the fortunes of individual households since 1991. This shows evidence of significant mobility. The real median incomes of those in the bottom fifth of the income distribution in 1991 rose from £129 a week (in April 1999 prices) to £179 a week in 1997. And half of those in the bottom fifth in 1991 had risen out of it by 1997.

Although many people experience temporarily low incomes, only 4% of the population were stuck in the bottom fifth for the whole seven years. The people most likely to be persistently poor were pensioners (especially single ones), unemployed people (including lone parents and those with disabilities), and people without educational qualifications. So ministers' Victorian remedy for avoiding persistent poverty looks spot on: study, work and save.'

'Poverty: a mobile society' in *The Economist*, 23 October 1999

1 According to the extract, what is the main cause of poverty? (3 marks)

2 Why are the children of lone parents more likely to be in households where no one works? (5 marks)

3 What is meant by income mobility? (4 marks)

4 Explain how studying might enable someone to move out of poverty. (5 marks)

5 Assess the arguments for and against raising benefits to reduce poverty. (8 marks)

Key concepts covered

- maintenance time
- merit goods
- tourism
- tourism income multiplier
- demonstration effect
- acculturation
- market failure
- carrying capacity
- consumption and investment benefits
- semi-public goods
- price discrimination

Introduction

Units 5–10 concentrated largely on work and income. However, people do not spend all their time working or seeking work. This unit shifts the focus and looks at the issue of how people spend their free or leisure time. It starts by defining leisure and examining different forms of leisure. It discusses the demand and supply of leisure and recent developments in the leisure market. The key features of two of the markets which make up the wider leisure market, the tourism market and the sports market, are then examined.

The meaning of leisure

Leisure is an experience that occurs outside working hours within the time when people are free to select what they do. People's time can be divided into three main categories:

- work/education
- **maintenance time**, for example time spent looking after children, sleeping, bathing, eating and undertaking domestic work – the activities necessary for existence
- leisure.

So leisure time is the time which people have left to spend in ways they wish after they have completed their work/educational and maintenance commitments.

Of course, it is not always clear cut as to what constitutes leisure. Someone may regard time spent gardening as maintenance time while another person may regard it as leisure time. Similarly, one person studying an A-level subject might be doing so for 'leisure reasons' while another might be doing it as part of a course with the intention of using the qualification to gain access to higher education. In addition, while some people, for example, play football for fun, others are paid to play.

Leisure time is not evenly distributed between people. The retired have the most free time while women working full time have the least.

Table 11.1 shows that men have slightly more free time than women and that people aged 45 and over have more free time than those aged 16–44.

Choice between work and leisure

A key determinant of how much leisure time many adults have is how long they spend working. This is affected by the income and substitution effects which

Table 11.1 Time use: by age, Great Britain, May 1995

	Hours and minutes					
	Males			Females		
	16–44	45 and over	All aged 16 and over	16–44	45 and over	All aged 16 and over
Average daily hours spent on						
Sleep	8.25	8.54	8.40	8.33	9.03	8.48
Free time	5.22	6.48	6.06	4.54	6.15	5.35
Education/paid work	5.13	2.39	3.54	3.15	1.23	2.18
Domestic work	0.33	0.51	0.42	2.03	2.45	2.24
Personal care	0.37	0.42	0.39	0.46	0.49	0.47
Household maintenance (including DIY and gardening)	0.36	1.11	0.54	0.16	0.34	0.25
Free time per weekday	4.44	6.07	5.24	4.28	6.11	5.20
Free time per weekend day	7.32	8.56	8.19	6.02	6.42	6.22

Source: Table 13.2, *Social Trends 29*, 1999, Office for National Statistics

were discussed in Unit 5. The trade-off between work and leisure also explains why overtime rates are usually above the standard pay rates. If employers ask their workers to work longer hours they are also asking them to have less leisure time. The fewer the hours of leisure that people have the more valuable those hours become to them and the more they have to be compensated to give them up.

Forms of leisure

Leisure activities can be divided into categories in a number of different ways. One is into home-based activities such as reading, listening to CDs and gardening, and activities away from the home such as eating out, visiting a disco and going to the cinema. In the UK the most popular home-based activity is watching the television. On average, in 1997 people spent 25 hours a week watching television. The most common leisure activity outside the home in the UK is visiting the pub.

Leisure can also be divided into broad categories, for example educational and cultural, sporting, social and caring, and nature and environmental. The most detailed form of categorisation is into particular activities, for example music, film, **tourism**, theatre.

Demand for leisure

The key influences on demand for leisure are as follows:

■ The amount of disposable income available. Leisure is a normal good. As incomes rise demand for leisure increases.

■ The price of leisure. The demand for leisure is influenced by its opportunity cost, i.e. what has to be given up to gain the free time.

■ The pattern of working hours. Over time the standard working week in most countries has tended to decline, giving rise to more free time.

■ Technological developments in domestic appliances. The increased efficiency of washing machines and vacuum cleaners, for example, has reduced the amount of time people have to spend on domestic tasks.

■ The range and quality of leisure activities and equipment. The development of new forms of leisure activities such as home videoing and surfing the Internet have increased demand for leisure.

■ Population size and age distribution. Obviously, a rise in population size increases demand for

leisure. An increase in the proportion above retirement age may also increase demand for leisure.

The supply of leisure

Leisure is supplied by the following sectors:

■ The private sector. Private-sector firms supply a range of leisure activities through, for example, health clubs, travel agents, cinemas, theme parks and professional football clubs. The most common aim of these firms is to maximise profits so a rise in price will usually result in more being supplied.

■ The public sector. Local authorities and agencies acting on behalf of the government, for example the Arts Council, also supply directly a range of leisure activities, including libraries, public playing fields, sports centres, museums and art galleries. They charge either no price or more commonly a low price for these activities. The state also subsidises some leisure activities by giving grants, including grants from National Lottery funds to private-sector companies supplying leisure services. The motive behind the state's intervention is linked to the **merit good** nature of many leisure activities and the question of equity.

■ The voluntary sector. A number of voluntary organisations supply leisure services such as tennis clubs, angling clubs and craft societies. These are usually self-financed through subscriptions and charges.

ACTIVITY 1

The number of visitors to the Millennium Dome at Greenwich in the first few months of 2000 was disappointing. On some days attendances were as low as 5000 instead of the projected 20 000. The New Millennium Experience Company was employing 2000 people and had intended to take on more staff in the summer to cope with the expected rise in visitors to 55 000 a day.

a Why was the number of visitors expected to rise in the summer?

b Why might the number of visitors have been lower than anticipated?

c What could the New Millennium Experience Company have done to raise attendance in the first few months?

Factors influencing demand for a particular leisure activity

- The price of the activity. Some leisure activities are provided free to the consumer such as walking, watching hockey on local playing fields and making use of public libraries. Other activities involve fixed and marginal costs. For example, someone who plays tennis has to buy rackets and balls and may pay belong to a tennis club (fixed costs). They may also then have to pay each time they use a court (marginal cost).

- The price of complementary goods and services. Someone who enjoys visiting the theatre may also have to pay to get to the theatre in which case a taxi or bus service, etc. is a complementary good.

- The price of substitutes, including not only other leisure activities but also work.

- Tastes. Tastes in leisure activities change over time. For example, in recent years the popularity of line dancing has increased while the popularity of ten-pin bowling has declined.

- Age composition. The increase in the average age of the population has led to a rise in the demand for holidays specially designed for the over-50s and an increase in spending at garden centres.

- Gender composition. For example, a higher percentage of men engage in DIY and gardening than women and a higher percentage of women read books and knit than men.

- Advertising. Advertising can be a potent force. Advertisements for films and concerts can help to raise attendances.

- Major events. A major event can generate demand for related activities. For example, attendances at football matches usually rise after a World Cup and a concert by a band can help sell its CDs.

- Exchange rate. A fall in the exchange rate makes the country or area's products more price competitive in terms of other countries' currencies. This can result in a rise in the number of tourists visiting the country/area.

Changes in the leisure market

In recent years there has been a number of changes in the market, including the following:

- A rise in the proportion of home-based leisure activities. For example, the ownership of home computers has increased from 16 per cent in 1986 to 26 per cent in 1996–97 and more people now order deliveries of, say, pizzas and Chinese food to their homes.

- A rise in gambling. This is largely accounted for by the introduction of the National Lottery in November 1994. It has been estimated that 94 per cent of the adult population have bought a lottery ticket.

- A rise in expenditure on leisure activities. This has been the result of rising income and more leisure time. Some of this rise in expenditure has gone on merchandise associated with leisure activities. For example, anglers buy magazines on angling and football supporters buy team strips sold by their clubs.

- An increase in the influence of the USA. Trends in leisure activities in the UK and the EU are increasingly being influenced by developments in the leisure industry in the USA. For example, theme parks and private health clubs have spread from the US to Europe.

ACTIVITY 2

Table 11.2 Percentage of UK households participating in the National Lottery, by social class of head of household

	Percentages		
	1995	1997	1998
Professional	63	54	43
Managerial and technical	70	62	58
Skilled non-manual	82	67	58
Skilled manual	89	80	75

Social Trends 29, 1999, Office for National Statistics

a What does the extract suggest about the income elasticity of demand for National Lottery tickets?

b What might explain the change in the participation of households in the National Lottery between 1995 and 1998?

Tourism

Tourism involves people moving from their usual place of residence to a destination in which they make use of facilities and undertake activities. People can be tourists in their own countries and in other countries.

Table 11.3 shows the most popular places for people to visit in the UK.

Table 11.3 Top attractions: annual visitors (fee-charging sites)

Alton Towers	2.8m
Madame Tussauds	2.7m
Tower of London	2.5m
Natural History Museum	1.9m
Chessington	1.6m
Science Museum	1.6m
Legoland	1.5m
Canterbury Cathedral	1.5m
Windsor Castle	1.5m
Edinburgh Castle	1.2m

The Sunday Times, 9 January 2000

People visit these sites from the UK and from a wide range of other countries, including the USA, Japan and Germany.

In the UK and most other countries tourism has grown significantly in the last two decades and is now the largest industry in the world. Nevertheless, its market is volatile, with significant fluctuations in demand according to the time of the year, the type of weather experienced and changes in income levels.

Much of the economic analysis of tourism focuses on its effects on income, employment, the balance of payments and the environment.

The growth of tourism
The tourist industry has increased because of:

■ an increase in disposable income

■ a reduction in working hours

■ early retirement

■ a reduction in the time spent on domestic tasks

■ improved transport

■ increased advertising

■ increased awareness of the benefits of holidays and travel.

The effects of tourism
Income and employment
The growth of the tourist industry has increased income and employment in a number of countries. This effect can be greater than it first appears. Obviously, tourists create income and employment directly for the hotels, restaurants and attractions which cater for tourists. But they also create income and employment in a wide range of other industries. Some of these are ones which supply goods and services to the tourist industry such as insurance firms, farms and taxi firms. Others are ones which benefit from spending by local people and firms arising from the income brought in by the tourists. So an initial rise in income of, say, £30 million in an area and the creation of 2000 extra jobs may eventually lead to a rise in income of £90 million and 5000 more jobs. This knock-on effect on income and employment is referred to as the **tourism income multiplier**.

However, the initial jobs created in the tourist industry may not be of a very high quality as many are unskilled. Workers in the tourist industry also tend not to be very well paid. In addition, the effect on income and employment will not be very great if a significant proportion of the goods and services used in the tourist industry are bought in from abroad. For example, a hotel in Petra in Jordan run by a UK company may buy some of its furniture and linen from the UK. Some of the senior staff it employs may also come from the UK.

The balance of payments
The effects on the country's balance of payments position will also be influenced by where the firms in the tourist industry obtain their materials and food from and the national origin of the firms. The UK firm running the hotel in Petra will send profits back to the UK.

Countries not only have tourists visiting them but also their own citizens are tourists in other countries, so in the trade in services section of the balance of payments there is both a credit and a debit item.

Culture
Where there are notable differences in the income levels and culture of the tourists and the local inhabitants social tensions may arise. Tourists may act in a way, for example, getting drunk and gambling, which upsets the sensibility of the locals, and their greater spending power may result in resources being switched from meeting the needs of locals to meeting the needs of the tourists. For example, houses for locals may be demolished in order to build hotels.

Local culture may be threatened by the presence of tourists in a number of ways. One is referred to as the **demonstration effect**. This is where the locals, particularly the younger locals, copy the culture of the tourists, especially in terms of clothes, films, music, food, drink and social attitudes. The presence of tourists, especially wealthy ones, changes the types of goods and services demanded and thereby changes the skills and working patterns of the locals. The process whereby contact with tourists actually changes the culture of a county is called **acculturation**.

Environment

Tourism may damage the environment in a number of ways including:

■ visual pollution – the building of hotels, funfairs, etc. can reduce the visual attractiveness of an area

■ noise and air pollution caused by, for example, the planes and coaches transporting the tourists

■ waste generated by the tourists

■ congestion arising from the influx of tourists and people catering for the needs of tourists

■ destruction of the natural environment, for example to build golf courses and ski slopes for tourists

■ heavy use of water supplies, often in areas where the locals are short of water.

The ability of an area to cope with tourists in a way that does not damage the features that attract the tourists in the first place is referred to as its **carrying capacity**.

Sport

Sport is another major component of the leisure industry. It covers a range of activities, including games, outdoor pursuits, dance and movement and keep-fit. It can also be divided into participatory and

spectator sports. For example, far more people watch football, including both at games and on the television, than actually play football.

Table 11.4 shows that the main physical exercise which people in the UK participate in is walking and that not many adults regularly play sport.

Consumption and investment benefits

Those people who take part in physical activity gain both **consumption and investment benefits**. People may enjoy, for example, playing hockey. It can give them a sense of well-being and the competitive element may provide them with mental stimulation and satisfaction. This is the consumption benefit.

The investment benefit refers to the increased productivity and income potential which results from the improvement to health. Those who take regular exercise live longer, feel fitter and have fewer days off work. This increases the amount they are capable of earning. In the case of professional sportsmen and sportswomen there is a clear investment benefit as an increase in the quality and quantity of their training should improve their performances and hence their earnings.

Of course, the benefits vary between different activities. For example, walking provides high investment benefits but, for some, low consumption benefits. In contrast snooker provides high consumption benefits for some but relatively low investment benefits.

There are also possible disbenefits from sport in the form of injuries and deaths but for the vast majority of people the benefits exceed the disbenefits.

Table 11.4 Participation in most popular sports, games and physical activities, by gender, Great Britain

| | Percentages | | | | | |
| | Males | | | Females | | |
	1987	1990–91	1996–97	1987	1990–91	1996–97
Walking	41	44	49	35	38	41
Snooker/pool/billiards	27	24	20	5	5	4
Cycling	10	12	15	7	7	8
Swimming	–	14	13	–	15	17
Darts	14	11	–	4	4	–
Soccer	10	10	10	–	–	–
Golf	7	9	8	1	2	2
Weight lifting/training	7	8	–	2	2	–
Running	8	8	7	3	2	2
Keep fit/yoga	5	6	7	12	16	17
Tenpin bowls/skittles	2	5	4	1	3	3
Badminton	4	4	3	3	3	2
At least one activity	70	73	71	52	57	58

Table 13.18, *Social Trends 29*, 1999, Office for National Statistics

Market failure and sport

Governments encourage and sponsor participation in sport and indeed some make it compulsory in schools. This is because they believe that participation in sport would be below the allocatively efficient level if left to market forces. Sport may be regarded as a merit good. Some people undervalue the investment benefit it provides. In addition, sport provides not only private benefits but also external benefits. By raising the productivity of workers it increases the output and the income of the country. It also has the net effect of reducing the burden on the NHS, and some commentators suggest that it reduces vandalism.

Another reason for government intervention is that some sporting activities may be regarded as **semi-public goods**. For example, participating in water sports on a large lake may be non-rival until the number of participants reach a certain number.

Spectator sport

People watch a range of sporting activities. One sport which has become more popular in recent years has been watching football. The three football clubs which had the highest average attendances in the 1999/2000 season in England were Manchester United, Liverpool and Arsenal and in Scotland, Rangers and Celtic.

League football clubs raise revenue in a variety of ways:

- Through merchandise sales. They have sold items such as strips and scarves for some time but now most have branched out into a whole range of items which have the club's name attached to them such as duvets and wrist watches.

- Through sponsorship. League football clubs are sponsored by firms and their players wear the sponsor's name on their shirts. The competitions they play in are also sponsored.

- Through selling TV coverage. In recent years the amount of money received by top clubs from TV companies paying for the right to screen their games has increased dramatically. This has enabled the clubs to raise their players' wages to unprecedented levels.

- Through ticket sales. Clubs are faced with the problem of a fixed supply of seats. In recent years a number of the top clubs have built new stadiums but nevertheless demand for tickets still frequently exceeds the supply. To increase

their profits clubs charge different prices according to:

- the age of the spectators

- where people sit in the stadium

- the quality of the seating, for example charging people more to hire a box

- the expected quality of the game, for example charging their fans more for watching their team play a high-placed team than a low-placed one.

- The first example may be regarded as **price discrimination** but it could be claimed that in the case of the last three a different service is being provided to the different groups.

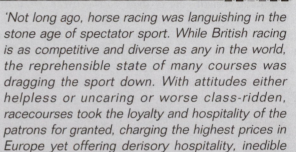

ACTIVITY 3

'Not long ago, horse racing was languishing in the stone age of spectator sport. While British racing is as competitive and diverse as any in the world, the reprehensible state of many courses was dragging the sport down. With attitudes either helpless or uncaring or worse class-ridden, racecourses took the loyalty and hospitality of the patrons for granted, charging the highest prices in Europe yet offering derisory hospitality, inedible catering and primitive facilities.'

'Can Britain's courses meet new demands?' in *The Times*, 5 January 2000

a Assess what the extract is actually suggesting about the competitiveness of the British race horse industry.

b Discuss in a group what the consumption and investment benefits of attending a race meeting might be.

Summary

Leisure is what people do in their free time. A key influence on the demand for leisure is income, and demand for leisure has increased as incomes have risen. Leisure activities can be divided into those based at home and those undertaken outside the home. In recent years there has been a rise in the proportion of home-based activities. Leisure activities are supplied by both the private and public sector. One of the leisure activities which the government promotes is sport. This is because of the positive externalities which participatory sport creates. Of course, people not only play sport, they also watch it with tens of thousands going to watch, say, Manchester United each week during the season and even more watching at home on television. Tourism, the largest industry in the world, generates not only positive but also negative externalities. The presence of tourists in an area can result in ecological damage and can have an adverse effect on the native culture. Tourism does generate income and employment but the jobs are often ones requiring low skills and paying low wages.

Data response question

'By the year 2000 tourism will be the world's biggest industry. Estimates by the World Tourism and Travel Council put the annual value of trade in world tourism at over $2.5 trillion (thousand billion) dollars – a staggering 5.5% of world GDP. Receipts from international tourism (about 20% of all tourism expenditure) have expanded at an annual growth rate of over 13% between 1970 and 1992. The UK has been a major beneficiary of this massive growth in international tourism. Our share of world arrivals in 1992 was 3.9% and we captured 5% of all international tourism receipts.

In the ten years to 1992, UK tourism recorded better foreign exchange earnings growth than all other leading export sectors apart from transport and electrical equipment manufacturers. Tourism's share of Gross Domestic Product in 1992 was 3.4% (excluding day visitor spending) and tourism-related purchases accounted for around 5.3% of all consumer spending in Britain. Transport, petroleum, retailing and other industries benefit from purchases directly allied to tourism. Tourism stimulates further indirect spending elsewhere in the economy, equivalent to an estimated 50 – 70% of direct tourism-related expenditure.

There are well over 220,000 tourism related businesses in Britain employing almost 1.5 million people – around 6% of the entire workforce – and embracing a further 183,000 self-employed jobs.

On the other hand, the large number of tourists visiting London caused considerable external costs for those who live and work in the capital.

It is inevitable that the British will wish to experience the cultures and climates of other countries. As a result, expenditure by UK residents on holidays abroad increased by 40% in the 1980s, while expenditure on holidays at home declined. Many of the factors influencing travel decisions, such as exchange rates, are out of our control.'

Adapted from A Bliss, 'Tourism: a major contribution to Britain' in *Public Policy Review*, 1994

1 Examine the importance of tourism to the UK economy. (10 marks)
2 Discuss *two* arguments you could use in support of the case for the UK government promoting the tourism industry in the UK. (6 marks)
3 It has been argued that the growth of tourism has an adverse effect on the local environment. Examine *two* policies which the UK government could adopt in recognition of this problem. (12 marks)
4 Analyse *three* factors that affect the demand for travel abroad by UK residents. (9 marks)

Section 2 questions

Essay questions
1 a Discuss what could cause the marginal revenue product of airline pilots to increase. (10 marks)
  b Explain why airline pilots are more highly paid than hospital porters. (15 marks)
2 a Explain what is meant by labour market failure. (12 marks)
  b Assess three measures a government could take to reduce labour market failure. (13 marks)

Project
Prepare a report on the extent of discrimination against a particular group in an occupation or on a national scale.
  This should cover:
- a definition of discrimination
- a comparison of employment, pay and promotion of the group with the rest of the employees
- an analysis of the possible causes of differentials
- an analysis of the effect of government anti-discrimination legislation
- a discussion of the possible consequences of the discrimination
- a list of sources.

You should make use of appropriate economic theory throughout your report.
C3.1a, C3.1b, C3.2, N3.1, N3.2, IT3.1, IT3.2, IT3.3

Section 3
The national and international economy

Introduction

Increasingly, economies throughout the world are becoming more integrated. So what happens in one economy and the firms based in that economy has implications for other economies. This section looks first at the international environment in which economies work and then focuses on three key aspects of the working life of the national economy. It builds on AS Units 20–26.

The key development in recent years in the international environment has been globalisation. This, linked to the basis of international trade, forms the topic of the Unit 12. Unit 13 discusses the ways in which countries can seek to protect their industries from foreign competition and the arguments for and against doing so. In Unit 14 different types of exchange rate systems are described and the question of the possible entry of the UK into the European single currency is examined. Issues relating to the balance of payments, including the impact of foreign direct investment and possible measures to reduce a balance of payments deficit are covered in Unit 15. Performance in international trade influences a country's economic growth and this is the topic of Unit 16, in which the causes of economic growth and the new economic paradigm are discussed. In Unit

17 the attention is on the causes of unemployment and differences between Keynesian and new classical economists on whether most unemployment is involuntary or voluntary. Unit 18 concentrates on inflation and examines the causes of inflation and the possible link between unemployment and inflation.

Before reading this section, check that you can recall the meaning and use of the following concepts:

- opportunity cost
- multinational companies
- speculation
- fixed exchange rate
- floating exchange rate
- balance of payments
- current account
- economic growth
- unemployment
- inflation
- cost-push inflation
- demand-pull inflation.

UNIT

12 Globalisation

Key concepts covered

- globalisation
- multinational companies
- fragmentation of production
- newly industrialised countries
- transnational companies
- World Trade Organisation
- International Monetary Fund
- absolute advantage
- comparative advantage
- opportunity cost ratios

Introduction

The UK is operating in a global economy. Advances in technology and reductions in transport costs are enabling UK consumers to access markets throughout the world. UK firms are selling their products throughout the world and locating separate parts of their production processes in a range of countries. However, as the demonstrations at a meeting of the World Trade Organisation held in Seattle in 1999 showed, some people are concerned about the effects of globalisation.

This unit explores the meaning of globalisation. It discusses the features, causes and consequences of globalisation. The principle of comparative advantage and its limitations are discussed and then related to globalisation.

The meaning of globalisation

Globalisation is the development of the world into one market place. National barriers are being broken down in terms of where firms make their products and in terms of where people buy their goods and services from. Countries have always traded with each other but now the scale of the movement of goods and services, ideas and capital investment between countries is increasing rapidly. The production processes and patterns of consumption are becoming more and more integrated. Consumers in, for example, China, France and Nigeria buy more and more of the same products, for example Manchester United strip and Coca-Cola. Parts of products, including cars and toys, are being assembled in a number of industrial and developing countries.

Features of globalisation

Globalisation is manifesting itself in the following main forms:

- Through the rapid increase in international trade. This is growing faster than world output.
- Through an increase in foreign direct investment which is the movement of physical capital between countries.

Other periods, for example the end of the nineteenth and start of the twentieth centuries, have witnessed rapid increases in international trade and international capital movements, but this time these have also been accompanied by the following:

- The growth of **multinational companies** (MNCs) which are increasingly thinking and operating globally, not only owning plants in different countries but also engaging in the **fragmentation of production**. This involves MNCs spreading different stages of production around the world, sometimes using their own plants and sometimes a combination of their own plants and other firms' plants. So when the managers of MNCs plan their production processes they do not simply consider producing a product in one location. Instead they think transnationally – they consider assembling parts in a range of countries and they use a decentralised management structure.
- An increase in the number of countries producing manufactured goods for export.

Causes of globalisation

Globalisation is occurring due to the following:

- Improved communication. Advances in information and computer technology are increasing the ease with which consumers can find out about and buy products from other countries and the ease with which producers can coordinate production throughout the world. For example, consumers in the UK now regularly order CDs, books and other items from the USA and other countries over the Internet. Managers of UK MNCs keep in touch with their staff in other countries using a range of information and computer technology, including e-mail and teleconferencing.
- Reduced transport costs. Over time, with the development of containerisation and increasing

use of larger ships and planes, transport costs have been falling.

■ Trade liberalisation. Since World War II the barriers to the free movement of goods and services and capital have been reducing.

■ Increased competition in manufactured goods. This is coming from developing countries, particularly from the **newly industrialised countries** (NICs) of South East Asia such as South Korea and Singapore.

■ Rise in skill levels throughout the world. This is enabling multinational companies to assemble parts not only in industrial but also developing countries.

Consequences of globalisation

Globalisation is having a number of significant effects, including the following:

■ It is changing the nature of international trade. An increasingly higher percentage of international trade consists of the exchange of similar products from the same industries (for example different makes of computers from China to the USA and from the USA to China) and a smaller percentage consists of different products from different industries (for example textiles from India to France and cars from France to India). At the start of the twentieth century manufactured goods were being exported from Europe and the USA to developing countries in return for raw materials. Now, at the start of the twenty first century Europe and the USA are still exporting manufactured goods to developing countries but in return for manufactured goods.

■ It is causing more and more firms to think globally. As already noted, advances in technology and transport are enabling firms to target consumers throughout the world and to operate in a range of countries.

■ It is increasing foreign direct investment. This is linked to the point above. Multinational companies are seeking out the lowest cost countries in which to locate production and parts of the production process. Indeed, some are now being referred to as **transnational companies** as they have substantial operations in a large number of countries and have a decentralised management structure.

■ It is increasing the susceptibility of countries to external crises. The increased integration of economies means that problems in one part of the world quickly spread to other countries. This was seen during the East Asian Crisis of 1997–99. The difficulties faced by financial institutions and other countries in Japan, Thailand, Indonesia and other East Asian countries resulted in a slow down in world growth and reduced aggregate demand in the west and caused problems for USA and European firms and banks with links to the Far East.

■ It is increasing the role of international organisations in overseeing world trade, including the **World Trade Organisation** (WTO) and the **International Monetary Fund** (IMF). The WTO was formed in 1995, replacing the General Agreement on Tariffs and Trade (GATT). It seeks to reduce tariffs and other restrictions on international trade and provides a means by which countries can settle their trade disputes. (The WTO is discussed in more detail in Unit 13). The IMF was established in 1947 with the main aim of encouraging world trade. It acts as an international bank offering assistance to countries in financial difficulties.

■ It is changing countries' **comparative advantage** (see below). The rise in the level of competition coming particularly from the newly industrialised countries is causing a shift in resources in Europe and the USA.

■ It is reducing price differences between countries. A market is said to be completely integrated when identical products sell at the same price in different countries.

Absolute advantage

In the past some international trade could have been explained in terms of absolute advantage. A country is said to have an **absolute advantage** in producing a product when it is better at producing it than other countries. Putting it in more technical terms, it means that a country can produce more of the product from each unit of resource than other countries – it has a greater productivity.

Table 12.1 is based on the assumption that there are ten workers in the USA and ten workers in Malaysia. Initially, each country divides its workers equally between car and rubber production. It is

ACTIVITY 1

'British industrial countries remain highly competitive even at the present exchange rate. An update of the annual survey by the US Bureau of Labor Statistics, using current exchange rates, suggests that if the total cost of employing an hour of manufacturing labour in Britain is set at 100, the comparable cost is 115 in America, 105 in France and 170 in Germany. For companies capable of attaining international productivity standards, Britain remains a profitable manufacturing location.'

Anatole Kaletsky, 'Structural fears undermine Britain's economic miracle' in *The Times*, 2 November 1999

a Why are comparative costs in the USA, France and Germany significant for the UK's trade position?

b Why might a country have a low cost of employing labour per hour but still have high unit wage costs?

c Discuss the evidence you might examine to determine whether a country is a profitable location.

further assumed that each worker in the USA can make either six cars or ten units of rubber and each worker in Malaysia can make either two cars or 60 units of rubber.

Table 12.1 shows that the USA has the absolute advantage in the production of cars as it can make three times as many cars per worker as Malaysia and Malaysia has the absolute advantage in rubber production as it can make six times as much rubber per worker as the USA.

Table 12.1 Position before specialisation and trade

	Output	
	Cars	Rubber
USA	30	50
Malaysia	10	300
Total	40	350

In this case it is clear that the USA should specialise in the production of cars and Malaysia in the production of rubber. Both countries would gain as a result of specialisation and trade. In our simplified example if the USA now specialised in cars and Malaysia in rubber, output would rise to the levels shown in Table 12.2.

Table 12.2 Position after specialisation

	Output	
	Cars	Rubber
USA	60	–
Malaysia	–	600
Total	60	600

The USA could export 20 cars to Malaysia in return for 200 rubber units and both countries would be better off in comparison to the situation before specialisation and trade.

Table 12.3 Position after specialisation and trade

	Consumption	
	Cars	Rubber
USA	40	200
Malaysia	20	400
Total	60	600

Comparative advantage

Although absolute advantage explains a small amount of current international trade, most is now based on comparative advantage. A large proportion of the UK's trade, for example, is with countries producing products the country is either making or could make in fairly similar quantities per worker. As implied earlier, globalisation is also increasing the imports of manufactured goods from the NICs.

Comparative advantage, as its name suggests, is concerned with relative efficiency. A country is said to have a comparative advantage in a product when it is even better at making that product or not so bad at making the product. This can also be expressed in terms of opportunity cost – a country has a comparative advantage if it can produce it at a lower opportunity cost than another country.

The principle or theory of comparative advantage states that both of two countries will benefit from specialisation and trade even if one country is more efficient at making both products as long as there is a difference in its relative efficiencies.

Table 12.4 again assumes there are ten workers in the USA and in Malaysia and that the workers are divided equally between the two products. In the USA each worker can make either six cars or 120 toys. In Malaysia each worker can make either two cars or 80 toys.

Table 12.4 Position before specialisation and trade

	Output	
	Cars	Toys
USA	30	600
Malaysia	10	400
Total	40	1000

The USA has the absolute advantage in the production of both of the goods. Its comparative advantage, however, lies in the production of cars. It can produce three times as many cars as Malaysia but only one and a half times as many toys. The opportunity cost of one car in America is lower than in Malaysia, 20 toys as opposed to 40 toys.

Malaysia's comparative advantage is in toys. It can produce two-thirds as many toys as the USA but only a third as many cars and it has a lower opportunity cost in the production of toys.

Table 12.5 shows the situation if the USA concentrates mainly on car production, devoting eight workers to car production and two to toy production and Malaysia specialises completely in toy production.

Table 12.5 Position after specialisation

	Output	
	Cars	Toys
USA	48	240
Malaysia	–	800
Total	48	1040

Specialisation has caused total output to rise. Countries will benefit from trade if the exchange rate lies between their respective opportunity cost ratios. If it is not the countries would gain more of a particular product by switching its own resources. For example, if the USA wanted more toys and it could only exchange one car for ten toys through international trade, it would be better moving workers from car to toy production. However, if the exchange rate does lie between the opportunity cost ratios both countries can gain. Table 12.6 shows the position if the exchange rate is one car for 30 toys and the USA exports 13 cars.

Table 12.6 Position after specialisation and trade

	Consumption	
	Cars	Toys
USA	35	630
Malaysia	13	410
Total	48	1040

ACTIVITY 2

Look at Table 12.7 and answer the questions below.

Table 12.7

	Output per worker	
	TVs	Vacuum cleaners
Germany	4	20
Greece	3	6

a Which country has the absolute advantage in the production of both goods?

b What is the opportunity cost ratio of one TV in Germany and in Greece?

c Which country has the comparative advantage in TV production?

Limitations of the principle of comparative advantage

While the principle of comparative advantage highlights the importance of differences in relative productivity it does have its limitations in explaining the pattern of international trade which actually occurs.

It is often expressed, as here, in terms of a few countries and a few products. Of course, in the real world, as there are many countries, many products and as situations are always changing, it is more difficult to work out where comparative advantages lie.

The principle ignores transport costs that may outweigh any comparative advantage particularly in terms of heavy products. However, as noted earlier, one feature of globalisation is reduced transport costs.

The principle also assumes constant opportunity cost ratios and productivity as resources are shifted. So that in the example shown in Table 12.5, when Malaya doubled the number of workers producing toys, the output of toys doubled. However, in practice increased specialisation may mean higher output per worker. It may on the other hand mean lower output per worker. This is because the workers most suited to toy production are likely to be employed first so that when more are employed these are likely to be less productive. This would mean that the opportunity cost of increasing toys would rise and so the returns from specialisation would be reduced.

The benefits of specialisation and trade are also

reduced in the real world by the existence of import restrictions and, for some countries, by differences in bargaining power. A country may have a comparative advantage in a particular product but may have difficulties exporting it because other countries impose tariffs, quotas or other trade restrictions on it. Developing countries may also find that exchange rates are set in a way which disadvantages them.

In addition, a country may not specialise to the extent that the principle suggests because it may wish to keep a more diversified industrial structure in order to reduce the risks arising from sudden shifts in demand and supply. There are a number of other reasons why a country may seek to maintain industries in which it does not currently have a comparative advantage including strategic industries and new industries. (These reasons are examined in more detail in Unit 14.)

ACTIVITY 3

'On the whole, the industries in which Britain has become most competitive are those, such as pharmaceuticals, business services and computer software, with a strong emphasis on "knowledge" and with strong prospect for long-term growth. The industries in which Britain is least competitive are those dependent on heavy capital investment or cheap labour, and in many of these industries global demand is growing relatively slowly and competition from Third World producers is becoming more intense.'

Anatole Kaletsky, 'Bank's critics could end up right for the wrong reasons' in *The Times*, 13 December 1998

a What are the advantages of having a comparative advantage in knowledge-based industries?

b What is enabling competition from third world producers to become more intense?

Globalisation and comparative advantage

As noted earlier, globalisation is changing countries' comparative advantage. Developing countries are becoming more efficient at producing manufactured goods. Their comparative advantage at the moment is mainly in manufacturing industries which make use of low-skilled labour. They have a large supply of low-skilled workers and so their wage rates are lower. In the past this did not result in a comparative advantage since while wages were low so was productivity and, as a result, unit wage costs were high. However, now with rises in productivity,

particularly in NICs, unit wage costs have been falling. Some commentators have expressed the concern that this will result in a rise in unemployment and a fall in wages in industrial countries. Their fear is that multinational companies will locate more of their processes in developing countries and that developing countries' firms will gain a larger share of the market for manufactured goods.

This, however, is only part of the picture. What is happening is not so much that industrial countries are facing a fall in demand for their output but a shift in demand from some products towards other products resulting from changes in relative efficiencies. Resources will have to shift to reflect these changes and this process is already under way. Average wages are not falling in most industrial countries but the wages of unskilled workers are falling relative to skilled workers. Industries producing goods and services requiring high-skilled labour are experiencing rises in demand while some relying on low-skilled labour are facing lower demand. In the case of the UK some processes are being relocated to lower-production cost countries but, at the same time, foreign direct investment is being attracted by the high-skilled labour force of the country.

So while jobs requiring low skill levels are declining, jobs requiring high skill levels are increasing. To ease the shift in resources, educational and vocational qualifications need to rise.

Of course, the situation is always changing and economies and their citizens have to be adaptable. Currently, the UK has a comparative advantage in, for example, oil, financial services, business services and scientific instruments, but in a few years' time, with skill levels rising throughout the world and patterns of demand and supply changing, this may alter.

Summary

Globalisation is the creation of world markets in goods, services and capital. This movement is resulting from advances in information and computer technology, reduced transport costs, trade liberalisation and advances in the economic performance of NICs. As a result of globalisation, international trade is becoming more intense in manufactured goods, multinational companies are assembling products in a range of locations throughout the world, foreign direct investment is increasing and countries are becoming more susceptible to external shocks. Globalisation is altering countries' comparative advantages. A country has a comparative advantage in the production of a product in which it has a lower opportunity cost than another country. There are however a number of limitations to the principle of comparative advantage. The principle does not take into account transport costs, import restrictions and the risks of over specialisation. It also assumes constant opportunity cost ratios. With the improved performance of NICs, the comparative advantage of industrial countries is shifting from low skilled labour intensive industries to high skilled labour intensive industries.

Data response question

For its proponents, globalisation describes a dream of opportunity and prosperity. For its opponents, it denotes a nightmare of greed and inequality. Both sides agree that technological change and economic liberalisation are creating something new and important. But how new is today's global integration? And, more important, how is it to be governed?

The integration of computers with telecommunications is creating a far more sensitive nervous system for the world economy. Cheaper transport acts, similarly, as a healthier blood stream. Companies are, in consequence, able to integrate production and address customers, worldwide, as never before.

Nevertheless, today's integration is not unprecedented. On some measures, capital flowed more freely across frontiers in the late nineteenth century than in the late twentieth. One reason for the good performance was the gold standard, which created a global monetary stability.

Yet even if not more integrated than ever before, the world economy has become progressively more integrated over the past half-century. Moreover, the potential for further integration is vast. It is necessary only to contrast the intensity of transactions within borders with that going across them.

Yet what may be possible is not inevitable, as the collapse of international trade and capital flows between the two world wars demonstrated. Bad policy can thwart good outcomes. Happily, extremes of bad policy seem unlikely. For much of the century, many believed in economic self-sufficiency. Today, that view is discredited by painful experience. The failure of alternatives is then the chief explanation for the widespread of liberalisation over the past two decades.

Global economic integration is at least as much an opportunity as an inevitability. However strong the technological forces pushing the world towards it, progress can be slowed, if not halted. If it is to proceed smoothly in the twenty-first century, policymakers will have to perform two clever tricks: agree and implement the minimum of global regulation needed to make integration work; and help their societies cope with changes integration will bring about. It will be hard to pull both off. But there is no sane alternative.

'Challenge of globalisation', editorial in the *Financial Times*, 28 December 1999

1 Explain in what sense globalisation may lead to both 'prosperity' and 'inequality'. (7 marks)
2 What are the causes of globalisation? (5 marks)
3 How new a phenomenon is globalisation? (4 marks)
4 What is meant by 'economic self-sufficiency'? (3 marks)
5 Discuss the 'changes that integration will bring about' in demand for labour in an industrial country and in a developing country. (6 marks)

13 Free trade and protectionism

Introduction

In Unit 12 we discussed how one of the causes of globalisation is the liberalisation of world trade. In this unit we examine in more detail the benefits and costs of free international trade. The means by which countries can limit imports and their reasons for seeking to are explained. Then the significance of trade blocs and their possible conflicts are discussed. Finally, the role of the World Trade Organisation is examined.

International free trade

As the term suggests, international free trade occurs when there are no restrictions imposed on the movement of goods and services into and out of countries. The fewer the restrictions on imports and exports, the greater the value of international trade is likely to be.

Benefits and costs of international trade

As Unit 12 showed in theory, if countries specialise and trade, total output will be greater. The resulting rise in living standards is the main benefit claimed for free international trade.

Consumers can benefit from the lower prices and higher quality that result from the higher level of competition which arises from countries trading internationally. They also enjoy a greater variety of products, including a few not made in their own countries.

Although firms will face greater competition in their domestic markets, they will also have access to larger markets in which to sell their products (enabling them to take greater advantage of economies of scale) and from which to buy raw materials.

However, despite all these advantages and increasing trade liberalisation, restrictions on exports and more particularly imports still exist. This can be because governments are concerned that, for example, certain undesirable products may be imported, that the continued existence of new and strategic industries may be threatened and other countries will not engage in fair competition. (These points are examined in more detail below.)

International trade faces countries with challenges. Competition from other countries and access to their markets results in some industries contracting and some expanding. This requires the shifting of resources which can be unsettling and may be difficult to achieve due to, for example, occupational immobility of labour.

Protectionism

Protectionism refers to the deliberate restriction of the free movement of goods and services between countries and **trade blocs**. A government engages in protectionism when it introduces measures to protect its own industries from competition from the industries of other countries.

Methods of protection

The methods of protection can be divided into **tariffs** and non-tariff measures.

Tariffs

Tariffs (also known as customs duties or import duties) are taxes on imported products. They can be imposed with the intention of raising revenue and/or discouraging domestic consumers from buying imported products. For example, the European Union's (EU) common external tariff, which is a tax on imports coming into the EU from countries outside, does raise revenue but its main purpose is to encourage EU member countries to trade with each other.

Tariffs can be ad valorem (percentage taxes) or specific (fixed sum taxes). The effect of imposing a tariff is to raise prices to domestic consumers and, in the absence of any retaliation, shift demand from imports to domestically produced products.

Figure 13.1 shows the effect of a specific tariff. Before the country engages in international trade price is p and the quantity purchased is q, all of which comes from domestic suppliers. When the country engages in international trade the number of producers in the market increases significantly. The increase in competition drives price down to p_1.

The quantity demanded extends to q_1. Of this amount qx is now bought from domestic suppliers and qx-q_1 from foreign firms. So domestic supply falls from q to qx.

The imposition of a tariff causes the world supply to decrease to wS_1. It raises the price to p_2 and causes the quantity to be purchased on the domestic market to fall to q_2. Domestic supply rises to qy and imports fall to qy-q_2. Domestic producers gain but this is at the expense of domestic consumers.

Non-tariff measures
These include the following.

Quotas. A quota is a limit on the supply of a good or service. It can be imposed on exports. For example, a developing country may seek to limit the export of food during a period of food shortages. However, quotas on imports are more common. For example, a quota may place a restriction on the imports of cars to, say, 40 000 a year or to £400 000 worth of cars. The effect of a quota is to reduce supply. This is likely to push up price. Foreign firms will experience a reduction in the quantity they can sell but they may benefit from the higher price if demand for their products is inelastic and if the quotas are not operated via the selling of import licences.

Voluntary export restraint or restriction (VER). This is similar to a quota but this time the limit on imports arises from a voluntary agreement between the exporting and the importing countries. A country may agree to restrict its exports in return for a similar limit being put on the exports of the importing country or to avoid more damaging import restrictions being imposed on its products. VERs have been used frequently by the EU and the USA. For example, the EU entered into several VERs with Japan which restricted the sale of Japanese cars.

Exchange control. A government or an area may seek to reduce imports by limiting the amount of foreign exchange made available to those wishing to import goods and services or to invest or to travel abroad. This is a measure which was used by a number of European countries, including the UK, in the 1960s and 1970s and is still found in some developing countries.

Embargoes. An embargo is a ban on the export or import of a product and/or a ban on trade with a particular country. For example, a country may ban the export of arms to a country with a poor human rights record, may prohibit the importation of hard core pornography and is likely to break off trading relations with a country during a military conflict.

Import deposit schemes. The UK made use of import deposit schemes in the 1960s. These schemes involve requiring importers to deposit a given sum of money with a government before they can import

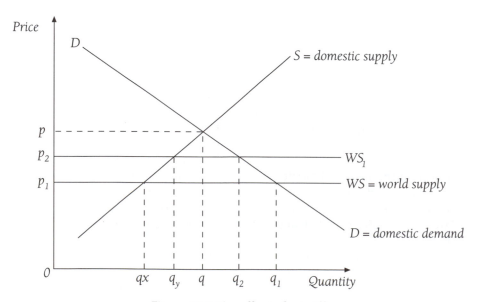

Figure 13.1 The effect of a tariff

products. The intention is to increase the cost, in terms of time and money, of importing.

Time delaying customs procedures. These are designed to have a similar effect to import deposit schemes. If it takes time to complete long and complex customs forms it will be more expensive to import products.

Quality standards. A government may use quantity standards as a means to limit imports. They may set high and complex requirements with the intention of raising the costs of foreign firms seeking to export to the country.

Government purchasing policies. A government may try to reduce imports by favouring domestic firms when it places orders, even when the domestic firms are producing at a higher cost or lower quality.

Subsidies. Those given to domestic firms may be used as an indirect way of protecting them. The subsidies may enable relatively high cost domestic firms to undercut more efficient foreign firms in the domestic market.

Arguments for protection

There are a range of arguments put forward for imposing restrictions on free trade. These include arguments for raising revenue, protecting the whole industrial base of the country, protecting particular industries and recently for protecting domestic standards of, for example, food safety, environment and labour market conditions.

Revenue raising

The imposition of tariffs enables governments to raise revenue. This is no longer a major motive behind industrial countries imposing import duties but the revenue received by some developing countries is a significant proportion of their tax revenue.

Arguments for protecting the whole industrial base

■ To protect domestic employment. This was an argument which was used by a number of governments in the 1930s when countries in the west were going through a depression. It was thought that if a country imposed import restrictions it would mean that its citizens would purchase more domestic products and thereby raise domestic employment. This concentration on domestic employment at the expense of other countries led to such measures being referred to as 'beggar-my-neighbour' policies. However, imposing import restrictions is likely to result in

a reduction in other countries' ability to buy the country's exports and may provoke retaliation. So the country's exports may decline and any jobs created by reducing imports may be offset by jobs lost due to the fall in exports. Indeed, the level of unemployment may rise if the imposition of tariffs results in a trade war, with governments raising their tariffs higher and higher – building 'tariff walls' round their countries. There will also be a welfare loss resulting from countries not being able to specialise to any great extent in those products in which they have a comparative advantage.

■ To improve the country's balance of payments position. One reaction to a situation where expenditure on imports exceeds revenue from exports is to place restrictions on imports. The intention is to switch domestic expenditure from imports to expenditure on domestic products. However, the same risks and disadvantages apply to this argument as to the one above, i.e. it may provoke a price war and it reduces the degree of specialisation. In addition, simply imposing import restrictions in the absence of any other policy measures does not solve the cause of the balance of payments deficit. If domestic consumers are purchasing imports because their quality is higher, for example, they may still continue to buy imports even after the restrictions have been imposed.

■ To protect the country's industries from 'unfair low wage competition' from abroad. This would involve putting restrictions on the imports from certain countries. Some commentators argue that if the wages paid to workers in developing countries are very low, then firms in industrial countries will not be able to compete unless they reduce wages to unacceptably low levels. However, low wages do not always mean low unit wage costs. Due to a lack of capital equipment and education, labour productivity in a number of countries is low.

Being able to sell products without restrictions to industrial countries may enable income levels to rise in developing countries. This may result in their levels of investment, education, wages and purchases of products from industrial countries rising.

The competition from low-wage countries may also reflect the fact that those countries have a comparative advantage in low-skilled labour-intensive industries, in which case unemployment in certain industries may rise, but the rise in unemployment may be a temporary situation if that labour can move into the industries in which the country does have a comparative advantage.

Where the case for imposing restrictions has more justification is where the wages being paid are being held below the equilibrium rates, the working conditions are poor and child or slave labour is employed.

■ To maintain a diversified industrial base. Import restrictions may be imposed on a range of products in order to ensure that a number of domestic industries survive. The intention would be to avoid the risks which arise with a high level of specialisation. For example, if a developing country's employment and income is dependent on a few industries there is a risk that world fluctuations in demand and supply-side problems can result in significant falls in economic activity.

■ To improve the **terms of trade**. The terms of trade refer to the relationship between a country's export and import prices and are measured by:

$$\frac{\text{Index of export prices}}{\text{Index of import prices}} \times 100.$$

If a country is a dominant buyer of a product or products (monopsonist or oligopsonist), then placing restrictions on imports may force the sellers to lower their prices in order to remain competitive on the domestic market. If this occurs the country will be able to purchase its imports more cheaply. The fall in the price of imports will improve the terms of trade.

Arguments for protecting particular industries

■ To prevent **dumping**. Dumping occurs when firms sell their products at less than cost price. Foreign firms may engage in dumping because government subsidies permit them to sell at very low prices or because they are seeking to raise profits by price discriminating. In the latter case the initial reason for exporting products at a low price may be to dispose of stocks of the good. In this case consumers in the importing country will benefit. However, their longer-term objective may be to drive out domestic producers and gain a strong market position. In this case consumers are likely to lose out as a result of the reduction in choice and the higher

prices which the exporters will feel able to charge.

■ To enable **infant industries** to grow. Infant industries (which are also called sunrise industries) are newly established industries. The firms in such industries may find it difficult to develop because their average costs may be higher than their well-established foreign competitors. However, if they are given protection in their early years they may be able to grow and thereby take greater advantage of economies of scale, lower their average costs and become competitive. At this stage the protection could be removed. The infant industry argument is thought to be particularly strong in the case of high technology industries which have high fixed costs and which have a potential comparative advantage. There is a risk, however, that the industries may become dependent on protection.

■ To permit **declining industries** to go out of business gradually. Declining industries (also called sunset industries) are likely to be industries which no longer have a comparative advantage. However, if they go out of business quickly there may be a sudden and large increase in unemployment. Protection may enable an industry to contract gradually, thereby allowing time for resources, including labour, to move to other industries.

■ To enable industries to regain their comparative advantage. Industries may have lost their comparative advantage due to a lack of investment. A case may be made to protect them temporarily while additional investment is made.

■ To protect **strategic industries**. This is more of a political than an economic argument. Many countries believe it is important to have a degree of self-sufficiency in certain industries, including arms and agriculture in case disputes or military conflicts cut off supplies.

Arguments for protecting domestic standards

Governments have traditionally placed restrictions, including embargoes, on demerit goods, for example drugs and pornography. However, in recent years domestic regulations on food safety, labour conditions and environmental standards have increasingly been acting as trade restrictions. Although countries may be keen on free trade in theory, in practice many are reluctant to compromise

ACTIVITY 1

'Trade protection costs the European Union between 6 and 7 per cent of its gross domestic product or the equivalent of the annual economic output of Spain, according to a forthcoming study. The study, by Patrick Messerlin, a leading French economist, claims to be the first attempt to measure the impact of all types of protection, including anti-dumping measures, non-tariff barriers and subsidies, as well as tariffs.'

Guy de Jonquieres, 'Protection "is costing EU 6% of GDP"' in the *Financial Times*, 10 November 1999

a In what sense may trade protection impose a cost on a country or trade area?

b Explain what is meant by anti-dumping measures.

domestic policy in sensitive areas such as genetically modified foods. As mentioned in Unit 12, economies are becoming more closely connected through trade and investment, so a government policy can have a discriminatory impact on foreign firms. For example, the EU has banned all hormone-treated beef largely because of public concern about food safety. This has hit US farmers in particular as there is widespread use of hormones in US beef farming.

Trade blocs

The break down of trade barriers has actually occurred mainly within groups of countries operating as trade blocs. There are four main types of trade blocs with increasing degrees of integration:

- A **free trade area**. Countries within a free trade area remove restrictions between each other but are free to operate whatever trade restrictions they wish on non-members. The members have to make some provision, usually via maintaining customs points, to prevent imports into the area coming in via the country with the lowest tariffs. Examples of free trade areas include the North American Free Trade Area (NAFTA), consisting of Canada, the USA and Mexico, and ASEAN (Association of South East Asian Nations), consisting of Brunei, Indonesia, Malaysia, the Philippines, Singapore and Thailand.

- A **customs union**. The members of a customs union not only remove trade restrictions between each other but also agree to operate the same import restrictions on non-member

countries. An example is Mercosur which consists of Brazil, Argentina, Paraguay and Uruguay, and operates a common external tariff.

- A **common market**. This not only has no import restrictions between member countries, a common external tariff but also permits the free movement of labour and capital between its members. In 1986 the Single Market Act was signed which moved what was then the EC, but since has become the EU, towards a single market.

- **Economic and monetary union** (EMU). This takes integration several stages further by introducing a single currency, similar labour market policies and some degree of tax harmonisation. The Maastricht Treaty of 1992 started the movement of the EU towards EMU.

ACTIVITY 2

In October 1999 the World Trade Organisation ruled against Canada in a complaint brought by Japan and the European Union over Canadian import duties on finished motor vehicles. Most of the Canadian vehicle market is supplied by US car companies.

a Discuss why most of the Canadian vehicle market is supplied by US producers.

b Explain the effect that the imposition of an import duty will have on the market for a product.

Trade blocs and conflicts

As the EU has become more integrated and a more powerful economic force it has come into more conflict with the USA and NAFTA. The USA complains particularly about the EU's protection of its farming and film industries. In 1997 and 1998 the USA protested to the **World Trade Organisation** (WTO) about the privileged market access given to the exports of bananas from former British and French colonies in Africa, the Caribbean and Pacific under the Lome convention, at the expense of cheaper Latin American bananas. In 1999 it imposed retaliatory tariffs of over $190 million on a range of European goods after the EU failed to comply with a WTO ruling requiring it to restructure its banana import regime to prevent the discrimination against Latin American exporters.

The EU, in turn, is concerned about the noise levels caused by US aeroplanes, hormone-treated beef and genetically modified food.

So while the EU and the USA are keen to open markets for their exporters they are much more reluctant in practice to open their own markets.

Countries outside trade blocs, particularly developing countries, feel discriminated against. They do not obtain the benefits of belonging to a trade bloc but have restrictions imposed on their products by the EU, USA and other countries.

The role of the WTO

The WTO, which currently has 136 member countries, seeks to promote trade liberalisation through a series of negotiations (which are often referred to as rounds). For example, the Uruguay Round achieved agreement to reduce trade barriers in textiles. It also operates a trade dispute settlement mechanism which is binding on member countries.

The role of the WTO has been criticised by developing countries which argue that the rounds have benefited mainly industrial countries by devoting more attention to reducing the tariffs imposed mostly by developing countries. For example, tariffs on tobacco have been reduced to 4 per cent while tariffs on tobacco products remain at 40 per cent. Developing countries argue that the differential has nothing to do with health concerns but is concerned with keeping industrial processing, where higher profits are made, in the west. They also claim that the WTO, by allowing industrial countries in certain circumstances to impose restrictions to prevent dumping, is often merely enabling them to protect jobs in sensitive industries which would prove politically unpopular to allow to decline.

A C T I V I T Y   3

'The rise of post-war global prosperity has been driven by trade liberalisation. If 1930s protectionism gave us the depression, those who saw that sustained recovery from the depression would need global free trade and set up the General Agreement on Tariffs and Trade (GATT), the WTO's predecessor, deserve our thanks.'

David Smith, 'Trade talks hit stormy weather' in *The Sunday Times*, 28 November 1999

Using CD-ROMs of, for example, *The Times*, the *Daily Telegraph* and the *Guardian* and the Internet, research views of the performance of the WTO and produce a brief summary of these.

Summary

Free international trade provides a number of benefits. The main one is higher world output which arises from allowing countries to specialise in those products in which they have a comparative advantage. Other benefits include more choice, more competition and greater opportunity to take advantage of economies of scale. However, it can also pose problems for countries, especially if they cannot trade on equal terms. Countries impose a range of import restrictions, including tariffs and quotas in order to protect their economies and industries. Countries may be seeking to protect most of their industries or particular industries, for example infant industries, declining industries and those industries facing dumping. A large part of the trade liberalisation which has occurred has taken place within trade blocs. The two most dominant trading areas are now the EU and the USA which are regularly in conflict over trade restrictions. The WTO polices world trade.

Data response question

'The US was given permission yesterday to impose 100 per cent import duties on $116m worth of European goods. The sanctions, about half the level the US had asked for but twice that sought by Europeans, reflect the damage the trade body thinks has been inflicted by an illegal EU ban on North American hormone-treated beef.

Goods from a preliminary list which included Danish ham, Belgian chocolates and motorcycles could be affected as early as next week. Canada also won permission to apply sanctions worth C$11m ($8m) on goods from a hit-list including beef, gingerbread, gin and vodka.

But EU officials still hope that 11th hour talks will persuade the US to accept compensation in the form of greater market access for other US goods instead of imposing tariffs, which will effectively close the US market to the designated goods.

It was the second such finding against the EU in recent months. The WTO also gave the US permission to apply $191m of sanctions in the long-running dispute over Europe's rules on banana imports, which it found discriminated unfairly against US producers.

Charlene Barshefsky, the US trade representative, said yesterday: 'The EU must pay a price for failing to comply with its WTO obligations.'

The WTO approved the principle of EU sanctions in May after Brussels failed to meet a deadline to comply with a ruling against its ban on imports of hormone-treated beef. The EU maintains some hormones may cause cancer and is conducting further studies on their safety. It has refused to lift the ban, even though it has been ruled illegal.'

Diane Coyle, 'WTO gives go-ahead to US tariffs' in *The Independent*, 13 July 1999

1 Explain what is meant by '100 per cent import duties'. (4)

2 How might EU citizens benefit from the EU giving some US goods greater access to its market? (6)

3 In what sense had the EU's rules on banana imports acted in a discriminatory way? (4)

4 Why was the EU banning imports of hormone-treated beef? (3)

5 Assess two arguments for imposing import restrictions. (8)

UNIT 14 Exchange rates

Key concepts covered

- fixed exchange rate
- floating exchange rate
- parity
- speculation
- European single currency
- euro area
- convergence criteria
- transparency
- asymmetrical policy sensitivity

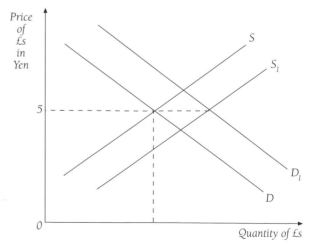

Figure 14.1 The exchange rate

Introduction

As noted in Unit 13 a country may seek to limit imports by imposing import restrictions. It could also reduce imports by lowering its exchange rate. This presumes that the country is not operating a floating exchange rate and that the government is content to have a lower exchange rate. In this unit the difference between fixed and floating exchange rates and their respective advantages and disadvantages are discussed. After considering the factors influencing exchange rates and the consequences of their movements, the European single currency is examined. The criteria for joining the single currency, set down both by the EU and by the UK government are outlined, and the effects of joining and not joining are discussed.

Exchange rate systems

A country or area can operate a **fixed**, managed or **floating exchange** rate system.

A fixed exchange rate

This is one where the parity (exchange value, for example £1 = US$1.5) of the currency is pegged against other currencies. If the **parity** comes under threat by market forces the central bank, acting on behalf of the government, will step in to maintain the value by either buying or selling the currency and/or changing its rate of interest. For example, Figure 14.1 shows an exchange rate set at £1 = 5 Yen.

If, perhaps, due to a rise in demand for the country's exports, demand for the country's currency increases the government would intervene by selling

its currency and/or reducing its interest rate. Figure 14.2 shows the effects of these events.

A managed exchange rate

A government may not set a particular parity but it may seek to influence the general direction of exchange rate movements in order to prevent changes that are too large and perhaps to prevent the rate rising too high or too low. Again, its central bank would influence the value of the exchange rate by buying and selling the currency and changing its interest rate.

Floating exchange rate

This is one determined by market forces. If demand for the currency rises this will raise the exchange rate, whereas if the supply of the currency increases, the exchange rate will fall in value.

Figure 14.2 Maintaining a fixed exchange rate

Advantages and disadvantages of a fixed exchange rate

The main advantage claimed for a fixed exchange rate is the certainty it provides to traders, investors and consumers. A firm buying raw materials from abroad will know how much it will have to pay in terms of foreign currency, a firm selling products abroad will know how much it will receive in terms of its own expected return from their investment, and consumers going on holiday abroad will know how much they will have to pay.

Another advantage claimed is that a fixed exchange rate imposes discipline on government policy. For example, if the country is experiencing inflation a government could not rely on the exchange rate falling to restore its international competitiveness, it would have to tackle the causes of the inflation.

However, to maintain the parity other policy objectives might have to be sacrificed. For instance, if the exchange rate is under downward pressure, the government may raise its interest rate which could slow down economic growth and cause a rise in unemployment.

There is also no guarantee that the parity set will be at the long run equilibrium level. If it is set too high, this will put its firms at a competitive disadvantage since exports will be relatively high in price while its imports will be relatively low in price. In this case the rate would not be sustainable and the value of the currency would have to be reduced.

In addition, reserves of foreign currency have to be kept in case the central bank has to intervene to increase demand for the currency. This involves an opportunity cost – the foreign currency could be put to alternative uses.

Advantages and disadvantages of a floating exchange rate

Operating a floating exchange rate means that the exchange rate no longer becomes a policy objective. The government does not have to sacrifice other objectives and does not have to keep foreign currency to maintain it.

Also, in theory, a floating exchange rate should move automatically to ensure a balance of payments equilibrium. For example, if there is a deficit, demand for the currency will fall and supply will rise. This will cause the exchange rate to fall, exports to become cheaper and imports to become more expensive.

However, in practice, the balance of payments position is influenced not just by the price of exports and imports. A country could have a deficit on its balance of payments but speculation may actually lead to a rise in the exchange rate.

A floating exchange rate can create uncertainty, with traders being unsure how much the currency will be worth in the future. Some may seek to offset this uncertainty by agreeing a price in advance but this involves a cost. The degree of uncertainty will be influenced by the extent of fluctuations in the currency.

Factors affecting exchange rates

A number of factors influence the value of a floating exchange rate and put upward or downward pressure on a fixed exchange rate. These include the following:

- Relative inflation rates. A country which is experiencing an inflation rate above that of its competitors is likely also to experience a decrease in demand for its exports and a rise in demand for imports. This would cause demand for the currency to fall and supply of the currency to rise. This would put downward pressure on a fixed exchange rate. Figure 14.3 shows the effect on a floating exchange rate.

- Income levels. Rises in income levels abroad will tend to increase a country's exchange rate. This is because foreigners will have more income to spend on the country's exports.

- Relative quality. If a country's products rise in quality relative to its competitors, demand for its products both at home and abroad will increase. This will cause a rise in a floating exchange rate

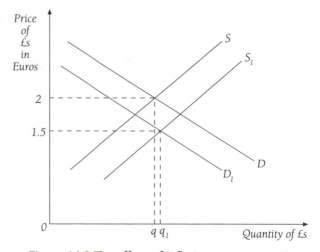

Figure 14.2 The effect of inflation on a country's floating exchange rate

and put upward pressure on a fixed exchange rate. Improvements in marketing and after-sales service will have a similar effect.

- Relative interest rates. If a country's interest rate rises relative to other countries it is likely to attract an inflow of funds from abroad into its financial institutions. This will increase demand for the currency and raise the exchange rate or put upward pressure on it. As noted earlier, a government seeking to influence its currency may use changes in its interest rate to achieve its objective.

- Levels of foreign direct investment (FDI). A country which attracts more investment from foreign multinational companies than its own multinational companies invest abroad will experience an increase in demand for its currency and upward pressure on its exchange rate.

- Speculative capital flows. A high percentage of the dealing in foreign exchange markets is now accounted for by speculation. Speculators buy and sell currency hoping to make a profit from movements in interest rates and exchange rates. **Speculation** can have a stabilising or a destabilising effect on exchange rates. If speculators respond to a falling exchange rate by selling some of their holdings of the currency this will drive the rate down even further. However, if they think the rate will soon start to rise they will purchase the currency, thereby preventing a large fall. Speculation is something of a self-fulfilling principle – by their action speculators bring about what they expect to happen.

The effects of exchange rate movements

A rise in the exchange rate will raise the price of the country's exports in terms of foreign currencies and reduce the price of imports in terms of the domestic currency. This will put downward pressure on inflation. This is because the price of imported raw materials will fall, thereby reducing the cost of production and the price of imported finished products which count in the calculation of the country's inflation. In addition, domestic firms, facing cheaper imported rival products at home and facing the prospect of their products becoming more expensive abroad, will be under pressure to cut their costs in order to keep their prices low.

A rise in the exchange rate will improve the terms of trade. The sale of each export would enable more imports to be purchased. However, the change in prices will affect demand. If demand for exports is elastic, the revenue earned from selling exports will fall, thereby reducing the overall purchasing power of the country.

Higher priced exports and cheaper imports may also reduce the industrial base of the country. Some firms may not be able to compete at home and/or abroad as a result of the higher exchange rate and some may go out of business. This will reduce the rate of economic growth and cause unemployment.

ACTIVITY 1

The high value of the pound sterling at the end of the 1990s led to some concern among economists and business people. One of their worries was that the value of sterling would fall suddenly and abruptly. While exporters would benefit from a lower exchange rate a large fall would raise the price of imported raw materials significantly and could feed through to domestically generated inflation.

a Explain why a fall in the exchange rate may create inflation.

b Discuss the advantages and disadvantages of a floating exchange rate.

ACTIVITY 2

The high value of the pound sterling in 1999 led to British farmers complaining that they could not export at a profit. In December 1999 the German owner of Rover warned that the car maker would halve its spending on components bought in the UK.

a Explain the concern expressed by the farmers and the comment made by the German owner.

b Discuss why the volume of exports may still rise despite a high exchange rate.

c Research, using recent newspapers, whether the value of the pound sterling is currently thought to be too high, too low or about right.

The European single currency

The **European single currency**, the euro, is currently operated under a floating exchange rate system.

However, the European Central Bank (ECB) reserves the right to intervene if it considers it to be necessary. In addition, the changes to its interest rate, which it makes mainly to control inflation, have an impact on the value of the euro.

The single currency came into existence on 1 January 1999. So far, 11 out of the 15 members of the EU have joined. This group is referred to as the **euro area**, euroland or the euro zone. The four countries which have not joined are Denmark, Greece, Sweden and the UK. Denmark, Sweden and the UK chose not to join at the start. Greece did not meet the criteria set down in the Maastricht treaty which are referred to as the convergence criteria.

Convergence criteria

To join the single currency (sometimes referred to as joining EMU), a country has to show that its economy is operating at a similar stage of the economic cycle as the rest of the members. The convergence are:

■ the government budget must not exceed 35 per cent of GDP

■ government debt should not be above 60 per cent of GDP

■ the inflation rate should not exceed the average of the three members with the lowest inflation rates by more than 1.5 percentage points

■ long-term interest rates should not be more than 2 percentage points above the average of the three members with the lowest inflation rate

■ a stable exchange rate.

Those members in the single currency have to continue to meet the limits on the fiscal deficits.

The UK government's criteria

Gordon Brown, the Chancellor of the Exchequer, has set down five conditions which have to be met before the UK government will consider entry. These are as follows:

■ There must be sustainable convergence between the UK economy and the economies of the euro area countries.

■ There must be flexibility within the euro area for coping with economic change.

■ Entry will be beneficial for promoting foreign direct investment in the UK.

■ Entry will benefit UK financial services.

■ Entry will be good for jobs and growth.

The effects of belonging to the single currency

Joining the single currency would have a number of effects for the UK, some potentially beneficial and some potentially harmful.

Benefits

■ A reduction in transaction costs. UK firms and consumers would no longer have to spend money and time converting pounds into euros.

■ The elimination of exchange rate risk with the euro area. For example, UK firms would no longer be caught out by unexpected changes in the value of the pound against the euro.

■ Increased **transparency**. This is thought to be an important advantage. Having one currency makes it easier for firms and consumers to compare prices throughout the EU. Consumers and firms will not have to spend time and effort converting prices into pounds before they decide which are the best offers. Competition should increase and price discrimination decrease. For example, the price difference between car radios in EU countries and in the UK should diminish. In 1999 car radios were 36 per cent higher in price in London than in Rome.

■ Increased influence within the EU. Being part of the single currency would give the UK more say in the future direction of the EU. It would also make the EU a stronger economic power.

■ Lower interest rates. The EU, since its inception, has had a lower rate of interest than the UK. A lower interest rate may stimulate investment and growth in the UK.

■ Increased foreign direct investment. Some claim that membership of the euro would attract more multinational companies to set up in the UK. It is argued that the UK would become a more attractive location because of the reduced transaction costs and reduced exchange rate uncertainty.

Disadvantages

There would be transitional costs. These are the costs of changing over from using the pound to using the euro. For example, firms would have to convert their information and computer technology systems, show for a period of time prices in both pounds and euros and train staff.

However, transitional costs are one-off costs and are not a major consideration in deciding whether to join or not. More significant are the disadvantages which may be more long lasting, including the following:

- Reduction in independence of macroeconomic policy. The European Central Bank sets the rate of interest in the euro area. In addition to no longer being able to operate its own interest rate, the UK government would lose the exchange rate as a policy tool and would have constraints imposed on its use of fiscal policy.

- **Asymmetric policy sensitivity**. The UK economy differs from the rest of the EU in three main ways which may mean that it would be affected more significantly than other members by changes in policy. More UK borrowing is undertaken on variable interest rate terms than in most EU countries. So if the euro area's interest rate were to rise, this would affect UK home buyers and firms more than those in other EU countries. However, there is an increasing tendency for loans to be taken out on fixed interest rate terms. The UK trades more with the USA than other EU countries and so is affected more than the other countries by changes in the level of economic activity in the USA and changes in the value of the dollar. The UK is also still a major exporter of oil so its economy is influenced more, and in a different way, to the other EU countries, which are importers of oil, by changes in the world price of oil.

The effects of staying out

The UK government has not yet decided on entry. Staying out of an arrangement which most EU members have joined may have a number of effects on the UK economy, including the following:

- A tendency for its exchange rate to be high because of its higher interest rate

- A risk of loss of foreign direct investment. The euro area has formed a large market which may prove more attractive to foreign direct investment than the UK. This may particularly be the case if companies decide to locate close to each other to benefit from external economies of scale. Currently, FDI is very important for the UK. Indeed, the UK is the third largest recipient of FDI, after the USA and China.

- A risk that some of the UK's financial institutions may move to the euro area to be closer to the main financial dealings.

ACTIVITY 3

'The one obvious and inescapable consequence of Emu membership is the elimination of exchange rate risk within the zone (provided Emu is irrevocable). But it is wrong to conclude that foreign exchange risk will be eliminated for British business. The UK received just 43 per cent of its total credits on the current account from members of the euro-zone in 1997. It follows that membership of the euro-zone cannot eliminate currency instability.'

Martin Wolf, 'Emu's small reward' in the *Financial Times*, 26 May 1999

a Explain how entry into the single currency affects exchange rate risk.

b Why would the impact on exchange rate risk be different for the UK than for the current members of EMU?

c Assess whether the UK economy currently meets the convergence criteria.

Summary

A fixed exchange rate is one set and maintained by the government, whereas a floating exchange rate is determined by market forces. A fixed exchange rate provides certainty but to maintain it, measures may have to be taken which have an adverse effect on employment and growth. A floating exchange rate frees a government to concentrate on other objectives but it may discourage trade if it fluctuates too much. The level of an exchange rate is influenced by relative interest rates, relative inflation rates, income levels, relative quality, foreign direct investment and speculation. A rise in the exchange rate tends to reduce inflation but raise employment. The UK is still considering whether to enter the single currency. Benefits would include reduced transaction costs and increased transparency but there are also costs, including reduction in macroeconomic policy independence and asymmetric policy sensitivity.

Data response question

In macro-economic terms, the euro-zone will be judged not just by how well it performs on average, but by divergences in performance across member states.

How might this be assessed? First, how well does the 'one size fits all' monetary policy work? Does it give roughly the right monetary policy for all member states or are there widely divergent macro-economic conditions, with over-heating in some economies and recessions in others? Second, are member states able, in practice, to use fiscal policy to stabilise their economies as and when needed?

Success will mean that the citizens of each member state are content with the outcome for themselves – or at least happy enough for there to be no serious talk of recession.

One of the most important by-products of monetary union should be structural reforms, particularly in labour markets.

With the exchange rate safety valve closed, adjustment pressures will fall elsewhere, particularly on workers. Exchange rate certainty will increase the attractiveness of moving production towards member states with relatively low labour costs. The result is likely to be strong pressure on the more inflexible and higher cost labour markets. This, in turn, will generate resistance, with efforts being made to create euro-zone wage bargaining and raise labour standards to those of the highest cost countries.

Martin Wolf, 'Testing the euro's mettle' in the *Financial Times*, 22 January 1999

1 Which countries are members of the euro zone? (3 marks)
2 What problems would be caused if some members of the euro zone are overheating and some are experiencing recessions? (6 marks)
3 Explain what is meant by exchange rate certainty. (3 marks)
4 What is meant by inflexible labour markets and why might they be high-cost labour markets? (5 marks)
5 Discuss whether the UK economy would benefit from membership of the euro zone. (8 marks)

Introduction

In Unit 13 one reason given for imposing import restrictions was to improve a country's balance of payments position and in Unit 14 the effect of a change in the exchange rate on the balance of payments was touched on. In this unit issues relating to the balance of payments are examined in more detail. The influences on and effects of foreign direct investment are discussed. The determinants of a country's international competitiveness and the measures a government can take to increase it are explored. Finally, the measures a government can take to restore a balance of payments equilibrium are examined.

The section of the balance of payments

As noted in AS Unit 20, the balance of payments account consists of a number of sub-groups. These are the current account, the capital account, the financial account and the International Investment Position. The current account is influenced by the international competitiveness of the goods and services produced and by the amount of income earned and paid on overseas investments and financial assets and liabilities. The financial account covers the flow of investment into and out of the UK including direct investment, a significant amount of which is carried out by multinational companies.

Foreign direct investment

UK multinational companies invest abroad and foreign multinational companies invest in the UK. This investment includes the establishment of new plants, the expansion of existing plants and the purchase of existing plants and firms.

Multinational companies seek the highest return on their capital. So the amount of **foreign direct investment** (FDI) attracted by a country is influenced by the productivity and flexibility of its workers, its tax rates, the stability of its economic policies, its rate of economic growth, the size of its market and the perception of its future economic prospects.

The UK is currently an attractive location for FDI because of the following:

- Government grants, especially for multinationals setting up in the poorer regions of the UK.
- Its flexible labour force.
- Its time zone advantage in financial services.
- Its membership of the EU. Setting up in the UK gives a Japanese or US multinational company, for example, access to the EU market without having to pay the common external tariff. However, as noted in Unit 14, some economists believe that if the UK continues to stay out of the single currency, FDI may be reduced.
- The use of the English language. This is the main language of the Internet and is frequently used in international business. In addition, it is obviously spoken by Americans and is the most popular foreign language learnt by the Japanese and South Koreans.

ACTIVITY 1

'[Kit Juckes (currency strategist at NatWest GFM)] rejects the argument that Britain's current account deficit, which may have reached £12bn last year as exports failed to keep up with imports, is now a serious problem. He notes that the attraction of UK assets has kept money flowing into the country and that, as long as foreigners are buying, there is no current account crisis.'

Martin Essex, 'Industry must live with the strong pound' in *Sunday Business*, 16 January 2000

a What is the connection between foreign direct investment and the current account?

b What may cause a current account deficit?

The effects of foreign direct investment

- An initial inflow of investment which will appear as a credit item in the financial account. However, in the longer run money will flow out of the country in the form of investment income (profit, interest and dividends) which will appear in the current account. The goods and services that the multinational company (MNC) sells abroad will count in the country's exports. The net effect on imports is rather more uncertain. Some goods and services which had previously been bought abroad from the MNCs may now be purchased from their plants in the home country. However, the MNC may purchase some of its raw materials and services from its home country.

- MNCs may cause a rise in employment. This is one of the key reasons that governments give grants to MNCs to set up in their country. They hope that the MNCs will increase employment directly by taking on workers and indirectly by increasing economic activity and demand in the area in which they are based. However, some of those employed by the MNCs, particularly in top management posts, may be brought over from the home country. Even more significantly, if the competition from MNCs leads to domestic firms going out of business, they will not be creating employment, merely replacing jobs.

- MNCs, especially in developing countries, can help to spread knowledge and understanding of recent technological advances. A high proportion of MNCs are high tech, capital intensive firms.

- MNCs can bring in new ideas of management techniques. The establishment of Japanese and South Korean MNCs in a range of countries has resulted in their host countries reviewing their management styles.

- MNCs' output counts in the home country's GDP, and in many cases their contribution to output and growth is significant.

- MNCs tend to have high labour productivity. This is mainly because of high capital/labour ratios. This may encourage domestically owned firms to raise their productivity levels and may reduce inflationary tendencies.

- A rise in tax revenue may occur but some MNCs try to reduce their tax payments by moving revenue around their plants in different countries in order to minimise their payments.

- Pollution levels may rise. This is particularly the case in developing countries where MNCs may locate in order to get round tighter environmental regulations at home. MNCs may also be attracted by less strict labour market policies in terms of working hours, health and safety, minimum wages and lowest working age.

ACTIVITY 2

A significant number of plants in the UK are owned by foreign multinational companies – for example Ford at Dagenham, Nissan at Sunderland and Honda at Swindon. These companies can have a large impact on the surrounding area.

In a group, research the impact that multinational companies have in your area.

International competitiveness

Multinational companies that do introduce new technology will help to raise the **international competitiveness** of a country. International competitiveness can be defined as the ability of a country's firms to compete successfully in international markets and thereby permit the country to continue to grow.

Sometimes, referring to a country as being internationally competitive is taken to mean that it can produce products more cheaply than most other countries. However, it is more commonly taken by economists in a wider context to include also competitiveness in terms of quality and marketing.

Indicators of international competitiveness

In assessing how internationally competitive an economy is, economists examine a range of indicators:

- Growth rates. Competitive economies tend to grow faster than non-competitive ones because their products are in high world demand.

- Productivity levels. Higher productivity levels increase the country's productive capacity and allow long-term growth to occur.

- Unit labour costs. This is obviously linked to productivity levels. If output per worker rises more rapidly than wages and other labour costs, unit labour costs will fall.

- Share of exports in world trade. It is becoming increasingly difficult for an industrial country to maintain its share of world trade in the face of increasing competition from a number of developing countries, particularly the newly industrialised countries.

- Balance of trade in goods and services. This is linked to the point above. A competitive country is not likely to have a large deficit on its trade in goods and services balance.

- Investment as a proportion of GDP. Investment is seen as an important cause of economic growth.

- Education and training. As with investment, these are thought to be very important indicators. A country with high-quality education and training is likely to have a flexible, high-skilled and highly productive labour force.

- Investment in research and development (R & D). High levels of expenditure on R & D are likely to develop and encourage the implementation of new technology.

- Communications and infrastructure. Good communications and infrastructure will increase the efficiency of firms by lowering their costs and increasing their speed of response to changes in market conditions

- Industrial relations. Good industrial relations increase the quantity and quality of output.

- Composite indicators. The Swiss-based International Institute for Management Development (IMD) each year publishes a global league table for international competitiveness. This ranks 46 countries on 259 criteria designed to measure factors providing a good business environment. These include economic performance, infrastructure, the role of government, management, the financial system and technological competence. Two-thirds of the criteria are based on statistical data and one-third comes from an opinion survey of more than 4000 business executives worldwide. The USA has, so far, always come top of the league table.

UK's international competitiveness

The UK's position in the IMD league table fluctuates but in recent years the trend has been upwards. On certain of the criteria used to measure competitiveness the UK has been performing well in recent years. These include economic growth (where the trend economic growth rate has improved), a reduction in strikes and high levels of FDI. However, investment and productivity levels still remain below some of the UK's main competitors and the high value of the pound has been putting pressure on the price competitiveness of exporters.

ACTIVITY 3

'By May of this year, sterling unit labour costs in manufacturing had risen 13 per cent above 1995 levels. The sterling nominal exchange rate had appreciated by 23 per cent over the same period. So the rise in domestic unit labour costs – over which UK producers have control – accounted for more than a third of the overall increase in their unit labour costs in foreign exchange.'

Martin Wolf, 'Sick man of Britain' in the *Financial Times*, 2 August 1999

a What could cause unit labour costs to rise?

b What could cause an appreciation (rise) in the exchange rate?

Government measures to promote competitiveness
These include:

- maintaining price stability and general economic stability

- promoting FDI

- increasing the quality and quantity of education and training

- encouraging investment.

New classical economists also favour privatisation and deregulation as they believe that these measures increase the efficiency with which industries work.

Balance of payments disequilibrium

A country which lacks international competitiveness may experience a deficit on its current account – a **balance of payments disequilibrium**. It will earn less from the sale of its exports of goods and services than it spends on imports of goods and services if its products are more expensive and/or of a lower quality than its rivals.

The UK usually has a deficit on its current account. As its trade in services and its investment income are usually in surplus, this suggests that the UK has a competitive weakness in its trade in goods.

Export performance

International trade is significant for the UK. The country exports approximately 24 per cent of all the goods it produces and imports approximately 25 per cent of all the goods it consumes.

In terms of **export intensity** (the ratio of exports to domestic production) the UK has a similar record to other EU countries. However, this masks a decline in its performance in manufactured goods. This is partly because of the contribution of the oil industry to UK exports.

Import penetration

When the UK economy is growing, it tends to suck in imports. Since World War II UK imports of primary products such as food and tobacco have declined in importance while imports of finished manufactured products such as TVs, cars and washing machines have increased. **Import penetration** (the ratio of imports to domestic consumption) has increased more in the UK than in most other industrial economies and more rapidly than its export intensity ratios.

Causes of a poor trade performance

■ Inflexibility. Some countries produce products that are not in high and increasing world demand. Market conditions change and if resources are not reallocated quickly and smoothly, a country may find itself producing inappropriate products for its own consumers and for foreign buyers.

■ High relative prices. If a country's prices are high relative to its competitors it will lose some of its market share. A key influence here is unit labour costs since a country with high unit labour costs is likely to have high prices.

■ High income elasticity of demand for imports. For example, the UK's income elasticity of demand is high and currently higher than the income elasticity of demand for UK exports. This means that when world income rises, UK imports increase by more than UK exports.

■ Poor quality in terms of design, reliability, lifespan, inclusion of new technology, etc. This, in turn, is influenced by research and development, technology and labour skills which is linked to income elasticity of demand (YED). A country which produces low-quality products is likely to have high YED for imports and low YED for exports.

■ Poor marketing and sales. This includes advertising, delivery dates, packaging and after-sales service.

Balance of payments policy measures

If a country continues to have large deficits on its current account its government may decide to take action to increase its export revenue and/or reduce its import expenditure. There are a number of measures which it might consider taking.

Exchange rate adjustment

A country may seek to devalue its exchange rate if it believes that its current level is causing its products to be non-price competitive against rival countries' products. A devaluation will cause export prices to fall in terms of foreign countries' currencies and import prices to rise in terms of the domestic currency. The immediate effect may be to worsen the balance in trade in goods and services. This is because in the short run demand for exports and imports may be inelastic as it takes time for firms and consumers to recognise the price changes and to change their orders. In the longer run it will be hoped that the trade position will improve. This tendency for the trade position to get worse before it gets better is known as the **J curve effect** and is illustrated in Figure 15.1.

However, whether the position does improve or not will depend on the following:

■ The price elasticities of demand for exports and imports. The **Marshall-Lerner condition** states that for a devaluation to be successful in improving the trade position the combined price elasticities of demand for exports and imports must be greater than one.

■ The reaction of other countries. If other countries devalue, the effect will be negated.

■ Import restrictions. If other countries increase their import restrictions the devaluation may not be successful in increasing the volume of exports.

■ Elasticity of supply. If demand for exports rises as a result of the fall in their price it is important that more can be produced. So devaluation may

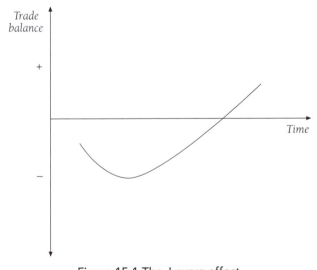

Figure 15.1 The J curve effect

not be considered to be an appropriate measure to take at a time of full or near full employment.

- Low propensity to import. If a high proportion of the extra income resulting from higher export earnings is spent on imports the beneficial effect on the trade position will be reduced.

By increasing demand for the country's products a devaluation usually helps to raise employment and economic growth for a period of time at least. However, by increasing demand for the country's products and raising import prices it may lead to inflationary pressures.

Independent devaluation is not a policy option for a member of the European single currency.

Demand management

To discourage expenditure on imports and to encourage some products to be switched from the home to the export market a government may adopt deflationary measures. These are measures designed to reduce aggregate demand, for example higher taxation, lower government spending and/or higher interest rates. These are more likely to be adopted when an economy is experiencing supply constraints.

However, there is the risk that the resulting fall in aggregate demand may cause unemployment. In addition, if there are other causes of the deficit, for example the poor quality of domestically produced products, the problem is likely to reappear.

Import restrictions

A country may seek to reduce import expenditure by imposing import restrictions such as tariffs and quotas. However, in the absence of other policy measures, these may not tackle the cause of the deficit. Such measures may also have inflationary effects. For example, imposing tariffs will increase the price of some products bought in the country, raise the cost of imported raw materials and reduce competitive pressure on domestic firms to keep costs and prices low.

Placing restrictions on imports also runs the risk of provoking retaliation. In addition, membership of a trade bloc such as the EU and of the WTO limits the independent action that a country can take on import restrictions.

Supply-side policies

If the cause of the deficit is thought to be a lack of competitiveness a government may seek to improve economic performance through supply-side policies. These are measures which seek to increase aggregate supply by improving the quality and quantity of economic resources.

To raise competitiveness there are a number of measures a government may take, including:

- cutting corporation tax to stimulate investment
- cutting income tax to encourage enterprise and effort
- privatising industries if it is thought that firms will operate more efficiently in the private sector
- deregulating markets to promote competitiveness
- promoting education and training to increase productivity and reduce labour costs.

How effective these measures are depends on how firms and workers respond. Most economists agree that promoting education and training will increase international competitiveness. However, there is some disagreement about the best way to improve education and training.

Other measures

A government may give subsidies to infant industries in the belief that in the future they will be internationally competitive. It may also increase funds for research and development at universities and give awards to top exporters.

Current account surplus

A balance of payments disequilibrium may also arise because of a current account surplus. A government may seek to reduce or remove a surplus in order to avoid inflationary pressures and to raise the amount of imports it can enjoy. To reduce a surplus a government may revalue its currency (i.e. raise its value), adopt reflationary measures and/or reduce import restrictions.

Summary

The UK attracts a large amount of foreign direct investment. The multinational companies that come to the UK contribute to its output and introduce new technology and new working practices. They have also helped the UK to compete in international markets. The UK's international competitiveness is also influenced by its productivity and investment levels. A lack of international competitiveness is likely to result in a current account deficit. Among the measures a government may employ to correct such a deficit are deflation, devaluation, the imposition of import restrictions and supply-side policies.

Data response question

Economic recovery

When the UK left the exchange rate mechanism (ERM) the value of the pound fell. Some economists argued that the fall in the exchange rate would provoke inflation and would not result in a long run increase in output and employment. However, the performance of the economy picked up by more than even those in favour of the exit from the ERM anticipated. Output did increase and both inflation and unemployment fell.

In the second half of the 1990s the strength of the UK economy led to a rise in the value of the pound. This time some economists claimed that the higher value of the pound would lead to a fall in output and a rise in unemployment. Whilst some manufacturers did experience problems, output continued to rise and unemployment continued to fall

1   Explain what effect a fall in the value the currency has on export and import prices. (4 marks)
2   Explain why some economists through that the devaluation 'would provoke inflation and would not result in a long run increase in output and employment'. (8 marks)
3   Discuss two causes, other than the strength of the economy, which can cause a rise in the value of currency. (6 marks)
4   Explain the effect that a rise in the value of currency may have on the current account position. (7 marks)

Economic growth and business cycles

Introduction

This unit examines in more depth the topic of economic growth which was discussed in AS Unit 20. Different causes of rises in aggregate demand and the role of investment, education and training are examined. The nature, causes and effects of business cycles are explored and the question of whether business cycles may be a thing of the past is posed.

Causes and effects of economic growth

The causes and effects of economic growth were discussed in AS Unit 23. Here we examine how the effects of economic growth are influenced by their causes.

Demand-led growth

As noted in AS Unit 21, the main cause of increased output in the short run is increases in aggregate demand (**demand-led growth**). These increases may be caused by rises in investment, government spending, consumption or exports or a combination of these components of aggregate demand. All would shift the aggregate demand curve to the right but their effects differ.

An increase in investment may involve an opportunity cost in terms of forgone consumption goods in the short run, especially if the country is operating near full capacity. However, the higher investment will increase the productive capacity of the economy (**investment-led growth**) and thereby raise the potential output of capital and consumer goods. Investment and output are closely linked since an increase in investment raises output which, in turn, tends to stimulate a further rise in investment.

Consumption-led growth, by its very nature, does increase the consumer goods and services which households enjoy and so raises living standards in the short run. Such growth may result in increases in productive potential if firms respond to the higher demand by raising investment to increase output. However, if they are unable to increase output due to supply constraints or if they seek higher profit margins, the effect may be to create inflationary pressures and balance of payments difficulties.

In a situation of low output one of the measures Keynesian economists advocate to increase output is increases in government expenditure. However, the effect of increased government spending depends on what it is spent on and how it is financed. Economists also disagree about the merits of government spending.

Rises in government spending on education, training, research and development, infrastructure and investment subsidies are likely to have a more direct and long lasting influence on economic growth than spending on welfare benefits. Government spending is financed either by taxation or borrowing. In the short run taxation is likely to reduce private sector spending. So to boost economic activity Keynesians tend to advocate financing increased government spending by means of borrowing. However, new classical economists believe that a rise in borrowing will crowd out private sector spending by raising interest rates and reducing funds for borrowing. As new classical economists argue that private sector spending results in a more efficient allocation of resources than public sector spending, they do not favour **government expenditure-led growth**.

Export-led growth tends to raise more support across different groups of economists. This is, in part, because it is taken as an indicator of international competitiveness. It is also because at least some of the revenue earned can be used to finance the increase in imports which is likely to result from the subsequent higher level of economic growth. However, an increase in demand for exports when the economy is operating at a high level of capacity utilisation may be inflationary. In addition, export-led growth is vulnerable to changing world market conditions.

Supply-led growth

In the long run increases in output can only continue if the productive capacity of the economy increases. For this to occur the quality and/or quantity of resources have to increase (**supply-led growth**).

One significant resource is capital goods. Replacement of existing capital goods may increase productive potential if the new capital goods embody advanced technology. Net investment, however, will have a greater impact on productive capacity. The extent of the effect will depend on both the amount of net investment, its type and how efficiently it is used. **Capital deepening** will be more effective than capital widening. Capital deepening involves increasing the amount of capital per worker. This should raise labour productivity. **Capital widening** occurs when investment increases to keep up with increases in the supply of labour.

Not all investment results in higher output. Investment in industries which are in high demand should lead to increases in output but spending on capital goods in declining industries is likely to be ineffective.

Business investment is likely to have a more immediate effect on productive capacity than investment in social capital. Higher spending in houses and hospitals does not directly lead to further increases in output but indirectly they are likely to by the improved productivity which results from the improved health standards. However, this benefit may take some time before it has a significant impact on the productive capacity.

Nevertheless, to use capital efficiently it is important to have educated and healthy workers. One way of measuring the efficiency with which investment is used is the **capital/output ratio**, which is the extra value of capital needed to produce a given value of extra output.

Investment in human capital should increase the productive capacity of the economy but again the extent to which this occurs is influenced by the appropriateness and the quality of the investment. For example, the function of training and one of the functions of education should be to develop the skills needed in the competitive world market. These include not only numeracy and literacy but also communication and interpersonal skills and information and computer technology skills. While the increases in the quality and quantity of training and secondary education in a number of countries, including the newly industrialised countries, has come in for praise, the UK has been criticised for its low levels of training, educational standards and staying-on rates. UK employers have been critical of the skill levels, particularly the communication and interpersonal skills, of the school leavers they employ. They, in turn, have been criticised in a number of reports for the poor quality and insufficient training which they provide.

Stable growth

In seeking to promote economic growth most governments aim for stable growth. Their objective is for actual growth to match trend growth and for that trend growth to rise over time.

They try to avoid aggregate demand increasing faster than the trend growth rate permits since this can result in the economy overheating, with inflation and balance of payments difficulties arising. They also try to stop aggregate demand rising more slowly than the trend growth rate since this would mean an output gap developing with unemployed resources. So what most governments are trying to avoid is destabilising fluctuations in economic activity. The Labour government when first elected in 1997 gave as one of its objectives, the end of 'boom and bust'.

ACTIVITY 1

"*Treasury economists hold out the hope of future revisions to the trend growth rate if evidence of a permanent improvement in productivity does emerge. Even a small improvement in productivity compounds into a big change in living standards after a number of years. During the past 20 years productivity – GDP per worker – has grown on average by just under 2 per cent a year.*'

Diane Coyle, 'Economy growth trend rises as Brown prepares for Budget' in *The Independent*, 8 November 1999

a Explain why an improvement in productivity would increase the trend growth rate.

b What other factors would cause a government to revise its trend growth rate?

Business cycles

Business cycles, which are sometimes referred to as trade cycles, describe the tendency for economic activity to fluctuate outside its trend growth rate, moving from a high level of economic activity to negative growth. The last two decades of the twentieth century witnessed two recessions in the UK, 1980–81, and 1990–92. There were also periods of rapid growth and falling unemployment, for example 1987–89 when a consumer boom took place.

Phases of the business cycle

Four phases of the business cycle are recognised and these are illustrated in Figure 16.1.

■ Upturn. This can also be referred to as the upswing or recovery phase. At this time, economic activity is increasing because of a rise in optimism about the future. Consumers increase their spending and entrepreneurs increase their investment. As a result, employment rises which further stimulates spending and output. Bank lending will increase to finance some of this extra consumption and investment.

■ Boom. During this phase, which can also be called the peak, economic activity reaches its highest point. Unemployment is low and economic growth is high as existing firms expand and new firms are set up. However, a point comes where it is not possible for output to continue to rise to meet the increasing levels of aggregate demand. A supply constraint is met, the economy overheats and the excess aggregate demand results in inflation and balance of payments difficulties.

■ Downturn. This can also be called a downswing. This is the period when economic growth starts to slow below its trend growth rate. The high level of inflation will result in a loss of international price competitiveness causing some domestic firms to cut back their output and some to go out of business. The government may also respond to the problems of inflation and balance of payments deficit by introducing policies to cut back on aggregate demand. The fall in economic growth and rise in unemployment is likely to make consumers and firms more pessimistic about the future and so reduce their spending and investment plans. This will further contribute to the slow down in economic activity.

■ Recession. A recession, which can also be referred to as a trough, is a period of negative growth which lasts for at least six months. In this period aggregate demand falls and unemployment reaches high levels. The economy may even move into a depression or slump which is a prolonged period of falling output. This decline in economic activity comes to an end and the economy moves into an upturn phase. There are two principal reasons why this reversal in economic activity occurs. One is that there is a demand constraint. However pessimistic consumers and firms are about the future a point comes when they have to raise their spending in order to replace such items as worn-out washing machines, cars, office equipment and machines. Another is the role of the government. During a recession net government spending is likely to rise. This may occur automatically as the lower level of economic activity will cause tax revenue to fall while government spending, especially on unemployment benefit rises. It may also be the result of a deliberate rise in government spending and/or cut in tax rates designed to stimulate economic activity.

Types of business cycles

Economists have identified a number of different types of cycles, differentiated by their duration from boom to boom and their cause.

■ **Kitchin cycles**. These last between three and five years and are thought to be caused principally by firms changing their levels of stock.

■ **Juglar cycles**. These last slightly longer, eight to

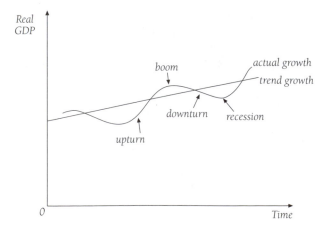

Figure 16.1 The business cycle

ten years, and are caused mainly by changes in net investment.

- **Kuznets cycles**. Due to their emphasis on changes in activity in the construction and associated industries these are sometimes called building cycles. Their duration is thought to be between 16 and 20 years.

- **Kondratieff** (sometimes spelt Kondratiev) **cycles**. These are long run cycles which leads to them being called long waves. Kondratieff argued that shorter run cycles occur within long run cycles which can last for 50 years or more. His work was built on by the Austrian economist, Joseph Schumpeter, to link long run changes in economic activity to technological changes, with time being taken to apply new technology and for it to influence the whole economy. For example, the introduction of electrical power resulted in several completely new industries, new types of capital goods and components and changed productive processes and managerial techniques.

ACTIVITY 2

'... *we are at the beginning of one of the long cycles or Kondratiev waves that last 50 years or so. The last upswing lasted roughly 1948–73, the one before that 1898–1929. Each is triggered by a cluster of innovations and commercial and cultural changes. Each is marked by a great risk and upheaval, the making of new fortunes and the breaking of old ones.*'

Diane Coyle, 'A new model of thought is needed to understand the networked e-commerce' in *The Independent*, 14 December 1999

a How does the Kondratiev cycle differ from the Kitchin cycle?

b Discuss in a group whether advances in information and computer technology are:

 i creating new fortunes

 ii causing commercial and cultural changes.

Explanations of business cycles

The different types of cycles outlined above touch on some of the causes of fluctuations in economic activity. Most are related to changes in investment. Economists have developed explanations for not only why changes in investment but also changes in the other components of aggregate demand and changes in aggregate supply may lead to alterations in the rate at which the economy grows.

- The Keynesian explanation. This suggests that business cycles arise because of the multiplied effects of changes in spending and investment. A small change in spending has a knock-on or multiplied effect on GDP as the extra spending generates a rise in incomes, some of which, in turn, is spent creating even more income. The higher level of demand encourages consumers and firms to be optimistic. Firms increase investment by a greater percentage. When full employment is reached and the government introduces measures to restrict aggregate demand, spending starts to slow down, causing firms to cut back on their investment plans and a downward process occurs. In this Keynesian explanation changes in investment and expectations play a key role.

- The monetarist explanation. Monetarists believe that fluctuations in economic activity arise because of fluctuations in the money supply. They argue that if the money supply grows faster than output, consumption will rise as people feel better off. However, this extra spending causes inflation. This results in a fall in spending as consumers realise they are not better off in real terms and foreign demand declines due to the reduction in international competitiveness.

- Shocks. Unanticipated changes in aggregate demand or aggregate supply can set off a business cycle. These shocks may be positive or negative. An example of a negative aggregate demand shock would be a decline in world demand and a positive aggregate supply shock would be a fall in the world price of oil.

- Political cycle. This is also sometimes called an election cycle. A government may raise its spending and cut tax rates before an election to win political support. Such reflationary policy is likely to stimulate economic activity. However, after the election, if its pre-election policy has resulted in inflation and balance of payments difficulties it may introduce measures to reduce aggregate demand. This explanation can be linked to the monetarist explanation since changes in government spending and taxation can result in changes in the money supply.

Business cycles and government policy

The traditional policy response to the existence and potential existence of business cycles was to operate counter cyclical policies in a bid to maintain the economy on the trend growth path. This could be by the deliberate increasing of government spending and/or cutting taxation during a recession and cutting government spending and/or increasing taxation during a boom. It might also be by allowing government spending to rise on benefits, particularly unemployment benefit, and tax revenues to fall automatically during a recession and government spending to fall and tax revenue to rise automatically during a boom.

One way the Labour government is seeking to achieve greater economic stability is by creating a stability of government policy. It has given the Bank of England independence to determine interest rates (subject to its need to meet the government's inflation target), sets three-year spending plans for government departments and has put limits on public sector debt.

Effects of business cycles

Governments seek to dampen down cyclical fluctuations because of the harmful effects they can have on the performance of the economy. When it is uncertain that aggregate demand will continue to rise this will tend to discourage both domestic and foreign direct investment. It may also mean that firms do not employ the optimum level of workers. During an upturn some may be wary about taking on workers for fear that the increased level of activity will not last while during a downturn some may hoard labour.

The new economic paradigm

The **new economic paradigm** holds out the hope that the business cycle may be a thing of the past, at least for a long period of time. This new model was outlined in AS Unit 22.

The belief that economies may be entering a new era in which it is possible for output to rise at a high rate without encountering a supply constraint and without provoking inflationary pressures was initially based largely on the performance of the US economy. In the 1990s the USA grew at a rapid rate with both unemployment and inflation falling to low levels. Then it was found that the underlying performance of other industrial economies, including the UK, was also improving.

Reasons for the improved performance

The main reasons advanced for the improved performance and increased stability of industrial economies are as follows:

- Improvements in information and computer technology and communications. These have increased productivity and, as with the introduction of electrical power and the car in the past, have created new products, new industries, new methods of production and new management techniques.

- Globalisation, which has increased competition and facilitated the spread of new technology.

- Reduced expectations of inflation following a period of low inflation.

- More flexible labour markets in which the hours worked can be adjusted smoothly to changes in aggregate demand.

- An increase in the participation rate of previously marginal workers, including lone parents, college students, older workers and married women. The USA in particular has been successful in increasing not only the number of jobs but also the supply of labour. In the period 1996–2000 the US economy grew on average by 4 per cent a year. Two-thirds of this was attributed to increased productivity and one-third to increases in the number of workers.

- Increased growth and flexibility of venture capital (finance for new high risk firms) markets, again particularly in the USA. This has facilitated the start up of new firms which are exploiting the new technology.

Views on the new economic paradigm

Some economists believe that economies have really changed and have entered a 'golden age' of high growth, low inflation and low unemployment. They think that the advances in information and computer technology will have a larger and more prolonged impact than previous innovations. Others are more cautious and some are sceptical. The latter raise questions about the accuracy of the productivity figures, questions whether inflationary pressures are likely to remain low, and argue that economies are enjoying a short run increase in economic activity rather than a long run and smooth upward trend.

Implications of the new economic paradigm

The debate about the new economic paradigm is an important one since if the way in which economies work has changed, it will have a number of significant implications. The three main ones are that in industrial economies:

- economic growth can be sustained at higher rates

- government spending can be higher and/or taxation rates lower since government revenue will rise and expenditure on unemployment benefit will fall with economic growth

- the need for governments to restrain rises in aggregate demand to counter inflationary pressures will be removed or reduced.

Summary

In the short run economic growth is caused by increases in aggregate demand. This may be the result of higher investment, consumer spending, government spending and/or exports. Investment-led growth has the benefit of shifting both aggregate demand and long run aggregate supply. Shifts in long run aggregate supply increase the productive potential of the economy. Investment which is capital deepening will have a greater impact on output than capital widening. Fluctuations in investment combined with changes in consumption, are thought to be one of the reasons why business cycles occur. It is also claimed by different groups that the movement from an upturn, to boom, to downturn, to recession and back again can be caused by an excessive growth of the money supply, aggregate demand and supply shocks and changes in pre- and post-election government spending. Governments seek to avoid cyclical fluctuations. The new economic paradigm suggests that economies may be able to continue to grow without hitting a supply constraint or causing inflationary pressures.

Data response question

Could there really be another year of boom for the US economy? If today is the day when the American boom officially becomes the longest in US history, the boom is pretty elderly. While there is no inevitable law that declares that a recession must follow, the fact remains that all booms eventually come to an end.

The consensus view of economists is very simple: that 2000 will be another year of growth, albeit at a slower pace than 1999. But not very much slower; say about 3.5 per cent instead of the 4.0 per cent which the economy looks to have reached last year. Is that credible? After all, however much you stretch the estimates of the long-term growth potential of the US economy, you would be pushed to claim that it can manage much more than 3 per cent growth. So the consensus is forecasting not just another year of growth, but another year of above-trend growth too. And the US economy is expected to do that during a year when interest rates are clearly going to rise.

Let's start by looking at the reasons why the long boom has been so long, the things that differentiate it from previous booms. We are still far too close to be able to make a measured assessment but there are a couple of things that stand out. One is the ability of the US economy to create new jobs and fill them; the other, the way in which hi-tech America has outpaced the middle-tech economy of before.'

Hamish McRae, 'Longest economic boom in US history will race on – for now' in *The Independent*, 28 January 2000

1 Explain what is meant by a boom. (4 marks)
2 Why might it be argued that all booms must come to an end? (4 marks)
3 What factors influence the long-term growth potential of an economy? (5 marks)
4 Explain why the writer thought that the forecast growth rate for the US economy in 2000 was unexpectedly high. (6 marks)
5 Explain what was happening to US labour markets in the 1990s. (6 marks)

Key concepts covered

- frictional unemployment
- seasonal unemployment
- casual unemployment
- search unemployment
- structural unemployment
- regional unemployment
- technological unemployment
- international unemployment
- cyclical unemployment
- NAIRU
- hysteresis
- replacement ratio

Introduction

In the last unit we discussed cyclical fluctuations in economic growth and the new economic paradigm. During a recession actual output will be below potential output and unemployment will be high, whereas during a boom unemployment will be low and if, for example, workers work overtime and machines are not rested for normal maintenance, actual output may exceed potential output. The new economic paradigm suggests that economies will be able to operate with lower unemployment in the future.

In AS Unit 25 the way unemployment is measured and the costs of unemployment were covered. The causes of unemployment were also touched on. In this unit different types of unemployment are discussed and their causes are examined in more detail. This involves distinguishing between voluntary and involuntary unemployment and cyclical unemployment and NAIRU (the non-accelerating inflation rate of unemployment). Particular attention is paid to explaining the meaning of NAIRU and the factors that influence its level.

Types of unemployment

Unemployment can be categorised according to its cause. The three main categories are frictional, structural and cyclical.

Frictional unemployment.

This includes workers who are between jobs and young people who are seeking their first job. What determines how long these people are out of work is principally the mobility of labour. The more geographically and occupationally immobile workers are, the longer they are likely to be out of work.

There are three particular forms of **frictional unemployment**:

- **Seasonal unemployment**. The seasonally unemployed are people who are out of work for a short period because of falls in demand which occur at particular times of the year. For example, the hotel and catering industry and the construction industries tend to employ fewer workers in the winter than in the summer.

- **Casual unemployment**. Some people work on an occasional basis, most noticeably actors.

- **Search unemployment**. This is a form of frictional unemployment that economists pay particular attention to. Some people who are out of work do not necessarily accept the first job on offer. Instead they spend time searching for a congenial and well-paid job. The length of search unemployment is influenced by the savings the unemployed have, the level of benefits and how society views unemployment.

Structural unemployment

Structural unemployment is usually more significant than frictional unemployment as it is often more long run, largely because geographical and occupational immobility are likely to be more important factors. It arises from changes in the pattern of demand or supply which cause a change in the structure of the economy's industrial base and a change in demand for labour. At any time it is likely that some industries will be declining and some will be expanding. This will require workers to move from one industry to another industry. However, some of those workers may lack the necessary skills or may find it difficult to move from where they currently live to where the expanding industries are. The main forms of structural unemployment are as follows:

- **Regional unemployment**. This arises when the declining and expanding industries are in different parts of the country. For example, some of the towns and cities in the south of the UK have shortages of labour while some of the towns and cities in the north have significantly higher than average unemployment.

- **Technological unemployment**. This occurs when the introduction of new technology reduces demand for workers in particular jobs and industries. For example, the development of cash points and electronic banking have reduced the demand for bank cashiers. However, as well as reducing demand for workers in certain industries and occupations, technological change can also result in an increase in demand for workers employed in other occupations and industries. For example, the mobile phone industry is continuing to employ more workers, including people to work on the development of mobile phones which incorporate facilities giving access to the Internet and e-mail.

- **International unemployment**. On a world scale changes in comparative advantage can lead to changes in the demand for labour in terms of quantity and type in different countries. For example, while demand for British steel has declined in the last two decades, demand for steel from Brazil has increased as Brazil has become more efficient in its production.

Cyclical unemployment.

This is linked to the business cycle. It is the unemployment that begins to develop during a downturn in economic activity and can grow to very high levels of unemployment during a recession. It arises because of a lack of aggregate demand – this is why it is also known as demand deficient unemployment.

Voluntary and involuntary unemployment

Voluntary unemployment occurs when there are vacancies but the unemployed do not take them up because they are not prepared to work for the going wage rate. New classical economists believe that a significant proportion of unemployment may at any time consist of voluntary unemployment. For example, they argue that if unemployment benefit is high some of the unemployed may take their time looking for a good job (search unemployment) and some may decide that they are better off being unemployed.

In contrast Keynesians believe that most unemployment is involuntary. They think that most of the unemployed are willing to work at the going wage rate but are unable to find employment because of a lack of vacancies. The shortage of vacancies, in turn, is caused by a lack of aggregate demand (cyclical unemployment).

ACTIVITY 1

'Arm Holdings, the designer of microchips for mobile phones and palmtop computers, is suffering from staff problems, which means that it cannot satisfy demand, the company said yesterday.

Arm said the problem was not recruiting "raw" engineering graduates, but having sufficient staff within the organisation to coach new recruits.'

Chris Hughes, 'Staff shortage hits Arm as demand for chips soars' in *The Independent*, 1 February 2000

'Invensys, the engineering group formed last year from the merger of BTR and Siebe, yesterday said it planned to step up its job-shedding programme. The group said it expected to cut an extra 2000 staff on top of the 9500 worldwide cuts announced in May. About 200 of the extra job losses are expected to fall in the UK.'

Saeed Shah, 'Invensys plans to cut 2,000 more jobs' in *The Independent*, 1 February 2000

a What type of unemployment is being discussed in the second extract?

b Explain why workers made unemployed by Invensys might not find employment with Arm Holdings.

Disequilibrium unemployment

As noted above, cyclical unemployment can be referred to as demand deficient unemployment and, as implied above, it can also be called involuntary unemployment. There is yet another term which is disequilbrium unemployment. This term emphasises the fact that cyclical unemployment arises when there is disequilibrium in the labour market with the aggregate supply of labour exceeding the aggregate demand for labour at the going wage rate. Figure 17.1 shows that the number of people wanting to work at the wage rate w is qS while the number of workers firms want to employ is qD, resulting in unemployment of qD-qS.

Disequilibrium unemployment can arise if the aggregate supply of labour grows more rapidly than the aggregate demand for labour or if the wage rate rises above the equilibrium level. New classical economists argue that disequilibrium unemployment can occur if trade unions or minimum wage legislation drives the wage rate above the equilibrium level. This is referred to as real wage or classical unemployment.

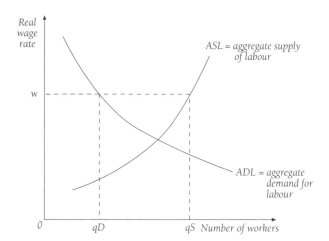

Figure 17.1 Disequilibrium (cyclical unemployment)

However, cyclical unemployment is related to disequilibrium unemployment which is caused by a shortage in aggregate demand. When aggregate demand for labour falls the real wage rate may not fall because workers are likely to resist cuts to wages. Indeed, if the wage rate did fall it may actually make the situation worse. This is because a fall in wages is likely to reduce demand for goods and services that, in turn, will cause a further fall in demand for labour – there is a risk that a downward spiral may develop. Keynesians favour trying to reduce cyclical unemployment by raising aggregate demand via cuts in taxation or interest rates or increases in government spending.

ACTIVITY 2

'Unemployment tumbled to a 20-year low in the final month of 1999, fuelling fears that interest rates will rise again next month. Official data showed that the number of people claiming unemployment benefit in December fell by 21 900 – double expectations – to reach 1.164 million. This was the lowest level since the beginning of 1980.'

Lea Paterson and Alasdair Murray, 'Jobless level drops to 20-year low' in *The Times*, 20 January 2000

a In 1999 the level of economic activity in the UK was rising. Illustrate the effect this had on unemployment, as discussed in the extract, using an aggregate demand and supply of labour diagram.

b Research what is currently happening to national unemployment and unemployment in your area and the reasons why it is rising, falling or staying largely unchanged.

NAIRU

NAIRU (the non-accelerating inflation rate of unemployment) is the level of unemployment which exists when the aggregate demand for labour is equal to the aggregate supply of labour at the going wage rate. This is why it is also sometimes referred to as equilibrium unemployment. As the name NAIRU suggests, it is consistent with the level of unemployment at which there is no upward pressure on the wage rate and inflation. If unemployment falls below this level, perhaps because a government raises aggregate demand in a bid to reduce unemployment, the rate of inflation increases. In contrast if unemployment rises above NAIRU, this time perhaps because the government is seeking to reduce inflation, the wage rate and the inflation rate will fall.

NAIRU consists of frictional and structural unemployment. These are the people who are not in employment because they are unaware of vacancies, unsuited to take up the vacancies or are unwilling to take up the vacancies. Some economists argue that all these are voluntarily unemployed because they could put more effort into finding out about job vacancies, could be more prepared to move to find employment and be more prepared to accept, for a period of time at least, a lower paid job than they ideally would like.

NAIRU can be illustrated on a diagram that shows the aggregate labour force (ALF) but separates out from the labour force those prepared to work at the going wage rate (the aggregate supply of labour, ASL). The gap between the aggregate labour force and the aggregate supply of labour consists of those who are not prepared or feel unable to work at the going wage rate. The gap between ASL and ALF narrows as the wage rate rises as more of the labour force is prepared to work the higher the wage rate.

Figure 17.2 shows that the labour market is in equilibrium at q. However, there are still unemployed workers, q-qz, consisting of those not willing to work at the going wage rate.

Views on NAIRU

NAIRU was originally referred to as the natural rate of unemployment and was almost exclusively associated with new classical economists. This group believes that the real wage adjusts quickly and smoothly to change in labour market conditions so that any unemployment which occurs must be of an equilibrium level. It is now more frequently referred to as NAIRU, in part because the term 'natural'

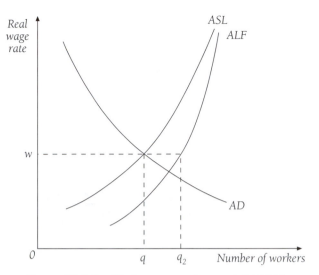

Figure 17.2 Equilibrium unemployment (NAIRU)

implies that a certain level of unemployment should exist and also because it emphasises the connection with inflationary pressure.

Keynesians also argue that while during a recession the main cause of unemployment is a lack of aggregate demand, at any time unemployment can include both equilibrium and disequilibrium forms as illustrated in Figure 17.3.

Figure 17.3 shows that at the going wage rate unemployment is qx-qz, consisting of qx-qy disequilibrium unemployment and qy-qz equilibrium unemployment.

Keynesians, however, believe that real wages do not adjust smoothly to changes in labour market conditions to eliminate disequilibrium unemploy-

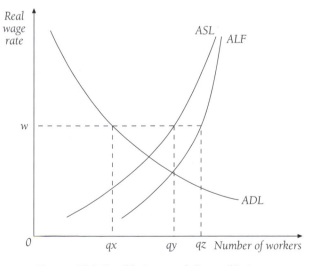

Figure 17.3 Equilibrium and disequilibrium unemployment

ment. They also argue that those experiencing frictional and structural unemployment may be experiencing real difficulties in gaining employment. For example, the longer someone is unemployed, the more problem they may find in gaining a job because their skills have become out of date and perhaps because they have lost the habit of working and some of their confidence. This tendency for unemployment to generate longer-term unemployment and to push up NAIRU is called **hysteresis**.

Factors affecting the NAIRU rate

A number of factors are thought to affect the rate of unemployment which is consistent with stable inflation, including the following:

■ Hysteresis – as discussed above. This can be influenced by government policy. If a government, seeking to reduce inflation, reduces aggregate demand and causes a rise in unemployment the level of unemployment may not return to the former NAIRU rate because of hysteresis.

■ Educational standards, training and skills of the labour force. The higher the quality and quantity of education, training and skills the more occupationally mobile workers are likely to be and the easier they are likely to find it to move from one job to another.

■ Unemployment benefits. New classical economists argue that if there is only a small gap between wages and job seekers' allowance there will be little incentive for the unemployed to seek work. So they favour widening this gap, which is called the **replacement ratio**, and tightening up the eligibility criteria for receiving benefit.

■ Flexibility of labour. The more flexible labour is in terms of the hours worked, the length of employment contract, the type of tasks undertaken and location, the lower NAIRU is likely to be.

■ Trade unions. New classical economists argue that trade unions can increase NAIRU by engaging in restrictive practices.

■ Income tax rates. Lower income tax rates increase the return from working.

■ Labour market regulations. New classical economists argue that the more government controls there are on the employment of workers, the higher NAIRU will be. This is why they opposed the signing of the Social Chapter which, for example, puts a limit on the number of working hours per week and gives male workers paternity rights.

Policies to reduce NAIRU

As noted above, new classical economists favour measures which increase the flexibility of labour markets, make work more attractive relative to unemployment by cutting income tax rates and job seekers' allowance, remove labour market regulations except for 'essential' health and safety rules and reduce trade union power.

In contrast Keynesian economists favour more interventionist policies, including increased government spending on education and training and regional policies. The latter seek to reduce regional unemployment largely by moving work to workers. This policy approach is based on the view that social ties can make labour immobile, that firms do not always seek the optimum location sites and moving people out of areas of high unemployment can depress them further and waste social capital.

The Labour government elected in 1997 sought to reduce NAIRU in a number of ways as follows:

By raising spending on education and setting higher performance standards.

- By widening the gap between the amount that low-paid workers receive and the amount that the unemployed receive. It did this by introducing the working families' tax credit which is a top-up payment given to the low paid. Once in work it is anticipated that most of the recipients will move up into higher paid jobs and so no longer require the subsidy. The introduction of the national minimum wage has raised the pay of the very low paid – although this is a measure opposed by new classical economists who argue that it creates a labour market imperfection.

- By introducing the New Deal. This has been financed by a £5.2 billion windfall tax on the privatised utilities. The intention is to reduce hysteresis by developing the skills and work experience of the unemployed. Initially, it was targeted at those aged between 18 and 24 and then extended to all unemployed adults. Under the scheme the unemployed have to take up the offer of a job subsidised by the government, a place on an educational or training course or on the government's environmental task force

- By introducing compulsory job advice interviews for those receiving benefit, including those

receiving income support and housing benefit. For example, lone parents are made aware of how they might be able to combine working with bringing up their children, including undertaking part-time employment. Again the intention is to maintain the habit of work and keep skills up to date. First-time claimants refusing three calls to interview are refused benefit and those already receiving benefit who refuse have their benefit reduced.

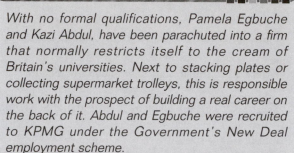

ACTIVITY 3

With no formal qualifications, Pamela Egbuche and Kazi Abdul, have been parachuted into a firm that normally restricts itself to the cream of Britain's universities. Next to stacking plates or collecting supermarket trolleys, this is responsible work with the prospect of building a real career on the back of it. Abdul and Egbuche were recruited to KPMG under the Government's New Deal employment scheme.

Ultimately though, it is hard to see the New Deal making more than a token difference. KPMG last year took on six unemployed people – and 590 university graduates.'

Jon Ashworth, 'New Deal gives new hope to unemployed youngsters' in *The Times*, 12 January 2000

a Explain how the New Deal aims to reduce unemployment in the long run and comment on how successful the extract suggests it is.

b As a group, try to come up with one measure you would recommend the government should introduce to reduce unemployment.

The new economic paradigm

In the light of apparent changes in the structure and performance of the US and UK economy economists have revised down their estimates for the countries' NAIRU. The factors that have led them to do this include:

- reduced inflationary expectations
- increased flexibility of the labour market
- increased competition via globalisation and advances in information technology
- tightening up of eligibility criteria for benefits.

Summary

Unemployment may be frictional, structural or cyclical. Frictional unemployment arises when workers are between jobs, structural unemployment arises due to changes in the pattern of demand or supply and subsequent changes in the industrial structure of the country and cyclical unemployment is caused by a lack of aggregate demand. Keynesians believe that most of the unemployed are involuntarily unemployed while new classical economists believe that most are voluntarily unemployed. NAIRU is the level of unemployment which exists when the aggregate labour market is in equilibrium and there is no upward pressures on inflation. Its rate is influenced by the existence or otherwise of hysteresis, the flexibility and skills of the labour force and unemployment benefit, among other factors. Keynesians favour reducing NAIRU by improving the skills of workers and potential workers and implementing regional policy measures. New classical economists advocate free market policy, including reducing labour market regulations and unemployment benefit. The Labour government is seeking to get marginal workers into employment through improving education and training, raising the income the low paid receive, the New Deal and compulsory job interviews. Economists believe that the UK's and USA's NAIRU have fallen.

Data response question

Structural reforms and technological advances mean that the so-called 'natural rate' of UK unemployment may have fallen significantly during the 1990s, a member of the Monetary Policy Committee (MPC) argued last night.

Sushil Wadhwani, the newest MPC member, said the natural rate of unemployment – a measure of how far the economy can expand before inflation picks up – could fall still further during the next decade as e-commerce takes off.

But he added that the UK still has some way to go before it matches the 1960s 'golden age' of low inflation and high employment growth.

If correct, Mr Wadhwani's arguments mean that the Chancellor's recent pledge to return Britain to full employment may be achievable over the medium term.

A sustained fall in the natural rate could also mean that interest rates have to rise less than in previous cycles. However, speaking to the Society of Business Economists, Mr Wadhwani cautioned that the natural rate was just one of a number of factors studied by the MPC.

He said: 'A belief that the NAIRU (the natural rate of unemployment) has fallen and is likely to fall further does not, of course, necessarily imply that one might be complacent about inflation.'

A drop in trade union membership, the New Deal and moves to tighten benefit availability may be behind the drop in the natural rate, Mr Wadhwani said. Looking forward, e-commerce could be expected to take the natural rate lower, he argued.

Greater competition would put downward pressure on costs and wages, and if wages fall, the economy would be able to support more jobs without generating inflation.

Lea Paterson, 'Wadhwani sees fall in natural jobless rate', in *The Times*, 3 December 1999

1 Explain why advances in technology may reduce NAIRU. (5 marks)
2 Discuss the other reasons the writer gives for the fall in NAIRU. (6 marks)
3 Why might a fall in wages reduce the number of unemployed? (4 marks)
4 Discuss the benefits of full employment. (5 marks)
5 What might cause a rise in NAIRU? (5 marks)

Key concepts covered

- cost-push inflation
- wage-price spiral
- profit-push inflation
- demand-pull inflation
- incomes policy
- deflationary policy
- the Phillips curve
- the expectations-augmented Phillips curve
- NAIRU
- the Fisher equation
- the velocity of circulation
- the Quantity theory

Introduction

In AS Unit 24 we discussed the meaning of inflation, how it is measured, its causes and the effects of inflation. In this unit we build on that discussion to explore the topic in more depth. Further aspects of the causes of inflation are explored, including the 'excessive growth of the money supply', and measures to reduce inflation are discussed. The relationship between unemployment and inflation is examined by making use of the Phillips curve and the expectations-augmented Phillips curve. The Fisher equation and the different views of monetarists and Keynesians on it are discussed. The causes of the recent low inflation rates are also outlined.

The causes of inflation

In AS Unit 24 we divided the causes of inflation into cost-push and demand-pull. It is also possible to separate them into cost-push, demand-pull and monetary, although monetary is really a particular category of demand-pull.

Cost-push inflation

Cost-push inflation occurs when the price level is pushed up by increases in the cost of production, independently of the level of demand. Higher costs of production shift the aggregate supply curve to the left and will result in inflation if they affect a large part of the economy and set in train a series of rises in the price level.

The causes of cost-push inflation can be further broken down into:

- a rise in wages
- higher raw material costs
- an increase in profit margins.

If workers in key industries get a pay rise this will be likely to encourage workers in other industries to press for pay rises. Higher wages, not matched by increases in productivity, will reduce profits and encourage firms to pass on, at least, some of the cost in the form of higher prices. In turn, the higher prices will be likely to stimulate workers to press for higher wages in order to maintain their real wages. So a **wage-price spiral** may be set in motion with prices continuing to rise. In the UK changes in wage rates are a significant factor since they account for approximately two-thirds of total costs.

Higher import prices could result from a fall in the exchange rate. The higher costs of finished imported goods and services would directly increase the Retail Prices Index (RPI) and the other measures of inflation. In addition, the higher cost of imported raw materials will raise costs of production which may be passed on to consumers in the form of higher prices. Domestic producers, facing less fierce price competition from overseas, may be more inclined to raise prices. If workers respond to the rise in the price level by demanding and receiving higher wages, prices will rise still higher. These higher prices will reduce the country's international price competitiveness. The resulting fall in demand for exports may reduce the exchange rate further. This will again raise the general price level and again encourage workers to press for wage rises.

Higher raw material costs may also result from shortages of raw materials due to, for example, a failure of a crop or a hurricane or from producers forming a cartel and exerting their increased market power. It is also possible that profit push inflation may occur with prices being forcrd up as a result of firms raising their profit margins.

Policies to reduce cost-push inflation

To reduce cost-push inflation a government must obviously seek to reduce increases in the costs of production. If it believes that the main cause of inflation is increases in wage rates it may introduce an incomes policy. An **incomes policy**, in this sense, involves the government controlling wage rises. For instance the government may place a limit on wage increases of 5 per cent or £1000 a year.

This measure does seek to reduce inflation without causing unemployment. However, in practice, a number of problems arise with the operation of incomes policies – employers and employees often find ways round the limit by, for example, changing workers' job titles in order to give them a higher than permitted wage rise. A limit on wage rises also introduces a degree of inflexibility in labour markets, with firms wishing to attract more labour being unable to raise wage rates as much as they would like. Groups of workers are likely to press to be made exceptions on the grounds of, for example, low pay, rises in productivity and comparability of work with better-paid workers.

Even if an incomes policy does hold down wage rises it may not succeed in reducing wage pressure. So once the incomes policy is lifted wage rates may rise significantly.

Alternatively, a government could seek to reduce cost-push inflation by reducing firms' costs via cuts in corporation tax and/or interest rates. The danger here, though, is that while reducing firms' costs, such measures are likely to increase aggregate demand which may itself raise the general price level.

The government could reduce firms' imported raw material costs by raising the exchange rate. This measure would not raise aggregate demand but would put pressure on the country's firms to keep their costs low in order to remain competitive at home and abroad.

Demand-pull inflation

Demand-pull inflation occurs when aggregate demand exceeds aggregate supply at the current price level. The excess of aggregate demand pulls up prices. In AS Unit 24 we discussed one particular cause of demand-pull inflation which was a consumer boom. Another possible cause is demand for exports increasing when the economy is either at full employment or near full employment. If more exports are not offset by more imports, there will be more income coming into the country with fewer goods and services on which to spend the income.

Demand-pull inflation may also be initiated by an increase in government spending. One of the reasons why governments impose taxation is to try to ensure that their spending does not cause inflation. For example, a government may believe that its economy is capable of producing £120 billion worth of goods and services. It estimates that, in the absence of

taxation, private sector spending will be £110 billion. If it wants to spend £40 billion on education, health and other public services, it will reduce private sector spending via taxation by £30 billion to ensure that total spending does not exceed £120 billion. Of course, in practice, it is difficult to get these estimates right. There is also the problem of time lag. A government may decide to increase its spending when private sector spending is low and unemployment is high. However, by the time public sector spending is increased the economy might have picked up anyway and the extra government spending may result in an excess of aggregate demand and hence demand-pull inflation.

Policies to reduce demand-pull inflation

To reduce demand-pull inflation a government may adopt **deflationary policy** measures. These are ones which seek to reduce inflation via decreasing aggregate demand, or at least the growth of aggregate demand. For example, it could raise income tax. This would reduce people's disposable income and their ability to spend. It could also reduce aggregate demand directly by cutting its own spending. Alternatively, it could raise interest rates. This measure may reduce aggregate demand by raising the cost of borrowing, reducing the ability to spend of those who have already borrowed and encouraging saving.

Figure 18.1 shows aggregate demand falling from AD to AD₁. This does reduce demand-pull inflation. However, if aggregate demand falls too far, for example to AD₂, deflationary policies may result in unemployment.

There is also the risk that raising income tax rates and interest rates may provoke workers to press for wage rises to compensate for their reduced spending

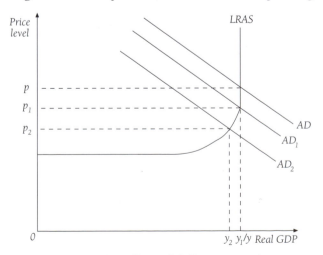

Figure 18.1 The effect of deflationary policies

power. If they do gain wage rises and if these are not matched by rises in productivity, firms' costs will increase.

An alternative approach to the problem of excessive aggregate demand is to seek to increase aggregate supply. New classical economists favour measures to increase incentives such as reducing corporation tax and income tax rates. Keynesians may also support cuts in corporation tax and giving grants to firms to expand their output. To be successful these measures would have to increase aggregate supply by more than aggregate demand.

The main short-term anti-inflationary measure being employed in the UK is currently changes in interest rates. The government is also seeking to reduce the possibility of inflation in the future by raising long run aggregate supply via education, training and increased incentives. If successful these measures should also reduce firms' costs of production.

ACTIVITY 1

'The beneficial effect of the rise in sterling is already being reflected in producer prices, with firms' raw materials prices dropping by 7½% in the year to March …

But raw materials account for only about one-seventh of a typical firm's costs compared with about three-quarters attributed to labour costs. Therefore wage inflation trends are more important, at the margin, then changes in raw materials prices as drivers of future retail prices. Worryingly, whole economy earnings inflation has accelerated, from an underlying annual 4% in November last year to 5% in February.'

Trevor Williams, 'The UK outlook – unbalanced growth' in Lloyds Bank, *Economic Bulletin*, May 1997

a What does the extract suggest would be the main cause of inflation in 1998?

b Did the inflation rate in 1998 rise or fall in contrast to the previous year?

c Explain what factors have accounted for the change in the inflation rate over the past three months.

The Phillips curve

One measure of the pressure of aggregate demand, in particular the demand for labour, is the **Phillips curve**. This is named after Bill Phillips, a New Zealander, who started his working life as an engineer. After World War II he came to study sociology at the London School of Economics (LSE). During his course he became interested in economics and, in particular, in studying the effect of changes in unemployment rates on money wages. He stayed on at the LSE and studied unemployment rates and wage increases for the period 1861 to 1913. He found an inverse, non-linear, relationship between unemployment rates and wage increases. This means that as unemployment falls, rises in money increase but not at a proportionate rate – they accelerate. When unemployment falls to low levels money wages rise rapidly, whereas when unemployment rises to high levels workers resist cuts in their money wages.

The Phillips curve was developed by two US economists, P. Samuelson and R. Solow in 1960, with changes in money wages being taken as an indicator of inflation to show the expected relationship between unemployment and inflation. Figure 18.2 shows the inverse relationship between unemployment and inflation.

When demand for labour rises, unemployment is likely to fall. The increased competition for workers is likely to bid up wage rates. Higher pay for workers can increase the price level via increased costs of production and higher aggregate demand as the workers spend their wages.

Economists had drawn up Phillips curves for most countries by the mid-1960s. In this period the Phillips curve was interpreted by economists and politicians to suggest that policy makers could trade off inflation and unemployment to reach a desired combination. For example, a reduction in unemployment from, say, 6 per cent to 4 per cent might have to be 'bought' at the price of a rise in inflation from, for example 3 per cent to 5 per cent.

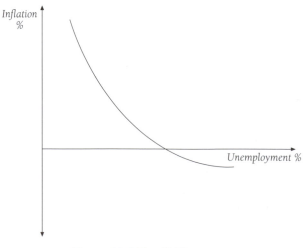

Figure 18.2 The Phillips curve

The expectations-augmented Phillips curve

In the 1970s the Phillips curve came in for criticism. Some economists argued that the relationship it predicted still existed but that the curve had shifted to the right, indicating that a higher level of unemployment would be combined with any level of inflation. They suggested that in the 1970s workers had got used to higher levels of unemployment and so did not modify wage claims to the same extent when unemployment rose.

Milton Friedman, the most famous monetarist economist, went further. He questioned the accuracy, in the long run, of the traditional Phillips curve in predicting the effect of changes in aggregate demand on the level of unemployment and inflation. He argued that while a Phillips curve relationship may exist in the short run between unemployment and inflation, in the long run changes in aggregate demand would influence inflation but leave output and unemployment unaffected. Figure 18.3 shows the economy initially operating on the short run Phillips curve 1 (SPC_1) with 0 per cent inflation and 5 per cent unemployment.

An increase in aggregate demand may, in the short run, encourage firms to expand their output and take on more workers. Unemployment falls and the economy is at point a. However, the rise in demand for goods and services and the resources to produce them will result in inflation. The economy now moves to point b. When producers and workers realise that inflation has eroded their real profits and wage levels they adjust their behaviour. Producers reduce their output and demand for labour. This, combined with some workers leaving their jobs because of the fall in real wages, causes unemployment to return to the NAIRU level. The economy now moves to point c on the long run Phillips curve (LPC) where there is no trade-off between unemployment and inflation. However, the economy is also on a higher level short run Phillips curve since now expectations of inflation have been built into the system. Producers and workers have experienced 5 per cent inflation and so will base their future prices and wage claims on the assumption that prices will continue to rise. Any future increase in aggregate demand, not accompanied by an increase in long run aggregate supply, will result in acceleration in inflation.

ACTIVITY 2

'The improved performance of the jobs market could justify "testing the water" with interest rates by allowing unemployment to fall further, Sushil Wadhwani of the Monetary Policy Committee argued last year.

He said the unemployment rate below which a tight jobs market triggers inflation – the "non-accelerating inflation rate of unemployment" or NAIRU – is lower now than during the economic golden age of the 1960s.'

Diane Coyle, 'Little inflation risk from falling jobless rate, says Wadhwani' in *The Independent*, 3 December 1999.

a Why may a change in the rate of interest lead to inflation?

b Explain why a fall in the unemployment rate below a certain level might trigger inflation?

Monetary inflation

Monetarists argue that the cause of inflation is the money supply growing faster than output. They argue that if the supply of money increases faster than the demand for money the value of money will fall. In support of their view, monetarists make use of the **Fisher equation**. This is MV = PY (or MV = PT) where M is the money supply, V the **velocity of circulation** (i.e. the number of times money changes hands in a given period of time), P is the general price level and Y the level of output. T stands for transactions and is equivalent to output. As it stands, it is a truism. One side represents total expenditure and the other the value of goods sold so, by definition, they must be equal. However, monetarists developed the equation into the **quantity theory**. They did this by insisting that V and Y are constant. They argue that V is relatively stable and that Y does not change in the long run as a result of a change in aggregate demand. This leads them to

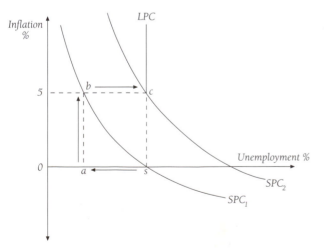

Figure 18.3 The expectations-augmented Phillips curve

conclude that a change in M will have a direct and pro-portional effect on P.

The monetarists' explanation can also be illustrated by a shift in the aggregate demand curve to the right. In the short run the higher demand resulting from an increase in the money supply will lead to an increase in output and the economy will move to point B on the short run aggregate supply curve as shown on Figure 18.4.

However, the increased demand for resources will bid up their prices and thereby increase costs of production. So the SRAS curve shifts to the left. The economy in the long run moves to point c as workers and firms adjust to the rise in costs and prices. Output and employment return to their previous levels and aggregate demand again equals long run aggregate supply. However, the price level has risen and firms and workers will now expect the price level to continue to rise.

Keynesians, however, disagree with the monetarist explanation of inflation on two main grounds:

■ They argue that V and Y can change in both the short and long run. An increase in M may be accompanied by a fall in V and/or a rise in Y and hence have little effect on P. They believe that the shape of the long run aggregate supply curve will vary according to the level of economic activity. So that an increase in aggregate demand resulting from a rise in the money supply, or any other cause, may not be accompanied by a proportionate rise in P. Indeed, at low levels of economic activity P may not rise at all. So they do not think that the equation MV = PY can be used as the basis for any predictions.

■ Keynesians accept that inflation is indeed a monetary phenomenon in the sense that inflation will be accompanied by a rise in the money supply. However, they argue that a rise in P leads to a rise in M and not the other way round. Inflation will cause firms and households to demand more money in order to cover higher costs and prices.

Policies to reduce monetary inflation

As monetarists argue that the cause of inflation is the money supply growing at a more rapid rate than output, they favour reducing the growth of the money supply to a level where it matches the change in output. The main measure they advocate to achieve such a reduction is to decrease any government borrowing which is financed by increasing the money supply.

ACTIVITY 3

a Distinguish between the Phillips curve and the expectations-augmented Phillips curve.

b Using the latest data, plot unemployment and inflation rates and comment on your findings.

Recent trends in inflation

Recent years have witnessed a period of low inflation in many countries. It is thought there are a number of reasons why inflation is remaining low in the UK, including:

■ advances in information technology which are raising productivity levels, reducing costs and increasing competition by lowering barriers to entry (the new economic paradigm)

■ globalisation which is increasing competition in many markets

■ reduced expectations of inflation – having experienced a number of years of low inflation, consumers, workers and firms no longer expect high inflation and so do not act in ways which create inflation

■ privatisation and regulation of utility firms which are driving down utility prices

■ high value of sterling which lowers import prices, reduces costs of production and puts pressure on UK firms to keep their costs low

■ more flexible labour markets which permit output to change more rapidly and smoothly to meet changes in demand.

There has also been an improved unemployment-inflation combination. Both have been at low levels

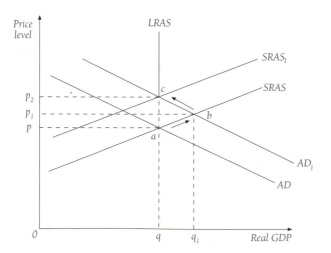

Figure 18.4 The effect of an increase in the money supply

suggesting that a trade-off may no longer be necessary and that NAIRU has fallen.

Summary

Inflation can be caused by cost-push or demand-pull factors. Among the causes of cost-push inflation are increases in wages, raw material costs and profits. Demand-pull inflation can be caused by an increase in any or a combination of the components of aggregate demand, including exports and government expenditure. The Phillips curve examines the relationship between unemployment and inflation. It suggests an inverse relationship with, for example, a fall in unemployment being associated with a rise in inflation. The expectations-augmented Phillips curve was developed in response to criticism of the Phillips curve. It suggests there is no long run trade-off between unemployment and inflation. Monetarists who support the expectations-augmented Phillips curve also argue that the main cause of inflation is the money supply growing by more than output. In support of their arguments they make use of the quantity theory. However, Keynesians argue that it is increases in inflation which generate inflation and not the other way round. The UK and many other industrial economies have been experiencing low inflation because of increases in productivity, rises in competition and reduced expectations of inflation, among other causes.

Data response question

Table 18.1

Year	Annual change in RPI %	Annual change in money supply (M4) %	Balance of payments current balance (£m)
1992	3.7	4.1	−9661
1993	1.6	3.1	−10 309
1994	2.5	5.2	−1425
1995	3.4	7.5	−3211
1996	2.4	9.8	136
1997	3.1	8.6	7427
1998	3.5	6.3	557

National Institute of Economic and Social Research, *National Institute Economic Review*, October 1999

Inflation can be caused by demand-side or supply-side factors. An increase in aggregate demand may be caused by a rise in consumption, investment, government spending or net exports. If there is excess demand in the product and factor markets demand-pull inflation will occur.

Changes in the supply side of the economy can also cause inflation. An increase in wages, the price of imports or profits, independent of aggregate demand will raise the costs of production and shift the aggregate supply curve (upward) to the left.

1 Discuss how easy it is to distinguish between demand-pull and cost-push inflation. (4 marks)
2 Do the data suggest the existence of a relationship between the growth of the money supply and inflation? (5 marks)
3 What economic explanation might there be for a relationship between the money supply and inflation? (6 marks)
4 Describe and comment upon the nature of the relationship between inflation and the UK's balance of payments current account performance. (7 marks)
5 Identify three other variables it would be useful to examine to assess the causes of inflation. (3 marks)

Section 3 questions

Essay questions

1 a Explain the main factors that influence the rate of economic growth. (20 marks)
  b The economy of the Republic of Ireland is growing at a faster rate than the UK. Does this necessarily mean that the citizens of the Republic of Ireland are better off than the citizens of the UK? (30 marks)
2 a Explain the advantages of free international trade. (10 marks)
  b Discuss the reasons why countries impose import restrictions. (15 marks)

Project

Prepare a report which investigates and analyses the validity or otherwise and the implications of the new economic paradigm.
  This should cover:

■ a discussion of traditional theory

■ an explanation of the new economic paradigm

■ an investigation and analysis of statistical and theoretical evidence

■ a discussion of the implications of the paradigm, if true, for the performance and management of the UK economy

■ a list of sources.

You should make use of appropriate economic theory, including aggregate demand and supply analysis, throughout your report.
C3.1a, C3.1b, C3.2, N3.1, N3.2, N3.3, IT3.1, IT3.2, IT3.3.

Section 4
Government Policy

Introduction

AS Units 19 and 27 discussed government policy. In this section the main forms of government policy are explored and appraised. Governments can employ a range of policies, including incomes policy, which is influencing pay and trades policy and includes import or lifting restrictions on imports. The latter was discussed in A2 Unit 13. Aspects of incomes policy were touched on in A2 Unit 18. In this section the focus is on fiscal, monetary and supply-side policies. The first two have traditionally been very important policies widely used by governments throughout the world. The last one has increased in importance in the last two decades.

In Unit 19 fiscal policy is examined. Various aspects of taxation and government expenditure are considered and then the relationship between the two is explored. A government seeking to achieve a number of objectives is likely to make use of a range of policies including monetary policy. This is the topic of Unit 20 where the process by which monetary policy affects the economy is discussed and monetary policy is discussed in its current context. In Unit 21 supply-side policies, which have come to

prominence in recent decades, are discussed in terms of different approaches to raising the productive potential of the economy. Unit 24 discusses the possible shortcomings of government policy and some of the advantages and disadvantages of fiscal, monetary and supply-side policies.

Before reading this section, check that you can recall the meaning and use of the following concepts:

- fiscal policy
- direct taxes
- indirect taxes
- progressive taxes
- proportional taxes
- regressive taxes
- the Budget
- monetary policy
- exchange rate
- Monetary Policy Committee
- supply-side policies
- policy conflicts.

UNIT 19 Fiscal policy

Key concepts covered

Introduction

Fiscal policy was defined and briefly explored in AS Unit 27. This unit looks in more detail at taxation and government expenditure and then examines the relationship between the level of government expenditure and taxation. It also covers a number of the key issues of fiscal policy, including the relative merits of direct and indirect taxes, the question of hypothecated taxes and tax harmonisation.

Fiscal policy

Fiscal policy is concerned with changes in taxation and government policy. It can be used to influence the efficiency of particular markets and to influence the overall level of economic activity. The current government is using fiscal policy to increase incentives in a bid to raise the long-term growth potential of the economy and reduce particular market failures while largely leaving the short-term management of economic activity to monetary policy in the form of interest rate changes (see Unit 20).

Tax burden

Most governments seek to reduce or at least prevent the **tax burden** rising. The tax burden refers to the total amount of tax that people and firms pay to the government. It is usually expressed as a percentage of GDP. When Margaret Thatcher came to power in May 1979 with the promise of cutting taxes the tax burden was 33.3 per cent, but by the end of her first government it had risen to 39.1 per cent. From then until she left office in 1990 it did fall – to 36.2 per cent. Under John Major it fell further to 35.2 per cent. In the first three years of the Labour government the tax burden rose, up to 37 per cent.

Types of taxes

The main forms of UK taxes were outlined in AS Unit 27. Most tax revenue comes from income tax, followed by value added tax (VAT). Income tax is a direct and progressive tax – as income rises both the amount and the percentage that a person pays in tax rises. VAT is an indirect and largely regressive tax. It is imposed on goods and services at different rates. The standard rate is 17.5%, domestic fuel and power, and sanitary protection are taxed at 5%. Some products, for example most foods, children's clothing, medicines on prescription, books and newspapers are zero-rated. This means that the firms selling the products cannot charge VAT but can reclaim any VAT paid on their inputs. Others are VAT exempt, including education, finance, and health services. In this case the firms do not charge VAT but cannot claim back any VAT they have paid.

Other taxes include capital gains tax and inheritance tax. Capital gains tax is a tax on the increase in the value (difference between purchase and selling price) on items such as shares, second homes and paintings. A large number of assets are exempt, including agricultural property, private motor cars and winnings from gambling. Inheritance tax is a tax on transfers of wealth above a certain amount.

Qualities of a good tax

Four qualities of a good tax were identified by Adam Smith, who wrote *The Wealth of Nations* (1776) and is sometimes referred to as 'the father of economics'. A good tax should be equitable, certain, convenient and economical.

- Equitable. This means that the amount of tax that a person or firm pays should be fair. Economists now discuss horizontal and vertical equity. **Horizontal equity** occurs when people or firms with the same income and financial circumstances pay the same amount of tax. **Vertical equity** occurs when the amount that people and firms pay is based on their ability to pay, so that people with high incomes pay more than those with low incomes.

- Certain. This means that it should be clear to people and firms how much tax they will have to pay.

- Convenient. The tax should be easy for taxpayers to pay and for the government to collect.

- Economical. An economical tax is one which, relative to the revenue raised, is cheap for people or firms to pay and for the government to collect.

Since Adam Smith's time economists have added two additional criteria – flexible and efficient.

- Flexible. This means that it must be possible for the tax to be changed relatively quickly in the light of changing market conditions.

- Efficient. An efficient tax is one that increases efficiency in markets. An example of an efficient tax is a **Pigouvian tax**.

Pigouvian tax

A Pigouvian tax was named after Arthur Pigou (1877–1959) who wrote extensively about economic welfare. It is one with the prime aim not of raising income but correcting a negative externality. The tax is imposed to turn the external cost into a private cost and thereby achieve allocative efficiency. However, for the tax to be efficient it must be possible to measure the external costs accurately. Figure 19.1 shows that the tax imposed is equal to the external cost and so does improve the allocation of resources.

Direct and indirect taxes

In the last two decades there has been a shift in the UK and other European Union (EU) countries from direct to indirect taxes. In the UK income tax rates have been cut, in the case of the top rate dramatically so – from 83 per cent to 40 per cent, while VAT and excise duty rates have increased.

Direct taxes are progressive and, depending on their rates, contain a degree of equity. They also help to make the distribution of income more equal. In addition, they help to stabilise economic activity since revenue from direct taxes rises automatically during a boom since incomes and profits rise and falls automatically during a recession when incomes and profits fall. However, governments have reduced their reliance on direct taxes mainly because they believe that they can be a disincentive to work and effort. The argument is that high marginal rates of income tax may discourage some workers from working overtime, some from

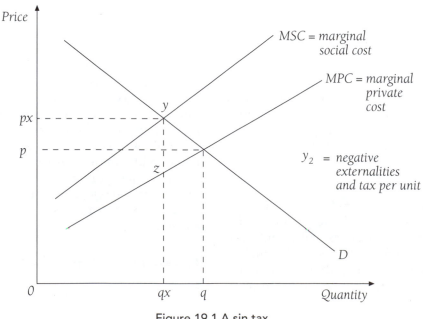

Figure 19.1 A sin tax

taking promotion and some marginal workers from entering the labour force. It is also thought that high marginal rates of corporation tax discourage entrepreneurs from expanding their firms and high marginal tax rates on savings reduce the incentive to save. There can also be the problem of saving being taxed twice effectively, once when the income is earned and again when it is saved.

Direct taxes can also take some time to change. For example changes in income tax rates can take some time to implement since PAYE codes have to be adjusted. Changes in indirect tax can usually be implemented more quickly. It is also claimed that indirect taxes have less of a disincentive effect since they are based on spending rather than earnings and, in part, because they are thought to be less obvious to the payers. They are also difficult to evade.

In addition, taxes can be used to influence the consumption of particular products. For example, demerit products can be taxed highly. Indirect taxes, as well as direct taxes, have a stabilising effect since spending rises in line with the trade cycle.

However, indirect taxes tend to be regressive. The zero rating of VAT on some products reduces the regressive effect but some claim that combined with differences in excise duty, it results in horizontal inequity. For example, two families of the same size and with the same amount of income will pay different amounts of tax if one family enjoys walking and reading (which are not taxed) and the other enjoys driving and drinking (which are taxed).

Indirect taxes can be inflationary if the rise in indirect tax stimulates a further rise in prices. This is thought to be a particular risk with taxes on fuel that feed through to increased costs of production.

Indirect taxes also reduce consumer surplus and distort the pattern of consumption. Indirect taxes may be introduced to eliminate negative externalities. However, unless negative externalities can be measured accurately, there is a danger that indirect taxes will result in a less efficient allocation of resources.

Hypothecated taxes

A **hypothecated tax** is one that is raised, or raised in part, for a specific purpose. So the revenue, or some of the revenue, is 'ring fenced'. In November 1999 the Chancellor of the Exchequer, Gordon Brown, announced that more than £300 million a year raised from tobacco duty would be earmarked for the National Health Service to spend directly on fighting smoking-related diseases. It was the first time that he

ACTIVITY 1

Sin taxes are taxes designed to discourage unhealthy living and thereby reduce negative externalities. One example of a sin tax is the excise duty imposed on alcohol.

a   Identify two other examples of sin taxes.
b   What negative externalities are caused by the consumption of alcohol?
c   Discuss, in a group, the arguments for and against cutting tax on wine.

had specifically earmarked revenue for public spending, although later that month he also said that any further future increases in petrol and diesel duties will be devoted to spending on transport.

Hypothecation gives consumers some choice, can give some idea of how much people are prepared to pay for particular services and can be used to take money from those creating negative externalities and using it to compensate those who suffer from the negative externalities.

However, hypothecation reduces the Chancellor's flexibility in changing tax revenue and government spending to influence economic activity. The revenue earned is also itself subject to changes in economic activity. It is debatable whether many people would want spending on the NHS to fall during a recession, for example. There is also the question of financing categories of government spending which are less popular than education and health and, if adopted on a large scale, the technical problem of aggregating individual preferences.

Forms of government spending

Government spending can also be referred to as public expenditure. It includes spending by both central and local government and public corporations. It can be divided into:

- capital expenditure – on hospitals, schools and roads, etc.

- current spending – on the running of public services and includes teachers' pay and the purchase of medicines to be used in the NHS

- transfer payments – money transferred from tax payers to receipts of benefits, for example pensioners and the unemployed.

- debt interest payments – payments made to the holders of government debt, for example holders of National Savings Certificates.

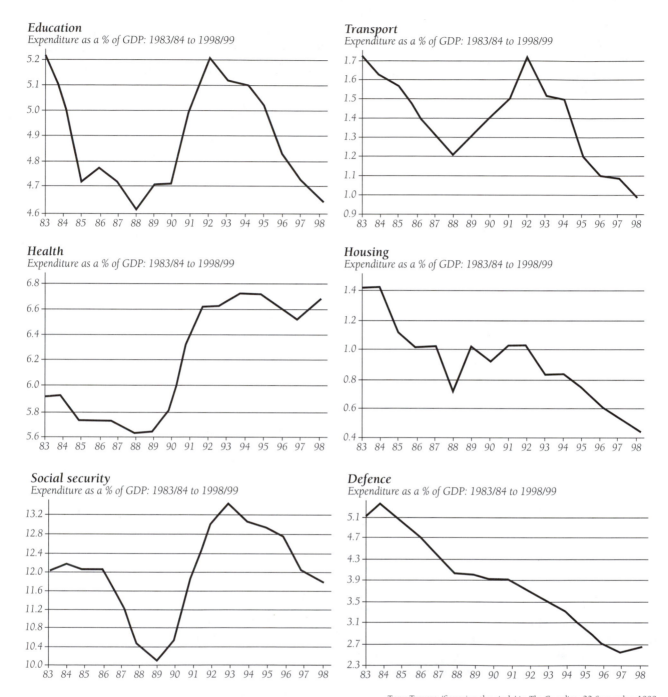

Education
Expenditure as a % of GDP: 1983/84 to 1998/99

Transport
Expenditure as a % of GDP: 1983/84 to 1998/99

Health
Expenditure as a % of GDP: 1983/84 to 1998/99

Housing
Expenditure as a % of GDP: 1983/84 to 1998/99

Social security
Expenditure as a % of GDP: 1983/84 to 1998/99

Defence
Expenditure as a % of GDP: 1983/84 to 1998/99

Tony Travers, 'Squaring the circle' in *The Guardian*, 22 September 1999

Figure 19.2

Capital and current expenditure are sometimes referred to as **exhaustive expenditure** as they make use of resources directly. When the government builds a new school it is paying for the use of the land, materials and other resources. On the other hand, transfer payments and debt interest are **non-exhaustive** forms of **expenditure**. In their case the government is not buying the use of resources but enabling others to do so and it is the recipients of the benefits and interest that will determine the use of resources.

The main forms of government spending were outlined in AS Unit 27. It was noted the four most important areas of government spending are social security payments, health, education and debt interest. The amount and proportion spent on different items is influenced by a number of factors. For example,

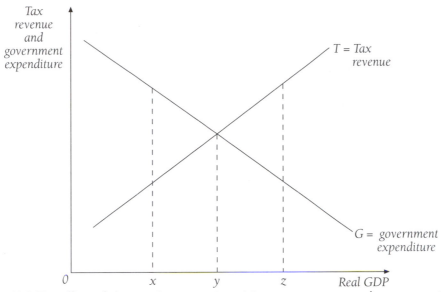

Figure 19.3 The effect of changes in economic activity on tax revenue and government spending

spending on social security, while influenced by benefit rates, is much more significantly affected by economic activity. It rises during periods of increasing unemployment and falls during periods of falling employment. Expenditure on health and education are affected by government priorities, government policies (for example the replacement of student grants with loans) and changes in the age composition of the population, among other factors. Debt interest is affected by the level of government debt and interest rates. Spending on two other categories have tended to decline in recent years. One is defence where expenditure has been cut back in the light of the end of the perceived threat from eastern Europe. The other is housing where spending has declined in importance with the rise in owner occupation, the sell off of council houses and with housing associations taking over the prime role in social housing.

The Labour government has introduced a comprehensive spending review that decides on the amount that departments can spend over the next three years.

ACTIVITY 2

The charts in Figure 19.2 show government spending on six major categories of expenditure as a percentage of GDP.

Study the charts and comment on the trends in spending shown.

The Budget

The Budget is presented by the Chancellor of the Exchequer in March of each year. Prior to this date in November the Chancellor sets out his or her plans for taxation. The Budget is now just concerned with taxation, as the spending plans are presented separately.

However, to calculate the country's budget position, tax revenue and central government spending are compared. A budget surplus arises when tax revenue exceeds government spending and a budget deficit occurs when government expenditure exceeds tax revenue. A budget deficit will increase demand in the economy as the government is adding more to spending than it is taking out of circulation. In contrast a budget surplus reduces aggregate demand.

Fiscal stance

Fiscal stance refers to whether the government is seeking to raise or lower aggregate demand through its fiscal policy measures. A reflationary fiscal policy is one which is increasing demand, whereas a deflationary fiscal policy aims to reduce aggregate demand. However, it is harder to assess a government's fiscal stance than might initially appear to be the case. A government may be trying to raise aggregate demand but may end up with a budget surplus. This is because the budget position is influenced not only by government policy but also by changes in the level of economic activity.

Figure 19.3 shows how tax revenue rises and government expenditure falls with GDP. At income level x there is a **cyclical deficit**, at income level y there is a balanced budget and at income level z there is cyclical surplus.

As noted earlier, a number of forms of government expenditure and taxation adjust automatically with economic activity to dampen down the fluctuations. These are referred to as **automatic stabilisers**. For example, spending on job seekers' allowance falls when economic activity picks up. Of course, some forms of government expenditure and taxation are not automatic stabilisers. For example, spending on child benefit is not linked to the business cycle.

Full employment budget position

To try to assess how a budget's position is influenced by cyclical fluctuations economists sometimes make use of the full employment budget concept. This plots the budget position which would occur taking into account only cyclical factors achieving a balanced position at full employment. This is shown in Figure 19.4 by line A. Then the government's actual budget position is plotted on line B. If GDP is at s, there is a budget deficit of st. Of this sr is the cyclical deficit component and rt is the **structural deficit**. A structural deficit arises from government policy on taxation and spending and is the result of government spending being too high relative to tax revenues over the whole cycle.

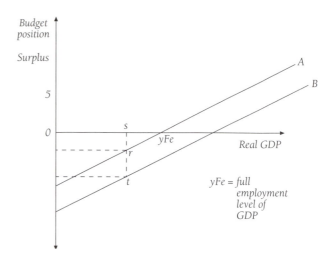

Figure 19.4 The full employment budget

Reflationary and deflationary policy

A government may implement a **reflationary fiscal policy** by increasing government expenditure and cutting taxation during a recession. Once the economy starts to pick up it is likely to try to seek to reduce its level of spending and/or raise taxes (**deflationary policy**). However, this may not be that easy as people and firms get used to higher levels of spending and do not like tax rises.

Seeking to influence the level of aggregate demand in the economy is referred to as **demand management**. Governments do this to create greater stability. So they act counter-cyclically, injecting extra demand when private sector demand is thought to be too low and reducing its own demand when private sector demand is thought to be too high.

In the past governments frequently engaged in **fine tuning**. This involved short-term changes in government spending and/or taxation with the aim of achieving a precise level of aggregate demand. However, governments now accept that fiscal policy cannot be used so precisely. They may be said to engage in **coarse tuning**. This is less frequent changes in policy designed to move the economy in the right direction.

The Public Sector Net Cash Requirement

The **Public Sector Net Cash Requirement** (PSNCR) is the excess of public sector (central government, local authority spending and the net trading surplus or loss of nationalised industries and public corporations) over revenue. To finance the gap between revenue and

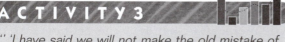

" 'I have said we will not make the old mistake of confusing a cyclical surplus with a structural surplus," the Chancellor said, "I can therefore report that based on prudent and cautious assumptions, audited by the National Audit Office, we are on course to balance the current budget over the cycle."

Analysts said that the Chancellor was right not to take the improvements in the public finances at face value, which had been the mistake in the late 1980s.' ''

David Smith, 'Brown's good battle plan' in *The Sunday Times*, 14 November 1999

a Distinguish between a structural and a cyclical deficit.

b What might be the consequence of a government 'confusing a cyclical surplus with a structural surplus'?

spending the government will borrow either from the banking sector (high street banks or the Bank of England) or the non-bank private sector (insurance companies and individuals, etc.). The government borrows by selling, for example, government bonds and National Saving certificates, on which it pays interest.

New classical economists are concerned that government borrowing can lead to **crowding out**. This means that the extra government spending does not add to total expenditure, it merely replaces some private sector spending. The thinking is that the higher borrowing used to finance the increased spending pushes up demand for scarce funds and thereby raises the rate of interest. The higher rate of interest discourages private sector consumption and investment. It may also cause a rise in the rate of interest which will further reduce demand for the country's output. However, Keynesians argue that increased government spending can cause a rise in private sector spending – **crowding in**. They believe that higher government spending will encourage firms to increase their output, either because the government is buying directly from them or because the recipients of benefits will buy more from them. The higher incomes which arise will result in increased savings which can finance the borrowing.

A negative PSNCR means that revenue exceeds expenditure. This would enable a government to repay past debt.

Fiscal policy and the EU

If the government decides to enter the single currency it would have to accept a limit on any budget deficit to 3 per cent of its GDP. Its fiscal policy is already influenced by its membership of the EU. Under the Conservatives the UK entered into an agreement linking its VAT rates to those in the EU. There are calls for greater **tax harmonisation** (i.e. the standardisation of tax rates) within the EU. The main argument behind such a move is that for the area to operate as a single market similar, if not the same rates, of taxes must operate in the different countries. Without such a standardisation countries can gain a comparative advantage in products, labour and capital markets by operating lower rates of taxation. For example, workers may be tempted to work in countries with low income tax rates, consumers to buy in countries with low excise duty and firms to locate in countries with low corporation tax. For example, UK citizens make regular day trips to France where tax rates are lower to stock up on alcohol and cigarettes.

The current government's fiscal policy

The government has stated that its aims for fiscal policy are to raise sufficient revenue to pay for the services which its policies require, to pay necessary interest on the national debt while keeping the burden of taxation as low as possible, to promote fairness and to encourage work, saving and investment.

It has also sought to increase greater stability in fiscal policy by introducing the comprehensive spending review and fiscal policy rules. The first rule is called the golden rule. This is a commitment that over the economic cycle the government will only borrow to finance investment spending and will not borrow to finance current spending. The second is the public debt rule. This is the requirement to keep public sector debt at 40 per cent over the period of the economic cycle. The motives behind promoting stability of government policy is to make it easier for government departments, firms and consumers to plan.

Summary

A good tax is one which is certain, equitable, convenient, economical, efficient and flexible. Direct taxes are progressive but have disincentive effects. Indirect taxes are regressive but are thought to have fewer disincentive effects. Recent decades have witnessed a shift from direct to indirect taxation. Hypothecated taxes are ones raised for a specific purpose. The main items on which the government spends are social security payments, health, education and debt interest. A government which spends more than it raises in tax is said to have a budget deficit. A budget deficit will contribute to a PSNCR which is the gap between public sector spending and revenue. A PSNCR can be financed by borrowing from the bank or non-bank private sector. An excess of government spending over tax revenue can arise as a result of government policy designed to increase economic activity or as a result of changes in the level of economic activity itself. Demand management may seek to be very precise (fine tuning) or to achieve a movement in the right direction (coarse tuning). Countries within the EU are being encouraged to harmonise their tax rates. The UK government is seeking to provide greater stability to fiscal policy.

Data response question

During the 1970s and 1980s, not only did fiscal fine-tuning fail, but budget deficits rose alarmingly. In recent years most governments (with the notable exception of Japan) have accordingly focused almost exclusively on trimming or eliminating their deficits. Governments in the euro area have, under their stability pact, set a limit on budget deficits of 3% of GDP. Some American economists favour strict balanced-budget amendments.

But by reducing the ability of fiscal policy to respond to developments in the economy, such constraints could put an excessive burden on monetary policy to prevent economies from either overheating or diving into recession. Central banks may enjoy their new powers, yet it could be argued that monetary policy is not well suited to this role, as its effects on the economy are felt only after long and variable lags. Some studies suggest that fiscal policy is better suited to steering nominal demand, because once implemented (where the delays currently lie), it affects the economy more swiftly than changes in interest rates. Furthermore, the effects of monetary policy tend to be spread less evenly across the economy than those of fiscal policy. For example, high interest rates and hence a stronger exchange rate squeeze manufacturers more than other producers.'

'Fiscal flexibility' in *The Economist*, 27 November 1999

1 What is fine tuning? (4 marks)
2 Explain what could cause a budget deficit to arise. (6 marks)
3 What fiscal policy measures might be taken to prevent an economy overheating? (5 marks)
4 What fiscal policy measures may not be spread across the economy? (5 marks)
5 Discuss what you think is the government's current fiscal stance. (5)

UNIT 20 Monetary policy

Introduction

In recent years there has been a shift away from relying on fiscal policy to influence aggregate demand in the short run to greater reliance on interest rate changes. This is one of the monetary policy tools. The other two are changes in the money supply and changes in the exchange rate. In this unit the operation of monetary policy is examined with particular attention being paid to interest rates. This is because it is the main form of monetary policy currently being used in the UK, the USA and many other industrial economies. However, the effects of changes in the money supply and exchange rates are discussed. The type of monetary policy which a government operates, the arguments for and against Bank of England independence and European monetary policy are also examined.

Monetary policy

As explained in AS Unit 27 monetary policy can be taken to include changes in the money supply, interest rates and the exchange rate (some economists separate out the exchange rate as a separate policy). It includes the measures which influence the quantity and price of money. Its prime aim has been to try to achieve price stability. However, it is also used to achieve the other main government objectives, i.e. full employment, economic growth and balance of payments equilibrium.

Recent history of monetary policy

When the Conservatives came to power in 1979 their main priority was to reduce inflation. As they believed that inflation is caused by excessive growth of the money supply they sought to reduce the growth of the money supply. They found this very difficult to achieve and statistical evidence for the period suggested that there was not a clear link between growth in the money supply and inflation. So in 1990 the emphasis of monetary policy switched to the exchange rate. In 1990 the UK joined the **ERM** (the Exchange Rate Mechanism). This is a pegged exchange rate system in which currencies can vary only by a small amount relative to the other member currencies. The UK went in at a high exchange rate in the belief that this would put downward pressure on domestic inflation. However, the rate was not sustainable and the UK left the ERM in 1992. It then decided to target inflation and to use the rate of interest to influence its level. (It is thought that setting an inflation target may itself reduce inflationary pressure by persuading firms and consumers that the government is taking a determined approach to reducing inflation.) This is still the approach of the government, although the operational determination of the rate of interest has been given to the Bank of England.

The exchange rate

If a government operates a fixed exchange rate it becomes largely a policy objective rather than a policy tool. However, as noted above, if the rate is set above or below the equilibrium level it can be used to influence inflation and economic activity although it is unlikely to be sustainable. Changes in a fixed exchange rate can also be used. For example, a devaluation, by making exports cheap and imports expensive, is likely to help the balance of payments position, employment and economic growth although it may result in inflationary pressures.

If a government is prepared to allow an exchange rate to fluctuate more frequently the exchange rate can be a more active policy tool. However, it is thought that frequent changes in the exchange rate can be destabilising for traders.

Changes in the money supply

Measures of the money supply became prominent when the Conservative government started to target the growth of the money supply. Measures are still produced today and, while they are not given the prominence they once were, they are still taken into

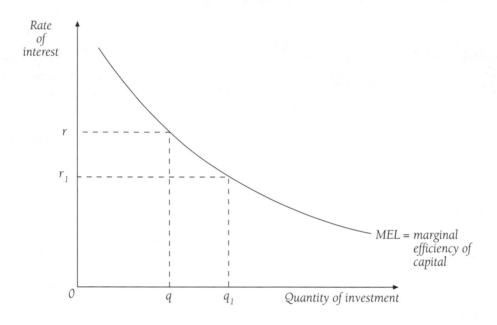

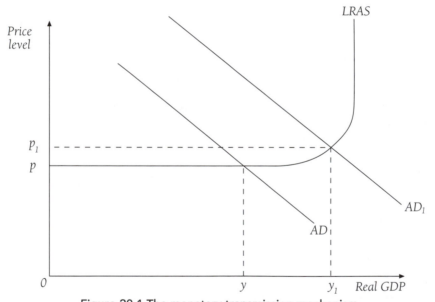

Figure 20.1 The monetary transmission mechanism

account by the Monetary Policy Committee (see below). The two main measures of the money supply are **M0** and **M4**. M0 includes notes, coins and high street banks' accounts at the Bank of England. M4 covers the items in M0 and bank and building society deposits (accounts).

The amount of money in existence is heavily influenced by the lending policies of the high street banks. When banks lend they open up deposits for the borrowers. As these deposits can be spent they are money and are included in the M4 measure of the money supply. Banks lend when they are able to

back up their loans with liquid assets (assets which can be turned into cash quickly and without loss) and when demand for loans is high.

Measures to reduce the growth of the money supply

The Bank of England, acting on behalf of the government, can seek to reduce the growth of the money supply either by reducing the ability of the banks to lend and/or by reducing demand for loans. There are a number of policy measures they can implement to achieve this including the following:

- **Open market operations**. This involves buying and selling government bonds. If the Bank of England is seeking to restrict bank lending it will sell government bonds. The intention is to use up some of the banks' liquid assets and thereby reduce their ability to lend.

- **Funding**. This involves converting government debt from short term to long term with the intention of reducing the value of liquid assets that banks can get hold of.

- **Moral persuasion**. This involves the Bank of England asking banks to lend less.

- **Interest rates**. Raising interest rates works on the demand for loans by increasing the price of the loans. This is thought to be the most effective way to control bank lending.

The monetary transmission mechanism

The **monetary transmission mechanism** is the process by which changes in the money supply come to affect output, employment, inflation and the balance of payments. For example, an increase in the money supply will mean that people will have more money to spend on financial assets. This will raise the price of financial assets. The price of financial assets and the rate of interest are inversely related. For example, a government bond issued for £1000 may pay £100 interest (i.e. 10 per cent). If the price of the bond rose to £2000 the £100 interest would now be 5 per cent. So a rise in the price of financial assets results in a fall in interest rates. Lower interest rates stimulate consumption and investment. They also tend to reduce demand for the currency, thereby lowering its value, and increase demand for exports and lowering demand for imports. So three components of aggregate demand are likely to rise. The effect of the shift to the right of the AD curve will depend on at what level of output the economy was initially operating. If, for example, the economy was operating close to full employment the effect is likely to be to raise both output and the price level. The monetary transmission mechanism is illustrated in Figure 20.1.

The role of the Monetary Policy Committee

The Monetary Policy Committee (MPC) sets the rate of interest with the prime objective of achieving the government's target rate of inflation of 2.5 per cent with a 1 per cent point margin either side. Subject to meeting that objective it has been instructed to support the economic policy of the government, including its objectives for employment and economic growth. The MPC consists of five members drawn from employees of the Bank of England, including the Governor of the Bank of England and four economists nominated by the Chancellor of the Exchequer. It meets monthly to review evidence on the performance of the economy and indicators of changes in inflationary pressure. This information includes figures on the current and predicted growth of the money supply, the exchange rate, wage rates, employment, productivity, retail sales and surveys of business and consumer confidence. If the MPC believes that the information points to the risk that inflation will rise above the target it will raise interest rates.

ACTIVITY 1

'Business and homeowners yesterday faced the grim prospect of a new year hike in interest rates after it emerged that a majority of the MPC now favours a rise – possibly next month.'

Philip Thornton, 'Bank of England signals rate rise at start of the millennium' in *The Independent*, 23 December 1999

a Would a rise in interest rates be a grim prospect for all homeowners?

b Discuss four factors that would cause the MPC to consider raising interest rates.

The independence of the Bank of England

The government gave the Bank of England operational independence to set interest rates in May 1997. In January 2000 the shadow chancellor, Michael Portillo, stated that the Conservative Party accepted that the Bank of England should remain independent, so now there is agreement between the two main political parties on the issue.

The arguments for permitting the Bank of England to decide on the appropriate level of interest rates are that it has considerable experience in financial markets, is more likely to take a longer-term perspective, will not be tempted to lower interest rates just prior to an election to win popularity and doing so permits the government to concentrate on other policy measures. However, some argue that the Bank of England is too concerned with price stability and is sometimes prepared to sacrifice jobs to pay for it. The independence of the members has also been questioned as the Governor of the Bank of England and the four economists are appointed by the Chancellor of the Exchequer.

Monetary policy stance

A **tight** (or restrictionist) **monetary policy** is one which aims to reduce aggregate demand, or at least the growth of aggregate demand, usually in a bid to lower inflation or improve the balance of payments position. In contrast an **expansionary monetary policy** approach (loosening monetary policy) is one which encourages a growth in aggregate demand. So reducing the rate of interest would be regarded as an expansionary approach.

Monetary policy and the EU

Entry into the European single currency means that a country loses autonomy over its monetary policy since the euro area operates one exchange rate and one interest rate. The European Central Bank (ECB) sets the interest rate and can influence the exchange rate. The governing council of the ECB includes the central bank governors of the euro area. The target set for the ECB is to maintain price stability as defined by an increase in HICP (the harmonised index of consumer prices) of below 2 per cent. Some commentators have expressed concern that the rate of interest chosen by the ECB and the value of the

euro may not benefit the UK economy, but this is the reason why it is important that a country's economy converges with that of the area before it considers membership.

Even outside the euro area the UK's monetary policy is influenced by the ECB's actions. If, for example, the euro falls in value relative to the pound sterling the UK's price competitiveness against its main trading partners declines. In addition, if the UK's interest rate falls below that of the ECB's, money may flow out of UK financial institutions into those of the euro area which would put downward pressure on the value of the pound.

Summary

Monetary policy measures are changes in the money supply, interest rates and the exchange rate. A high exchange rate will tend to reduce economic activity. The main measure currently being used is changes in interest rates. Higher interest rates and a reduction in the growth of the money supply also tend to reduce aggregate demand and are a sign that the Bank of England is implementing a tight monetary policy. The Bank of England has operational independence to determine and introduce the appropriate interest rates to achieve the government's inflation target. Should the UK join the euro area, control of monetary policy will pass to the ECB.

Data response question

The Bank of England's monetary policy committee meets today to set interest rates, in the elegant octagonal committee room designed by Sir Robert Taylor in the 18th century. Its members will be conscious that, to some of its critics, the MPC's attitudes are almost as antiquated as the surroundings.

The committee is trying to hit a target – inflation – that has been an obsession for decades, using a policy instrument that has been in use since 1833.

In the US, seismic structural changes are taking place in the economy, leading to talk of a technology-led 'New Economy'.

These signs of an economic transformation are gaining some influence on the MPC's thinking, largely through the advocacy of DeAnne Julius, the committee's most enthusiastic proponent of the New Economic hypothesis. She argues that British companies are becoming global price-takers, rather than price-setters.

The Bank of England has – somewhat grudgingly – accepted that the emerging trends in the economy are significant. In its last Inflation Report, in November, the Bank cut 0.2 percentage points from the forecast for this year's inflation, and the same again for next year, to reflect 'competitive forces'.

That revision is by no means negligible; the rough rule of thumb relating interest rate changes to inflation suggests interest rates could be set one or two percentage points lower than they would otherwise have been.

But to some proponents of the New Economy, the change in attitude does not go far enough. 'The Bank is being a bit unimaginative about New Economy effects,' says Roger Bootle of Capital Economics, who was early into this area with his book *The Death of Inflation* in 1996. 'They ought to take an a priori decision that the internet is really big, and its effect will be to unleash a series of price reductions right across the economy.'

If the British economy is being changed in a way that is holding down prices and delivering a significant improvement in productivity, it would mean the Bank could afford to let growth run for many years above its trend of the past few decades.

The problem is that policy-makers cannot yet be certain that this is what is happening. The structural changes that have begun to affect the economy have occurred at the same time as other temporary, ephemeral phenomena.

British businesses' perceptions of intensified international competition over the past few years owe a lot to the strength of sterling. The currency markets do, of course, regularly defy any attempt at forecasting, but all logic suggests the pound cannot stay as high as it is now forever.

Ed Cooks, 'Britannia's new rules' in the *Financial Times*, 13 January 2000

1 What is meant by the New Economy? (3 marks)
2 What target for inflation does the MPC seek to hit? (2 marks)
3 What implications does the New Economy have for interest rate setting and why? (6 marks)
4 What are the dangers of the Bank of England being too optimistic about the extent of the development of a new economy in the UK? (6 marks)
5 What effect would a fall in sterling have on employment and inflation? (8 marks)

UNIT 21 Supply-side policies

Key concepts covered

- Laffer curve
- poll tax
- neutral tax
- privatisation
- deregulation
- regional policy

Introduction

Supply-side policies were discussed in AS Unit 27. In this unit we examine this area of policy in more depth, including the rise in importance of supply-side policies and differences in approach to supply-side policies. In discussing free market supply-side policies, reducing tax rates, reducing benefits, re-forming trade unions, privatisation and deregulation are covered. Grants to industries, education and training and regional policy are examined in connection with interventionist supply-side policies. The approach of the Labour government elected in 1997 is touched on.

Nature of supply-side policies

Supply-side policies include measures designed to shift the long run aggregate supply curve to the right by increasing the quantity and quality of resources via improving the efficiency of product and labour markets. A number of the measures are concerned with changes in taxation, but their aim, unlike with fiscal policy, is not to influence aggregate demand but to increase incentives. Supply-side policies are micro as opposed to macroeconomic policy, working through particular markets.

The rise in importance of supply-side policies

Supply-side policies came to the fore in the UK and USA mainly in the 1980s. The Conservative government, elected in May 1979, implemented a number of significant supply-side policies in the 1980s and 1990s. Initially, supply-side policies were very much identified with new classical economists. Keynesians were associated with demand management policies. However, in the 1990s there

was an increased consensus that governments needed to be concerned not only with the level of aggregate demand but also aggregate supply. The Labour government, elected in 1997, has also been using supply-side policies in an attempt to raise the long run growth performance of the economy.

Approach to supply-side policies

While there is increased agreement that governments should seek to increase aggregate supply, there are still differences in opinion about how this is best achieved. New classical economists advocate free-market supply side policies. These are measures that seek to increase the country's productive potential by increasing incentives, the level of competition and reducing government intervention. Keynesians, on the other hand, favour raising the efficiency of markets by means of interventionist supply-side policies.

Free market supply-side measures

Reducing direct taxes

As discussed in AS Unit 27 supporters of supply-side policies argue that a cut in direct taxation will result in a rise in the number of hours worked and the amount of investment undertaken. They also argue that lower tax rates can actually increase tax revenue. In support of this argument they make use of the **Laffer curve**. This shows the relationship between marginal tax rates and tax revenue as shown in Figure 21.1.

At 0 per cent tax rate and 100 per cent tax rate there is no tax revenue. It is obvious why there is no

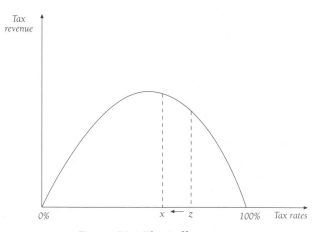

Figure 21.1 The Laffer curve

revenue at 0 per cent and fairly obvious that at 100 per cent there would be no incentive to work. If, however, the tax rate is at the high point z, a cut in the rate to x would raise revenue. This is not only because a greater incentive to work is created but also because the incentive to evade tax is reduced. So new classical economists argue that cutting taxation not only increases output but also enables a country to gain a more accurate picture of the size of the output – the black economy is reduced. However, the importance of the Laffer curve has been questioned in terms of whether the shape he drew was accurate (some claim it may be linear for part of its length) and because, in practice, it is difficult to assess where a country is on the curve.

Simplifying the tax system

New classical economists favour making the tax system more straightforward and less time consuming to reduce the costs imposed on firms and workers from participating in markets. The simplest, but controversial, tax is a **poll tax**. This is a tax per head of the population. The benefit claimed for the poll tax is that it is a **neutral tax**. This means that its imposition does not distort the behaviour of firms, workers and consumers as the amount they pay is not influenced by, for example, the amount of income they earn, the amount they spend or where they live. However, as it is the same tax for everyone it is very regressive. The Community Charge that was introduced in Scotland in 1989 and England and Wales in 1990 contained elements of a poll tax. It proved to be very unpopular and was also not very efficient as there was significant evasion. It was replaced by Council Tax in 1993.

ACTIVITY 1

In the November 1999 pre-budget report the Chancellor of the Exchequer, Gordon Brown, announced his intention to cut dramatically capital gains tax on the profits of entrepreneurs selling their businesses within five years of setting up.
a   Explain what is meant by capital gains tax.
b   Why might the measure outlined above stimulate a rise in output?

Cutting benefits

New classical economists argue that benefits can discourage the incentive to work if they are too high or if people's claims are not checked carefully. So they favour increasing the replacement ratio (the gap between paid employment and job seekers' allowance), making the criteria for receiving benefits such as disability benefit more rigorous, checking more regularly that the recipients are still unable to work and cutting down on fraud. They are keen to reduce a 'dependency culture'.

ACTIVITY 2

Discuss in a group:
a   how a government could seek to assess whether benefit claimants are genuine
b   whether a cut in job seekers' allowance would lower or raise unemployment.

Privatisation

Privatisation is one of the best known free market supply-side policies. As mentioned in AS Unit 27 new classical economists believe that firms work best in the private sector where they have greater freedom and where they face more competitive pressures. If they do face more competition they will be forced to keep their costs low and their quality high which may raise their international competitiveness. The reduction in government interference may enable the firms to respond more quickly to changing market conditions.

Deregulation

Deregulation is the abolition or reduction of government rules, regulations and laws that restrict the free workings of markets. The intention is to raise efficiency by increasing competition. In the UK a number of industries have been deregulated, including the building society and banking industry (1986) and the local bus service industry (1986). Deregulation has sometimes occurred simultaneously with privatisation such as with the privatisation of British Telecom when the barriers to entry into the industry were reduced. However, at the same time various regulatory agencies such as OFTEL (Office of Telecommunications) were established to check that the privatised firms do not abuse their market power. The setting up of such agencies is opposed by some new classical economists who argue that all that is necessary is to ensure that the markets are contestable.

Reform of trade unions

Again, as noted in AS Unit 27, new classical economists favour passing legislation to reduce the power of trade unions. They believe that reducing the monopoly power of trade unions will restrict the extent to which unions can push the wage rate above the equilibrium level and enforce restrictive practices such as demarcation (workers being prepared only to undertake certain tasks). They also think that trade union reform will increase the flexibility of wages, including permitting local wage negotiations which would lead to wage differentials developing in different areas of the country to reflect differences in the level of demand for labour.

Interventionist supply-side policies

Education and training

There are two key arguments advanced in favour of government intervention in education and training. One is that they are merit goods and are likely to be under-consumed if left to market forces. Consumers may not appreciate the true value of education and training, may take a short-term view and in the case of firms may be discouraged from spending large amounts on training for fear that their trained workers will be poached by other firms. Consumers will also not take into account the positive externalities that arise. The other main argument is equity. Education and training, if left to market forces, would not be equally available to all. Indeed, some children might have to leave school, for example, at 10 years old. Wide disparities in access to education and training would have a significant impact as education and training are key determinants of future income levels.

ACTIVITY 3

In 1999 the Labour government announced nearly £200 million worth of new investment in schools and training, including an extra £150 million in a school improvement programme, £25 million on giving up to 50 000 people basic computer training through a network of local learning centres, £10 million to boost enterprise skills in schools and £12.5 million on expanding child care within FE colleges.

a   Why do you think the government places so much emphasis on information and computer technology training?

b   Explain the benefits to the economy of increasing child care provision.

Grants to industries

A government may consider that some industries should receive financial assistance for a period of time. For example, governments throughout the world give financial assistance to infant and declining industries. One reason for this is to allow the economy to adapt more smoothly to changes in comparative advantage. There are also non-economic arguments such as the protection of strategic industries.

Regional policy

Regional policy seeks to influence the distribution of people and industries. Problems can arise if a country has congested areas and depressed areas. A depressed region is one which is likely to have relatively high unemployment, poor-quality jobs, low GDP per head, a shortage of entrepreneurial talent, net outward migration and a high proportion of the population reliant on benefits. New classical economists argue that if markets work efficiently these regional differences would be eliminated by a combination of wage adjustments and factor mobility. Workers would move to the more prosperous areas which would be paying higher wages and firms would move into the depressed regions attracted by the ready availability of low-cost labour. However, Keynesians argue that the unemployed, because of social ties and because they cannot afford the costs of moving, are often immobile and that firms tend to move not to the depressed regions but to the prosperous ones – success attracts success. Those who do move out of depressed areas are usually the young, ambitious and the most educated and skilled. When these people move out of the area they deplete it even further. Keynesians believe that it is easier and more effective to move firms than workers. They think that most firms are 'footloose'. This means that their costs do not vary significantly in different areas and that they can be based anywhere. If they relocate to depressed areas, it is argued, there is no reason why they should not be a success there. To encourage them to move a government may make use of regional investment grants, improve the local infrastructure and place limits on expansion in the congested areas.

Current government approach

The current Labour government regards the use of supply-side policies as an important part of their drive to improve the performance of the economy. It is making use of a range of free market and interventionist policies. For example, on the free market side it has cut income tax and corporation tax rates and has introduced a welfare-to-work programme designed to get people off benefit and into work. On the interventionist side it is increasing spending on education and training and does provide financial assistance to industries setting up in areas of high unemployment.

Summary

Supply-side policies are microeconomic policies designed to raise the productive potential of the economy. Their use has increased in recent years. Supply-side policies can be separated into free market and interventionist policies. The former seek to increase the efficiency of markets by reducing government intervention and raising incentives, for example via privatisation and cutting income tax. The latter seek to achieve the same objective but by means of government intervention, for example government spending on education and training. The present government is employing both free market and interventionist supply-side policies.

Data response question

Every adult long-term unemployed person aged 25 and over will be brought within the government's welfare-to-work programme from April 2001.

The chancellor said the move to extend the New Deal would bring their rights and responsibilities into line with those for the young long-term jobless.

'Our long-term economic ambition over the next decade for employment is to achieve a higher percentage of people in work than ever before,' he added.

Gordon Brown's latest reforms will take the UK closer to the workforce system now in force in the US.

Mr Brown also announced a crackdown on the abuse of the benefit system by the bogus unemployed.

The Chancellor said billions of pounds were being drained away in unpaid taxes and fraudulent benefit claims. 'This cannot be allowed to continue, especially when there are jobs that benefit claimants could take,' he added.

Lord Grabiner, a senior judge, is to head a taskforce to investigate the scale of the problem and devise a plan of action with a strict timetable.

'He will examine ways to move economic activity away from illegitimate to legitimate businesses. He will consider increased fines for fraud and new requirements specifically for those suspected of being in the hidden economy – to sign on for benefit not every fortnight but every single day,' said Mr Brown.

Under the extension of the welfare-to-work programme, every adult long-term unemployed will be offered a job with a private-sector employer; self-employment; work-based training or work preparation. They will not have the option of doing nothing without facing a loss of benefit. Fortnightly job search reviews will be introduced.

Under tough new rules New Deal personal advisers will identify suitable vacancies and job-seekers will be required to apply for them. If unsuccessful, they will have to improve their employability skills.

Robert Taylor, 'New Deal extended to jobless adults over 25' in the *Financial Times*, 10 November 1999

1 What type of unemployment, voluntary or involuntary, was the Chancellor seeking to reduce with the measures discussed in the article? (5 marks)

2 What is meant by the term 'hidden economy'? (4 marks)

3 Are the policy measures discussed, free market or interventionist supply-side policies? Explain your answer. (5 marks)

4 How could an unemployed person improve his or her 'employability skills'? (5 marks)

5 Discuss two other supply-side policies designed to promote output and employment. (6 marks)

Introduction

In Units 19, 20 and 21 we discussed three of the main forms of government policy. In this unit we briefly assess each of these policies in turn. However, we first examine the general problems faced by government policy, including inadequate information and time lags.

Views on government policy

Keynesians believe that markets do not work efficiently. They think that market failure is a real problem. They also think that governments have the appropriate knowledge, skills and tools to intervene and improve the performance of the economy. In contrast new classical economists argue that markets work efficiently and that there is a real risk that government intervention will make the situation worse. They believe that governments should remove some past policies, laws and regulations which are hampering the smooth working of free market forces, should keep tax low and should concentrate on creating a low inflationary climate which will provide the basis for achieving the other three macroeconomic objectives.

Government failure

Government failure occurs when government intervention instead of improving the performance of markets makes it worse. As noted above, new classical economists believe that government failure is a more significant problem than Keynesians do. There are a number of possible causes of government failure.

Poor quality of information

If a government lacks information or has inaccurate information it may make the wrong policy decisions.

For example, if the Bank of England wrongly believes that aggregate demand will rise too rapidly in the future it may raise interest rates now. If the economy is actually on the brink of a recession this will reinforce the downturn in demand. Also, as noted in Unit 21, if a government estimates the extent of negative externalities inaccurately and imposes a tax on this basis, it will reduce economic welfare.

The government employs a large number of economists who supply it with analysis and advice. The government also receives advice from other economists working in academia, the media and industry. Some of these economists now use very sophisticated models, but the accuracy of these models is influenced by the information and theories fed into them and how the predictions are interpreted.

In assessing the expected effect of changes in government policies on the economy, economists make use of the concept of the **multiplier**. This is the relationship between an initial change in aggregate demand and the final change in income. For example, the government may increase its spending by raising the state pension. Pensioners receiving more money will spend some of the extra. The shopkeepers who benefit from the rise in spending, in turn, will spend some of the extra revenue they receive and so on. The size of the multiplier can be measured as either:

$$\frac{\text{Final change in GDP}}{\text{Initial change in AD}} \quad \text{or}$$

$$\frac{1}{1 - \text{proportion of extra income which is spent}}$$

For example, if people spend 80% or 0.8 of extra income, the multiplier would be:

$$\frac{1}{1-0.8} \quad = \quad \frac{1}{0.2} \quad = \quad 5.$$

Keynesians believe that it is possible to calculate the multiplier reasonably accurately while new classical economists do not think it is. So the latter group believe it is difficult for a government to assess, in advance, the effect that changes in government spending and taxation will have.

New classical economists also argue that markets provide higher quality information and provide it more quickly. In a free market, in theory at least, an increase in demand will result in a rise in price which will automatically inform producers that they should expand production of the product.

Economic theory

The policies adopted are influenced by the economic theories followed by politicians and their economic advisers. However, there are disagreements as to which are the appropriate theories to follow. For example, there are different theories on interest rate determination. The view widely held for the first part of the twentieth century was that the rate of interest is determined by demand for loans and the supply of savings. This theory is known as the loanable funds theory. It led its supporters to advocate a rise in saving during the depression of the 1920s and 1930s. The thinking was that more savings would increase the supply of loanable funds, lower the rate of interest and encourage spending and investment.

Keynes argued that the economists were following an incorrect theory and that by encouraging saving, and thereby discouraging spending, they made the depression worse. He developed the **liquidity preference theory** of interest rate determination. This argues that the rate of interest is determined by the demand and supply of money. Keynes believed that there are three reasons why people choose to hold their wealth in a money (liquid) form, i.e.

■ the transactions demand – money held to spend on goods and services

■ the precautionary motive – money held to meet unexpected expenses and take advantage of unexpected spending opportunities

■ the speculative motive – money held to take advantage of changes in the price of financial securities and interest rates.

He argued that an increase in the money supply will lower the rate of interest as shown in Figure 22.1

Time lags

By the time some government policies take effect the situation which caused them to be implemented has changed. For example, a government may cut income tax to increase consumer spending but by the time the tax rates are changed the economy may be entering a boom period. There are three main time lags involved with government policy:

■ **Recognition lag.** This refers to the time it takes for a government to recognise there is a problem.

■ **Implementation lag.** It can take time for a government to decide on the appropriate policy measure and implement.

■ **Behavioural lag.** This is the time it takes for

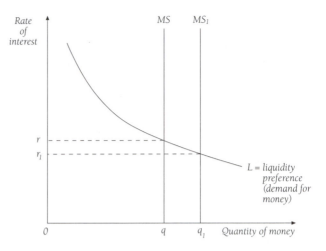

Figure 22.1 The effect of an increase in the money supply

people and firms to change their behaviour in the light of government policies. For example, a government may cut income tax but people may take time to adjust their spending.

Unexpected responses

Economics is a social science; it deals with people, and people and the firms they run do not always react in the way the government expects or wants. For example, the Japanese government, in 1998, cut

---

ACTIVITY 1

'Supporting our understanding of the economy is an immense wealth of theory. It is important in this context to understand the word "wealth" as meaning "an abundance of" rather than "the state of being rich". The great majority of economics theory reflects the attempt to formulate a fixed set of rules that describe how an economy functions. Most of it is worthless. The problem lies in a desire to set up economics as a quasi natural science – as something that has its own fundamental laws. But economics is the very antithesis of this. It is a behavioural science with no fixed laws.'

Richard Jeffery, 'Reading the runes is a salutary business for an economist' in *Sunday Business*, 16 January 2000

Discuss in a group:

a whether you think that most economic theory is 'worthless'

b the implications for the formulation of government policy of the comments above.

interest rates and income tax hoping to stimulate a rise in aggregate demand. However, this failed to materialise because consumers and firms were pessimistic about the future and so actually saved more.

Economists have also noted that targeting can itself alter the behaviour of what is being targeted. This phenomenon was identified in **Goodhart's law**. This states that any measure of the money supply behaves differently when it is targeted.

Complexity

The world is a complex, increasingly integrated and constantly changing place. Economic growth of a country can be knocked off trend by sudden and unexpected events abroad such as the East Asian crisis of 1997–99.

Conflicts of objectives

This problem was discussed in AS Unit 27. Policy instruments affect simultaneously a number of objectives. So a rise in income tax designed to reduce inflation may also raise unemployment. However, it is interesting to note that new classical economists argue that policy objectives do not need to conflict. They think that if the government keeps inflation low, largely by avoiding the temptation for itself to increase aggregate demand, the other three objectives will be achieved. The new economic paradigm also holds out the promise of increasing the ease with which all four major objectives can be achieved simultaneously.

Government self-interest

The recommendations and decisions made by politicians and civil servants may be influenced by their own self-interest. For example, a government may receive advice from economists that now would not be an appropriate time to cut income tax. However, if it is approaching a general election, it may go ahead with such a change. Ministers and civil servants might resist cuts in the spending of their department for fear that a smaller department will reduce their status and, in the case of civil servants, their pay. Economists also recognise the risk of **regulatory capture**. This arises when regulators of industries become unduly influenced by the managers of the industries they are regulating, perhaps because of their frequent contacts with the managers or perhaps because of the superior knowledge of the managers and in some cases because of perks offered.

ACTIVITY 2

When the Chancellor of the Exchequer set up the MPC he decided to appoint four independent high-grade economists to join the five Bank of England members. However in 2000 three of the four economists were working more or less full time for the Bank of England and the other one part time. The salaries paid by the Bank of England exceed the salaries paid in academia and in some industries.

a   How might the change in the occupational status of the 'independent' economists affect the quality of their advice?

b   What effect would a decision by the MPC to raise interest rates have at a time when the economy is just beginning to enter a downturn?

c   Why might the MPC not have recognised that a downturn was forthcoming?

Rigidities

As noted above, while market conditions are constantly changing it is difficult to change some aspects of government policy. For example, laws take time to change. Some forms of public expenditure are difficult to change. Once a government has started to build a hospital it is difficult and costly to stop.

If governments are reluctant to admit their mistakes they may continue to spend money on a project which does not have long-term viability.

However, where consumers and firms need to make long-term plans frequent and large changes in government policies can cause problems. For example, a decision to remove grants to firms which have located in a depressed region three years after they were first announced may put the viability of their firms in question. A doubling of the rate of interest would also cause major problems for those with mortgages.

Policy constraints

Membership of international organisations and increasing globalisation limit the autonomy of national government policy. The UK government cannot impose tariffs on EU members and its rate of interest cannot be significantly out of line with that of the EU and the USA.

Assessment of fiscal policy

The aims of fiscal policy include:

■   reducing the inequality of wealth and income distribution

■ altering the allocation of resources towards a more efficient allocation

■ stabilising the economy.

Fiscal policy has a number of advantages. The provision of benefits in cash and kind and progressive taxation can be used to redistribute income and wealth. If a government wants to raise economic activity it can do so by directly changing its own spending or indirectly by lowering taxation. As mentioned in Unit 19, a number of taxes and forms of spending also adjust automatically to offset cyclical fluctuations.

Fiscal policy can be used to discourage the consumption of demerit goods, encourage the consumption of merit goods and finance the provision of public goods. It can also be employed to affect the distribution of industries, to protect infant industries and encourage investment.

However, fiscal policy has a number of drawbacks. Much of fiscal policy is subject to time lags and some of it is inflexible.

Assessment of monetary policy

Monetarists have traditionally placed more emphasis on monetary policy than Keynesians. This is because they believe that inflation is caused by an excessive growth of the money supply. Controlling the money supply is not easy, especially as banks have a strong profit motive to increase bank lending. The main policy instrument currently being used to influence short-term economic activity is the rate of interest. However, interest rate changes are, like fiscal policy, subject to time lags. In addition, their effects are more concentrated on certain groups than changes in income tax, for example, tend to be. For instance, a rise in interest rates will hit firms which export a high proportion of their output more than other firms, as they will be affected not only by higher costs but also by a likely fall in demand resulting from a rise in the exchange rate. A government's ability to change its interest rate is also limited by the need for it to remain in line with other countries' interest rates, unless it is prepared to experience an inflow or outflow of funds.

Supply-side policies

Supply-side policies are now widely used. They have the advantage that they are selective, targeted at particular markets and are designed to raise efficiency. However, there is disagreement about

ACTIVITY 3

In 1999 the UK economy enjoyed high economic growth, low inflation and falling unemployment. Government's finances were in good order. Still, many commentators argued that all was not perfect. Exporters were hoping that the pound would fall from its high value and some regions in the north of the country were hoping to see an upturn in the local housing and labour market.

a Explain why all regions of the country may not benefit equally from a fall in unemployment.

b Discuss the implications that regional differences have for the operation of economic policy.

whether a free market or interventionist approach should be adopted. There are differences of opinion about how workers respond to cuts in income tax, how potential workers respond to cuts in benefits and whether firms operate more efficiently in the private or public sector. Some of the policies also take a relatively long time to have an effect, for example increased spending on education and regional development grants.

Summary

In assessing government policy it is necessary to consider the costs and benefits of government policy. Keynesians believe that the need for, and effectiveness, of government policy is greater than new classical economists do. Both groups acknowledge that government policy may fail to improve welfare, although new classical economists believe this is more of a risk than Keynesians do. There are a number of reasons why government failure occurs, including time lags, lack of accurate information and inflexibility. Some fiscal, monetary and supply-side policy measures can all take time to take effect.

Data response question

Monetary and fiscal policy

The Treasury's responsibilities include setting the framework of monetary policy, making forecasts of the economy, setting interest rates, and handling EMU matters. After discussion with Ministers, we decided that the overall aim of the Treasury was 'to promote rising prosperity based on sustained economic growth'.

This overall aim is then fleshed out in a two-part mission. The first part of this requires us to 'maintain a stable macroeconomic environment'. The second part of the mission to 'strengthen the long-term performance of the economy', is associated with a range of supply-side policies. Macroeconomic policy has been targeted on stability, in particular low and stable inflation and stable public finances. The clear consensus around the world now is that monetary policy is the most effective way of regulating inflationary pressures and that short-term interest rates are the main instrument of monetary policy. Short-term rates seem to have a clear effect on spending, even if the effect can be delayed at times.

Fiscal policy is, by contrast, a blunter weapon. It is called upon to perform two tasks, firstly to maintain sound public finances and secondly, to control the level of demand. It cannot effectively do both jobs at the same time. The main task of delivering low and stable inflation falls to monetary policy and in particular to the setting of short-term interest rates. On the one hand, this sounds rather easy and yet we know from experience that, in practice, it is intensely difficult. Essentially there are two reasons why mistakes are made: time lags and conflicts of objectives.

One common source of conflict over the past 20 years has been the behaviour of the exchange rate. A conflict can arise because the main instrument of policy, short-term interest rates, affects many people. In particular it can be very discriminatory in its impact. It has a big impact on the housing market and may also lead to a higher exchange rate, so that exporters will be hit disproportionately hard. Meanwhile, other parts of the economy remain relatively untouched.

Adapted from T. Burns, 'The conduct of monetary and fiscal policy' in *Economic Trends*, no. 509, March 1996

1   Describe the mechanism by which 'short-term [interest] rates seem to have a clear effect on spending, even if the effect can be delayed at times'. (6 marks)

2   Discuss why the author suggests that fiscal policy is a less effective method of influencing spending than monetary policy. (6 marks)

3   Explain why 'a conflict can arise because the main instrument of policy, short-term interest rates, affects many people'. (6 marks)

4   Examine the significance of the interest elasticity of demand for the operation of monetary policy. (6 marks)

5   Evaluate the extent to which supply-side policies 'strengthen the long-term performance of the economy'. (12 marks)

Section 4 questions

Essay questions

1 a Explain how both fiscal and monetary policy can be used to influence the level of aggregate demand. (20 marks)

  b Should governments aim to influence aggregate demand, or should they concentrate on the supply-side of the economy? (30 marks)

2 a Explain what is meant by supply-side policies. (10 marks)

  b Discuss how supply-side policies can be used to increase the rate of economic growth and reduce the rate of inflation. (15 marks)

Project

Prepare a report assessing the effectiveness of interest rate policy in keeping inflation within the government's target range.

  This should cover:

■ an explanation of how interest rate policy can affect the inflation rate

■ a discussion of how the MPC determines interest rate changes

■ an analysis of how successful interest rate changes have been in maintaining inflation within the margins of the government's target

■ a discussion of any effects interest rate changes have had on the government's other macroeconomic policy objectives

■ a list of sources

You should make use of appropriate economic theory, including aggregate demand and supply analysis, throughout your report.

C3.1a, C3.1b, C3.2, N3.1, N3.2, N3.3, IT3.1, IT3.2, IT3.3

Section 5
Topical economic issues

Introduction

In this section three key topics are explored. Unit 23 covers transport economics. Rail privatisation was discussed in A2 Unit 4. In this unit attention is paid to the increased use of the private car and the costs this imposes on society, including the cost of congestion. Government transport policies are discussed, including the controversial policies of road pricing, privatisation and deregulation. The meaning of a suitable transport policy is explained.

The idea of sustainability is also an issue in economic development. This is the topic of Unit 24. Particular attention is paid to the characteristics of developing countries and how they seek to achieve sustainable development and the obstacles they face in this attempt.

The European Union provides some financial assistance and advice to developing countries. It is also seeking to help potential entrants into the EU raise their economic development. In Unit 25 the challenges that the economies of the former communist countries of eastern Europe and the countries which previously made up the former Soviet Union are facing in making the transition from planned to market economies and in some cases, in preparing for entry to the EU are examined. Several of the issues facing the EU are also discussed including reform of EU agricultural policy and economic monetary union. The issue of the single currency was discussed in A2 Unit 15.

Before reading this section, check that you can recall the meaning and use of the following concepts:

- derived demand
- externalities
- privatisation
- contestable markets
- cost benefit analysis
- sustainable development
- economic growth
- trade blocs.

UNIT 23 Transport

Key concepts covered

- transport
- derived demand
- modes of transport
- private transport
- public transport
- negative externalities
- congestion
- road pricing
- privatisation
- deregulation
- contestable markets
- cost benefit analysis
- sustainable transport policy

Introduction

In this unit some aspects of transport economics are covered. Transport, its derived demand and various modes are explained. Recent trends in transport are discussed, with the main focus being on the rise in the use of the car and the relative decline in the use of bus travel. Then the consequences of the increased use of cars are examined. One of these is congestion and the costs that congestion imposes, and possible solutions to the problem are explored. A measure that some economists advocate is to improve public transport via privatisation and deregulation. The nature and effects of these measures are examined, with particular reference being made to rail privatisation and deregulation of bus services. The way in which the government assesses transport projects and the meaning of sustainable transport policy are also discussed.

Transport

Transport is the movement of goods and people. Goods are moved from points of production to points of distribution. People move for a variety of reasons, including to get to and from work (commuting), to visit shops, to go to the cinema and other places of entertainment, to visit friends and relations and to go on holiday.

Demand for the vast majority of transport is, like the demand for labour, a derived demand. It is not wanted for its own sake but for what it enables firms and households to do. So demand for transport is influenced by, for example, the distance people live away from their work, the number of holidays they take and the number of goods firms sell.

The **derived** nature of the **demand** for transport explains the significant fluctuations in demand which occur during the day and between seasons. For example, demand for a number of forms of transport is much higher between 7.30 am and 9 am and 3.30 pm and 6 pm than at other periods of the day because a high number of people are taking their children to school or going to work at these times.

Categories of transport

Transport can be categorised as follows:

- According to what is being transported. Freight transport is the movement of goods. Demand for freight transport is usually measured in terms of tonne kilometres or number of journeys. Passenger transport is the movement of people and is measured in terms of passenger kilometres or, again, number of journeys.

- **Modes of transport**. Modes of transport are the methods or forms of transport. The modes can be divided into road, rail, sea, inland waterways and in the case of freight only, pipeline. Road transport can be further broken down into transport by lorry, van, car, taxi, bus, coach, motorbike, bicycle and walking.

- **Private and public transport**. Private transport is usually taken to include transport by lorry, van, car, taxi, motorbike and bicycle. Public transport is transport by rail, bus and coach, all of which involve moving freight and people in 'bulk'.

Trends in transport in the UK

In recent decades there have been two major trends. One is a continuing increase in demand for transport reflecting a variety of factors, including people living further away from their place of work and relatives, people undertaking more holidays and holidays further afield, hypermarkets and places of entertainment being built outside of city centres and increases in output.

The other major trend is a shift from public to private transport. The most noticeable feature is the rise in travel by car and fall in travel by bus. Figure 23.1 shows the rapid growth in car, van and taxi transport and the fall in bus and coach transport (as a percentage of total passenger transport).

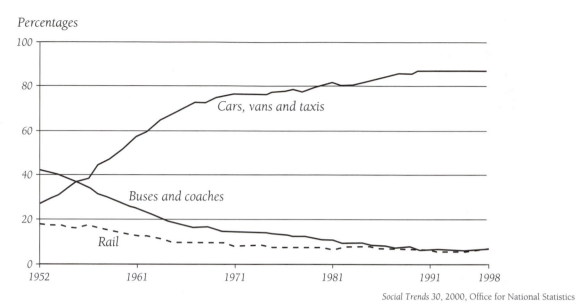

Percentages

Figure 23.1 Passenger transport by mode

Social Trends 30, 2000, Office for National Statistics

Car transport

This dominates passenger transport and its dominance is increasing. In 1961 only 30 per cent of UK households had a car and only 2 per cent had two or more. However, by 1998 70 per cent had at least one and 25 per cent had two or more. Cars now account for 60 per cent of all journeys, whereas in 1975 they accounted for only 25 per cent.

The following reasons account for the rise in demand for car transport:

- A fall in the price of car use relative to other forms of transport. This has occurred because the cost of using a car has risen less than bus, coach and rail fares.

- A rise in real incomes. Car use has a high income elasticity of demand. Car travel is regarded as the most flexible, comfortable and convenient of all the transport modes. It enables people to travel when they want, from door to door and in some cases to areas not served by other forms of transport, apart perhaps from taxis.

- Increase in the car orientation of society. People are increasingly more likely to drive than to walk or cycle. There are a number of reasons for this. One is concern about risks to safety. For example, more children are now taken to school by car and fewer walk or cycle than ever before. This is because parents are worried about the higher risk that cyclists and pedestrians face of a road accident and the fear of child molesters.

More members of a household now expect to own their own car rather than share a 'family car'. Some households containing two parents and two children, aged 17 plus, now have four cars.

People are also more likely to use their cars for short journeys and for more purposes. For example, more people now shop in bulk at hypermarkets and this requires the use of a car.

In addition, more leisure time has increased demand for a variety of activities for which car use is a complement. These include not only shopping but also watching and playing sport, visiting theatres and clubs and many other activities.

Bus transport

Bus travel is an important form of public transport. However, the number of bus journeys has declined considerably since the 1950s. In recent years the number of journeys has stabilised but, as a percentage of passenger transport, it continues to fall in importance. Again, there are a number of reasons behind this trend, including the following:

- Rise in real incomes. Bus transport is perceived as an inferior good. Passengers are restricted by timetables. Buses are perceived as providing a low quality of service. They do not usually carry passengers from door to door, which is a particular disadvantage during bad weather, passengers are not guaranteed a seat, there can be delays and buses are not always as clean and comfortable as passengers would like.

- Rise in price. Bus fares have risen more in real terms than the cost of using a car.

- Increase in the length of journeys undertaken. People are more likely to undertake long journeys by car, rail or coach because of the greater speed and comfort.

ACTIVITY 1

The Deputy Prime Minister announced a range of new measures yesterday to persuade motorists to abandon the car and take the bus.

John Prescott and representatives of the industry have agreed the first national targets for reliability and for reducing the age of the 76 000-strong UK bus fleet.

The image of the bus as a "second-rate, second-class form of transport" must be left behind, Mr Prescott told representatives of local authorities and bus companies.'

Barrie Clement, 'Prescott promises new image for bus services' in *The Independent*, 16 November 1999

As a group:
a Keep a record of the journeys you make during a week and the modes of transport you use
b Analyse your findings.
c Discuss what would encourage you to make more use of buses.

Consequences of increased car and lorry use

Governments have become increasingly concerned about the continuing rise in demand for road space by private motorists and haulage firms. This is because of the **negative externalities** caused by road transport. These include the following:

- Pollution. Road traffic creates air, noise and visual pollution. Gaseous emissions from cars and lorries make buildings dirty, damage the environment and health. More children than ever are suffering from respiratory diseases as a result of pollution. Road traffic, particularly lorries, creates noise and in some areas of heavy volumes of traffic the noise levels can create stress and disrupt lives. The roads which are needed to carry the traffic can also destroy the natural beauty of an area.

- Accidents. While car travel is safer than riding a motorbike (the most dangerous form of transport), cycling and walking it carries a higher risk of accidents than rail, air, bus and coach travel. Accidents impose high costs on society including loss of output and use of health service resources.

- Damage to buildings. As well as pollution making buildings dirty, the vibrations caused by transport can damage the foundations of buildings. For example, a considerable amount has had to be spent rebuilding the foundations of Worcester Cathedral which have been undermined by the high volume of traffic passing close by.

- Destruction of wildlife. Road traffic kills animals and destroys their natural inhabitant.

- **Congestion**. In 1998 traffic levels were 455 billion vehicle kilometres and are projected to rise to 524 billion vehicle kilometres by 2006. As a result, the speed at which vehicles are travelling is declining. For example, in 1995 motor vehicles travelled at an average of 63 miles an hour. By 1998 this was down to 56 miles. Congestion is thought to be a major problem.

Congestion

Congestion occurs when the actual journey time taken is longer than the normal expected time. Congestion gives rise to a number of costs, including the following:

- Higher household costs. People spend more in fuel and time getting to their destination. The time they lose has an opportunity cost. The effect on the cost of driving is illustrated in Figure 23.2.

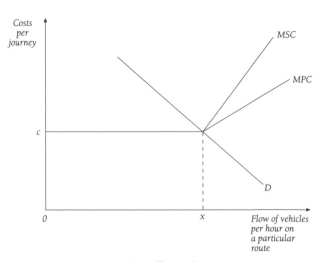

Figure 23.2 The effect of congestion

- When the number of journeys on a particular road reaches a certain level, traffic is slowed down and negative externalities occur. In Figure 23.2 this occurs at a flow of x. In peak periods the negative externalities are likely to be very high.

- Higher costs to transport firms, for example haulage firms, bus and coach companies. The increased time it takes reduces the productivity of vehicles. They will carry a lower volume of goods or passengers per hour.

- Higher costs to other firms. Firms which use haulage companies or use their own vehicles to transport their goods will experience higher costs which they are likely to pass on, at least in part, to consumers in the form of higher prices. This reduces international price competitiveness. It also reduces the price competitiveness of those domestic firms based near to highly congested roads relative to those based near less congested ones. For example, in 1999 an excavating firm, Smith and Sons of Bletchingdon, estimated that it lost £200 000 as a result of delays on the congested A40 between Witney and Oxford. Firms also experience increased costs arising from their staff arriving late for work. A RAC report published in 2000 put the total cost of congestion in the UK at £23 billion a year.

- Stress-related illnesses which, as with accidents, reduce output and increase the demand on health service resources.

- Road rage. This is thought to be becoming an increasing problem. It again can lead to stress and uses up police time.

- Pollution. The amount of air pollution is greater when vehicles are stuck in traffic jams.

Policy approaches

Congestion arises because the demand for road space grows more rapidly than the supply. The government can respond to this problem in a number of ways. It can increase the supply of road space by, for example, building more roads, widening existing ones or freeing up space on roads by discouraging on-road parking through parking charges and yellow and red lines. It could also do nothing hoping that high levels of congestion will, by themselves, encourage firms and private motorists to switch to other routes and to public transport. However, increasing supply of road space tends, by initially speeding up the flow of traffic, to generate higher demand and creates environmental problems.

Congestion also does not seem to be self-correcting.

Demand for car use is price inelastic and higher levels of congestion on particular routes simply tend to shift the problem on to other routes.

So governments usually try to reduce congestion by measures designed to reduce demand for road space.

Policy measures

A number of measures are advocated to reduce congestion by means of lowering demand for road space. These include the following:

- Charging people to park at work. The intention is to discourage people from taking their cars to work. This is a measure that is used in California in the USA. The State runs a 'parking cash out' scheme. Employers charge a market price to any of their employees who use the car parking they provide and pay every employee an amount which, after tax, is equal to the charge. This gives the workers the financial incentive to find cheaper ways of getting to work. The UK Labour government has given local authorities the right to make workers pay a levy for office or factory parking.

- Creating pedestrian-only zones.

- Providing park and ride schemes. These are designed to reduce congestion in city centres.

- Encouraging the use of public transport. One way is by making public transport cheaper by means of subsidies. However, it is thought that a more effective way of raising the attractiveness of public transport is to increase the quality of the service. There are a number of measures which can be undertaken to achieve this, including creating bus lanes, subsidising the public transport companies to increase the frequency of their journeys, the quality of their vehicles, and to create a more integrated system.

- Taxing car ownership and petrol. This raises the entry price on the road system and probably does reduce demand for road space. The tax on petrol use does have the advantage of taxing heavy vehicles and fuel-inefficient firms more, thereby reducing pollution. However, the effect may not be very significant since, as mentioned earlier, demand for car use is relatively price inelastic and it does not discriminate between when and where people use their cars. So the effect on congestion is thought to be small.

- **Road pricing**. This is a measure that is

advocated by a number of economists. This is because it addresses the problem of the negative externalities caused by vehicle use. When people drive their cars the cost to them (the private cost) is less than the cost to society (social cost) because of the external costs they create such as pollution and congestion. So the quantity of road space used is greater than the socially optimum level. Drivers gain at the expense of non-drivers. Road pricing is said to be a market solution as it is based on working through the price mechanism and making that system work more efficiently. This is because the prices charged are, in theory, based on the negative externalities generated and so depend on time and place. So they should make drivers think about whether the benefits from, for example, travelling into a city centre at peak time is worth the cost and that cost would be the true (social) cost. However, to ensure the socially optimum use of road space it is necessary that externalities and price elasticities of demand can be measured accurately. Road pricing also fails to distinguish between income levels and so may have a regressive element to them.

There are two main forms of road pricing. One is tolls. However, these are only feasible on roads on which non-payers can be excluded. These must have limited entry and exit points, for example motorways and tunnels. There is also the risk that tolls merely shift the problem of congestion by encouraging drivers to use alternative routes.

The other method, which is now receiving increasing support, is by use of smart electronic cards and detectors that identify the time when a car uses a particular road. The revenue, or at least some of it, received from road pricing could be used to fund improvements in the quality of public transport.

There have been a number of trials on road pricing in the UK and a number of countries run road-pricing schemes. One which has received considerable attention is the scheme operated in Singapore.

Singapore and congestion
Singapore has been very successful in reducing congestion in its towns and cities. It has achieved this by a combination of policies, including:

- electronic road pricing, whereby those driving into town and city centres pay a large fee.

- a quota and auctioning system, whereby people have to pay a large amount for the right to buy a certificate of entitlement which gives them the right to own a car
- a high rate of taxation on fuel
- the provision of a good alternative form of public transport. This is the subsidised, high-quality transit system.

Privatisation

The Conservative governments of the 1980s and 1990s sought to improve the quality of public transport by moving them from the public to the private sector and opening them up to a greater amount of potential competition. The Labour government has continued this approach of moving more of state-owned transport to the private sector.

Those in favour of **privatisation** of transport argue that it results in a more efficient use of resources, provides consumers with higher quality, lower price and possibly more choice and encourages additional investment by the private sector. However, some argue that public transport should remain in state ownership. Their arguments include that the state is more likely to base its decisions on social costs and benefits than the private sector where the prime motive is profit, is in a better position to integrate transport modes the more it controls, can help the poor by keeping fares low and can ensure that natural monopolies benefit consumers.

Among the transport industries which have been privatised are the National Freight Company (1982), Associated British Ports (1983–84), British Airways (1987), municipal bus companies (1988), British Rail (1994–96) and Railtrack (1996).

Rail privatisation

British Rail was divided into four for privatisation. Railtrack took over the running of the track, signalling and stations. It receives its revenue from charging the users of track and from income earned from the leasing of stations. Railtrack is a natural monopoly – that is an industry that has to be run as a monopoly to take full advantage of the economies of scale on offer. It would be inefficient and impractical to have a number of separate firms being responsible for the provision and maintenance of track. To take account of the dominant market position of Railtrack the government has appointed a regulator, OPR (Office of Rail Regulator), to ensure that it does not exploit its market power. Nevertheless, Railtrack, which has earned high profits, has come in for criticism for not investing sufficiently to improve safety and the quality of track.

Then there was the sale of train operating companies, freight companies and rolling stock companies. The train operating companies, again regulated by OPR, are carrying more passengers but have been criticised for delays, cancelled services and overcrowded compartments.

Deregulation

Deregulation is the removal of government regulations which act as barriers to entry into and exit from a market. For example, in the case of transport markets central government or local authorities may prohibit other firms competing with a sole provider or may limit entry by giving out only a few licences to operate a particular route. **Deregulation** involves removing these restrictions and thereby opening up the market to greater potential competition.

The arguments in favour of deregulation include that the higher potential competition will result in more choice for consumers, greater pressure to be competitive and to innovate and a reduction in the need for state subsidies. However, some economists argue that deregulation can result in duplication of provision on some routes, neglect of other routes, rise in fares and increased market concentration.

Deregulation in the UK appears to have had mixed results. For example, the deregulation of long-distance coach services has generally been considered to be a success. Fares have fallen and the quality of service has risen through increased frequency of services and innovation, for example in the form of including waiter/waitress services, computer points and television monitors. However most consider that bus deregulation has been less successful.

Bus deregulation

A number of problems have arisen since deregulation. One is the development of 'bus wars', with two companies racing from bus stop to bus stop on a busy route competing for customers. This can disadvantage customers by placing their safety at risk and because drivers may miss out less frequented stops to reach the more popular stops before their rivals.

Fares on a number of routes have also risen by more than the rate of inflation and the provision of services on some rural routes and at off-peak times has declined.

Particular concern has been expressed about the increased concentration of the market into the hands of a few companies. Three large groups (Arriva, First Group and Stagecoach) provided almost half of the local mileage in Britain in 1999. These companies continue to buy up smaller companies and have been investigated by the Office for Fair Trading (OFT) for restrictive practices.

Concerns about the outcome of the deregulation of local bus services have caused the government to shelve the proposed deregulation of bus services in London and prompted them to promote partnerships between local authorities and bus companies to facilitate improvements in the quality of service.

ACTIVITY 3

In 1998 the Office of Fair Trading investigated the allegation that Stagecoach was operating a secret agreement to rig the school bus market in Hull. It was claimed that it had formed a cartel with other bus companies to fix prices and carve up the market. Kingston-upon-Hull City Council informed the OFT that after it put its school bus service out to tender, the bus operators had met secretly in a hotel and agreed on minimum prices which they would tender for the business and which routes each operator would bid for.

a   What is the principal motive behind the formation of a cartel?

b   Discuss who may have gained and who may have lost as a result of Stagecoach's alleged actions.

Contestable markets

The concept of contestable markets lies behind the move to privatise and deregulate transport markets. The idea is that what matters in terms of promoting efficiency and consumer sovereignty is not the actual level but the potential level of competition. So, for example, only one train company may operate a route but the market can be made contestable by selling it a short-term franchise which will only be renewed if the service it provides is of a better quality and lower price than that which could be offered by other companies. The bus service market is claimed by some to be a contestable market. If profits rise on a particular route bus companies operating on other routes may switch some of their fleet to the profitable route. Consumers may reap double benefits from contestable markets. They may be able to benefit from the lower costs which a sole firm can gain because of economies of scale while also benefiting from the absence of supernormal profits because of the possibility of entry of competitors into the market

However, mergers may reduce the number of potential competitors, restrictive practices may occur and consumers may not benefit if there are significant negative externalities.

Investment projects

One of the arguments of state ownership of transport infrastructure and transport operating firms is that the state is more likely to base its resource allocation decisions on social costs and benefits rather than just private costs and benefits.

When UK governments consider whether to undertake a major investment project they make use of **cost benefit analysis**. This involves identifying all the costs and benefits involved – private and external. Monetary values are then placed on the costs and benefits. This is not an easy task in the case of external costs and benefits. The costs and benefits have to be discounted. This means adjusting future costs and benefits to current values. For example, £50 000 to be earned in ten years' time must be valued down in comparison to £50 000 to be earned this year. Money now is worth more than money in the future as it can be invested and earn interest. When the costs and benefits have been identified and measured they are then compared, and the project recommended if the social benefit is greater than the social cost and if the net benefit is greater than alternative projects.

A sustainable transport policy

Taking into account social costs and benefits is a major stage in developing a **sustainable transport policy**. A sustainable transport system is one which can meet the current needs of people and firms in a way which does not threaten the environment and the ability to meet the transport needs of future generations. Some transport economists argue that a sustainable transport policy is one which discourages the use of the car and promotes other more environmentally friendly modes of transport such as rail, bus, coach, cycling and walking. To develop sustainable transport, transport policy has to be coordinated with a range of other policies, including education, health, environment and land use planning. For example, building schools further than walking distance from the children attending and away from local routes will negate measures to reduce car use.

Summary

Transport is the movement of people and goods. The main way people travel is by private car. Car use continues to increase largely at the expense of bus use, cycling and walking. This increased use generates considerable negative externalities, including pollution, damage to the environment, accidents and congestion. Governments seek to reduce congestion because of the costs that congestion causes, including fuel costs, time costs and stress-related illnesses. A number of policies to reduce congestion have been advocated. The one currently receiving most attention is road pricing. Conservative governments sought to encourage some people to switch from car use to public transport by raising the efficiency of public transport. The two main measures they implemented were privatisation and deregulation. These measures had mixed outcomes. A longer established feature of government transport policy is the use of cost benefit analysis in assessing transport projects. When deciding on whether a particular project should go ahead, governments are increasingly recognising the need to develop a sustainable transport policy. This is one which meets both current and future transport needs.

Data response question

'In Britain, where traffic congestion has become a troublesome political issue, the response of governments has been to try to price motorists off the roads. The country already has some of the world's highest fuel taxes and John Prescott, the deputy prime

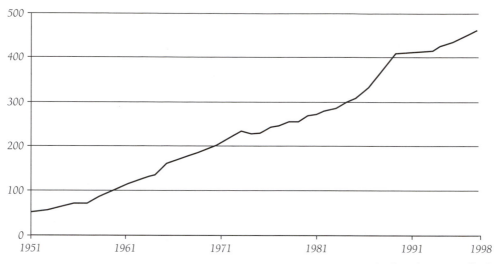

Billion vehicle kilometres

Social Trends 30, 2000, Office for National Statistics

Figure 23.3 Road traffic, Great Britain

minister, is proposing further levies, such as charging for the use of the roads on a pay-as-you-go basis.

The idea of using price to regulate people's behaviour grew in popularity in the 1980s, when – at least in the US and UK – free market economies replaced government regulation as the favoured means of achieving social objectives.

As traffic congestion worsened, economists in the UK started arguing for a "market" solution. Congestion imposed heavy costs on society, they said, and in a socially efficient market, motorists should meet these costs directly.

But there is no magic bullet that will end traffic jams. Congestion is part of modern life; we find it at the supermarket, the airport, the burger bar and the hospital, and the art of modern life is to learn how to deal with it.

Motorists are already doing this quite well. No new roads have been built in central London for decades, yet traffic speeds have not fallen greatly. Instead, the rush-hour has expanded to the point where it lasts all day, and is now stretching into the night.

Drivers themselves are the best judges of how to deal with congestion. They will adjust their journey times to maximise the use of the available road space, or they will change their lifestyles to minimise their travel needs.

Richard Tomkins, 'Taxation road to nowhere' in the *Financial Times*, 2 September 1999

1 Describe the trend in road traffic from 1951 to 1998. (3 marks)
2 Discuss two methods, other than road pricing, a government could implement to 'price motorists off the roads'. (4 marks)

3 In what sense is road pricing a market solution to the problem of congestion? (6 marks)
4 Discuss two costs congestion imposes on society. (4 marks)
5 Assess whether drivers 'are the best judges of how to deal with congestion'. (8 marks)

UNIT 24 Economic development

Introduction

In a world in which a high percentage of people are absolutely poor the question of economic growth is crucial. Economics can be used to gain an insight into why poverty levels are so high in some countries and how economic development can be achieved to improve the quality of their lives. In this unit a range of issues surrounding economic development are discussed. Economic development is defined and compared with economic growth, and levels and indicators of economic development and the characteristics of developing countries are covered. The factors that can hinder development, theories of development and policy approaches are also considered.

Economic development and economic growth

Economic development occurs when a country improves the economic welfare of its population through, for example, reducing poverty. It has sometimes been regarded as synonymous with economic growth. However, while the two are likely to be closely associated they are not the same and it is possible for economic growth to take place without economic development occurring. For example, a country may produce more goods and services but if these are very unevenly distributed and if they are produced at the cost of damage to the environment, it can be questionable whether economic development has occurred.

Indicators of economic development

A number of factors may be considered when deciding on the level of economic development a country has reached, including the following:

- Real GDP. However, care has to be taken in deciding whether high GDP means the population are enjoying a high quality of life (see AS Unit 20). Problems of interpretation are even greater in those developing countries where there is a high degree of non-marketed output (for example subsistence farming) and where it is difficult to obtain accurate information because of low levels of literacy.

- The nature of the economic growth being experienced. For economic growth to take place the economic growth must be sustainable, i.e. achieved in a way which does not reduce future populations' ability to produce more.

- Level of, and access to, health and education services.

- Literacy rates.

- Life expectancy.

- Consumer durables per head.

- Compound measures. The two best-known ones are the UN's human development index (HDI) and the human poverty index (HPI) (see AS Unit 20).

Categorisation of countries

Countries are grouped in a number of different ways. The World Bank and the United Nations classify countries into high, middle and low income countries. The middle income group is further divided into upper middle and lower middle. The UN, using the HDI, also groups countries into high human development, medium human development and low human development. In addition, it and a number of other organisations such as the International Monetary Fund divide countries into least developed, developing and industrial. Economists also sometimes discuss the north-south divide. This refers to the gap between rich countries which are mainly in the northern hemisphere and poor countries which are located mainly in the southern hemisphere.

General characteristics of developing countries

- Low GDP per head. This is one of the key characteristics. The least developed countries experience a high level of absolute poverty.

- A high degree of income inequality.

- High population growth. This is usually the result of a natural increase in population (the birth rate exceeding the death rate) caused by high birth rates. Indeed, developing countries tend to have not only a high birth rate but also relatively high death rates and low life expectancy.

- Poor industrial infrastructure. Developing countries tend to lack good quality infrastructure, for example roads and communications.

- A high proportion of the population employed in the primary sector. As economies develop workers tend to move from the primary to the secondary sector (manufacturing) and then from the secondary to the tertiary (services) sector.

- A concentration on a narrow range of exports, most of which are primary products.

- Poor-quality natural resources. Although these countries often have a high proportion of their workforce employed in agriculture they are often working with low-quality land, sometimes in unfavourable weather conditions.

- Poor-quality investment in physical and human capital which leads to low levels of labour productivity.

- Low levels of saving. This contributes to the low level of investment.

- High levels of unemployment and underemployment. The latter occurs particularly in agriculture where a number of members of a family may work on a small family plot.

Differences between developing countries and regions

Of course, not all developing countries share all the characteristics listed above. The most notable exceptions are the **newly industrial countries (NICs)** of East Asia, including Singapore, South Korea and Thailand. In the early 1990s these countries achieved the fastest growth rates in the world. Although they experienced difficulties in 1997–99, in part because of an over-rapid

development of their financial sector, it is thought that they are likely to resume their economic development.

While East Asia contains a relatively more prosperous group of developing countries, Africa contains some of the poorest countries in the world. However, here again there are differences in performance. For example, between 1990 and 1996 Uganda experienced a high rate of economic growth, 7 per cent per annum, which reduced the proportion of the population below an absolute line from 56 per cent to 40 per cent.

A C T I V I T Y 1

'Three billion people – half the world's population – live on less than $2 a day (at international purchasing power parity) and 1.3bn are on less than a dollar a day. Helping these destitute people to escape from their plight is humanity's most urgent challenge. The question is how to achieve this desired end.'

Martin Wolf, 'Danger of well-meaning ambition' in the *Financial Times*, 6 October 1999

As a group:

a convert US$2 and $1 into pounds sterling and discuss what you could buy for this in terms of basic necessities in the UK.

b consider why the quantity of goods and services which people living on this income can consume is likely to be higher in developing countries

c discuss how the UK could help 'these destitute people to escape from their plight'.

Obstacles to development

Achieving economic development is not easy. There are a number of factors that make it difficult for developing countries to improve the economic welfare of their citizens, including the following:

- Poor natural resources. This results in low productivity in the primary sector. However, while good natural resources are beneficial they are not a necessary requirement for development. For example, Israel has relatively poor natural resources but is a rich country.

- Lack of investment. This is thought to be a significant factor. A country that has low levels of investment is likely to have low output and low productivity. Low output will mean low incomes. When incomes are low it is difficult for

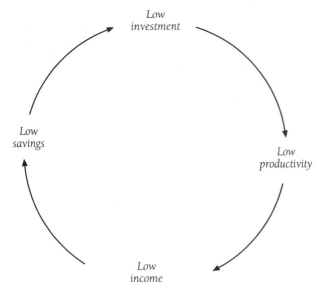

*Low
investment*

*Low
savings*

*Low
productivity*

*Low
income*

Figure 24.1 Vicious cycle of poverty

people to save. So investment continues to be low. A **vicious circle of poverty** develops as shown in Figure 24.1.

■ It can be difficult for a country to break out of this circle without outside help. This is because persuading or forcing people, through taxation, to save more may result in them experiencing, albeit possibly, for the short run, real deprivation.

■ Lack of a developed financial market. A shortage in terms of number and range of financial institutions tends to discourage saving and makes it more difficult to channel funds from savers to borrowers.

■ Lack of infrastructure. Lack of, or poor quality of, for example roads, railways and utility services, will increase firms' costs and discourage foreign direct investment (FDI).

■ Lack of investment in human capital. As with lack of physical investment, this can arise because of low incomes and will again reduce productivity and incomes. In addition, it will make it more difficult for the country to take advantage of foreign direct investment (see below).

■ High population growth. A country with a continually high birth rate will have to devote resources which could have been used to increase productive potential to provide hospitals and schools to cater for the children.

■ Disadvantages in international trade. Developing countries tend to concentrate on exporting primary products. This has two main disadvantages. One is that primary products

have income inelastic demand so that as world income rises developing countries see only a small rise in demand for their products. The other is that supply of primary products is volatile due to changes in weather conditions and, in the case of agricultural products, diseases. This volatility results in fluctuations in export earnings. In addition, the concentration on a narrow range of exports makes the countries vulnerable to changes in market conditions. Developing countries also experience problems in gaining access to the markets of the industrial countries because of the tariffs and subsidies the countries use to protect their own industries, including agriculture.

Theories of development

■ **Balanced growth theory**. This suggests that countries develop most rapidly when their industries and sectors grow at a similar rate. This enables markets to be created and for inputs and outputs to be coordinated. This theory has led some economists to argue that governments should seek to increase investment across a wide range of industries simultaneously.

■ **Unbalanced growth theory**. This contrasts with the theory above by suggesting that governments should promote investment in a narrow range of key industries.

■ **Dependency theory**, also called exploitation theory. It suggests that developing countries' economic development is controlled and restricted by industrial countries and by international organisations, such as the International Monetary Fund (IMF) and the World Trade Organisation, which are dominated by industrial countries. The developing economies are unable to gain equal access to the markets of the industrial economies and multinational companies buy up domestic industries, sending profits back to their home countries and purchasing raw materials from their home country rather than from the host countries. However, economists debate the relative advantages and disadvantages that multinational companies provide for their hosts.

■ **The Harrod-Domar model**. This is one of the best-known theories. It was developed independently by a UK and a US economist in 1948. It argues that the key driving force behind economic growth and development is a high savings ratio. This is because it permits high investment to occur (by shifting resources in the short run from making consumer to capital goods) which, in turn, increases both output and productivity. However, a high level of saving does not guarantee investment as this will depend on a number of factors, including the range and quality of financial institutions in the country and, in the private sector, the optimism, of entrepreneurs. High levels of investment, while usually they are an important factor, may, however, not generate development if the investment is in inappropriate sectors.

■ **Rostow's stages of growth theory**. This is another well-known theory. Rostow argued that countries have to pass through five stages on the path of development. These are:

- the traditional society
- the pre-conditions for take-off into self sustaining growth
- the take-off
- the drive to maturity
- the age of mass consumption.

In the second stage, which is the transitional stage, again high levels of saving permit investment to occur and raise the productivity of the country. The same qualifications apply to this theory as to the Harrod-Domar model. In addition, some economists question whether it is necessary for a country to have to pass through all the stages.

■ **The Lewis model**. This suggests that development can be increased by transferring workers from low productivity agriculture into the higher productivity manufacturing and service sectors. W. Arthur Lewis argued that in some developing countries with a large number of underemployed people working in agriculture some of the workers have zero marginal productivity. For instance, a small farm with three family members working on it might not experience an increase in output if an additional family member started work on the farm. If there are workers not contributing anything to agricultural output that could be moved into other sectors, then national output would increase. However, this presupposes there are job vacancies in the other sectors. In practice, in a number of developing countries the migration from rural to urban areas can cause problems. These include pollution, congestion and under-used social capital in rural areas and a shortage of social capital in urban areas.

ACTIVITY 2

'For ten years, Thailand was the world's fastest growing economy. From 1985 to 1996, the whole shape of the Thai economy changed from one based on agriculture to one where 80 per cent of exports were manufactured goods. The urban population of Bangkok doubled.'

Jon Ashworth, 'Thais pin hopes on tourism for economic resurgence' in *The Times*, 17 December 1999

a Which theory, or theories, of development might the change in the Thai economy outlined above support?

b Discuss the problems that may have been caused by the rise in the population of Bangkok.

Policy approaches

A government can adopt a number of policies to promote development.

Increasing agricultural productivity

The role of agriculture in improving economic development has tended to be overlooked in the past. This was, in part, because of the income inelastic demand for food and the volatility of supply, discussed above. However, increasing productivity in agriculture, as part of a development strategy, can stimulate demand for manufactured products, for example tractors, increase the nutrition of the population, reduce costs to any food processing and other firms in the country, for example textiles and tobacco firms, and increase export earnings, some of which could be spent on imported foreign capital goods.

Export-orientated industrialisation

Export-orientated industrialisation (EOI) involves an outward orientation of development, opening up the country to international trade by removing trade barriers. The thinking is that the increased competition from industrial countries will force the developing country's firms to become more efficient. The NICs followed an EOI approach from the 1970s. However, prior to this they built up their industries behind tariff walls.

Import-substituting industrialisation

Import-substituting industrialisation (ISI) refers to the strategy that the NICs were pursuing in the 1950s and 1960s. So an ISI strategy involves protecting infant industries by means of tariffs until they have built up a comparative advantage. In this case imports are gradually replaced by domestically produced products and a more diversified industrial structure is built up.

Attracting foreign direct investment

The presence of multinational companies (MNCs) may bring a number of benefits to a developing country. For example, they may bring in up-to-date technology and modern management techniques which indigenous firms can copy. They also provide employment, train domestic workers, contribute to the country's output and exports and may improve the country's infrastructure. Care has to be to be taken to check the net effect on employment and output as their presence may mean that some domestic firms go out of business. In practice, most are not competing directly with domestic firms as MNCs are mainly high technology, capital-intensive firms, although of course this means that the number of jobs they create are not that high.

Indeed, the benefits of the presence of MNCs may be more limited than they first appear. If, for example, the MNCs deplete natural resources and create pollution they may contribute to economic growth but not to sustainable economic development. While the introduction of new technology holds out the promise of increased growth through imitation, the technology may not be appropriate for the resources of the country.

To assess the effect on the host country's balance of payments a number of effects have to be taken into account. The items which result in more money coming into the country or less going out are the initial investment, the products the MNC exports and the products which are no longer imported because they are now produced by the MNCs. More money going out of the country arises from the repatriation of profits made, imports of raw materials and services purchased by the MNCs from abroad and the repatriation of wages by workers brought over from the host country, often to fill management posts.

Developing the tourist market

Tourism is the fastest growing industry in the world. It also benefits from having high-income elasticity of demand. However, tourism tends to create low income and low-skilled jobs. There are also a number of potential disadvantages of building up a tourist industry. It can damage the environment, result in clashes with the native culture and can displace local industries.

Population control

A high birth rate results in a high dependency ratio (i.e. a high proportion of non-workers dependent on the labour force). Not only do the children have to be supported but so do the mothers (or less commonly, in developing countries, fathers) for the time they are raising their children on a full-time basis. Also as noted above, it creates a high need for social capital. However, population control programmes, including the provision of information on contraceptive methods and incentives to limit family size, are not always easy to operate because they frequently come up against opposition on the grounds of religion and culture.

When countries experience economic development there is usually a time lag before population growth slows. Indeed, in the short run population growth may accelerate. This is because infant mortality falls but it takes some time for people to adjust the number of children they have to take into account that more of them will survive.

Borrowing from abroad

A developing country may borrow from industrial countries in order, for example, to spend on investment, both in capital goods and human capital. It may look to foreign banks because the supply of domestic funds is low due to low savings. If the money borrowed does result in the development of new industries and increases in productivity, sufficient income may be generated to repay the interest on the loans. However, there is a risk that some of the money borrowed may be used for non-productive purposes such as military programmes, that some projects may prove to be unprofitable and that interest rates rise. There are a number of other reasons why developing countries may experience difficulties in paying interest (servicing the debt) and repaying the capital sum. These include natural disasters and changes in exchange rates. Many developing countries, for example Brazil and Mexico, have significant levels of debt. This can result in more money flowing out of the developing countries into industrial countries than the other way around – a redistribution of income from the poor to the rich. This restricts development.

Applying for aid

Foreign aid (grants, loans at concessionary rates and the supply of, for example, educational, technical services) can assist development if it is used in high productive projects which take into account the resource endowment of the country. Untied aid is thought to be more beneficial than tied aid. The latter requires the recipient to buy goods and services from the donor country. These may be at a higher price and of a low quality than available from other sources. Aid may also be bilateral (from one country to another) or multilateral (from international organisations to developing countries). The latter is provided, for example, by the IMF, the World Bank, the UN and the EU. The IMF and its sister institution, the World Bank (also called the International Bank for Reconstruction and Development – its original name), provide loans to developing countries designed to improve their infrastructure, education and health services, restructure the economy and cope with aggregate demand and supply shocks. For example, the World Bank operates the extended structural adjustment programme (ESAF) which aims to reduce poverty and increase growth by supporting specific programmes. It also runs the Heavily Indebted Poor Countries initiative (HIPC). This has got major lenders, including western governments, the IMF and the World Bank itself, to agree to write off up to 80 per cent of their loans to developing countries with unsustainable debts.

The World Bank and, in particular, the IMF have, however, been criticised on the grounds that their assistance is insufficient, often inflexible and largely based on the economy theories pursued in, and policy interests of, the United States which is a dominant member of both institutions.

ACTIVITY 3

In August 1999, Herbert Murerwa, finance minister of Zimbabwe, admitted that the country had fallen behind with foreign debt payments with arrears reaching US$32 million in May. Of this, $11 million, owed to multilateral creditors, was cleared by August.

As a group, discuss the benefits to industrial countries of writing off the debts of developing countries.

Summary

Economic development is associated with an improvement in the lives of most of a country's population, most noticeably by a fall in poverty. Countries can be divided into industrial and developing ones, although within these categories there are differences. Developing countries tend to have low incomes, high birth rates, a high proportion of the labour force employed in the primary sector, low levels of investment and saving and a concentration on a narrow range of exports. These features, combined with disadvantages in international trade, make it difficult for the countries to improve their position. A number of theories are advanced to explain economic development, two of which, the Harrod-Domar Model and Rostow's stages of growth theory emphasise the role of saving. Countries employ a range of policies in a bid to improve their economic development. These include developing particular industries, export-orientated industrialisation, import-substituting industrialisation, attracting foreign investment, borrowing, accepting foreign aid and population control policies.

Data response question

Almost one in five Ghanaians are now under five, half are under 15 and 62% under 25. The momentum in this country of the young is unstoppable, and will define Ghana in the next century. At best, the government can reduce the long-term numbers but it expects there to be 30m by 2025, perhaps as many as 38m. The national plan is to reduce the birth rate to 4.0 by 2003 and then bring it, as fast as possible to 3.5. That doesn't sound that difficult but it represents a Herculean task in educating people and providing contraception. The culture in the countryside, where 70% of people live, is still to see children as assets, conferring status, wealth and recognition.

Cosmos Offei works with the Ghanaian family planning association and is in the personal and professional frontline. He is the youngest of eight children, and his brothers and sisters have 26 children between them. He has just two and is unlikely to have more, he says, because prices are high, and life hard in Accra.

The national rate of natural increase, he says, is falling, but despite working with churches, schools, hospitals, villages and chiefs, birth control is only practised by 15% of couples. There is no problem with the growing numbers, says Offei, if the economy and the environment on which people depend keep up with the needs. It's a big if. More than 12 000 teachers should be employed just to cope with today's burgeoning school numbers. Training colleges for the next generation of professionals must be built soon, the country needs to invest in infrastructure, education, health and agriculture now to avoid massive problems later.

It can't. Ghana may be one of Africa's most economically successful and peaceful countries, but the average wage is just over £600 a year, and it depends heavily on US and Japanese aid for help with population control. Social services are falling behind and unless the economy picks up, the future is rocky. It's hard enough to service a population of 20m but 18m more over the next 20-odd years means work must be found for millions more when a third of the country is now unemployed. So people leave the villages, adding to pressures on the cities. Accra is now bursting out of its boundaries, 10 times the size it was 40 years ago and a magnet for thousands of illiterate people each year.

John Vidal, 'Population explosion' in the *Guardian*, 20 September 1999

1 Why was Ghana experiencing problems in limiting its population growth? (4 marks)
2 Explain what is meant by a natural increase in population. (3 marks)
3 What are the disadvantages of a rising population? (5 marks)
4 Why were people migrating to Accra? (4 marks)
5 Discuss whether Ghana is a typical developing country. (9 marks)

UNIT 25 Economics of Europe

Key concepts covered

- transitional economies
- central and east European countries (CEE)
- Commonwealth of Independent States (CIS)
- Comecon
- trade creation
- trade diversion
- Common Agricultural Policy (CAP)
- EU budget
- Agenda 2000
- Lome conventions
- Treaty of Rome
- Single European Act
- Maastricht Treaty
- European Central Bank (ECB)
- European System of Central Banks (ESCB)

Introduction

This unit discusses the key issues facing different groups of countries within Europe. These include the problems being experienced by those countries which are developing market economy systems, the effects of an enlargement of the European Union for the new and current member countries and the process of increased integration.

Transitional economies

Transitional economies are those economies which have moved away from operating planned economies and which are developing market economies. In Europe transitional economies are divided into two groups:

- **Central and east European countries (CEE)**. This group includes former communist countries that previously had close links with the former Soviet Union. It consists of Albania, Bulgaria, Croatia, the Czech Republic, Estonia, Hungary, Latvia, Lithuania, Macedonia, Poland, Romania, the Slovak Republic and Slovenia.

- **Commonwealth of Independent States (CIS)**. This consists of the 12 countries that used to make up the former Soviet Union: Armenia, Azerbaijan, Belarus, Georgia, Kazakhstan, Kyrgy-

stan, Moldova, Russia, Tajikistan, Turkmenistan, Ukraine and Uzbekistan.

The CEE and CIS countries used to be members of **Comecon**. This was the Council for Mutual Economic Aid which was a trade bloc, set up in 1949 and dissolved in 1991. It sought to encourage trade between members, to provide technical and financial assistance and to coordinate state planning across the area.

To date, the performance of the CEE economies has been stronger than that of the CIS countries although all have experienced difficulties in changing their economic systems.

The process of transition

The CEE and CIS countries were motivated to move away from a planned economy system because of the shortcomings of the system, including high levels of bureaucracy, inefficiency, shortages, lack of choice and lack of consumer sovereignty. However, in this transitional stage they are experiencing some of the problems of trying to operate a market system before they have got the necessary governmental, legal, regulatory, social and financial infrastructure in place and before they have developed the required entrepreneurial skills and markets.

When they were planned economies the state ensured that everyone was employed and had access to basic health and education services and housing. It also kept prices low and discouraged the consumption of demerit goods. When many of the state concerns were privatised and state intervention in the running of the economy significantly reduced there was a major upheaval in economic activity. Some industries did expand but others, deprived of state subsidy, collapsed. Many workers, used to working for the same state concern throughout their working life, found it difficult to change their jobs. Unemployment rose at a time when a welfare system to match the new economic situation had not been adequately established. The removal of price controls and increases in the money supply led to high levels of inflation. Social problems also occurred with a rise in crime and the sale of demerit goods, including drugs and pornography.

Some of the countries, most notably Poland, have now built up some of the necessary infrastructure and their economic performance is improving.

Extension of the European Union

In 1957 six countries, Belgium, France, Italy, Luxembourg, the Netherlands and West Germany, signed the Treaty of Rome to form the European

	Population (millions)	Income per head (US $s)
Slovak Republic	5	3700
Slovenia	2	9760
Turkey	63	3160
And some already in the EU		
Denmark (highest)	5	33 260
UK	59	21 400
Portugal (lowest)	10	10 690

The Independent, 13 December 1999, based on World Bank figures

It is currently thought that the first six entrants will be Poland, Hungary, the Czech Republic, Slovenia, Estonia and Cyprus who may join as early as 2003.

Effects of joining the EU

Countries that do join the EU will experience a number of effects, some of which may be advantageous and some potentially disadvantageous. The effects include the following:

- A change in the pattern of trade. The absence of barriers within the EU and a common external tariff on products from outside the EU will encourage the new entrants to trade more with fellow EU members. **Trade creation** or **trade diversion** may occur. The first occurs when membership of the trading bloc enables the countries to specialise, produce more and lower costs. Trade diversion involves the members having to buy more from high cost firms within the bloc rather than from cheaper suppliers outside. So the effect on new members will depend on the cost of the products they bought prior to entry, the price of EU products without the common external tariff (CET) on them and the impact that the countries' entry will have on EU countries' performance.

- Access to EU funds. The countries will be entitled to receive grants from the regional and social funds and assistance from the **Common Agricultural Policy (CAP)** (see below).

- Access to a large single market. This may enable the countries' firms to take greater advantage of economies of scale, although there is also a risk that diseconomies of scale will occur.

- Increased competition. This may stimulate the countries' firms to modernise and increase their performance in terms of productivity, quality and price. However, if the firms are unable to respond to the challenge they may go out of business causing output to fall and unemployment to rise.

Economic Community (EEC) which came into existence on 1 January 1958. This was a customs union. The name changed to the European Community (EC) in 1967. Nine countries joined later – Denmark, Ireland and the UK in 1973, Greece in 1981, Spain and Portugal in 1986 and Austria, Finland and Sweden in 1995. In addition, in 1990 East Germany merged with West Germany to form Germany. The area's name was changed again in 1992 to the European Union (EU) to reflect the greater degree of integration that was occurring.

Currently, there are 13 countries waiting to join the EU. Table 25.1 shows the population and income per head of the 11 largest applicants. The other two are the smaller economies of Cyprus and Malta.

Table 25.1 Potential EU members

	Population (millions)	Income per head (US $s)
Bulgaria	8	1230
Czech Republic	10	5040
Estonia	1	3390
Hungary	10	4510
Latvia	2	2430
Lithuania	4	2440
Poland	39	3900
Romania	22	1390

■ Reduction in sovereignty of macroeconomic policy. National governments will have to give up some of the control of their economies to EU institutions.

ACTIVITY 2

'To qualify for the single currency, Italy had to reduce its budget deficit swiftly. It did so by sharply increasing taxes rather than cutting back spending.

A second effect of euro entry was to end the competitive advantage of frequent lira devaluations that periodically boosted the export performance of Italian industry.'

James Blitz, 'The end of la dolce vita' in the *Financial Times*, 12 October 1999

a Explain which convergence criteria Italy was seeking to achieve by increasing taxes.

b Discuss the effects that the rise in taxes may have had on the Italian economy.

c Discuss the economic measures the transitional economies may have to take before they can meet the convergence criteria.

Effects on the EU of new entrants

The EU is concerned that before the applicants can join their economic performance, infrastructure and environment protection systems should be improved. The greater the extent they can do this, the smoother the transition will be. A larger EU may create greater political stability in Europe. It will also have the economic advantage of increasing the size of the trading bloc, thereby giving it greater bargaining in negotiations with, for example the World Trade Organisation and the USA. However, it will have to make adjustments to its procedures and policies to cope with the new entrants. The first will arise because it is more difficult to coordinate up to 28 than 15 countries. For example, more decisions will have to be taken on the basis of majority decisions rather than unanimous decisions. The need for the latter will arise mainly because the new members will have lower income levels than the current members. This is likely to mean the need for an increasing contribution to the **EU's budget** from a number of the current members, including the UK and the possibility of large movements of labour from the low income, high unemployment new entrant countries to the current member countries. There is also the potential problem that most of the potential members have large agricultural sectors. This is currently putting pressure on the EU to reform its Common Agricultural Policy.

The Common Agricultural Policy

The CAP seeks to raise agricultural productivity, protect the incomes of farmers, make the area self-sufficient in agricultural produce and ensure supplies to consumers at reasonable prices. While it has been fairly effective in terms of the third objective mentioned here it has been criticised for its performance on the first, second and fourth objectives.

The CAP is an interventionist policy based on setting a target price that is usually above the world equilibrium price. This price is maintained by buying up surpluses and placing a variable import levy on food supplies from outside the area to prevent them threatening the target price. This policy results in a number of disadvantages. Consumers have to pay higher prices for food and costs are incurred in buying up and storing the surpluses. It also disadvantages exporters of food that lie outside the EU.

The EU budget

As noted above, the entry of new members will have an impact not only on the EU's agricultural policy but also its budget.

The EU receives revenue from the proceeds of the common external tariff, the variable import levy on agricultural products and contributions based on member countries' GDP and VAT revenue. Its main items of expenditure are CAP and structural funds (including the regional and social funds). The European Social Fund spends money on developing human resources and improving the workings of the labour market by means of providing financial assistance for training and educational projects. Some countries are net beneficiaries of the budget, for example Greece, Ireland and Spain. This means that the countries receive more from EU spending in their country than they contribute to the EU budget. Others, for example the UK, Germany and the Netherlands, are net contributors.

To cope with the implications of the enlargement for the EU's budget, **Agenda 2000** has been introduced. This programme is seeking to place a limit on expenditure in enlargement and to reform the CAP and other spending programmes.

Assistance to non-members

Some of the EU's budget is spent on assisting countries outside the EU. These countries include potential entrants who receive help to prepare for entry through, for example association agreements which provide technical assistance and reduce trade restrictions. Help, in the form of finance and advice, is also given to other transitional economies and developing economies.

The **Lome conventions** provide favourable trade terms (exemption from most industrial tariffs and reduced agricultural tariffs) and financial aid to a number of developing African, Caribbean and Pacific countries (ACP), some of which had former colonial links with EU members.

Increasing integration

Over time the economies of the EU members have become increasingly integrated. There have been a number of significant stages in this process including the original Treaty of Rome, the Single European Act, the Maastricht Treaty and the introduction of the single currency.

The Treaty of Rome

The **Treaty of Rome** set out the basic aims of the EU. These include the elimination of tariffs and quotas on the import and export of goods between member states, the establishment of a common customs tariff, the abolition of obstacles to the free movement of people, services and capital between member states and the establishment of common policies for agriculture and transport. It also stated that the EEC would seek to increase trade and development with overseas countries and territories.

The Single European Act

The **Single European Act** was signed in 1986 and came into force a year later. Its main aim was to end all internal barriers in order to create a single market by 1992. Members agreed to remove non-tariff barriers on the movement of goods and services and barriers on the movement of workers and firms within the area.

These barriers included, for example, technical barriers on product standards and frontier controls. It was also agreed that there would be a move towards the harmonisation of taxes and the Act required the member countries to impose a minimum standard rate of VAT of 15 per cent.

The Maastricht Treaty

The **Mastricht Treary** is also known as the Treaty on European Union. It was signed in February 1992 and set out a timetable table for EMU (economic and monetary union) to be achieved in three stages. Stage 1 was already in progress, with the creation of a single market. The main features of stage 2 were to be increased coordination of national monetary policies and governments seeking to achieve greater similarity of economic performance (convergence). If economies had, for example, similar inflation, unemployment and growth rates it would be easy to operate a single European economic policy and hence make the third stage more achievable. The third stage was to be the introduction of the single currency and the establishment of the European Central Bank.

The Treaty also set out a common foreign and security policy and a common social policy. This is sometimes known as the Social Chapter. The objectives of the Social Chapter include improving working conditions and employment and improving the dialogue between management and workers. Among its provisions are equal pay for men and women, extending many of the rights of full-time workers including sick and holiday pay to part-time workers, and a minimum wage.

EMU

Economic and Monetary Union started on 1 January 1999 with the introduction of the single currency and the operation of monetary policy being moved to the **European Central Bank (ECB)**. The single currency was discussed in Unit 14. The ECB is based in Frankfurt. Its prime objective is to maintain price stability within the euro area. It implements monetary policy and foreign exchange and reserve policies. In undertaking this role it has been given a high degree of independence of political control. It is directed by a Governing Council consisting of the members of the Executive Board and the governors of the member countries' central banks. The Council sets the main lines of monetary policy, for implementation by an Executive Board. The Bank decides on the interest rate, is not obliged to finance government deficits or lend to EU institutions and does not depend on government finance to cover its running costs. The European System of Central Banks (ESCB) consists of the ECB and all the central banks of the euro area which have to be independent of their government. The national central banks implement the policy of the ECB.

In addition to monetary union, the EU is also seeking to achieve greater convergence of fiscal policy, particularly tax rates (see Unit xx).

ACTIVITY 3

'For those of you who think that whether or not the UK adopts the euro is the single most important issue facing us in Europe today, I have just one word: tax. And, for those who think that Emu stands for European monetary union here is a reminder: it stands for Economic and monetary union.

Harmonising taxes is the key to economic union. If Europe is to become a single economic unit, then taxes must be harmonised.'

Martin Essex, 'Cut taxes for true EU harmonisation' in *Sunday Business*, 30 May 1999

a Explain what is meant by 'harmonising' taxes.
b Discuss whether harmonisation of taxes is a necessary condition for the EU to become 'a single economic unit'.

Summary

The geographical area of Europe includes transitional economies, members of the EU and other countries. Transitional economies have experienced a number of problems in moving from a planned economic system to a market economic system, including inflation, unemployment and falling output. These problems have arisen in part because the appropriate infrastructure to run a market system is not fully in place. Some of the transitional economies have applied for membership of the EU. They are hoping to gain access to the markets of the EU, to receive financial aid and to become part of a large trading bloc consisting of economies that have experience of running market economies. Their imminent entry is increasing pressure to reform the EU's CAP. When the countries come in it will also have an impact on the EU's budget. To assist the transitional countries' preparation for entry the EU is providing assistance. As well as getting ready for enlargement the EU is coping with the last move towards increased integration.

Data response question

The Common Agricultural Policy
Article 39 of the Treaty of Rome called for the creation of a common policy for agriculture. The objectives of the policy were:

- to stabilise agricultural markets;
- to raise agricultural productivity
- to increase farm income;
- to assure the availability of supplies;
- and to ensure reasonable prices for consumers.

The CAP, adopted in the 1960s, was based on a system of price support backed up by variable import levies, intervention buying, export refunds and a structural policy. It is funded through the European Agricultural Guidance and Guarantee Fund (EAGGF).

During the 1980s concern about the economic and financial cost of the CAP mounted, both within and outside Europe. For example between 1981 and 1991 total EAGGF expenditure increased by approximately 72% in real terms to almost 31 billion ECUs, 60% of the total EC budget. These concerns led to a series of measures to reform the CAP.

Figure 1 and Table 1 show the trends in agricultural prices and surpluses for selected agricultural commodities supported by the CAP.

1 a Use Figure 1 to compare EC producer prices of agricultural commodities with world market prices from 1979 to 1991. (2 marks)
  b Which commodity listed in Table 1 showed the greatest relative decline in intervention stocks between 1985/6 and 1988/9? (1 mark)
2 a Explain *two* reasons why EC producer prices might be higher than world market prices. (4 marks)
  b Briefly explain the implications of CAP support for the world market prices of agricultural commodities. (3 marks)
  c Why might some countries outside the EC have benefited from the operation of the CAP and others suffered? (4 marks)
3 Discuss whether price support is the best way of achieving the objectives of the CAP as set out in the treaty of Rome. (6 marks)

Section 5 questions

Essay questions
1 a Explain why traffic congestion is regarded as a misallocation of resources. (10 marks)
  b Discuss three policies which could be introduced to reduce congestion. (15 marks)
2 a Discuss the obstacles to development which developing countries face. (10 marks)
  b Assess three policies a developing country could adopt to increase its rate of economic development. (15 marks)

A comparison of EC producer prices[1] and world market prices[2] of agricultural commodities (1979–91), in real terms.

Index of prices

Figure 1

Notes:

[1]EC producer price index $= \dfrac{\text{EC producer prices}}{\text{World market prices}}$

[2]World market price index in 1979 = 100

Table 1: Stocks of selected commodities held in EC intervention stores, thousand tonnes 1985/6–90/91

Marketing year	Common wheat	Barley	All cereals	Butter	Skimmed milk powder
1985/86	10 312	5296	18 502	1122	646
1986/87	7319	4235	14 271	1188	765
1987/88	4567	3916	11 748	640	240
1988/89	2906	3242	9146	64	7
1989/90	5521	3320	11 795	820	21
1990/91	8520	5538	18 729	324	354

Source: Q1, *Economics of Europe Paper*, June 1998, UCLES

Project

Prepare a report which investigates and analyses the proposition that 'the UK should join the European single currency sooner rather than later'.

This should cover:

■ a discussion of the nature of the single currency

■ an assessment of the performance of the single currency

■ an evaluation of the arguments for and against membership

■ an assessment of whether the UK currently meets the criteria for entry

■ an evaluation of the costs of remaining out

■ an assessment of how smoothly entry could be undertaken

■ a list of sources.

You should make use of appropriate economic theory throughout your report.

C3.1a, C3.1b, C3.2, N3.1, N3.2, N3.3, IT3.1, IT3.2, IT3.2

Multiple choice questions – answers

Section 1

1 **Answer B:** Opportunity cost is what has to be forgone. In this case, the car is now worth £3500, which is what the man sacrifices by owning the car – irrespective of whether or not he uses it.

2 **Answer C:** As more and more arms are produced, more and more production of kidney beans has to be sacrificed. As the production possibility boundary is a straight line, the number of kidney machines sacrificed as more arms are produced remains constant.

3 **Answer C:** The key concept underpinning economics is that people's wants are greater than the world's resources.

4 **Answer C:** A production possibility frontier indicates the maximum that can be produced when all resources are fully used. It follows that an outward shift can only occur if ways are found to produce more goods.

5 **Answer B:** As indicated, earlier opportunity costs is what has be given up.

6 **Answer D:** A demand curve shows the relationship between the effective demand (that is, peoples' wants) backed up by the ability to buy, and the price of that good. In almost all cases, demand will rise if price falls and vice versa.

7 **Answer D:** Falls in consumption, output, and the demand for factors of production are all associated with falling incomes. It follows that rising incomes are likely to be associated with rising levels of consumption.

8 **Answer A:** The essential characteristic of a subsistence economy is that people live a 'hand to mouth' existence. They will tend to consume all that they produce, and in the unlikely event of the production of a surplus, barter would be used.

9 **Answer C:** The BSE crisis tended to depress the demand for most beef related products, which lead to falling prices. However, the demand for organic products has risen, as people seek healthier alternatives.

10 **Answer C:** Command economies involve a high level of government intervention, combined with shortages of products in demand, causing the likely creation of black markets. All resources are owned by the state. Hence, share ownership is very unlikely.

Section 2

1 **Answer C:** If the co-efficient of income elasticity of demand is positive, then an increase in income is associated with an increase in demand, and vice versa. However, if the value is smaller than 1, it means that the rise or fall in income has been relatively larger than the rise or fall in demand.

2 **Answer C:** If a change in the price of one good has an effect on the demand for another, the two goods in questions will either be substitutes or complements. If the price of product X rises, there will be a fall in the demand for that product, and as the demand for Y is said to have fallen, they must be complements.

3 **Answer D:** If the price elasticity of coffee is –0.7, and its price increases by 10%, sales will fall by 7%. Similarly is the cross elasticity of demand between tea and coffee is +1.1, an increase in the price of coffee by 10% will result in an increase in demand for tea by 11%

4 **Answer D:** If a rise in bus fares of 80% is associated with a fall in demand of 22%, the price elasticity of demand for bus journeys is –0.275, which is relatively inelastic. This is backed by the information that bus company revenue has risen.

5 **Answer B:** If income elasticity of demand for x is +0.5, and income rises by 10%, demand will rise by 5%. If at the same time the price of Y falls by 10%, and the cross elasticity of demand of X to Y is +0.5, the demand for X will fall by 5%, leaving the demand for X unchanged.

6 **Answer C:** A shortage of skilled workers is most likely to lead to higher incomes, whereas the other factors are likely to contribute to lower incomes.

Section 3

1 **Answer A:** If supply were perfectly inelastic, it would not change at all, leading to a larger fall in price than any of the other scenarios.

2 **Answer C:** Normal and inferior goods are associated with income elasticity of demand, and normally one would expect the demand for a good to rise as income rises and vice versa, giving a positive income elasticity of demand

3 **Answer A:** Elasticity of supply is a measure of the responsiveness of supply to changes in price. If elastic, an industry would be able to raise supply in response to higher prices. All the options except that mentioning excess capacity would act as constraints to changing supply.

4 **Answer D:** PeS + Percentage change in quantity supplied/percentage change in price. An increase in price by £2 represents a 10% rise, substituting into the equation will give $.75 = x/10, = 7.5\%$. A 7.5% increase on 2000 tones = 150, hence the correct answer is 2150.

5 **Answer A:** E1 is given by the intersection of D1 and S1, D2 represents and increase in demand, and S 2 and increase in supply which could only be accounted for by a fall in the price of a raw materials. This would lead to an increase in supply and the rise in the price of a substitute, leading to an increase in demand.

6 **Answer D:** If the supply of butter rises, then its price is likely to fall. This will probably lead to an increase in demand for butter, and a fall in demand for substitutes such as margarine, whose price is likely to fall.

7 **Answer C:** If consumers switch to synthetic rubber, the demand for natural rubber will fall, leading to a fall in its price and out.

Section 4

1 **Answer D:** Public goods are those goods having positive externalities, which a freely operating market would under supply. The police are an example. It would be hard to work out exactly who benefits from the police, and harder still to devise some system whereby those who benefitted would be made to pay. Hence, the government intervenes.

2 **Answer B:** Merit goods are those which a government judges to be socially desirable, but which freely operating markets would not supply. The National Health Service is an example.

3 **Answer C:** Harmful third party effects, such as damaging effects of waste disposal, are classified as negative externalities.

4 **Answer C:** If private costs are less than social costs, negative externalities are occurring. Government intervention in the form of a tax on the polluter might be justified, to ensure that the actual price charge for the good reflects the true cost to society of its production.

5 **Answer C:** If a guaranteed minimum price is imposed above the market equilibrium, supply is likely to exceed demand and in this case, the government might be forced to purchase the whole of the excess supply to maintain the higher price.

6 **Answer A:** The imposition of indirect taxes will have most effect on the actual sales of a product or service, if the demand is highly elastic. If it is not, many people would be prepared to pay much more, in order to continue to purchase the (undesirable) good.

7 Answer D: If the government wishes to hold a minimum price above the equilibrium, it will have to purchase the whole of the excess demand (20 million tonnes) at the going price (£15 per tonne), and keep it off the market by holding in a buffer stock.

8 **Answer B:** The provision of public transport is generally considered to generate positive externalities. Subsidies will therefore help to increase the provision of public transport. Their removal will result in less provision, and those using public services (and others) will suffer as a result.

Section 5

1 **Answer A:** Over time, governments seek to balance the money entering and leaving the country. The other major macroeconomic objectives are high employment, sustainable economic growth and low but not zero inflation.

2   **Answer C:** Tinbergen's rule states that a government should implement a separate policy measure for each objective it is seeking to achieve. For example, to increase employment a government may increase spending on training and to reduce inflation its central bank may raise the rate of interest.

3   **Answer D:** If pollution increases, the quality of life may fall. The answer cannot be A or B, since if real GDP per head has increased, the rise in output must have outstripped any rise in the price level and population. The answer also cannot be D, since a rise in life expectancy will increase and not reduce the quality of life.

4   **Answer A:** Production is output, whereas productivity is output per worker hour. If employment falls but output is unchanged, it means that each worker must be producing more. In the situations described in B, C and D productivity is falling.

5   **Answer B:** A decrease in the rate of income tax will raise disposable income. This will increase consumption, and hence aggregate demand. A and D would reduce aggregate demand and C would increase aggregate supply.

6   **Answer A:** A shift to the right of the SRAS curve represents an increase in aggregate supply. SRAS increases if costs of production fall and wages are, of course, one of firms' main costs. B and C would lead to a decrease in SRAS, and so a shift to the left of the SRAS curve. D would cause a shift to the right of the long run aggregate supply curve.

7   **Answer A:** An increase in aggregate demand is represented by a shift to the right of the aggregate demand curve. As Figure 1 shows in the case described this will cause a rise in the price level.

8   **Answer B:** New classical economists believe that changes in aggregate demand can affect the price but, in the longer run, have no effect on output. This is because they believe that wage rates and prices will change to restore full employment. Figure 2 shows a decrease in aggregate demand reducing the price level from P to P1 but leaving output unchanged at Y.

9   **Answer B:** A shift to the right of the production possibility curve represents an increase in a country's productive capacity – potential economic growth. However, because the production point remains at t, it means that the country is not making use of this extra capacity. Output remains unchanged, and so actual growth has not occurred.

10 **Answer B:** If an economy is experiencing full employment, it will only be able to increase its output of capital goods by reallocating some

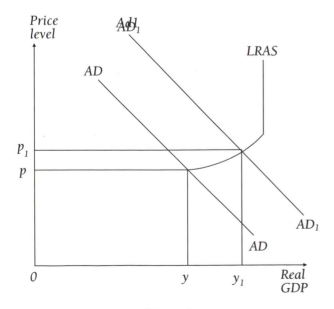

Figure 1

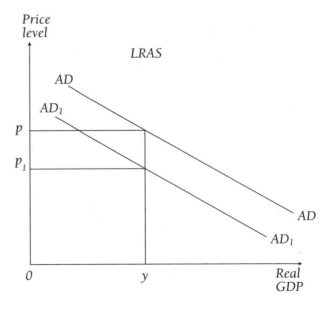

Figure 2

resources from making consumer goods to capital goods. In the short run, this would result in fewer consumer goods being made. However, in the longer run the extra capital goods will raise the productive capacity of the economy, and will enable more capital and consumer goods to be made.

11 **Answer A:** A cut in income tax rates will raise disposable income, which in turn is likely to increase consumer spending, and hence aggregate demand. If the economy is operating at or near full capacity, this will cause demand-pull inflation. B would reduce aggregate demand, and C and D would cause cost-push inflation.

12 **Answer B:** The key word here is "must". B, C and D could, but may not, result from inflation. However, a rise in the price level must result in a fall in the value of money. Each e.g. £ will buy less if prices are higher.

13 **Answer D:** RPI, known as the headline rate of inflation, includes mortgage interest payments, whereas RPIX, the target rate, does not. A, B and C are included in both RPI and RPIX, although A and B are not included in RPIY.

14 **Answer B:** The most significant item forgone as a result of inflation is output. Tax revenue will also be lost but not on the same scale as the loss of output. More significantly, during a time of unemployment, a fall in tax revenue may be seen as an advantage rather than a disadvantage. This is because lower tax revenue will stimulate economic activity. C and D are financial costs resulting from unemployment. They are incurred rather than forgone.

15 **Answer B:** The labour force consists of those working and those seeking employment – the economically active. A, C and D are economically inactive groups.

16 **Answer D:** If people are unemployed but there are job vacancies available, it suggests that people are unaware of the vacancies, unable to move to where the jobs are, unwilling to work for the wages on offer or, as in this case, lacking the skills need to do the jobs on offer. A, B and C would all tend to result in the unemployed filling the vacancies.

17 **Answer D:** The current account of the balance of payments includes trade in goods, trade in services and investment income. A and B would appear in the capital and financial accounts. D is shown as a separate section.

18 **Answer B:** Sea transport covers the cost of using foreign ships to transport UK goods and people and the revenue earned by UK ships transporting foreign goods and people. It is a service and so appears in the trade in services section.

19 **Answer C:** Monetary policy covers changes in the money supply, the interest rate and the exchange rate. A and B are fiscal policy measures and D is a supply-side measure.

20 **Answer A:** The Phillips curve suggests there is an inverse relationship between unemployment and inflation with e.g. a rise in unemployment being accompanied by a fall in the inflation rate.

Glossary

absolute advantage the ability to produce output using fewer resources than other regions or countries

absolute poverty the inability to purchase the basic necessities of life

aggregate demand the total demand for a country's goods and services at a given price level

aggregate supply the total amount a country's producers supply at a given price level

allocative efficiency a situation in which resources are producing what consumers want

average revenue total revenue divided by output i.e. price

average (total) cost total cost divided by output

automatic stabilisers forms of government spending and taxation that reduce fluctuations in aggregate demand

balance of payments a record of flows of money coming in and out of a country

barriers to entry restrictions on the entry of new firms into a market

barriers to exit restrictions on firms leaving a market

barter the direct exchange of goods and services

black economy undeclared economic activity

black market an unofficial market in which a product is sold for a price above the set price

budget a statement of government's planned spending and tax changes

business cycles fluctuations in economic activity

capital assets that are used in producing goods and services

circular flow of income flows of money and resources between firms and households

claimant count a measure of unemployment which includes those receiving job seekers' allowance

command economy an economy in which resources are owned by the state

comparative advantage relative efficiency – ability to produce a product at a lower opportunity cost than other regions or countries

competition a situation in which a number of producers are contesting for customers

Competition Commission a government body that investigates and reports on mergers, anti-competitive practices, the utilities and public sector bodies

complements products demanded to be used together

concentration ratio a measure of the share of the output of the leading firms in a given market

consumer sovereignty a situation in which consumer preferences determine what is produced

consumer surplus the difference between what consumers are willing to pay and what they actually pay

consumption household spending on goods and services

contestable market a market in which there are no barriers to entry and exit

cost benefit analysis a method of assessing a project which takes into account social costs and benefits

cost-push inflation a rise in the price level caused by increases in the costs of production

costs of production payments made in order to produce a product

cross elasticity of demand the responsiveness of demand for one product to changes in the price of another product

current account deficit expenditure abroad and income paid abroad exceeding revenue earned and income received from abroad

cyclical unemployment unemployment arising from a lack of aggregate demand

deflationary policy a policy which reduces aggregate demand

demand the willingness and ability to buy a product

demand-pull inflation a rise in the price level caused by increases in aggregate demand

demergers the splitting up of a firm into two or more separate firms

demerit goods products which if left to market forces would be over-consumed and which have negative externalities

deregulation the abolition of government rules, regulations and laws

demand-side shocks unanticipated events that shift the aggregate demand curve

derived demand demand for something depending on the demand for another item

direct taxes taxes on the income of firms and people

diseconomies of scale factors which cause rising long run average costs

discrimination treating one group differently than other groups

disposable income income after the deduction of direct taxes plus state benefits

division of labour the specialisation of labour on particular tasks

dumping the sale of products at less than cost price

economic development the improvement in the economic welfare of a country

economic growth an increase in real GDP

economic rent a surplus paid to a factor of production above what is needed to keep it in its current occupation

economically active those in employment and those seeking employment

economies of scale factors which cause decreasing average costs

elasticity of supply responsiveness of supply to changes in price

enterprise the process of organising the other factors of production and taking risks

equilibrium a state of balance

equity fairness

Euro area the 11 EU countries that have adopted the single currency

expectations-augmented Phillips curve a diagram implying there is no long run trade off between unemployment and inflation

external growth firms growing by means of mergers and takeovers

externalities third part effects of any transaction between a consumer and a firm

factors of production resources used to produce goods and services

finite resources resources which are in limited supply

fiscal policy the use of government spending and taxation

Fisher equation MV = PT (money supply × velocity of circulation = price level × output)

fixed costs costs that do not change with output

fixed exchange rate an exchange rate fixed against other currencies that is maintained by the government

floating exchange rate an exchange rate determined by market forces

free market economy an economy in which resources are owned by individuals

frictional unemployment unemployment arising because workers are in between jobs

game theory the view that the behaviour of oligopolists is influenced by assumptions about their rivals' behaviour

geographical immobility barriers to the movement of workers between different areas of the country

gross investment total spending on capital goods

Harrod-Domar model the view that the driving force behind development is a high savings ratio

HICP harmonised index of consumer prices – a measure of inflation used throughout the EU

hypothecated tax a tax raised for a specific purpose

hysteresis the view that unemployment generates unemployment

imperfect competition a market situation in which firms have some influence over price

income elasticity of demand responses of demand to changes in income

indirect taxes taxes on spending

inflation a sustained rise in the general price level

inferior goods products which decrease in demand as income rises

inputs factors of production

internal growth firms growing by opening new outlets

investment spending on capital goods

investment income profits, interest and dividends

J curve effect the tendency for a devaluation of the exchange rate to make the trade position worse before it gets better

kinked demand curve a model of oligopoly that suggests firms follow price cuts but not price rises

labour human effort used to produce goods and services

Labour Force Survey a measure of unemployment based on a survey using the ILO definition of unemployment

Laffer curve a diagram showing the relationship between marginal tax rates and tax revenue

land natural resources used in production

law of diminishing marginal returns a situation in which extra units of a variable factor of production result in a fall in the addition to output

liquidity preference theory the view that the rate of interest is determined by the demand and supply of money

Lorenz curve a diagram showing the inequality of income and wealth

macroeconomics the study of economics at a national and international level

marginal cost the change in total cost resulting from the production of one more unit

marginal productivity theory the view that demand for a factor of production depends on its marginal revenue product

marginal revenue the change in total revenue resulting from the sale of an extra unit

marginal revenue product of labour the change in a firm's revenue resulting from employing one more worker

market an arrangement for exchanges between buyers and sellers

market clearing the process by which markets are brought into equilibrium

market failure undesirable outcomes of the working of market forces

Marshall-Lerner condition the view that for a devaluation to be successful in improving the balance of payments the combined elasticities of demand for exports and imports must be greater than one

merit goods products which if left to market forces would be under-consumed and which have positive externalities

microeconomics the study of individual markets

mixed economies economies in which resources are owned by the state and individuals

monetary policy the use of the money supply, interest rates and the exchange rate

money transmission mechanism the process by which changes in interest rates affect prices, output and employment

monopolistic competition a market structure in which there are a number of firms selling a similar product

monopoly a single seller

monopsony a single buyer

multiplier the relationship between an initial change in aggregate demand and final change in income

Nairu the non-accelerating inflation rate of unemployment – the level of unemployment which exists when the labour market is in equilibrium

natural monopoly a market in which full advantage of economies of scale can be achieved only if there is one firm

net exports the value of exports minus the value of imports

net investment spending on extra capital goods

new economic paradigm the view that economies are entering a new era of high, sustained growth, low unemployment and low inflation

normal goods products which increase in demand as income rises

normal profit the level of profit needed to keep a firm in the industry in the long run

occupational immobility barriers to workers changing occupations

oligopoly a market structure which is dominated by a few sellers

oligopsony a market in which there are only a few buyers

opportunity cost the cost of a particular activity in terms of the best alternative forgone

perfect competition a market structure with many buyers and sellers, free entry and exit and an homogeneous product

Phillips curve a diagram suggesting a trade off between unemployment and inflation

price discrimination the practice of charging consumers different prices for the same product

price elasticity of demand responsiveness of demand to changes in price

privatisation the transfer of resources from the public to the private sector

producer surplus the extra paid to producers above what they were willing to accept to supply the product

production possibility curve a diagram showing all the possible combinations of two types of products that can be made with given resources and technology

productive efficiency achieved when production takes place at the lowest average cost

productivity output per worker hour

profit maximisation the highest level of profits possible, achieved where MC = MR

protectionism the restriction on the free movement of products between countries

public goods products which are non-rival and non-excludable

PSNCR public sector net cash requirement excess of public sector spending over revenue

quantity theory the view that an increase in the money supply causes a direct and proportionate affect on the price level

quota a limit on the supply of a product

regional policy measures designed to influence the location of firms and people

relative poverty a situation of being poor in comparison to others

RPI the Retail Prices Index – a weighted consumer price index

Rostow's stages of growth theory the view that countries have to pass through five stages on the path of development

social benefits private benefits plus external benefits

social costs private costs plus external costs

specialisation the concentration on particular tasks or the production of particular products

structural unemployment unemployment arising from changes in demand and supply affecting particular industries

substitutes products which are considered to be alternatives for each other

sunk costs fixed costs attributable to capital that cannot be transferred to other uses

supernormal profit profit earned where average revenue exceeds average cost (which includes normal profit)

supply the willingness and ability to sell a product

supply-side policies policies used to increase aggregate supply by raising the efficiency of markets

supply-side shocks unanticipated events that shift the aggregate supply curve

tariffs taxes on imports

tax burden the total amount of tax paid as a percentage of GDP

tax harmonisation the standardisation of tax rates between countries

terms of trade the ratio of export to import prices

transfer earnings the amount a factor of production could earn in its next best paid occupation

trend growth expected increase in potential output over time

variable costs costs which change with output

velocity of circulation the number of times money changes hands in a given period

wage differentials differences in wages

Index

ACKNOWLEDGEMENTS

The publishers gratefully acknowledge the following for permission to reproduce copyright material. Every effort has been made to trace copyright holders, but in some cases has proved impossible. The publishers would be happy to hear from any copyright holder that has not been acknowledged.

Pg. 6 Cheltenham and Gloucester Logo. Used with permission of Cheltenham and Gloucester, Gloucester; Pg. 15 '47 nations still ban our beef' by Ian Kirby, from *Mail on Sunday* 14 November 1999. Used with kind permission of the *Mail on Sunday*; Pg 27. Estate Agents adverts, reprinted with permission of Steve Gooch Estate Agents, Coleford; Pg. 32/33 'EMI attracts some upbeat attention' by Mark Milner (and graph), from *The Guardian*, 18 January 2000 © *The Guardian*; Pg. 38 Table B Tonne-Kilometres carried by commodity and means of Transport 1984 and 1990, from Central Statistical Office, Transport Statistics 1992; Pg. 45 Telewest Advert, reprinted with permission of Telewest; Pg. 50 Viglen Advert, reprinted with permission of Viglen Limited; Pg. 57 Futon Company Advert, reprinted with permission of Futon Company; Pg. 57 Distribution of Earnings as a percentage of median pay, from Dept. of Employment New Earnings Survey 1997, Part A HMSO, Office for National Statistics © Crown Copyright 2000; Pg. 65/66 Extract from Cadbury Schweppes Interim Report 1999; Pg. 67 'No Quick Fix for ailing Marks' by Alister Osborne in *The Electronic Telegraph*, 3 November 1999. © Telegraph Group Limited; Pg. 82 'Housebuilding in the SE' by Charles Clover, in *Daily Telegraph*, 9 October 1999 © Telegraph Group Limited 1997; Pg. 82 'Surge in oil prices has governments over a barrel' by Anthony Barnett, in *The Observer*, 20 October 1996. © *The Observer*; Pg. 83 'Opec over a barrel' adapted from articles in *The Observer*, 1 April 1998 and *The Guardian*, 13 December 1998 by Dan Atkinson. © *The Observer/The Guardian*; Pg. 91 'Up to 50% off the price of your new car' from Eurobuyers Guide. Used with permission of Insiders Limited; Pg. 100 'Future going underground' from *Financial Times,* 9 January 1997; Pg. 101 'Road Traffic Growth' and 'Passenger transport'. Crown copyright is reproduced with the permission of the controller of Her Majesty's Stationery Office; Pg. 108/9 'In Love with the job' from *The Times* © Times Newspapers Limited 9 May 1991; Pg 110 'Rail users face £660 county line penalty' by Paul Martson, from *The Electronic Telegraph,* 12 January 1999'; Pg. 111 'Tesco to sell 'label' wear worth £8m' from *The Electronic Telegraph*, 18 July 1998; Pg. 112–113 'Unions urge fight to save jobs at Ford', from *The Observer*, 23rd April 2000; Pg. 128 'Ease up before the workforce cracks up', b;y Larry Elliott, in *The Guardian*, 23rd August 1999 Pg. 129 extract from 'Human Development Report 1998' United Nations Development Programme. Published by Oxford University Press New York; Pg. 130, extract from 'Outlook Darkened by waste and congestions' by Paul Brown, *The Guardian*, 9 December 1999. © *The Guardian*; Pg. 135 'America goes shopping and growth hits 5.5 per cent' by Nancy Dunne, *Financial Times*, 25 November 1999; Pg. 141 extracts from 'World economy fires on all cylinders' by David Smith, *The Sunday Times,* 28 November 1999 © Times Newspapers Limited; Pg. 144. 'Brave New World' by David Smith, *The Sunday Times* © Times Newspapers Limited 14 November 1999; Pg. 145 'Hurdles on the road to sustained growth' by Diane Coyle, *The Independent*, 10 November 1999; Pg. 146 'UN report warns of Earth's unsustainable future' by Michael McCarthy, *The Independent*, 16 September 1999; P. 149 'Fun-loving Britons splash out more on leisure' by Julia Hartley-Brewer. © Julia Hartley-Brewer, first published in *The Guardian,* 25 November 1999; Pg. 154 'Industry's heroes engineer a productivity miracle' by David Smith, *The Sunday Times* © Times Newspapers Limited 21 November 1999; Pg. 157 'Unemployment rates in the EU (per cent)' from 'National Institute Economic Review' October 1999, published by National Institute Economic and Social Research; Pg. 158 extracts from 'Pay rises and fall fall in jobless spark fears over inflation' by Philip Thornton, *The Independent*, 16 September 1999; Pg .159 extracts from 'Richer and poorer: Britains cities have their own north-south divide' by Diane Coyle, *The Independent*, 23 August 1999; Pg .160 'Jobs galore but in the wrong place' by David Smith, *The Sunday Times* © Times Newspapers Limited 3 October 1999; Pg. 161/2 'Trade goods, 1998' from 'UK balance of payments' in 'The Pink Book 1999 Edition' Office for National Statistics. © Crown Copyright 2000; Pg. 162 'Trade in services' and 'Main destination of UK exports and main source of imports 1998' from 'UK balance of payments' in 'The Pink Book 1999 Edition' Office for National Statistics. © Crown Copyright 2000; Pg 163 'UK is world's second biggest services exporter' by Christopher Adams, *Financial Times*, 12 February 1999; Pg. 179 'Low inflation and the property market' adapted from an article in 'The British Economy Survey – Autumn 1996'; Pg. 182 'Input and output analysis applied to environmental degradation' from 'Environmental Economics' by Turner, Pearce and Bateman, published by Harvester in 1994. Used with permission of Pearson Education, UK; Pg. 183 'What a load of Rubbish' is adapted from 'Bottle Bank dilemma – recycling economics are being challenged' in *Financial Times*, 18 November 1994, and from an article in *The Observer*, 28 July 1996; Pg. 186 'The football economy' by John Duncan, *The Guardian*, 18 February 1998. © The Guardian; Pg. 187 'Tackling monopolies' © *The Economist*, London 7 February 1998; Pg. 211/212 'New car registrations' and 'EU car price differences' from *Financial Times*, 12 November 1998; Pg. 219 'The UK Brewing Industry – Table and Text' from *Mail on Sunday*, 19 February 1995. Used by kind permission of the Mail on Sunday; Pg. 229 'Economic activity rates by ethnic group, gender, and age, Great Britain' from Social Trends 29, 1999, Office of National Statistics © Crown Copyright 2000; P. 230 'UK employees by gender and occupation, 1991 and 1998' from Social Market Trends 29, 1999, Office of National Statistics © Crown Copyright 2000; Pg. 230 'Workers urgently wanted: employees switch jobs for yet another bonus' by Christopher Bowe, *Financial Times*, 17 December 1999; Pg. 235 'Tough job for the referee as more workers pick a fight' by Christine Buckley © Times Newspapers Limited, 2 September 1999; Pg. 238 'Female/Male Employees' from 'National Earnings Survey' Office for National Statistics © Crown Copyright 2000; Pg. 238 'Women still bottom of earnings pile', *The Guardian*, 13 December 1999; Pg. 240 'Incentives boost workplace training' by Kevin Brown, *Financial Times*, 12 January 2000; Pg. 242 'Universities underpay women' by John Carvel, *The Guardian*, 6 May 1999; Pg. 246 'IT is transforming the world of work' by Roger Trapp, *The Independent*, 13 May 1999; Pg. 247

'Older but no wiser' by Martin Wolf, *Financial Times*, 4 January 2000; Pg. 247 'Workers still losing out on minimum wage'by Paul Kelso, *The Guardian*, 2 October 1999; Pg. 249 'Distribution of wealth in the UK' from Social Trends 30, 2000, Office for National Statistics. © Crown Copyright 2000; Pg. 250 'Boom makes Mr. Average worth £72,000' by David Smith and Trushar Barot, *The Sunday Times* © Times Newspapers Limited 9 January 2000; Pg. 252 'Regional comparison of GDP per head in 1997' from Social Trends 30, 2000, Office for National Statistics. © Crown Copyright 2000; Pg. 254 'Redistribution of income through taxes and benefits UK 1997-1998' from Social Trends 30,2000 table 5:18, Office for National Statistics. © Crown Copyright 2000; Pg. 254 'There is inequality, but hand-outs will not solve the North's problems' leading Article, The Independent, 7 December 1999; Pg. 254/255 'Income in different regions in 1995-98' from 'Regional Trends 1999' Office for National Statistics. © Crown Copyright 2000; Pg. 256 'Percentage of households that did not feel that they could afford certain items: EU comparison, 1995' from Social Trends 29, 1999, Office for National Statistics. © Crown Copyright 2000; Pg. 257 'Gap between rich and poor widened during Labour's honeymoon months' by Nicholas Timmons, Financial Times, 15 October 1999; Pg. 258 extract from 'Human Development Report 1998' United Nations Development Programme. Published by Oxford University Press New York; Pg. 259 'Incentives to boost workplace training' by Kevin Brown, *Financial Times*, 12 January 2000; Pg. 259 'Poverty: a mobile society' from The Economist © The Economist 23 October 1999; Pg. 260 'Time use: by age, Great Britain May 1995' from 'table 13:2 Social Trends 29, 1999' Office for National Statistics' © Crown Copyright 2000; Pg 262 'Percentage of UK households participating in the National Lottery, by social class of head of household' from 'Social Trends 29, 1999' Office for National Statistics. © Crown Copyright 2000; Pg. 263 'Top attractions: annual visitors (fee charging sites)' from The Sunday Times © Times Newspapers Limited 9 January 2000; Pg. 264 'Participation in most popular sports, games and physical activities, by gender Great Britain' from 'table 13:18 Social Trends 29, 1999' Office for National Statistics. © Crown Copyright 2000; Pg. 265 'Can Britain's courses meet new demands' from *The Sunday Times* © Times Newspapers Limited 9 January 2000; Pg. 271 'Structural fears undermine Britain's economic miracle' by Anatole Kaletsky, *The Times* © Times Newspapers Limited 2 November 1999; Pg. 273 'Bank's critics could end up right for the wrong reasons' by Anatole Kaletsky, *The Times* © Times Newspapers Limited, 13 December 1998; Pg. 274 'Challenges of globalisation' from *Financial Times*, 28 December 1999; Pg. 279 'Protection is costing EU 6% of GDP' by Guy de Jonquires, *Financial Times*, 10 November 1999; Pg. 280 'Trade talks hit stormy weather' by David Smith, *The Sunday Times* © Times Newspapers Limited 28 November 1999; Pg. 280 'WTO gives go-ahead to US tariffs' by Diane Coyle, *The Independent*, 13 July 1999; Pg. 286 'Emu's small reward' by Martin Wolf, *Financial Times*, 26 May 1999; Pg. 288 'Industry must live with the strong pound' by Martin Essex, *Sunday Business*, 16 January 2000; Pg. 290 'Sick man of Britain' by Martin Wolf, *Financial Times*, 2 August 1999; Pg. 295 'Economy growth trend rises as Brown prepares for Budget' by Diane Coyle, *The Independent*, 8 November 1999; Pg. 297 'A new model of thought is needed to understand the net worked e-commerce' in *The Independent*, 14 December 1999; Pg. 299 'Optimism of 1900 returns' by David Smith, *The Sunday Times* © Times Newspapers Limited 26 December 1999; Pg. 299 'Longest economic boom in US history will race on' by Hamish McRae, *The Independent*, 28 January 2000; Pg. 301 'Staff shortage hits Arm as demand for chips soars' by Chris Hughes, *The Independent*, 1 February 2000; Pg. 301 'Invensys plans to cut 2,000 more jobs' by Saeed Shah, *The Independent*, 1 February 2000; Pg. 302 'Jobles level drops to 20-year low' by Lea Paterson and Alasdair Murray, *The Times* © Times Newspapers Limited 20 January 2000; Pg. 304 'New deal gives new hope to unemployed youngsters' by Jon Ashworth, *The Times*, © Times Newspapers Limited 12 January, 2000; Pg. 305 'Wadhwani sees fall in natural jobless rate' by Lea Paterson, *The Times* © Times Newspapers Limited 3 December 1999; Pg. 308 'The UK outlook – unbalanced growth' by Trevor Williams, 'Economic Bulletin May 1997'; Pg. 309 'Little inflation risk from falling jobless rate, says Wadhwani' by Diane Coyle, *The Independent*, 3 December 1999; Pg. 311 'Table 18.1 from National Institute Economic Review October 1999' published by National Institute of Economic and Social Research; Pg. 318 'Squaring the circle' by Tony Travers, *The Guardian*, 25 September 1999; Pg. 320 'Brown's good battle plan' by David Smith, *The Sunday Times* © Times Newspapers Limited 14 November 1999; Pg. 322 'Fiscal flexibility' from *The Economist* © The Economist 27 November 1999; Pg. 325 'Bank of England signals rate rise at start of the millenium' in *The Independent,* 23 December 1999; Pg. 326 "Anglo Saxon" central banks put Europeans in the dock' by Anatole Kaletsky, *The Times* © Times Newspapers Limited 9 February 1999; Pg. 326 'ECB boosts euro by lifting interest rates' by George Trefgarne, *Daily Telegraph*, 4 February 2000. © Telegraph Group Limited 2000; Pg. 327 'Britannia's new rules' by Ed Cooks, *Financial Times*, 13 January, 2000; Pg. 331 'New Deal extended to jobless adults over 25' by Robert Taylor, *Financial Times*, 10 November 1999; Pg. 333 'Reading the runes is a salutary business for an economist' by Richard Jeffrey, *Sunday Business*, 16 January 2000; Pg. 336 adapted from 'The conduct of monetary and the fiscal policy' by T. Burns in 'Economic Trends 509 March 1996'. Office for National Statistics. © Crown Copyright 2000; Pg. 340 'Passenger Transport by mode' from Social Trends 30, 2000. Office for National Statistics. © Crown Copyright 2000; Pg. 341 'Prescott promises new image for bus services' by Barrie Clement, *The Independent*, 16 November 1999; Pg. 343 'Road tolls 'will cut costs and boost economy' by Philip Thornton, *The Independent*, 10 January 2000; Pg. 345 'Taxation road to nowhere' by Richard Tomkins, *Financial Times*, 2 September 1999; Pg. 346 'Road Traffic, Great Britain' from Social Trends 30, 2000, Office for National Statistics. © Crown Copyright 2000; Pg. 348 'Danger of well-meaning ambition' by Martin Wolf, *Financial Times*, 6 October 1999; Pg. 350 'Thais pin hope on tourism for economic resurgence'by Jon Ashworth, *The Times* © Times Newspapers Limited 17 December 1999; Pg. 352 'Population explosion' by John Vidal, *The Guardian*, 20 September 1999; Pg. 356 'The end of la dolce vita' by James Blitz, *Financial Times*, 12 October 1999; Pg. 358 'Cut taxes for true EU harmonisation' by Martin Essex, *Sunday Business*, 30 May 1999; all AQA examination questions are reproduced by permission of the Assessment and Qualification Alliance; all OCR examination questions are reproduced with the kind permission of OCR; all WJEC examination questions are reproduced with the kind permission of WJEC. Used with permission; all Edexcel examination questions are reproduced by permission of London examinations, a division of Edexcel Foundation.